'To meet ... ... e in the Baede... ... by a person of enthusiastic and individual views, Collins's Companion Guides have appeared miraculously on the scene.' *Angus Wilson, Observer*

'The best travel-guide formula in Britain since the war—a formula combining informative detail à la Baedeker with seductive readability.'
Times Educational Supplement

'The Companion Guides provide the traveller with an expert and sympathetic cicerone, exactly the kind of expatriate Englishman one often longs for but never meets, who can be relied on to talk well and knowledgeably about a place and shut up when not required.' *New Statesman*

Also in Fontana:

LONDON *David Piper*

'It has strong claims to be among the best guide-books ever written.' *Sunday Telegraph*

VENICE *Hugh Honour*

'The best guide-book I have ever encountered.'
Angus Wilson, Observer

THE COMPANION GUIDE TO

Rome

❧

GEORGINA MASSON

FONTANA · COLLINS

First published by Wm. Collins 1965
First issued in Fontana Books 1970

The cover painting by Sir C. L. Eastlake, P.R.A., shows
The Trajan Forum, Rome, and is reproduced by courtesy
of the Victoria and Albert Museum.

Maps by Charles Green
Set in Monotype Times
© Georgina Masson, 1965
Printed in Great Britain
for the publishers, Wm. Collins Sons & Co. Ltd.,
14 St. James's Place, London, S.W.1.
by Richard Clay (The Chaucer Press), Ltd.,
Bungay, Suffolk.

Contents

❧

To the memory of Gunhild Bergh,
who was herself a part of Rome.

Illustrations

❧

Between pages 192 and 193

The Forum
Statues of Vestal Virgins in the Forum
A model of the Palatine
A street in Trajan's market
*Sansovino's 'Madonna and Child'
The Appian Way
Pinturicchio's fresco of the Delphic Sybil (*Anderson*)
Mosaic in the Villa Borghese (*Anderson*)
Piazza del Campidoglio
Piazza Navona
S. Maria in Trastevere
Raphael's 'Fornarina' (*Anderson*)
*The nympheum in the Villa Giulia
*A garden court in the Museo delle Terme

Between pages 400 and 401

Trajan's Column
The Arch of Constantine
*Palazzo Farnese
*Palazzo della Cancelleria
*Palazzo Spada
The Doria picture gallery
Detail from the ceiling of the Sistine Chapel (*Anderson*)
*Etruscan terracotta sculpture
*The Ludovisi Throne
Statue of Augustus in the Vatican Museum (*Anderson*)
Michelangelo's 'Pietà' (*Anderson*)
Cloisters of St. Paul's Without The Walls
*Cloisters of S. Giovanni dei Genovesi
The Piazza of St. Peter's

All photographs are by the author except where otherwise indicated. Those marked with an asterisk are reproduced by kind permission of Thames & Hudson Ltd., chiefly from the author's 'Italian Villas and Palaces' and 'Italian Gardens'.

Suggested plan for walks

❧

Rome

yards in hundreds.

——————— *Principal bus or train routes*

Numbers in bold refer to chapters
which describe the areas indicated.
More detailed maps will be found
at the chapter openings.

Foreword

❦

Roma, non basta una vita (Rome, a lifetime is not enough) is the name of the last book written by the eminent Italian author and journalist Silvio Negro, who had indeed devoted his own life to its study. So the reader must be warned that this book does not pretend to cover every aspect of a city which has, after all, some 2,500 years of history, and contains buildings and art treasures representative of much of that time. Rome is moreover an introvert and secretive place that hides its treasures; even after living there for twenty years it can spring surprises. Few people have known it better than Augustus Hare, or were more able to interpret its fascination, and for him this lay in the discovery of 'ancient cloister and sculptured fountain, of mouldering fresco and medieval tomb—of mosaic-crowned gateway and palm-shadowed garden—and the gradually acquired knowledge of the wondrous story which clings around each of these ancient things'. It is with the intention of starting the traveller on the way to his own personal discoveries, and perhaps providing the key to some of their associations, that this book has been written. A list of books for further reading is given on p. 558.

WALKING has always been the best way in which to explore the historic centre of old Rome, where each crooked street and narrow alley is so filled with historic and artistic interest that otherwise half of what there is to be seen would be missed. Moreover, within the last few years the chaotic traffic situation (it is estimated that some 7000 new cars come into circulation every month) has made walking imperative, and by far the quickest means of locomotion. In view of this it is a considerable economy in time and money to stay in a hotel in the centre of the old city (these are marked with an asterisk on the hotel list in the Appendix).

For these reasons the itineraries in this book have been divided into morning and afternoon walks, beginning and ending at some central and easily recognisable spot. The names of some conveniently placed restaurants of various categories, for luncheon or a snack, have been given, and the use of public transport has been kept to a minimum except for outlying districts. The walks themselves have been designed to fill a fortnight's holiday in the hope that this minimum will conform to the needs even of the hurried traveller of today. As most people now come to Rome by air (the alternatives of train or car from London take more than twenty-four hours and four days respectively; a car is also more of a liability than an asset in Rome today, though almost indispensable for sight-seeing in the surrounding country), and many of them arrive by week-end flights during Friday night or on Saturday morning, the walks are planned to begin with a visit to the Capitol on Saturday evening, when the museum is open. Stalwart spirits who do not require some rest and recuperation after a night flight can very profitably fill in Saturday morning or afternoon by a trip to the excavations of Ostia Antica (reached in half an hour by the Metropolitana). As Ostia is some way outside Rome it does not come within the scope of this book, but its ruins give a clearer idea than anything else of what the remains of ancient Rome, buried beneath the streets and squares of the modern city, must be like, while the sculptures in the museum are exhibited as the excavators found them, not restored and polished as they are in most old Roman collections.

The walks can, of course, be treated in any order, and many will prefer to pick and choose among the sights themselves. In fact the timing of the itineraries has been based on the assumption that not everyone shares the same enthusiasm for, say, paleo-Christian sites and baroque art, and may well want to skip one in order to examine the other in detail. However, in making one's selection, it must always be borne in mind that *the Roman lunch 'hour' lasts from 1 to 3.30 p.m. at least, and that then, especially in summer, many museums and art galleries are shut; while all the year round most churches, except the great basilicas, are closed from midday to 3.30 p.m. or even later.* In fact the highly complicated system of OPENING AND CLOSING HOURS, which vary in winter and summer and almost for each individual museum, gallery, monument and church, make sight-seeing in Rome more complicated probably than in any other European capital. Basic facts to remember are that on Sundays nearly all state and municipal museums, monuments and galleries are open only in the morning, and on

Mondays are closed all day, also that the smaller ones do not open even on all the other days. The Vatican museum on the other hand is closed on Sundays and open on all weekday mornings. In addition certain privately owned palaces are open to the public, usually only for very limited periods. In order to assist the traveller to see as much as possible by suiting his itineraries to the appropriate days, a plan covering a fortnight is given on p. x. **A list of some principal opening and closing hours is given on p. 561.**

The above has, however, by no means exhausted the problems of timing one's sight-seeing; there are in addition a bewildering number of PUBLIC HOLIDAYS in Italy (no less than seventeen, of which a list is given on p. 547) when banks, offices and many sights are shut for at least half the day. To this may be added, often for months' duration, the unexpected closure of a building or part of a museum for restoration; no wonder *pazienza* (patience) is a word frequently to be heard on Roman lips.

Many foreign travellers will also be surprised to find that one has to pay to enter state owned museums and monuments as well as all the rest, though sometimes on Sundays or on a specified date each month entry is free. Therefore, a CULTURAL IDENTITY CARD, issued to those entitled to it who belong to the countries which are members of the Council of Europe, can prove a considerable saving, as it gives free entry at least to state owned museums, etc. Although a card can usually be obtained through the various nationals' official channels in Italy, it saves considerable time to procure it beforehand. The list of those entitled to this privilege is too long to give here, so travellers should apply to their professional organisations in their own countries to find out if they qualify—university students of more than two years' standing, engaged in research, can get theirs through the British Council in London. Direzione Generale delle Antichità e Belle Arti, 18 Piazza del Popolo in Rome, between 11 a.m. and midday, will often also issue temporary free passes to state owned museums, etc., to students and those culturally engaged *who bring their credentials with them.*

The IDEAL SEASONS in which to visit Rome are from mid-March to mid-June and especially October. Most people coming for the first time usually have no idea of what the Roman climate is like, and as Augustus Hare said: 'Nothing can be more mistaken than the impression that those who go to Italy are sure to find a mild and congenial temperature.' The mean average temperature of Rome in January is only 5 degrees Fahrenheit above that of London while in August it is 13 degrees, and Rome gets eight and a half more inches of rain in a year than London. It is not an easy climate, being subject to rapid changes of temperature in less than an hour, so suggestions for what to bring in the way of clothes and, very important, shoes, are given on p. 546, also recommendations on how to deal with that common traveller's complaint —Rome tummy.

As in France, STAMPS can be bought in any TOBACCONISTS, who generally stock both English and American cigarettes; the local one which most closely resembles English cigarettes is the Virginia. LETTERS from Italy do not automatically go air mail for the normal foreign stamp of 90 lire, to this another 15 lire has to be added. A good deal of time can be saved by posting at the Central Post Office in Piazza S. Silvestro or at special boxes in the Stazione Termini. This and the large Post Office near the station and one or two others are open all day, but local ones close at 1 p.m. All BANKS are closed on Saturdays and on weekdays open from 8.30 a.m. to 12.30 p.m. and from 3.30 to 4.45 p.m. except savings banks or Casse di Risparmio, which open from 8.15 a.m. to 12.45 p.m. At the height of the tourist season they are very crowded, and as a time-saver it is well worth cashing travellers' cheques in your hotel if possible.

TRANSPORT is one of the worst problems of Roman life, at the rush hour buses and trams are almost unbelievably crowded; the struggle to get one's ticket as one enters and work one's way forward to the front, in order to get out at the right stop, is something of an ordeal; also it is necessary to beware of pickpockets. Transport is, however, cheap, the normal fare is 50 lire for buses and trams. For tourist purposes the most useful ones are the 64, which goes from the Station to St. Peter's, and the 56 and 60, whose terminus is just beside the Piazza Belli in Trastevere. The 56 goes along the Corso, up the Via del Tritone, and part of the Via Veneto, continuing along the Via Po, near the Villa Borghese, and ending up in a remote suburb near the Villa Chigi. The 60 pursues the same route as far as the Piazza Barberini, branching off from there up the Via Barberini, continuing along the Via XX Settembre to the Porta Pia and running the whole length of the Via Nomentana to the garden suburb of the Monte Sacro. Taxis do not cruise for hire, but can be called by telephone from the nearest rank. When taking a *carrozza*, which is the ideal way of seeing the Villa Borghese or the less crowded parts of Rome, be sure that the meter is down and in working order. The Metropolitana (underground) is really only useful for going to the E.U.R. or Ostia.

The best MAP OF ROME is that produced by the Guida Monaci, via Francesco Crispi 10; it can also often be bought at the Central Post Office and, together with a street guide, costs 2,500 lire. The WEEK IN ROME is a useful guide to what's on in the city, while the local English language paper, *The Rome Daily American*, provides a lively commentary on local current events.

PAPAL AUDIENCES. Once a week when he is in residence in the Vatican, and sometimes twice a week when he is in residence in the summer in Castelgandolfo, the Pope gives general audiences. Permission to attend may be obtained by any U.K. or Commonwealth citizen (except Indians, who have their own diplomatic representation) at the British Legation to the Holy See at 91 Via Condotti, *bringing their passport*. Legation hours to obtain audience permits are from 9.30 a.m. to 12.30 p.m. No special dress is required for these audiences, except that women must wear long sleeves, and a veil or a scarf is preferred to a hat.

Finally, in order to enjoy Rome to the full, follow the age-old adage and do as the Romans do, in other words relax and enjoy the tempo of the city which does not run to the precise time-table of the northern world. Do not be surprised if plans fail to work out as expected—*pazienza*—go and sit in the sun with a glass of wine and watch the world go by. This is the advice of all the old Roman friends who with their knowledge, time and patience have so greatly helped me with this book.

CHAPTER ONE

The Capitol

❧

'THE Capitol was the head of the world, where the consuls and senators abode to govern the earth. The face thereof was covered with high walls and strong, rising above the top of the hill, and covered all over with glass and marvellous carved work' . . . thus in the twelfth century the author of the *Mirabilia Romae*—the earliest guide-book to ancient Rome—described the hill that in his own day was largely a desert, a poor place of pasturage for goats. Few things could better illustrate the legendary fame of this little hill whose glory had survived the dark ages—when its monuments crumbled to dust—which still at the time when our author was writing was associated in men's minds with ideals of civic liberty. So that in 1143 when the Romans revolted against the domination of the popes and the misery produced by their unending struggle with the emperors, they called a meeting on the Capitol to re-establish the Senate and revive the sovereign glory of their city.

From that day to this the legend of the Capitol has, if one may phrase it so, gathered fresh laurels. Petrarch, who more than any man of his time rekindled the love of the ancient world, received there in 1341 the poet's laurel crown; to Europeans of the Renaissance its history was part and parcel of their own inheritance, and men like Montaigne could truthfully say that they were more familiar with the temples which once stood there than with the existing palaces of their own kings; here it was in 1764 that Gibbon was inspired to write his immortal *History of the Decline and Fall of the Roman Empire*, and in succeeding centuries it has given its name to the seats of government of the new nations that have come into being.

Thus, more than anywhere else in Rome, the Capitol provides a link between the ancient world and our own, and as such is the ideal place from which to start our exploration of

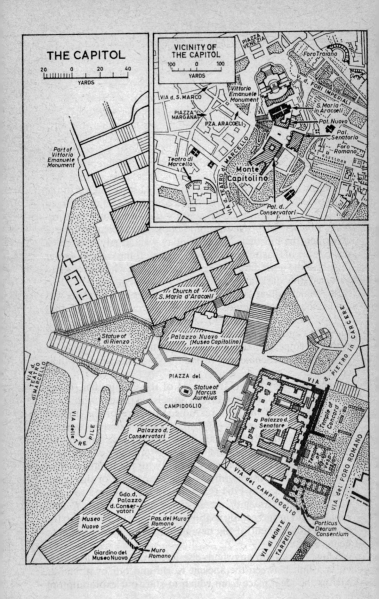

THE CAPITOL

20   0   20   40

YARDS

VICINITY OF THE CAPITOL

100   0   100

YARDS

PIAZZA VENEZIA

Foro Traiano

VIA D. S. MARCO

d. FORI IMPERIALI

Vittorio Emanuele Monument

S. Maria in Aracoeli

PIAZZA MARGANA

Pal. Nuovo

PZA. ARACOELI

Pal. Senatorio

Teatro di Marcello

Foro Romano

Monte Capitolino

Pal. d. Conservatori

Part of Vittorio Emanuele Monument

Church of S. Maria d'Aracoeli

Statue of di Rienzo

Palazzo Nuovo (Museo Capitolino)

VIA d. TEATRO di MARCELLO

VIA delle TRE PILE

PIAZZA del

Statue of Marcus Aurelius

CAMPIDOGLIO

Palazzo d. Senatore

VIA S. PIETRO in CARCERE

Temple of Concord

Palazzo d. Conservatori

VIA del CAMPIDOGLIO

VIA del FORO ROMANO

Museo Nuovo

Gdo. d. Palazzo d. Conservatori

Pas. del Muro Romano

Giardino del Museo Nuovo

Muro Romano

VIA di MONTE TARPEIO

Porticus Deorum Consentium

the city. So let us begin with the Capitol, let us time our first visit—this is a very important point—to coincide with the hour after sunset, when the sky on a fine night is a translucent shade of green and the monuments imperceptibly lit by a master hand are beginning to glow softly in the gathering darkness.

Viewed thus for the first time this sight of the Capitol is an unforgettable experience, fixed for ever in one's memory, which can then better withstand the subsequent inevitable shock of seeing it of a morning as a parking place for the Vespas and Seicentos of the municipal employees. For the Capitol, or Campidoglio as it is now called, is still the seat of the Roman municipality, whose cipher—the immortal letters S.P.Q.R., representing the words *Senatus Populusque Romanus* —today appears, to the horror of some purists, on such mundane municipal property as buses, lamp posts and drain covers. All this is something of a shock, but when one stops to think about it one realises that it is in just this curious mixture of ancient and modern that the secret of the city's extraordinary fascination chiefly lies.

Rome is most emphatically not a museum city, preserved in a vacuum as an *objet d'art*; for one thing its inhabitants would render this impossible, for, appallingly and terrifyingly at times, they have the habit of treating the grandeur of their inheritance with complete insouciance. All through the centuries they have ruthlessly destroyed the old to build up something new, with the same indifference with which Roman housewives have hung out their washing upon imperial ruins or the terraces of the princely Renaissance villas and palaces which rose above them, and Roman children play football or hop-scotch among the baroque splendours of fountains and piazzas that stand upon the site of classical circuses.

For all Rome, architecturally, as in its way of life, is a palimpsest. At first glance parts of the city may appear to belong wholly to today or to some other easily recognisable period of history, but once one begins to look beneath the surface a bewildering series of strata appear that lead one backwards through the centuries. Nowhere in Rome is this more plainly evident than upon the Capitol, which is endowed with something of the same qualities as Wells's Time Machine; rising as it does like an island of peace out of the strident roar of the Piazza Venezia in the heart of the city, it can lead us backwards by gradual degrees through the centuries to the time when Rome first emerged from a collection of pastoral villages set upon seven hills.

Starting off, then, from the Piazza Venezia, the best way to approach the Capitol is to skirt the Palazzo Venezia and make for the little garden which lies between the Via di S. Marco and the Piazza d'Aracoeli, as it is from here that the fascinatingly contrasting staircases leading to the church of S. Maria d'Aracoeli and the piazza of the Capitol itself appear in all their grandeur—the first soaring upward like the side of a mountain, the second ascending gradually to an elysian world of golden-hued palaces silhouetted against the translucent aquamarine of the twilight sky. The difference between the two epochs that produced them is implicit even in this first glimpse of these two staircases; the 122 steps of the Aracoeli suggesting the medieval concept of life as a weary pilgrimage leading ultimately to heaven, while the *cordonata*, the gentle inclined ramp before the Capitol, is very much of the splendour and glory of this world. It is understandable that this should be so, as the Aracoeli stairs were built in 1348 as a thank-offering for Rome's delivery from the black death, while the *cordonata* was originally designed by Michelangelo in 1536 for the reception of an emperor.

According to a popular tradition Cola di Rienzo—the self-styled tribune whose grandiose dreams envisaged Roman sovereignty re-established over all Italy under his own leadership—inaugurated the Aracoeli steps by being the first man to walk up them. In actual fact Cola had fled from Rome some seven months before they were completed, leaving his silver crown and steel sceptre as pious offerings in the church above, after his first brief reign, begun in a tumult of popular enthusiasm, had ended in anticlimax. His return after six years' wandering culminated in his ignominious death on the spot where his statue now stands in the grass between the two staircases.

Michelangelo designed the *cordonata* and the palaces and piazza of the Capitol as, with a few exceptions, we see them today, for the arrival in Rome of a man who did indeed rule over one of the most extensive empires of modern times—the Holy Roman Emperor Charles V. Although, in recognition of his victory over the infidel in North Africa, Pope Paul III accorded Charles the signal honour of a triumphal procession modelled upon those of the Caesars of old, he did not inaugurate the *cordonata*—it was only completed a century later. But Charles's procession followed the time-honoured route used by so many of his classical predecessors—passing under the Arch of Titus, traversing the Forum (buried deep under the debris of centuries) by a specially constructed road. The procession then passed under the Arch of Septimius Severus and ascended the Capitol, not, however, by the same route as the victors of ancient times. With the passage of the centuries the city's centre had shifted from the classical Fora to the area of the Campus Martius (now called the Campo Marzio), in the bend of the Tiber, and since the Middle Ages the main approach to the Capitol had changed from the south to the north-eastern slope, where the *cordonata* now stands.

Even so, when approaching the Capitol from this side, Charles V (like ourselves) traversed the site of an old Roman road which was believed to cross a spot hallowed by one of Rome's most ancient traditions—the Asylum proclaimed by Romulus himself as a place of refuge for all who wished to call on the protection of the first King of Rome and so help to swell the population of his newly-founded city. Today it is almost impossible to imagine that this was once probably a wild gully leading to a hollow between the two crests of the hill, for as we ascend the *cordonata* one of the most splendid scenes in Rome, or in the world for that matter, is gradually revealed before us, like a stage as the curtain rises.

The theatrical comparison at once leaps to one's mind, and rightly so; as Michelangelo's conception of the Capitol was quite evidently that of a stage set for the magnificent pageantry of Renaissance ceremonial, with consummate mastery he did not leave it empty, but brought an emperor of the ancient world to greet the one of his own day. For sheer drama there can be few sights to compare with the scene he thus evoked, as the dark figure of **Marcus Aurelius** appears riding forward on his horse, with hand outstretched, silhouetted against the golden Palazzo del Senatore.

No wonder that this dramatic statue—the most famous equestrian bronze of the ancient world, which survived unburied through the centuries—has become the centre of legend and prophecy. It is said that Michelangelo was himself so fascinated by the sense of life and action which it conveys that when it had been placed on the pedestal he designed for it (practically the only part of his plans completed for Charles

V's arrival) he stood in front of the horse and commanded it to walk! But most of the tales told about Marcus Aurelius and his horse date back to the Middle Ages when it stood by the old Lateran Palace, and the rider was believed to be Constantine, the first Christian Emperor, a mistake to which the statue owed its escape from the melting pot of religious vandalism that swallowed up most of its companions. The legend relates that when the statue again appears covered, as it originally was, with gold, the end of the world will come and the Last Judgment be announced by a voice speaking from the horse's forelock. Such forebodings bore little weight with Cola di Rienzo, who converted the horse into a fountain for a banquet, with wine flowing from one nostril and water from the other, nor for one of the more energetic popes, who hung a rebellious city prefect from the statue by his hair.

Already, like the Time Machine, the Capitol has begun to work its spell, taking us backwards through the centuries, leaving the splendour of its Renaissance trappings far behind and plunging us into the blood-soaked memories of medieval Rome, when the present piazza was used as a market and a place of execution. On a winter night when the freezing *tramontana* whistles through its colonnades, it is somehow easier to imagine the hill as it then was, with the fortress of the Corsi huddled among the ancient ruins, and wolves fighting in the streets below, as Adam of Usk saw them still at the beginning of the fifteenth century in the sacred precincts of St. Peter's. Nor is this period of the Capitol's existence simply a grim memory recorded for us by the medieval chroniclers; we have only to take a few steps to the left or right, away from the shimmering floodlit waters of the fountain, round either of the corners of the **Senator's Palace**, to see the dark towers of the medieval building which is concealed behind the Renaissance façade.

The towers we see today date from the fourteenth and fifteenth centuries, but they rise on the site of older ones that had defended the senatorial palace, built as a meeting place for the fifty-six senators who were elected as a result of the popular uprising of 1143. This dream of civic freedom was short-lived, however. Its first check came from the forceful English Pope Hadrian IV, who refused to recognise the Senate and for the first time in history placed Rome under an interdict. The *coup de grâce* came at the hands of that great statesman Innocent

III, who produced the compromise that killed it. After 1204 only one, or at the most two, senators were elected annually and assisted by councillors or *conservatori*. In 1358 even this shadowy municipal freedom ceased to exist and a single senator was appointed by the pope; thus emasculated the office survived until the unification of Italy. It is for this reason that the central palace on the Capitol is called the Palazzo del Senatore in the singular, and the one on the right the Palazzo dei Conservatori.

Thus ended one phase of the dream, recurrent through the centuries, of reviving the city's ancient greatness. But, whether they were aware of it or not, the senators of 1145 chose a site which linked their palace with the glory of republican Rome, for just as the remains of the medieval building survive beneath the Renaissance façade, so it in its turn rose above the ruins of the *Tabularium* or Record Office, dating from the year 78 BC. By climbing the few steps on the left-hand side of the Palazzo del Senatore, we can look through a glass door into a gallery, leading into this the only building on the Capitol which, unlike its fabulous gold-roofed temples, has defied sack, fire, earthquake and, most damaging of all, the pillage of centuries. Particularly at night, when the lights concealed by great terracotta urns illuminate the vaults, this is an extra-ordinarily evocative sight, and one has the eerie sensation of looking into a passage that leads backwards into the very heart of time.

But already from the steps we catch a glimpse of the scene which makes a night visit to the Capitol one of the most enthralling sights in the world, for stretched out beyond it are the ruins of the Roman Forum and the Fora of Julius Caesar, Augustus and Trajan, with the Colosseum towering up behind them in the distance. Seen by day it requires something of the knowledge of the archaeologist and the imagination of a poet to conjure up what this prospect must once have been. But at night, especially when a rising moon adds its magic to the diffused glow of the illuminations[1] and stark reality is clothed in mysterious shadows, it is not nearly so difficult to picture the stately ranks of colonnaded temples crowned with gilded statues and the basilicas rearing their great bulk against the night sky. Or to imagine the faint glow of the sacred fire

1. Unfortunately not always possible when *Son et Lumière* is on in the Forum.

warming the marbles of the Temple of Vesta, and above them all the vast palace of the emperors on the Palatine overshadowing the whole scene, as it then dominated the civilised world.

Night after night for years one can walk upon the Capitol looking at the same scene, and always it seems to suggest some different aspect of Rome's history, for it is a place of many moods that never seem to repeat themselves. In winter it is the stark ruin of medieval Rome, when the Forum was called the Campo Vaccino (the cow field) and the Capitol the Monte Caprino (hill of the goats), that comes closest. But the classical world seems to waken with the summer heat; when the nightingales answering each other from the ilex groves bring back memories of the Roman poets. In the whirlwind heat and dust of the scirocco and the air heavy with the scent of sun-baked cypresses and oleander blossom, it is not difficult to conjure up the ferocious pageantry of a Roman triumph, with the laurel-crowned victor in his chariot, the prisoners in their chains, and the tramp and shouts of the legionaries approaching along the Sacred Way.

With the cool stillness of autumn the seething life of Rome as the centre of the ancient world seems to recede and instead there come to mind memories of the time when the early humanists came like us to wander on the Capitol—men like the Florentine Poggio Bracciolini who was there in 1431 and described what he saw in his *de Varietate Fortunae*. It is quite possible that Poggio stood on almost exactly the same spot as we, at the top of the steps leading off from the Via S. Pietro in Carcere that winds down the hill from the left-hand side of the Palazzo del Senatore to the Forum of Julius Caesar. Or in the little garden beside it, from where we can now look over the ruins of Caesar's Temple of Venus to the Fora of Trajan and Augustus, dominated by the illuminated Renaissance loggia of the Casa dei Cavallieri di Rodi and the vast bulk of the Torre delle Milizie, glowing red against the night sky. A rough road and a garden with a palm tree appear in the same place as they exist today in an early sixteenth-century drawing of the Capitol, but the hill on the other side of the Palazzo del Senatore is shown as a series of amorphous mounds. Still, then as now, it was probably one of the best vantage points from which to look at the Forum, where today the Via del Campidoglio joins the Via di Monte Tarpeio. As the name indicates, this road runs below the precipitous face of the Capitoline Hill that is most generally believed to have been the place of execution for traitors, the famous **Tarpeian rock**, called after Tarpeia who betrayed the citadel to the Sabines and was killed by them.

The supposed site of such legendary events probably held a greater fascination for the men of Poggio Bracciolini's generation than for our own, as then they were wrapped in an aura of mystery which a century of scientific excavation has done much to dispel. But as a result we can now actually walk on the stones of the ancient Clivus Capitolinus, followed by the victors in their triumphs, which Julius Caesar lined with forty torch-bearing elephants for his Gallic triumph (it runs beside the modern Via di Monte Tarpeio), and identify most of the famous buildings in the Forum. Though as a matter of fact the outstanding landmarks of the Forum are still the same as they were in Renaissance times. Looking down from the Capitol, from left to right, they are: the **Arch of Septimius Severus**, the three columns of the **Temple of Vespasian** right under the slope of the Capitol, the portico of the **Temple of Saturn**; in the middle distance the **Column of Phocas**, Byron's famous 'nameless column with a buried base', and farther away on the left the high steps and portico of the **Temple of Antoninus and Faustina**, and on the right the three columns and fragment of the architrave of the **Temple of Castor and Pollux**.

Poggio Bracciolini's visit to Rome was a landmark in the history of art, as he was the first man to look at the ancient monuments as works of art and not simply as marvels in the sense of the *Mirabilia* and the Middle Ages. Poggio was also the first man of his day to collect classical statues and use them for the decoration of his house and garden (he had been anticipated in this by the thirteenth-century 'Stupor Mundi', the Emperor Frederick II of Hohenstaufen). One cannot help wondering if this idea of Poggio's came to him during his wanderings on the Capitol; it would have been particularly appropriate if this were so, as the famous **Capitoline Museum** was the first public collection of classical sculpture in the modern world. It is more likely, however, if Poggio's idea originated in Rome, that it came to him in the Lateran, as the wonderful ancient bronzes—the **She-Wolf**, the **Boy with the Thorn** and the colossal head of **Constantius II**—were all there until 1471, when Pope Sixtus IV gave or 'restored' them to the

Roman people, as the inscription in the Capitoline Museum gracefully phrases it.

Like the Capitol itself, the **Capitoline Museum** should if possible be seen for the first time at night, and certainly before visiting the Forum and Palatine. It is open regularly every Saturday throughout the year from 9 to 11.30 p.m. (see Appendix for other opening times) so if you can time your arrival in Rome for that day, you will be able to enjoy the best possible introduction to your exploration of the city. From the very beginning, however, it is as well to remember that the average mind—and feet—can stand just so much sight-seeing at a time, and enthusiastic efforts to drive them beyond this limit will only end in disaster. So after exploring the Capitol itself, take time off for a really good Roman dinner in one of the colourful *trattorie* in the neighbourhood. Angelino's in the Piazza Margana is one of the nearest and is delightful for eating out in the picturesque piazza. The Hostaria SS. Apostoli in the piazza of the same name caters for serious eaters, and makes a speciality of duck and original hors d'oeuvres including *scapece*, of which more hereafter. Il Buco in the Via S. Ignazio also serves *scapece* and excellent Tuscan food.

Returning to the Capitol, we find that the darkness has increased its theatrical aspect and the classical statues surrounding it look like actors in some antique drama of gods and men. At the top of the *cordonata* the giant figures of Castor and Pollux dwarf even the famous 'trophies of Marius', let alone such mere mortals as the Emperors Constantine and Constantius II who stand farther along the parapet; while beneath the Palazzo del Senatore the porphyry-robed 'Goddess Rome' appears like some ancient seeress illuminated by the eerie flickering light of the illuminated fountain, guarded by the huge recumbent figures of Nile and Tiber.

Another river god confronts us as we enter the **Palazzo del Museo Capitolino** on the left. For centuries he has been known as Marforio, Pasquino's companion in the famous dialogues of the 'talking' statues from which our word pasquinade is derived. The Capitoline collection, which was founded by Sixtus IV's gift of 1471, has been continually added to ever since and is now housed in three palaces. The one in which we stand contains most of the older part of the collection, including such famous works as the **Capitoline Venus** (not numbered), the **Dying Gaul** (No. 15 in room called after it) and

the **Marble Faun** (No. 7 in same room), which gave its name to
Hawthorne's famous Roman romance. In the Palazzo dei
Conservatori, opposite, stand the ancient bronzes given by
Sixtus IV; this palace also houses some beautiful Greek
sculpture, a picture gallery and collections of coins and porcelain. Connected to the Palazzo dei Conservatori is the Palazzo
Caffarelli, formerly the German Embassy, which contains the
newest additions to the vast collection, mostly sculptures and
inscriptions discovered during excavations and building
operations resulting from the vast expansion of Rome since
it became the capital of unified Italy in 1870.

With a collection as old as the Capitoline—and indeed in
most Roman museums—it should be borne in mind that it
reflects not only the changing taste of ancient Roman and
Greek civilisation but also that of generations of collectors
from the Renaissance onwards, who often 'restored' and
polished up their finds, adding heads, limbs and sometimes
whole bodies. To many of us today there is something cold,
almost intimidating, about ranks of statues ranged in long
galleries; but this, it should be remembered, reflects the taste of
later collectors rather than that of the artists and patrons, who
originally created and commissioned the sculptures for very
different settings. Singly or in groups many of them were
intended as ornaments for monuments and buildings, and
their brilliant colours—for most of the statues were originally
painted—would have stood out vividly in the sunlight. Others
may have completed the decoration of some elegant salon,
standing in niches adorned with mosaics or painting, a style
which was later imitated by the great Renaissance architects.
Very many of the statues would have been surrounded by the
verdant green of gardens or have stood in porticoes by rippling
fountains—as the delightfully gay 'Drunken Faun' (No. 1 in
Sala del Fauno) and the rose-coloured Centaurs from Hadrian's Villa (Nos. 2 and 4 in the Salone of the Palazzo del
Museo Capitolino) probably originally did. All the sparkling
life of the Hellenistic world has survived even in these copies
of the second century AD, but they were the work of Greek
sculptors from Aphrodisias, not of Romans.

There is an intentional solemnity, an almost hieratic quality,
about most Roman sculpture; it reflects an attitude of mind
which the Romans evidently shared with the collectors of the
eighteenth and early nineteenth century when the classicism of

Canova was so much appreciated. It is said that when Canova himself in his later life first saw the Elgin marbles he exclaimed: 'If only I could begin again.' This point of view is shared by our own generation, for whom the surging life of Greek sculpture and even the dramatisation of the Baroque holds a greater appeal. But one aspect of the art of Roman sculptors holds a supreme fascination for us even today—their portraits, which have rarely been equalled, and the Capitoline museum contains some of the most famous examples of their kind.

This is one of the reasons why a visit to the museum makes such a wonderful introduction to the exploration of ancient Rome, particularly the Forum and the Palatine, as with these images fresh in one's mind it is so much easier to people what are now deserted ruins with the men and women who once lived and worked, loved, hated, worshipped and ruled there. It is a pity from the point of view of chronological order that the earliest portrait in this marvellous series is in the Palazzo dei Conservatori, which comes second in the itinerary. By some miraculous chance of survival, this bronze, which for long was identified as Lucius Junius Brutus, the founder of the Republic and avenger of Lucretia, but is in fact the head (the only antique part of the bust) of an unknown man of the third or second century BC, typifies all that one imagines an outstanding Roman of the Republic to have been. No doubt the early Romans differed from one another just as much as you and I, but nearly all of us have a mental image of what they were like, and here this vision stands personified in the austere features, direct gaze and stern mouth that indicate a man of immovable determination, outstanding in any age, but surely one who was untouched by the gentler aspects of life.

There is no face like this among the serried ranks we see in the famous Sala degli Imperatori in the Palazzo del Museo Capitolino. The closest in time is that of Augustus in his old age (No. 6), but there seems to be no doubt that in the two hundred years which separated the austere republican from the first of the emperors the Roman type had changed and softened. This portrait of Augustus is arresting in its beauty and its humanity, and there is no reason to suppose that the artist was unduly flattering, for even the malicious Suetonius admitted that Augustus was remarkably handsome still in his old age. Looking at it one can well believe the stories Suetonius recounts of the Gallic chieftain who planned to murder

Augustus but found himself unable to do so 'because the sight of that tranquil face softened my heart'. Or of Augustus amusing himself sometimes on holiday from ruling an empire, by playing dice and marbles with cheerful small boys.

Still one cannot help feeling that if Augustus lived in a world far removed from that of the stern republican, with his homespun clothes made for him by his wife, his world was separated by an even greater gulf from that of the other most strikingly beautiful person in the room. This is a lady, sometimes believed to have been Julia the daughter of the Emperor Titus (No. 15), but in any case one who lived at the end of the first century of our era. Distinguished, and as obviously sophisticated as her own elaborately curled hair, piled high in the form of a diadem, she corresponds to the luxurious type of beauty that the elder Pliny described frequenting fashionable dinner parties, with some half-million pounds' worth of emeralds and pearls distributed about her person. One can easily imagine her setting out for the baths, accompanied by her slaves, carrying her green parasol, peacock feather fan and elaborate cosmetics in an ivory make-up box, and lingering in the jewellers and other luxurious shops that lined the Sacred Way on the Velia.

For the student of human nature the Sala degli Imperatori is surely one of the most fascinating rooms in Rome. Though now some of the traditional attributions are no longer accepted, it makes little difference, as these were the men and women of the Roman Empire even if they did not rule it. Some of the faces are admittedly terrible—Caracalla (No. 40), whose cruelty did not shrink from the murder of his own brother, and his successor Elagabalus (No. 55), whose weak and vicious face is easily distinguishable for its sideburns and strange air of Teddy-boy modernity. No wonder he amused himself with parties where the guests reclined on cushions filled with crocus petals, while Julia Maesa, his terrible old Syrian grandmother, ruled the Empire with her friends.

Among so many emperors and empresses there is one face which rivets attention and it is simply that of an unknown man (No. 58) of the third century AD. Looking at it one has no doubt that it is a speaking likeness, the whimsical expression, the sidelong glance and the humorous mouth are so vividly portrayed and the whole is so infused with life that it seems that this is someone we know and not an anonymous man who died some 1,700 years ago. But he lived, this humorous man, in one of the most troubled centuries of ancient history, when Rome was menaced by schism from within and barbarian invasion from without, when eight emperors were murdered in eighty years. Looking at him, one is tempted to think that he was the typical man in the street or Forum in Rome of the decadence, who whiled away his time among pleasant company in the baths and theatre. Nothing could be more different from the grim Republican of four hundred years before, but just as that one face seems to personify the early Rome, so this equally anonymous man represents the disillusionment of his own epoch. This amiable cynicism does not conceal the alert intelligence which makes such a vivid impression, and we have an uneasy feeling that perhaps his shade stands mockingly watching us as earnestly, with guide-book in hand, we try to piece together a picture of the world he once inhabited.

But we must hurry on if we are to see the Palazzo dei Conservatori and all the rest before the museum closes. In the courtyard of this palace are the great head and hand of a colossal statue of Constantine, originally about 40 feet high, that once stood, or rather was enthroned, in the apse of the huge basilica beside the Forum which, begun by Maxentius, is usually called by the Romans the Basilica di Massenzio after him, though it was completed by the first Christian Emperor. The courtyard contains another fragment, so unimpressive that many people pass it without realising what it is, but the letters BRIT of the mutilated inscription afford a clue—it once formed part of the triumphal arch erected to celebrate Claudius's conquest of Britain. The inscription recorded the capture of the proud chieftain Caractacus, who according to Tacitus, even as a prisoner faced up to the pomp of Caesar, and Claudius pardoned him. What would they both have thought if they had known that 1,756 years later the Union Jack was to be flown from the Capitol? That was in 1799, when a squadron under Captain Troubridge's command freed Rome from the French, and incidentally saved many of the ancient sculptures from the Vatican from being shipped to Paris, an action for which the captain was accorded the unusual privilege of adding the keys of St. Peter to his arms.

Mounting the stairs, on the landing we are faced by some fine Roman reliefs. One of these, showing Marcus Aurelius making a sacrifice, is of particular interest, as in the back-

ground there is the best surviving representation of the
Capitoline Temple of Jupiter, whose ruins we will shortly see.
The principal rooms of the Palazzo dei Conservatori are still
used for official receptions by the Mayor of Rome; seeing them
thus at night they appear to have almost the intimacy of a
private house, with antique bronzes, pictures and tapestries
displayed as they are in so many old Roman palaces. It is, of
course, a matter of personal taste, but among so many
beautiful things, including the 'Boy with the Thorn', which
stands in the same room as the republican 'Brutus', to the
writer the **Capitoline wolf** is the greatest treasure of them all
(none of these statues are numbered). No photograph or
drawing ever seems to do it justice—one has to see it for oneself to appreciate the mastery with which the Estruscan
sculptor—believed to be the famous Vulca of Veii—portrayed
this animal in which fear, intelligence and ferocity are so
fascinatingly mixed. The wolf dates from the end of the sixth
or the beginning of the fifth century BC; the figures of the
twins from 1509, and although they are the work of Pollaiuolo, they are banal by comparison. Indeed, the bronzes of
eagles (Sala delle Aquile not numbered) and geese (Nos. 12
and 14 Sala delle Oche), and the superb marble dog which
stand in the adjoining rooms demonstrate the curious fact
that, like our own Victorians, the artists of ancient Rome
excelled at animal sculpture as they did in portraiture.

It would require several books to describe in detail the vast
collections of the Palazzo dei Conservatori and Palazzo
Caffarelli, but five groups in the former stand out from the
rest—those of the Orti Lamiani, which include the exquisite
'Venere Esquilina'; the two Sale dei Monumenti Arcaici,
containing some wonderful Greek archaic sculpture; the Sala
dei Bronzi and the Sala degli Orti di Mecenate, this last a
fascinatingly eclectic and possibly personal collection from
the famous gardens of Maecenas. In the Palazzo Caffarelli, or
Museo Nuovo, apart from the ravishing 'Polymnia' (No. 24)
in room IV, room V contains a superb Minerva or Athena of
the fourth century BC (No. 16) and an Aphrodite in the style of
Praxiteles (No. 9).

But it is as well to pause and take a rest between the two
museums; on a fine summer night the perfect place is the
delightful little courtyard garden that opens off the long gallery of the Palazzo dei Conservatori. We are now approaching

the spot which was once the most sacred in the whole of Rome, and according to Livy its first beginnings were like this—an open space of grass and trees. Still in the early part of the sixth century BC the Romans had no temples and no personified images of gods, but simply turf altars in the open. According to Livy, the shepherd soldiers of early Rome brought the spoils of war and deposited them under a sacred oak tree that grew on the Capitol. This is legend, but it is a historical fact that the kings of Rome started to build the first great temple on the Capitol, calling Etruscans—including the famous Vulca—to help in its construction and adornment. The last king had fallen and the Republic was born before the temple was consecrated in 509 BC; it was dedicated to Jupiter, Juno and Minerva, though it was known as the Capitoline Temple of Jupiter, and was the centre of Roman religious life. The Senate, which frequently met in religious buildings, held its first session there each year, and for centuries the temple was the setting of the culminating scene of Roman triumphs.

One curious aspect of a triumph was that in early times the victorious general's body was painted red like the original image of Jupiter, and he was dressed in similar robes. These consisted of a purple flowered tunic and a gold-embroidered purple toga, while on his head he wore a laurel wreath and in his hands he carried an ivory sceptre and a laurel branch. Julius Caesar and Augustus were given the right to wear these robes whenever they wished, and in later imperial times they also became the official dress of consuls. Thus attired as a god, the general offered up a sacrifice to Jupiter and, except on the rare occasions when he spared their lives, his vanquished enemies were executed just beforehand in the Mamertine prison in the hill below.

The earliest Temple of Jupiter stood on a high podium of grey volcanic stone; it had Tuscan columns and a low wooden entablature adorned with terracotta sculptures. Changes came with the centuries, the floor was paved with marble, the ceiling was gilded and bronze statues substituted for the original terracotta ones; but still the old original temple stood until it was burnt down in 83 BC. Its successors, and there were several of them, grew richer and richer, the doors, roof tiles and the gods within were all ablaze with gold, and from this splendour the phrase 'the golden Capitol' originated. The temple became a treasure house of votive offerings, like Pompey's gift of

King Mithridates's fabulous collections of gems looted in
Asia Minor; but as in Roman churches today, the temple also
contained tablets, banners, medallions and inflammable tinsel
draperies—hence the fires that necessitated the constant rebuilding of Roman temples.

But through all its vicissitudes and rebuilding the podium of
the earliest Capitoline temple still stood, as enduring as a rock,
and we can now see some of its great roughly-hewn grey stone
blocks as we enter the Passaggio del Muro Romano. After the
silence of centuries when no one knew where the most famous
temple in the world had stood—the temple that had witnessed
the triumphs of the consuls who had unified Italy and defeated
Pyrrhus and Hannibal, and of Julius Caesar—this fragment
has again come to light. But the gold and the jewels and the
marbles have vanished, plundered by the Goths and the
Vandals and the Romans of later centuries, and now all that
remains are these grey stones of the original temple built
nearly two thousand four hundred years ago.

This is the temple that we saw in the relief of Marcus
Aurelius making a sacrifice, the last to be built on the old
podium; it appears there with a portico of four rows of
columns (whereas in actual fact there were six) of magnificent
Pentelic marble brought from Greece. In this same relief an
ox is portrayed in the middle of the group, and it serves to
remind us that in the midst of all the gold and marble and all
the priceless works of art, one of the main forms of worship
was the sacrifice of animals, and that these same wonderful
temples must often have reeked of the smell of blood and the
roasting flesh of a holocaust. What the aftermath of one of the
great Roman sacrifices—like the solemn *suovetaurilia* made at
triumphs, when a pig, a goat and a bull were all slaughtered—
must have been like beggars description.

It would be pleasanter not to dwell on these scenes, but they
must nevertheless be borne in mind if we are to arrive at a true
picture of life in ancient Rome. Crossing the garden of the
Palazzo Caffarelli, on the other side of the wall of Jupiter's
temple, which must have witnessed so many of these sacrifices,
we come to room IV, where 'Polymnia' stands entranced,
listening to what must surely be the 'music of the spheres'.

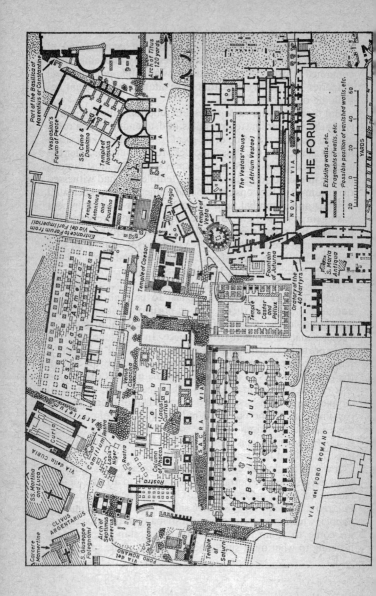

THE FORUM

Existing walls, etc.
Fragments of walls, etc.
Possible position of vanished walls, etc.

YARDS
20 0 20 40 60

CHAPTER TWO

The Forum

❧

IN all but the great heat of summer, which usually lasts from about mid-June to mid-September, the ideal programme for the rest of our exploration of the Capitol, Forum and Palatine is to begin the day with the church of S. Maria d'Aracoeli, going on, if we have not been able to see it the night before, to the Capitoline Museum. Then make our way by the Clivus Argentarius, the Mamertine prison and the church of SS. Cosma and Damiano, to the Forum. This will take us roughly from 9 a.m. to 12.30 p.m. If it was possible to visit the Capitoline Museum the night before, by 12.30 p.m. we should also have 'done' the Forum. As this is most convenient, we will treat our itinerary in this order; though in the great summer heat it is advisable to reverse the process, as in the middle of the day the Forum is stifling. This would mean our seeing the Capitoline Museum afterwards, if it was not possible to go there the night before. In July and August, therefore, go straight on from the Church of S. Maria d'Aracoeli to the Forum by the same route as before, leaving the cool rooms of the Capitoline museum, which is open till 2 p.m. on weekdays, also Tuesdays and Thursdays from 5 to 8 p.m. (and on Saturdays from 9 to 11.30 p.m.) until the afternoon which is the hottest time of the day. As always in Rome a sharp eye must be kept on opening and closing hours, which make the timing of sight-seeing something of a fine art.

We set off then from the Piazza Venezia, and if our courage fails at the sight of the Aracoeli's 122 very steep steps, we can take the easier way round by the *cordonata* and the Piazza del Campidoglio up the graceful and less breathtaking ones on the right of the Palazzo del Museo Capitolino. These, and the loggia above, are all that remain of the old Franciscan monastery of the Aracoeli since the building of the Victor Emanuel monument. Here in Augustus Hare's day the friars, who were famous dentists, still performed their useful but unaesthetic operations gratis every morning!

The **Church of the Aracoeli**, as it is usually familiarly called, is one of the most venerable foundations in Rome. Already in AD 574 a church standing on this site was considered old; attached to it was a Greek monastery (at that time Rome was governed by the Byzantine exarchs), which passed to the Benedictines in the tenth century and to the Franciscans in the thirteenth, and they restored and enlarged the existing church, which has probably changed little in its outward aspect since that day. Its surroundings would then have been much the same as in the previous century, when a bull of the Antipope Anacletus II (1130–8) confirmed the monastery's possession of 'the Capitol with its houses, crypts, cells, courts, gardens and trees . . . with its walls and columns'—a description which would have delighted Piranesi. But in the midst of these ruins something of the hill's ancient greatness still lived within the walls of the Church and Monastery of S. Maria in Capitolio, as it was then called, where the city elders met to discuss their affairs in the now vanished cloister, as the Senate had done each year in the Temple of Jupiter.

The twelfth-century *Mirabilia* tells the legend which accounts for the church's change of name. It states correctly that it was built on the site of the Temple of Juno Moneta (this housed the early Roman mint and from it our word money originated), but added to this both the Temple of Jupiter and an imperial palace. It was to this palace that according to the legend the Emperor Octavian, or Augustus, summoned the Tiburtine Sibyl in order to consult her because, 'to his consternation,' the Senate wished to honour him as a god'. The Sibyl prophesied that 'there are signs that justice will be done, soon the earth will be bathed in sweat and from the sun will descend the King of future centuries'. While she was speaking the emperor saw the heavens open and the Virgin robed in light standing on an altar, holding the Christ child in her arms; two voices called out from heaven: 'This is the Virgin who will receive in her womb the Saviour of the world—this is the altar of the Son of God.'

According to the legend, on the spot where he had seen the vision Augustus raised an altar—the *Ara Filii Dei* or *Ara Coeli*. Several medieval chroniclers mention the existence of the altar in the church, though the existing one of that name only dates from the thirteenth century. Further confirmation of the legend was seen in an antique column inscribed with the words

'*a cubiculo Augustorum*'—really signifying a domestic attendant of the imperial bedchamber. This column is the third on
the left in the nave of the church, and may have been brought
from the imperial palace on the Palatine, as all the columns
come from what must have been important classical buildings.

The legend probably owes its origin to the very early
medieval concept that the Roman Empire arose in order to aid
the spread of Christianity, and fell because instead it had protected idolatry. This was the explanation advanced by St.
Augustine in his *De Civitate Dei*, in order to combat the pagan
view which attributed the barbarian invasions to the abolition
of the old gods and the Palladium that had protected the city.
The identification of the legend with the Capitol and the
Emperor Octavian or Augustus may be attributed to the fact
that still in the eleventh century there was some quite large
building on the hill in the area of the Aracoeli known as the
camera or *palatium Octaviani*, where an emissary of the
Emperor Henry III was festively received.

The Aracoeli is perhaps the most typically Roman of all
Roman churches. Rising above the ruins of a temple dedicated
to a pagan mother-goddess and now consecrated to the
Madonna—a transformation which is far from rare in Italy—
its interior provides a perfect illustration of the continuity of
Roman life, with its magnificent columns that once graced
classical temples and palaces, and its cosmatesque pavement
and monuments gleaming with brilliant fragments of marbles
taken from the ancient ruins. The floor is chequered with the
tombstones of famous men who lived and worked in Rome
throughout the centuries, the walls are lined with the votive
chapels of historic Roman families, and the magnificent gilded
ceiling commemorates the papal fleet's participation in the
victory of Lepanto, which ended Turkish naval expansion in
the Mediterranean.

Simply to walk round the church is like turning the pages of
a history of Rome. Here we see the porphyry urn said to
contain the remains of S. Helena, the mother of Constantine,
resting upon the thirteenth-century altar, for long believed to
be Augustus's original Ara Coeli. Near by, in a corner of the
nave, is the funerary tablet of Felice de Fredi, discoverer of
the Laocoön. Farther down the nave is the Della Valle chapel,
where Pietro of that name, known from his travels as *il
pellegrino*, finally buried the body of his beautiful Persian wife

in 1626, after carrying it with him during five years' wanderings through Asia. The last chapel but one contains the most famous *presepio* or Christmas crib in Rome where, from Christmas Eve to Epiphany, the miracle-working figure of the Holy Child—the *Santo Bambino*—stands in all his glory. His swaddling bands are covered with jewels from top to toe, and there he receives the homage of Roman children, who recite 'sermons'—speeches and poems—from the small pulpit opposite.

On the other side of the church, just to the right of the door, is the Bufalini chapel, which contains the Aracoeli's greatest artistic treasure, Bernardino Pinturicchio's wonderful frescoes of the life and miracles of his patron S. Bernardino of Siena. In the cool light of morning these pictures glow with all the freshness of the Renaissance world; the piazza where S. Bernardino lies on his bier could well be a scene in any Italian city of the time, filled with human incident. The portrait of the donor, dressed in his best, stands in the left-hand corner of this masterpiece which he gave to posterity.

A Byzantine Madonna of the twelfth century looks out from among the baroque decoration of the high altar, while in the apse Augustus and the Tiburtine Sibyl are portrayed among the saints and angels, surely a rare occurrence for a pagan emperor, though this particular sibylline prophecy was one of the most influential in qualifying the sibyls to take their place in the decoration of Christian churches.

Before leaving the Aracoeli we must pay our respects to the 'Santo Bambino', that curious little figure said to have been carved out of the wood of one of the olive trees of the Garden of Gethsemane, which is so revered and loved by the Roman populace. Except at Christmas, he stands in a glass case above the altar of a small chapel of the sacristy when he is not out bringing comfort to the sick and dying in the hospitals of Rome. For although he no longer has his own personal coach but travels today in a prosaic taxi, the Bambino still carries on his mission as he has done since the seventeenth century or earlier. Reactions to him have been varied, from a nineteenth-century Frenchman who described him as 'a doll who most irreverently represents the divine Infant' to the Italian soldiers who stopped a cardinal's car when Mussolini was making a speech in the Piazza Venezia, but let it through instantly when they knew it was carrying the Bambino to a sick-bed. Count-

less tales are told about the Bambino. It is said that once early
in the eighteenth century a woman tried to steal him by pretending she was ill, asking for him to be left with her, and
exchanging him for a copy which she dressed in his clothes.
Nothing was suspected until the middle of the night when in
the midst of a furious storm the bells of the church rang and
there was a knocking at the door; the monks opened it and
found the Bambino naked on the threshold. Not long ago his
jewels were stolen—but within a week he was covered with
new ones. Nor is the Bambino's fame limited to Rome, for he
receives letters from all over the world often addressed just
to 'Il Bambino, Rome'. We can see them lying in front of
the altar—they are left there for a while, then burnt, un-
opened.

Midnight on Christmas Eve is the greatest occasion of the
year at the Aracoeli. Then its precipitous steps are thronged
and the crisp air resounds to the tune of bagpipes as the
pifferari, who before the unification of Italy used to come
down from their mountains to serenade the street-side shrines
of the Madonna in Advent, still come to play their old pastoral
airs to the 'Santo Bambino'. These shepherd pipers look as if
they had stepped out of a picture by Pinelli or Roesler
Franz, in their traditional dress of sandals with criss-cross
leather thongs, short breeches with sheepskin chaps, velvet
jackets and billycock hats. They present a striking contrast to
the glittering gold and blazing chandeliers of the church's
interior, but they have formed part of the Roman Christmas
scene for centuries, as a reminder of those other shepherds who
watched their flocks on the hills round Bethlehem.

On a sunny morning, seen from the little garden behind the
church, the ruins of the Forum are apt to look very stark after
our first sight of them in the kindly darkness the night before.
But the impression is a momentary one. Once we are in their
midst, their broken columns and roofless walls appear in
another perspective and the sheer human history of every
stone makes the whole thing live. So let us take the quickest
way down the steps of the Scala dell' Arce Capitolina, cross
the Via di S. Pietro in Carcere, and so find ourselves at once
in an ancient Roman street, the Clivus Argentarius. The word
Clivus implied a steeply rising street—hence our word decli-
vity for a downward slope—and this one led to the Campus
Martius past the Basilica Argentaria, the banking centre and

Stock Exchange of ancient Rome, when its worn paving must have been as crowded as Threadneedle Street.

From here we emerge into the Via del Tulliano, called after one of the oldest relics of early Rome. The Tullianum was formerly believed to have been a prison built by Servius Tullius, but now generally recognised as a water cistern, probably built after the Gauls sacked Rome in 387 BC. The Tullianum did indeed later serve as a prison; it was the lower vault of the dread Mamertine, where the enemies of Rome—vanquished chieftains and soldiers like Jugurtha, Vercingetorix and Simon Bar Giora—died of starvation or were strangled, and state prisoners such as the Catiline conspirators and Tiberius's fallen favourite, Sejanus, were executed.

Today the prison is a chapel, **S. Pietro in Carcere**, as according to legend Nero had S. Peter imprisoned there. It stands on the corner to our right, beneath the church of S. Giuseppe dei Falegnami. A double modern stair leads down to the entrance of this chapel-prison, whose consecration has not robbed it of its horror. The upper trapezoidal chamber, the Mamertine prison proper, was in ancient times only connected to the Tullianum by a hole in the floor, through which prisoners were flung to await death by starvation or at the hands of an executioner in the charnel house below. Here Vercingetorix was thrown and later strangled, and Jugurtha fell naked. Defiant to the end, he laughed and exclaimed: 'Oh, Hercules, how cold your bath is'; he died of starvation after six days. The only other exit from this place of horror, darkness and stench was a drain leading to the Cloaca Maxima which was used for the disposal of the corpses. A modern stair now leads into the Tullianum, where an altar has been erected with a relief representing S. Peter baptising his gaoler. When Charles Dickens was in Rome the curious custom obtained of hanging in this gruesome place the instruments of violent crimes, and the walls were covered with rusty daggers, knives, pistols and clubs.

From the horror of ancient Rome we now turn to the scene of her greatness, but before we reach the Forum we pass the fine baroque church of SS. Martina and Luca, built over the secretariat of the Senate, and then make our way to **SS. Cosma e Damiano**. This church was built in what was the library of Vespasian's Forum of Peace and was dedicated in the sixth century to the Arabian doctors martyred under

MUSEI E MONUMENTI COMUNALI

TARIFFA GIORNI FERIALI

Tassa d'ingresso
L. 100

SERIE VI

№ 212137

I.G.E. CORRISPOSTA
COME DA SPECIALE CONVENZIONE

CONSERVARE IL BIGLIETTO
PER IL CONTROLLO

Diocletian. It is reached by way of the short flight of steps beyond the Forum entrance, crossing Via in Miranda and the small grass patch beyond, and turning right into the monastery building, whose cloister has to be traversed in order to enter the church. The sixth-century mosaic in the apse of SS. Cosma e Damiano is one of the finest and earliest in Rome and has been used as a model for many others; what particularly distinguishes it from the rest, however, is that here something of the mastery and style of the Hellenistic tradition have survived. SS. Peter and Paul and the two martyrs, attired in sumptuous red and violet robes, stand out as living persons against the dark blue mosaic of the sky, while the figure of Christ, swathed in golden draperies and holding in his hand the scroll of a classical orator, appears to be descending a stairway of purple clouds. Palm trees and flowers glitter with gold, but the bees hovering above those in the left-hand corner indicate that this part of the mosaic was restored in the seventeenth century by the Barberini Pope, Urban VIII, whose family coat of arms bears three bees.

It is a great pity that the model reconstruction of imperial Rome has been removed to the distant modern suburb of the E.U.R. instead of being kept, as it formerly was, near the Capitol, where it was of more practical use to the sight-seer. But in its absence we must try to reconstruct in our mind's eye the Forum as it was, not only in imperial times, but at different periods in its history. In doing this we will not examine all the monuments in detail or trace their often very complicated and debatable building history, as admirable archaeological guide-books exist for this purpose, but rather by the selection of individual buildings try to evoke a picture of the part the Forum played in the life of ancient Rome, and its influence upon succeeding generations. This will not always be very easy as so much has been overlaid by buildings of the imperial era, though the heroic days of the Forum, when it was the real centre of the city's life, were those of the Republic. And one is sometimes apt to forget that the Republic lasted almost as long as the Empire—482 years from the expulsion of the kings in 510 BC to the beginning of Augustus's reign in 28 BC as compared with the western Empire's 504 years, ending with the deposition of the shadowy figure of Romulus Augustulus in AD 476—though after the foundation of Constantinople in AD 330 Rome was but a capital in name.

Just for a moment as we enter **the Forum** from the Via dei Fori Imperiali, let us try and picture something of its early days and the people who made it what it was. The Forum was originally a marshy valley or *marrana*, like many to be found in the *Campagna*, with a cemetery beside a rough highway. This last probably belonged to the Iron Age hut village that existed on the Palatine between the end of the ninth and the beginning of the sixth century BC. The Romans identified the beginnings of the Forum with the legendary founding of their city by Romulus in 753 BC when the war with the Sabines of the Quirinal—touched off by the rape of their women—had ended. According to Roman tradition two of the places which we can still see in the Forum dated from this period, the Vulcanal—sacred to the protector of the forge, where Romulus and the Sabine leader Titus Tatius made their peace—and its earliest meeting place, the Comitium.

About this time a village of rough thatched huts, like those which shepherds still build in the *Campagna*, had probably grown up along the highway, and also a market. The people who met in this market—Latins and Sabines—were of pastoral farming stock, men who counted their wealth in head of cattle, *pecunia*, and made offerings of milk to their gods. They were deeply religious people, recognising a mysterious power or *numen* in every aspect of the world around them, which they named and personified—thus Jupiter represented the sky and sunlight; Mars, who later became the God of War, was the spirit of the fields. Religion entered into every aspect of their daily life, so there were presiding deities of the house and store-cupboard, Lares and Penates, Janus the guardian of doors and gates and, of course, Vesta the protectress of the household fire.

These early Romans were a sober purposeful people, admiring the stoic virtues of discipline, industry and frugality, but from the first they seem to have possessed what we would call a community spirit, and also an aptitude for reasonableness and conciliation. *Clementia* was their word for it—and no doubt it was this *clementia* that brought about the peace between the Latins and the Sabines. Thus, as we would expect from such a people, the earliest identifiable sites in the Forum were of a religious and social nature—the Vulcanal and the Comitium; to these were added the Temple of Janus whose site has been lost, and whose doors were only opened in time of war—for these farmers who transformed Mars into a God of War were also born soldiers. To Numa the second King of Rome's reign, tradition dates the building of the Regia and the Temple of Vesta; this accords with his reputation in later times as the alleged founder and co-ordinator of Roman state religion, and it is significant that the Regia continued to be associated with the high priest or Pontifex Maximus right through the Empire. The building of the earliest Curia, the official meeting place of the Senate beside the Comitium, is attributed to Tullus Hostilius, the third king, and the final draining of the Forum by means of the Cloaca Maxima to one or other of the Tarquins, the last of the kings.

These, then, were the earliest buildings in the Forum, and it is interesting to note that they already delimited the area which right until the end continued to be regarded as the hub of the city—the Comitium or small square before the Curia and the larger open space, or Forum proper, beside the Via Sacra, bounded at its east end by the Regia and Temple of Vesta. Great temples and basilicas subsequently rose around these spaces, commemorative monuments were erected in them, and the name Forum Romanum came to apply to the whole of the valley, but its heart and core still always remained these two small squares and the ancient sacred sites grouped around them.

It is remarkable that although we are inclined to think of Rome as the Eternal City and of the Romans as citizens, they for long continued to regard themselves as men of the soil. The anecdotes which they cherished about their early heroes illustrate this—one has only to think of old Cincinnatus in the first half of the fifth century BC, ploughing a field in his shirt, and his wife hastily wrapping on his toga in order to receive the senatorial delegation announcing his nomination as dictator. Or of Manius Curius Dentatus some hundred years later, found by the Samnite ambassadors in his cottage eating turnips, but who nevertheless expounded to them his astonishing view of life: 'I don't want gold, what I want is to govern the men who own it.' This attitude was typical of the early Roman leaders. G. Fabricius Luscinus, who went to Tarentum to negotiate with Pyrrhus in 280 BC, reacted in the same way to the king's offers of money and attempts to frighten him by the sudden appearance of an elephant: 'Your gold does not attract me nor does your monster frighten me,' he said. But he opened Pyrrhus's eyes to the power wielded by men like himself when he refused the king's invitation to remain with him and help him by replying: 'If I come to help you, your subjects will end by preferring me to you—and where will you be then?' Fabricius was a plebeian statesman who served twice as Consul, three times as a tribune, once as a censor and once as an aedile, all elective offices, so he knew what he was talking about. Such then were the men who made the Forum what it was and received their training in statesmanship there in the Senate House and the Assembly of the people—the men who gave the letters S.P.Q.R. their meaning and later carried them to the ends of the known world.

Though they revered it as the cradle of their institutions, the Romans continued to alter, add to and rebuild the temples and other buildings in the Forum. This was partly due to damage by fire and earthquake but also to their desire to make it worthy of the growing power of Rome. Augustus's pride in having found Rome a city of brick and transformed it into one of marble is typical of this attitude; the idea is still alive in Italian minds today—things are considered worthy or unworthy of the '*decoro della città*'.

The first building on our right as we enter the Forum, the **Basilica Aemilia**, affords a perfect illustration of this point of view that changed a market into a meeting place surrounded by palaces, for the porticoes and basilicas where the ordinary Roman men in the street met and did business were as rich in marbles and sculpture as any king's house. In the early days of the fifth century BC the site of the Basilica Aemilia was occupied by a row of butchers' shops. According to the legend it was from one of these that Virginia's father seized the knife which he plunged into her heart rather than allow her to be seduced by the Decemvir Appius Claudius. The precise spot is said still to be marked by the circular shrine of the Venus Cloacina, built where the Cloaca Maxima enters the Forum in the portico of the Basilica Aemilia.

In time the butchers' shops were replaced by the more aesthetically pleasing ones of the money changers, and these in their turn were concealed by the portico built on the Forum side of the basilica, which Pliny considered to be one of the three most beautiful buildings in the world. It was the second of its kind to be built in Rome in 179 BC—the first was the Sempronia on the other side of the Forum—and it came to be called after M. Aemilius Lepidius, one of the censors who built it. But it is interesting to note that the building of the splendid new basilica did not result in the money changers being ousted: their shops remained lining its outer wall—camouflaged later by a portico—and the basilica became their centre, but the whole layout was now much more consonant with the dignity of the Forum of a great republic than simply a row of shops.

As basilicas are generally considered to be a peculiarly Roman contribution to architecture and certainly played a large part in Roman life, later even being taken as models for the great Christian churches, it is well worth our while to pause for a moment and study what they were really like. Basically they were great halls, with 'aisles' divided by one or two rows of columns from the central 'nave' which had a higher ceiling than the rest of the building and was lit by clerestory windows. Porticoes usually lined one or more of the outer walls of the building and were often connected to the great hall by an open colonnade. Caesar's Basilica Julia, on the other side of the Forum on the site of the old Sempronia, was built in this style; the Aemilia had an open portico at one end and the row of money changers' shops incorporated into the portico on the side facing the Forum. Later basilicas often had one or more apses in the side or end walls, like the last to be built in Rome, begun by Maxentius and completed by Constantine. The building in Rome today which gives us the clearest picture of what the interior of these ancient basilicas was like is the Christian one of St. Paul's Without the Walls.

The basilicas were built as general meeting places for business transactions, as in the case of the Aemilia, but also for use as law courts, like the Basilica Julia, and in time any city of the Empire worthy of the name had at least one basilica. The name basilica was, of course, derived from the Greek, and some eminent authorities consider that the building too was inspired by the Greek peristyles, but so far no one has explained why the Romans evolved the particular form they did; my personal belief is that the airless summer heat of the Forum supplies the explanation.

On a stifling August day buildings like the Basilica Aemilia would have been much cooler than any Roman tenement house, or than anything that exists in Rome today except their Christian counterparts. Perhaps it was this coolness combined with the belief that Rome was eternal—whatever happened in the world outside, Rome would continue—that persuaded the money changers to carry on business as usual on that fateful 23 August AD 410 with a Gothic army at the gates. Relics of their misplaced optimism can still be seen in the green stains which mark the Basilica Aemilia's marble pavement, for they are copper coins fused into the stone by the heat of the fire when the Goths, who entered the city during the night, sacked Rome. Nowhere else in the city is the scene brought so vividly before our eyes as by these few scattered coins. For six days the savage tribesmen sacked imperial Rome, the mistress of the world, and it must have seemed as if civilisation itself was crashing into ruins with the great basilica on that sultry August night.

Plenty of inflammable material was lying close at hand, as the **Argiletum**—the paved street at the far end of the Basilica Aemilia—was the Paternoster Row of ancient Rome, the centre of the booksellers and copyists. It was also the haunt of a much less respectable brotherhood, the pickpockets, who must have mingled with the crowds coming from the populous Suburra, to which the street ultimately led. Crossing the Argiletum we find ourselves in a small open space—it seems very small to have seen so much history: this is the **Comitium**. Admittedly in Republican times it was larger, and in it stood the original Rostra or platform from which orators addressed the people, that took its name from the *rostra*, or beaks of ships, captured at the battle of Anzio in 338 BC. This Rostra was built so that speakers could address people standing in the Comitium on one side or in the Forum on the other, and it came to be regarded as a sign of democratic independence for an orator to turn and address the less select crowd standing in the Forum. The Comitium also contained the *Graecostasis*—the predecessor of our distinguished strangers' gallery—where foreign ambassadors sat while the Senate was in session in the **Curia**, the austere red brick building on our right.

The Curia was rebuilt many times after its legendary foundation by Tullus Hostilius and the one which we now see dates from Diocletian's reign (AD 284–305). According to tradition, Romulus first summoned the 100 *patres*, or heads of families, from which the Senate originated, and throughout twelve centuries of Roman history it endured, long after the People's Assembly had ceased to exist. But before the rise of Julius Caesar the Senate's glory had departed and after the first century AD it had no control over affairs. Still, as we have seen, the magic of its name was such that it could kindle men's imagination in the Middle Ages with dreams of ancient glory.

Something of this aura of past greatness is transmitted to us as we enter the Curia. The stark simplicity of the great hall conveys the same atmosphere of majesty which we feel in the Pantheon. It is useless to remind ourselves that the senators who met in this third-century building were mere ciphers, for our minds fly back to their predecessors—the magistrates who remained to face the invading Gaul, wrapped in their purple-bordered robes, ivory wand in hand, seated on their curule chairs. They perished, but their story is immortal, as is Pyrrhus's ambassador's description of the Senate of his day— 'it is an assembly of kings', he said.

Sad to relate, the one great struggle that the Curia which we see today really did witness was that of the last leaders of pagan Rome against newly-triumphant Christianity. It was fought over the removal of the golden statue of the 'Goddess of Victory', which stood on an altar at the far end. Before the statue the senators took the oath of loyalty to the Empire and at the beginning of each session they performed the ancient rite of offering her wine and incense. The statue was removed by imperial edict in AD 357; to the conservative senators who saw the temples of the gods being closed around them in the Forum, this must have seemed the ultimate blow. Their feelings were voiced by their leader Symmachus in four petitions to the emperor. Speaking in the name of Rome, in one of them he wrote: 'This religion has reduced the world under my laws. These rites have repelled Hannibal from the city and the Gauls from the Capitol.' The goddess was returned to her place for two years in AD 392 but in 394 she disappeared for ever, and the conservative pagan element in the city saw in Alaric's sack of Rome the pagan gods' revenge. In the seventh century the Curia was converted into the church of S. Hadrian, and one wonders what Symmachus would have felt if he had known that it would be under the aegis of a Christian saint that the last Senate House would survive practically intact into the twentieth century, as Professor Bartoli found it when it was restored in 1937.

If in the Curia we see the end of ancient Rome, under a strange-looking shed on the opposite side of the Comitium we see what may be a monument to its founder. For the famous black marble pavement, or Lapis Niger, was evidently laid down over ruined monuments that were regarded as particularly sacred and are certainly exceedingly ancient; for one thing they contain the oldest known inscription in Latin, written in characters that still resemble the Greek alphabet. The general consensus of opinion is that these were funerary monuments built about the end of the sixth century BC and that possibly one of them was the tomb or cenotaph of Romulus; but after so many years of learned battle on the subject, it would be a brave man indeed who ventured upon a more definite opinion.

Dominating the whole of this area stands the triumphal **Arch of Septimius Severus**. According to the inscription which appears on both sides, it was erected in AD 203 in his honour and that of his sons Caracalla and Geta. After the murder of his brother, however, the guilty Caracalla had his name erased and the words '*optimis fortissimisque principibus*' added after his own, but the original lettering can still be traced in the fourth line of the inscription. Like the basilica the triumphal arch was a peculiarly Roman contribution to architecture; of the many which once stood in Rome, only three have survived in anything like their original state, but their influence has been widespread—we have only to think of the Arc de Triomphe and the Marble Arch as the most obvious examples.

The Arch of Septimius Severus, however, appears to have exercised a greater influence than either that of Titus or Constantine. The reclining gods in the spandrels on the side facing the Capitol were the prototypes of hundreds of such figures sculptured or painted above the doors of Renaissance palaces and country houses throughout Europe. A replica of the arch formed the entrance of the imperial palace in Berlin, while in its partly buried state it plainly inspired the 'ruined' gateway of the Archangelskoe, the Yusopovs' country seat on the far-away plains of Russia. Septimius Severus's arch was also a favourite subject of the French eighteenth-century artist Hubert Robert—Robert des Ruines as he was called—whose exquisite drawings were such a potent influence in spreading the taste for 'picturesque' ruins throughout Europe.

The Arch of Septimius Severus did not bestride the Via Sacra. The stage-managers of the Holy Roman Emperor Charles V's triumph therefore made a mistake in building the road for his procession through it, a road incidentally which resulted in the destruction of two churches, 400 houses and a good deal of damage to the ancient monuments of the Forum. But they acted in good faith, as for centuries the popes had followed a similar route in their stately cavalcade known as '*il possesso*' when they rode from their coronation at St. Peter's to the Lateran to 'take possession' of the temporal power. The circuitous route they followed must have been specially designed to take them past many of the ancient monuments of Rome, no doubt in order to link the Christian Pontifex Maximus with his imperial predecessors—for the Roman Emperors automatically assumed the office of Pontifex Maximus until the Christian Emperor Gratian (reigned 373–82) refused the title.

Looking across the modern road which separates the Forum from the Capitol, we can see a rough rubble platform, partly faced with stone, all that remains of the **Temple of Concord**. Dedicated in 367 BC, the temple was built to commemorate the end of what was probably one of the toughest political battles in Roman history—a real case of diamond cut diamond—between the Senate and the Plebs. It is said that for five years the Tribunes of the Plebs held up the government of Rome by using the paralysing tribunician veto—no Russian could do better today!—but in the end, under the leadership of the Tribunes Licinius and Sextius, the Plebs won, the Senate gave way, and the Licinio-Sextian laws were passed, the most important clause of which permitted plebeians to be elected as consuls.

Beside the Temple of Concord stand the three beautiful Corinthian columns of that of Vespasian, one of the landmarks of the Forum throughout the centuries of decay. The low colonnade to the left is the reconstructed **Porticus Deorum Consentium** another reminder of the last days of paganism, as an inscription tells us that it was restored by the prefect of the city in AD 368. This would have been during the reign of Julian the Apostate, whose passion for Homer and ancient literature generally caused him to start a pagan reaction.

Just to the left of the Arch of Septimius Severus and covered by a protective roof is the famous **Vulcanal**, or Altar of Vulcan, dating according to tradition from the time of Romulus. All that we can see now is a block of living rock surrounded by a rough wall of the same tufa. Originally the Vulcanal seems to have been something like Livy's description of the sanctuary of the oak tree on the Capitol, for Pliny records that in his day an ancient lotus tree (probably the *Celtis australis* or nettle tree) grew there. This was believed to be older than Rome itself and had roots reaching right to the other side of the Curia under the Forum of Caesar; the Vulcanal also contained statues and honorary monuments, including one said to be of Romulus, and a quadriga dedicated by him.

The superb fourth-century portico of the **Temple of Saturn** which soars up by the Vulcanal may well have had equally ancient beginnings, as according to legend the god was welcomed to Rome by Janus, and took up his residence at the foot of the Capitol. This description would correspond with the position of the existing temple ruins and an earlier temple is known to have been inaugurated upon the same site in 497 BC. Saturn's name was derived from the verb 'to sow', and the Romans believed that he had taught them agriculture; his statue in the temple was filled with olive oil and he was represented holding a pruning knife in his hand.

It was no doubt the connection of ideas between agriculture and riches that resulted in Saturn's temple being used as the state treasury. The treasure was kept in a room excavated in the side of the steps leading up to the portico, and here, after he had seized power, Julius Caesar found fifteen thousand gold bars, thirty thousand silver ones and thirty million sestertii. Part of this treasure was earmarked as a special emergency fund to be used only in the event of a Gallic invasion; with dry humour the conqueror of Gaul said that he felt he was entitled to break into this as he had ensured that there would be no more Gallic invasions!

The Temple of Saturn was naturally the centre of the six days' celebrations of the December festival of the Saturnalia, or what was in effect the pagan Christmas. During this time schools were closed, all rank and formality were laid aside, and slaves sat at table with their masters or were even waited on by them. It was indeed a time of good will to all men, and presents were exchanged between people of all classes; the commonest were candles and, for children, clay dolls. A special fair was held by the makers of these during the festive season, which must have closely resembled the Advent fair in the Piazza Navona today, where the small clay figures for the Christmas cribs are sold.

Turning our backs on the Temple of Saturn, we walk down

the western branch of the Sacred Way and find ourselves in the square which was the **Forum** proper. It is almost as difficult for an English man or woman to understand what the Forum meant in the lives of the Romans as it is easy for a modern Italian, whose piazza is descended directly from it and plays very much the same part in his life. A few years ago an architectural critic said that Italians today pay little attention to the interior planning of their houses and, like the ancient Romans, have the smallest bedrooms, because they have the largest and finest 'parlours', in the sense that a parlour is a place to meet and talk in, and that is exactly what a piazza is and what the Forum was, especially under the Empire. In Republican times the square had been the centre of every aspect of the city's life both grave and gay: the great religious ceremonies were held there, it was the scene of triumphs, sacrifices and important funerals, and was also a law court where the praetor, seated on his tribunal, gave judgment in full sight of the people. The early gladiatorial games were held there and sometimes sacrificial banquets, later it was the scene of elections and orators addressed the crowds, official communications of all kinds were posted up in it—edicts, prescription lists, the results of lawsuits and so on. But at the same time the Forum was the meeting place of everyone, from the briefless barrister in search of a client to the farmer up for a day from the country to sell his produce.

Today we see the Forum as an empty open space with grass growing among the paving stones and a few columns soaring up to remind us of what must have been. But let us half close our eyes and picture it surrounded with tall buildings and colonnades. It is not so difficult if we look at the temples at the far end, on the left that of Antoninus and Faustina, with its magnificent flight of steps which were the distinguishing feature of Roman temples as opposed to those of Greece, and on the right the three remaining columns of the Temple of Castor and Pollux. If we imagine the Basilica Aemilia on our left and the Basilica Julia on our right rising to a similar height, and the temples on the Capitol towering up behind us, we will quickly realise how small the open space of the Forum actually was, and readily understand why until the end of the Republic it was kept jealously clear.

Until the end of the Republic the only monuments the open-spaced Forum contained, if we can call them so, were in a

small piece of open ground, which still exists, planted with a
fig tree, an olive and a vine—the traditional trees of Italian
agriculture (they have recently been replanted). In their midst
stood a statue of Marsyas, suspended from a tree awaiting his
punishment for having had the temerity to challenge Apollo to
a musical contest. This statue was regarded as a warning
against presumption and as a symbol of the citizen's liberty. A
little farther on, the pavement of the square is interrupted by
an irregular triangular area containing a well-head, known as
the Lacus Curtius. This was enclosed by a railing and was
regarded as a sacred spot. According to legend, a bottomless
fissure appeared here and was only closed when Marcus
Curtius jumped into it on his horse. The area was, however,
certainly preserved as a reminder of the days when the Forum
was a marsh.

This then was how the Forum appeared when Julius Caesar
started to put into effect his plans for its enlargement and
embellishment. He reorientated the square slightly towards
the north-west and began building the Basilica Julia on its
south-western side and a new and splendid **Rostra**, whose
remains we see today, at the Capitoline end. In order to relieve
congestion Caesar transferred the electoral meetings, which
had been held in the Forum instead of the Comitium since
145 BC, to the Saepta Julia which he had specially built for the
purpose in the Campus Martius, and built a new Forum of his
own behind the Curia.

All these plans and innovations of Julius Caesar's were no
doubt well-intended and a change of some kind was probably
long overdue. Nevertheless, like his own meteoric career, they
marked the end of an epoch and constituted the first step in the
Forum's decline from being the living centre of a community
into the place of idle gossip that it became under his successors. We have only to recall Horace's 'as I was walking idly
down the Sacred Way', and his evening stroll in the Forum to
watch the fortune-tellers, and the idle games played in the
Basilica Julia which have left their traces in the pavement, and
contrast this world with all that the Forum had stood for in
the great days of the Republic, to realise the transformation
that had come about even in Augustus's reign. Already the
reins of power were in the hands of the *Princeps* and his
advisers 'the friends of Caesar', whereas before they had been
in the firm grasp of the Senate and the people.

It is significant that as the Forum ceased to have any real purpose its area shrank as more and more monuments encroached upon it. Augustus completed the Basilica Julia and the fine new Rostra that Julius Caesar had begun; incidentally it was from here that Mark Antony made his famous speech after Caesar's murder. The dictator's body had been brought to lie in state in the Forum after his murder in Pompey's theatre and, stirred by Mark Antony's oration, the sorrowing crowds piled up chairs and benches to make an improvised pyre. We can see the actual spot, where the base of the altar of his temple still stands at the south-eastern end of the Forum. Suetonius described the scene in all its drama, with women flinging their jewels on the fire, veterans the arms they had borne in Caesar's campaigns, and the professional mourners tearing the robes he had worn for his four triumphs and throwing them into the flames. Afterwards the enraged crowds seized brands from the pyre and rushed to try and set fire to the houses of Brutus and Cassius.

In that fire the Republic perished and Caesar emerged from it as something more than human. A column was erected on the spot—the first monument to mortal man to be built within the sacred precincts of the Forum; during Augustus's reign Caesar's altar and temple replaced the column and he was officially deified. Although the ancestral cult had long formed an important part of Roman life, this deification of a man and the institution of his temple and cult in the area so long and jealously preserved as the centre of civic life and liberty is an outward sign of the profound psychological change that the Romans had undergone since the great days of the Republic. Afterwards the deification of dead emperors was to become almost as automatic as their assumption of absolute power, and the Palatine replaced the Forum as the real centre of the Roman world.

As the imperial palace on the Palatine grew so the Forum shrank, physically as well as morally. Triumphal arches to Augustus and Tiberius were built along its fringes, and Domitian even dared to set up his own equestrian statue in it —he earned the Senate's 'damnatio memoriae' for that and other things. In Diocletian's reign mere citizens were commemorated there by seven honorary columns and Constantine, who resuscitated that Roman anathema, a hereditary monarchy, also erected his own equestrian statue. Three hundred years later, in AD 608, its last monument was added to the Forum—one which would have shocked Symmachus more perhaps than the removal of the Goddess of Victory—a column placed in the centre of the square in honour of a Byzantine usurper, Phocas, who had made a gift of the Pantheon to Pope Boniface IV. Ironically enough this was for centuries one of the Forum's most conspicuous monuments and one of the earliest to be excavated, with funds provided by the Duchess of Devonshire.

Turning our backs on the Forum and walking east, with the whispering clump of bay trees that marks the site of Caesar's temple on our left, we are confronted by the ruins of a small circular white marble temple whose rites remained immutable for over a thousand years in a changing world—the **Temple of Vesta**. The ruin that we see today has been recomposed from the fragments of the temple rebuilt after the fire of AD 191 by Septimius Severus and Julia Domna. Several previous temples on the same site had been destroyed by fire, but from reproductions on coins and literary descriptions we know that the temple had always been round, though its style and building materials had changed through the ages. According to Ovid it had originally been thatched and had walls of woven osiers. This is confirmed by the general archaeological opinion of today that the temple's circular shape dates right back to the huts of primitive Rome, like the thatched 'house of Romulus' which was kept in continual repair beside the marble walls of the palaces on the Palatine.

The preservation of the original hut-form of the temple was consonant with the archaic simplicity which surrounded every aspect of the cult of Vesta and of the lives of the Vestal virgins who ministered to it. For the sanctity of the fire that burnt continually on the altar, and symbolised the perpetuity of the State, no doubt had its origins in far distant times when fire was a precious thing to be carefully tended and guarded—a task which naturally fell to young girls, the daughters, probably, of the king or tribal leader, in whose house it would have been kept for greater safety. This, at any rate, was the opinion of Frazer, author of *The Golden Bough*. It is borne out by the fact that the temple and the house of the Vestal virgins stand just beside the Regia, which was traditionally supposed to have been the house of the Priest-King Numa Pompilius and was certainly closely associated, possibly as a sort of office, with the Pontifex Maximus, who stood *in loco parentis* to the Vestal virgins.

The Vestals' house, or *Atrium Vestae* as it was called, owing to its being built in the patrician style round a rose-filled court or atrium, is without doubt the most evocative place in the whole of the Forum today. A short flight of steps beside the white marble shrine, which contained the statue of the goddess, leads us directly into what must have been a long and elegant garden court, surrounded by marble colonnades, with three pools in the centre. The existing house dates from the second century AD but it was built over an earlier and simpler one and there is no doubt that the origins of the Vestals' home date right back to the beginnings of the Forum. In atmosphere it must have resembled those austere convents for ladies of rank which grew up in Christian Rome, great walled enclosures grouped around tranquil cloisters, to which the noise of the city hardly penetrated. But even these cannot have equalled the style and grandeur in which the Vestals lived, at least in later times; the ground floor alone of their house comprises some fifty rooms and closets, and there were two or possibly even three upper floors. As in Roman palaces today, the Vestals probably lived on the first floor, while the ground floor would have been mainly given over to store-rooms and domestic offices—we can still see the remains of what were a kitchen, flour mill and bakery.

Its very spaciousness must have added to the sombre grandeur of the Vestals' house, for only six priestesses lived there, two of whom would have been quite young, even small, girls, as Vestals were recruited between the ages of six and ten. Like certain orders of nuns today, their hair was cut off when they entered the sisterhood and hung on the sacred lotus tree as an offering. When it grew again it was dressed in archaic style with six pads of artificial hair divided by narrow bands and adorned with a fillet resembling a diadem with pendent strips on either side. The Vestals were always dressed in long white robes, but when sacrificing had a curious insignia of their own—a white hood bordered with purple which was fastened on the breast with a brooch. This was the only ornament they were allowed as they were expected to be as austere in their dress as in their lives—Livy mentions the case of a Vestal being denounced and rebuked by the Pontifex Maximus for giving way to her taste for personal adornment.

The Vestals' lives were a curious mixture of extreme austerity and great privilege, but the benefits of the latter seem to have out-weighed the former, for although they could officially resign and marry, very few of them ever did so. For one thing they were very well off, being maintained by the State which provided them with a large dowry that they could spend as they wished. Socially they had precedence over everyone except the empress and only she and they were allowed to drive in Rome in carriages. The highest authorities—even consuls and praetors—made way for them in the street and special places were reserved for them in the theatres and at the gladiatorial games. They enjoyed enormous influence: a condemned criminal could be reprieved simply by their asking if they passed him in the street, and their intercessions in general bore tremendous weight—for instance they saved Julius Caesar from Sulla's prescription—and wills and important documents of all kinds were entrusted to them for safe-keeping.

On the other side of the medal there was the penalty of being entombed alive if they transgressed their oath of thirty years' virginity, and the long intricate ritual that governed their whole existence and took ten years to learn. We do not know how long the watches were that the Vestals kept over the sacred fire, but it could never have been left for one instant, as its extinction was a national calamity which earned the attendant Vestal a scourging by the Pontifex Maximus. In the violent storms of wind and rain to which Rome is subject, its care could have been an anxious task in a small temple whose roof was pierced by a vent hole. In some secret hiding place in their house or temple the Vestals kept the sacred pledges of Rome's sway, one of which was the Palladium, reputedly a small wooden figure of Pallas Athene brought by Aeneas from Troy, another dire responsibility in a city so subject to devastating fires as ancient Rome.

Apart from these awe-inspiring responsibilities, the sacred duties of the Vestals were of a curiously housewifely character; they had to fetch water, carrying it on their heads from the fairly distant fountain of Egeria, and depositing it in a special marble tank. When used for ritual purposes this water was purified with salt, itself purified by being baked in an earthen jar in an oven. The Vestals also had the job of cooking special sacrificial salt cakes called *mola salsa*, used in sacred ceremonies; these were made from the very first ears of ripened grain, pounded in archaic style in a mortar. The ritual cleaning of the temple with special mops was naturally one of their functions, also its decoration with bay or laurel which was changed once a year, on 1 March when the sacred fire was rekindled by the ancient method of rubbing a piece of wood against a plaque cut from a fruit tree. All these tasks had to be performed with the simplest of utensils, such as ordinary undecorated clay ware of the humblest kind.

The archaic simplicity of the Vestals' duties and their homely character confirms the supposition that their ritual was probably a survival of the domestic routine of early times. This is borne out by the fact that the religious functions at which they had to assist were connected with the oldest rites of primitive Italian agriculture, such as the harvest and vintage festivals and the Lupercalia.

So austere were the lives the Vestal virgins led and so great the esteem in which they were held that their order survived until AD 394, long after Christianity had become the religion of the emperors. Although the order was abolished by an imperial decree of Theodosius, there is good reason to suppose that feminine influence was at the root of the summary treatment the Vestals then received. At this time the Emperor's niece Serena (who was also the foster-mother of his son and successor Honorius) was in Rome, and the wife of the Vandal general Stilicho, the *de facto* ruler of the Western Empire. Both husband and wife were violent, and not altogether disinterested, enemies of paganism and were instrumental in having many of the Roman temples closed. By Stilicho's orders the Sibylline books were burnt and the gold removed from the doors of the Capitoline Temple of Jupiter, and part at least of the loot is said to have found its way into his pockets. Serena seems to have taken a particularly active part in the suppression of the Vestals, and is said to have robbed the goddess of a fabulous necklace, for which she was cursed by one of the virgin priestesses. The hatred Serena evidently inspired found its outlet fifteen years later when, during Alaric's second siege of Rome, she was strangled by order of the Senate for alleged communication with the enemy.

Some evidence of the hatreds involved in this last struggle between the triumphant Christians and the conservative pagan element is still to be seen in the house of the Vestals. The name and inscription have been erased from one of the Vestals' statues standing in the atrium. It is believed that this may have represented the Vestal Claudia, who about AD 364 was converted to Christianity. Her face has a look of calm determination and one feels that her change of faith cannot have been determined by reasons of political expediency, as was often the case at that time. But to her sister priestesses Claudia was a traitor, and the bitterness of their hatred is evidently reflected in their decision not simply to remove her statue but to leave it standing there, nameless, as a perpetual reminder of her ignominy. Thus she was found when the Vestals' house was excavated in the last century. Some traces were also found of the house's subsequent tenants—imperial and, later, papal officials—in two hidden hoards of gold coins (one of them strangely enough Anglo-Saxon), buried no doubt during later sacks of Rome. But in spite of all the archaeologists' hopes that some light might be cast upon the holy of holies where the Palladium and other sacred objects once lay hidden, not a clue was found—true to their tradition the last of the Vestals had evidently carried the secrets of their order with them to the grave.

Emerging from the House of the Vestals and skirting the temple, we turn left along a narrow paved street which is dominated by the three remaining beautiful Corinthian columns of the **Temple of Castor and Pollux**. This is also one of the very ancient sacred sites in the Forum, originally dedicated in 484 BC to the brothers of Helen of Troy who, according to legend, brought the news of the victory of Lake Regillus to Rome. This victory, which ended the hopes of the deposed Tarquin dynasty of ever regaining their sovereignty over the city, was believed to have been won owing to the divine intervention of Castor and Pollux. On their heavenly white steeds the brothers then covered the twenty-odd kilometres that separated the lake from the city, bringing the glad news to the populace before mere human messengers had time to arrive.

Castor and Pollux were first seen watering their horses at the **Fountain of Juturna** which still stands on the opposite side of the narrow street and, all questions of divine intervention aside, this part of the legend at least has the ring of truth as in those early days the fountain of Juturna was the fountain of Rome, the natural gathering place for news and gossip, as the village pump used to be in England.

If we continue along the narrow street that leads to the foot of the Palatine, we find ourselves in the oldest centre of Christian worship in the Forum. On our left stands the little oratory of the forty martyrs of Sebaste in Armenia, and before us lies the church of **S. Maria Antiqua**. This imperial building, whose original function is the subject of learned argument, was converted for use as a church in the fifth or sixth century, or possibly even earlier, and was restored and embellished early in the seventh century by Pope John VII, son of Plato the Byzantine curator of the palaces on the Palatine.

The great interest of S. Maria Antiqua lies, however, in its remarkable and exceedingly rare frescoes of the eighth century which reflect the passions aroused by the iconoclastic struggle then in progress in the eastern Empire, from which many priests and monks had fled to sanctuary in Rome. These represent a species of artistic counter-propaganda to the iconoclastic persecutions, by honouring the oriental saints whose images were then being destroyed in Constantinople— martyrs and theologians like SS. Quiricus and Julitta, S. John Chrysostom, S. Gregory Nazianzen, S. Basil, S. Athanasius and many others. It is remarkable that the style and iconography of many of these paintings closely resemble those of the rock churches of Cappadocia, and it is generally believed that they were the work of oriental refugees who thus introduced their native art, which was destined to exercise a profound influence upon church decoration, as they display some interesting innovations to western Christian art.

The frescoes, of which there are several superimposed layers, can be precisely dated as three popes—S. Zacharias, S. Paul I and Hadrian I—are represented with the square halo of the living, and were therefore painted during their reigns. Unfortunately, since their discovery in 1900 many of the paintings have faded or disappeared almost completely, but those in the chapel to the left of the presbytery are fairly well preserved. Here there is a Crucifixion with Christ portrayed in a long blue robe in the Syrian style, while to the right appear SS. Quiricus and Julitta to whom the chapel was dedicated by Theodatus, the first consistorial advocate, who appears beside them with a square halo. On the right wall an unusual scene is represented, probably of Theodatus and his wife presenting their two children with square haloes to the Virgin, and in the corner Theodatus is seen kneeling before SS. Quiricus and Julitta. This last is of particular interest as it is the earliest example of a donor shown kneeling, as later became the customary practice, instead of standing. Other frescoes in the same chapel portray in detail scenes of the martyrdom of SS. Quiricus and Julitta, another innovation in western religious art.

In spite of its tremendous artistic interest, it is with a certain feeling of relief that on a fine day we emerge from the shadows of S. Maria Antiqua and, retracing our steps past the Temple of Vesta, find ourselves on the **Sacred Way.** Here oleanders of every imaginable shade of crimson, rose, apricot and yellow blossom in the summer months, and the Forum cats sit washing themselves on slabs of marble warmed by the sun. About midday many of them will be found making their way, like ourselves, towards the Arch of Titus. At that time one of the monks of S. Bonaventura on the Palatine, with truly Franciscan spirit, comes down to this end of the Sacred Way to feed them every day, bringing with him in hot weather also a *fiasco* of water, with which he fills the crevices in the marble to provide them with little drinking bowls. He is one of Rome's anonymous and unsung animal lovers who, every day among the ancient ruins and in back alleys of the city, have a regular rendezvous with their cat friends. Many of them are poor, lonely old men and women who make a round of the *trattorie* asking for scraps, or who, like the monk, spend quite a considerable sum during the year to feed the cats which have been abandoned in the ruins. For in Rome it is considered to be extremely unlucky to have even a sick and aged cat humanely put to sleep.

This is the part of the Forum where we can best give ourselves over to the romantic enjoyment of a superbly picturesque scene, in something of the same spirit as the eighteenth-century Grand Tourists, uninhibited by too much precise archaeological information which, although it greatly increases the interest of what we see, does tend to limit the imagination that plays so great a part in the enjoyment of ancient ruins. Except for the vast pile of the Basilica of Maxentius or Constantine that towers up above us on the left, most of the buildings in this part of the Forum are the subject of considerable debate. The charming little circular temple, for instance, which with its porphyry columns and the dark green patina of its ancient bronze doors (whose automatic lock is still in perfect working order) lends a touch of colour to the scene, has never been definitely identified. It is called the Temple of Romulus, and may have been dedicated by Maxentius to his son of that name who died in boyhood, but the only things we definitely know about it are that it was designed by an exceedingly able architect to mask an awkward angle of Vespasian's Forum of Peace in relation to the Sacred Way, and for centuries it served as the vestibule of the church of SS. Cosma e Damiano.

We can let our fancy wander even more freely among the amorphous mass of ruins on our right that in spring rise out of a lush green mass of wild fennel and acanthus, interspersed with aromatic bays. Here Nero built the portico of his fabulous Golden House, but twenty years after his suicide Domitian converted part of it into markets, shops and storehouses. Subsequently it became the Bond Street of ancient Rome, where exotic spices and scents were sold and silversmiths and jewellers plied their trade, and was much frequented by the fashionable world—ladies like Titus's daughter Julia, whose bust we saw in the Capitoline Museum.

The **Arch of Titus** stands on top of the Velia, a spur of the Palatine that juts out towards the Esquiline, closing the Forum valley at its south-eastern end. It is a superb site, and the view from the arch was for centuries a favourite subject of the *vedutisti*—the painters of small views of Rome, whose work was eagerly bought as souvenirs by the Grand Tourists. The arch, erected in AD 81 to commemorate the capture of Jerusalem eleven years before, in medieval times was called the 'Arch of the Seven Lamps' from the relief representing the spoils of the temple, including the seven-branched candlestick. The silver trumpets and the golden table of the shewbread are also shown.

The sacred objects from the Temple of Jerusalem were kept, with innumerable other treasures, in the Temple of Peace, and in spite of many fires are believed still to have been there when the Goths sacked Rome in AD 410. According to one source they were then seized by Alaric and buried with him in the bed of the River Bucento; according to another they were looted by the Vandals, taken to North Africa and retrieved by Belisarius, who sent them to Constantinople. The Jews on the other hand believed that they had been thrown into the Tiber. The twelfth-century author of the *Graphia Aurea Urbis Romae* stated, rather surprisingly, that they were then kept in the Lateran. This seems to have been extremely unlikely, and a very interested contemporary—the Rabbi Benjamin of Tudela—who was in Rome about this time described in his itinerary a cave near the church of S. Sebastian where 'Titus son of Vespasian kept the sacred vessels of the Temple' but makes no mention of their still existing in the Lateran.

But as a matter of fact the very observant rabbi also completely ignored the Arch of Titus itself, which is described in detail by both the contemporary authors of the *Graphia* and the *Mirabilia*. In this, however, he was following the custom of his people, who throughout the centuries have given the arch a wide berth; a fact which was commented upon by the Roman vernacular poet Belli in the last century and still holds good today. According to Augustus Hare, until Pius IX put a stop to it, during the nineteenth century in the course of the procession of the '*possesso*' a representative of the Jewish community stood beside the Arch of Titus to present the pope with a copy of the Pentateuch and to take the oath of fealty.

By now, whichever way we arranged our itinerary, it will be past midday and we will be ready for a break and a rest. Twelve-thirty is very early for luncheon in Rome, but it has its advantages in uncrowded restaurants and swifter service. Strategically sited right in or near the imperial Fora are two excellent restaurants—the Ulpia at 2 Piazza del Foro Triano, whose downstairs room is actually built into the Roman ruins, and the more simple Trattoria Angelino ai Fori in Largo Corrado Ricci, at the beginning of the Via Cavour. On a fine day, however, there is nothing more delightful than taking a picnic lunch up on to the Palatine, but this must be done with discretion as it is frowned on by the authorities for fear of litter. The ideal place to buy a picnic lunch is a *rosticería* or *tavola calda* where they will make it up into a neat parcel for you to take away.

CHAPTER THREE

The Palatine

❧

IF we have brought a picnic with us, we can continue straight on from the Forum for our exploration of the Palatine. From the Arch of Titus we turn right up the little path that ascends the hill, paved in places with the original stones of the ancient Clivus Palatinus. The dappled sunlight and shade falling on the grass and weathered stone make this a worthy approach to what is one of the most romantic sites in Rome—the **Palatine**, the hill that has given its name to all the palaces in the world, and the only place in the city where we can still see 'a classical landscape with ruins'. Here marble columns rise out of a coloured carpet of field flowers and fragments of antique reliefs lie half-concealed among the feathery fronds of fennel and the curling acanthus leaves from which so much of their decoration was derived.

Although of course it is at its best in spring, at any time of year the Palatine is a place of enchantment. Simply by wandering there without any knowledge of its ancient remains, but drinking in its atmosphere, enjoying its marvellous views and letting our imagination run riot, we can gain as much enjoyment as from a serious study of its past. One feels as if one has strayed into the midst of a landscape by Claude Lorrain or Hubert Robert, which is as it should be, as in their day so much of Rome—all the area between the old city in the bend of the Tiber and the vast enceinte of the Aurelian walls—must have looked very much like this, and such was the fascination this scene held for them that it remained an inspiration for the rest of their lives. For 250 years, from the end of the sixteenth century, when Paul Brill and other Flemish artists first began to paint their small pictures of the classical ruins, until the first half of the last century, when Corot made Rome the subject of so many of his wonderful canvases, this particular type of landscape was the inspiration of the artists of half Europe, painted and loved by our own Richard Wilson,

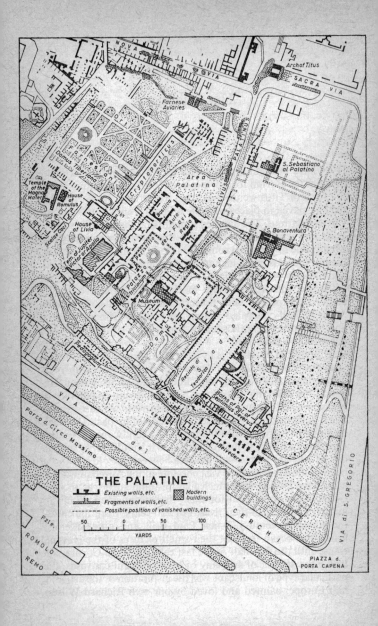

THE PALATINE

Existing walls, etc.	Modern buildings
Fragments of walls, etc.	
------- Possible position of vanished walls, etc.	

50   0   50   100
YARDS

Gavin Hamilton, Marlow, More and a host of others. This is partly why it holds an instant and magic appeal for us, remembered and yet half forgotten like a melody heard long ago. But there is another reason why the landscape of the Palatine fascinates us as something half familiar; it was from the pictures by these artists and the taste of the English eighteenth-century connoisseurs and travellers who bought them that the creators of the English landscape garden drew their inspiration, which changed the face of the English countryside, filling it with vast parks where 'classical ruins' and 'temples' stand among bosky clumps of trees and are reflected in spacious waters.

So if as we walk around the Palatine, conscientiously trying to trace out the pattern of its history, we sometimes lose the thread and instead find ourselves simply sitting on a fallen column and enjoying the view, we should not feel that we are wasting our time, as many a better man has done just this before us. It is in fact no easy matter to decipher the building history of the Palatine for, as one of the most famous living archaeologists once told me, 'it presents a very complicated archaeological problem.' For like the rest of Rome, the Palatine is an architectural palimpsest—perhaps it would be more correct to say an archaeological one—as its building history begins earlier and, partly owing to the enormous bulk of the ruins of the imperial palaces, it was less built over in later ages than some other areas of the ancient city. As a result, even more than in the Forum, one is sometimes apt to forget the Palatine's earlier history, and even its greatest claim to fame —that it was the birthplace of Rome itself.

The Romans, however, never forgot that the Palatine was the cradle of their civilisation, and still in the fourth century AD a shrine stood by a cave that was believed to be the famous Lupercal where the she-wolf suckled Romulus and Remus. This is known to have been on the south-west side of the hill and to have contained an ancient bronze statue of the wolf and the twin brothers, but the site has never been redis-covered. Fourth-century authors such as Dionysius of Halicarnassus and Dion Cassius also described as still existing in their day a primitive thatched wattle hut, known as the House of Romulus, which stood on the south-west part of the Palatine and was constantly kept in repair. Excavations car-ried out during this century have confirmed the veracity of this

Roman tradition, for on the spot indicated by the ancient authors traces of early Iron Age huts have come to light, and their date—at some period between the beginning of the eighth and seventh centuries BC—coincides with that traditionally ascribed to the founding of Rome.

Romulus, if indeed it was he as the famous legend asserts, who drove the plough round the *pomoerium* or sacred enceinte of the newly-founded city, already displayed a typically Roman eye for the practical military advantages of his choice of site. With its three crests—the Germalus, Palatium and Velia—the hill was quite a large one, but easily defended because of the steep slopes and marshy valleys that surrounded it; moreover it commanded the easiest crossing of the river by the Tiber island. The word city is, however, altogether too ambitious a one to be applied to this Rome of the seventh century BC, which was probably nothing more than a large hut village defended by an agger or earthworks.

Somewhere about 600 BC a great change began in this primitive settlement. Down in the valley of the Forum below, the cemetery and huts beside the Sacred Way were demolished and a simple type of gravel pavement laid down over their remains. From this and other archaeological evidence it is apparent that about this time the village settlements were being transformed into the semblance of a town on the Greek and Etruscan pattern. This process was so rapid that already ninety years later the first great stone blocks of the Temple of Jupiter were being placed in position on the Capitol, and by the time the Republic was declared in 509 BC Rome was a city in fact as well as name.

During the Republic the Palatine became what estate agents today would call 'a desirable residential quarter'. Thanks to its favoured situation above the Tiber and its exposure to sea breezes, houses there were much sought after, and men of great families like the Scauri, Crassi and Flacci lived there, and ambitious ones like Cicero aspired to do so. It was therefore quite natural that Julius Caesar's great-nephew, Gaius Octavius, should be born there, on 23 September, 63 BC. When Gaius Octavius became Augustus the *Princeps*, or first Roman Emperor, he saw no reason to move from the dignified private house on the Palatine, which he had bought from the orator Hortensius after the defeat of Pompey in 36 BC. Probably he was attached to the quarter where he had grown up, but he was also a man of simple personal tastes and a consummate statesman. Though he had achieved absolute power Augustus had no intention of being ostentatious about it and thus wounding delicate Roman republican susceptibilities, so for the rest of his life the first emperor continued to live quietly in a few modest rooms of the house of a private citizen.

It was only as a result of a series of family tragedies, and *faute de mieux* as far as Augustus was concerned, that the eccentric Tiberius succeeded as the second Roman emperor. Although it is obvious from his subsequent retirement to Capri that Tiberius preferred living out of Rome, something had evidently to be done about a suitable imperial residence in the city. The fact that Augustus's redoubtable widow Livia was still living in his house, but that during his long reign the Palatine had come to be associated with the residence of the emperor, probably decided Tiberius to build his own residence there, so on the north-west part of the Palatine he proceeded to build the Domus Tiberiana—the first of the imperial palaces which were subsequently to cover practically the whole of the hill.

Thus from being the cradle of Rome itself, after a period of centuries of comfortable quiescence as a select residential quarter, the Palatine again became the most important centre in Roman life and indeed the world. For centuries the fate of nations was dictated from this hill, and so tenacious was the tradition that this was the seat of power that even after the foundation of Constantinople, in a period when the emperors rarely came to Rome, the Palatine was still officially their residence. The tradition survived into the early Middle Ages. In the seventh century representatives of the Byzantine emperors still lived in the palace, in 686 one of them repaired the grand staircase, and later some of the popes lived there. In the year 1241, for the last time in history, the ruins of the imperial palaces were associated with the accession of a sovereign, when the cardinals who elected the short-lived Pope Celestine IV were virtually imprisoned in the Septizonium for the conclave. This was the last brief interlude in the part the Palatine had played in world history. For the next three hundred years it was little more than a vineyard and vegetable patch, cultivated by the monks who had established themselves among the ruins. But in the sixteenth century great Roman families like the Farnese laid out their pleasure gardens on the hill, and humanist cardinals, whose 'purple' robes recalled those of the emperors and consuls, strolled along its spacious terraces, discussing the works of the classical poets, as their predecessors must have done more than a thousand years before.

By far the largest portion of the Palatine as we see it today is covered by the vast palace which Domitian's architect, C. Rabirius, built for him between AD 81 and 96. In order to make room for this enormous edifice, which comprised the emperor's official residence, his private dwelling and a vast stadium, many private houses were taken over and buried, and whole sections of the hill levelled so that the original crests of the Germalus and Palatium could no longer be differentiated. Both the public and private palaces, which adjoin each other, were built in the characteristically Roman style as a series of rooms ranged round peristyles or garden courtyards, but whereas in the Palazzo dei Flavi, or official residence, these huge halls opened off a single court, the private house, or Domus Augustana, was designed in a far freer style with rooms of varying sizes and shapes grouped round two garden courts at different levels. The predominating characteristic of the whole palace was the close association—interpenetration is a better word—of house and gardens. The great open courtyards, with their fountains and flower beds, were evidently used as out-of-doors salons merging, through porticoes and colonnades, into the rooms themselves, and there is some doubt among the archaeologists as to whether the great stadium adjoining the Domus Augustana was not just another sunken garden, as the 'hippodromes' of the great Roman villas so often were.

All of this is very much easier to follow from a plan than when walking through the ruins themselves as, owing to the richness of the marbles which adorned them and the consequent treasure-hunting excavations of the Renaissance, the imperial palaces suffered even greater depredations than many other great Roman ruins. As a result, to the layman at any rate, their component parts are difficult to identify. This confusion is rendered even greater by the fact that the various paths lead us into the palaces from the sides, so that we are confronted by a jumble of ruined walls and the overall plan is almost impossible to distinguish.

Curiously enough the general plan of the palaces is most easily understood if we enter by one of the least frequented paths, which branches off to the right from the Clivus Palatinus, crosses the open grassy slope known as the Area Palatina and joins a broader path coming from the gardens of the Casino Farnese. Here we turn left and after a short distance find ourselves standing beside the remains of an ancient terrace bordered with the stumps of vast columns; this was once the portico that led into the Basilica and Aula Regia of the **Palazzo dei Flavi**. Mounting a short flight of steps we cross the portico and enter the ruins of the Basilica by a side door, where a fragment of the corner wall, standing as gaunt as a chimney stack, is all that remains to tell us of the vast height of the emperor's hall of justice, while a single column of *giallo antico* reminds us of its former marble splendour.

After a brief glance at the adjoining Sala Regia, where stark ruin now mocks the ancient authors' descriptions of statuary and purple marbles, we make our way behind the apse of the Basilica into the great peristyle of the Palazzo dei Flavi. In the centre we can still trace the pathetic remains of a vast fountain pool, surrounding a curious octagonal brick maze. It is believed that this is the courtyard where, according to Suetonius, the walls of the surrounding porticoes were lined with highly polished Cappadocian marble that reflected like a looking-glass. Here Domitian, the emperor whose whim could command the splendours of this vast palace, walked in hourly terror of assassination, for ever watching among the brilliant sunlit reflections of flowers and fountains, grass and trees, for the hand armed with a dagger that got him in the end.

Domitian enjoyed giving large banquets, and even in its ruined state, with part of the floor excavated to show the remains of one of Nero's palaces beneath, we can still perceive something of the charm as well as the splendour of the triclinium which Rabirius designed as a setting for them. This vast dining-room and its annexes fills the whole of the far side of the peristyle. Its walls appear to have been covered with pale pink marble, and the same tone is repeated in the magnificent pavement, inset with motifs of red and green porphyry in the apse. But the most charming aspect of the room was that the diners could look through windows on either side into two nymphaeums where oval fountains, rising out of pools of water, were decorated with pots of flowers and caged song birds that hung in niches.

In Domitian's day, at any rate, this triclinium was not the scene of the type of banquet which degenerated into a drunken orgy lasting far into the night, as was all too common in Imperial Rome. Suetonius is emphatic about this, also that these entertainments, which usually began about two or three in the afternoon, ended at the respectable hour of sunset. For banquets such as these the guests wore a light muslin robe or *synthesis*, were heavily scented and crowned with flowers. As far as we know ladies did not take part in banquets; until Augustus's reign they sat at private dinner parties while the men reclined in threes on cushioned couches or triclinia, from which the dining-room took its name; later women also reclined at dinner. Although spoons were provided, nearly everything was eaten with the fingers, from the hors d'oeuvres, through the five main courses which consisted of three entrées and two roasts, to the dessert of fruit and cakes and creamy puddings. Individual courses would be ushered in with music and dancing and for the dessert the original tables were cleared and new ones brought in their place.

Apart from exotic fantasies like larks' tongues and peacocks' brains, the Roman gourmets appreciated many of the same delicacies as ourselves; their hors d'oeuvres, for instance, consisted of olives, hard-boiled eggs, salads and salted fish. They were very fond of oysters, lobsters and sea-food generally—one of the most famous dishes of Apicius, the renowned gourmet and culinary expert, was an early form of lobster a l'Américaine. Wild boar and game of all kinds, plump chickens and beccaficos, were among the most sought-after dishes, accompanied by mushrooms, truffles, asparagus and other vegetables cooked in complicated ways. At least one of these vegetable dishes, attributed to Apicius himself, has survived. It is known as *scapece* and is made of baby vegetable marrows fried and then marinated in a spiced sauce; it makes a very good hors d'oeuvre and is still served in some Roman restaurants.

Domitian's triclinium is really the only part of the Palazzo dei Flavi to retain any evidence of its past splendour, and unfortunately the upper level of the **Domus Augustana**, which stands parallel to it, is even more bleak. We reach the main peristyle of this private palace by passing in front of the museum, whose chief interest lies in the wall paintings which are gradually being collected there after their removal from the excavations in the houses of the Republican era that were filled in when the imperial palaces were built. The famous graffito of the crucified donkey, from the Pedagogium, is now also housed in the museum.

To the left of the museum are the only appreciable remains of the Domus Augustana standing at this level; they were preserved by having been incorporated into the sixteenth-century Villa Mattei, which was later furbished up in the Strawberry Hill style of mock Gothic by an Englishman of the name of Mills who lived there at the beginning of the last century. Passing through the central arch of this part of the Domus Augustana, we are confronted by a considerable drop and find ourselves looking down into the lower peristyle of the palace. Until the last war it was possible to descend into this garden court by an ancient staircase behind the museum. It is a great pity that the responsible authorities have not reopened this part of the palace to the public, because it is the only place in which the layman can visualise something of what it once looked like. Many of the rooms and nymphaeums are remarkably complete, right up to their domed and vaulted ceilings, and if the peristyle was tidied up and replanted, as in Pompeii, with even the simplest Roman flowers like roses, violets and acanthus, it would present a really charming sight. Furthermore the reopening of the passage leading from the peristyle into the adjoining stadium would enable the tourist to appreciate how this vast sunken arena formed an integral part of the whole palace layout, and would spare the elderly and footsore the long trek round nearly to the baths of Septimius Severus, to the nearest entrance now available.[1]

However, until the powers that be make up their minds to let us explore this most interesting part of the palace, we must console ourselves with the picturesque aspect of the Palatine, of which the view of the church of S. Bonaventura seen through the arch of the Domus Augustana and across its peristyle is a delectable example. Retracing our steps through the arch and turning sharply to the right, a path leads us shortly to a fine vantage point overlooking the **Stadium**, which

1. No doubt this would entail the services of an extra watchman but, given the importance of the place, surely the Belle Arti purse strings might be loosened to this extent.

is the most imposing relic of the whole palace. There is a good
deal of argument as to whether this arena, which was surrounded by double porticoes, was really used as a hippodrome
for races or not. The large niche on its far side known as the
imperial box seems to indicate that originally it was, but at
some later date a portico was built across it near the centre
which would have precluded this. The oval enclosure at the
rounded end is of a very late date and is generally attributed
to the Gothic King Theodoric, who repaired the palace and
lived there in the middle of the fifth century; a later tenant was
the Byzantine General Narses who is said to have died in the
palace towards the end of the sixth century.

We make our way across the ruins of the Domus Augustana
and, skirting the straight northern end of the Stadium,
descend some curved steps to a little *rond-point* on the edge of
a magnificent grove of stone pines. The slope below us is
carpeted with acanthus, and in May and June when its
lavender-coloured spikes of flowers rise in stately ranks this is
one of the most charming corners of the whole of the Palatine;
indeed from now on it is the picturesque landscape aspect
of the hill which dominates. (One entrance to the lower
level of the Stadium is reached by steps farther along the
slope.)

Turning to our right we follow the broad path that skirts
behind the imperial box of the Stadium and, passing through
the ruins of Septimius Severus's baths, make our way on to the
great terrace known as the **Belvedere**, which this emperor
built out on vast supporting arches from the south-eastern
corner of the hill. Beyond its eastern end stood the Septizonium, a decorative structure like the *scenae frons* of a Roman
theatre, destroyed in the sixteenth century. A Roman writer
somewhat snobbishly attributed its creation to Septimus
Severus's desire to impress his African compatriots arriving in
Rome by the Appian Way. Nevertheless the views from his
Belvedere terrace are superb. Pacing along we can look backwards on our left over the pine trees to the Colosseum, then
farther on to the medieval and Renaissance churches and
gardens of the Coelian, the obelisk of Axum and, typical of
Rome today, the ultra-modern glass-fronted building of the
Food and Agriculture Organisation of the United Nations,
while in the distance the Alban Hills stand out blue against the
evening sky. It is touching and revealing to recall that this

area of the Palatine was the favourite walk of Napoleon's mother, who ended her days in Rome.

Retracing our steps and turning to our left, after a slight scramble through the ruins we find ourselves in the imperial box overlooking the Circus Maximus; this is now planted with pink oleanders, and the spina is marked by the dark spires of cypresses. Lentiscus, laurustinus and myrtle grow among the ruins, and in the crevices of the bricks of the imperial box itself rue and capers—all of them plants that were grown in Roman gardens and one wonders if their forebears were once clipped into the fantastic topiary, or *nemora tonsilia*, shaped in formal parterres, or cultivated to flavour the imperial sauces. Looking down from the imperial box the possible continuity of this plant life does not seem so improbable as just below is a typical kitchen garden, one of the last of its kind that once flourished everywhere among the ruins of the Palatine, with its fig tree, vine pergola and neat rows of vegetables.

We must retrace our steps through the ruins of the Baths of Septimius Severus, taking the path that leads to the right, which will in the end bring us to an ancient brick staircase that leads down to the lower levels of the ruins, where the vast brick arches supporting the Belvedere tower up above us, fráming delightful glimpses of the Coelian and Aventine. From here we can at last enter the Stadium and, while resting on one of its broken columns, watch the lizards darting in search of flies upon the sun-warmed marble, while brimstone or peacock butterflies plane down to rest upon the spring flowers. A path leading through a narrow exit in the far corner of the rounded end of the Stadium takes us out on to the stony base of what was once a colonnaded exedra facing towards the Circus Maximus. In the centre is a door (also blocked) leading into the lower peristyle of the Domus Augustana—this was originally its main entrance. Below us to the left lies the Pedagogium, which, from the number of schoolboy type of graffiti found there, is thought to have been the training school for the imperial pages; it can be reached by taking the path to the left winding down the hill.

Continuing along our original path, in the grateful shade of an old ilex we find a curved flight of steps that brings us back up on to the higher level of the hill. This is one of the most charming spots of the whole Palatine, with an elegant file of Corinthian columns on our right, great masses of acanthus growing on the slope below, a little loggiaed casino of the Farnese in front of us, and to our left a wonderful distant view of the dome of St. Peter's, with the much disputed ruins of either the Temple of Jupiter Victor or of Apollo in the foreground. Skirting round the edge of these and leaving them on our right, a path leads us to the direction of a shed which shelters the so-called **House of Livia**.

According to some authorities this was the actual home of Augustus and his empress, according to others it is simply a fine and well-preserved house dating from the same period. Whichever it is, it conveys better perhaps than anything else in the city what the home of a rich and cultivated Roman family was like just before the beginning of the Christian era. What surprises us most, after the monumental ruins that we have seen, is the smallness and intimacy of the rooms and the vivacity and delicacy of their painted decoration. Light and fantastic are the best words with which to describe the architectural settings of the mythological scenes in the so-called *tablinum* or drawing-room. But the prize for sheer grace and beauty is won by the painted garlands of fruit and flowers that festoon the walls of the adjoining room on the right; the spontaneous freedom of execution bespeaks a great artist and the style is reminiscent of the famous sculptures of Augustus's Ara Pacis.

Though it is not visible at the time of writing, very shortly another house of the Augustan era, which has lately been discovered, will be open to the public. It too is remarkable for its delightful paintings, and again there is a room decorated with garlands—of fir branches and cones this time —which makes one wonder why no modern interior decorator has ever taken a leaf out of his Roman predecessors' book.

On the slope of the hill to the west of these two houses, partly sheltered by a shed, are the remains of the first village upon the Palatine—an archaic cistern and the traces of huts of the Iron Age. These last consist of holes cut in the rock to support the timber framework which supported the thatch and wattle of the roof and walls; the actual construction is much easier to understand after an examination of a reconstructed hut in the museum. Beside the huts are the remains of a tufa wall of the fourth century BC and a gate giving on to a steeply descending road. This was the Scalae Caci, the only one of the three primitive entrances to the fortified hill that can be definitely identified.

If these very ancient remains are more than a little difficult of interpretation to the layman, behind them on the hill rise the ruins of the temple of the Magna Mater, presenting a scene whose charm requires no archaeological science to be appreciated. Fragments of ancient tufa columns are ranged along a weathered wall, and the statue of the goddess enthroned in majesty is half hidden in the shade of an enormous ilex, while beyond a series of vaulted rooms support the grassy terrace of the Farnese gardens, where cypresses wave against the bright blue sky. The temple dates from 191 BC and the vaulted rooms were probably added to the Domus Tiberiana in the first century.

Nero's famous cryptoporticus, which was only excavated in 1870, is entered on the other side of the Casa di Livia (here it retains some of the exquisite stucco decoration of the ceiling) and runs along the whole of the eastern side of the Domus Tiberiana, which lies buried under the Farnese gardens. On a bright day its gloom is pierced by shafts of sunlight from the windows placed high up in the vaulting on the right and, ignoring the invitation of the first staircase on the left, we pass on to the second, which leads us into the centre of the Farnese gardens.

Created in the first half of the sixteenth century by Vignola for Alexander Farnese, nephew of Pope Paul III, the Farnese gardens, or Horti Farnesiani, were among the earliest botanical gardens in Europe. They were designed in the typically Roman tradition of the '*vigna*', originally a vineyard and later a pleasure garden, not as a residence—there was no house, simply two aviaries and a casino. Thus they reflect an age of luxury, almost as far removed from the hard realities of our own as that of the Caesars, when a man could buy up half the Palatine and spend a fortune on laying it out just as a place to stroll, and occasionally dine, on summer evenings. These formal gardens where the *Acacia Farnesiana* was first grown in Europe and the *Sprekelia* introduced into Italy early in the seventeenth century are now little more than a memory, for all but a small fraction of them disappeared with the systematic excavation of the Palatine in the last century. Only the stately avenues of cypresses and shady groves of bay and ilex which wave in the wind above the buried palace of

Tiberius recall that here too was once the pleasance of a family of whose palaces and villas even a Roman emperor would not have been ashamed.

On a summer evening when the last rays of the setting sun gild the Forum's columns the view from the terrace is of a beauty and fascination beyond compare. But as the sky darkens and the *ponentino*—the gentle little breeze from the west—stirs among the leaves, like a voice whispering of ancient hates and loves, we are reminded that if few places in the world have been more favoured by nature, fewer still have been so coveted by man, for, as the medieval author of the *Graphia Aurea Urbis Romae* phrased it, this was once 'the Palace of the Monarchy of the Earth'.

CHAPTER FOUR

Piazza Venezia to Piazza Colonna

❧

ALTHOUGH it is perhaps the least beautiful in the city, the **Vittorio Emanuele Monument** serves the very useful purpose of providing a conspicuous landmark. English soldiers during the war christened it the 'wedding cake', and indeed its blindly white columns of Brescian marble stand out like some elaborate piece of confectionery, towering above the mellow Roman townscape, whose predominating tones range from the honey colour of travertine—surely one of the loveliest building stones—through every imaginable shade of faded rose and sienna to the weathered terracotta of the old tiled roofs. Startlingly in the midst of these monochrome vistas, one suddenly catches sight of the monument, which also serves as a reminder of the recent date of Italian unity—for no period other than the late nineteenth century could have produced it. In fact the monument was begun in 1885 and finished in 1911 and was built in honour of the unification of Italy, and her first King Vittorio Emanuele II. After the First World War the tomb of Italy's Unknown Warrior was placed in front of the Altare della Patria.

Apart from serving as a landmark, the monument fulfils several other useful purposes. Its mountainous mass of marble houses the archives of the Istituto per la Storia del Risorgimento Italiano, a police station, large water tanks for supplying the fountains, and other useful offices, which are all too rare in Rome. Thus all told the Vittorio Emanuele Monument will serve as a convenient starting point for this and many of our other expeditions through Rome, especially as the Piazza Venezia which lies in front is one of the nodal points of the city's bus services.

The **Piazza Venezia** today is the least Roman of all the great squares, but even the ruthless nineteenth- and twentieth-century town planners, who destroyed so much that was beautiful and picturesque to create their conception of a

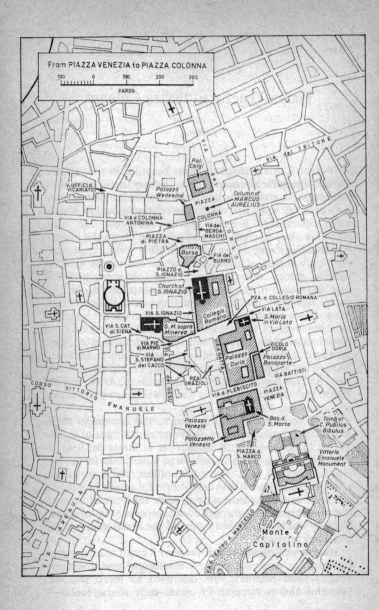

From PIAZZA VENEZIA to PIAZZA COLONNA

100   0   100   200   300

YARDS

VIA del TRITONE

Pal. Chigi

V. UFFICI d. VICARIATO

Palazzo Wedekind

PIAZZA

Column of MARCUS AURELIUS

VIA d. COLONNA ANTONINA

COLONNA

VIA dei BERGAMASCHI

PIAZZA di PIETRA

Borsa

VIA del BURRO

PIAZZO d. S. IGNAZIO

Church of S. IGNAZIO

PZA. d. COLLEGIO ROMANA

VIA LATA

S. Maria in Via Lata

VIA S. IGNAZIO

Collegio Romano

VIA S. CAT. di SIENA

S. M. sopra Minerva

VICOLO DORIA

VIA PIE di MARMO

Palazzo Doria

Palazzo Bonaparte

VIA S. STEFANO del CACCO

VIA BATTISTI

PZA. GRAZIOLI

CORSO

VITTORIO

VIA d. PLEBISCITO

PIAZZA VENEZIA

EMANUELE

Tomb of C. Publius Bibulus

Palazzo Venezia

Bas. d. S. Marco

Palazzetto Venezia

Vittorio Emanuele Monument

PIAZZA d. S. MARCO

VIA ARENULA

VIA d. TEATRO d. MARCELLO

Monte Capitolino

suitable setting for the monument and the classical ruins in the vicinity, spared two fragments which remind us of its past. On the right of the marble mountain are the remains of an Insula, or block of flats, of the first century AD. The church of S. Biagio del Mercato was built into the Insula in the Middle Ages—we can still see its campanile and some frescoes and these in their turn were submerged beneath the seventeenth-century church of S. Rita and ordinary dwelling houses. These classical and medieval buildings were only rediscovered during the Mussolini excavations of 1927.

On the left of the monument, standing isolated in the midst of the grass, is a fragment of Roman wall pierced by a door. This is all that remains of the **Tomb of C. Publius Bibulus**, a plebeian aedile of the first century BC, but it is a key point to students of the topography of ancient Rome as it is known to have stood at the beginning of the Via Flaminia, one of the great consular roads which led, and still leads, to Fano on the Adriatic. In fact Bibulus's tomb has always been a landmark. Petrarch mentioned in a letter that he had written one of his sonnets leaning against it, and today it reminds us of a Rome which seems almost as remote—that of the Papal States and the famous Roman Carnival. Then the tomb formed part of a house which stood just beyond the narrow end of the Corso known as the *Ripresa dei Barberi*, because it was here that the riderless horses, or Arab Barbs, of the race which was the climax of the carnival, were halted at the end of their wild career by the folds of a great white sheet suspended across the street.

It was the Venetian Pope Paul II, builder of the Palazzo Venezia, who really created the carnival in all its glamour and excitement when, in 1466, he decreed that it should be held in the Via Lata, instead of—as previously—on the Capitol or Monte Testaccio. Although he was Venetian born, Pietro Barbo's temper was well suited to the Romans, and already as a cardinal his personal charm and generosity had made him a popular figure. As Pope his love of splendour and the good things of life appealed to the pleasure-loving Renaissance populace. Pope and people were at one in their enjoyment of the carnival and the races for young and old, Christians and Jews, and the *Barberi*, which for them re-evoked the splendour of the ancient Roman games and chariot races. The pope himself assisted at the spectacle, awarding prizes and presents to the contestants. Probably it was for his convenience, so that he could watch the races from the windows of the walled garden of his newly-built Palazzo Venezia (or di S. Marco as it was then called), that Paul II ordered the carnival to be held in the Via Lata. By so doing he gave its name to what is still the main thoroughfare of Rome—the Corso, where the carnival *corse* or races were run. Previously the Corso had been called the Via Lata at the Piazza Venezia end and the rest went by its ancient name of Via Flaminia.

In succeeding centuries the Roman Carnival became the most famous in Europe. Particularly in the eighteenth and nineteenth centuries, it was one of the sights that were *de rigueur* for the fashionable grand tourist; Roman princes and English *milords* then rivalled one another in the entertainments which they gave during the eight days of riotous celebration.

As we stand prosaically by the car parks of Piazza Venezia it is difficult to conjure up this colourful past, or to imagine the square as it was right up to 1870, when it was less than half its present size and enclosed on two sides by Palazzo Venezia and Paul II's walled garden, which stood at right angles to the palace and was connected to the tower by an arch. The garden was removed to provide an open space in front of the Vittorio Emanuele Monument and its beautiful enclosing double loggias were reconstructed inside the building, known as the Palazzetto Venezia, adjoining the palace on the other side of the Piazza di S. Marco. This lovely cloistered garden can now only be seen by special permission (to be obtained from the Director of the Palazzo Venezia Museum).

The **Piazza di S. Marco**, which is really not a square at all but a small public garden and the stop for the buses to the Aventine, lies on the left-hand side of the Palazzo Venezia and takes its name from the **Basilica di S. Marco**, one of the ancient titular churches of Rome. A *titulus* or titular church is, correctly speaking, one of the original twenty-five Roman churches administered by priests whose origins date from early Christian times. Ever since the fourth century the churches have been associated with cardinal priests, and throughout the ages cardinals have taken their titles from them—thus Pietro Barbo was the Cardinal of S. Marco until his election as Paul II.

Since Paul II's day S. Marco has been the national church of the Venetians in Rome; it is dedicated to their patron St. Mark, who according to tradition wrote his Gospel while living in a house on the slopes of the Capitol, where he founded an oratory; also to his namesake another St. Mark who was Pope in AD 336. Recent excavations under the Basilica have confirmed its traditional foundation in the period of this pope's lifetime, whose relics still rest under the main altar in company with those of SS. Abdon and Sennen. This first church, the earliest Roman parish church to be built on the plan of a classical basilica, had incorporated in its pavement the mosaic floor of a late third- or early fourth-century house; possibly part of a Christian meeting place which belonged to St. Mark before he became Pope. This church was burnt and another built above it in the sixth century; in the ninth century the third, and existing, church was built by Pope Gregory IV, whose dedicatory inscription appears in the beautiful mosaic in the apse.

S. Marco was restored by Paul II and, although most of its interior decoration dates from subsequent restorations of the seventeenth and eighteenth centuries, his superb gilded ceiling and elegant Renaissance portico still survive unchanged. This double portico—which is one of the finest of its kind in Rome—owes its size and importance to the fact that Paul II used the adjoining palace as an official residence, and the portico had to be large enough to accommodate him and his retinue when he gave his benediction to the crowd assembled in the piazza; a ceremony which today we are apt to associate only with St. Peter's. On the right-hand wall on the ground floor of this portico is the funerary inscription of Vanozza Cattanei, the mistress of the Borgia Pope Alexander VI, and mother of his children—the murdered Duke of Gandia, Lucrezia and the notorious Cesare—who are also mentioned in it. The inscription is known originally to have been in S. Maria del Popolo and to have disappeared; by what mysterious means this large block of stone was subsequently conveyed and buried under the portico of S. Marco, where it was recently discovered, is unlikely now ever to be revealed.

In the corner by the Basilica di S. Marco, attached to the wall of the Palazzetto Venezia, is a somewhat damaged classical bust of Junoesque proportions; this has long been known to the Romans as Madama Lucrezia, one of the city's famous talking statues who took part in the dialogues of Pasquin and Marforio. The origins of the name are obscure, but in the sixteenth century some houses in a nearby street, where the bust then stood and which subsequently came to be called after it, were owned by a certain Signora Lucrezia, and some authorities believe that local appreciation of this lady's notable vital statistics resulted in the Junoesque bust being called after her.

Before beginning our exploration of **Palazzo Venezia** and its delightful museum, let us for one moment take a glimpse at its great garden court, which, unlike the erstwhile private garden of Paul II in the Palazzetto, is open to the public. The entrance is through an arch beside the Basilica di S. Marco, and in this tranquil oasis of shade and greenery we find a charming eighteenth-century fountain presided over by a Doge of Venice. This reminds us of the fact that in the latter half of the sixteenth century the palace was given to the Most Serene Republic as her embassy and as the residence of the Cardinal of S. Marco, who was always a Venetian. Thus it continued until Venice became an Austrian province during the Napoleonic wars, after which the palace was used as the Austria Embassy until the First World War. The only relic of this Austrian occupation is a small plaque beside a door on the left of the courtyard, marking Canova's studio. As a Venetian Canova was an Austrian subject, and as the most celebrated sculptor in Europe of his day any embassy would have been proud to give him house room. *The* sight of the garden, however, is the exquisite Renaissance loggia, built between 1467 and 1471 but never completed, which extends along part of two sides of the court. Like the palace itself, the design of the loggia has been attributed to L. B. Alberti, Giuliano da Maiano and other great architects, but, as frequently happens with Roman fifteenth-century buildings, this is a subject upon which the experts are unable to agree.

From its comparatively modest beginnings as the residence of the cardinal, built beside his titular church in 1455, the Palazzo Venezia grew during Paul II's reign to become the first great Renaissance palace of Rome; architecturally, however, it plainly reflects the period of transition in the city's life in which it was built. Though the garden loggias and many details are in the Renaissance style, with its great tower and machicolations the palace itself recalls the medieval strong-holds of the Roman nobles who made the city their battleground. A glance at the Piazza Venezia façade of the palace affords us a clue to its growth. The windows on the left of the door are closer together than those on the right and belong to Pietro Barbo's original residence; the rest of the main block and part of the Via del Plebiscito side were built after he became Pope, though they were only finally completed in the sixteenth century.

Strangely enough the door in the imposing Piazza Venezia façade of the palace is not the principal one; it leads to a mezzanine (now occupied by the Biblioteca Nazionale di Archeologia e Storia dell'Arte), and on the floor above to rooms of the palace which are often used for art exhibitions, though they form part of the **Palazzo Venezia Museum**. The museum itself is entered by the old ceremonial door in the Via del Plebiscito, where a vast vaulted hall leads to a magnificent state staircase; this, however, is a modern reconstruction. Like the state staircase, a great deal of the interior decoration of the palace had to be reconstructed or restored in 1916, but on the whole this work has been very well carried out, and a visit to the museum also affords an excellent opportunity, rare in Rome, of seeing the inside of a Renaissance palace.

Paul II was one of the greatest collectors of his day and we know from contemporary descriptions that then the palace was hung with magnificent tapestries and brocades and filled with objets d'art and dressers laden with gold and silver plate. Thus its present use as a museum chiefly devoted to the arts and crafts of medieval and Renaissance times is a singularly happy choice. The Palazzo Venezia collection also includes much fine sculpture, ranging from such early works as Arnolfo di Cambio's figure of a pope and the famous thirteenth-century polychrome wooden Madonna di Acuto, to the superb Barsanti collection of Renaissance bronzes. Pictures, porcelain, furniture, textiles and plate of varying periods, and from countries other than Italy, have come to swell the original collection. So that now as we walk through the vast Renaissance rooms, which Mussolini once used as offices, or pause to examine the bibelots in some velvet-lined cabinet, we are reminded more of a collector's paradise in some great private house than of a state museum. In fact this is not so strange as a large proportion of the beautiful and precious things assembled in the Palazzo Venezia have come as gifts or bequests from private collections, and it is from this sense of intimacy and discerning personal taste that the palace and its contents derive their extraordinarily human charm.

If an exhibition is being held in the Palazzo Venezia, we emerge by a secondary exit in the arch leading into the Piazza di S. Marco—otherwise we can make the complete round of the palace and leave by the door in the Via del Plebiscito. In this street, which takes its name from the plebiscite of 2 October 1870 by which Rome became part of united Italy, we are confronted by Paolo Amali's graceful mid-eighteenth-century façade of the immense Palazzo Doria and on the right, in a small enclave formed by the Vicolo Doria, the Palazzo Bonaparte, now Misciatelli. It was in this last palace that Napoleon's mother came to live after Waterloo, and here she died in 1836.

Though it is one of the smallest and least conspicuous in Rome, the **Vicolo Doria** well illustrates how much of the changing life of different epochs in its history can be reflected in the naming of a single street. Until 1871 the Vicolo was called Via della Stufa, after one of the city's many *stufe* or public baths, one of which must have stood there at some period. The name was changed, in common with all others of the same denomination, because these baths, which were of the ancient Roman or Turkish type, had since the Renaissance also become brothels, like the 'stews' in England.

For some sixty years the Vicolo continued to bear the name of the great family palace which stands beside it, then during the Fascist period it was changed again to Vicolo della Fede; the word *fede* in Italian means both faith and a wedding ring. In order to whip up popular feeling at the time when economic sanctions were applied to Italy by the League of Nations during the Abyssinian war, Mussolini organised a 'voluntary' collection of wedding rings to augment the country's gold reserve. The late Princess Doria, who was a Scotswoman, refused to give up hers; nor would the prince, who was anti-fascist, fly a flag on his palace in celebration of the collection. As a result of their courageous action, the Doria palace was broken into by demonstrating Fascists and the family name was removed from the adjoining street, only to be quietly put back again after the fall of Mussolini.

As we turn the corner of the Vicolo Doria into the Corso, the left-hand side of the street, right up to the church of S.

Maria in Via Lata, is taken up by the immense **Palazzo Doria**, which here again presents a graceful eighteenth-century face to the world, but this façade, added about 1734 by Gabriele Valvassori, masks much earlier buildings. As this is the first Roman family palace that we have come across, and because these great princely houses are such a dominating feature of the city, it is worth our while to pause for a little and examine not only its architecture but how people have lived in it, and others like it, during the centuries.

The first thing that usually surprises foreigners about these great palaces is that although their owners were, and often are, Princes of the Holy Roman Empire, the ground floors of their homes are usually lined with shops which are quite obviously not modern additions. This is evident in the Via del Plebiscito façade of Palazzo Doria, and even in a great fifteenth-century palace like the Cancelleria, and was evidently a well-established Roman custom.

According to the famous Swedish archaeologist, Axel Boethius, this practice may well have been handed down through the centuries as a tradition surviving from the *insulae* or blocks of flats of classical Rome, which were constructed in the same manner. Although they were built for a single owner these Roman palaces were, like the *insulae*, divided up into separate apartments, of which the grandest on the first floor, known as the *piano nobile*, were reserved for the most important members of the family. The rest would be allotted to aged aunts and impoverished relations; but also to dependants, ranging from 'gentlemen of the household' (in eighteenth-century Rome princes and cardinals still had gentlemen-in-waiting like royalty), and artists and musicians employed by the family, gradually descending the social scale to servants and plain hangers-on.

Thus a great Roman palace was, and still is, a little world of its own, sheltering under the same roof a prince who may live in state with liveried footmen to wait on him and, usually under the eaves, impoverished but colourful families, who do their shopping by letting a market basket down on a string into the street for friends or itinerant vendors to fill. During the immediate post-war years when I lived in Palazzo Doria, an aged neighbour kept chickens and a pig on her terrace and routed all our landlord's efforts to dislodge them!

Like any self-respecting Roman building, Palazzo Doria's

foundations are sunk among ruins of classical times, for long believed to have been Caesar's Saepta Julia, but now according to the latest archaeological opinion simply one of the great store-houses of the ancient city. At the end of the fifteenth century Cardinal Fazio Santorio built himself a fine palace on the site, the renown of which was such that the great Della Rovere Pope, Julius II, asked to visit it. The pope was full of admiration, but the poor owner well understood what was required of him when his august visitor said that his palace was so fine that it was more suitable for a duke than a cardinal. Bowing to the inevitable Santorio made it over to the Duke of Urbino—Julius II's nephew—whose Roman embassy it then became. The palace subsequently passed to the Aldobrandini and, by marriage, to the Pamphilj and then the Doria family of Genoa, who added Pamphilj to their name. It is still owned by the same family.

If we have dwelt rather long upon the history of this single palace, it is not only because it is so typical of its kind, but also because it is the only great Roman palace in private possession whose magnificent picture gallery, as well as its state and private rooms, are now all open to the public.

As we pursue our way along the Corso, we catch a glimpse, through the main door, of the beautiful Bramantesque cloistered garden of the palace—once converted into a ballroom for the Emperor of Austria. A little farther on we pause for a moment to admire the façade that Pietro da Cortona designed in 1660 for the ancient church of **S. Maria in Via Lata** on the corner. According to legend this church was built over the house of the centurion who guarded St. Paul on his Roman journey, but in actual fact its lowest levels are rooted in a paleo-christian structure built into ancient store-houses formerly believed to have been part of the Saepta Julia. Turning the corner we find ourselves in a short street now known as the Via Lata, which contains one of the oldest fountains in Rome—the *facchino* or porter who also took part in the dialogues of Pasquino and Marforio. The Facchino was a real person, Abbondio Rizzi, the head of the porters' guild who lived in the fifteenth century and was famous for the weights he was able to carry; the fountain was made as a monument to him after his death.

The Via Lata leads into the **Piazza del Collegio Romano**, which is dominated by the fine building of this famous school,

whose foundation stone was laid by Gregory XIII in 1582.
The Collegio Romano also houses the National Vittorio
Emanuele library, but no longer all the Pigorini prehistoric
museum, of which the most famous exhibit, the 'Treasure of
Praeneste', has been transferred to the Etruscan Museum in
the Villa Giulia and some other exhibits to the Museo Preistorico e Protostorico del Lazio, Piazza G. Marconi in the
distant suburb of the E.U.R.

The whole of the left-hand corner of the piazza is enclosed
by two wings of Palazzo Doria, the earliest and perhaps the
finest, designed by Antonio del Grande in the seventeenth
century. The entrance to the **Doria picture gallery** is by an
inconspicuous little door (No. 1a), in the angle of the building.
From here a narrow stair leads to an ante-room, where it is
advisable immediately to notify the attendant that one also
wishes to visit the state and private apartments; these are only
opened at intervals to individual groups and for them a
separate ticket is necessary. The picture gallery consists of
four long salons, or *braccia*, built over the porticoes surrounding the garden courtyard which we saw from the Corso, and a
series of rooms running the whole length of the palace on that
side. To this is added the Salone Aldobrandini, containing
antique sculptures, most of which were found on the family
estates, as well as pictures and tapestries.

The great treasure of the Doria gallery is, of course, Velas-
quez's famous portrait of the Pamphilj family Pope, Innocent
X (kept together with his bust by Bernini in a small cabinet
at the end of *braccio* 3). This, in a way, may be said to set the
tone of the whole gallery as it is pre-eminently a family collection that, both in content and in the style of presentation,
reflects the taste of a great Roman house of the seventeenth
century. As one might expect, the setting is magnificent.
Seventeenth-century consoles, settees and chairs, gilded with
real gold and upholstered with Genoese velvet, line the walls,
alternating with superb portrait busts by Algardi and Bernini.
Notable among these is Algardi's one of Innocent X's redoubtable sister-in-law, Donna Olimpia (No. 1, just by the
door of the Sala dei Marmi), who was the butt of so many
pasquinades. In the first *braccio* of the gallery hang two
magnificent Titians—'La Spagna Soccorre la Religione', an
unfinished allegory, (No. 10), and a 'Salome' or 'Erodiade'
(No. 29). Three pictures by Caravaggio on the same wall

illustrate his evolution as an artist from the simplicity of his early days—shown in the 'Maddalena' (No. 40) and the 'Riposo durante la Fuga in Egitto' (No. 42)—to the chiaroscuro effects of his later development, as seen in 'S. Giovanni Battista' (No. 44). Into the composition of these last two pictures, the artist has introduced the mullein plant (*Verbascum broussa*), which is so characteristic a feature of Caravaggio's exteriors and those of his followers, as to constitute almost a signature of the Caravaggesque school.

The four rooms which lead out of the second *braccio* of the gallery on the right contain many fine Flemish paintings, which were very popular in seventeenth-century Rome; these include J. van Schorel's exquisite portrait of his mistress 'Agatha van Schoonhoven' (No. 279) and Pieter Breughel the Elder's famous 'Bay of Naples' (No. 317). Four pictures hanging in room IV cast a curious reflection on seventeenth-century taste; several figures from David Teniers's 'Banchetto Campestre' (No. 277) have been copied and enlarged by J. B. Weenix (?) to form whole pictures on their own (Nos. 236, 248 and 254). The small octagonal cabinet at the far end of this series of rooms contains a charming series of small landscapes, including one of the Roman Forum, which are of particular interest as they are all the works of Flemish artists of the early sixteenth century, whose influence played such a large part in the foundation of the Roman landscape school. The Doria Gallery, with its five superb Claude Lorrains (Nos. 343, 346, 348, 351 and 352) and its seven Dughets (Nos. 344, 358, 395, 398, 400, 402 and 407), has, perhaps, the most representative collection of the pictures of this school in Italy, which is of outstanding interest to the English as the inspiration of our landscape style of garden.

The state apartments of Palazzo Doria include a baroque family chapel, a ballroom and a series of reception rooms. Among these last, three small salons—decorated and furnished right down to the smallest detail in the second half of the eighteenth century—are one of the most delicious sights in Rome. 'Off with the old and on with the new' is so deeply ingrained a Roman characteristic—if it were not the Colosseum might still be complete today!—that these three charming little rooms are probably unique. The first, the yellow salon, is lined with twelve exquisite Gobelin tapestries made for Louis XV. The second, the Venetian or green salon, is redolent of the gay and frivolous life of eighteenth-century Venice, as illustrated by the pictures attributed to Pietro Longhi which hang on its walls; while one can imagine some Venetian belle reclining on the exquisite chaise-longue to drink her morning chocolate. The third or red salon is more sober, as befits a room in which hangs a picture where Sir Isaac Newton and Lord Gravesend are seen conversing with Britannia; also portraits of a Roman senator and the Old Pretender. This room also contains a superb Gobelin tapestry made for Louis XIV with his personal cipher of the sun as well as the lilies of France; this hangs between Jan 'Velvet' Breughel's allegories of the elements and seasons.

The private apartment of the palace, which is still lived in, contains personal mementoes of the family, whose history dates back to the beginning of the twelfth century. These include the great sealed title deeds of the Doria estates, collars of the Golden Fleece awarded to different members of this race of seafarers, and tapestries recording their participation in the victory of Lepanto, all preserved in the Andrea Doria room. Sebastiano del Piombo's superb portrait of this astute admiral and statesman hangs in the large green drawing-room, in company with Gothic tapestries, a Filippo Lippi Annunciation, a Memling Deposition, a Bronzino family portrait and a host of other treasures.

A certain amount of will-power has to be exercised in order to tear ourselves away from the treasures of Palazzo Doria, but it must be done if we are to manage to see the interior of the church of S. Ignazio before it closes. There will, we hope just be time for a quick glimpse down the **Via della Gatta**, which leads from the Piazza del Collegio Romano to the Piazza Grazioli, in order to see the curious little stone figure of a cat, standing on the cornice of Palazzo Grazioli at the far end. This was found during the excavations of the nearby temple of Isis and has given rise to the popular legend that a treasure lies buried nearby, under the spot at which the cat is looking, but so far no one has been successful in discovering exactly where that is. The area to the right of Piazza Grazioli and Piazza del Collegio Romano was in ancient times devoted to the worship of Egyptian deities, and was filled with obelisks and ancient statues brought from Egypt. The curious little three-pronged street of **S. Stefano del Cacco**, which connects Piazza Grazioli with the Via del Gesù and the Via Piè di

Marmo, owes its name to the fact that a statue of the dog-faced god Anubis was found there. This was mistaken for a baboon, so the word *macacco* (baboon) was added to its original name; this in time has been abbreviated to *cacco*. The **Via Piè di Marmo**, leading from the Piazza del Collegio Romano to the Via S. Caterina da Siena, also derives its name from an antique relic, in this case an enormous marble foot, possibly of a colossal statue of Isis. Formerly this stood on the corner of the Piazza del Collegio Romano, but was removed to its present position at the corner of S. Stefano del Cacco to make way for King Vittorio Emanuele's funeral procession on its way to the Pantheon in January 1878.

Our quickest way from here to the **church of S. Ignazio** is by the street of the same name. In it we pass the great Casanatense library, where a covered passage bridges the street, connecting what were once the headquarters of rival camps—the Jesuit headquarters of the Collegio Romano and the Dominican priory of S. Maria sopra Minerva. The restrained and massive façade of the church of S. Ignazio seems well-suited to the character of the soldier-saint, S. Ignazio or St. Ignatius of Loyola, who founded the Jesuit order. But what, one wonders, would he have made of Raguzzini's deliciously frivolous rococo piazza, so like an operatic set, which was laid out in front of it in 1727? The church itself, which was built between 1626 and 1685, is largely the work of two priests— Orazio Grassi the architect, and Andrea Pozzo who executed the tremendous frescoes in the interior. To gain the full effect of Pozzo's *trompe l'oeil* ceiling representing the 'Entry of S. Ignatius into Paradise', one should stand on the small disk half-way up the nave. His virtuosity in creating the effect of a dome over the transept can be appreciated from any angle. The richness of the interior decoration of S. Ignazio reaches its zenith in the resplendent baroque altar and *lapis lazuli* urn containing the relics of S. Luigi Gonzaga. This baroque taste is now very fashionable, but there may still be some who would appreciate Gregorovius's and Augustus Hare's definition of it as 'the drawing-room style of church decoration'.

From the Piazza di S. Ignazio we make our way by the curiously named Via del Burro, which winds through Raguzzini's operatic set. The street name is definitely a corruption of the word '*bureau*', but no one is sure whether it is derived from the bureau-like shape of the rococo buildings themselves, or from the fact that the *bureaux*, or offices, of the French administration were situated there during the Napoleonic occupation. The street leads us into the picturesque Piazza di Pietra, the whole of one side of which is lined with the vast stone columns of the **Temple of Neptune**; in reality the Hadrianeum, or temple dedicated to the deified Emperor Hadrian. Some idea of the tremendous rise in the ground level which has occurred in this part of the city since classical times can be gathered from the fact that the temple was then raised above the ground on a high podium, and now its columns are half sunk below street level. The building incorporated into the temple is, incongruously enough, the Roman Stock Exchange; but this, in its way, is almost as interesting a historical relic as the temple, as it is one of the most extensive examples of a Roman architectural palimpsest to have survived the archaeological fervour of the Fascist period. The Via dei Bergamaschi leads us now into the **Piazza Colonna**, dominated by the famous **Column of Marcus Aurelius**. Like the Column of Trajan, this owed its survival through the Middle Ages to ecclesiastical ownership; it belonged to the monks of S. Silvestro in Capite, who derived a considerable income by charging the pilgrim-tourist an entrance fee. The column was built to commemorate Marcus Aurelius's triumphs over the Marcomanni, Quadi and Sarmathians, and although the reliefs which spiral up it are less fine than those of Trajan's column they provide a vivid picture of the life and costumes of the time. Originally the column was surmounted by a statue of the emperor, but in 1589 the existing one of St. Paul was placed there by Domenico Fontana, who at the same time restored the base of the column, placing there the inscription attributing it, erroneously, to Antoninus Pius, Marcus Aurelius's uncle and adoptive father. It was perhaps a pardonable mistake as the column rose in the centre of an area filled with monuments of the Antonines, and a column dedicated to Antoninus Pius had stood close by, in the centre of what is now the Piazza Montecitorio. This vast monolith was rediscovered in the eighteenth century and sawn into pieces.

The dominating building in the Piazza Colonna is the **Palazzo Chigi**. Begun in 1562 by Giacomo della Porta for the Aldobrandini, it was bought by the famous Sienese banking family during the reign of the then Pope, Alexander VII, and completed by the architect Vincenzo della Greca. For long the seat of the Italian Foreign Office, Palazzo Chigi now houses the Cabinet offices. The palace is one of the few in the square that was not radically changed in the last century, when Palazzo Wedekind (where the *Tempo* offices now are) was built, incorporating some of the columns found in the excavations of the ancient city of Veii. The character of the piazza itself has changed out of all recognition since the eighteenth and nineteenth centuries; in the eighteenth century the Column of Marcus Aurelius was surrounded with stoves where the entire city's supply of coffee was roasted. This extraordinary practice was dictated by law, and was due to the curious foible, then fashionable in Rome, of detesting any kind of scent or aroma, even flowers. Then, too, the piazza was filled with booths selling fruit and cooling drinks; in time these were gradually replaced by the smart cafés which were the rendezvous of the nineteenth-century bloods of the town, especially in the evening when all the rank and fashion of Rome drove along the Corso in their carriages.

Today, like any other city square, Piazza Colonna is a car park, but by now this should be emptying, and the whole of Rome bent on one single thought—the midday meal. We are well placed, however, to begin thinking of our own, as the piazza lies in one of the best restaurant centres in the city. There is such an embarrassment of choice that suggestions are difficult; but for an elegant luncheon with first rate Italian food, '31' at 31 Via Uffici del Vicariato is excellent. For Valpolicella wine on draught and succulent Venetian home cooking, try Battaglia's Ristorante della Colonna Antonina (at No. 48 Via della Colonna Antonina). If all you want is a quick snack and more time to stroll during the siesta hour, have a pizza in the Pizzeria at 42 Piazza di Pietra and top up with an ice and coffee at Giolitti (at No. 40 Via Uffici del Vicariato), among Romans the most famous ice-cream shop in the city.

CHAPTER FIVE

Piazza Montecitorio to the Tiber Island

❧

If we have lunched in the neighbourhood of the Piazza Colonna, the **Piazza Montecitorio** is the ideal place from which to begin our afternoon's stroll. Though various theories have been advanced as to the origin of the square's name—a corruption of *Mons Acceptoris*—none of them really explain it. Nor has anyone ever been able to discover how the *mons*, or mound, upon which a medieval Colonna fortress preceded Bernini's existing Palazzo Montecitorio came to exist; the palace is now used as the lower house of the Italian Parliament.

The most interesting monument in the square, however, is the **Obelisk of Psammeticus I**, originally brought by Augustus from Heliopolis and erected as the gnomon of a sun-dial in the Campus Martius. Pliny gives a detailed account of it in his *Natural History* and says that the ships used by Augustus to bring the first two obelisks to Rome, probably this and the one in Piazza del Popolo, excited so much curiosity that they were kept on permanent exhibition in the docks of Pozzuoli. This is the fourth biggest of the thirteen obelisks now standing in Rome, surviving from classical times; then apparently there were no less than forty-eight. All of the thirteen have since been re-erected—a process which began with Sixtus V, who put up three of them, and continued until the last century. Most of these obelisks are surmounted by crosses, stars or the arms of popes; only two—those of the Villa Mattei and Montecitorio—have the gnomon and ball enabling them to cast the clearly defined shadow necessary for a sun-dial, as described by Pliny. The Montecitorio obelisk, which was found in a fragmentary state after centuries of oblivion, was restored during Pius VI's reign at the end of the eighteenth century with pieces of granite from the commemorative column of Antoninus Pius, and erected on the spot which this monument had formerly occupied. Probably it was in

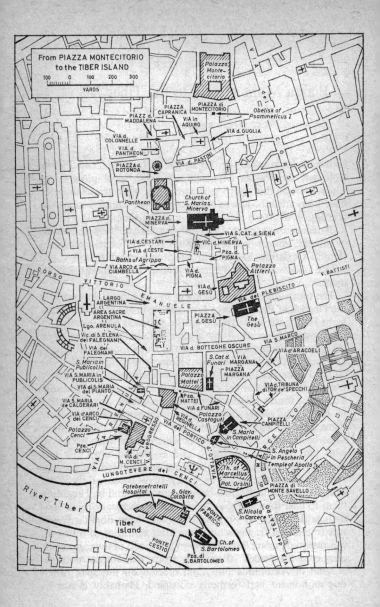

From PIAZZA MONTECITORIO
to the TIBER ISLAND

100   0   100   200   300
YARDS

Palazzo Monte-citoria

PIAZZA di MONTECITORIO

Obelisk of Psammeticus I

PIAZZA CAPRANICA

PIAZZ. d. MADDALENA

VIA in AQUIRO

VIA d. GUGLIA

VIA d. COLONNELLE

VIA d. PANTHEON

VIA d. PASTINI

PIAZZA d. ROTONDA

CORSO

Pantheon

Church of S. Maria s. Minerva

PIAZZA d. MINERVA

VIA S. CAT. d. SIENA

VIA d. CESTARI

VIC. d. MINERVA

VIA d. CESTE

Pza. d. PIGNA

Baths of Agrippa

VIA ARCO d. CIAMBELLA

VIA d. PIGNA

Palazzo Altieri

V. BATTISTI

CORSO

VITTORIO

VIA d. GESÙ

VIA dei PLEBISCITO

LARGO ARGENTINA

EMANUELE

AREA SACRE ARGENTINA

PIAZZA d. GESÙ

The Gesù

Lgo. ARENULA

VIA d. BOTTEGHE OSCURE

VIA S. MARCO

Vic. di S. ELENA dei FALEGNAMI

VIA d'ARACOELI

VIA dei FALEGNAMI

S. Cat. d. Funari

VIA MARGANA

S. Maria in Publicolis

Palazzo Mattei

PIAZZA MARGANA

VIA S. MARIA in PUBLICOLIS

VIA d. TRIBUNA di TOR de' SPECCHI

VIA di S. MARIA del PIANTO

Pza. MATTEI

VIA S. MARIA de CALDERARI

VIA d. FUNARI

VIA d'ARCO dei CENCI

VIA d. REGINELLA

Palazzo Castaguti

PIAZZA CAMPITELLI

Palazzo Cenci

VIA d. PROGRESSO

VIA dei PORTICO

S. Maria in Campitelli

Pza. CENCI

VIA d'OTTAVIA

S. Angelo in Pescheria, Temple of Apollo

VIA di M. CENCI

VIA d. TEATRO

LUNGOTEVERE dei CENCI

Th. of Marcellus

PIAZZA di MONTE SAVELLO

River Tiber

Fatebenefratelli Hospital

S. Giov. Calabita

Pal. Orsini

S. Nicola in Carcere

Tiber Island

PONTE FABRICIO

PONTE CESTIO

Ch. of S. Bartolomeo

Pza. di S. BARTOLOMEO

memory of Pliny's description of its original use that the obelisk was then surmounted by its existing bronze ball and point.

The area which we are going to explore this afternoon is in fact the one where more obelisks have been found than in any other part of Rome, three besides the Montecitorio one, but all the others were small and were evidently used for the adornment of the temples of the Egyptian gods, the existence of which in the area we have already noted. Two obelisks still stand near the place of their discovery, that in the Piazza della Minerva and the one in the centre of the fountain in front of the Pantheon. This last was found in the street we now take out of the Piazza Montecitorio, which is called Via della Guglia (the street of the obelisk) after it.

We now turn instead to the right out of the Via della Guglia and by way of the Via in Aquiro arrive in the **Piazza Capranica**. This takes its name from the Collegio Capranica, an ancient religious foundation originated by Cardinal Domenico Capranica who, in the sixteenth century, built the beautiful palace which houses it. **Palazzo Capranica**, which is now a cinema, is one of the exceedingly rare survivals in Rome of a palace built in the transitional period when Gothic and Renaissance styles met and mingled. The tower and crossed mullioned windows on the left remind one of Palazzo Venezia, but the three *bifore* on the right are clearly medieval in style and probably belong to the earliest part of the palace. Incidentally it is interesting to note that although the palace is of an earlier date than Palazzo Venezia, the tower is not machicolated like a medieval fortress, but is furnished with a loggia; this is a prototype of the characteristic Roman palace *belvederi* of later times that were designed for taking the air on hot summer evenings.

Passing by way of the Via delle Colonnelle, so-called from seven small columns set up there to prevent passing carts from damaging the houses in the narrow street, we find ourselves in the **Piazza della Maddalena**. This small square, dominated by the delightful eighteenth-century rococo façade of the church of the same name, is the centre of one of the liveliest and most colourful districts of old Rome, which, here at least, has preserved its own inimitable character unchanged. Hardly a building exists that has not some association with the past, but this—and it is one of the great charms of Rome—

does not mean that it is treated as a museum piece, for instead it forms part and parcel of the surging and vivacious life of the city today.

No. 63 of the street we now follow—the Via del Pantheon— is a case in point; it is a hotel, the Albergo del Sole, that already in the early years of the sixteenth century was known as the Albergo Montone. Here the great poet Ariosto went on an evening in the spring of 1513 after he had been affec- tionately received by the humanist Pope Leo X; later he recorded how he ate his supper there 'with a heart full of hope, but my clothes spoiled and soaked by the heavy rain that was falling'. Parts of the original sixteenth-century building exist, but no tablet records the fact that here in 1768 young Giuseppe Balsamo, who later styled himself Count Cagliostro, was arrested for hitting one of the inn servants and went to cool his heels in the Tor di Nona prison. Twenty years later he was again imprisoned in Rome, but the dread Inquisition did not so easily relinquish its prey, and Cagliostro paid for his mis- deeds by ending his days in the papal fortress of San Leo.

The history of few squares in Rome illustrate more pro- foundly the insouciant Roman attitude to their great monu- ments than the Piazza della Rotonda that lies before the **Pan- theon**. The fame of this marvellous building was already well- established in antiquity and is celebrated in a popular Roman proverb which, making an untranslatable play on the word *rotonda*, says that anyone who comes to Rome without seeing the Pantheon 'goes and comes back an ass'. Yet, in spite of the edicts of successive popes (and the provision of an alternative site) the populace persisted in using the piazza, with its charming Renaissance fountain surmounted by Rameses II's obelisk, as a fish market until 1847.

There is no doubt that the Pantheon was only saved by the Byzantine Phocas having made a gift of it, for it was imperial property, to Boniface IV in 608, and its having been conse- crated as a church dedicated to St. Mary and All Saints or Martyrs. The accepted Christian conversion of pagan cults is reflected in the *Mirabilia*'s erroneous description of the building as having been 'dedicated to Cybele, mother of the gods' and the pope's subsequent consecration of it 'to the blessed Mary, ever virgin, that is mother of all saints'. Even this, however, did not prevent the portico from becoming encrusted with the booths and huts of a poultry market, whose roofs were supported by poles inserted into still visible holes cut in its columns; these accretions were only removed after Eugenius IV's return from Avignon in 1431.

Just about a century later, in 1549, William Thomas described the Pantheon in his *History of Italy* as 'the perfectest of all the antiquities', and admired the wonderful engineering of the dome; remarking rather prosaically that it is 'vaulted like the half of an egg'. The curious thing about the Pantheon is that although it has been perhaps the most admired monument in Rome for close on two millennia, its building history was something of a mystery until 1892. Then the French architect, Georges Chedanne, discovered that the bricks in all of it, even the foundations, bear stamps dating from the years between AD 120 and 125. In other words, in spite of Agrippa's dedicatory inscription which appears on the trabeation of the portico 'M. AGRIPPA. L.F.COS. TERTIUM FECIT' (Marcus Agrippa, son of Lucius, Consul for the third time, built this), the whole of the Pantheon we see today was built in the reign of Hadrian; though it was later restored by Septimius Severus and Caracalla. Agrippa did indeed originally build the first Pantheon, or 'temple of all the gods', as part of an enormous layout of temple, baths and public gardens in the redesigned Campus Martius, between 27 and 25 BC. But Hadrian rebuilt them entirely, and such was the emperor's modesty (he never had his name inscribed on any of his buildings) and Agrippa's fame that the original inscription was repeated on the new building. The latest expert opinion also designates Hadrian, who is known to have designed Rome's largest temple, that of Venus and Rome, as the architect of the Pantheon, as he probably also was of his famous Tivoli villa.

Hadrian's architectural ideas were dominated by his love of Greece and a native daring in trying out new effects and theories of what might be achieved from the solid basis of old Roman building and engineering techniques; his innovations in this field in the Tivoli villa might almost be said to presage the Baroque. In the Pantheon, however, although the Greek influence is evident in the superb pedimented porch supported by eighteen monolithic Corinthian columns of grey and red Egyptian granite, it is Rome which dominates in the vast circular hall or *cella* that lies behind. But it was Hadrian's original genius that made this temple unique among those of classical times. Unlike all the others where it was the exterior that dominated architecturally (the *cella* or shrine being small and reserved for a limited number of adepts), here it is the *cella* which is the cynosure of the whole building. It is roofed with what was still the greatest dome in the world until this century[1] (the diameter is 43·30 metres; St. Peter's, the second largest, is 42·52 metres; St. Paul's in London, the seventh, is 31 metres). The wonderful sense of harmony engendered by the proportions is due to the fact that the diameter of the dome is equal to the height of the building.

Aesthetics apart, the design of the Pantheon is also an engineering feat of the first order; even a layman can guess at the intricacy of the calculations and the profound knowledge of construction techniques that were required to create a building which would withstand the thrust of the great dome. This was achieved by a complicated system of relieving arches embedded in the huge mass of concrete that forms the core of the whole building, from its foundations to the summit of the dome. The concrete was mixed with travertine, tufa, brick and pumice stone in successive layers, with the heaviest materials at the lower levels, the lighter tufa and pumice mixture being used at the top of the dome. The concrete for the dome was poured on a framework which bore in reverse the outline of the coffering and its thickness diminishes from 5·90 metres at the base to 1·50 metres at the summit. The great central *oculus*, which lights the whole building, has a diameter of 8·92 metres and was originally ringed with bronze. In spite of the infinite care and attention that went to its construction, subsequently there was some settlement within the enormous mass of the Pantheon. Cracks appeared, and the builders reinforced the foundations and built retaining walls behind and on either side; so that in antiquity the great circular building, except for the dome, cannot have been seen in its entirety as it is today.

In ancient times the dome of the Pantheon was covered with sheets of gilded bronze; these were plundered by the Byzantine Emperor Constans II in 655, and were replaced with lead by Gregory III in the eighth century. The bronze removed by the Barberini Pope, Urban VIII, came instead from the beams of

1. The prefabricated concrete dome of the Palazzo dello Sport, built for the 1960 Olympic Games in Rome, has a diameter of 100 metres, and there are other modern domes whose diameter is greater than that of the Pantheon.

the portico, its use for the *baldacchino* of St. Peter's and the cannons of Castel S. Angelo provoking the famous pasquinade '*quod non fecerunt barberi, fecerunt Barberini*' (what the barbarians didn't do, the Barberini did). During the sixteenth and seventeenth centuries the portico was used as an exhibition hall on St. Joseph's day (19 March) for pictures painted by members of the artists' club known as the *Virtuosi del Pantheon*; these included such famous painters as the Carracci, Pietro da Cortona and Salvator Rosa. Curiously enough this was a revival of an ancient custom; Agrippa had exhibited pictures—including a Venus which cost him 300,000 denari—in the original Pantheon.

The Pantheon is one of those monuments whose appearance is so well known to us before we ever see it that we cannot help wondering beforehand if it will come to us as an anticlimax. The answer, speaking from personal experience of nearly twenty years and having taken countless people to see it, is decidedly to the contrary; the Pantheon not only far exceeds all one's previous conceptions, but the tremendous impression it makes grows on one with time. To me there is always something comforting about catching even a glimpse of it in passing; solidly planted there, as witness that a work of man's endeavour can survive the wreckage of centuries. But as I pass through the great bronze doors, the largest of the three Roman ones to have survived, this comfortable feeling of human companionship is transformed into the awe which one experiences when confronted with a manifestation of that universal aspiration towards the sublime which is common to all creeds, though each one interprets it after its own fashion. The Altar of Heaven in China (which I have never seen) perhaps best represents this in the eastern world, just as the great Gothic cathedrals seem to me to do so for the Christian one. But here in the Pantheon it is the calm and majestic spirit of the classical world which lives, perhaps as nowhere else, in the vast sweep of the dome and the light diffused from above as from the all-seeing eye of heaven; the symbol, it is said of a divinity which was superior to all others. This was no personal god, however, nor one to inspire human warmth or any mystical searching of the soul, but rather a feeling of omnipotent and detached calm, well-suited to the stoic philosophy of ancient Rome.

The interior of the Pantheon has, surprisingly enough,

changed little since ancient times. Though restored, the design of the pavement is the same; so is the coffering of the dome, which originally would have been adorned with stucco ornament. The main difference lies in the decoration of the attic between the two entablatures; a small portion of this, on the right of the apse, has been restored to its original state, with groups of porphyry pilasters alternating with square-headed false windows, ranged above a high white marble plinth. The great apse, the six recesses and the eight *aedicole*, with their columns of precious marbles, have not changed since classical times. Then the apse and recesses would have housed the statues of the seven great gods—the *aedicole* the minor ones—with Mars and Venus, the protecting divinities of the Julian house, standing in the place of honour. According to Pliny the statue of Venus wore as ear-rings the two halves of the famous pearl that Mark Anthony took from Cleopatra, after she had drunk its twin dissolved in vinegar in order to win a bet with him. The statues of goddesses in classical temples were adorned with jewels, like the figures of saints in many Roman churches today. The breast of Julius Caesar's 'Venus Genetrix' for instance was covered with British pearls, while the famous 'Diana of Nemi' had a crown studded with twenty-one topazes and eighty carbuncles, a diadem, nine ear-rings, eight necklaces and bracelets ornamented with beryls and other gems, of which an inscribed catalogue still exists.

Unfortunately it cannot be said that all the religious pictures, statues and tombs in the Pantheon today are aesthetically worthy of their magnificent setting, though the latter contain the remains of some of Italy's great artists. The most famous is, of course, that of Raphael (in the *aedicola* between the second and third chapels on the left), inscribed with his friend Cardinal Bembo's celebrated epitaph '*Ille hic est Raffaello Sanzio, timuit quo sospite vinci Rerum magna parens et moriente mori*' (Here lies Raphael: while he lived the great mother of all things [Nature] feared to be outdone; and when he died she feared too to die). Raphael was known to have commissioned Lorenzetto to make the 'Madonna of the Stone' which stands in the *aedicola*, but for centuries his tomb itself was lost and was only discovered in 1833. He died on Good Friday 1520, at the age of 37 and, by his own wish the name of Maria Bibiena, to whom

he was engaged for six years, is commemorated in a plaque
on the right of the tomb. Maria died before Raphael, and their
relationship was apparently a matter of formal arrangement
(she was his patron's niece); possibly the charms of the
famous Fornarina had something to do with the length of
the engagement, and on his deathbed Raphael repented of it.
Two of Raphael's favourite pupils lie near him, Perin del
Vaga and Giovanni da Udine, and another contemporary
Baldassare Peruzzi; also artists of later generations such as
Flaminio Vacca, Taddeo Zuccari and Annibale Carracci.

After the unification of Italy, the Pantheon was chosen as
the mausoleum of her kings, of which the first two—Vittorio
Emanuele II and Umberto I—lie buried in the smaller apses,
to right and left. The design of their tombs makes one regret,
especially in this magnificent setting, that Italy was united at
the particular period artistically that she was. But perhaps the
manes of Hadrian may derive consolation from the thought
that some at least of the bronze robbed by Urban VIII has
returned to its original home: the ornaments on the tomb of
Vittorio Emanuele were, for symbolic reasons, made from the
melted-down cannons of Castel S. Angelo.

If we have contented ourselves with a light lunch, over by
2 p.m., and taken about three-quarters of an hour to stroll
from Piazza Montecitorio and see the Pantheon, we will now
find ourselves with more than an hour on our hands before
the church of S. Maria sopra Minerva, the next great sight on
our list, opens at 4 p.m. In this case we would do well to
continue our exploration of the *vicoli* down to the Tiber
Island, and return to see the church and that of the Gesù
before they close at 7 p.m. If our lunch has been a typically
Roman one, lasting to 3 p.m., then the Minerva, as it is
popularly known, will be open shortly after we emerge from
the Pantheon and we can fill in the odd quarter of an hour
locally; leaving the rest of our exploration till afterwards. As
Roman habits are very insidious, soon exercising their influence upon the stoutest northern resolution, we will treat our
itinerary in this order.

Thus, before entering the church, we pass through the
Piazza della Minerva. In the midst of the square stands the
third of the obelisks found in the area, mounted upon the
back of Bernini's famous elephant. This monument, which is
one of the most appealing in Rome, was the result of long and

earnest consultations between Pope Alexander VII and the artist, who made many alternative sketches for the design. The inspiration for the motif of the elephant and the obelisk comes from a curious fifteenth-century romance, the *Hypnero-tomachia* of Poliphilo, describing lovers who pursue an imaginary journey through a dream garden filled with strange devices. Twenty years earlier Bernini had designed a similar monument for the Barberini gardens, which was never put up, and from a still existing copy of the *Hypnerotomachia*, annotated in Alexander's own hand, it is evident that the pope too had studied the story. Alexander wanted the monument to glorify his reign, as the famous Bernini fountain with the obelisk in Piazza Navona had done that of Innocent X, and he himself composed the inscription on the base, which says that the elephant was chosen to show that it requires a robust intelligence to uphold solid wisdom; the monument was un-veiled in 1667.

From the Piazza della Minerva we take the Via dei Cestari, part of which formerly went by the name of Via dei Calcarari, or the street of the lime kilns; a sinister reminder of the fate of heaven only knows how many sculptural masterpieces of antiquity whose marble was there reduced to lime. Half-way down the street, turning to the right down the **Via Arco della Ciambella**, we come to the remains of an apse of the Baths of Agrippa. Formerly part of a circular hall, these ruins re-sembled a stone ring and were popularly called after a ring-shaped cake or bun known as a *ciambella*; or, according to some other sources, the street and an inn which stood there derived their name from a great antique bronze ring or crown which was found there. A little *trattoria*, called the Ciambella, still stands, and old houses cling to the ruined apse like barnacles. The whole scene is a synthesis of Roman life, brought up to date, with caper plants flowering in the stone-work of the ancient apse, a Madonna in a lovely Renaissance frame set into it, two Siamese cats basking among the flower-ing window boxes, and the whole thing surmounted by a TV aerial.

Leading out of the Via dei Cestari, on the opposite side, is the **Via della Pigna**, on the right of which stands the fine Palazzo del Vicariato; on the left, through a dark old door (No. 19) we can penetrate into the courtyard of the house of Stefano Porcaro. This member of an ancient Roman family and ardent collector of antiquities, who in the fifteenth century revived the dream of restoring the Roman Republic, paid with his life for his ideas. Justifiably it must be admitted, as, inspired by the examples of Brutus and Catiline, he planned to burn down the Vatican and to imprison the gentle humanist Pope Nicholas V. Gregorovius, and many others, believed that Stefano's house was destroyed, all but the fine portal which is to be seen on the other side of the block in Via delle Ceste (No. 25), but in actual fact the beautiful early Renaissance stairs and doors which we see in this neglected courtyard once formed part of it, as is evident from the Porcaro arms and inscriptions.

The Via della Pigna leads us into the piazza of the same name, both of which are called after the famous antique bronze *pigna* or pine cone from which the whole surrounding *rione* also takes its name. This probably adorned a fountain in the temple of Isis in the vicinity but its discovery in this area gave rise to the story that it had once surmounted the dome of the Pantheon. In the Middle Ages the *pigna* was removed to the piazza in front of St. Peter's and later to the Cortile del Belvedere. The Piazza della Pigna has also played its part in modern history, for the first conversation between Cardinal Gasparri and Mussolini, which paved the way to the Conciliation between the Church and the Italian State, took place in secret in the house at No. 6 in 1923. At the far end of the square (actually numbered as 85 Via del Gesù) is an exquisite portal in classical style. Taking the narrow little Vicolo della Minerva, at whose corner stands the charming little church of S. Giovanni della Pigna, we make our way back to the Piazza della Minerva.

To those who have been told that the church of S. **Maria sopra Minerva** is the only Gothic one in Rome, and who expect to see grey stone tracery, the church will come as something of a surprise. The façade, dating from 1453 and attributed to Meo da Caprino, is in the severe style of the early Renaissance, while the interior (which was most unfortunately restored in the last century) has polished marble Corinthian columns and flattened vaulting, scarcely consonant with the usual conception of Gothic architecture; but it has a beauty of its own when flooded with the golden afternoon light from the rose windows. Although the appellation '*sopra Minerva*' would lead one to suppose that the church is a very ancient foundation, in fact this is not so; both it and the adjoining monastery were built in 1280 among the ruins of the precinct of the Temple of Minerva, as the centre of the Dominican Order in Rome.

During the seven centuries of its existence, the Minerva has become a veritable museum of art treasures. The existence of so many chapels and tombs of great Roman families, and monuments to popes and cardinals, would in itself have been sufficient to explain this, but there, in addition, lies the body of St. Catherine of Siena. This mystically inspired Dominican sister, who played such a part in the political life of her time, and was largely responsible for the return of the popes from Avignon, died in a house in the nearby Via S. Chiara (the room where she died was bodily transported to the sacristy of the Minerva). In memory of this, until 1870, the popes came in solemn procession to the church each year on the feast of the Annunciation. Owing to the plethora of treasures which the church contains, only the most important, or those of outstanding human interest, will be mentioned in our itinerary.

The fourth chapel on the right of the nave contains a charming but curious 'Annunciation', now attributed to Antoniazzo Romano. Against a gold background is portrayed not only the Biblical scene, but the Virgin is also represented in the act of handing small bags to three young girls, kneeling before her in company with Cardinal Torquemada (uncle of the Inquisitor). This commemorates a charitable institution founded by the cardinal for providing poor girls with dowries, which were presented to them by the pope himself in the course of the Annunciation Day ceremonies. The Venetian diarist, Marin Sanudo, saw the papal procession and ceremony in 1504, Augustus Hare during the last century, and both described it as one of the solemn sights of Rome, with the Host being borne aloft through decorated streets on the back of the white papal mule. The girls were drawn up in two rows in front of the church to receive their dowries; those wearing white wreaths received a double portion, because they were going to become nuns, and 'money placed in the hands of religion bears interest for the poor'.

Continuing our progress down the church, in the sixth chapel on the right we find one of the finest Renaissance tombs in Rome, made during his lifetime for the Spanish

Cardinal de Coca (who died in 1477) by Andrea Bregno. Perhaps by an association of ideas, in the next chapel (the first on the right in the transept) we find a twentieth-century revival of this old custom of erecting the funerary monument of a living person. The tomb of Cardinal Micara, formerly titular of the church, stood here complete with its inscription —only the date of his death was lacking during his lifetime and added after death. In the same chapel is a beautiful wooden crucifix, formerly attributed to Giotto.

At this end of the transept stands the **Carafa Chapel**, one of the greatest artistic treasures of the church, and indeed of Rome. After many years of patient restoration, Filippino Lippi's wonderful frescoes (executed in 1489) are again visible, and are now expertly illuminated (the light switch is on the left wall), so that the full effect of this exquisite chapel can be clearly seen. It is best to view it first from well back in the transept, as here the wonderful composition of Lippi's soaring 'Assumption', filling the whole of the main wall, can be fully appreciated. Above the altar, set in a beautiful Renaissance frame attributed to Giuliano da Maiano, is another Annunciation. Here again the figure of the donor, Cardinal Olivieri Carafa, has been introduced, being presented to the Virgin by St. Thomas Aquinas, to whom the chapel is dedicated. On the right wall of the chapel, St. Thomas is represented in triumph, confounding the heretics, shown here as two central figures usually identified as Arius and Sabellius. Rather curiously in this context, the two small boys shown standing nearby are the future Medici popes, Leo X and Clement VII. In the left-hand corner of the painting is a very rare contemporary view of the old Lateran palace with the equestrian statue of Marcus Aurelius before it was moved to the Capitol. Against the left wall of the chapel stands the tomb of the Carafa Pope, Paul IV, the great inquisitor, who enclosed the Jews of Rome in the Ghetto and who was so hated by the people that they beheaded his statue on the Capitol after his death in 1559. It is related that this pope's aspect was so terrifying that even the proud and fearless Spanish commander the Duke of Alva quailed at the sight of him; and with Renaissance veracity Pirro Ligorio has conveyed something of this dread even on his tomb. With relief one turns to look up at the vaulted ceiling of the chapel where Raffaellino del Garbo's Sybils of Tibur, Delphi, Cuma and

Hellespont, recall a more tolerant world. Just beside the Carafa chapel on the left is the exquisite cosmatesque tomb of Bishop Durand of Mende, with a beautiful mosaic of the Madonna and Child, dating from 1296.

On the left-hand side of the high altar is the other great treasure of the church, Michelangelo's 'Christ bearing the Cross'. Commissioned by Metello Vari and Pietro Castellani, and executed between 1514 and 1521, it recalls the pure beauty of Greek sculpture. The gilded drapery and the sandal are later additions, the latter to preserve the foot from being worn away by the kisses of the faithful. Under the altar, which is modern, are preserved the relics of St. Catherine of Siena.

Behind the altar are the monuments of the two Medici popes; that on the right is of Clement VII, by Raffaello da Montelupo; on the left of Leo X, by Nanni di Baccio Bigio. Nearby in the pavement is the tomb of the humanist Cardinal Bembo, friend of popes and princes, and particularly of Leo X, to whom is attributed the phrase 'Let us enjoy the Papacy, since God has given it to us'; they both lived in the heyday of Renaissance Rome. In the next-door chapel, which leads to a back entrance of the church, is the tomb of a Dominican friar, a rare monument as friars who died in priories did not usually have individual tombs, but the Giovanni da Fiesole which it commemorates is better known to the world as the Blessed Fra Angelico. A little farther on a door leads into the sacristy and a passage into the monastery itself, where two fifteenth-century popes—Eugenius IV and Nicholas V—were elected, and where the famous trial of Galileo took place. The Dominicans were the executants of the Inquisition and as a result of their abuses under Paul IV the Roman populace tried to storm the monastery at the time of his death. The chapels to the left of the nave are of less artistic interest than those on the right, but before leaving the church we should not miss Mino da Fiesole's exquisite tomb of the young Francesco Tornabuoni, who died in Rome in 1480; it stands at the end of the wall near the door.

From the Piazza della Minerva we now pursue the little street of S. Caterina di Siena on the right of the church and, taking the second turn to the right, find ourselves in the **Via del Gesù**, which in its turn leads us to the piazza of the same name. The whole of the last part of this street, on the left-hand side, is occupied by the vast block of the **Palazzo Altieri**, built

in the second half of the seventeenth century for the family of
the Altieri Pope, Clement X. Its size, and the speed with which
this palace grew, provoked a pasquinade which was a repeti-
tion of what the Romans said when Nero was building the
Golden House—'Rome will become a single house. Quirites,
emigrate to Veii, if Veii has not also been occupied by this
house.' Nevertheless, Clement controlled the building activities of his family to a certain extent; he would not allow them
to dislodge an old woman who refused to sell her little house
which stood in the way of the growth of the great palace.
Instead the palace was built over and around it, and its small
window can still be seen on the ground floor to the right of the
palace's main door in the Via del Plebiscito.

The dominating monument in the Piazza del Gesù is,
naturally enough, the Gesù, the great Jesuit church after
which it is called. The piazza is supposed to be the windiest
place in Rome and this fact is accounted for by a curious
legend. The devil and the wind were once walking there and
the devil asked to be excused for a minute to go into the
church; he never emerged, and the wind has been waiting for
him ever since. The Gesù, the mother church of the Jesuits in
Rome, was begun in 1568 and consecrated in 1584; the rich
façade is the work of two Jesuits, G. B. Tristani and Giovanni
de Rosis.

The observant may notice a curious thing about this façade;
it bears, as all churches in Rome do, the arms of the reigning
pope, painted on a wooden shield on the left, and on the right
another with the S.P.Q.R. of the Roman Commune. This last
is a very rare privilege, shared only by the Aracoeli, which
belongs to the people of Rome, and S. Marco which includes
the Capitol within its parish boundaries. The reason is that
the church is under the special protection of the Roman people
and, as a sign of this, the mayor presents a golden chalice to
it annually. Much incidental history may be learnt about the
churches of Rome by looking at these painted coats-of-arms
which appear on their façades; the stone ones of popes and
cardinals architecturally incorporated into the building indicate the founder or restorer. In general these painted shields
bear only the arms of the reigning pope and the titular cardinal, but there are notable exceptions to this rule. S. Marco,
as the church of the Venetians, bears the arms of Venice as
well as those of the pope, titular cardinal and S.P.Q.R. S.

Luigi dei Francesi, as the national church of France, carries the arms of the French Republic; these are encircled by the collar of the Légion d'Honneur, a most unusual circumstance as it does not in fact form part of the arms of the Republic. The church of S. Agnese in the Piazza Navona is also unique in that it bears not only the arms of the pope and protecting cardinal, but also those of the Doria Pamphilj family who actually own it. A rather costly privilege this, as they are responsible for its upkeep; in return members of the family enjoy the right of being censed with incense when they enter.

But to return to the Gesù; it was the prototype of the large congregational churches that were built in Rome as a result of the Counter-Reformation. The single broad nave and short transept are ideally suited for preaching to the large congregations which were drawn to it, and other churches of its kind, by the new orders who attracted so much religious fervour. The object of the Jesuits was to go out and conquer the world, and as a result their churches, including the Gesù, are worldly, splendid, magnificent. One is overwhelmed by the gold and precious stones; the columns of St. Ignatius of Loyola's tomb, in the left transept, are covered with *lapis lazuli* and it is surmounted by a globe of this semi-precious stone which is the largest piece in the world. Such riches naturally provoked criticism. Pasquino was not dumb on the subject, but the unkindest cut of all came from the Grand Duke of Tuscany who translated the society's device, the letters I.H.S., as representing '*Iesuiti habent satis*' (the Jesuits have enough). These letters form the central motif of Giovan Battista Gaulli's great painting of 'The Adoration of the Name of Jesus' in the ceiling of the nave; this, together with his frescoes in the dome, are considered to be his masterpiece. The paintings were executed between the years 1672 and 1685, and are typical of the vast decorative works in the late baroque style which filled Roman churches at this period. Here the *trompe l'oeil* is carried to its ultimate extreme, with the painting spreading over the adjoining architectural features and coloured stucco figures in the round employed to complete the illusionary effect.

From the Piazza del Gesù we take the Via d'Aracoeli, which leads diagonally across the **Via delle Botteghe Oscure**, the Street of the Dark Shops, now widened and no longer corresponding to its picturesque name. This was formerly believed to have been built into the remains of the Circus Flaminius, but the latest archaeological opinion now places the circus nearer the Tiber. The first turn to the right after the Via delle Botteghe Oscure brings us into the **Via Margana**, leading to the picturesque piazza of the same name, called after the tower, of the Margani family, who were very powerful in the fourteenth century. Beside the tower is a picturesque gateway made out of fragments of an ancient Roman cornice and embedded into it is an ancient Ionic column. At the far end of the piazza, the Via della Tribuna di Tor de' Specchi leads past the *tribuna* or apse of the Church of the Annunziata, which forms part of the famous **Convent of the Tor de' Specchi** (Convent of the Tower of Mirrors), owned by the Order of Oblates, founded by S. Francesca Romana in 1425.

The convent is called after a tower which was a landmark until it was knocked down in 1750; according to some authorities part of it is still incorporated into the convent, whose entrance is in the Via del Teatro di Marcello. Although many theories have been expounded to explain the curious name, it is generally believed that it is associated with the medieval legends woven around the Capitol and the buildings in its vicinity. According to one of these, this tower was surmounted by magic mirrors, in which the ancient Romans could see all that went on in the world, and thus discover if any of their subject peoples plotted against them. From the Via della Tribuna di Tor de' Specchi, by way of the Piazza and Via Capizucchi, we make our way to **Piazza Campitelli**, one of the most attractive small piazzas in Rome, with a charming baroque church, fountain and palaces. In Palazzo Cavalletti (No. 1 on the corner), at the end of the last century, died Marchese Francesco Cavalletti, the last Senator of Rome. The church of S. Maria in Campitelli was built in 1667 by C. Rainaldi to house a much revered medieval icon of the Madonna; she is represented against a background of oak branches and some authorities believe that this represents the survival of a pagan cult.

The **Via dei Funari**—opinion is divided as to whether this street derives its name from a family of that name or from the *funari* or rope-makers who plied their trade there—now leads us past the fine façade of the church of S. Caterina dei Funari (founded in the twelfth century and rebuilt by Guido Guidetti in the sixteenth) to the delightful Piazza Mattei. Here stands the famous **Fontana delle Tartarughe**, executed in 1585 by Taddeo Landini, probably to the design of Giacomo della Porta. Even in a city of fountains such as Rome, this probably holds the palm for sheer delight; and what other country but Italy could have produced it? It was made simply to be beautiful, and the joy of life is implicit in every line of the four graceful boys, who in one hand hold a dolphin, from whose mouth water gushes into marble shells, and with the other support little bronze tortoises to drink in the fountain above.

On the right side of the piazza (No. 31) is the oldest of the group of **Palazzi Mattei**, which were built by this rich and powerful family during the sixteenth and seventeenth centuries. During the troublous times of papal elections they then enjoyed the right of occupying militarily, with their own men-at-arms, the whole of the area between these palaces and the Tiber. When we enter the courtyard of this oldest palace, with its beautiful external staircase and double loggias, we feel as if we were in Florence, not in Rome; it is not a mistaken instinct as the palace was built by the Florentine Nanni di Baccio Bigio in the first half of the sixteenth century. The next door (No. 17) leads into the double courtyard of another Mattei palace; beautiful too, but belonging to another world, that of the pomp and scenic effects of baroque Rome. This palace, which is considered to be Maderno's best, was begun in 1595 and finished in 1618: in it the architect made skilful decorative use of the Duke Asdrubale's famous collection of antique sculpture, which is here arranged as in an open-air museum. This type of decoration is continued on the singularly fine state staircase, where antique reliefs are combined with contemporary stucco work; an amusing detail is the use as seats of small antique altars, to which stucco tasselled cushions have been added.

We now take the narrow Via della Reginella, the only one of the old Ghetto to survive, to which it was added as late as the reign of Leo XII; after the Napoleonic wars, the popes again confined the unfortunate Jews within the Ghetto. The history of the Jews of Rome is a long and sad one, and all the more tragic because although in medieval days they enjoyed very considerable freedom, it was in later and what should have been more enlightened times that they were persecuted. During the Middle Ages their industry, financial capacity and renown as doctors commended the Jews to the

popes, who even at this early date allowed them to build a
synagogue in the city; an example of religious toleration which
was not later extended to any of the reformed Christian
creeds. In the eleventh century, one famous Christianised
Jewish family—the Pierleoni—even produced a pope, or at
least an anti-pope, Anacletus II. In the thirteenth century
Innocent III first made the Jews wear a distinguishing mark—
a yellow O—but it was really with the Renaissance, and
especially with the Counter-Reformation, that their tragedy
began. As we have seen Paul IV enclosed them in the Ghetto,
even imposing a curfew, and subsequent popes forbade the
Jews to practise any kind of trade but that in old clothes and
scrap iron. As a result they fell back upon such dubious
practices as astrology and the brewing of love philtres, though
usury was always practised surreptitiously. Right up to 1870
the Jews were debarred from owning land, practising any of
the professions or taking any part in public life; though under
Napoleon and during the brief Roman Republic of 1848 they
had enjoyed freedom.

In classical times the Jewish colony was established in
Trastevere, but by the Middle Ages it had crossed the river,
and Paul IV's choice of the site for the Ghetto was evidently
dictated by the fact that this was the area in which most Jews
lived. That it was already a quarter with a sinister reputation
is evident from the accounts of the Duke of Gandia's murder;
after dining with his mother Vanozza and his brother Cesare
Borgia, he went under cover of darkness to keep an appointment in the now vanished Piazza del Pianto in the Ghetto.
He was never seen again alive. His body was afterwards
recovered from the Tiber, pierced by nine dagger wounds, and
as his father, Alexander VI, suddenly stopped all efforts to
discover the murderer all Rome was convinced that it was
none other than his brother Cesare.

We are now approaching the scene of the tragedy as just
to the right of where the Via della Reginella enters the Via
del Portico d'Ottavia is the Via di S. Maria del Pianto, which
formerly led into the Piazza del Pianto. The site is easily
identified as the house on the corner is distinguished by a fine
inscription in antique style, announcing that Lorenzo Manili
(in its latinised form of Laurentius Manlius), from love of his
native city, at a time when its ancient beauty was being
restored built this house for himself and his descendants in

the year 2221 since Rome's foundation (1467). The **Via del Portico d'Ottavia** is one of the most colourful in Rome. Many of the houses on the left-hand side date from the early Renaissance, as is evident from their fine windows and the traces of loggias on the top floors; but the real fascination of the street lies in the stumps of classical columns, relics of the famous Portico of Octavia, rising out of the pavement at the far end. Nowhere else in Rome is one so acutely conscious of the ancient city which lies buried beneath.

The Portico d'Ottavia was originally built by Quintus Metellus in 149 BC but it was rebuilt by Augustus and dedicated to his sister Octavia in 23 BC, and later restored by Septimius Severus and Caracalla. The rectangular portico (measuring 135 by 115 metres) enclosed temples dedicated to Jupiter and Juno, libraries and public rooms and was intended as a foyer or meeting-place for the adjacent Theatre of Marcellus. Among its three hundred columns stood many masterpieces of Greek sculpture, including the famous Medici Venus (now in the Uffizi), which was found under piles of rubbish in the fish market which grew up in the portico in the Middle Ages. As late as 1878 the inscribed pedestal of a statue of the mother of the Gracchi was found in like condition.

A church, now known as **S. Angelo in Pescheria**, was built into the ruins of the portico in very early times. This is said to have been rededicated to St. Michael the Archangel by Pope Boniface II in the sixth century; in the eighth century it was certainly rebuilt by the same Theodatus who commissioned the frescoes of S. Maria Antiqua. A surviving inscription dates the rebuilding with complete assurance to the six thousand two hundred and seventy-third year since the creation of the world! and describes Theodatus as 'formerly Duke, now *primicerius* of the Holy Apostolic Seat'. A *primicerius* was the highest papal official of those days, a kind of prime minister, so Theodatus had no reason to regret the loss of what had probably been a Byzantine dukedom, especially as the reigning Pope, Hadrian I, was his nephew

The church of S. Angelo in Pescheria, as it has been called for centuries owing to the portico fish market, was again rebuilt in 1869 and, apart from the above inscription, is now of little interest; except, that is, for a curious inscribed plaque let into the brickwork on the right side of the portico. The Latin legend states that the head and body, up to the first fin, of any fish longer than the plaque had to be given to the conservators. This may be considered a curious part of a fish to exact as tribute, but, of the umber especially, this was considered a great delicacy.

It was from under the medieval arches, built to support the tympanum of the portico, that the fish must have begun its journey, as it was here that the slabs of the fishmongers' stalls were placed. It was also from this insalubrious corner of old Rome that Cola di Rienzo set out on 19 May 1347 to the Capitol in his abortive attempt to refound the glories of the Roman Republic. We ourselves now continue by the little alley to the right of the church, the Via del Foro Piscario, which separates it from two charming medieval houses (Nos. 28 and 29 of the Via Portico d'Ottavia), now used as the administrative office of the *Belle Arti* of the Commune. The old house on our left, with its little garden of vines, oleanders and pomegranates growing among the classical ruins, still looks today much as it did when Roesler Franz painted it in the last century. Beyond it stand the two beautiful Corinthian marble columns of the Temple of Apollo, built by Augustus's old enemy C. Sosius, on the site of an earlier temple, in 32 BC. The setting of the **Theatre of Marcellus**, whose vast bulk now looms before us, has, however, changed out of all recognition in the last forty-five years. Previously its arches were filled with small shops, and the surrounding Piazza Montanara was as lively a market as the Foro Olitorio of ancient times, which stood at its far end. During the Fascist period this side of the theatre was stripped of these accumulations of centuries, and its fine double order of semi-columns now stand out against the green slopes of the Capitol.

The theatre was begun by Caesar, completed by Augustus in AD 13, and dedicated to Marcellus, his sister Octavia's son who died at the age of 25. This theatre and the Castel S. Angelo are the only two survivors of the once numerous group of ancient monuments which were converted into fortresses in the Middle Ages. But whereas S. Angelo, though luxuriously appointed inside, always remained a fortress, the Theatre of Marcellus was converted into a Renaissance palace by Peruzzi for the Savelli family in the sixteenth century. The architect had plenty of space for his conversion, as the theatre had been designed to hold 20,000 spectators; internally it is now a maze of apartments, one of which even has a spacious hanging garden. During the German occupation, in 1943-4, this labyrinthine character of old Roman palaces saved the lives of many of their occupants; as it did in this particular case that of the late Duchess of Sermoneta, when the Gestapo came to arrest her as a hostage. The palace is usually known as Palazzo Orsini, after the famous family who owned it for two centuries (to the Sermonetas' mere forty years), and their device of a bear (*orso*) appears on the gateway in the Via di Monte Savello, where the stage of the Theatre of Marcellus formerly stood.

To reach this side of the palace and Theatre of Marcellus we make our way over an empty piece of ground, left bare by the clearance of the area in 1932. On our left is the church of S. Nicola in Carcere, another wonderful example of a Roman architectural palimpsest. Opposite the entrance to the Palazzo Orsini, beyond the tram lines and the newspaper kiosks, the Ponte Fabricio, built in 62 BC and the oldest in the city, spans the river to the Tiber island. The bridge is popularly known as Ponte dei Quattro Capi (bridge of the four heads) from the two herms of the four-headed Janus on the parapet.

The Tiber island, which is one of the most charming and picturesque places in the city, was believed by the ancient Romans to have accumulated on the grain stores of the Tarquins which the people flung into the river after their expulsion. The island has long been associated with the art of healing; a Temple of Aesculapius was built there after the great plague in 291 BC. Consultation of the Sibylline books at this time of national disaster had resulted in an embassy being sent to Epidaurus to bring back the statue of the god. As the ship bearing the statue sailed up the Tiber, a great serpent was seen to leave it and swim to the island. Believing that this was an incarnation of the god himself, the Romans proceeded to erect a temple to Aesculapius and to give part at least of the island the form of a ship to commemorate the occasion. The temple was very large and constructed with porticoes where sick people could sleep the night in the hope that the god would visit them in their dreams and prescribe a cure. Several pits containing *ex votos*, models of human arms and legs made as thank-offerings for cures, were found there in the last century. Various other temples existed on the island and a statue of the deified Caesar, which, according to legend, turned from facing west to east during the reign of Vespasian; sacred statues that move are no new thing in Italy.

At the end of the tenth century the Emperor Otto III built a church, which he dedicated to his friend St. Adalbert, on the site of Aesculapius's temple. Otto also brought there the relics of St. Paulinus and St. Bartholomew. Somehow poor St. Adalbert has been forgotten, and the church, which has been rebuilt many times, has now been known for centuries as the church of S. Bartolomeo. However, an inscription of 1113, above the main door recalls Otto's translation of the relics, and the curious little sculptured wellhead standing on the chancel steps is probably a survival of his original church; possibly it even marks the site of the healing spring of the temple of Aesculapius. In the Middle Ages a pilgrims' hospice grew up on the Tiber island and, according to tradition, it was here that Henry II's jester, Rahere, had the vision which resulted in his founding the Hospital of St. Bartholomew in London.

The dominating features of the Tiber island, as we approach it today, are the great mass of the modern hospital of the Fatebenefratelli on the right, built possibly on the site of the medieval hospice, and on the left a medieval tower. This tower formed part of the Pierleoni fortress in the eleventh century, but it is popularly known as the Torre della Contessa, after the redoubtable Matilda of Canossa, who stayed there in 1087. Urban II also took refuge in the tower from the Anti-Pope Clement III, and such was the power of the Pierleoni that the island withstood all attack. Later, island, tower and fortress came into the possession of the Caetani family, who lived there till the beginning of the sixteenth century.

The **Piazza di S. Bartolomeo** is emphatically one of those corners of old Rome that invite contemplation. Even if, unlike our eighteenth-century predecessors such as Boswell and Robert Adam, we may not describe our meditations as 'sublime thoughts' we can rest here for a while and watch the waters of the Tiber as they swirl past the Ponte Cestio. This Roman bridge, originally built in the first century BC, but many times restored, connects the island with the right bank of the river and the quarter known as Trastevere, or across the Tiber. Although the famous wooden bridge, the Pons Sublicius, defended by the immortal three—Horatius, Herminius and Spurius Lartius—was a little farther down the river, Trastevere was then the Etruscan shore where Porsena had his camp. It was from here that Cloelia and her girl companions escaped from being held as hostages by swimming the river; only for her to be sent back by her stern parents for fear that Rome might suffer. Here too, in the sacred grove of Furrina, Gaius Sempronius Gracchus and his servant Philocrates were killed by the emissaries of the Senate after the failure of his plans for reform.

Before we leave the island, however, we must make our way through the arch on the left of the church of St. Bartholomew (no one seems to pay any attention to the notice saying no entry) under a vine pergola and down the steps beside the establishment of the river police to the embankment. Here we can still see a fragment of the old Roman travertine wall representing the prow of a ship with Aesculapius's serpent climbing up it. There is also a fine view of the Ponte Rotto, a fragment of the bridge built in 179 BC by M. Aemilius Lepidus who also built the Basilica Aemilia in the Forum.

We now return over the Ponte Quattro Capi and pursue the Lungotevere dei Cenci till we reach the **Via del Progresso**. A thoroughly modern street this, which somewhat surprisingly leads us to a vast conglomeration of old buildings which, as Archibald Lyall said in his excellent book on Rome, 'still seems to reek of ancient evil and nameless crimes'—it is the **Palazzo Cenci**. Most people are surprised to learn that Beatrice's murder of her monstrous father did not occur here, but in the Castle of Petrella in the Sabine Mountains, also that a branch of the family still exists—the Cenci Bolognetti.

Fully to appreciate the enormous size of the Cenci palace, we must turn sharp left through a narrow alley leading into a little square (Piperno, the restaurant in it, is the most famous place in Rome for eating artichokes—*Carciofi alla giudea*). We then continue by the Via di Monte Cenci and turn right into the Via Arco dei Cenci, named after the dark archway at the far end, whose sinister appearance somehow makes one's blood run cold.

From here we emerge into Via S. Maria de Calderari; on the left the fragment of Roman wall incorporated into a house is probably a relic of the Theatre of Balbus. Continuing to the right, we find ourselves back in the Via del Progresso. Here we turn sharp left into the Via di S. Maria del Pianto and

right into **Via S. Maria in Publicolis**. This derives its name
from the fact that the Santacroce family (whose palace is in
the street) claim descent from the Valerian gens of ancient
Rome, whose most famous member earned the name of
Publicola for his assiduous cultivation of popular support.

The Santacroce tombs are in the family church of S. Maria
in Publicolis, on the left of the street. On the right is the small
Piazza Costaguti, enclosed on two sides by the Palazzo Costaguti, whose main entrance is in Piazza Mattei. We continue
up the Via di S. Maria in Publicolis, cross the Via dei Falegnami (street of the carpenters), and, by way of the brief
Vicolo di S. Elena dei Falegnami, find ourselves in a piazza
usually called Argentina *tout court* but whose official name is
Largo di Torre Argentina. This provides the clue to the fact
that the square is not, as is usually supposed, called after the
South American Republic, but after a tower built by the
fifteenth-century German Bishop Burckhard of Strasbourg;
the Latin name of the diocese being *Argentoratum*. The tower
is no longer visible as it was truncated and now forms an
indistinguishable part of his palace in a neighbouring street;
incidentally he was that Burckhard who wrote the famous
diaries which reveal the secrets of the Borgia Pope Alexander
VI's court.

It is difficult to believe that until some thirty-five years ago
the open space of the Largo di Torre Argentina was a warren
of alleys and old houses. The only reminder of those days is
the old brick tower, on the right of the sunken space in the
middle, which belonged to the Papereschi family and still goes
by the name of Torre Papito; beside it is a graceful loggia,
formerly part of a neighbouring palace, which was reconstructed here in 1933. The reason for the extensive clearance
of the area in 1926 lies in the discovery of the republican
temples, whose ruins can be seen in the sunken area in the
middle of the square. Although very little is really known
about them and even their dedication is a mystery, these four
temples are among the earliest Roman buildings existing in
the city. The temple on the extreme left (viewed from the
loggia) is the latest of the group, but the one next to it probably dates from the fourth or third century BC. The circular
temple in the middle, also of a later date, had, however, already
been altered and enlarged in republican times. The temple on
the right, the best preserved of the group, was restored in

imperial times. In the Middle Ages a church dedicated to S. Niccolò was built into the ruins (two of its apses can still be seen), and in the eighteenth century another church was built above this, at the level to which the city had then risen. Although one may not always be in sympathy with the fascist predilection for razing subsequent strata of Rome to the ground in order to lay bare the vestiges of classical ruins, in this particular case one cannot but feel that justice has been done. The church of S. Niccolò was called alle Calcari as it stood at the other end of the Via dei Calcari we have already mentioned, where the marbles of ancient Rome were reduced to lime; now in their turn all memory of the infamous lime kilns has been erased and the ancient monuments brought to light.

As we walk round the square to catch a bus, we look down into the extreme right-hand corner of the excavations and see what appears to be the remains of a long narrow passage, filled with marble. This was in fact an enormous public lavatory of imperial times; its size and splendour indicate the fact that the ancient Romans also used their public lavatories as friendly meeting-places, where they could have a pedicure and even sit and listen to an orchestra. On the other side of the street rises the eighteenth-century façade of the Teatro Argentina, where one of the world's most popular operas, the *Barber of Seville*, was actually booed and whistled off the stage at its first performance.

CHAPTER SIX

S. Andrea della Valle to Palazzo Spada

❧

So far our expeditions have taken us to see classical Rome, also something of the great baroque churches and palaces; but we have touched very little upon the life of Rome of the Renaissance. Although owing to its special character as an architectural palimpsest, covering 2,500 years of history and artistic development, it is not possible conveniently to explore Rome according to periods, the itineraries in this chapter can fairly be described as an expedition into the Renaissance. We shall see two of the finest palaces of the period, and many smaller ones, standing in what was the commercial hub of the city in the fifteenth and sixteenth centuries.

Setting out again from Piazza Venezia, we continue on familiar ground down the Via del Plebiscito and cross the northern end of the Largo di Torre Argentina; only beginning our exploration when we reach the **Corso Vittorio Emanuele** on the other side. This wide thoroughfare was made after 1870 to open up a convenient route to St. Peter's; it cuts across the maze of ancient narrow streets which had grown up among the masses of decaying classical ruins. This fact is immediately brought home to us by the name of the first notable monument we see on our left, the church of S. Andrea della Valle. (N.B. On this expedition our attention will be exclusively devoted to the buildings on the left of the Corso Vittorio Emanuele as those on the right will be covered in the next day's itinerary.) Long before the church was begun in 1591, according to the latest authorities by Giacomo della Porta, the whole of this area was known as the '*valle*' or valley. In classical times the low-lying marshy ground had been excavated by Agrippa to form an artificial lake, the **Stagnum Agrippae**, as part of the landscape setting of his famous baths. This was probably connected with the Euripus, a large canal which flowed nearby; the remains of these extensive classical waterworks had given the locality its name.

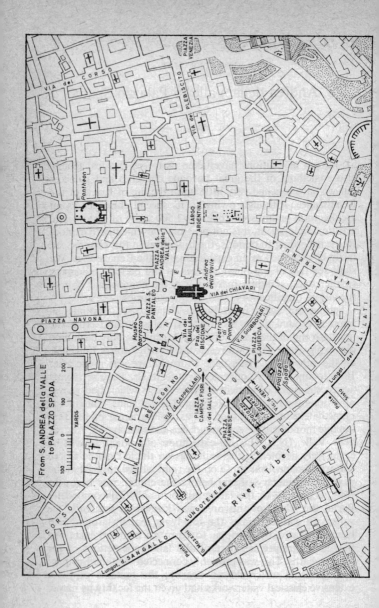

From S. ANDREA della VALLE to PALAZZO SPADA

YARDS
100   0   100   200

A charming Renaissance fountain (originally designed for the Piazza Scossa Cavalli near St. Peter's, removed to make way for the Via della Conciliazione and re-erected here in 1957), in the midst of the Piazza di S. Andrea della Valle, is the only sight which reminds us of the fact that once this whole area was a sheet of glittering water, surrounded by woods and pavilions. It was here, Tacitus relates, that Nero and his friend Tigellinus enjoyed one of that emperor's most notorious orgiastic entertainments. They floated on a raft adorned with gold and ivory, while the surrounding groves were filled with musicians and exotic animals and birds, and in the pavilions noble Roman ladies rivalled naked *hetaerae* in the exercise of their trade. The piazza has, happily, a better reason to be remembered; it was here in the eighteenth century that the philosopher Gravina heard an unknown boy, Pietro Trapassi, reciting improvised verses. Recognising his genius, Gravina adopted and educated the boy, even re-editing his name in its Greek form; thus founding the fortunes of one of Italy's greatest poets—Pietro Metastasio.

To the musical world the splendid baroque church of S. Andrea della Valle is best known as the scene of the first act in *Tosca*. The church was completed in the second half of the seventeenth century by Maderno, Rainaldi and Fontana; Maderno's dome being the second highest in Rome after St. Peter's. The impressive façade was the result of the successive labours of the three Carlos—Maderno, Rainaldi and Fontana. It has one curious defect, however; the symmetry is disturbed by the single angel on the left having no partner to counter-balance it; but thereby hangs a tale. The Chigi Pope, Alexander VII (1655–67), criticised the sculptor Fancelli's work; to the fury of the artist, who exclaimed: 'If he wants another he can make it himself!' and nothing would induce him to produce another angel. Domenichino painted the choir and pendentives of the dome; to his chagrin, the decoration of the dome was given to his successful rival Lanfranco. Other points of interest are the tombs of the two Piccolomini popes high upon the left of the nave (removed here from St. Peter's in 1614), and the Barberini and Lancellotti family chapels. But now we must hurry on down the Corso Vittorio Emanuele to see one of the most interesting and little-known museums of Rome.

The **Museo Barracco**, stands on the left of the Corso

where it widens to form the Piazza S. Pantaleo. As it is so near the Palazzo Farnese, which can only be seen by the public on Sunday mornings, and the Palazzo and Galleria Spada, also open on Sunday mornings (the palace is sometimes closed on weekdays), this is the most convenient time of the week in which to visit this area.

The Barracco collection is housed in one of the most delightful small Renaissance palaces in Rome, known as the Piccola Farnesina, though in actual fact it never had any connection with the Farnese. The name is instead derived from the popular misinterpretation of the heraldic lilies which figure prominently in the palace's external and internal decoration; but they are the lilies of France not of the Farnese, the propinquity of whose great palace gave rise to the misnomer. The Piccola Farnesina was begun in 1523 for the Breton prelate Thomas Le Roy, who played a large part in negotiating the concordat between Pope Leo X and François I. In recognition of his services the French king awarded Le Roy the honour of incorporating the Fleur de Lys into his coat of arms. No doubt it was due to the personal instructions of his patron that, in designing the palace, Antonio Sangallo the younger made such free use of this motif; combining it with the ermine tail, the heraldic device of Le Roy's native Brittany. The palace was completed by Le Roy's nephew in 1546; subsequently it passed through the hands of many different owners before it was bought by the Roman commune in 1887. At this time many old houses were being destroyed in order to make way for the Corso Vittorio Emanuele, including some adjoining the Piccola Farnesina. This necessitated additions to the Via dei Baullari side of the palace and the creation of a complete new façade on the Corso. It is by a door (No. 168) in this modern addition that we now enter.

The Museo Barracco was the personal collection of Barone Giovanni Barracco, intended to illustrate the history of sculpture in ancient times, and given by him to the city of Rome in 1902. Although there is some variation in the actual quality of the exhibits, they include fine works of Assyrian, Babylonian, and particularly Egyptian and early Greek sculpture, rare in Rome. Presented in the limited compass of a personal collection, these make the evolution of ancient art particularly easy to assimilate for the ordinary person. Unfortunately the catalogue on sale in the museum is difficult to follow; the rooms on the plan are numbered differently to the text, and in certain cases the exhibits themselves have been moved. Moreover, owing no doubt to a shortage of staff, one room on the first floor (numbered 4 on the guide book plan and III in the text) is shut and a guardian has to be asked to open it. One must be quite firm about this, however, as it is one of the most interesting in the whole museum.

To see the collection in its correct consecutive order, on reaching the top of the stairs we turn left along the first-floor gallery and begin with the vestibule (numbered 1 on the plan) From here we continue into the room on the right (numbered 2 on the plan). This last contains some exquisite Assyrian reliefs, remarkable for their treatment of natural settings. Especially notable is the one representing three warriors fleeing through a cane brake (No. 50), which might have served as the inspiration of a Japanese print. The large room next door, devoted to Egyptian art, also contains some exquisite reliefs; No. 1 is the oldest Egyptian sculpture in Rome; it shows the court dignitary Nofer with offerings made to a pharaoh of the third dynasty and dates from the period 2778–2432 BC. But the outstanding feature of this part of the collection is the wonderful series of portrait heads, illustrating Egyptian mastery in this branch of art from 1,500 years BC up to Roman times. These range from a prince of the eighteenth dynasty (No. 15) and a head of Rameses II as a young man (No. 21) to that of a priest (No. 31, formerly believed to be Julius Caesar). A painted stucco portrait from a woman's mummy found in the Fayum, with an elaborate ringleted style of hair-dressing, illustrates the pervasive influence of Roman fashions.

The attendant in the Egyptian room has the key to the room on the left of the stairs (numbered 4 on the plan). This contains some beautiful works up to the first half of the fifth century BC and a fascinating group of Cypriot limestone sculptures of the same period. What strikes one on entering this room, however, is a statue at the far end, which so resembles the famous 'Good Shepherd' of the Lateran Museum that one feels that a copy of this early Christian work has strayed here by mistake. In actual fact it is a statue of Hermes Kriophoros, a copy of Kalamis's votive bronze of the god made at Tanagra about 480 BC, portraying him carrying a ram on his shoulders. There is little doubt, however, that this representation of Hermes, and possibly this actual statue which was found near Rome, inspired the sculptor of the 'Good Shepherd'. Though small, the room is so rich in objects of such beauty that one can only single out a few. The head of a boy (No. 80), dating from the end of the sixth century BC, with curly hair and enigmatic smile. A herm of the blind Homer (No. 123). The head of Marsyas (No. 97); copied at the end of the fifth century BC from Myron's bronze masterpiece on the Acropolis. Then, last but not least, the bearded heads of Cypriot priests; one of the sixth century BC (No. 66), and another of the fifth century BC (No. 64). In this last the colours of the painted red rosebuds and white myrtle flower and green leaves of the diadem are perfectly preserved.

We now retrace our steps to the loggia at the top of the stairs which contains a collection of Etruscan sculpture. Most remarkable is an exquisite head of a woman (No. 204), whose distinctive features and elaborate jewels and hair-style suggest that this was the portrait of some beauty of Orvieto (where the head was found) of the third century BC. We now ascend the stairs to the second floor and enter the large room opposite the top of the stairs (numbered 1 on the plan and IV in the text); this is devoted to Greek art of the fifth and fourth centuries BC. Here again so much that is beautiful is contained in so small a space that selection is difficult. But few could forget the grace of the young athlete crowning himself after his victory (No. 99 in the centre, probably a copy of Poly-cletus's lost work of the fifth century BC representing Kyniskos of Mantinea), or the majestic tranquillity of the head of Apollo (No. 92, believed to be a copy of a work of Phidias dating from before 450 BC).

The most remarkable and interesting sculpture in the next room is that of a wounded bitch (No. 139); it is a marble copy of Lysippus's bronze which was one of the most prized works of art in ancient Rome. Pliny referred to the bronze in his *Natural History*, saying it was kept in the *cella* of Juno in the Capitoline Temple of Jupiter and that its custodians were punishable by death if any harm came to it.

The small adjoining room, which is dedicated to Hellenistic art, contains some beautiful reliefs, notably one of dancing maenads (No. 124), and a delightful votive plaque in archaic style (No. 176) showing three nymphs in Pan's cave. We now pass into the last room containing a small collection of

Roman sculpture. Here again, it is the portraits that rivet our attention. In this case, the remarkable likenesses of two boys: one a coldly elegant youth who lived in the reign of Tiberius (No. 190); the other a delightful head of a small boy, a princeling of the Julio-Claudian house (No. 194). But for all its rounded childishness there is something sinister about this last face, and it is not surprising to learn that it was previously believed to represent Nero. As we pass through the gallery leading back to the stairs on our way out we see two funerary portraits of the third century AD from Palmyra, whose richness of dress and ornament strikes a curiously exotic note (Nos. 249 and 250). So no doubt did their Queen Zenobia when she walked in golden chains, almost fainting under the weight of her jewels, in the triumph of Aurelian.

Emerging from the Museo Barracco we turn right down the **Via dei Baullari**, pausing for an instant to look to the right down the Vicolo dell' Aquila at the delightful original Renaissance façade of the Piccola Farnesina. The Via dei Baullari, or the Street of the Trunk-makers, is the first which we enter in this area where so many of the street names are derived from the trades that were formerly practised there. These include the Via dei Cappellari (the hat-makers); Via dei Giubbonari (the jerkin-makers); Via dei Chiavari (the locksmiths); and even Via dei Balestrari (the crossbow-makers). Although this custom of artisans practising the same trade congregating in a single street, as in an oriental bazaar, dates from the Middle Ages, the great commercial development of this area only began in the second half of the fifteenth century. At this time the recent return of the popes (absent from Rome since their residence in Avignon, 1305–77, and during the Wars of the Schism) had brought new life to the city. But such was the decay and destruction that the intervening period had brought about in the old Lateran Palace, as in the rest of Rome, that Nicholas V had been obliged to make the Vatican the principal papal residence. Thus this area lying between the two great city centres—of the papacy in the Vatican and the Commune on the Capitol—achieved an importance it had never known before. From 1450 onwards successive popes had undertaken the widening and improvement of the two great thoroughfares—the Via Papalis and the Via Peregrinorum (or dei Pellegrini)—and the surrounding streets; also the paving of the Campo dei Fiori.

In preparation for Holy Year 1475, Sixtus IV had built his new bridge—still known as the Ponte Sisto—connecting the area with Trastevere.

Thus this roughly triangular stretch of land in the bend of the Tiber, now bounded to the north and east by the Corso Vittorio Emanuele and Via Arenula, came to be the heart of Renaissance Rome. Here in that turbulent period lived so many of the figures whose very names conjure up for us the light and shade—the artistic brilliance and the sinister intrigue —of the vast canvas which we call history. Foremost among them were Rodrigo Borgia, later Pope Alexander VI (1492–1503) and his beautiful mistress Vanozza Cattanei, mother of Cesare, Lucrezia and the Duke of Gandia, all of whom were born here. Here also Benvenuto Cellini fought and brawled with boon companions and created his masterpieces; here Imperia, most famous of the Renaissance courtesans, poisoned herself. Here also magnificent papal nephews and cardinals like Raffaele Riario and Alessandro Farnese (later Pope Paul III, 1534–49) built their superb palaces which still dominate the scene. By day these streets are now filled with the roar of a modern city. But at night it is not difficult to picture the Corsican assassin lying in wait for Cellini in the shadows of the Via Giulia; the murderous duel fought for the favours of the beautiful courtesan La Grechetta in the Piazza del Biscione; or the gambling parties where fortunes changed hands overnight, like the one where Riario won 60,000 scudi with which he built the Cancelleria Palace.

It was through this area, too, that the magnificent processions—which in Renaissance times took the place of the 'circuses' of ancient Rome—passed on their way to and from the Vatican: the popes proceeding to the Lateran to take 'possession' of the temporal power or the holy relics borne in state on feast days and special occasions, like the memorable entry of St. Andrew's head when it was rescued from the Saracens in 1462. Ambassadorial cortèges also wended their way through these narrow streets. Burckhard recorded the passage of Henry VII's plenipotentiary on his way to present his letters of credence in 1487, while every Holy Year throngs of pilgrims of all nations poured down the street called after them— the Via del Pellegrino—on their way to the shrine of the Apostle in St. Peter's. One wonders how many of them realised that the very dust beneath their feet was part of history. For deep down under these same streets still slumber the remains of ancient Rome; the Theatre of Pompey in whose halls Caesar was murdered, and the barracks and stables of the 'Greens', the chariot-racing team which was the idol of the Roman mob, whose defeat or victory in the circus caused many a riot.

Although today the inhabitants of Trastevere claim to be the only true descendants of the ancient Romans—forgetting that in imperial times their area was more or less a foreign colony—it seems to me that the most truly Roman types are to be seen in the Campo dei Fiori and the surrounding streets. If we look closely at the passing crowd on our way down the Via dei Baullari, it is astonishing how many of the faces recall those we have seen on ancient statues, particularly among the women and girls, some of whose fine profiles would not look out of place upon an ancient coin. It is comforting too to find that at least one trunk-maker's shop has survived to preserve the tradition of the street's name. Though at one time this trade was practically ousted by the umbrella makers; particularly specialists in the enormous green ones, still used by peasants and shepherds, which are called 'basilicas' because of their monumental size.

The street leads us into the great open space of the **Campo dei Fiori**, on weekday mornings and all day on Saturdays the scene of one of the busiest and most picturesque fruit and vegetable markets in Rome. On Sunday morning, however, the square is empty; and the grim figure of Giordano Bruno in its midst recalls the fact that he was burnt here for heresy on 17 February 1600. For long after that the square was used as a place of execution. A true son of his age, John Evelyn went to witness some of these when he was in Rome in 1644. He saw a gentleman murderer hanged in his cloak and hat; the man was already dead, having been rendered senseless by a blow, before his throat was cut. Ten years previously the piazza had been the scene of one of the most sensational executions in Rome; a triple one of two renegade monks and their accomplice, who by the means of black magic had tried to bring about the death of the Barberini Pope, Urban VIII (1623–44). Shocking as it may seem, practitioners of the black arts in Rome seem on several occasions to have been monks or priests; the wizard with whom Benvenuto Cellini said he passed a terrifying night in the Colosseum was a priest.

Urban VIII's efforts to extirpate this evil are recorded in the *Malleus Maleficarum*.

The Campo dei Fiori only began to be used as a place of execution in 1600; before that it had resembled rather the Via Veneto of today—the centre of a select residential and business district and of the hotel trade. The towering building that we see at the far south-eastern end was once the palace of the Orsini and Cardinal Condulmer, the last of its kind to be built as a fortress in the midst of classical ruins. Far less conspicuous is a building in the opposite corner, on the angle between the Vicolo del Gallo and the Via dei Cappellari; but in the sixteenth century it was one of the best known inns in Rome. This was La Vacca, owned by no less a person than Vanozza Cattanei. After her relationship with Rodrigo Borgia had ended and she had retired into respectability with her third husband, this shrewd business-woman invested part of her not inconsiderable fortune in what we would call today the hotel trade; she bought no less than four inns. The documents relating to Vanozza's purchase and her plans for alterations to La Vacca are still preserved in the Capitoline Archive. But a more surprising survival is the shield bearing her arms quartered with those of her third husband *and* the Borgia pope. This is still to be seen at No. 13 in the Vicolo del Gallo today. At the time of Alexander VI's death in 1503, evidently fearing expropriation, Vanozza made a faked sale of the inn and her house in the Via del Pellegrino; but by 1513 she had so far recovered her confidence as to blazon, in the literal sense of the word, her relationship with a former pope on the front of an inn.

The Vicolo del Gallo leads us into the **Piazza Farnese**, an outstanding example of the consummate art with which Italian architects of all periods have achieved dramatic settings for their masterpieces; for the **Palazzo Farnese** on the far side of the piazza is without doubt the finest palace of the high Renaissance in Rome. But before we enter we should pause for a moment to look at the two beautiful fountains. Here glistening threads of water fall from the stone Farnese lilies into great baths of Egyptian granite from the ruins of the baths of Caracalla. The simple little modern church and convent on the right of the square (No. 96) were built where the Swedish St. Bridget died on 23 July 1373.

Since 1871 the Palazzo Farnese has been the French Embassy. By a remarkably economical arrangement between the French and Italian governments, the palace was exchanged against the Hotel Galiffet in Paris for a rent of one lira payable every ninety-nine years. One wonders what the palace's creator, Alessandro Farnese (later Pope Paul III, 1534-49), would have thought of this bargain. Even his vast fortune was so strained by the costs of the palace's erection that, after it was begun in 1514, construction ceased—provoking the pasquinade: 'Alms for the building of the Farnese', which was attached to the scaffolding.

Alessandro owed his prosperity to the charms of his sister Giulia (wife of Ursino Orsini and known as Giulia Bella), which so captivated the Borgia Pope, Alexander VI, that she replaced Vanozza in his affections. Like his papal patron and namesake, Alessandro Farnese did not trouble to disguise his affection for his children Pierluigi and Costanza as mere nepotism; he endowed both them and his grandsons Alessandro and Ottavio with plenty of this world's goods. But it must be recorded to their credit that the family taste for magnificence ultimately left Italy the richer; not only by this magnificent palace, but also the superb Farnese villa at Caprarola, and the famous collection of antique sculpture which is now the glory of the National Museum of Naples.

As might be expected of such a man, Alessandro Farnese called in the greatest artists of the age to design his palace: Antonio Sangallo, until his death in 1546, then Michelangelo. It was only finally completed for his descendants by Giacomo della Porta in 1589. The main façade and great courtyard are in their lower two-thirds the work of Sangallo; in the upper storey that of Michelangelo, who is believed also to have designed the famous cornice and central loggia window above the Piazza Farnese entrance. Michelangelo also entertained grandiose ideas for the riverside wing and gardens of the palace. He intended to connect them with the Villa Farnesina in Trastevere by a bridge across the Tiber; but the work was completed by Giacomo della Porta on a much diminished scale. However, a single arch of the viaduct, which was to connect the palace with the bridge, still spans the Via Giulia.

One of the most beautiful features of the Palazzo Farnese is the vestibule by which we enter. The sober magnificence of its quadruple rows of columns and semi-columns, and its exquisite stuccoed ceiling, make this a fitting prelude to the famous porticoed courtyard. Recent research has revealed that it owes the perfect harmony of its proportions to Vitruvius. A detail which often passes unnoticed is Sangallo's ingenious use of *trompe l'oeil* above the smaller side entrances leading from the vestibule into the portico; this preserves the symmetry of the whole. Look at the skilful foreshortening of the decorative mouldings in the portico, and you will see for yourself.

For all its grandeur, a certain dissonance is noticeable in the courtyard between the sober classical style of Sangallo's first two storeys and Michelangelo's top one; evidently the great man could not bring himself to follow obediently in the footsteps of his predecessor. Before leaving the courtyard we should spare the time to look at the charming little garden at the back, laid out in the Renaissance manner.

The great state staircase brings us to the door of the famous *Salon d'Hercule*, so called from the gigantic statue of Hercules standing to the right of the entrance. This is only a copy of the original signed by Glycon of Athens and found in the ruins of the Baths of Caracalla in 1540; it was the pride of the Farnese collection, and is now in the National Museum of Naples. The salon itself is of enormous proportions, filling two storeys of the palace. The recumbent statues of Piety and Abundance on either side of the monumental fireplace were designed by della Porta for Paul III's tomb in St. Peter's but were never used. Viewing the room on a cold morning, one cannot but sympathise with Queen Christina of Sweden, who, wintering in the palace after her arrival in Rome in 1655, insisted upon keeping the fires blazing. This northern passion for comfort astonished the hardy Romans, just as it does to-day. They were more shocked than surprised, however, when the eccentric queen insisted on the removal of the fig leaves and modest draperies from the Farnese marbles. Furthermore, instead of retiring into pious seclusion after her recent conversion, she made the palace the centre of the brilliant intellectual and social life of the day.

From the *Salon d'Hercule* we follow the long galleries surrounding the courtyard to the famous Carracci gallery used on state occasions as the Embassy dining-room. Surely few ambassadors in the world today can entertain their guests in surroundings of greater splendour; for high above the glittering silver and candles on the table, Annibale Carracci's magnificent painted ceiling glows in a riot of exuberant colour. Even in the cold light of morning the tremendous vitality of the composition strikes one instantly; one feels that few artists could have been better suited—technically and temperamentally—to portray the chosen theme of the loves of gods and goddesses from Ovid's *Metamorphoses*. The triumph of Bacchus and Ariadne in the central panel conveys to an extraordinary degree the pagan voluptuousness of the scene. Nor is this surprising as we know from the preparatory drawings which have survived that the artist made a prolonged study of classical reliefs. With some assistance from his brother Agostino, the ceiling occupied Annibale Carracci from 1597 to 1604; it exercised a tremendous influence upon subsequent decorative painting in Rome. But, sad to relate, it is said to have hastened the artist's death; in disappointment at the fee he received, he took to drink and died at the early age of 49.

When we emerge into the Piazza Farnese, we turn right down the Vicolo dei Venti, taking care to look high up on the wall above the door of No. 5, where there is a beautiful small Renaissance shrine. This must be one of the earliest of its kind existing in the city, as it bears the Della Rovere arms. It was probably put up during the reign of the family's first Pope, Sixtus IV (1471–84), who was responsible for many public works in the area. The house opposite has some fine doors and windows, possibly dating from the tenancy of Francesco Fusconi, the celebrated doctor of Hadrian VI (1522–3), the last non-Italian pope.

We now find ourselves in the delightfully irregular Piazza della Quercia, which is dominated by the **Palazzo Spada**. After the sober magnificence of Palazzo Farnese, the exuberant stucco decorations of Palazzo Spada strike an unexpectedly frivolous note, presaging the baroque; and it is difficult to believe that less than fifty years separate the beginnings of the two palaces. The original building date for Palazzo Spada is now given as 1550; it was begun for the Camera Apostolica. From 1555 to 1559 it belonged to Cardinal Capodiferro, then to the Mignanelli family. In 1632 they sold it to Cardinal Bernardino Spada, whose family owned it until its sale to the Italian state in 1926; it is now the seat of the Consiglio di Stato. The architect is most generally believed to have been Giulio Mozzoni or Mazzoni, who was famous for the type of stucco decoration which is such an outstanding characteristic of the whole palace. The façade is somewhat overloaded with inscriptions, grotesques and figures of Roman heroes; but in the courtyard delicate festoons and reliefs of centaurs and tritons are beautifully contrasted with the deep shadows of the porticoes.

The most celebrated architectural feature of Palazzo Spada is, however, the *trompe l'oeil* perspective in the garden gallery. This was designed by Borromini, who was a friend of Cardinal Bernardino Spada's brother; he was thus a natural choice for the extensive renovations and additions undertaken in the palace when the cardinal bought it. The perspective was originally intended to be seen from the courtyard through the doors of one of the ground-floor rooms; this distance would have greatly enhanced its remarkable effect. Now we must ask the porter to take us by back ways into the garden to see it; but even so Borromini's optical illusion is extraordinary. We see what appears to be a gallery of considerable length, terminating in a courtyard adorned by a large statue. In actual fact the distance covered between the entrance to the gallery and the statue is some 10 metres; the statue itself is a pygmy. The trick is soon revealed to the spectator when anyone takes a few paces down the gallery; he suddenly appears as a giant sandwiched between the rising floor and the descending ceiling, which is supported by rapidly diminishing columns.

From the garden we retrace our steps to a door marked GALLERIA SPADA; after climbing the stairs we find ourselves in the smallest, but what Italians would call the most *caratteristico*, of Roman galleries. The collection, filling only four rooms, was probably largely the personal one of Cardinal Bernardino Spada. It is believed to have been bought chiefly while he was legate in Bologna about 1630; though he may have added to an existing nucleus of family pictures dating from the fifteenth and sixteenth centuries. The gallery has a unique character and charm; it is the only survivor of the once numerous small Roman family collections, and it is housed in its original setting. The décor and furnishing of all the rooms are contemporary; room III, for example is a perfect period piece. This, one imagines, was the setting of many a seventeenth-century conversazione; where aristocratic dilettanti like Vouet's portraits of gallants in blond wigs (Nos. 130 and 135), met and discussed the arts with elegant ladies typified by Vouet's other portrait (No. 123). The furnishing of this room includes two very rare Dutch seventeenth-century globes, some unusual Italian sixteenth-century painted stools, and delicious gilded eighteenth-century consoles, riotously decorated with cupids and swags of fruit and flowers.

Many of the pictures in the gallery have been re-hung since the war in order to make the most important easier to see. Among those in room I are two portraits of Cardinal Bernardino Spada, by his friends Guido Reni (No. 25) and Guercino (No. 38). The earlier pictures, dating from the fifteenth and sixteenth centuries, are grouped in room II; they include a wonderful unfinished portrait of a 'Musician' by Titian (No. 38) and a 'Visitation' by Andrea del Sarto (No. 53). The frieze of this room (on the two side walls) was painted by Perin del Vaga as an interim covering for the wall below Michelangelo's 'Last Judgment' in the Sistine Chapel. It was to have been replaced by tapestries which were being specially woven in Flanders, but was not completed when the artist died in 1547. The outstanding pictures in room III are Jan 'Velvet' Breughel's 'Landscape with Windmills', signed and dated 1607 (No. 138); Rubens's portrait of 'A Cardinal' (No. 121); and Francesco Furini's masterpiece, a most delicate and original rendering of 'The Martyrdom of S. Lucia' (No. 118). In room IV are grouped works illustrative of the influence of Caravaggio. These include Michelangelo Cerquozzi's 'Revolt of Masianello' (No. 149); an allegory of 'Architecture' by an unknown seventeenth-century artist (No. 140); an exquisite Baugin still life (No. 156); and 'The Madonna and St. Anne' by G. A. Gallo (No. 162).

As the gallery and the state apartment close at 1 p.m. on Sundays, we must hurry if we are to see the whole palace before it closes, but our visit to the state rooms of **Palazzo Spada** will only occupy a very short time, perhaps twenty minutes; the two principal objects of interest being the 'statue of Pompey' and the curious *meridiana*, really a celestial sphere and not a sun-dial. If the Consiglio di Stato is not in session the porter of the palace will usually conduct one round (no charge is made but a tip is acceptable); he begins with the *sala del trono*. It is a bit mystifying to most foreigners to find a throne room in what was a private house, even a princely one; but this is explained by the fact that until 1870 the popes might honour the houses of princes, dukes, and four privileged marquesses with a visit. As a sign of this signal honour, and so as to be ever ready properly to receive the sovereign pontiffs, the palaces of these nobles always contained a throne room, complete with a throne standing under a *baldacchino* or canopy. Though the custom has fallen into disuse for nearly a century, palaces belonging to the princely and ducal families and those of the marquesses Costaguti, Patrizi, Teodoli and Sacchetti still possess such rooms. From the enjoyment of this privilege, the latter are known as the '*marchesi del baldacchino*'.

The throne room of Palazzo Spada is now used for meetings of the *Consiglio di Stato*; providing a particularly appropriate setting for the 'statue of Pompey', if only the story of the origins of this famous heroic figure were true. At the time of its discovery in 1550, in the Via dei Leutari (Street of the Lute-makers), the statue was believed to have been the one of Pompey which stood in a hall of his theatre where the Senate met on the fatal ides of March in 44 BC. In actual fact it is more likely to have ornamented the barracks of the chariot-racing 'Greens', as in those days the Via dei Leutari reached to the Cancelleria palace which was built on the site. But so firm was contemporary opinion that this was the actual statue at whose feet Julius Caesar had been murdered that a battle for its possession was only eventually settled by its being bought by Pope Julius III and presented to Cardinal Capodiferro, who installed it in his palace. Nor has the verdict of modern archaeologists, that this could not possibly be the famous statue, entirely robbed it of its glamour. For some twenty years, until the last war, an elderly Frenchwoman appeared punctually every year on the ides of March and deposited a bunch of scarlet carnations at its feet.

Though the installation of the statue dates from Cardinal Capodiferro's tenancy of the palace, the decoration of the room in which it now stands was carried out in the middle of the seventeenth century for Cardinal Spada by two Bolognese artists. One wonders if their deliciously frivolous *trompe l'oeil* paintings, including a cage of little birds, ever raises a smile during the austere meetings of the *Consiglio di Stato*. On leaving the throne room, we pass through a very fine series of reception rooms and a gallery, notable particularly for their seventeenth-century stucco decoration in high relief and their superb gilded ceilings. These finally lead us to the gallery of the *meridiana*, where the ceiling displays an outstanding seventeenth-century example of the art of *trompe l'oeil*, executed by Domenichino's pupil, G. B. Ruggeri.

In order to view this properly we must stand in the middle of the centre window. Looking upwards we will see that the artist has succeeded in creating the illusion of a celestial sphere projected on to the barrel vault. This curiously scientific form of decoration resembles the famous illuminated clock in Piccadilly Circus underground station. For, with Rome in the centre, it gives the differences in time from Dublin in the west to Pegu in Burma in the east, as well as that of many intervening places such as Crete, Bengal and so on. Cardinal Bernardino Spada must have been something of an amateur astronomer, for one of the end walls of the gallery bears tables referring to the positions of the planets. There is also a curious disk, a nocturnal, used for telling the time by the stars at night. Let into the gallery walls are eight celebrated Hellenistic reliefs of mythical subjects dating from the first century AD. Ten of these were found in 1620 near the church of S. Agnese on the Via Nomentana. The fact that they were found lying face downward and being used as a pavement accounts for the remarkable state of preservation of their high relief. They are notable for the realistic natural detail of their backgrounds. Two of the ten reliefs are now in the Capitoline Museum, but facsimiles of these complete the set in the *meridiana* gallery. We can now lunch either very simply at the little *trattoria* in the Piazza della Quercia; or, more grandly, at Pancrazio's in the Piazza del Biscione, whose downstairs room is built into the ruins of Pompey's theatre.

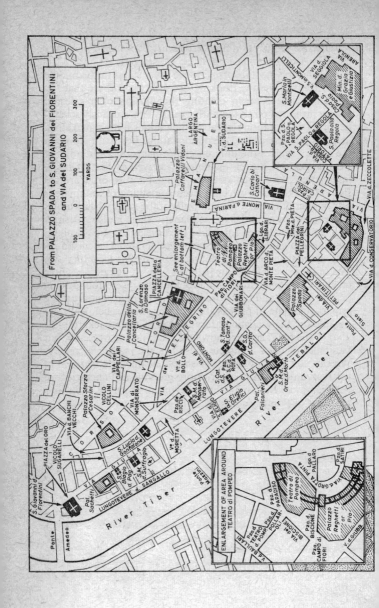

From PALAZZO SPADA to S. GIOVANNI dei FIORENTINI and VIA del SUDARIO

YARDS
100   0   100   200   300

River Tiber

Ponte Amedeo

S. Giovanni d. Fiorentini

PIAZZA dei ORO

VIA d. BANCHI VECCHI

VICOLO SUGARELLI

Palazzo Sforza Cesarin

VICOLO CELLINI

VIA dei CAPPELLARI

VIA di MONSERRATO

Palazzo d. Cancelleria

PIAZZA della CANCELLERIA

S. Lorenzo in Damaso

VIA d. PELLEGRINO

See enlargement at bottom left.

VIA d. MONTE d. FARINA

Palazzo Caffarelli Vidoni

LARGO ARGENTINA

v.d. SUDARIO IL

S. Carlo bi Catinari

Teatro Argentina

VIA di Pompeo

Pal. Righetti R. Pio.

Psa. CAMPO di FIORI

VIA di GIUBBONARI

VIA d. ARCO d. MONTE PIETA

Pzo. d. Mte d'Pietà

PIAZZA dei PELLEGRINI

Palazzo Spada

VIA d. PETTINARI

Sato

Ponte

River Tiber

LUNGOTEVERE

VIA d. CONSERVATORIO

VIA d. ZECCOLETTE

S. Maria in Monticelli

VIA ARENULA

S. Paolo alla Regola

VIA di S. PAOLO alla REGOLA

Min. d. Grazia e Giustizia

VIA MONTEVERDE

Pza. d. S. PAOLO alla Regola

VICO D'ORO

Pza. d. CAIROLI

VIA d. MONSERRATO

VIA d. MORETTA

S. Maria d. Monserrato

Pal. RICCI

VIA GIULIA

S. Cat. d. S. Rota

VIA di MORETTA

S. Eligio d. Orefici

S.G. d. Carità

S. Tomaso di Cant'y

Pal. Falconieri

S. Maria d. Orazio d. Morte

River Tiber

LUNGOTEVERE

LUNGOTEVERE d. SANGALLO

Pal. Sacchetti

S. M. d. Suffragio

Biagio d. Pag.

S. Lucia d. Gonfalone

VIA d. BOLLO

VIA del TORRE

VIA MONTORO

ENLARGEMENT OF AREA AROUND TEATRO di POMPEO

Psa. d. Teatro di Pompeo

Pzo. d. BISCIONE

VIA d. BISCIONE

VIA d. TEATRO di POMPEO

VIA d. POLLAROLI

VIA d. GROTTA PINTA

Pza. d. PALLARO

Pzo. d. PALLARO

Teatro di Pompeo

Palazzo Righetti Pio

VIA d. GIUBBA

Psa. d. CAMPO di FIORI

CHAPTER SEVEN

Via Capodiferro to Via del Sudario

❧

WHEREVER we have lunched, our afternoon's walk now begins with the Via Capodiferro which leads out of the Piazza della Quercia. On the right of Via Capodiferro is the fine but dilapidated original palace of the Spada family (No. 7); variously attributed to Vignola or Peruzzi, it is now known as the Palazzetto Spada. A little farther along on the left, some Ionic columns and part of an ancient trabeation appear imbedded in the wall of a house (No. 31). These classical fragments had probably been re-used in the Middle Ages to make the street side porticoes which were then common in Rome, as they still are in Northern Italian cities. Many of the Roman ones were walled in by order of Sixtus IV after 1475. King Ferrante of Naples had then warned him that it was impossible to keep order in a city whose dark porticoes providing hiding places for thieves and rebels.

We now find ourselves in the square variously known as **Piazza Trinità dei Pellegrini** or simply Piazza dei Pellegrini, after the church and hospice of the same name which stand there. The hospice was founded by S. Filippo Neri for the reception of pilgrims during Holy Year 1575, when more than 170,000 were lodged there. It continued for centuries as one of the greatest centres of hospitality, especially in 1625 for English and Scots pilgrims, whose expenses were defrayed by their protecting Cardinal, Francesco Barberini. In the same year his august uncle, Pope Urban VIII (1623–44), came to witness the ceremonial washing of the pilgrims' feet by Roman grandees. This custom endured right into the nineteenth century and Augustus Hare, who then witnessed it, wickedly remarked 'here the washing is a reality, the feet not having been prepared beforehand'. The hospice was used as a hospital for the wounded Garibaldini during the 'Hero's' defence of the Roman Republic; here in 1849 the gallant poet Mameli died of his wounds.

We now take the Via dell'Arco del Monte di Pietà and come to the piazza called after the Monte di Pietà, the Roman municipal pawnshop. This is familiarly known as 'il Monte' to impoverished Romans or, to sarcastic ones, as the 'Monte d' Empietà' (the Mount of Impiety as opposed to Piety or Pity); an allusion to its (indeed!) very high rates of interest. The origins of this institution date back to 1439, when a cardinal and a Franciscan friar founded its first predecessor in the Via dei Banchi Vecchi. Sixtus IV (1471–84) transferred it to Via dei Coronari, and Clement VIII (1592–1605) to its present site. Those who enter, by necessity or choice, can ask to see Carlo Maderno's fine chapel.

The short remaining tract of the Via dell'Arco del Monte di Pietà leads us into the Largo dei Librari, the old Paternoster Row of Rome. From here we turn left down the Via dei Giubbonari, where the jerkin-makers have now been replaced by rather flashy dress shops.

In Campo dei Fiori we turn right, and then right again, into the irregular space where the **Piazza** and **Via del Biscione** meet.

On week-day mornings the Piazza del Biscione is a market; and in it and the surrounding streets are several 'junk,' shops where one may still pick up a bargain. The Albergo del Sole al Biscione, in the Via del Biscione, is the oldest hotel in Rome, known to have existed since the beginning of the fifteenth century. It was evidently a grand one, as Burckhard noted that the French Ambassador was staying there in 1489. In the far corner of the Piazza del Biscione is one of the rare Roman houses still possessing a delightful painted façade. But the dominating building in the square is the Palazzo Righetti or Pio, whose origins go right back to republican Rome. It is built over part of the ruins of Pompey's Theatre, owned by the Orsini in the twelfth century. Then because of its rounded shape it was called *il Trullo*, in its midst rose the towering fortress even more oddly named *l'Arpacata* (the significance of the word is unknown). Some fragments of ancient brick walls, still to be seen at the summit of the Palazzo Righetti from the Campo dei Fiori, may be relics of this.

A dark arch in the corner of the Piazza del Biscione leads us through a narrow passage into the semi-circular Via di Grottapinta, whose outline still follows that of the auditorium of Pompey's Theatre. The adjoining **Piazza dei Satiri** probably occupies part of what was once the stage. It is comforting to observe that the theatrical tradition still survives here: the modern Teatro dei Satiri has been built into a courtyard of the Palazzo Righetti. Nor has all trace of the Orsini connection with the area been lost; the arms of the Dukes of Bracciano appear on the façade of the derelict chapel of S. Maria di Grottapinta on the corner.

The discovery in 1864 under one of the courtyards of the Righetti Palace of the famous bronze Hercules (now in the Vatican museum) recalled the splendour of the theatre which Pompey built in 55 BC. It was Rome's first stone theatre and was so famous that it was known simply as 'the Theatre' or 'the Roman theatre'. Its design was inspired by the Greek one on the island of Mitylene, where splendid spectacles had been staged in Pompey's honour after his victory over King Mithridates. Nevertheless Pompey had to employ a ruse in order to win conservative Roman opinion over to his building of this oriental luxury. He did this by erecting a temple to Venus Victrix at the top of the auditorium, thus giving the theatre the character of a sacred building. The celebrations connected with its inauguration lasted for five days, with concerts alternating, incongruously to us, with the savage games beloved of the populace. Five hundred lions and eighteen elephants were slaughtered to make this Roman holiday. More pleasing, but still characteristic of the ancient world, was Nero's gesture of having the entire theatre gilded in a day, inside and out, for the reception of King Tiridates of Armenia in AD 66.

But the most memorable part of Pompey's Theatre was its portico, the famous *Hecatostylon* of a hundred columns, where Brutus administered justice from the Praetor's bench on the fatal ides of March. It was in one of the halls of this vast architectural layout that the Senate was called to meet that day. Caesar, when he entered, actually held in his hand a short message of warning, put there by a Greek, Artemidorus. If he had only read it, he might have saved his life. The conspirators at once gathered round him, as if to urge the petition being made by Tillius Cimber. As they pressed closer, Caesar cried 'this is violence', and the first blow was struck; he fought them off until his body was riddled with twenty-three dagger thrusts. Suetonius says that as Brutus stabbed him for the second time Caesar uttered in Greek the famous words: 'You, too, my son?' Then, covering his face with his robe, he fell dying at the base of Pompey's statue.

After Caesar's murder, the Senate ordered the room where it happened to be walled up. Who knows, it may still have remained sealed five hundred years later, when Theodoric the Goth ordered the theatre to be restored. Or even in the eighth century, when the anonymous Swiss monk from Einsiedeln transcribed the inscriptions on the theatre walls for his list of the 'marvels' of ancient Rome. Perhaps the statue still lies buried deep in the soil of Rome, which has hidden so many treasures; its chances of survival appear to have been better than most. If it does, then some spot near the Monte della Farina conceals a mute witness of one of the world's greatest dramas.

Leaving the Via di Grottapinta, we turn left into the Largo del Pallaro and left again into the Piazza del Paradiso and continue through the Piazza Pollarola. Then, crossing our old friend, the Via dei Baullari, we come to a long elegant square, the Piazza della Cancelleria, which has not changed since it was laid out in 1673. Here rises one of the most superbly beautiful palaces in Rome—the **Palazzo della Cancelleria**—majestically filling the whole of the far side. The heraldic stone roses above the windows of the *piano nobile* indicate that the palace was built for Raffaele Riario, nephew of Sixtus IV (1471–84). If ever there was a monument to nepotism surely it is this. The famous 60,000 scudi which went to its building were won in a night's gambling from another papal nephew, Franceschetto Cibo, whose uncle was to become Pope Innocent VIII (1484–92). Whatever the sober-sides of fifteenth-century Rome may have thought of the matter, we are bound to admit that no one who has broken the bank at Monte Carlo has ever left the rest of the world so much richer in beauty.

The Medici Pope, Leo X (1513–21), confiscated the palace from the Riario family, who had plotted against him. Subsequently he installed there the presiding cardinal and the offices of the papal chancellery, hence its name of *Cancelleria*. The palace is still the property of the Vatican, housing one of the ecclesiastical courts; but it has passed through many vicissitudes. In 1798–9 it was the seat of the Tribune of the Roman Republic; in 1810 of the Imperial Court, and in 1848 of the first Roman parliament. It was on 16 November of that year that Pius IX's minister, Count Rossi, was murdered on the stairs, allegedly by medical students who had experimented on a corpse to discover the exact spot at which to strike for the jugular vein. But to the British the period of greatest interest in the palace's history is the eighteenth century, when no less than three members of the exiled Stuart family lived there. As Vice-Chancellor of the Roman church, it was Cardinal Henry's official residence; he gave his sister-in-law, Louise Stolberg, a suite of rooms there, after she had fled from his brother Charles Edward. Louise's stay terminated abruptly when the horrified cardinal learnt from his brother's lips—what all Rome already knew—that Louise was the poet Alfieri's mistress. After Bonnie Prince Charlie's death in 1788, the patient cardinal received another of his female relatives in the Cancelleria. This was Charlotte Stuart, Duchess of Albany, Charles's illegitimate daughter by Clementina Walkenshaw, whom he had met in Scotland during the '45.

Although we know so much about the people who lived in it, the palace's own history is obscure; all documents concerning it seem to have been destroyed in the sack of Rome in 1527. On Vasari's authority the Cancelleria was long believed to have been designed by Bramante; but as research has revealed that he did not come to Rome till 1499, only the great courtyard is now somewhat doubtfully assigned to him, the rest of the palace is now generally attributed to Andrea Bregno.

To us, seeing it on a fine Roman afternoon, it seems to be enough that the Cancelleria is there. In the golden light its delicately wrought façade resembles some ancient casket of mellowed ivory, hoarding as a treasure the most beautiful court in Rome. To the writer this has only one rival in Italy, its near contemporary, Laurana's masterpiece in the Ducal Palace of Urbino. It is said that the ruins of Pompey's *Hecato-stylon* were plundered to provide the forty-four superb granite columns which adorn the porticoes; the grace with which these were incorporated into their Renaissance setting is perhaps unparalleled. The only decorations are Riario's roses, appearing in the spandrels of the arches, in miniature on the corner pillars, and as the central motif of the courtyard pavement. After this splendour, the interior decoration of the palace comes as something of an anti-climax, and to see it a special permit is necessary. Suffice it to say that Vasari's boast to Michelangelo, that he and two assistants had painted the vast salon in the brief space of a hundred days, elicited the retort: 'It looks like it!'

Built into the fabric of the palace is the church of S. Lorenzo in Damaso. One of the ancient titular churches of Rome, this was founded by the thirty-seventh Pope, St. Damasus (366–84). The existing church, however, only dates from the same period as the palace. Nor does it occupy the site of the original one, which faced on to Via del Pellegrino. Inscriptions recording St. Damasus's foundation of the first church, and the libraries housed in its porticoes, still existed in the eighth century. The design of this original church appears to have been unique; it had a transept *behind* the apse, and the whole building was surrounded by porticoes. Possibly as a reminder of these, the interior of the existing Renaissance church is also surrounded by a portico, doubled in front of the entrance to form a vestibule. The effect is dignified if somewhat ornate; the Riario roses again adorn the gilded coffering of the ceiling. Apparently the only surviving relic of the original church is the monument of Cardinal Scarampo, whose palace was knocked down to make way for the Cancelleria. The grim features of this martial churchman, who served both as an admiral and general and defeated the Turks at Belgrade, were realistically portrayed by Paolo Romano. The tomb stands near the end of the left nave. In the chapel at the far end hangs a black Byzantine Madonna of the ninth century, transferred from S. Maria di Grottapinta by Sixtus IV (1471–82). Both the church and the Cancelleria were damaged by fire in this century. It was during the consequent restorations that inscriptions were found indicating that this was indeed the site of the barracks of the Green Company of Charioteers. Another ancient name of the church, S. Lorenzo in Prasino (*Prasinus* in Latin is leek green), indicated the possibility.

We now turn round the left corner of the Cancelleria into the **Via del Pellegrino**, the only tract of the ancient medieval Via Peregrinorum to have been restored to its old name. Today the Via del Pellegrino is one of the few places in Rome to preserve the old custom of artisans practising the same craft congregating in a single street; the small shops on either side of the beginning of the street are jewellers. At the end of the seventeenth century all the jewellers in Rome were required not only to practise their business here, but also to live in the street; giving it yet another name, that of Via degli Orefici, or goldsmiths.

Two blind alleys off the left of the Via del Pellegrino afford a glimpse of the fast vanishing picturesque Rome. One of these (entrance at No. 19), leading under the Arco degli Arcetari, terminates in a small court where the houses have outside staircases leading to the first floor; a characteristic still to be seen in many Italian villages, but rarely in Rome. On the left corner of the second blind alley, the Arco di S. Margherita, is a splendid baroque street shrine or *edicola*, supported by eagles. Rather surprisingly an inconspicuous house in Via del Pellegrino (No. 58) has Borgia associations. It was bought on 12 July 1469 by Vanozza Cattanei for 500 ducats, 310 of these coming from her dowry; apparently she had recently married her first husband, Domenico Gianotti. Possibly Vanozza's only legitimate child, Michele Angelo Gianotti, was born here before her relationship with Rodrigo Borgia began about 1470. The house is a short distance from the palace which he had begun to build in 1458, and was certainly living in by 1462; this is now owned by the Sforza Cesarini. A short way beyond Vanozza's house we turn to the left down the narrow Vicolo del Bollo. This took its name from the office for stamping the hallmark on gold or silver (in Italian a *bollo* is a stamp or seal) which was established here in the eighteenth century for the convenience of the jewellers in the neighbouring street.

We now find ourselves in the **Via dei Cappellari** (the Street of the Hat-makers), one of the most picturesque though least salubrious in Rome; narrow and dark, it seems to be eternally festooned with washing—one wonders how this ever dries except at the height of summer. A little way down on the left the street is spanned by a dark and sinister-looking arch; in its shadow, on the wall of the houses on the right (Nos. 29 and 30), is an inscribed marble plaque. This is difficult to read, but it relates that Pietro Trapassi, the boy who recited his verses in the Piazza S. Andrea della Valle and became the famous poet Metastasio, was born here in 1698.

Just to the right of the arch, a passageway opens out of the street; it terminates before a shrine with a curious dark old picture of the Crucifixion. To the left of this a gateway leads into a picturesque courtyard where a splendid fig tree flourishes on the first-floor terrace of a house on the right. The old walls and small grated windows on the left of this court are said to be relics of the Corte Savella. One of the grim medieval prisons of Rome, this was placed under the jurisdiction of the Savelli, who were created hereditary Marshals of the Conclave in the thirteenth century. Formerly the prison reached to the Via di Monserrato (then called Via di Corte Savella); it was only closed by Innocent X in the seventeenth century. Most famous of its prisoners was Beatrice Cenci who, with her mother and brother, were executed by the Ponte S. Angelo in 1599.

We now return to the cross-roads where the Vicolo del Bollo enters the Via dei Cappellari, and take the street opposite, the Via di Montoro. As we traverse this short street the whole atmosphere of our surroundings changes completely. We leave behind us the grim memories of medieval Rome and the narrow dark alleys of the fifteenth century and find ourselves in the Via di Monserrato; a street of fine old palaces, baroque churches and quite a number of antique and junk shops. To the English this street is best known for the **Venerable English College** (No. 45), which was established here in 1362; it claims to be the oldest English institution abroad.

The English College of the Via di Monserrato began as a hospice for English pilgrims, founded by a seller of rosaries, John Shepherd, and his wife Alice. According to an anonymous source it owed its existence to 'national pride, national piety, and a national distaste for being fleeced by foreigners'. By the reign of Henry VII the hospice had so risen in the world as to have the royal arms on its seal, and for the office of its *custos* to be a crown appointment. Cardinal Bainbridge, Henry VIII's first Ambassador to the Holy See, who died in Rome in 1514, lies buried in the College Church of St. Thomas of Canterbury. This was restored by Cardinal Howard in 1575, four years before the hospice became a college, Henry VIII's break with the Church in the intervening years having put an end to the numerous pilgrimages. But already by 1638 the college was a centre frequented by English Protestant visitors; Milton dined there on 30 October of that year, his first night in Rome, and Evelyn in 1644. Six hundred years' existence in a foreign capital have not in any way diminished the national character of the college. The energy of its fresh-faced young seminarists seems to withstand even the insidious Roman climate; one can pick them out anywhere by that unmistakable gait, dubbed '*il passo nordico*' by some Italian wit, and their prowess on the cricket field is practically unchallenged.

Almost opposite the English College is the little **Piazza di S. Caterina della Rota**, probably unequalled even in Rome for the number of churches surrounding its small area. On the left in Via di Monserrato is S. Tommaso di Canterbury (the College church); on the far corner S. Girolamo della Carita; and at the far end the church of St. Catherine from which the square takes its name. Most interesting of these is S. Girolamo which, in the first chapel on the right, containing the tombs of the Spada family, is famous for Borromini's use of polychrome marbles. The usual balustrade is here replaced by two kneeling angels, holding stretched out between them what appears to be a swag of brilliant striped stuff; it is only when one touches it that one realises that this is also marble.

We now turn back along the Via di Monserrato, passing on our left the Spanish national church of S. Maria di Monserrato, from which the street now takes its name. Continuing along the Via di Monserrato, we see on our left Palazzo Ricci, standing at the far end of the piazza of the same name. This palace was once famous for its frescoed façade; but little now remains of these sixteenth century paintings of the legends of ancient Rome. Almost opposite, on the right (No. 20 Via di Monserrato), the door of the very simple Palazzo Corsetti leads us into an enchanting little court. The walls are covered with fragments of antique sculpture, and an iron gate affords a glimpse of a charming garden.

The Via di Monserrato ends in a rather desolate open space, used in the morning as a vegetable market. This was produced by demolitions during the fascist period. A plaque on the corner still gives the name as **Vicolo della Moretta**, though it is now officially Largo della Moretta. This area, where the Via di Monserrato meets the Via Giulia, Via del Pellegrino and Via dei Banchi Vecchi, is called after the famous pharmacy of the Moretta which had existed here since the fifteenth century. In Renaissance times it was known as *la Chiavica*, from the *chiavica* or sewer which passed near by; the neighbouring church of S. Lucia even being called S. Lucia della Chiavica. Benvenuto Cellini mentions it in his autobiography as the place where he killed his enemy, the Milanese jeweller Pompeo. He says that Pompeo entered the pharmacy 'on the corner of the Chiavica'; as he emerged Cellini attacked him. According to Cellini's account he killed Pompeo with a little dagger 'after only two blows'; but he himself got off scot free. However, in the pharmacy of the Moretta, which existed here with all its old fittings until just before the demolitions, there was an old bronze mortar. This was said to have been worked by Cellini and presented by him 'for assistance rendered after a duel fought in the Via Giulia, in which he was wounded'.

When wandering round this area of Rome, it is delightful to find how its history still lives in the minds of its inhabitants. In the Via dei Cappellari I had experienced some difficulty in finding the birthplace of Metastasio. I need not have bothered, the first comer I asked showed me the house. In the same way in the neighbouring courtyard, when I was trying to identify what might have been the remains of the Corte Savella, an old woman called out of a window to me: 'Beatrice Cenci was imprisoned underneath here.' So I was not surprised when I went to buy some aspirin in a chemist's at the beginning of the Via dei Banchi Vecchi and asked if they knew anything about the vanished Farmacia della Moretta; they told me that they are actually its successors, but they no longer possess any of its fittings. Cellini's bronze mortar was, alas, sold many years ago to 'a museum in London'.

Indeed the whole neighbourhood is so closely associated with the exploits, apocryphal or not, related by Cellini in his autobiography, that it is not surprising to find that a nearby street has been named after him. This is the Vicolo Cellini, leading to the right out of the Via dei Banchi Vecchi. The irrepressible Benvenuto never lived there, but it is said to have been the scene of one of his numerous love-affairs. This is quite possible, as several notorious courtesans lived there in the sixteenth century, when the street went by a very vulgar name indeed. The dilapidated but picturesque little house decorated with graffiti (Nos. 31, 32) may well be a survivor of this period.

Considering its brevity, the Via dei Banchi Vecchi contains as many interesting monuments as any street in Rome. Immediately upon entering it we find, on our left, the church of **S. Lucia del Gonfalone**. This church was restored in 1765 and again in 1886 and looks it. The chief interest does not lie in its antiquity, but in its being the station of the famous *Arcicon-fraternità del Gonfalone*. The history of this confraternity can be traced directly from its foundation by S. Bonaventura in 1263, when its eighteen members were called *raccomandati della SS. Virgine*. Then one of their chief functions was to take part in religious processions, wearing a white habit with a red and white cross, and wielding a discipline or scourge upon their own backs. This pious body had evidently grown in size and power by 1354 when, after the fall of Cola di Rienzi, its members played a great part as leaders of the people in oppos-ing the violence of the nobles. For this signal service they were awarded the name of *Confraternità del Gonfalone* (Confrater-nity of the banner or standard), because 'under the standard of liberty, of the fatherland and justice' they had given Rome back her liberty. In 1574, Gregory XIII made them the first *arciconfraternità*.

The only *arciconfraternita* in Rome which challenges the Gonfalone's antiquity is that of S. Spirito. This was in fact founded as early as 1198 but it remained a mere *confraternità* till 1612; then Paul V raised it also to the dignity of an *arcicon-fraternità*. These pious and charitable confraternities have existed in considerable numbers in Rome since the Middle Ages. Many of the small chapels and oratories tucked away in the back streets still belong to them, or to the trade and pro-fessional guilds and corporations known as *scholae* or *uni-versità*. According to the great Italian historian Muratori, the origins of the confraternities might be traced to late imperial times, or at least to the days of Constantine; while Gregoro-vius, in his *History of the City of Rome in the Middle Ages*, says that the professional corporations or *scholae* played a great part in the life of the city in the eighth century. Even then each one had its organisation for helping the poor and infirm and for paying for the funerals of members, like the ancient Roman burial clubs. As we continue our exploration of Rome we shall find other mementoes of the activities of these bodies.

For some peculiar reason the church of S. Lucia was used as the starting point for the Jews' race during the carnival; they ran from *la Chiavica* to the Piazza of St. Peter's. Burck-hard records it as taking place there in 1499 and 1501; later, 'out of respect for the blessed Apostles', Pius V (1566–72) ordered it to be held in the Corso. It was in this same short street that Imperia, the most famous Renaissance courtesan, died in 1511; she had come to live here while a new house was being built for her in the Borgo. For some reason which has never been explained, possibly a quarrel with her new lover Angelo del Bufalo, she poisoned herself at the age of twenty-six. She lingered for two days but all the efforts of Rome's greatest doctors—sent by her old love Agostino Chigi—could not save her. Imperia left all her possessions to her daughter Lucrezia, who also committed suicide, but for a very different reason; it was to save herself from the immoral advances of the governor of Siena.

An inscription on a house almost opposite the church of S. Lucia (No. 131) records the fact that a hospice for Bohemian pilgrims was founded here by the Emperor Charles IV (1346–78), and was rebuilt by the procurator, H. Borau, in 1457. A little farther along the street on the left is a palace known as the Palazzo dei Pupazzi (Nos. 22–24). The whole of the façade is covered with graceful Renaissance reliefs of trophies of arms and swags of flowers and fruit, supported by cupids.

The last interesting building in the street is the Palazzo Sforza Cesarini (No. 282). Though externally unremarkable today, in 1462 it was the residence of Cardinal Rodrigo Borgia and was once fulsomely compared with Nero's Golden House. On this occasion it was decorated with rich tapestries, objets d'art were exhibited under a canopy in its loggia, and it was surrounded by orchestras and singing minstrels. This remarkable display was staged as part of the general rejoicing to welcome the arrival in Rome of a revered relic, the head of St. Andrew, lately rescued from the Turks. If we wish to see the remains of the original Borgia palace, we must now turn to the right down the Vicolo del Pavone, and right again to the Corso Vittorio Emanuele. A new façade was added to this side of the palace when the Corso was built; but if we can evade the watchful eye of the porter at No. 282, we can catch a glimpse of the charming fifteenth-century porticoed court-yard inside. While curiosity of a less edifying kind may be satisfied by looking at the house in the corner of the adjoining Piazza Sforza Cesarini. According to the census of 1517, Vanozza lived for a while at No. 27, and here Cesare and Lucrezia may well have been born.

We now return to Banchi Vecchi and turn down the Vicolo

Sugarelli; which brings us into the **Via Giulia**, probably the most handsome street in old Rome. Looking left from where we stand, we see practically the whole of the kilometre's dead straight length of this sixteenth-century thoroughfare. Viewed thus it bears a strong resemblance to the artificial perspectives that formed the set scenery of Italian Renaissance theatres; like the famous 'streets of Thebes' in Palladio's Teatro Olimpico at Vicenza. Via Giulia is called after its creator, the great Della Rovere Pope, Julius II (1503–13). It formed part of his plan for creating a superb new approach to St. Peter's, which was to be carried out by Bramante. Funds ran out and the architect and then the pope died before the work could be completed; but later in the sixteenth century Via Giulia became the most important, and fashionable, street in the city.

In order to explore its full length we now turn right. Not far along this side we come to a small palace (No. 93), charmingly decorated with stucco reliefs. The Farnese lilies combined with the papal keys and umbrella feature prominently in the design; but in spite of the heraldic solemnity of these attributes, there is something appealingly light and feminine about the decoration. Apparently the palace was built by the Farnese Pope, Paul III, for his daughter Costanza, whose beauty was as legendary as that of her aunt Giulia Bella. Not many paces beyond this is another small palace (No. 86), with rusticated stonework on the ground floor; this is said to have belonged to Raphael.

The Via Giulia terminates in the **Piazza dell'Oro**, the centre of what in Renaissance times was the Florentine colony in Rome. The Via del Consolato, leading into the piazza on the right commemorates the fact that the Medici Pope, Leo X (1513–21), gave his compatriots the privilege of having their own court of justice. This was known as *il consolato*; the palace which housed it stands on the corner (No. 3). But the dominating building in the piazza is the church of **S. Giovanni dei Fiorentini**; though frankly this is a rather disappointing national place of worship for the people of a city so famous for its beauty. Nevertheless a galaxy of talents competed for the honour of designing it; Michelangelo, Peruzzi and Raphael are said to have submitted projects, but Pope Leo X selected Sansovino as the architect. The façade, only finally completed in the eighteenth century, is impressive and the interior of the church has a certain cold stateliness; but the only obvious link with Renaissance Florence is the small fifteenth-century statue of St. John the Baptist as a boy. This was transferred to its present position above the sacristy door, from an earlier church.

We now turn back along the Via Giulia, where the first notable building on our right is the Palazzo Sacchetti (No. 66), believed to have been begun by Antonio Sangallo for himself; an inscription to the left of the balcony which reads 'Domus Antonii Sangalli Architecti MDXLII'. It has now for centuries been the residence of the Sacchetti family, whose head is one of the *Marchesi del Baldacchino*.

Farther down the street, on the right, is the little church of **S. Biagio della Pagnotta**. S. Biagio was the Armenian Bishop St. Blaise, martyred in 316; he is protector of the throat. Rather suitably, on his feast day (3rd February), after a choral mass according to the Armenian rite, *pagnotte* (small loaves) are distributed to the congregation. As we continue down the Via Giulia, we see great travertine blocks protruding from the walls of the houses on our right. These look as if they were the relics of some classical ruin; but in fact they are the remains of the unfinished tribunal which Bramante was to have built for Julius II. They are now irreverently known to the local populace as the 'sofas of Via Giulia'.

A short way beyond the seventeenth-century church of S. Maria del Suffragio rises the forbidding brick pile of Innocent X's prisons, the **Carceri Nuove** (No. 52). These were built in 1655 by Antonio del Grande, and were for long considered to be models of their kind; as late as 1845 they were referred to as the most 'solid and salubrious' in Europe. The building now houses the Museo Criminale and is used as offices by the Ministry of Grace and Justice.

After passing yet two more churches—the dilapidated little chapel of S. Filippo Neri almost opposite the *Carceri* and farther down on the right the Neapolitan church of S. Spirito —we see a singularly beautiful dome appearing at the end of the short Via di S. Eligio on the right. This is the church of **S. Eligio degli Orefici**, attributed to Raphael and built in 1509 for the *università* or guild of goldsmiths. In 1601 the church was rebuilt or heavily restored, with baroque additions; it has lately been restored again. The damp of the low-lying site beside the Tiber makes itself felt in the somewhat gloomy interior; this is difficult of access even for Rome (the custodian usually leaves his address on a note pinned to the door). Continuing down the Via Giulia, on the left we come to the church of **S. Caterina da Siena**. This is the national church of the Sienese, built in 1526 and restored in 1767, when the existing façade was added.

As we approach the end of the Via Giulia, yet another fine palace, distinguished by large falcons' heads on the corners, comes into sight (No. 1). It was built for the Falconieri family by Borromini in the seventeenth century. Later it was the home of Napoleon's uncle, Cardinal Fesch; today it is the Hungarian Academy. Just beyond the palace is the rather macabre church of **S. Maria dell' Orazione e Morte**, whose door is adorned with stone skulls. This belongs to a pious confraternity founded in 1551 to collect the bodies of the unknown dead and give them Christian burial. The picturesque arch spanning the Via Giulia at this point is all that remains of Michelangelo's project for linking the Farnese palace, on our left, with the Farnesina across the river. Finally, on the right, at the very end of the street is a fountain which Augustus Hare described as 'the ugly fountain of the Mascherone'. This was once made to spout wine instead of water in celebration of the election of a Grand Master of the Order of Malta.

From the comparative tranquillity of the streets of old Rome we now emerge into the full blast of twentieth-century traffic roaring along the Lungotevere. It is only for a few minutes, and worth it, as the zebra crossing brings us to **Ponte Sisto** and one of the most charming views in Rome. It is said that before Sixtus IV became Pope in 1471 he lived in a monastery in the nearby Via dei Pettinari. Administrative affairs connected with his office often necessitated his going from here to the Vatican. Every time he looked regretfully at the ruins of the ancient Pons Agrippae and said that if ever he became pope he would rebuild it. Sixtus was as good as his word, in 1475 the bridge, which was to take his name, was built by Baccio Pontelli. Not everyone notices the charming and very human inscription on the parapet; roughly translated it reads as follows: 'You who pass, invoke the divine bounty so that Sixtus IV, excellent Pontifex Maximus, may be healthy and for long be preserved. You then, to whom this request is made, whoever you are, be healthy too.'

As we walk to the top of the rise on the old bridge, a view that no theatrical setting could equal appears before us. This comparison with the theatre is inevitable in Rome, where the love of display is inborn, as the love of beauty used (unfortunately the past tense is usually now operative) to be. But that beauty is an ideal to be pursued still survives as a relic of Italy's Renaissance heritage—the very word *bello* nearly always brings a smile. I found this true on this very bridge. Just after some one-way driving regulations had made it impossible to turn directly on to it from the Via Giulia I was stopped by a policeman and told to continue along the Lungotevere. 'But,' I said, 'this is very serious, you are robbing me of one of the most beautiful views in Rome which I always enjoy as I go home; that's why I come this way.' Although the traffic was streaming past, the policeman turned and looked himself; then he motioned me to wait at the side of the road, and I saw him consulting his book of rules. In a few minutes he was back, with a smile, and a route carefully worked out so that I could still enjoy my beautiful view.

For perfection one must look over the Ponte Sisto on a fine evening at sunset, when the sky is red behind the cypresses on the Janiculum and the faint glimmer of the floodlighting is just beginning to be perceptible in the twilight. Then the small fountain of the Acqua Paula on the Trastevere bank appears mellowed in the evening light, standing up against tier upon tier of the old russet-tiled roofs that climb the slopes of the Janiculum. These are broken on the right by a solitary umbrella pine, growing in the garden of the Arcadia. Above them all, glimmering silvery white against the sunset sky, towers the baroque magnificence of the Fontanone di Acqua Paola (the monumental fountain of the Acqua Paola, built by Paul V in 1612 to celebrate his restoration of the ancient acqua Traiana),

Retracing our steps, we recross the Lungotevere and enter the Via dei Pettinari, so-called after the wool-combers (a *pettine* is a comb) and carders who exercised their trade there until the last century. We now turn first right into the Via delle Zoccolette, then left into the Via del Conservatorio; which brings us to the piazza and church of **S. Paolo alla Regola**. The *regola* in this case does not correspond to the ordinary Italian word rule. It is a corruption of *reula*, which in its turn was a dialect abbreviation of *arenula* or sand, from the sandbanks formerly existing at this point of the Tiber, which gave their name to the whole district. Nor was the church, as is often stated, built over a house in which St. Paul once lived. It probably owes its origins to a guild chapel—of the leather-workers whose patron saint he is, because he earned his living by working the skins for tents. Documents prove that the Apostle's name was associated with this area as early as 1245; an old inscription in the church mentions a *schola Pauli* or guild of St. Paul. The existing building, however, only dates from the seventeenth century.

We now turn to the right out of the piazza, down the rump end of the Via di S. Paolo alla Regola. Immediately on our right, we find one of the very few surviving towered medieval houses in Rome, known as the **Casa di S. Paolo**. The house was formerly one of a group, but these precious relics of medieval Rome were torn down to make way for the sin-gularly unattractive Ministry of Grace and Justice, of which the Casa di S. Paolo is now an annexe.

The picturesque little street of **S. Maria in Monticelli** now opens out before us, broken half-way down by a small open space in front of the church of the same name. Although the existing façade is baroque, the charming little romanesque campanile beside the church indicates that it is an old one. It was in fact consecrated by Paschal II (1099–1118) and still contains the remains of a fresco and mosaic of that period. In this street we encounter, for the last time, traces of Vanozza Cattanei and her remarkable brood of children. She was living at No. 5 when she died, at the age of 76, on 26 November 1518. For many years before her death, Vanozza had spent her time in good works; she made over her inn, the Vacca, to three pious foundations, and the chapel where she was buried in S. Maria del Popolo was similarly endowed. Lucrezia, now Duchess of Ferrara, survived her by a year; but in Vanozza's will the chief beneficiary was her obscure legitimate son, Michele Angelo Gianotti. Michele Angelo did not do badly out of his mother's Borgia connections; when Cesare died in far-away Spain in 1507, he too left property in the Via S. Maria in Monticelli to his half-brother. It casts an unexpected light on Cesare's enigmatic personality to find that, after a life led among the great and famous of his day, in his last hours he remembered the insignificant Michele Angelo with whom he must have played as a child.

The Via S. Maria in Monticelli ends in the Piazza Cairoli, before the imposing baroque church of **S. Carlo ai Catinari**. This is not dedicated to some obscure saintly patron, but to S. Carlo Borromeo; the *catinari* were the bowl or dish-makers who plied their trade in the area. As we follow the **Via Monte della Farina**, on the left of the church, we gradually become aware of a most unusual building at the far end. This is the Palazzo Caffarelli Vidoni, whose design, at least in part, has been attributed to Raphael; it was begun in 1519. The ground floor, with its long strips of rusticated stone, reminds us in a curious way of the Piccola Farnesina, but the classicism of the windows and the twin columns of the first storey are of a far grander conception; the top floor is a later addition. This palace, where the Emperor Charles V is said to have lodged in 1536, juts out into the little Piazza Vidoni, confronting the somewhat battered statue of a Roman orator. Popularly known as Abate Luigi, this was another of the talking statues of Rome, which joined in the dialogues of Pasquin and Marforio.

We now turn right into the narrow **Vicolo del Sudario**, so called after the Chiesa del Sudario, or church of the Holy Shroud, the national church of Piedmont. A little farther along is the national church of the Belgians, dedicated to S. Giuliano dei Fiamminghi. Though rarely noticed by passers-by of other nations, this church is also of particular interest to the English. In 1717 William Kent executed one of his earliest known works there, a painting of the apotheosis of St. Julian. The church archive still contains the entry: '*Al Signor Guglielmo Chient Pittore, scudi ventiquattro*' (to Mr. William Kent, painter, 24 scudi).

There is just one more building of interest to see in this little street before our day's exploration comes to an end. This is the small and delightful but curiously un-Roman Renaissance palace known as the Casa di Burcardo (No. 44). This building has many of the characteristics of a German house of the late fifteenth century; the explanation lies in the fact that it was the residence which John Burckhard, Bishop of Strasbourg, built for himself in 1503. Burckhard was Master of Ceremonies to Innocent VIII (1484–92), Alexander VI (1492–1503), Pius III (1503) and Julius II (1503–13). His famous diaries—the *liber notarium*—in which, with true Germanic attention to detail, he noted the daily doings of the papal court over this long period are one of the great sources of Roman Renaissance history. Thus it seems particularly appropriate that our day's exploration of an area which is so closely bound up with that period, should end here.

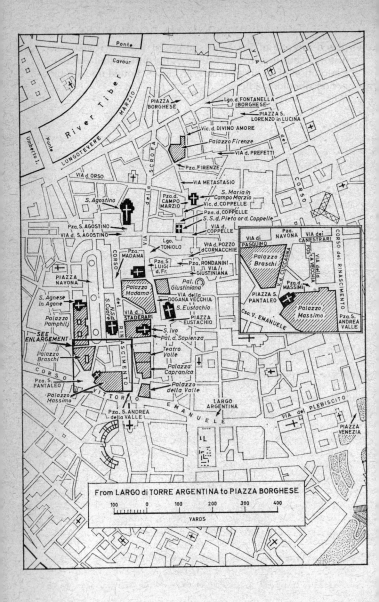

From LARGO di TORRE ARGENTINA to PIAZZA BORGHESE

100   0   100   200   300   400

YARDS

CHAPTER EIGHT

Piazza Argentina to Piazza Borghese

❧

AGAIN we set off from our familiar starting point of Piazza Venezia, continuing down the Via del Plebiscito and across the Largo di Torre Argentina to the Corso Vittorio Emanuele. But this time we are going to explore the area to the right of the Corso which in ancient times was the heart of the famous *Campus Martius*. In the midst of the area an inconspicuous little street and square—the Via and Piazza di Campo Marzio —are all that apparently survive to remind us of the immortal 'Field of Mars'. As always in Rome, however, we find as we begin to look beneath the surface, all is not so changed as it appears at first glance.

True, nothing could seem more different than the warren of narrow streets that now cover what was originally an open plain used for military and gymnastic exercises. The contrast is perhaps even greater with the *Campus Martius* of imperial times; then it was one of the great monumental centres of the city, where baths and theatres, porticoes and arenas stood in a park-like setting of public gardens. This was the aspect of Rome that most impressed the Greek geographer Strabo when he visited the city in 7 BC. 'Superior to all is the Campus Martius,' he wrote. 'The greatness of the plain itself is wonderful, all open for horse and chariot racing and for the great multitudes who take exercise in ball games; in the circus and in gymnastics. The ground is covered with grass, green all the year round, surrounded by buildings and hills that reach to the river's edge; it presents a scenic effect from which it is difficult to tear oneself away.'

It was Witigis the Goth who, all unknowing, sounded the death knell of the *Campus Martius* as it had been, when in 537 he cut the aqueducts while besieging Belisarius in Rome. Although attempts were made to restore them, gradually the populace deserted the now waterless higher residential districts and huddled in hovels built in and around the great monuments of the Campus, where water was more easily obtainable from the Tiber. Thus this area, which had never before been lived in, became the centre of Rome for many centuries to come. Still, through the dark ages, the memory of what had been was never quite lost; even today something of that memory remains in place names. We have already seen how the depression of Agrippa's lake gave its name to the Valle area. In medieval times, the church of S. Eustachio, whose origins date from the fourth century, was known as S. Eustachio *in platana* (St. Eustace among the plane trees); it stands on the site of the gardens of Agrippa which, in common with other Roman parks, was probably planted with planes, trees remarkable for their longevity. The name of another church, S. Salvatore in Lauro (St. Saviour among the bay trees), is believed by some to have similar origins; possibly even to commemorate the site of the famous groves of Europa; certainly its position near the Tiber bank would have been admirably suited for a public garden.

As we walk down the Corso Vittorio Emanuele, the first imposing palace on our right (No. 101) immediately provides us with a link with the medieval city that rose among the ruins of the *Campus Martius*. As the inscription above the door indicates, it is **Palazzo della Valle**; built by Cardinal Andrea, a sixteenth-century representative of the family who in the Middle Ages had established themselves in the *valle*, or valley, which was once Agrippa's lake, from which they also took their name. Cardinal Andrea played an important part in the struggle between Clement VII and the Emperor Charles V which ultimately led to the sack of Rome in 1527. Although he sided with the imperial party, during the sack he had to pay a large sum of money for the immunity of this palace and another Lorenzetto was building for him on the other side of the Largo del Teatro Valle (now Palazzo Capranica). By purchasing the protection of the soldier of fortune Fabrizio Maramaldo, Cardinal Andrea was able to save not only the lives of many Roman citizens, but also his own priceless collection of Roman antiquities. This included that treasure of the Uffizi now known as the Medici Venus, which was sold to Cardinal Medici in 1584.

As we continue down the Corso Vittorio Emanuele, standing on the gentle curve to the right we see the **Palazzo Massimo alle Colonne**, Baldassare Peruzzi's masterpiece, built for the brothers Pietro, Luca and Angelo Massimo after the sack of Rome in 1527. The palace takes its name from the great antique columns which were the distinguishing feature of its predecessor, burnt down in the sack. It was probably as a reminder of these that Peruzzi created the exquisite columned portico which is the principal feature of the façade. This forms a gentle curve, imposed upon the architect, by the line of the ancient Via Papale which, now much widened, is here followed by the Corso. Indeed the whole design of the palace is remarkable for Peruzzi's ingenuity in the use of an exceedingly narrow and difficult site. For centuries the loggia was allowed to be used as a shelter for homeless wanderers during the night; still today no eagle-eyed porter looks askance if one walks quietly in to admire the beauty of the stuccoed ceilings in the portico and vestibule and even the courtyard itself. Most unusually for a Renaissance palace, this is not centrally sited but is placed on one side so as to leave room for a magnificent series of reception rooms on the first floor. The painted portico leading to them is one of the few in Rome not to have been glassed in.

If one is so fortunate as to be in Rome on 16 March, even if unknown to its owners, one is welcome to enter the palace. Then Casa Massimo is 'at home' to the world in memory of the miracle performed by S. Filippo Neri on that day in 1583 when he recalled young Paolo Massimo from the dead. The saint talked to the boy for a while in the presence of his family, but upon Paolo declaring his readiness to die, S. Filippo said to him: 'Go and be blessed and pray to God for me.' The room where this event occurred is now a chapel; Masses are recited there continually on the morning of 16 March.

To the outside world, the name of Massimo is probably the best known of all the great Roman families, thanks to the ready wit of Camillo Francesco Massimo. When in 1797 this Marchese Massimo (the head of the family was one of the *Marchesi del Baldacchino* until 1826, when they were granted the princely title) was negotiating the Treaty of Tolentino with General Bonaparte, Napoleon asked him if it was true that his family was descended from Fabius Maximus. Camillo Massimo replied: 'I could not prove it, the story has only been told in our family for twelve hundred years.' Marchese Massimo had good grounds for his retort. Although they may not be descended from the famous 'Delayer', opponent of Hannibal, the family name is recorded in Rome at the beginning of the eleventh century, earlier even than the Colonna and Orsini. Like all old families, the history of the Massimo has patches of light and shade; perhaps the period of their greatest glory was in the second half of the fifteenth century. Then as humanists and patrons of the arts they received Conrad Sweinheim and Arnold Pannartz into their house, where in 1467 the first book was printed in Rome.

Just beyond Palazzo Massimo, the Corso Vittorio Emanuele widens out to form the little **Piazza S. Pantaleo**. This is called after the church dedicated to the patron saint of the medical profession, who suffered martyrdom by order of one of his patients, the Emperor Maximian. The great pile of **Palazzo Braschi** fills the whole of one side of the small piazza. Built in 1780 for the nephew of Pius VI, this was the last palace to be erected in Rome for the family of a pope; it is impressive rather than attractive. The palace now houses the municipal **Museo di Roma,** a modern collection but particularly interesting for the study of many aspects of Roman life. The collections of pictures, drawings, prints, and objects of daily use —ranging from weights and measures to Pius IX's personal train—illustrate the life of the city from medieval times until the last century. For the specialist, the print room is a rich source of research material, but permission must be obtained to consult this from the administration of the Municipal Museums at 28 Via Portico d'Ottavia.

A rapid tour of the museum, particularly the first floor, is most opportune before continuing our morning's exploration. No catalogue is available at the time of writing, but all exhibits are clearly marked; the most interesting for our purposes are easily recognisable, as they are principally pictures portraying scenes of Roman life, especially festivals. The third and fourth rooms on the first floor contain a remarkable series of these; outstanding among them are 'Il Torneo di Belvedere di 1565' and the 'Giostra del Saraceno' held in Piazza Navona in 1634. In this last we see the piazza we are shortly going to visit, decked out in all its glory for tilting at the quintain. In Italy this is usually called '*il Saraceno*', as the target at which the riders aimed their lances was made to represent a Saracen. From this and the other pictures exhibited it is evident that tilting, jousts and what can only be described as pageants on horseback were still very popular spectacles in seventeenth-century Rome. The fourth room contains a large canvas of a truly fabulous spectacle of this last type, staged by the Barberini for Queen Christina of Sweden's first Roman Carnival. In all these pictures the old Roman love of display is paramount; if we can only retain in our mind's eye the blaze of colour and the riotous good humour of these Roman holidays we will more readily be able to understand the theatrical quality of the baroque architecture, particularly that of Piazza Navona, which was designed to serve as their setting.

Leaving Palazzo Braschi, we turn left, then left again, down the little Via della Cuccagna, called after the *Albero della Cuccagna* or greasy pole, which was a prominent feature of the games held in the **Piazza Navona**. At the end of this street, the whole marvellous panorama of this, the most picturesque square in Rome, stretches out before us. This was Domitian's stadium for athletic displays—the *Circus Agonalis*—whose name, corrupted in time to *n'Agona*, lives on as the Piazza Navona. As late as 1450, the arena itself survived largely unchanged; the Florentine Giovanni Ruccellai described it then as the scene of jousts, witnessed by the populace occupying the ancient seats. For long afterwards the Piazza Navona continued to be used for shows and celebrations—almost in fact to within living memory, as Augustus Hare recalled having seen the curious summer water festival, when decorated carriages drove round the flooded square; describing it as 'a remnant of the pleasures of the *Naumachia*, once annually exhibited almost on this very spot'. The Piazza Navona still preserves the exact outline of Domitian's (AD 81–96) stadium; like the circuses, it resembles an elongated horse-shoe. It is perhaps the most Roman of all the city's squares—an architectural palimpsest if ever there was one; in the little Via del Circo Agonale, half-way up on the right, we can still see the ruined substructures of Domitian's circus. But it is more as the meeting place of past and present—as a site where the stream of history has flowed continually for more than two thousand years —that the piazza grips our imagination. Where the mellow ochre-washed houses that ring it round now stand drowsing in the sun, the excited Roman crowds once cheered themselves hoarse over the victory of one of their favourite athletes, though Domitian's arena never witnessed scenes of carnage like the Colosseum, and blood never flowed where Bernini's fountain now spouts rivulets of gleaming water among rugged rocks and wind-tossed palms. Nevertheless, St. Agnes's church raises its dome and belfries over the spot where the saint was stripped in a Roman brothel before a jeering crowd. Medieval pilgrims came to pray at this scene of her martyrdom; swashbuckling bloods of the Renaissance followed to take part in the jousting in the square; ambassadors, suave prelates and fine ladies of the seventeenth and eighteenth centuries lived in its palaces. The old piazza has seen them all; even in the grim days of the German occupation during the last war, it played its part in history; then a clandestine wireless transmitting set was hidden in one of the belfries of S. Agnese.

The modern history of Piazza Navona began in 1477, when Sixtus IV transferred the market from the foot of the Capitoline Hill to the ruined arena. In 1485 the central space was paved; by the end of the century the tiers of ancient seats had disappeared beneath the inns and eating houses that now surrounded what had become a public square. But the real glory of the piazza dates from the time of the Pamphilj Pope, Innocent X (1644–55); he made it a memorial to his reign and a family precinct rivalling if not surpassing that of his predecessor Urban VIII around the Barberini palace on the Quirinal.

Giambattista Pamphilj came of an Umbrian family who had established themselves in Rome during the fifteenth century, living in a modest palace in the Piazza Navona. In 1645, the new pope had already begun to put his ideas for the aggrandisement of his family home into action. In that year he planned to bring the waters of the *Acqua Vergine*—the best in Rome—to the piazza for the fountains. In the following year he called in Borromini to advise the aged Girolamo Rainaldi, who was already at work on the great new family palace. Not long after his accession he had seen Domitian's obelisk, which had stood in the centre of Maxentius's circus, lying in fragments by the Via Appia, and formulated the plan for erecting it in the Piazza Navona. In 1652 the foundation stone for the new church of S. Agnese was laid beside the family palace.

It is to this wonderful series of monuments that Piazza Navona owes its special character as the supreme baroque stage-setting for the pageantry of life in seventeenth-century Rome. Even two hundred years later when this style was regarded as the nadir of bad taste, and Jameson dismissed the interior of S. Agnese with the words: 'The works of art are all mediocre, and of the seventeenth century,' the great square with its fountains was still considered to be one of the sights of Rome.

The central **Fountain of the Four Rivers**, with the obelisk, is the only one to have been designed in its entirety by Bernini; the story of its creation is that of one of history's great artistic rivalries. Not for nothing does popular legend relate that the statue representing the Nile has its face covered (in reality an allusion to its unknown source), in order not to see Borromini's façade of the church of S. Agnese; while the 'River Plate' raises its hand as if to prevent the church from falling. As they say in Rome: '*Se non è vero è ben trovato*' (If it's not true it's to the point). By the brilliance of his design and, according to the Modenese ambassador of the day, by giving a silver model of it to the pope's sister-in-law Donna Olimpia, Bernini supplanted Borromini as the architect of the fountain. But this was unveiled in 1651, a year before S. Agnese was begun by Girolamo and Carlo Rainaldi, and two years before Borromini replaced them. The façade of the church was only ultimately completed in 1666, so the legends do not correspond to fact.

Although the design of the great fountain was by Bernini, many other hands contributed to its making. But according to an old tradition, upheld by Professor Wittkower, Bernini himself gave the finishing touches to the rocks, and executed the palm tree and the horse. What is not generally known is that this last is a portrait of the famous Montedoro, who belonged to Francesco Cecchini, a noted exponent of *haute école* of the day; or that the palm tree, rocks and plants growing in its crevices were originally coloured. Three of the allegorical figures of the rivers are also accompanied by emblems: the Plate, by a pile of coins, indicating riches, seen close beside him on the rock, also a rather curious rendering of an armadillo in the basin below; the lion and the horse symbolise respectively the Nile and Danube; only the Ganges lacks any representative of his native fauna.

The cost of making the fountain, 29,000 scudi, was raised by putting a tax, among other things, on bread. This called forth a storm of protest from the populace, often voiced in placards attached by unknown hands to the fragments of

Domitian's obelisk each night as they lay in the streets on their way from the Via Appia. The cream of these, obviously owing its inspiration to Holy Writ, was: 'God, if only these stones would turn into bread!' But the hated Donna Olimpia was the chief butt of savage pasquinades, the well-known '*Olim Pia*' (only roughly translatable as 'vanished piety)' being among the most gentle; many others were of unprintable virulence.

Bernini merely rearranged the 'Fountain of the Moro' (the Moor), at the southern end of the piazza. It was originally made by Giacomo della Porta in 1575; but the central figure of the 'Moro' holding the dolphin is by Bernini; the surrounding tritons are nineteenth-century copies of della Porta's original ones. Bernini had first designed a motif of dolphins and shells for the centre of the fountain. According to some this was not considered sufficiently impressive; according to others Donna Olimpia wanted it for the gardens of the Villa Pamphilj, where it stands today.

No one appears to have wondered why Bernini chose to introduce this exotic 'Moor' into the orthodox setting of tritons; nor, for that matter, why he personified the River Plate by an equally unsuitable figure from the ethnological point of view. There is a possible explanation for this. During the previous reign of the Barberini Pope, Urban VIII, King Alvaro of the Congo sent an embassy to Rome. The ambassador, an African in spite of his European-sounding name of Antonio Emanuele Marquis of Funta, died shortly after his arrival. But, it is said, not before Bernini had succeeded in taking a likeness of him.

According to pious legend, the church of **S. Agnese in Agone**, as it is still called, was originally built over the brothel, or some such infamous meeting place, in which the thirteen-year old saint began her martyrdom in the year 304 by being stripped of her clothes. It was then that the miraculous growth of her hair concealed her nakedness; a circumstance attested in the inscription which Pope S. Damasus placed upon her tomb near the Via Nomentana only sixty-two years later. In the vaults below the church some fragments of Roman pavement still exist. Although the walls have been plastered over and painted at various periods, there is no doubt that they once formed part of the substructures of Domitian's stadium; a building, in common with the baths and others of its kind, which would have attracted taverns and other less respectable establishments to the vicinity. The church itself is the work of Borromini, Girolamo and Carlo Rainaldi, all three of whom found favour with different members of the Pamphilj family; but the dramatic effect of its concave façade and towering belfries it owes to Borromini.

The adjoining **Palazzo Pamphilj**, now the Brazilian Embassy, has a surprisingly unimpressive exterior though the state rooms are fine. The showpiece is a magnificent gallery designed by Borromini, with a ceiling painted by Pietro da Cortona; in it the artist's genius is revealed in its full maturity. His work here has nothing of the cold pomp and circumstance which characterises the ceiling of the great saloon in Palazzo Barberini. The story of Aeneas is portrayed in wonderfully soft yet glowing shades of blue, pink, mauve and yellow, more suggestive of the eighteenth than the seventeenth century. This work occupied the artist for three years, from 1651 to 1654. The story of Aeneas was chosen as the subject because the Pamphilj claimed descent from him! According to some sources the dove in the family arms represents his mother, Venus's sacred bird; according to others it is a symbol of the purity of the Blessed Lodolfo Pamphilj. During the last century the state rooms were often open for concerts. The well-known conductor Vittorio Gui recalls as a child, some time about 1895, having heard sing there the famous soprano Maestro Mustafà, director of the Sistine Chapel Choir, and the last of the '*castrati*'.

In December, Piazza Navona is filled with booths selling the fascinating figures of shepherds in national dress, their wives and children, all the paraphernalia of inns and markets, the Magi and their train, reproduced in miniature, which in the Roman *presepio* or Christmas crib, surround the Holy Family. Today one is apt to find these representatives of a tradition—which in Christian eyes originated with St. Francis of Assisi, though it may well draw its origins from the small terracotta figures sold at a similar fair during the Saturnalia of pagan times—side by side with space suits and other delights of the twentieth-century child. This juxtaposition will probably shock the traditionalist; but in actual fact it demonstrates the age-old capacity of Rome and the Romans to take everything as it comes, and adapt it to their own way of life. In fact Alphonse Karr might well have coined his famous phrase '*plus ça change, plus c'est la même chose*' specifically to describe the survival of the ancient past in Rome.

Before we leave Piazza Navona, there is just time for a glimpse at Palazzo Lancellotti at its southern end (No. 114); this was designed by Pirro Ligorio. Then, taking the little Via della Posta Vecchia on the left-hand corner, we find ourselves in Piazza dei Massimi; at the back door of the Palazzo Massimo we saw in the Corso Vittorio Emanuele. This is the oldest part of the palace, with a painted façade executed by Polidoro da Caravaggio in the sixteenth century. An inscription records the existence of the first Roman printing press in Casa Massimo; though this is not now believed to have been set up in this actual house, but in another belonging to the family nearer the Campo dei Fiori.

Retracing our steps and taking the right-hand side of Piazza Navona, we pass before the church of **Nostra Signora del S. Cuore**, with fine rose windows. Formerly this was S. Giacomo degli Spagnoli, built by Nicholas V in 1450 as the Spanish church; during its recent restoration, however, all objects of national interest were transferred to S. Maria di Monserrato. We now turn right down the short Via del Circo Agonale, where the remains of Domitian's arena are visible beneath the houses on the right, and find ourselves in Piazza Madama.

This name is given to the slightly wider central part of the Corso del Rinascimento, which lies before **Palazzo Madama**, a fine seventeenth-century building now the seat of the Senate, the upper house of the Italian parliament. The palace takes its name from Margaret of Austria, the illegitimate daughter of the Emperor Charles V. Today Piazza Madama, as befits the seat of the Senate, has a certain quiet dignity. But in the eighteenth century, especially on Saturday mornings, it was the setting of scenes of wild excitement when the winning tickets for the national lottery were drawn on its balcony. The palace had been bought by the papal government in the seventeenth century and was used as the Ministry of Posts and Finance. Lottery enthusiasts were not the only people who formerly brought life to this area of the city; since the reign of Eugenius IV (1431–47) the University of Rome (founded in 1303) had been established in the neighbouring **Palazzo della Sapienza** (No. 40 on the same side of the street); it remained there until 1935. The building now houses the National Archives.

The Sapienza is an outstanding example of one of those architectural surprises which make the exploration of Rome a delight. Who for a moment would imagine that Giacomo della Porta's austere Renaissance façade conceals the dynamic vitality of Borromini's masterpiece, the church of **S. Ivo** (see Appendix for opening times). As we step into the shadows of the Sapienza door, we see St. Ivo framed by the central arch of the porticoed courtyard, its curious dome crowned by a golden-hued spiral soaring dramatically into the blue sky.

Borromini began his working life as a stonemason, and as a boy of 15 was employed in a humble capacity on the building of St. Peter's. He was an eccentric and difficult man, embittered by the way in which Bernini, who was the darling of the fashionable world, had for years made use of his technical skill. It was not until 1634, when he was about 30, that his big chance came; in that year he was commissioned to design the church and monastery of S. Carlo alle Quattro Fontane for the Spanish Discalced Trinitarians. The revolutionary character of his work was immediately recognised and Bernini, generously recommended him to Pope Urban VIII as architect for the Sapienza church.

Work was begun on S. Ivo in 1642, most of the building was finished by 1650, but the decoration was not completed until 1660. It is said that the star hexagon of the church's ground plan is derived from the outline of the heraldic Barberini bee; this unusual figure presents many technical problems and had been rarely used by Renaissance and post-Renaissance architects, though it is believed to have been employed in ancient Rome. In his treatment of this exceedingly difficult form, Borromini showed that he could surpass even Bernini in sheer architectural drama. Looking at the curves and angles of the body of the church as they soar upwards into the vast spaces of the dome, one can scarcely repress a gasp of admiration; to quote Professor Wittkower, 'Geometrical succinctness, and inexhaustible imagination, technical skill and religious symbolism, have rarely found such a reconciliation.' It is not surprising to find that experts consider that Borromini, who came from northern Italy, drew something of his inspiration from Gothic architecture. Especially in S. Ivo, there is a spirituality about this work which is rarely encountered in seventeenth-century Rome; though there are also points of resemblance between the daring innovations in the design of Borromini's churches and the garden pavilions of Hadrian's villa near Tivoli.

We now take the Via degli Staderari, the street of the weighing-machine makers, who formerly practised their trade near by, which brings us into Piazza S. Eustachio. This small irregular piazza takes its name from the very ancient church of S. Eustachio, that in its present guise appears as a mixture of medieval and baroque. The portico and campanile date from the twelfth century; the rest, and the interior, were rebuilt in the eighteenth. The church is recorded in documents of the eighth century as S. **Eustachio** in Platana; evidence of its even more ancient origin existed until the seventeenth century, in the form of funerary inscriptions. One of these was dated 399, another was composed according to a formula in use in the third century.

The stag's head, which appears on the façade, recalls the legend of St. Eustace, over whose dwelling the church is supposed to have been built. The fact that this first-century martyr, who is the patron of the chase, was a member of the same family as the Empress Octavia caused at least one noble Roman house to claim descent from him. In this they disregarded the facts of his entire family's martyrdom, as related in the pious legend. St. Eustace was a military man who owed his conversion to a vision of Christ, seen between the antlers of a stag while he was hunting near Tivoli. His baptism was followed by a series of misfortunes, but finally he was entrusted by Hadrian with the command of an army. Though St. Eustace covered himself with glory in his campaigns, this did not prevent the emperor from condemning him to death when he refused to make the customary sacrifice to Jupiter as a thank-offering for victory. The saint, together with his wife and two sons, Teopista and Agapito, were condemned to be roasted alive inside a brazen bull; their remains are believed to rest under the high altar of the church.

In the piazza opposite the church stands a fine palace built by Giulio Romano for the Maccarani (No. 83); this passed to the di Brazzà family, one of whose members was the famous African explorer after whom the Congolese capital of Brazzaville is named. To the right of the palace is a coffee bar, renowned among Romans for producing the best *Espressos* in the city; though rival connoisseurs claim that the palm is held by the Tazza d'Oro in the Via degli Orfani near the Pantheon.

We now take the **Via della Dogana Vecchia**, which runs to the left of S. Eustachio. This street is called after the old customs house, which was probably established here in the reign of Martin V (1417–31), and existed until 1625. The second street on the right, Via Giustiniani, takes its name from the family palace on the corner of the famous art connoisseur Marchese Vincenzo Giustiniani; it once contained a world-famous collection of sculpture and pictures.

We now find ourselves in the small piazza called after the national church of France, **S. Luigi dei Francesi**. This was begun in 1523 to the designs of Giacomo della Porta, and completed fifty-five years later; it has a dignified Renaissance façade. The interior is richly decorated, and the second chapel on the right has some fine frescoes of the life of St. Cecilia, by Domenichino. The great treasures of the church are, however, Caravaggio's famous paintings in the Chapel of St. Matthew (the last on the left). This is probably the largest area of canvas painted by Caravaggio, contained in the smallest space in the world. The three huge pictures of the 'Calling' and the 'Martyrdom of St. Matthew' and 'St. Matthew with the Angel' practically cover the walls of the little chapel; their vitality is riveting, almost overwhelming. So much has been written about Caravaggio's art during the last fifteen years that a description of these, his first great religious paintings, would be superfluous; but a biographical note may not be out of place as his life at this time was so closely bound up with the area we are now exploring.

Caravaggio came to Rome as a boy of 16, somewhere about 1589. The first years were hard, although a churchman, Monsignor Fantino Petrignani, gave him a room in his house in which to live and work. Here Caravaggio painted a 'Flight into Egypt' and a 'Magdalen', probably the ones we have already seen in the Doria Gallery. Apparently he sold his pictures through an art dealer, Signor Valentino, who lived or had his shop near S. Luigi dei Francesi. Here the artist met the powerful Cardinal Francesco del Monte, who bought some of his pictures, took him to live in his palace, and procured for him about 1597 the commission to paint the pictures for the St. Matthew Chapel in S. Luigi.

The life of Caravaggio's patrons and protectors was far from being a bed of roses. Though they recognised his genius, his use of realistic detail—such as portraying the Virgin or saints with dirty feet—roused many other people to fury at what they thought was a lack of respect. The priests of St. Luigi, for instance, refused Caravaggio's first painting of St. Matthew and the Angel for this very reason. It was bought by Marchese Vincenzo Giustiniani for the famous collection in his nearby palace; a second version now hangs above the altar. It is said that the priests wished to repudiate all three pictures, but on the advice of Giustiniani they gave way and hung the 'Calling' and 'Martyrdom of St. Matthew' in 1600. In the same way Caravaggio's 'Death of the Virgin' commissioned by the monks of S. Maria della Scala was refused because the body was represented as swollen. On Rubens's enthusiastic recommendation the picture was subsequently bought by the Duke of Mantua.

Nor was Caravaggio's private life any more helpful to his friends; armed with a large sword, he and his boon companions went looking for trouble through the streets of Rome. They found plenty. We know more about the artist from the police records of the time than from almost any other source. Once he was caught throwing stones at his former landlady's windows; on another occasion he threw a dish of artichokes at a waiter's head. There was a long quarrel with a notary about his girl friend Lena; she was evidently a prostitute, as she is described as 'standing in Piazza Navona'. Finally, after a ball game in Campo dei Fiori, Caravaggio killed a man in a duel and had to flee from Rome in 1606; he died four years later at the age of 37.

Just beyond S. Luigi, the street opens out to form the Largo Toniolo; this in turn leads into a street bearing the unusual name of **Via del Pozzo delle Cornacchie**, the Street of the Well of the Crows. Extraordinarily enough this is derived from the arms of Cardinal Wolsey, who built a palace, in which he never lived, where the street widens out to form Piazza Rondanini. A well in the courtyard apparently bore the cardinal's arms of two crows standing on either side of a rose; the palace was subsequently bought by the Rondanini family and then by the Aldobrandini.

On the corner of the Largo Toniolo and the Via Pozzo delle Cornacchie is one of the most charming shops in Rome. Although in the last ten years this has become sufficiently modern to call itself *Erborista* (Herbalist), as opposed to *Semplicista* (seller of simples), it has made no other concession whatsoever to the changing fashions of the last century and a half; but it still does a roaring trade in every kind of herb and spice. The fattest cloves, the longest sticks of cinnamon and the most aromatic lime tea are all to be found in the delightful old wooden boxes, with the names of their contents painted on fluttering blue ribbons, that line its walls. In the window, weird and wonderful-looking pods and roots, exhibited in glass jars, are grouped round charming old illustrated herbals.

Returning to the Largo Toniolo, we now take the **Via della Scrofa**. This is generally believed to derive its name from a fountain surmounted by a relief of a *scrofa* or sow which was made during the reign of Gregory XIII (1572–85). The relief still exists, let into the wall of what was formerly an Augustinian monastery, some way down on the left. But an inn called the Scrofa was already established in the street as early as 1445; so it seems more likely that the fountain was designed to conform with the already existing name. A short way down the Via della Scrofa we turn to the left into the little Via di S. Agostino, and find ourselves in a small piazza of the same name. On our right a steep flight of steps leads up to the only church in Rome dedicated to St. Augustine, Bishop of Hippo and author of the famous *Confessions*, not the sixth-century saint who converted England.

The church of **S. Agostino** was designed by Giacomo di Pietrasanta for Cardinal d'Estouteville, and built between 1479 and 1483 of travertine plundered from the Colosseum. The façade has the simple dignity of the early Renaissance, and is one of the few of this period still to be seen in Rome. It is particularly fortunate that the church should have retained its original character at least externally (the interior was redecorated by Vanvitelli in the eighteenth century) because it was then pre-eminently the centre of worship of the Roman humanists, intellectuals of the day: that charmed circle to which Castiglione, Sadoleto, Bembo and Raphael belonged, who used to dine out on summer nights in the gardens of their friends, especially John Goritz, or Coricio as he preferred to be called. These feasts were renowned for witty conversation, the company of the most beautiful courtesans and extemporised verses and speeches. Most famous of them all was the dinner given every year by John Goritz on the feast of St. Ann, 26 July, whom he regarded as his patron saint, when verses were hung on the garden trees and statues. Today these poems read as the most extraordinary mixture of paganism and Christianity, with the Virgin and saints apostrophised as classical goddesses such as Juno or Venus; they were however in accordance with the current of the times and the joy in the newly re-discovered classical ideal of beauty.

This pagan-Christian world was not then limited to garden festivals; some echoes of it even penetrated into S. Agostino itself. John Goritz commissioned Andrea Sansovino to execute a group of 'St. Ann with the Virgin and Child' for the church; before this he and his friends recited their odes on 26 July. The group now stands in the second chapel on the left; but in the sixteenth century it was placed under the fresco of Isaiah on the second pilaster on the left in the nave. This Goritz commissioned from Raphael, and he once complained to Michelangelo that he had been charged too much for it. He got short shrift: 'The knee alone is worth the price,' was Michelangelo's retort.

It is not surprising to find that S. Agostino was also the church preferred, in their moments of penitence, by the great courtesans who were the friends and companions of these artists and writers. Like the humanists themselves, these women imagined that they were modelling themselves upon their classical predecessors, the famous *hetaerae* of Greece and Rome. To this end they too composed verses, studied the classical authors, cultivated the art of conversation and excited the ridicule of contemporary satirists. Many went to S. Agostino to listen to the Lenten sermons; a letter written by one of them to Lorenzo de' Medici describes the scene and continues: 'I went to confession and gave the priest two golden ducats, gold I say. I now regret it to the bottom of my heart.' Cesare Borgia's mistress, the beautiful Fiammetta, had her own chapel in S. Agostino; other famous members of her profession, such as Tullia d'Aragona, Giulia Campana and Beatrice Pareggi, were buried there. The funerary inscription of this last recorded that she was 'a good mother cut off in the flower of her holiest (sic!) youth'. Such interments were, strictly speaking, contrary to the law; this prescribed that the members of the oldest profession should be buried in a desolate plot beside the Muro Torto.

Needless to say all sign of these ladies has now disappeared from the interior of S. Agostino; the walls are lined with monuments dedicated to the memory of blameless churchmen and noble Romans, and what is probably the largest collection of ex-votos in the city. Characteristically, these last aroused the disapproval of Augustus Hare, who quoted Alford's description of the church and the cult of the famous Madonna del Parto: 'The church of S. Agostino is the Methodist meeting-house of Rome, so to speak, where the extravagance of the enthusiasm of the lower orders is allowed freest scope. Its Virgin and Child are covered, smothered, with jewels, votive offerings of those whose prayers the image had heard and answered.'

Few would deny the classical affinity of this Madonna of Birth with the many goddesses who in ancient times were associated with the mother cult which still today plays such a large part in Roman life. Perhaps nowhere else in the city is one so clearly aware of the unchanging continuity of its life as when confronted with this 'Madonna and Child' by Jacopo Sansovino, which is enthroned in a niche before the closed central door. The group, dating from 1521, is a perfect example of the Renaissance adaptation of the classical style to the Christian cult. But why she, among all the Madonnas in Rome, came to be particularly associated with the most dramatic mystery of life is unknown. Possibly her situation in a church which was so closely associated with the pagan-Christian Rome, that existed before the Sack and the Counter Reformation, had something to do with it. Certainly Sansovino's Madonna is the personification of that world; with her Junoesque features and diamond solitaire blazing on her forehead, covered with gold and jewels she sits enthroned like some classical goddess of old. To see her surrounded by blazing candles and to watch her devotees touch the foot which has been worn smooth by the millions who have gone before is to realise that the cult of the mother strikes some deep atavistic chord in the Roman mind.

S. Agostino contains two other Madonnas which make a more direct appeal to the northerner. The first is a small but fine Byzantine one, brought from Constantinople shortly before its fall in 1453. This is framed in the high altar, which also supports angels designed, but not executed, by Bernini. The other, in the first chapel on the left, is Caravaggio's lovely 'Madonna of Loreto' or 'Madonna of the pilgrims'; it was painted between 1604 and 1605, shortly after the artist had been to the wild province of the Marche where the holy house

of Loreto—one of the great places of pilgrimage in Europe—
is situated. As usual, we know of Caravaggio's travels in the
Marche from the contemporary police reports: by what means
he managed to combine his rumbustious football-playing
bravado with the conception of a picture of such deeply
religious feeling is a mystery.

The probable reason why Cardinal Estouteville dedicated
his church to St. Augustine is hidden away in the chapel on
the left of the high altar. This is the tomb of his mother St.
Monica, whose relics were translated from Ostia in 1430. St.
Monica died there at the end of the fourth century, just
before her son embarked for Africa. The tomb, which stands
against the wall on the left, has been many times restored. The
figure of St. Monica on the cover is the work of the fifteenth-
century sculptor Isaia da Pisa; other of his sculptures which
formerly adorned it have been removed to the vestibule beside the left transept of the church.

Upon leaving S. Agostino we retrace our steps, cross the
Via della Scrofa and find ourselves in **Via delle Coppelle**. This
name is also given to a piazza, or *largo*, and *vicolo*; it denotes
the, evidently fairly extensive, area where the makers of small
barrels called *coppelle* exercised their trade. These were
originally used by the water sellers, later for wine and vinegar;
an inscription—which we will shortly see—indicates that the
trade was already established here in 1195. Palazzo Baldassini
(No. 35 Via delle Coppelle) is a charming early sixteenth-
century palace, recently restored, with a fine porticoed courtyard. Garibaldi stayed here on 26 January 1875 when, on his
return from the Chamber of Deputies, he was escorted home
in triumph by the Roman crowd carrying torches and singing
patriotic songs.

About half-way down the street, we turn left beside the little
church of **S. Salvatore della Pietà** or **delle Coppelle**. The church
was founded by the Orsini Pope, Celestine III, in 1195. An
inscription fairly high up on the wall on the right of the street,
which is one of the oldest in Rome still *in situ*, reads: *Chiesa
del S. Salvatore della Pietà. aler. de le Cupelle 1195*. Below this
is another inscription instructing all innkeepers to put a note,
giving details about the foreigners who fell ill in their premises, into the letter box above; this bears the date of Holy
Year 1750. In those days 'foreigners' would, of course, have
included travellers from other parts of Italy; they were then

looked after by the 'Confraternity of Perseverance', specially founded for the purpose.

This short tract of the Vicolo delle Coppelle now opens out into the piazza of the same name; a picturesque little square, used as a fruit and vegetable market, where, in typically Roman fashion, architectural styles range from classical columns, by way of the Renaissance, to some deliciously frivolous late baroque. The rump end of the Vicolo delle Coppelle now leads us out of the right-hand corner of the square into the **Piazza di Campo Marzio**.

How indeed are the mighty fallen! The Piazza di Campo Marzio of today is a small irregular space, little more than a street crossing. Even its name does not derive directly from the 'Field of Mars' of ancient times; it is only by the courtesy, as it were, of a neighbouring church—S. Maria in Campo Marzio—that it has come down to us. Both the piazza and a neighbouring street were called after the church; though it must be admitted that the surrounding area has always retained the ancient name. Some reminders of the classical past are, however, still visible; Ionic columns are embedded into the walls of the shops on the left of the piazza (Nos. 5 and 6); an ancient altar stands among the parked cars. These are not really direct survivors of classical ruins on the site; the columns probably formed part of a medieval street-side portico, while the altar has comparatively recently been placed here.

If we wished to see real relics of the ancient *Campus Martius*, we would have to dig down about seven feet. It was at this depth that the pavement of an old Roman road was discovered below the existing piazza in 1822. It led towards the church of S. Maria in Campo Marzio which, for all its modern appearance, is a very ancient foundation, dating probably from the reign of Pope St. Zacharias (741–52). About that time, Greek nuns fleeing from the iconoclastic persecutions established two convents among the ruins of the *Campus Martius*. One was S. Maria; the other was dedicated to the Greek theologian and saint, Gregory Nazianzen, whose portrait we have already encountered in S. Maria Antiqua in the Forum. The ancient church of S. Gregorio Nazianzen, built into a Roman ruin, still exists; the convent is now used as a depository for the National Archives, but a special permit is necessary in order to see both church and convent. However, as we make our

way down the Via Metastasio, if we turn right up the narrow
Vicolo Valdina, we can catch what the Italians would call a
very *suggestivo* glimpse of its medieval campanile.

The Via Metastasio, which had no connection with the poet
during his lifetime, brings us to the **Piazza Firenze**; so called
because from the eighteenth century until 1870 the Palazzo
Firenze standing in it was the seat of the Florentine embassy.
This fine early sixteenth-century palace was bought by the
Medici in 1577, Cardinal Ferdinando—who bought the Villa
Medici on the Pincio and Cardinal della Valle's collection of
sculpture—being the first of a series of Medici cardinals to live
there. Galileo stayed there in 1633. The palace now houses the
Dante Alighieri Society, who make no objection to strangers
pausing for a while to admire the fine porticoed courtyard and
small formal garden.

From here we turn right down the **Via dei Prefetti**, the Street
of the Prefects. The origins of this name are uncertain, but
must in some way have been associated with the office of the
Prefect of the city, as an old church in the street bears the same
name—S. Nicolò dei Prefetti. For nearly two hundred years,
from 1247 to 1435, the powerful De Vico family were hereditary prefects. They enjoyed, among other privileges, the right
of inheriting the possessions of anyone living in the Borgo
Leonino who died childless. The first turn on the left out of
this street, the Vicolo del Divino Amore, leads us into the
Piazza Borghese, filled with the picturesque stalls of the vendors of old prints, second-hand books and bric-à-brac
generally.

By this time thoughts of a meal and a rest will be looming
large in our minds. For really first-rate Tuscan food and wine,
the Fontanella Restaurant in the Largo di Fontanella Borghese on the right is the place (when ordering remember that a
bistecca alla Fiorentina is an ample meal for two; in winter try
fillet of turkey with white truffles). If we are willing to content
ourselves with a sandwich, coffee and luscious cakes, the Bar
Liberti at 33 Piazza S. Lorenzo in Lucina, a short way away,
is an excellent choice; especially as it has a small tea-room
where one can sit down. Or, pushing on a little farther with
the next stage of our exploration, we will find a gay little
pizzeria at 33 Via dell' Orso.

CHAPTER NINE

Piazza Borghese to Piazza di Pasquino

❧

THIS afternoon we will complete our tour of the old *Campus Martius* area, but this time our walk will take us into a different Rome from that which we have explored up to now. We will see no ancient ruins, spacious squares or spectacular baroque churches, but, what is much more rare in Rome, a prosperous bourgeois quarter of the late fifteenth century. Most of this delightful intimate townscape of narrow streets packed with small houses—which nevertheless reflect the architectural dignity of their day—came into being as a result of Sixtus IV's town planning policy, especially in connection with Holy Year 1475.

If we have lunched in the Largo della Fontanella Borghese, our first port of call will be the **Palazzo Borghese** that dominates it and the adjoining piazza—the one really sumptuous Renaissance palace of our itinerary. Owing to its curious shape, resembling a grand piano, the palace is known as '*il cembalo*' (the harpsichord); the keyboard being represented by Flaminio Ponzio's graceful portal near the river bank. The palace was begun in 1590 for a Spanish cardinal by Martino Longhi the Elder; the principal Fontanella Borghese façade is considered to be his masterpiece. In 1605, the same year as his election to the papacy as Paul V, it was bought by Cardinal Borghese, to whose family it still belongs.

The palace chiefly owed its fame to the Borghese's patronage of the arts; the pictures amassed by successive generations were so renowned as to be called 'the queen of the world's private collections'. Paul V's nephew, Cardinal Scipione Borghese, who was Bernini's first patron, founded the collection; it was housed in the palace until its removal to the Villa Borghese in 1891; in 1902 it was bought by the Italian state. Nevertheless the palace itself had provided a setting worthy of such treasures; though it is not open to the public, the glimpse we catch through the main door affords ample evidence of

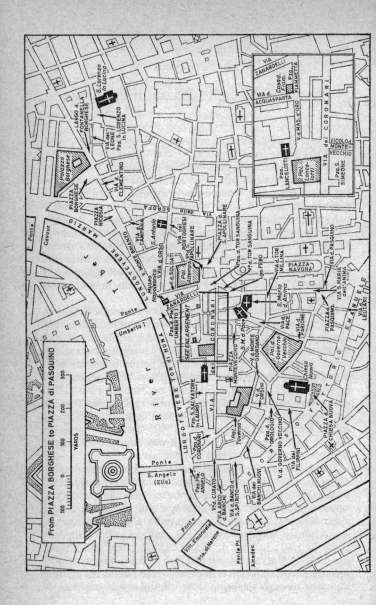

From PIAZZA BORGHESE to PIAZZA di PASQUINO

YARDS
100   0   100   200   300

this. The great court, with its ninety-six Doric and Ionic columns, ranged in pairs to support the double loggias, and the topiary and rushing fountains of Ponzio's enchanting garden, half hidden in the background, suggest a stage setting for the pageantry of life in seventeenth-century Rome. Here, one feels, is the theatre waiting for the first act, to be opened perhaps by the arrival of some great gilded coach, or possibly the entry of a cardinal accompanied by torch-bearers, still today the prerogative of princes of the Church upon entering any house.

In actual fact the most colourful personality who ever lived in Palazzo Borghese was a slim slip of a girl, aged 23 when she first came there. She was Pauline Bonaparte, Napoleon's favourite sister, who married Camillo Borghese in 1803. Pauline's personal suite, lit by the large windows on the fourth floor to the right of the main entrance, still bears the imprint of her fastidious taste; it was specially decorated for her in the French Empire style. A circular salon leads into her bedroom, which has a small window communicating with a tiny private chapel, designed apparently so that she could look into it from her bed. This piety is curiously at variance with the tales told of Pauline's way of life; the procession of lovers and the vanity that justified in her own mind her use of her ladies-in-waiting as footstools; also her curious habit of being carried to her bath by a gigantic negro. At balls Pauline never condescended to dance, but simply sat surrounded by her adorers. Still, seventy-five years after her death an old English lady could recall descriptions of Pauline recounted by those who had actually seen her on one of these occasions, radiant in a dress of pink gauze embroidered with huge diamonds —perhaps the selfsame ones as were found in Napoleon's coach after Waterloo. Tiresome and exacting as she no doubt was, Pauline was of the stuff from which legends are born.

Before continuing with the main part of our itinerary towards the Tiber, we must now turn for a moment in the opposite direction, along the short Via del Leone. This brings us into the **Piazza S. Lorenzo in Lucina,** called after the very ancient titular church of that name, on the right. Tradition ascribes its original foundation to the pious matron Lucina; although never substantiated, this corresponds to the early Christian meeting place origins of many titular churches. The first documentary mention of S. Lorenzo is dated 366; it occurs in an account of the reign of the thirty-sixth Pope, S. Liberius. During the first half of the fifth century the church was extended by Sixtus III (432–40), over ground given by the Emperor Valentinian III. Successive restorations—the last in 1650—have practically obscured the medieval character of S. Lorenzo; though fortunately they have spared the typical twelfth-century portico and campanile. Its interior is now completely baroque, though two early relics—the alleged gridiron of St. Lawrence's martyrdom and an ancient episcopal throne—are preserved in a closed recess behind the main altar.

The most notable monument in the church is the Fonseca chapel (the fourth on the right), designed by Bernini for Innocent X's doctor Gabriele Fonseca, whose bust (on the left of the altar) was executed by him. The unusually long midday closure makes it impossible for us now to see the interior of the church, but baroque specialists should make a return visit before 8 p.m. Gabriele Fonseca was not the only pope's doctor to be associated with S. Lorenzo. In the thirteenth century it was the titular church of Hugh of Evesham, created cardinal by Martin IV (1281–5) and summoned to Italy to act as his physician, but also to rid Rome of malaria. Hugh built himself a palace, where the Palazzo Fiano now stands on the left of the church; but unfortunately the author of the *Canones Medicinales* was not destined to forestall the discoveries of Manson and Ross in the thirteenth century, and himself succumbed to the dread Roman fever a few years later.

Returning to the Piazza Borghese we now take the Via Clementina to the Piazza Nicosia. Neither of them very remarkable today, but in ancient times somewhere in their area stood the altar of Mars which was the scene of one of the oldest and strangest Roman religious rites. This was the sacrifice of the 'October horse', performed on the ides of the month. After a chariot race in the *Campus Martius* (originally it was held in the Forum), the off horse of the winning *biga* was killed at the altar; his tail was taken to the Regia, some of his blood was sprinkled on the altar of Vesta and some kept for future rites. The populace of the Suburra and the Via Sacra contended for the head, which was then displayed in a prominent place in the area of the winning faction.

From Piazza Nicosia we continue by the Via della Campana, which joins with the Via della Scrofa just where it crosses the top of the **Via dei Portoghesi.** Looking down this narrow street, which takes its name from the Portuguese national church on the right, we are confronted by one of the most picturesque corners of old Rome—a medieval tower of a Frangipani fortress rises out of a welter of buildings of various periods. This is known as the Torre della Scimmia (the tower of the monkey). According to an old story, its owners once had a monkey which climbed to the top of the tower, carrying their baby in its arms. The anguished father returned home to find his neighbours in the street praying to the Virgin for the safety of the child. Uttering a short prayer himself, he called the animal with his customary whistle and, after carefully re-wrapping the baby in its swaddling clothes, it climbed down and entered one of the windows. As a thank-offering for this miraculous escape, the father raised a statue of the Virgin on top of the tower and vowed that a lamp should be kept burning in front of it in perpetuity. Electricity has made the vow easier to keep, but even this modern illumination appears as a glow on the dark tower at night, recalling the mystery of Nathaniel Hawthorne's Roman romance *The Marble Faun* or *Transformation*, in which he gives a graphic description of it as Hilda's tower.

A short way beyond the Torre della Scimmia, the Via dei Portoghesi becomes the **Via dell' Orso,** called after the famous fifteenth-century hostelry of that name at the far end, where Montaigne stayed when he was in Rome in 1581. In his day this picturesque old street (note the stone lion at No. 87 and the bears farther on the right) was the centre for the postillions and livery stables. By the early nineteenth century it had been taken over by the antique dealers, many of whose shops are still to be found in the area. Here that inveterate collector, Napoleon's uncle Cardinal Fesch, made the buy of all time. For a few pence he purchased part of a painted wooden board, which matched up with the remains of another he had bought previously; when put together and cleaned, they turned out to be Leonardo's 'St. Jerome', now hanging in the Vatican gallery.

An amusing anecdote is also related about the Osteria dell' Orso. The host once commissioned an artist to paint a fresco of bears on the walls. The artist asked eight scudi for painting two bears with chains on either side of the door, and six scudi for painting them without chains. The host naturally chose the cheaper design, but was furious when sometime afterwards the bears faded until they became indistinguishable. Calling the artist he expressed his views in forcible language, only to receive the reply: 'But I advised you to have them painted with chains, now you see they have run away!' Since the '30s the dell' Orso has been one of the smart restaurants of Rome, though during the last war it extended its hospitality to many less elegant guests. That redoubtable Under Secretary of the Holy Office, Mgr. O'Flaherty, to whom so many escaped Allied prisoners-of-war owed their lives and liberty, told me that when he was at his wits' end as to how to feed his protégés the late manager always contrived to provide them with a meal.

If we are Napoleonic enthusiasts and have lunched late or in a leisurely fashion and it is now three o'clock, on Tuesday, Thursday or Saturday afternoons this is the moment to visit the **Museo Napoleonico** (see Appendix for opening times). It is reached by climbing up the ramp on to the Lungotevere and turning left into Piazza di Ponte Umberto; the entrance is at No. 10. It should be emphasised, however, that this is pre-eminently a museum for the specialist.

If we have visited the Napoleonic Museum, the quickest way to continue our itinerary is down Via Zanardelli. If not, we should turn left from the end of the Via dell' Orso down the Via dei Soldati; another picturesque old street, with a charming small Renaissance palazzo at Nos. 28–39. Either way we end up in the **Piazza di Tor Sanguigna**, called after the tower on the left-hand corner (No. 8). This is all that remains of the medieval fortress of the once famous Sanguigni family, from which Pope Leo VI (who reigned in 928 for a few months) is said to have sprung.

From the Piazza di Tor Sanguigna we take the short Vicolo di S. Apollinare; a door on the left (No. 8) affords us a glimpse into the fine sixteenth-century courtyard of **Palazzo Altemps** (now a Spanish seminary); this is called after the Roman branch of the von Hohenems family, who thus italianised their name. The last great tournament held in 1565 in the Cortile del Belvedere in the Vatican (of which we have already seen a picture in the Rome Museum) celebrated the marriage of Pius IV's nephew and niece, Count Annibale von Hohenems or Altemps with Ortensia Borromeo, sister of S. Carlo.

We now find ourselves in the piazza which takes its name

from the Church of S. Apollinare; according to some authorities, this was built over the ruins of a temple of Apollo. We return to the Piazza di Tor Sanguigna; old book collectors and those who wish to see the fine Renaissance façade of the German national church of **S. Maria dell' Anima** are advised to make a short detour down the Vicolo di Tor Sanguigna on the left. In the picturesque triangle where this joins the Largo Febo (at Nos. 14, 15, 16) is a fascinating old book shop and just beyond it on the right stands S. Maria dell' Anima. Although there has been some learned argument on the subject, the soberly beautiful façade with the double-headed imperial eagle is now generally attributed to Giuliano da Sangallo; the campanile to Bramante; the three fine portals and the figures of the Virgin and two redeemed souls (soul in Italian is *anima*), from which the church derives its name, to Andrea Sansovino. These doors are nearly always closed, but the church can be entered through a convent, reached at a later stage in our itinerary.

Retracing our footsteps a short way up Via Zanardelli, we take the first turn to the left into **Piazza Fiammetta**. The word *piazza* is something of a misnomer, as in actual fact this is really a short street; at the far end, extending also round the corner into the Via degli Acquasparta (which to make things more complicated is wide and looks like a piazza), stands the Casa di Fiammetta. According to tradition, this delightful little fifteenth-century house was the home of Cesare Borgia's beautiful Florentine mistress Fiammetta. Beside the house, the Piazza Fiammetta narrows to become the Via della Maschera d'Oro; a short way down on the left (No. 9) is a rare and well-preserved example of a sixteenth-century house, entirely decorated with graffiti. On the top storey, *amorini* mingle with ladies 'noble and nude'; lower down, Roman cohorts parade in battle array; it is said that the inspiration for this part of the decoration was derived from the reliefs of Trajan's column. The house opposite (No. 21), whose façade was originally painted by Polidoro da Caravaggio, is Palazzo Cesi. Here Galileo stayed in 1603 as the guest of Prince Federico Cesi, founder of the famous Accademia dei Lincei (The Academy of the Lynx-eyed), which in Italy today corresponds to the Académie Française.

We now emerge into the **Piazza Lancellotti**, called after Carlo Maderno's somewhat forbidding Palazzo Lancellotti on the left corner. Apparently resembling in character the architectural style of his family palace, the Prince Lancellotti of the day grimly closed the main door of his palace in 1870 as a sign of his disapproval of the entry of the Italian troops into Rome; it is said never to have been opened again until the Conciliation between Church and State in 1929. We now turn left into the **Via dei Coronari** (the Street of the Rosary Makers), which today should really be renamed the Via degli Antiquari, as every other shop now sells antiques. Here one cannot hope to emulate Cardinal Fesch, as the dealers know their business and their prices are high, but they are usually *trattabile* (open to bargaining). We owe them a debt of gratitude, however; during the last fifteen years these antique shops have brought new life to what used to be a picturesque but somewhat dilapidated street and made it one of the most attractive in Rome.

In the fifteenth century, the Via dei Coronari was an important thoroughfare known as the Via Recta (the Straight Street); it stretched from what is now the Via di Banco di S. Spirito, in front of Ponte S. Angelo, to the present Corso. Its improvement, as one of the main pilgrim routes fanning out from the bridge leading to St. Peter's, was an important part of Sixtus IV's town plan, in pursuance of which he made special concessions to private persons who were willing to build alongside it. Thus the entire street, which has suffered remarkably little from the speculative builder of later centuries, presents a perfect picture of a flourishing business and residential centre of Renaissance Rome. Indeed, the whole area contains so many delightful buildings of this period that to mention each one individually would be tedious; nevertheless, we will note one or two in passing, especially if they happen to have particular human interest or to be hidden in a by way.

The **Vicolo di Montevecchio**, leading out of the Via dei Coronari opposite the Lancellotti palace to the small piazza of the same name is a case in point. It is so called because at one time Sixtus V established the Monte di Pietà pawnshop on the corner. The sad associations of this past still seem to linger here; the prosperity which has come to Via dei Coronari has passed it by. But the small piazza contains two really charming Renaissance palaces, the ground-floor rooms of which are now unfortunately used as a garage. Farther down the Via dei Coronari, in the minute Piazza S. Simeone, there is another delightful fifteenth-century house.

The not very promising looking **Piazza S. Salvatore in Lauro** has another, and even greater surprise in store for us. Roman topographers of the last century believed that the church of S. Salvatore, from which the piazza takes its name, was called *in Lauro* because in the Middle Ages either some relic or memory of the bay or laurel trees of the classical *Portico d'Europa* survived here. Modern authorities consider that the name had a medieval rather than an ancient origin; but it is a fact that a church called S. Salvatore in Lauro already stood on the site early in the thirteenth century. This has been rebuilt at least twice; the existing church of S. Salvatore has a neo-classical façade with a relief representing the miraculous flight of the holy house of Loreto. It is now the national church of the Marchigiani, in whose province Loreto stands.

The hidden jewel of S. Salvatore in Lauro is its cloister, entered by a small door on the left of the church. This is one of the most delightful in Rome; doubly so in this city of grandeur because of its smallness and absolute simplicity. The cloister was built in the second half of the fifteenth century by Cardinal Latino Orsini, who left his famous library of manuscripts to the canons of the church. Unfortunately they were burnt in the 1527 sack of Rome. A beautiful fifteenth-century door, surmounted by sculptured garlands and children's heads, leads from the cloister into a small garden court with a fountain, benignly presided over by a bust of Cardinal Orsini. The walls of the garden loggia are also covered with Renaissance reliefs, and another lovely sculptured door opens into the refectory. This contains Isaia da Pisa's monument to the Venetian Pope Eugenius IV (1431–47) which was brought here from St. Peter's (the *guardiano* in the porter's lodge on the left of the cloister has the refectory key; a small tip should be given).

Returning to the Via dei Coronari, the Vicolo dei Gabrielli opening off it affords us a picturesque glimpse of one of the courtyards of Palazzo Taverna, whose main entrance we see later. A little farther on (Nos. 148–9) is one of the most charming houses in the street, with an elegant Renaissance door and windows flanked by sculptured pilasters. Those by the door have what appear to be small portrait heads, heavily moustachioed, incorporated into the capitals. Above, a somewhat defaced inscription reads roughly as 'Regard as your own only what you create'. The house with graceful stucco decorations near the end of the street on the left (Nos. 122–3) is generally described as having belonged to Raphael; in actual fact it was bought by his executors with funds allocated in his will to provide an income for the upkeep of his tomb.

The Via dei Coronari terminates in the piazza of the same name, though the old Via Recta continued to the end of what is now the Vicolo del Curato. Having traversed this last we find ourselves in the **Via del Banco di S. Spirito**, which affords us a fine view of the Ponte S. Angelo. This street was formerly called Canale di Ponte, according to some authorities because the frequent Tiber floods often turned it into a waterway. The earliest existing inscription, written in Gothic characters and dated 1277, recording the height of flood water in Rome is to be seen low down on the left of the picturesque Arco dei Banchi, leading out of it. This was once the entrance to Agostino Chigi's 'the great merchant of Christianity' place of business, where for years he kept the papal tiara as security for a loan made to Julius II.

We now come to the **Piazza di Ponte S. Angelo**, which was created by Nicholas V (1447–55), when he knocked down the Arch of Gratian, Valentian and Theodosius at the entry to the bridge. This was in order to give freer access to it, after the terrible disaster of Holy Year 1450, when 200 pilgrims lost their lives through overcrowding; in the panic some were trodden underfoot, others were pushed into the Tiber. For the coronation of Leo X in 1513, Agostino Chigi had a facsimile of the arch made with real people standing in place of the original statues. The piazza was for long the place of public execution; here on 11 September 1599 Beatrice Cenci and her stepmother Lucrezia were beheaded and her brother Giacomo tortured before being killed with a mace and drawn and quartered. Both brothers had been imprisoned in the terrible medieval prison of Tor di Nona nearby; Bernardo was condemned to life imprisonment because of his youth, and later reprieved. All traces of the prison has now happily vanished; only its name survives in the neighbouring Lungotevere Tor di Nona. Benvenuto Cellini and Giordano Bruno were among the numberless unfortunates who were imprisoned there during the centuries.

But to return to Via del Banco di S. Spirito; this contains three fine Renaissance palaces—the Cicciaporci-Senni (No. 12), attributed to Giulio Romano; Niccolini-Amici (Nos. 41-2), where the sixteenth-century aesthete Annibal Caro lived; and finally Paul V's Banco di S. Spirito, after which the street is now called; this stands on the corner of Banchi Vecchi, and was built in 1605 on the site of Julius II's mint. The house where, according to his memoirs, Cellini lived and had his studio must have stood somewhere between the Cicciaporci-Senni palace and the Banco di S. Spirito; in this last, when it was the mint, he cast his famous medallions.

We now turn up the **Via dei Banchi Nuovi**, a rather gloomy street, which follows the line traced by the medieval Via Papale. During the Renaissance this was also a flourishing business and residential quarter. Pietro Aretino, the famous satirist of the period, lived there, exercising his caustic wit on the human material ready to hand. One of his chief butts was the bogus intellectualism of the fashionable courtesans who lived in the quarter. A mother, in one of his plays, advises her daughter on how to advance herself in the oldest profession, by leaving fashionable books such as *Orlando Furioso*, the *Decameron* and the works of Petrarch lying about her room, and employing some poor poet to ghost verses for her.

The Banchi Nuovi terminates in the **Piazza dell' Orologio**, named after Borromini's picturesque clock-tower surmounting the monastery of S. Filippo Neri's Oratorians. For a moment we must turn left, up the Via degli Orsini, at the end of which we are confronted by a dark arched portal, framing a view of one of the most enchanting fountains of Rome. From one chalice-like basin to another, the water descends like sparkling champagne, glittering in the sunlight against a sombre background of evergreens. This is the main entrance and courtyard of the Palace of Monte Giordano, now known as **Palazzo Taverna**, for centuries a stronghold of the Orsini. The *monte* (hill) is said to have been formed by a mass of ancient buildings collapsed into ruin after Robert Guiscard's incursion in 1084. Early in the thirteenth century it was known as Monte Johannis Ronzonis or Monte Johannis Bovis. The Boveschi or Boboni were the family from which the Orsini are believed to have originated; certainly by 1334 Giordano Orsini—from whom the place takes its name of Monte Giordano—already possessed a fortress there.

As the centre of the Orsini bailiwick, which at one time extended across the Tiber and included Castel S. Angelo, Monte Giordano suffered its full share in the struggles between the great families that turned Rome into a battleground. In 1485 it was taken and partly burnt, but in the years that followed the fortress was converted into a sumptuous Renaissance palace; here in 1506 another Giordano Orsini married Julius II's kinswoman Felice della Rovere, in a setting of unparalleled splendour. Later the palace passed out of Orsini ownership and was used as a residence for ambassadors and cardinals. Ippolito d'Este (creator of Villa d'Este at Tivoli) kept great state there, entertaining Bernardo and Torquato Tasso in 1554. The last cardinal to maintain the old tradition was Lucien Bonaparte (Napoleon's great-nephew); here also his sister entertained the Empress Eugènie. Of an evening the cardinal, who died in 1868, would invite his friend the famous anti-clerical poet Gioacchino Belli to read his poems. Apparently one of their favourites was 'Il Papa nun fa gnente?' (in Roman dialect 'The Pope does nothing?'); nevertheless the Cardinal was a great friend of Pius IX. Retracing our steps to the Piazza dell' Orologio, we continue down the Via dei 'Filippini' (S. Filippo Neri's own name for his Congregation of Oratorians) and turn left into the **Piazza della Chiesa Nuova**.

The Chiesa Nuova (or New Church) was the name popularly given to **S. Maria in Vallicella**, built by S. Filippo Neri as the centre of his reforming activities. This remarkable man, who founded the Congregation of Oratorians in 1551, was perhaps the most appealing figure among the saints of the Counter-Reformation. Charming, witty, possessed of a remarkable sense of humour allied to an innate shrewdness, and a first-rate judge of character, he was able immediately to distinguish genuine religious feeling from false piety. Some of the tales recounted of the humiliating acts he required his noble Roman postulants to perform reveal this clearly. One young Roman prince failed to qualify for admission to the Congregation of Oratorians because he refused to walk through the city with a fox's tail fastened to his posterior! Others were accepted after parading the city coatless, or in rags. S. Filippo expected these erstwhile spoilt and petted young gentlemen to set to work with bricks and mortar as common labourers in the building of his church, a requirement that

The Forum seen from the Tabularium on the Capitol. In the foreground are the three columns of the Temple of Vespasian and the Temple of Saturn. In the middle distance, the ruins of the Basilica Emilia, the Column of Phocas and the ruins of the Basilica Giulia. In the distance, the Temple of Antoninus and Faustina, the Colosseum, the Temple of Vesta and three columns of the Temple of Castor and Pollux

Vestal Virgins in the atrium of their house in the Forum, with the Church of S Francesca Romana in the background

The Palatine as it was in classical times — part of a model in the Museo della Civilta Romana. The colonnaded façade behind the Circus Maximus was of the Domus Augustana, the emperor's official residence. The large arch immediately behind this overlooked the sunken garden

Above A Roman street of shops in Trajan's Forum and market, designed by Apollodorus of Damascus early in the second century AD

Right Sansovino's Madonna and Child, in the church of S Agostino, was evidently inspired by some statue of Juno. Known as the Madonna del Parto — 'of birth' — this statue is covered with jewelled votive offerings, like the classical goddesses of old

The Old Appian Way, the earliest and most famous of the great Consular roads, built by Appius Claudius in 312 BC as far as Capua, and later continued to Brindisi

Top The Delphic Sybil, one of Pinturicchio's beautiful frescoes, painted against a trompe l'œil gold mosaic background, in the chapel behind the main altar in S Maria del Popolo

Bottom A third-century mosaic of gladiatorial and animal combats, now set into the pavement of the central hall of the Villa Borghese Gallery

Rome at Night

Top left   The Piazza del Campidoglio, with the statue of Marcus Aurelius silhouetted against Michelangelo's Palace of the Senator

Top right   The Piazza Navona, with Bernini's Fountain of the Four Rivers

Bottom   S Maria in Trastevere. The mosaics date from the twelfth or thirteenth century and are believed by some to represent the Wise and Foolish Virgins on either side of the Madonna

Raphael's 'Fornarina' in the Barberini Gallery. This is generally believed to be a portrait of the baker's daughter who was his mistress, though some maintain that it is a picture of a courtesan by Raphael's pupil Giulio Romano

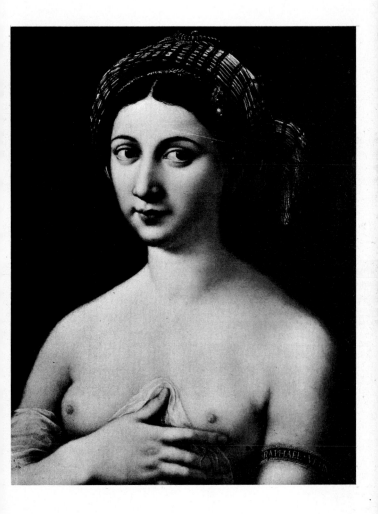

Roman Gardens

Above The nympheum of
Villa Giulia, designed by
Ammanati for Julius III,
one of the most perfect
Renaissance interpretations
of this aspect of Italian
garden architecture, which
was also a feature of
ancient Roman gardens

Right A garden court in
the Museo delle Terme,
with classical fountains and
garden sculpture and
planted with cypresses,
oleanders and box as in
ancient Rome

even in our democratic day would shock their modern counterparts.

S. Filippo's church rose on the site of a medieval one called *in vallicella*, because it stood in the valley formed by a small stream flowing into the Tarentum marshes of classical times; here the famous Altar of Dis and Proserpina then stood. The new church was begun in 1575 by Matteo di Città di Castello, continued by Martino Longhi, and consecrated in 1599; though the façade was only completed in 1606. S. Filippo had wished that the interior should be simply whitewashed, but in 1647 Pietro da Cortona was commissioned to execute the elaborate fresco decoration of the nave, dome and apse; it took him, working on and off, nearly twenty years to finish. Apart from this, the church's greatest artistic treasures are the three pictures by Rubens, executed in 1608, which hang above and on either side of the main altar. Of these S. Domitilla with SS. Nereo and Achilleo, on the right, is the most famous. In the sacristy there is an enormous statue of S. Filippo Neri; begun in 1640, it was one of Algardi's first important commissions. On the left of the church stands the famous Oratory with the curved façade which Borromini built for the Congregation between 1637 and 1662. This was not, as is often stated, the setting for the performance of the first oratorios; though this dramatical form of composition did indeed originate in S. Filippo's musical services. The actual oratory, which was built long after the saint's death in 1599, is on the ground floor of what was in fact a large monastery. This now houses the Capitoline archive and the Vallicelliana Library.

Returning to the Piazza dell' Orologio, we turn right down the **Via del Governo Vecchio**, which once formed part of the Via Papale. Its present name is derived from the fact that from 1623 to 1741 the fine fifteenth-century Palazzo Nardini or del Governo Vecchio (No. 39) was the seat of the papal governors of Rome. This is now a court of law, but nobody seems to object if one wanders in to admire the courtyard, with its distinctive fifteenth-century octagonal columns and graceful porticoes. Almost opposite the Palazzo Nardini is the charming little early sixteenth-century Palazzo Turci (No. 123), dignified by Doric pilasters alternating with round-headed windows. A little way farther on (on the same side No. 104) there is another attractive house whose façade is decorated with stucco medallions. By craning one's neck to look at the top storey one can see a rather faded but amusing *trompe l'oeil* conversation piece. It shows, painted in the recess of a blocked-up window, a churchman dictating to his secretary and is a portrait of a former owner.

Retracing a few steps, we now turn right up the **Via di Parione** a name once given also to the Via del Governo Vecchio and the whole of the surrounding *rione*, or ward of the city. This is another picturesque old street, with an attractive sixteenth-century palace on the right; usually known as the house of Sixtus V, it really belonged to his nephew. It has a charming courtyard with marble reliefs; the whole palace is excellently well kept by the Pio Sodalizio dei Piceni—an association of the natives of Ascoli Piceno resident in Rome. We now come to the **Via della Pace**, which ends in a delightful little piazza. This was designed by Pietro da Cortona as a setting for the lovely semicircular portico which he added to the church of **S. Maria della Pace** in 1656.

S. Maria della Pace (St. Mary of Peace) was originally built by Baccio Pontelli for Sixtus IV about 1480, to fulfil a vow and as a thank-offering for the peace which ended the war with Florence provoked by the Pazzi conspiracy. The church is curiously shaped, having a short nave terminating in an octagon surmounted by a beautiful coffered dome. Above the first chapel on the right of the nave is Raphael's famous fresco of the Sybils of Cuma, Persia, Phrygia and Tibur, each represented as receiving a revelation from an angel. The painting was commissioned by Agostino Chigi in 1514. The Cesi chapel, on the same side, affords a superb example of sculptured decoration of the high Renaissance. It was designed by Antonio da Sangallo the Younger, the decorative motifs being executed by Simone Mosca; the Cesi tombs on either side of the altar and the reliefs in the spandrels are by Vincenzo de' Rossi.

Above the main altar is an old picture of the Virgin, formerly hanging in a small chapel which stood on the site of the church. A drunken soldier is said to have pierced the painting with his sword, whereupon blood spouted from the Virgin's breast. Sixtus IV came in state to see the miraculous picture and vowed to build a church dedicated to the Virgin if she would grant an end to the war then raging. The chapel immediately on the left of the altar, containing the tabernacle of Innocent VIII (1484–92), is attributed to Pasquale da

Caravaggio. A door farther along this wall leads into Bramante's wonderful cloister, built in 1504. After coming to Rome in 1499, Bramante refused all commissions and spent four years studying and measuring the classical ruins. The effect upon his style was revolutionary—it is reflected in the sober classical dignity and serene beauty of this his first Roman building.

Emerging from S. Maria, we cross the Vicolo della Pace to the door of the German hospice opposite (No. 20); from here, upon request, we can enter **S. Maria dell' Anima** at any time of day. Although, for artistic treasures, this church cannot be said to equal S. Maria della Pace, it is, one feels, a living one, whereas the other is more like a museum. The atmosphere is not at all Roman; not only is the interior modelled on the German *Hallenkirche*, but the loving care and polish lavished on every piece of wood and marble bespeaks the northern temperament.

The most notable monument in S. Maria dell' Anima is the tomb of the last non-Italian Pope, Hadrian VI (1522–3), on the right of the presbytery. This handsome son of a ship's carpenter of Utrecht, who was tutor to the Emperor Charles V, tried during his short year's reign to reform the extravagances of the pontifical court. He would have no truck with humanists or poets and described the Laocoön as 'the effigies of heathen idols'. Hadrian would probably have disapproved of the beautiful tomb which his friend Cardinal van Enkevoirt commissioned Baldassare Peruzzi to design. Although this is appropriately adorned with allegorical figures representing Justice, Prudence, Force and Temperance, even in death Hadrian could not entirely escape the spirit of the age in which he lived. As Gregorovius noted with amusement, the pagan river god of Tiber appears in the corner of one of the reliefs.

Returning to the Via della Pace, we now take the **Via di Tor Millina** on the left; this brings us to the tower from which the street takes its name. The Tor Millina (No. 25) is not a medieval one, but—like those of Palazzo Venezia and Palazzo Capranica—a relic of the fifteenth-century custom for noble families to signify their state by adding a tower to their palaces. Later these reminders of feudal dignity were replaced by the more useful *belvederi*, convenient places from which to enjoy the view and breeze on summer nights.

We now turn right down the Via S. Maria dell' Anima, a rather dark but dignified old street, which brings us to the little triangular **Piazza di Pasquino**. In the course of our walks we have already encountered several of the 'talking statues' of Rome; but the battered clasical torso of Menelaus at the corner of Palazzo Braschi is the famous **Pasquino** himself— the originator of our own word pasquinade. The statue was apparently discovered during the re-paving of the nearby Via dei Leutari, and placed in its present position by Cardinal Oliviero Carafa in 1501. Although much mutilated, it dates from the third century BC and has considerable artistic merit; Bernini is said even to have gone so far as to describe it as the 'finest piece of ancient sculpture in Rome'.

According to popular legend, in the second half of the sixteenth century a prosperous tailor called Pasquino carried on his business in the area where the statue Pasquino now stands. He and his apprentices, who worked a good deal for the papal court, were very free with their comments on what went on there; with the result that in time it became the custom to attribute all salacious criticism of the papal government to Pasquino. After the tailor's death, the statue was set up beside his shop and came to be called after him; from this it was but a step for the *bon mots* of the day to be written up on placards and attached to it. Scribbling comments upon the events of the day is an immemorial Italian sport; writings of this kind have been found in the ruins of Pompeii, and frequently appear on the walls of Rome today. We have also seen how in the sixteenth century John Goritz and his friends extended this custom to hanging verses on the statues and trees of his garden.

According to the famous Roman topographer, Domenico Gnoli, however, Pasquino's function as the mouthpiece of popular criticism originated in a different manner. After placing the statue in its present position, each year on St. Mark's day Cardinal Carafa caused it to be temporarily restored with plaster head and arms, and dressed up to represent a classical divinity. The university lecturer who was entrusted with this work of restoration also instituted an annual competition for Latin epigrams; these were attached to the statue and the surrounding walls and left on exhibition for several days. Selections from these epigram exhibitions were printed in pamphlet form. A series dating from 1509 to 1525 still exists;

these, however, are notable more for their pedantry than for their wit. Possibly a sixteenth-century Bowdler was responsible for their publication, as already under Leo X (1513–21) Pasquino had become a great source of political satire. This reached its height during Hadrian VI's short reign—his reforming zeal was not calculated to arouse any Roman enthusiasm. Hadrian is even credited with wishing to have the offending statue thrown into the Tiber, and only to have desisted because he was advised that 'like the frogs Pasquino would croak louder in the water'. The Aldobrandini nephews of Clement VIII (1592–1605) are believed to have nourished a similar design, but were dissuaded by Tasso. It is a fact, however, that Marforio, Pasquino's partner in caustic repartee, was removed from his original site near the Forum in 1587, and finally enclosed in the Capitoline Museum. However, this did not bring about the hoped-for end of the notorious dialogues; the number of the talking statues grew, and Madama Lucrezia, Abate Luigi, Babuino and the Facchino swelled the chorus.

For the most part, the comments of Pasquino and his friends are untranslatable as their wit depends upon a play on words. But his savage dictum upon Queen Christina of Sweden as 'Queen without a realm, Christian without faith and a woman without shame' does not come into this category. Nor does the verse commenting upon a terrible storm occurring at the same time that many Roman works of art were seized by Napoleon's agents; roughly translated this reads as follows:

> The Highest above sends us a tempest,
> The Highest down here takes all the rest,
> Between the two Highest
> How badly we fare.

It once seemed as if Pasquino's famous 1870 interpretation of the letters S.P.Q.R. as *Sanctus Pater Quondam Rex* (The Holy Father Once a King), after the loss of the temporal power, was to be his swansong. But the muzzling of the Press and radio under Fascism showed that the old spirit was not dead. At the time when Mussolini was exhorting his compatriots to make more sacrifices in the interest of his imperial designs in Ethiopia, Roman bread became more and more uneatable. A worthy descendant of Pasquino then hung a loaf on the statue of Caesar in the then Via dell' Impero (now dei Fori Imperiali) with the following apostrophe written in Roman dialect.

> Cesare!
> Tu che ci hai lo stommico di fero,
> Mangete sto pane di l'Impero.

(Caesar! You who have a stomach of iron, eat this bread of the Empire!)

CHAPTER TEN

Piazza di Spagna to Villa Giulia

❦

WE have explored the Rome of the Romans, the old quarters in the bend of the Tiber where the people—and the princes— have lived entrenched since the Middle Ages. Now it is the turn of Rome of the foreigners, a mere parvenu of an area only some three and a half centuries old, dating from the reign of Sixtus V (1585–90). Rather unexpectedly for a Pope, Sixtus might fairly be called the father of modern town-planning; for he it was who first conceived the idea of ordered decentralisation. Unlike his predecessors, who contented themselves with improving the viability of the old city, Sixtus determined to extend it over the higher ground enclosed by the vast sweep of the Aurelian walls, thus repopulat-ing the ancient residential areas deserted since the Gothic wars.

Like any town planner today, Sixtus realised that a good water supply and road system must form the basis of his development. The first he provided by rebuilding Alexander Severus's aqueduct—the Acqua Alessandrina—renaming it after himself the Acqua Felice (before his election he was Cardinal Felice Peretti); thus supplying what is now the rail-way station area, and as far as the Villa Medici. The second he fulfilled by planning a network of roads, radiating star-fashion from S. Maria Maggiore, connecting it with the other great basilicas and places of pilgrim interest. The first of these to be completed was the Via Sistina (now passing under several names) connecting S. Maria Maggiore with Trinità dei Monti; this he intended to continue to Piazza del Popolo.

Writing at the time of the road's completion in 1587, the Venetian ambassador of the day prophesied: 'In three years all this area will be inhabited.' He was right. As so often in Italy, artists (many of whom still live in the Via Margutta) appear to have been the pioneers; shortly followed by the hotel trade, which seems to have transferred itself *en bloc* from

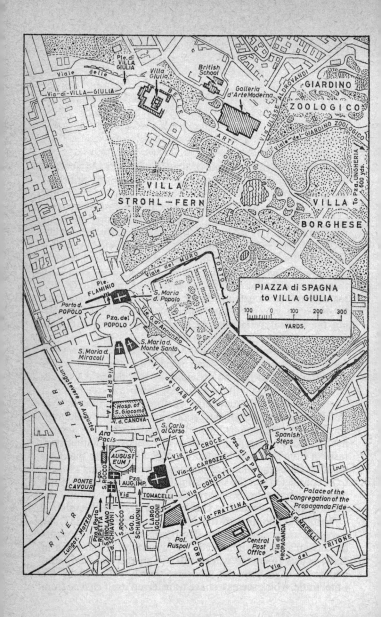

PIAZZA di SPAGNA
to VILLA GIULIA

100   0   100   200   300
YARDS.

the Campo dei Fiori area to that of what is now the **Piazza di Spagna.** Since the establishment of the Spanish embassy there early in the seventeenth century, the narrower end of the piazza has been called after it 'di Spagna'; though for long the main square with the fountain was known as Piazza di Francia, from the church of Trinità dei Monti built by the kings of France on the hill above. In any case, by the seventeenth century the 'Spanish Square' and its environs had become the great tourist centre in Rome. For the next three centuries there was hardly a foreigner of note who did not lodge there—from Rubens to Tennyson, Poussin, Angelica Kauffman, Robert Adam, Stendhal, Balzac, Gregorovius, Liszt, Wagner, Thackeray, Hans Andersen, Byron and, of course, Keats; not to mention fashionable English milords on the Grand Tour and even crowned heads. It was only after 1870, with the building of the Via Veneto, that the tide flowed up the hill to the Ludovisi quarter, still the great caravanserai of modern Rome.

In the eighteenth century the Piazza di Spagna area was known to the Romans as '*er ghetto de l'Inglesi*'; all rich foreign travellers being given by them honorary British citizenship and ennobled as '*milordi pelabili clienti*' (milords easily fleeced and excellent customers). In actual fact the English were drawn to Rome as to a magnet—the fashionable Dilettanti Club in London made at least one journey to Italy a condition of membership. Those were the days when the Via delle Carrozze off the Piazza got its name from the great touring carriages drawn up there for cleaning and repairs. The young eighteenth-century milord went on the Grand Tour in state; twenty-year-old Lord Burlington set out in 1714 with five gentlemen, six servants and his dogs—his first purchase in the Eternal City was 'a basket for Dye to pupp in'. Pictures by Carracci and Domenichino and porphyry vases followed; it is not surprising to learn that his lordship returned to England with 878 trunks and cases.

Still today the Piazza di Spagna is one of the first ports of call for any foreign traveller in Rome. It is the heart of the smartest shopping district, and those two venerable institutions the Caffè Greco (No. 86 Via Condotti) and Babington's Tea Room (No. 23 Piazza di Spagna) continue as general international rendezvous; to them might now perhaps be added a third, the English 'Lion Book Shop' (No. 181 Via del

Babuino) though here the fare is purely intellectual. The piazza, then, will be a suitable starting place for today's exploration.

It has always seemed most unfair to me that the famous **Spanish Steps**, which lead from the square to the church of Trinità dei Monti, should bear the name they do. Correctly speaking they should be the French steps, as they were first thought of by Louis XIV's great minister Cardinal Mazarin (admittedly only naturalised as a Frenchman), though his plan came to nothing. The question was again brought to the fore in 1660, after the death of the French diplomatic representative in Rome, Etienne Gueffier, who left 24,000 scudi for a chapel in Trinità dei Monti and a stair to replace the existing rough tree-lined paths leading up to the church. Clement IX (1667–9) and Innocent XIII (1721–4) both interested themselves in the question. During the latter's reign the matter was finally solved by Francesco de Sanctis's model for the existing stairs being approved both by the Pope and the French Chargé d'Affaires. Even so the first stone was not laid until 1723; the stairs were completed three years later. De Sanctis's own report which accompanied the project is still extant. It is interesting to learn from it what he himself considered to be the outstanding merits of what is perhaps the most famous street staircase in the world. First, its arrangement so that its whole extent could be seen from a distance; secondly, its division into three flights and three landings, an allusion to the church of the Trinity to which it leads; thirdly, its suitability for strolling and festive occasions; and finally, an efficient system of drainage preventing the staircase from being flooded even in a Roman cloud-burst.

Since the end of the last century flower sellers have been allowed to erect their booths at the bottom of the steps. During the last ten years, at the end of April and beginning of May, the staircase is banked with azaleas, presenting a wonderful spectacle of massed colour against the honey-coloured travertine and the blue of the sky. Charming though these floral additions to the staircase undoubtedly are, they are nothing like as amusing and picturesque as the 'fauna' which used to frequent it earlier in Dickens' day. He described the Spanish Steps as the rendezvous of all the artists' models, dressed in their colourful native costumes, waiting to catch the eye of the English tourist with artistic pretensions.

Today, somehow, this prosperous comfortable English middle-class world seems far farther removed from us than the 'Romantic Agony' of the poets of the previous generation. Keats would have had to be a very rich man indeed now to rent the rooms preserved as the Keats–Shelley Memorial (Piazza di Spagna No. 31) on the right of the Spanish Steps. But many of the spiritual successors of the romantic rebel poets—young men and women artists and writers attired in blue jeans and outlandish sweaters—still come to Rome for inspiration; though today their lodgings are more likely to be found in Trastevere or the older—and cheaper—quarters of the city. The room where Keats died on the evening of 23 February 1821 is tiny; but it faces out on to the sunlit spaces of the Spanish Steps. His death-mask, which is preserved there, has a gentle tranquil smile, showing that peace came to him in the end after the agony of the last terrible months. Apart from relics of the romantic poets, Keats's room contain a remarkable library composed of works devoted not only to himself, Shelley and Byron, but also affording a mine of information on the period and world in which they lived.

The oldest architectural feature of the Piazza di Spagna is the Fountain of the Barcaccia. This delightful 'old barge', sinking in its inadequate pool of water, was designed either by Pietro Bernini or his famous son the great Gian Lorenzo (modern art historians incline towards the latter). In any case it provides an ingenious solution of the problem posed by the lack of pressure in the aqueduct of the *Acqua Vergine*, which feeds it, that rendered the more customary jets and sprays of a higher fountain impossible. A little farther along in the narrow part of the square (No. 56) is the Spanish Embassy to the Holy See, from which the piazza takes its name. On 8 September 1857 this was disguised under a neo-classical front, complete with benediction loggia, erected for Pope Pius IX to bless the column commemorating his promulgation of the dogma of the Immaculate Conception three years earlier. The enormous monolith supporting the statue of the Virgin had been discovered in the Piazza di Campo Marzio in 1778, when there were plans to erect it in the Piazza Montecitorio, where the obelisk of Psammeticus now stands. Instead the column lay forgotten until Pius conceived the idea of thus commemorating the dogma; the work was entrusted to Luigi Poletti and its cost was defrayed by public subscription.

At the far end of the piazza, standing between the Via Due Macelli and the Via di Propaganda, is the vast Palace of the Congregation of the Propaganda Fide, an institution founded by Gregory XV in 1622. The exterior of the palace is the joint work of those notorious rivals Gian Lorenzo Bernini and Francesco Borromini. The Piazza di Spagna façade was rebuilt by Bernini in 1642–44; the strange Via di Propaganda one, with its concave and convex windows, was completed by Borromini not long before his death in 1667.

We now turn down the **Via Condotti**, so called from the conduits built by Gregory XIII (1572–85) to carry the waters of the *Acqua Vergine* to the lower part of the town. This is the Bond Street of Rome, specially famous for its jewellers, exquisite hand-embroidered table linen and lingerie, and luxury goods in general. Two streets running parallel to it, reached by numerous traverses, are also good shopping centres; the Via della Croce for its delicatessen (excellent for buying picnic lunches), and Via Frattina for boutiques, shoe shops, 'junk' jewellery, handbags, and fringes and tassels. This last may seem to be a curious speciality, but probably nowhere else in the world are such fascinating knotted silk fringes, tassels and galloons to be seen as at the famous Micci in Via Frattina (No. 68); nor is it the only establishment of its kind in the city.

The origin of this unusual Roman handicraft is more easily understood when one recalls the innumerable cardinals' hats, with their tremendously long tassels, portrayed on so many monuments. Still today it requires a week's work to convert a pound of pure silk thread into the sixty-four *fiocchi,* as they are called, which dangle in two half-yard-long 'orders' on either side of a cardinal's hat. These hats constitute the cardinals' insignia of office, and are never actually worn, even at their creation. The hats they really wear are simply scarlet editions of an ordinary priest's hat, with an embroidered gold band.

But to return to the Via Condotti, on the right we find the famous Caffè Greco (No. 86). This first opened its doors in the middle of the eighteenth century; some say it is the selfsame café mentioned by Casanova in his memoirs as the place where he waited long for an assignation in 1743. Certainly by the beginning of the following century it was the most famous establishment of its kind in Rome: the meeting place of Roman intellectuals and of the foreign artists and writers who flocked to the city. Goethe was an habitué, so was Gogol, who used to draw picturesque scenes of the Roman campagna on the marble table tops. Byron, Liszt and even— as a young priest—the future Pope Leo XIII all foregathered there. There, too, the American sculptor Story introduced Hans Andersen to Elizabeth Barrett Browning in 1861. The house across the street was a favourite lodging for English travellers; Tennyson and Thackeray both lived there; also Keats's friend Joseph Severn, who died there at the ripe age of 85 in 1879.

Everyone knows that Rome is the seat of the smallest sovereign state in the world, but most people think that this is the Vatican. In actual fact it is the palazzo half-way down on the right of the Via Condotti (No. 68) where the Sovereign Military Order of Malta has its headquarters and is there accorded sovereign extra-territorial rights by the Italian State. The order was founded in 1113 as the Knights of St. John of Jerusalem or Knights Hospitallers, to protect and succour pilgrims to the Holy Land. When this was overrun, in 1310, they seized and fortified the Island of Rhodes, which they held until at last in 1522, after a heroic defence, it too fell to the forces of Soliman the Magnificent. A few years later the Emperor Charles V granted the order the island of Malta as its new base; there it remained until Napoleon, on his Egyptian expedition of 1798, occupied the fortress. The British occupation of the island, and the recognition of her possession of it in 1814, left the Knights without a home. They finally settled in this palace which the famous archaeologist Antonio Bosio had bequeathed to them when he died in 1629.

In the palace courtyard visitors are sometimes mystified to see cars with number plates bearing the letters S.M.O.M. These are the initials of the order, which not only has its own licensing system, but issues passports—to a select few—its own diplomatic service, and a small merchant fleet. Austrian knights of 'honour and devotion' are required to have sixteen quarterings, other nationalities less. From the small élite of 'professed knights', who take the vows of chastity, poverty and obedience, the Grand Master is elected; in many Roman Catholic countries he is accorded the honours due to a reigning sovereign. Apart from this picturesque panoply of medieval state, with its hospitals, clinics and leper asylums, which are scattered throughout the world, the order still carries on the humanitarian work for which it was founded.

We now come to the **Largo Goldoni**, on whose left-hand corner stands the impressive Palazzo Ruspoli. With its massive rusticated quoins, this looks more like a Florentine than a Roman palace; indeed it was built for the Rucellai, by Ammannati in 1586, passing to the Caetani and then to its present owners. Taking the busy **Via Tomacelli**, half-way down on the right, through the brief Largo degli Schiavoni, we catch our first glimpse of the **Augusteum**. This vast tomb, built by Augustus as a mausoleum for himself and his family, was inspired by those of the Etruscans. Originally the enormous circular edifice was surmounted by a conical mound of earth—like the Etruscan tombs at Cerveteri—44 metres high and planted with cypresses.

The Augusteum suffered an even more varied career than most Roman ruins, before it was stripped to its classical foundations in 1936. In the twelfth century it was a Colonna fortress, seized and dismantled by Gregory IX in 1241— Cardinal Giovanni Colonna had supported the Emperor Frederick II at the height of his struggle with Gregory. Subsequently it was turned into a vineyard and later into a Renaissance garden. At the end of the eighteenth century the Augusteum was transformed into a bull ring, known as the Corea, where bullfighters in Spanish dress disported themselves before enthusiastic crowds. It was also used for firework displays, much frequented by the fashionable world; the last of these was held in 1870; after that the ruin was converted into a concert hall which survived until 1936.

Already, before Mussolini decided to restore the ancient mausoleum—it is said he intended it to be used as his own tomb—archaeologists had been at work exploring the old funerary chambers. In the very centre of the tomb they found a circular passage with three niches, one of which must originally have held Augustus's own ashes, laid there after his death in the year A.D. 14 on the 19th of the month renamed August in his honour. The other two niches would have contained the ashes of his wife Livia and his nephews Gaius and Lucius Caesar. Other members of his family, whose remains were laid to rest in the Augusteum, were Augustus's son-in-

law Agrippa, his stepsons Drusus and Tiberius, his grand-
daughter Agrippina and her husband Germanicus, his step-
grandson Claudius and Claudius's son Britannicus. Nerva
(AD 96–8) was the last emperor to be buried in the Augusteum;
his successor Trajan was buried in his column, and his successor, Hadrian, built another huge tomb across the river as
the imperial mausoleum of future generations.

Today, seen from a distance, the Augusteum preserves an
air of great dignity; massed cypresses surround its core of
mellow Roman brick. But on closer inspection it appears as a
desolate place, where the municipal street sweepers—the
unsung heroes of modern Rome—have a hard struggle to
keep pace with their fellow citizens' proclivity for turning any
open space into a rubbish heap. No wonder 'no litter' is the
leit motif continually reappearing through the centuries in
Roman street inscriptions!

On the far side of the Augusteum stands a most extraordinary piece of architecture, whose style can perhaps be
most realistically classified as 'Lenin funerary'; it is doubtful
if it resembles anything else this side of the iron curtain.
However, this strange erection shelters one of the most
beautiful classical monuments in Rome, the **Ara Pacis
Augustae**, the Altar of Augustan Peace. The building of the
Ara Pacis was decreed by the Senate to celebrate the peace
established in the Empire after Augustus's victories in Gaul
and Spain. It was consecrated on 4 July of the year 13 BC.
Built entirely of gleaming white marble, it consists of a
severely simple altar, rather resembling some oriental monarch's divan or throne, raised on a pyramid of steps. This is
enclosed, as in a small court, by a superbly beautiful screen;
open front and back, resting on a plinth and approached by a
flight of steps. The decorative reliefs on the screen are divided
laterally into two sections. The lower part is devoted to an
exquisite stylised representation of the acanthus and other
flowering plants. Flitting and nestling around them are birds
and butterflies, creeping under their leaves are lizards and
other reptiles. At the foot of the central acanthus plants a
snake is seen robbing a lark's nest of its fledglings. The spirit
of Virgil's Georgics and Horace's odes lives here still.

The frieze above is composed of figures sculptured in relief,
those on the front and back represent mythical scenes in the
history of Rome. The relief on the right of the main entrance,

showing Aeneas making a sacrifice, is considered to be the artistic masterpiece of the whole altar. The frieze on the side walls of the screen is of great iconographical interest; it portrays the procession of priests, great personages and members of the imperial family, led by Augustus himself, who took part in the consecration ceremonies on 4 July 13 BC. The lictors with their rods, though damaged, can be recognised at the very beginning of the frieze on the right-hand side wall of the screen. Unfortunately the figure of Augustus, which comes immediately after them, is also damaged. Tiberius stands immediately behind him, next to four figures, with the curious skull-caps with spikes on top; these are the priestly Flamines. The personages who follow have not been definitely identified, but the elderly man is believed to be either Agrippa or the Pontifex Maximus. The ladies are usually identified as Augustus's wife Livia, his daughter Julia and his niece Antonia, in that order; the children as Germanicus and the future Emperor Claudius. The figures in the frieze on the other side wall of the screen are also undoubtedly portraits, but of persons of less importance who brought up the rear of the procession. The only ornamentation on the inside walls of the screen is a series of exquisite garlands sculptured in relief; they resemble the painted ones in the House of Livia on the Palatine. This intentional simplicity serves to concentrate all attention on the altar itself; but one cannot fail to notice the extraordinary delicacy with which the components of the garlands—the ears of wheat, pine cones, pomegranates and other fruit and foliage—have been chiselled out of the marble.

The Ara Pacis did not originally stand on this site. Its excavation and reconstruction here was one of the most remarkable archaeological feats of modern times. Already in the sixteenth century, fragments of the frieze, including that representing Augustus and the Flamines, had been discovered during the building of a palace behind S. Lorenzo in Lucina. The remarkable quality of the sculpture was recognised; some of the fragments were bought by the Roman agent of the Grand Duke of Tuscany and dispatched to Florence; others passed through various hands, some of them ending up later in the Louvre. At this time no one suspected that they had formed part of the famous Ara Pacis; they were believed to have come from some triumphal arch.

Towards the end of the last century the work of Italian and foreign archaeologists revealed the fact that these beautiful fragments had once adorned Augustus's Altar of Peace. In 1894 Eugene Petersen embarked on the studies which resulted in the first theoretical reconstruction of the altar. In 1903 the first scientific excavation of the area was begun, revealing a great deal of the altar and some of the reliefs still *in situ*. The practical difficulties of the excavation were tremendous; they had to be carried on by means of underground galleries dug below existing buildings, and were finally abandoned owing to water seepage.

In 1937 it was decided to make another attempt. Almost immediately another part of the figure of Augustus was discovered, but again the excavations were flooded. With extraordinary ingenuity this recurrent problem was solved by the installation of an enormous refrigeration plant; this froze the spring waters at their source and the whole of the friable ground around them for a depth of ten metres. The palace above was under-pinned with a huge scaffolding of ferro-concrete; its foundations were gradually removed, together with the remains of the altar, and then solidly rebuilt. By the end of 1938 the work was finished. Then began the patient labour of re-assembling the altar. Fragments were brought back from Florence, some had already been bought back from foreign museums; reproductions of other missing pieces were made. In due course the whole marvellous monument stood revealed, probably as it had not been seen by human eyes since the fall of the Roman Empire.

We have now a few moments in which to examine the surroundings of the Augusteum. The modern square in which it stands is dominated by the apse and dome of the church of **S. Carlo al Corso**, dedicated to S. Carlo Borromeo. The main entrance is in the Corso, but its outstanding architectural feature is the dome, built by Pietro da Cortona in 1668. Turning our backs on S. Carlo, we walk under a modern arch linking the churches of S. Girolamo degli Schiavoni and S. Rocco. When Illyria and Slavonia were overrun by the Turks, many refugees from these countries found lodging with a pious compatriot, who lived the life of a hermit beside a ruined chapel on this spot. In 1453, Pope Nicholas V gave the land to them for a hospice; later Sixtus IV built them a church, which was dedicated to their compatriot S. Jerome. This was rebuilt by Martino Longhi the Elder for Sixtus V in 1587; it is still the national church of Yugoslav Catholics in Rome.

The neighbouring church of **S. Rocco** has a much more curious history, belied by its sober neo-classical façade, which was completed by Valadier in 1832. It began as the chapel of the confraternity of inn-keepers and bargees of the river port of the Ripetta, which stood where the Ponte Cavour now spans the Tiber. The confraternity was founded in 1500 under Alexander VI; its premises included a fifty-bed hospital for men. To this was later added, thanks to the munificence of Cardinal Salviati, a lying-in hospital for the bargees' wives who, owing to their husbands' vagrant occupation, had no proper homes in which to be cared for.

It is not known precisely at what time this part of the hospital came to be used by unmarried mothers; but the wandering lives of many of its patients naturally favoured a more irregular situation than would have obtained elsewhere. In any case this aspect of the hospital's life was actually recognised and sanctioned by Clement XIV in 1770. A special section of the hospital was reserved for expectant mothers who were not required to give their names—they were known only by numbers and could even wear a veil during the whole time they were there. They were cared for free of charge during their confinement and for eight days. If the mother did not wish to keep her child, it was sent to the orphanage of S. Spirito; if she or it died, they were buried in a nameless grave. For a small fee, women could stay in the hospital for several months beforehand. These hospital premises, which went by the name of the *Cellata*, were absolutely inviolate; no outside authorities—even the police—had any jurisdiction over them and, even less, were allowed to enter. The *Cellata* survived the unification of Italy and still functioned in 1878; somewhere about the turn of the century it ceased to exist. The hospital building was knocked down at the time of the excavation of the Augusteum; it stood just beside the church of S. Rocco.

The name of the **Piazza di Porto Ripetta** is practically all that now remains to remind us of Andrea Specchi's delicious curving water stairs. Built in 1703 on the site of some medieval steps they served as a quay for barges bringing produce from Umbria and the Sabina, and were barbarously destroyed to make way for a hideous iron bridge. Only the delightful rococo fountain, which stood at the top, was saved; it was reconstructed on a platform in front of the houses dividing the Via Ripetta from Lungotevere Marzio. We now turn back along the Via Ripetta, passing between the Ara Pacis and the Augusteum. Almost immediately upon our left, we find a large horse-shoe shaped building, appropriately known as the **Ferro di Cavallo**. This was built by Pope Gregory XVI (1831–46) to house various institutions, including the Accademia di S. Luca and its art schools. Though sponsored by the pope himself, the project aroused dismay among the respectable residents of the area, who feared that their daughters might be led into bad ways by such notoriously immoral people as artists and their models! On the opening day Gregory inspected every corner of the building, finally advancing to one of the windows in order to see the view. Across a very narrow street he found himself confronted by a Roman matron, standing in the window of her house surrounded by her daughters. In stentorian tones she cried out: 'Holy Father, save my daughters!' The pope took the hint, and had the windows of the rooms on this side walled up so that respectable Roman maidens might not be disturbed by the sight of art classes in progress. The building still houses the Accademia di Belle Arti.

A little farther along on the right is the Hospital of S. Giacomo, founded in 1339 by Cardinal Pietro Colonna. The **Via Antonio Canova**, to the right of this, is so called because at one time the famous sculptor had his studio there. This is the large building on the right (No. 17), with a bronze bust of the artist; its walls are covered with fragments of classical sculpture. At the Via Ripetta end of the street, let into the hospital wall, is the eighteenth-century equivalent of a 'no parking' sign. It is an inscription warning people not to put fodder down in the street, or to tie up their horses there, by order of the hospital authorities.

The Via Ripetta now brings us into the **Piazza del Popolo**, one of the most superb of its kind, even in this city of beautiful squares. The Via Ripetta was built by Leo X in 1518, with the intention of extending the then restricted old town towards the Piazza del Popolo. In spite of other legendary origins attributed to it, this is now most generally conceded to owe its name to the parish church of S. Maria del Popolo— in medieval times a parish was called a *populus*—built by

Gregory IX in 1227. The church replaced a chapel erected in 1099 by Paschal II, over what was popularly believed to be the site of Nero's tomb. In its turn, Gregory's church was replaced by the one built by Sixtus IV between 1472–7, which we know today.

In the fifteenth century the church and its adjoining monastery stood in the midst of vineyards and vegetable plots, reaching from the Aurelian wall to S. Lorenzo in Lucina. In spite of Leo X's efforts, the development of the area was slow. It was only in 1561 that Pius IV commissioned Nanni di Baccio Bigio to replace the ruined medieval gate in the Aurelian wall by the existing Porta del Popolo. This was the first step towards the creation of the wonderful monumental setting of the piazza. The next was taken by the redoubtable Sixtus V—who used to get up early in the morning personally to inspect the progress of his building schemes. In 1589 he re-erected the obelisk in the centre of the square, which came from the Circus Maximus. It is the second oldest obelisk in Rome, dating from the thirteenth century BC, and had been brought from Heliopolis to Rome by Augustus. It was the fourth to be re-erected by Sixtus, who employed these relics of antiquity more or less as punctuation marks at the crossings and terminals of his new road system. He originally intended also to use them as the gnomons of sundials; but, like his scheme for turning the Colosseum into a wool factory, this was never carried out.

As might be expected, during the following 'baroque' century, the importance of providing an imposing entrance into the city, which would be the first glimpse that most foreigners would have of it, was fully appreciated. This aspect of the matter was brought home to Alexander VII almost immediately upon his succession in 1655. He had to prepare for the all-important event of the arrival of Queen Christina of Sweden, the daughter of one of the great champions of the Reformed faith, who had abdicated her throne in order to be received into the Roman Catholic Church. According to a contemporary description, the queen was welcomed by the College of Cardinals at the Porta del Popolo. The inner face of this gate had been newly redecorated by Bernini in honour of the event; the pope himself had composed the inscription 'Felici fausto ingressui' (For a happy and blessed entrance), with the date 1655 which it still bears. The seventeenth-

century chronicler tells us that with these words Alexander
'wished, for the benefit of posterity, to allude to the fact that
this ornament had been made for the entry of the queen, but
not to stress it'. He goes on sagely to remark that 'the Pope
was very circumspect; restraining himself well within the
bounds of prudence, doing enough, but not too much!'

By 1660 Alexander had commissioned Carlo Rainaldi to
design the twin churches of **S. Maria di Monte Santo** and
S. Maria de' Miracoli; these stand between the Via Ripetta,
the Corso and Via del Babuino, where they fan out from the
piazza. By various ingenious devices, the architect succeeded
in providing exactly the dramatic effect desired by the pope;
making an architectural prologue, as it were, to the traveller's
entry into the city. The disposition of the three streets recalls
the architectural perspectives employed in Italian Renaissance
theatres, which disappear into the distance behind the proscenium. Here the proscenium itself is formed by the two
churches, whose façades are not quite straight, being inclined
slightly inwards towards the Corso, thus instinctively leading
the eye of the observer down its length. The difference in the
width of the sites of the two churches presented Rainaldi
with a difficult problem, as the appearance of symmetry had
to be preserved at all costs. This he achieved by the ingenious
idea of giving S. Maria di Monte Santo (on the narrower site
on the left as one faces the churches) an oval dome, S. Maria
de' Miracoli a round one.

The foundation stones of the two churches were laid in
1662; in 1673 Bernini was called in to complete S. Maria di
Monte Santo; it was actually finished by Carlo Fontana two
years later. Fontana also assisted Rainaldi with the other
church till its completion in 1679. What we may perhaps call
the 'tourist attraction' aspect of Piazza del Popolo was definitely appreciated by contemporaries. Writing in 1686, an
Italian author described the first impression made upon the
traveller as 'so majestic as to promise well from this beginning
how many marvels must lie within so famous a city'.

Thus the Piazza del Popolo remained for over a century; a
long irregularly wedge-shaped piazza, with a superbly effective baroque *mise en scène* at the far end. It was also the smart
meeting-place for evening carriage drives; the scene of tremendous gaiety during the carnival; and the stopping-place
for diligences arriving from the north. During the reign of

Pius VI, in 1794, Giuseppe Valadier first began the studies that were to result in the transformation of the piazza. In spite of his French-sounding surname, Valadier was Roman born. However, he entered the service of the French Prefect, Count de Tournon, soon after 1809; and there is good reason to believe he was the technical brain behind de Tournon's town-planning schemes for the 'second city' of the Napoleonic Empire. It is interesting to note that many of these plans were subsequently put into effect after the unification of Italy.

De Tournon's ideas included the creation of public parks on either side of the Piazza del Popolo, linking it with the then rural Pincian Hill on one side, and the Tiber bank on the other. For this typically nineteenth-century French conception, Valadier abandoned his original idea of an enclosed Italian-style piazza, and adumbrated the first outline of the present oval one with the ramps leading up to the Pincio. This was turned down, and two Frenchmen sent to prepare another. One of these, Berthauld, was a garden designer and decorator, who slightly modified Valadier's plan; this was only finally put into execution after Pius VII's return in 1814.

Such is the complicated building history of the Piazza del Popolo, but when looking at it, it is almost impossible to believe that so many hands, over a period of three centuries, have contributed to its perfection—a remarkable example of the mysterious workings of the *genius loci* if ever there was one. Appropriately enough, the only building in the piazza to have survived the various stages in its evolution has been the church of S. Maria del Popolo, from which it takes its name, the neighbouring monastery having been practically swept away to make room for the approach to the Pincio. This was not the actual building where Martin Luther lodged when he came to Rome in 1511, which was destroyed in the sack in 1527. But it was probably in Piazza del Popolo that on his arrival Luther—to quote his own words—'fell on my knees, held up my hands to heaven, and cried "Hail holy Rome, sanctified by the holy martyrs and by the blood they shed here".'

The reigning Pope at the time of Luther's visit was Julius II, who had done so much further to beautify the church of **S. Maria del Popolo.** Looking at it from the centre of the piazza, it is difficult to believe that this is still the church built by Sixtus IV in the fifteenth century; a neo-classical shell has been im-

posed upon this side in order to make it harmonise with the
other buildings flanking the gate. But as soon as we round the
corner, we are struck by the austere dignity of the early
Renaissance façade, generally attributed to Andrea Bregno.

S. Maria del Popolo is one of the artistic treasure-house
churches of Rome. Under the patronage of the two Della
Rovere Popes (Sixtus IV and Julius II), and members of their
family, Bramante, Bregno, Pinturicchio, Sebastiano del
Piombo, Raphael and Sansovino contributed to its decoration.
But such is the power of fashion that, standing in the church
today, one notices that the average tourist simply walks to the
chapel where Caravaggio's pictures of the 'Conversion of St.
Paul' and the 'Crucifixion of St. Peter' hang, missing all the
rest. These paintings are magnificent, but one is inevitably
reminded of the Victorians who raved about Guido Reni and
ignored Giotto.

Admittedly the church is badly lit and in parts badly cared
for; but with a little patience one can usually discover the
light switches. This is particularly important in the Della
Rovere chapel, the first on the right, where Pinturicchio's
lovely 'Adoration of the Child'—frescoed above the altar—is
otherwise exceedingly difficult to see; so are the lunettes,
painted by him and his pupils. (The light switch is on the left
wall just above the balustrade.) Bregno's fine tomb, with a
Madonna by Mino da Fiesole, of two Della Rovere cardinals
is on the left. The family arms—the *rovere* or oak tree—
appears on the low marble screen separating the chapel from
the body of the church. The relief here is exquisite, as indeed
is so much of the Renaissance decorative work of this type for
which the church is justly renowned; but the finest of all is by
Andrea Sansovino. In the third chapel on the right is another
Della Rovere tomb of similar style, and frescoes of the school
of Pinturicchio.

A small door on the right of the right transept opens into a
long narrow passage, with some interesting Renaissance
sculptures and tombs. This leads to the sacristy, where Andrea
Bregno's fine altar, executed for Alexander VI, was transferred
during the seventeenth century. Returning to the church, in
the chapel on the extreme right of the main altar Vanozza
Cattanei and her son the Duke of Gandia were buried. Their
funerary inscription, as we have seen, has since turned up
mysteriously in the Basilica of S. Marco. This was Vanozza's

personal chapel, for whose maintenance she had made ample provision; it is said that she served as the model for a picture representing S. Lucia which once hung there; it was removed by order of the Chigi Pope, Alexander VII (1655–67).

The main altar of the church is baroque, but it frames the famous Madonna, traditionally attributed to S. Luke; this was brought by Gregory IX from the Lateran and is a notable work of the early thirteenth century. We must now enter one of the low curtained doors on either side of the main altar; they bring us into the main chapel, which was extended by Vignola for Julius II. The chapel is very dark, and such subsidiary lighting as there is does not help us very much to see its treasures; (as in many Roman churches, the well-equipped traveller will come armed with binoculars in order to study the ceiling frescoes). This is partly due to the stained-glass windows, dating from 1509, the work of Guillaume de Marcillat and unique in Rome of that period. Beneath them, on either side of the chapel, stand the two superb tombs designed by Andrea Sansovino for Cardinals Girolamo Basso Della Rovere and Ascanio Sforza. The latter, who died in 1505, had supported Rodrigo Borgia's election to the papacy; in return it is said, for the Borgia-Sforza Cesarini Palace which we saw in Corso Vittorio Emanuele. He thus incurred the enmity of the future Julius II, but in the end Julius forgave him and erected this splendid monument in his memory. On the tombs, for the first time Sansovino represented the two cardinals reclining as if asleep, not lying in state as was the medieval custom. The reliefs on the tombs are among the most beautiful in Rome and are purely classical in subject and feeling. The lizards and garlands on the Sforza tombs on the left might well have featured on the Ara Pacis; the satyrs' heads garlanded with flowers and grapes on the Della Rovere one are also obviously inspired by some classical model.

But the greatest glory of this wonderful—but sadly ill-kept —chapel are Pinturicchio's frescoes on the vault. Here the Virgin, Evangelists and Fathers of the Church keep company with the Sibyls; all are framed in rich decoration in the 'grotesque' style characteristic of the artist and the period.

Returning to the body of the church, in the small chapel on the left of the main altar, hang Caravaggio's superb pictures already mentioned (the light switch is on the right wall just above a small offertory box). So much has been written about these, and they have been so frequently reproduced during the last fifteen years, that any comment seems superfluous. Suffice it to say, however, that even the best reproductions cannot convey the marvellous light effects, especially of the 'St. Paul'.

The outstanding monument on the left-hand side of the nave is the Chigi chapel, designed by Raphael for his friend and patron, the famous Sienese banker, Agostino Chigi. This is really beautiful, especially the dome, where Raphael's cartoons for the mosaics—with their wonderful shades of blue set in gold—were carried out by the Venetian Luigi di Pace in 1516. Raphael's conception of the chapel as a complete unit in itself—really a miniature church—was unique at that period; then such buildings were usually regarded simply as a suitable setting for religious pictures and family tombs. Very much of the period, however, is the curious mixture of sacred and profane subjects in the dome mosaics—God the Father surrounded by symbols of the sun and the planets. Of the same world is Lorenzetto's bronze altar frontal which, for all its sacred subject, is purely classical; it was in fact inspired by an ancient relief now in the Louvre. The 'Birth of the Virgin' above the altar is by Sebastiano del Piombo. The curious marble pyramids on either side of the chapel—the tombs of Agostino Chigi and his brother Sigismondo—were for long considered to have been the work of Bernini, replacing earlier monuments. However, it has now been ascertained that they formed part of Raphael's original design. It seems likely that they inspired Canova's monument of the Stuarts in St. Peter's; though, of course, both are derived from the pyramid of Cestius. Of the four prophets in the corners of the chapel, 'Habakkuk' (on the right of the altar), and 'Daniel and the Lion' (opposite), are really the work of Bernini. The two others, 'Jonah and the Whale' and 'Elias', were executed by Lorenzetto from Raphael's designs. The first of these two was inspired by a classical statue of a boy with a dolphin, which we will see later in the Villa Borghese.

On the left of the Chigi chapel is one of the most curious funerary monuments in Rome. It was erected in 1771 in memory of Princess Maria Flaminia Odescalchi, who died having her third child at the age of 20. A lion, a fair-sized tree, eagles and angels, in bronze and varicoloured marbles, support a portrait of the deceased, executed in black and white marble. Before leaving, we should pause to see, just to the left of the door, another curious monument: that of G. B. Gisleni, the friend of three Polish kings, who died in 1672. At the top is a portrait of Gisleni in life, with the inscription *Neque hic vivus* (Neither living here); at the bottom a hideous yellow skeleton, with the inscription *Neque hic mortuus* (Nor dead here). In between are two medallions showing a chrysalis and a butterfly as symbols of resurrection. A rare use of such a symbol, and a curious one to find in a church where Martin Luther must have worshipped, who also compared the after-life to a butterfly emerging from its chrysalis.

Now, for the first time in our exploration of Rome we must take a tram or bus, to get to the Villa Giulia, which houses the Etruscan Museum. The most convenient is the 67 bus, which stops in the Piazza del Popolo just in front of the Canova bar.

At the rush hours, travelling by Roman municipal transport is *not* conducive to sight-seeing *en route*; it requires the stamina of a commando and the patience of Job to board the vehicle, get one's ticket and gradually edge one's way to the front door, which is the only means of escape. However, if we have started off at 9 a.m. and been fairly brisk about our sight-seeing to date, we should have reached this stage of our exploration by 10.30 or a quarter to 11; generally a propitious and uncrowded hour at which to brave the rigours of Roman bus or tram.

With any luck, therefore, we should be able to see something of the few places of interest we pass *en route*; they are on the right-hand side of the road, so a seat, if available, on this side is indicated. The first thing we are likely to notice in the Piazzale Flaminio is the imposing gate on the right, flanked by two neo-classical porticoes; this leads to the Villa Borghese. What is not nearly so likely to draw our attention is the wide car road farther to the right, called the **Viale del Muro Torto**. Its very modern appearance may lead us to forget that it is associated with one of the most revered legends of Christian Rome. The Muro Torto, or crooked wall, which it skirts, is that section of the Aurelian wall which—according to Procopius—St. Peter himself assumed the responsibility of defending during the Gothic wars. From that day to this no one has dared to take upon himself the responsibility of repairing it.

In a few minutes we find ourselves deposited not far from a

dignified Renaissance building, enlivened by a delightful fountain at the corner. It was designed by Ammannati for Pope Julius III (1550-5); it once formed part of the extensive garden layout surrounding his villa. It is mentioned in contemporary descriptions of the villa as standing between the long pergola, covered with vines, jasmine and pink, white and red climbing roses, reaching to the river bank, and the path leading to the house itself, which was bordered with fruit trees. Pius IV's *palazzina* was for long also used as the stopping-place where newly-created cardinals or princes rested and changed into ceremonial attire, before making their state entry into Rome. It is now the residence of the Italian ambassadors to the Holy See.

From here we turn up the narrow **Via di Villa Giulia** on the right. After the first few yards, the tree-clad heights of the Villa Strohl-Fern come into view, affording the street something of the atmosphere of the country road which it was less than a generation ago. But the days of its glory are long past; then it led through Julius III's enormous park-like garden, planted with 36,000 elms, chestnuts, cypresses, bays, myrtles, pomegranates and other trees, in whose shade stood statues, fountains, grottes and pavilions. All that is now left to remind us of this splendour is the beautiful **Villa Giulia**, or to give it its old name, Villa di Papa Giulio.

Before his election in 1550, Julius III already owned a villa on this site. Immediately after his accession he consulted the leading architects of the day, including it is said Michelangelo, about his plans for enlarging it. Vasari always attributed the overall design to himself; but it seems that the major part of what we see today was the work of Ammannati and Vignola. It is generally considered that the house itself was designed by Vignola; the screen above the nympheum is certainly by Ammannati (as an inscription on the right-hand pilaster bears witness); while Vasari, Vignola, Ammannati and Baronio worked in collaboration on the nympheum. Viewed from the road, the villa presents the appearance of a dignified and massive country house. It is only on entering that we realise that it is little more than a screen, whose long porticoed arms reach out to enclose a garden. It is in fact the most perfect existing example of the Renaissance conception of house and garden as an inseparable whole, each one interpenetrating the other. But where, the stranger may well ask, did the pope and his numerous entourage actually live and sleep? The answer is that they did neither—except for the afternoon siesta—in this or practically any other of the great suburban villas (the term orginated in classical Rome, not Clapham) of Rome. These Roman country houses and gardens, which grew even grander and larger in the seventeenth century, were created purely for a day or an evening's enjoyment. Apart from anything else, malaria would have rendered most of them uninhabitable in summer—their pools and irrigation tanks were the breeding ground of the anopheles mosquito—when the rich and great sought refuge in their even larger villas in the Alban or Ciminian Hills.

Nevertheless Julius spent a fortune on his villa, filling it with classical statues (it required 160 boatloads to remove them to the Vatican after his death). Many of these probably stood in and around the garden courtyards we see today, surrounded by urns and vases filled with orange and lemon trees and rare flowers. We know that in the centre of the great horseshoe-shaped courtyard there stood the marvellous porphyry basin from the baths of Titus or Nero's Golden House (now one of the treasures of the Vatican museum). This was adorned with two shells of green marble and a statue of Venus and a swan from whose beak water gushed into the basin.

The pope used to come in a flower-decked boat up the Tiber to watch the progress of his villa (he was continually making alterations to it) and to dine there, entertained by dancers and musicians. Possibly on hot days he rested in the small underground rooms, especially designed for coolness like those of classical villas, which open out from the sunken nympheum. This, with its lily pools and fern-decked fountains, that fill the whole place with their gentle murmur, seems to have been expressly created for *dolce far niente*.

But we must not allow ourselves to fall victim to its spell, as in the **Etruscan Museum**. Julius's villa now houses what is undoubtedly one of the great collections of Rome and of the world. Founded in 1889, with objects discovered in the excavations at Civita Castellana, Satricum, Alatri and Segni, together with the Barberini collection, the Etruscan Museum was originally housed in old-fashioned style in the few rooms of the main block of the villa. Gifts, acquisitions and the fruits of many years of excavation over ever more widely extended areas resulted in the collection increasing so enormously in size and importance that some new provision had to be made for it. During the years 1950–60 the two great wings of the villa, which enclose the existing gardens and part of the first floor of the main block, were completely renewed inside; in this vast space the collection is now superbly displayed. The present arrangement is, however, provisional; further alterations have yet to be made, and until this is done no properly numbered catalogue listing the objects in precise room and case order is likely to be available. We will therefore proceed, picking out the most interesting exhibits as we come to them; though it is possible that within the next few years their position may have altered. (The existing catalogue, which costs two thousand lire and weighs a pound, is only now available in Italian and has some discrepancies in the numbering of rooms and so on.)

The vast majority of the exhibits in the Etruscan Museum have been found in tombs or on temple sites, both in the area north of Rome, between the Tiber and the Arno, which may be geographically termed Etruria proper, and in Latium and parts of central Italy, whose culture, prior to Romanisation, was dominated by that of the Etruscans. They consist of vases and pottery, some of great artistic value and some for ordinary household use; there are also arms, jewellery, toilet accessories, even kitchen equipment. Like the Pharaohs of Egypt, the dead Etruscan was buried with all the objects employed in his or her daily life, for use in the world beyond. Naturally in the early days, from the ninth to the seventh century BC, these were very simple; but already in the following century fine Greek vases were numbered among the contents of the tombs. In fact many of the most beautiful vases in the museum are Greek, not Etruscan. What is absolutely fascinating, however, is to observe the Etruscan interpretation and adaptation of Greek art forms. Sometimes this process involved the copying, in the characteristic black glossy pottery called *bucchero*, of Greek metal vessels such as vases, jugs and cups. Egyptian objects have also been found in Etruscan tombs; and several of them are included in the collection.

But the great glory of the Villa Giulia Museum, which singles it out from all the other collections of its kind in the world, are the stupendous sculptures in terracotta—some of them still retaining much of their polychrome colouring— which adorned the Etruscan temples. The most famous of

these are the Apollo and other figures from the temples at
Veii—the work, probably, of the renowned sculptor Vulca,
who was summoned to Rome by Tarquinius Priscus to make
the statues for the Capitoline Temple of Jupiter some time
before the year 509 BC.

With the exception of objects in the three 'antiquariums' on
the upper floor, the collection is arranged topographically. The
finds from each area are grouped together in one or more
rooms, where large maps and explanatory notices show clearly
the locality in which they were found. In the absence of an
efficient catalogue, these are a tremendous help towards understanding something about what one is looking at; also in
bringing home to the uninitiated the extent of Etruscan territory and influence. Starting the itinerary in its correct order,
from the door at the far end on the left of the semicircular
colonnade of the villa, the first three and a half rooms are
devoted to the territory of Vulci. To begin with, many of the
objects belong to the early or 'villanovan' period. Particularly
interesting are the roughly oval or circular hut-shaped funerary urns, undoubtedly modelled on the dwellings of the period.
In the last of these rooms, whose contents date from a later
period, we already find some fine Greek vases; also a curious
cup with painted eyes, originally probably regarded as a
charm; later this became quite a common form of decoration.
This room also contains the entire bronze armament of a
warrior. In the next one are small terracotta models of the
famous temple of Vulci and other votive offerings. In this
room a short flight of steps leads down into an Etruscan tomb,
discovered intact in the necropolis of Cerveteri, transported
here and reconstructed in its entirety.

The following room is devoted to objects found in the territory of Tarquinia so famous for its painted tombs. These include a most remarkable collection of metal objects, varying
from an elaborately decorated wheeled bronze trolley, used as
a scent burner, to a horse's bit and ordinary fire-irons and
kitchen implements—poker, tongs, grill, etc. We should not
be surprised at the amount of kitchen and cooking implements
which have survived among the objects found in Etruscan
tombs and are to be seen spread out through the museum.
In his fascinating book *La Vie Quotidienne chez les Etrusques*
(Paris 1961), Jacques Heurgon has explained the great importance of funeral and no doubt other banquets (the Ro-

mans despised the Etruscans for being fat) in Etruscan life. A painting in the Golini tomb at Orvieto shows the complicated preparation of such a meal, with the cook and his assistants working to the sound of music provided by the flute. Game, including venison, hare and what appear to be partridges, were evidently included in the menu. A slave is at work making something, which seems closely to resemble the sauce of pounded-up herbs, cheese and garlic, mixed with oil, called *pesto* in Genoa today. This is a close relation of the Roman sauces of Apicius. Eggs, black grapes and pomegranates, are among the easily recognisable foods in this Etruscan kitchen; others appear to be round biscuits and sweets of various kinds piled up in pyramids. In Etruria the diners, men and women (to the later scandal of the republican Romans) reclined together on couches; in the paintings a dog is sometimes also seen, waiting under the table for the scraps. Many of these banquets appear to have taken place in the open air, against a background of trees; others in houses at night, lit by tall candelabra. Usually, probably, the couples on the couches were man and wife; but Monsieur Heurgon has his doubts about the propriety of the banquet represented in the 'Tomb of the Leopards' at Tarquinia. Here the wine is served by a naked Ganymede and a gentleman is seen offering a lady an elaborate ring; according to Roman ideas Etruscan women were very immoral.

At the time of writing (though it is intended in future to move them to the upper floor) the following room in the itinerary contains the greatest treasure of the museum—the wonderful sculptures from Veii. Words cannot possibly convey the surging vitality that is still implicit in every line, even in their damaged state, of the two figures of Apollo and Hercules, on the right. It is believed that they were placed thus confronting each other, on the apex of the roof of the temple, at the end of the sixth century BC. They were the central figures of a group of at least four, representing the struggle for the possession of the Ceryneian Hind. The no less wonderful head of Mercury (the polychrome one with the ringlets in the case on the right) also belonged to a statue forming part of the group. The story of Hercules's and Apollo's struggle for the hind is Greek; so is the archaic smile on their faces. But these sculptures were the work of an Etruscan, almost certainly the famous Vulca; and he seems to have added something—a deeper vitality, a cruelty which is perhaps oriental—that is as mysterious as the origins of his people.

The Greeks hated the Etruscans for their cruelty in war. This same cruelty they appear to have transmitted to the Romans with the taste for such spectacles as men and animals fighting in the arena. Something of this spirit is also very evident in the ferociously smiling Medusa's head, on the polychrome antefix from the roof of the Veii temple, also standing in the room. But a very different aspect of Etruscan life is typified by the graceful figure of a goddess with a child in her arms—the recurrent theme of Italian art throughout the centuries—on the other side of the room. This was found beneath the altar in front of the temple, and is the work of the same sculptor or school as the other figures.

This more gentle spirit lives in the famous sarcophagus of the 'Bride and Bridegroom', which stands alone in the next room but one. That does not mean, however, that we should neglect the next room in passing. Apart from some beautiful polychrome antefixes and heads of Silenus from Cerveteri, it contains a superb portrait-head of a man, with bronzed skin and fair hair. Evidently a speaking likeness, this dates from about 80 BC when Etruria was rapidly becoming Romanised; it illustrates the great debt that the Roman art of portraiture owed to the Etruscans.

But to return to the 'Bride and Bridegroom'. There is an extraordinary gentleness in both their expressions, and touching affection in the young man's gesture of laying his hand protectively on his wife's shoulder. This, and the fact that they recline together on the banqueting couch, indicate the very different treatment of women and their position in Etruscan society as opposed to that of Republican Rome. Until Augustus's reign a Roman woman sat humbly in the presence of her lord, like children and other underprivileged persons; so as a matter of fact did Etruscan women in the later period when the austere Roman republican influence got going. The young couple, however, lived in Cerveteri in the second half of the sixth century BC. This is evident from the Bride's dress, particularly her curious domed headdress or *titulus*, later only worn on ritual or religious occasions, but at this time the characteristic headdress of Etruscan patrician women. Her curious buskins, with their pointed turned-up toes, were also a distinctive feature of Etruscan dress, though their origin was

Greek. Here, as in the tomb paintings, the reclining couple are portrayed as if participating at their own funerary banquet. We have no clue as to their names, or why they seem to have died together when so young. Were they, one wonders, some Romeo and Juliet of the sixth century BC or did some plague or other catastrophe carry them off?

The large room at the top of the small flight of steps is also devoted to objects found in the tombs of Cerveteri. The cases are arranged chronologically; beginning with objects found in tombs of the seventh century BC and ending with those of the first century BC. Here the museum authorities have hit on the helpful idea of placing photographs on the walls, showing the actual tombs in which many of these objects were found. The large number of superb Greek vases, some Egyptian scent bottles and even an ostrich egg indicate the prosperity and the extent of international trade existing in Etruria during these six hundred years. The country's own artistic development is also amply illustrated, particularly by fine black *bucchero* ware decorated with reliefs. An endearingly human touch is again provided by ordinary household implements, such as fire-dogs and spits; even the remains of a funerary meal, with eggs and small dishes, left to keep warm on a charcoal brazier. The shape of this last is not unlike those still in use in Italian country districts.

This room ends the part of the museum devoted to finds from what may be geographically termed Etruria proper. The 'antiquariums' which follow contain objects whose provenance is often unknown. The subsequent part of the museum is devoted to finds from Latium where, prior to Romanisation, Etruscan culture was dominant and in places there were even Etruscan kings. In the last room of all are objects showing Etruscan cultural influence, from the areas we know today as Umbria and the Marche.

We now ascend the staircase which brings us to the series of 'antiquariums' on the upper floor. The first four rooms are devoted to bronzes. Many of these come from the famous Castellani and Kircher collections; the latter was begun in the seventeenth century, and was formerly housed in the Collegio Romano. The bronzes are arranged as far as possible in chronological order; they date from the eighth to the first centuries BC. Among the fascinating statuettes in the second room is an appealing little group of the fourth century BC from Arezzo of a peasant ploughing with oxen. The next room contains helmets, greaves, horse bits, razors, strigils and the curious cage-like bags, carried by athletes, to hold the sand with which they rubbed themselves down. Following this is a room largely devoted to objects of feminine interest—the characteristic cylindrical-shaped cists were the equivalent of a modern make-up box. Many of these are beautifully decorated, as are also the bronze mirrors. Finally we come to the room containing a most delightful collection of candelabra; a particularly attractive one is supported by a dancing figure.

The last three rooms of this part of the antiquarium are devoted to objects made of glass, wood and terracotta. In the first of these are charming little wooden boxes in the form of animals and birds, used for their toilet by ladies of the fourth to the second centuries BC. There is even a wooden comb, and glass boxes for face creams. In a case on the left, among a collection of votive figurines, an enchanting little hedgehog begs the question, was it an ornament? a toy? or a votive offering of some kind? Among the terracottas in the next room are two fascinating plates painted with fish, of species easily recognisable to any Mediterranean under-water fishing expert. The small cavity in the centre suggests that these were designed for some Etruscan hors d'oeuvre or fish dish, served with a special sauce. The last room in this section contains five small funerary urns, resembling in miniature the sarcophagus of the 'Bride and Bridegroom'. The curious reproductions of parts of the human body, such as eyes, feet, etc., in a case in this room, were votive offerings at the shrine of some health-giving god or goddess.

A flight of stairs now leads us into a large semicircular gallery containing part of the wonderful collection of ceramics given by Augusto Castellani to the Italian State in 1919. So vast is the collection, including as it does painted and decorated vases, cups and ewers from Greece and many parts of Italy, and so beautiful almost every object in it, that selection is really too invidious a task. Looking at this bewildering array, our minds go back to Keats's small room with which we began our morning's walk. Inevitably so, because his 'Ode on a Grecian Urn', interpret the artists' genius and our own thoughts far better than the prosaic phrases of any catalogue.

A passage and more stairs now lead us into four large rooms devoted to objects found in the Falerii area; in the first of these, No. 25, we are again confronted with such an embarrassment of riches as to defy selection. For its historic interest, however, a note is indicated about the plate in the first case upon which a mother elephant and her baby are portrayed. On her back is a tower filled with soldiers; from her small size in relation to these, and the Phrygian cap of her 'mahout', it has been deduced that she is an Asian elephant (her ears are also small like those of Asian as opposed to African elephants). It is believed that this design may have been inspired by the elephants which Pyrrhus employed in his wars against the Romans, by means of one of which, as we have seen, he tried to frighten the redoubtable G. Fabricius Luscinus. The plate is dated to a period shortly after this event, the middle of the third century BC.

Making our way through these rooms, we are inevitably struck by the number of musicians and dancing scenes encountered in the decoration of the ceramics. Although the Falisci, the people who inhabited the area where they were found, constituted a buffer state between the Etruscans and the Latins, their culture was essentially Etruscan, and they evidently shared the Etruscan passion for music and dancing. We have seen how the Etruscans even cooked to the sound of the double flute; an instrument familiar to most of us from reproductions of the tomb paintings. After the flute, the zither and lyre seem to have been the preferred Etruscan instruments; but they also possessed three kinds of trumpets, whose use in war was adopted by the Romans.

The Romans, however, do not seem to have been so proficient with the unmartial flute. In any case the flautists in Rome, who accompanied with their music the ritual of the temple sacrifices, were all Etruscans. They enjoyed a monopoly of this art and even had their own 'college', or what today we would call a trade union. Trade unions do not seem to have differed much throughout the ages; on one occasion the Etruscan flautists' union struck—because they had been refused their traditional banquet on the Capitol. They departed in a body to Tibur, the modern Tivoli. Even the mighty Senate was driven to resort to a ruse; according to Livy, knowing the Etruscan partiality for drink, they persuaded the people of Tibur to invite the flautists to a banquet and ply them with wine. When they were all dead drunk, they were piled on to chariots, and only woke up when they were deposited in the

Forum. Rarely do we see an Etruscan banquet scene in which a musician is not portrayed. But what is much more odd, the Etruscans boxed and even chastised their slaves to the sound of music. They are said too to have charmed animals in the hunting field by this means. Inevitably one is driven to the conclusion that silence must have been as rare in ancient Etruria as in modern Italy, with its television and transistors.

Dancing is almost as frequently represented in Etruscan tomb paintings and decoration as are musicians. There were three kinds—sacred, profane and war dances. In the wild Bacchic dances, Silenus or satyrs and maenads are first portrayed dancing side by side before the maenad is finally carried off on her partner's shoulder. Women dancers used castanets and gestured with their hands much like the Balinese dancers of today. The names of two Etruscan dances have come down to us through the Romans; the *tripudium* which was danced in three time and the foot stamped thrice on the ground; and the *troia*, a war dance which was revived during Augustus's reign. Etruscan dancers who came to Rome called themselves in their own tongue *ister*; which became Latinised as *histrio*; from which our own word histrionic is derived.

We now come to the balcony, overlooking the room where fragments of terracotta sculptures and decorations from four temples of the Falerii area have been most skilfully recomposed on the opposite wall. Photographic panels showing a plan of the city and surrounding country, and the temples themselves, hang in the room. After the famous sculptures of Veii this is perhaps the most interesting exhibit in the museum. The terracottas are of extraordinary loveliness, especially the Hellenistic ones from the 'Temple of Apollo'. The exhibits are so well arranged and photographically documented as to be remarkably easy to follow.

We now come to three rooms devoted to the temples and tombs of the cities of Latium. They were all quite near Rome, and many of their ancient names have a familiar ring as they are not much changed today—Tibur (Tivoli), Praeneste (Palestrina), Aricia (Ariccia), Velitrae (Velletri), Ardea (Ardea). Only Satricum, now Conca, has completely changed; it stood near Anzio. The first two rooms, Nos. 30 and 31, are devoted to finds from this area generally; the third large one, No. 33, to Satricum and its great Temple of the Mater Matuta (the Dawn Mother). The temple apparently originated in the seventh century BC and existed until the end of the third or beginning of the second century BC, when it was destroyed by lightning. Even from the few surviving fragments of its terracotta decoration, it is possible to imagine the importance and beauty of this temple; while the vast number of votive offerings bear witness to the popularity of the mother-goddess cult. These include representations of doves and pomegranates (revealing the very ancient origins of both as religious symbols); also small family groups of devotees, usually represented sitting together—sometimes as many as seven—on a settee.

Room No. 33, the last but one of the itinerary, is devoted to finds from Praeneste. It contains the fabulous treasures in gold, silver and ivory, discovered there in two tombs of the seventh century BC, usually called after their former owners the Barberini and Bernardini. These, more than anything else in the museum, bring home to us the riches and luxury which were enjoyed at this early period in Italy. The jewellery bears witness to a remarkable technical knowledge of the goldsmith's craft—filigree, repoussé and granulation were all employed. The means whereby, in this last, thousands of tiny granules of gold were cemented on to ornaments is a secret to which even modern science has been unable to discover the answer. It is possible that these wonderful jewels were of Greek workmanship; but the ladies of Praeneste in the seventh century BC had the taste to appreciate and their husbands the means to buy them. Nor were gold and silver limited to personal adornment, as the magnificent cups and dishes bear witness. Ivory too was plentifully used for vessels and ornaments; it is believed that the curiously carved ivories representing human arms and hands served as handles for objects which must have perished. From the number of bronze mirrors, cists, bronze-covered wooden or make-up boxes, and pots and jars found in the Praeneste tombs, one receives the impression that the city was the Paris of the day. This is borne out by the fact that the cist was evidently a local speciality—first made at the end of the fifth or beginning of the fourth century BC—so also was a rather elongated type of bronze mirror. The compartments of some small wooden boxes, in the shape of a dove, a deer and a sandalled foot, still contain grains of rouge, tiny sponges and little sticks of charcoal for maquillage.

Hard though it is to tear ourselves away from these fascinatingly human treasures, we must now take a glance at the last room, where a beautiful bronze head of a girl, of the fifth century BC, stands out among other objects from the areas we now know as Umbria and the Marche. Harder still is the thought that we may have to leave Italy possibly without having had the opportunity of seeing something of the 'Etruscan Places' where these treasures were found. It is now, however, possible to make the journey in imagination at least, through the pages of the fascinating *Etruscan Culture, Land and People*, written in collaboration with the King of Sweden by nine Swedish savants. This brings to life the Etruscan civilisation and landscape in a way that no other learned work of its kind has ever done.

Probably by now we will be thinking of our well-earned luncheon. For this we have three alternatives; the first and best on a fine spring or autumn day, is to have come provided with a picnic; and to eat it by a fountain in some quiet corner of the neighbouring park of the Villa Borghese. If we feel like something more substantial, to be eaten in the open or indoors, the restaurant at the Zoo is a good (though more expensive) answer. For either of these we turn right after leaving the Villa Giulia, up the wide Viale delle Belle Arti; the park gates are at the far end. Once inside the park, a short walk up the Viale del Giardino Zoologico brings us to the Zoo entrance. In cold or wet weather we may prefer to take the ED bus, which brings us up the Via Ulisse Aldrovandi and the Viale Gioacchino Rossini. The last stop in this street, just before the Piazza Ungheria, will bring us almost to the door of the Pizzeria Carosi, on the corner of Via Guido d'Arezzo on the right; here we can have either a pizza or a full meal. For a snack and a cup of coffee the Hungaria Bar on the corner of Piazza Ungheria and Viale Liegi is also excellent.

CHAPTER ELEVEN

The Borghese Gallery to Via Vittorio Veneto

❧

As the **Borghese Gallery** is now open all the year round on weekdays from 9 a.m. to 4 p.m., our afternoon excursion will begin with this, one of the most famous sights of Rome. If we have lunched near the Piazza Ungheria, by taking the 53 or 39 bus from there to Via Allegri, a short walk down the Via Pinciana brings us to the gate of the **Villa Borghese Park** adjoining the Casino or Gallery building. After our tour is over we can return to the Via Allegri and take the 56 bus from the nearby corner of the Via Po. This brings us to the bottom of the Via Vittorio Veneto near the Cappucini church of **S. Maria della Concezione** with its macabre cemetery. In winter this last is open till 6.30 p.m. and the church all the year round till 7.30 p.m., so we have plenty of time to look around before finishing the day with an aperitif at one of the smart bars of the Via Veneto. In summer when the church of **Trinità dei Monti** is open from 4 to 6 p.m. we have the alternative of making our way there on foot, via the Via dei Cappuccini and the Via Sistina and then taking tea or a drink on the terrace below the Casino Valadier. On a fine summer day, a walk or a drive in a *carrozza* across the Villa Borghese Park direct to Trinità dei Monti, provides yet another alternative, this can be followed by a visit to the Cappuccini cemetery, which is then open till 7 p.m., by which time the fashion parade in the Via Veneto will be in full swing. As most people come to Rome in the summer we will treat the itinerary in this order.

From whatever direction we have approached the Borghese Gallery, we will have traversed part at least of the park, and some explanation of its history will not come amiss.

The Villa Borghese was primarily the creation of the nephew of Pope Paul V (1605–21), Cardinal Scipione Borghese, who shortly after his uncle's accession began to buy

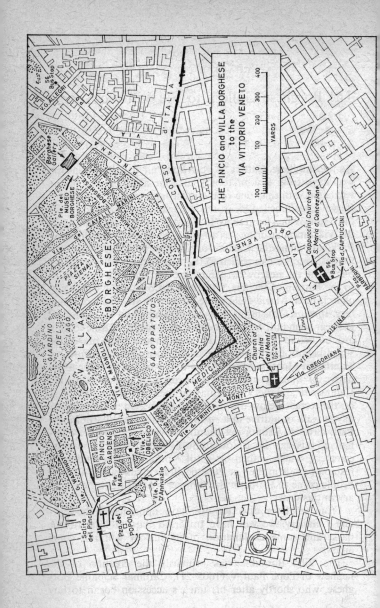

THE PINCIO and VILLA BORGHESE
to the
VIA VITTORIO VENETO

YARDS

100   0   100   200   300   400

56
Bus Stop
V.G. ALLEGRI

Borghese
Gallery

P.le del
MUSEO
BORGHESE

V. PINCIANA

Vle. del
MUSEO
BORGHESE

CORSO d'ITALIA

VIA d'ITALIA

Vle. CAVAL. MARINI

PIAZZA
di SIENA

VILLA   BORGHESE

GIARDINO
DEL
LAGO

Vle. d. MAGNOLIE

GALOPPATOIO

VIA VITTORIO VENETO

Cappuccini Church of
S. Maria d. Concezione

56
Bus Stop

Via d. CAPPUCCINI

BARBERINI

VIA SISTINA

Church of
Trinita
dei Monti

Via GREGORIANA

VILLA   MEDICI

Vle. d. TRINITA d. MONTI

PINCIO
GARDENS

Vle. d.
OBELISCO

P.le
NAP.

Vle. G.
D'Annunzio

Vle. d.
D'Annunzio

Vle. G. WASHINGTON

Salita del Pincio

Pza. del
POPOLO

the land. It was the first of the great Roman park villas, and there is little doubt that its vast layout (already by 1650 the circuit of the walls was some four kilometres) was inspired by that of the Emperor Hadrian at Tivoli. The Villa Borghese consisted in part of formal gardens, largely composed of hedged plots of trees, divided by walks and ornamented with herms and fountains, laid out around the casino and other buildings. But as in Hadrian's Villa there was no overall symmetrical plan; this is in direct contrast to the smaller Renaissance gardens which preceded it and the great parks Le Notre was later to design for Louis XIV. Already, however, the baroque conception of the formal layout gradually merging into the wild made its appearance in the Villa Borghese; also, significantly, by 1700 the first beginnings of an artificially contrived 'natural' landscape. Although conceived on so vast a scale and, in imitation of the classical Roman villas, containing enclosures for ornamental animals and birds—ranging from Indian sheep to lions, and peacocks to ducks—Cardinal Scipione's villa was also well furnished with flower gardens. There was a tulip garden hedged with Dutch roses; secret gardens planted with anemones, narcissus, hyacinths and exotic bulbs; beds of tuberose, carnations, amaranth, also of wild strawberries hedged with jasmine. In the seventeenth century Rome was one of the great horticultural centres of the world.

The gardens of the Villa Borghese today resemble an English landscaped park rather than a formal Italian garden. In fact, in 1773, the Prince Borghese of the day commissioned a Scottish artist, Jacob More, to redesign the layout of the garden in the English landscape style. More, who died in Rome in 1793, was greatly admired by his contemporaries, including Goethe and Reynolds, for his landscape paintings; the latter even comparing him with Claude Lorraine. More collaborated with Camporese in the conversion of the garden, and no doubt they did a good job according to their lights and the fashion of the day. Nevertheless, as a result, the *giardini segreti* on either side of the casino, the small stretch of land between it and the Viale dei Cavalli Marini, and isolated incidents such as the alfresco dining-room, and the 'theatre', are practically all that remain of one of the most interesting Italian baroque gardens ever to have been made.

Like his gardens, Cardinal Scipione modelled his casino on

the villas of classical Rome, using it as a museum for the display of his remarkable collection of antique sculpture; though, unlike the ancient Romans, he never intended it to be lived in, any more than Pope Julius III's Villa Giulia. Indeed the whole of this vast layout was simply meant to be used for a day or an evening's diversion and entertaining. After he had bought a sizeable piece of land, the cardinal commissioned the Flemish architect Ivan van Santen, who Italianised his name as Giovanni Vasanzio, to build the casino; it was begun in 1613 and completed three years later. The surrounding gardens and plantations must already have been well advanced by 1614, as in the summer of that year a banquet was given for the Spanish Ambassador in the alfresco dining-room; a circular building which still survives beside the Via Pinciana. After Cardinal Scipione's death, family interest in the villa and its collections waned somewhat until the middle of the eighteenth century. Then Marcantonio Borghese commissioned the architect Antonio Asprucci and a host of artists to restore and redecorate the casino, again filling it with sculptures. In fact the interior as we see it today is largely the work of this period. During the lifetime of Pauline Bonaparte's husband, Prince Camillo, the villa underwent another eclipse. Between 1801 and 1809 he sold many of the pictures to Napoleon, and exchanged 200 of the most famous classical sculptures for an estate in Piedmont; they are still in the Louvre. Another family collector, Francesco Borghese, reconstituted the collection in the first half of the nineteenth century, making good many of the gaps and introducing some colourful Roman mosaics, found near Tusculum, into the floor of the main hall. Finally in 1891, the pictures were brought from the famous gallery in Palazzo Borghese to the casino; and in 1902 the whole villa and its contents were bought by the State.

Although the façade of the casino was stripped of its reliefs early in the nineteenth century, and the balustrade, statues and fountains surrounding the *piazzale* in front of it are only copies of the originals (sold at the end of the last century to Viscount Astor for Cliveden), this part of the villa has changed less in appearance than most of the rest. In the portico there are two fragments of reliefs (numbered XXV), of particular interest to the English traveller; they once decorated the triumphal arch of Claudius, erected to commemorate his victories in Britain (they are the large pieces above the niches on the right and left)—the same from which we have already seen a fragmentary inscription on the Capitol. As well as numerous classical statues and reliefs, the portico contains a remarkably efficient coffee and snack bar. It is a pity that more Roman museum authorities do not follow this excellent example; it is remarkable how one's flagging aesthetic sense revives after a good *Espresso*.

The **Borghese Gallery**, apart from the Vatican Museum, is probably the collection we have heard most about before coming to Rome. Justifiably so, as it was probably the finest non-royal private collection in the world. It also has the enormous advantage of not being very large; thus, although the gallery contains many pictures of importance, one's artistic appreciation is not blunted by wandering past what seem like miles of second-rate ones, before arriving at what one really wants to see. The great treasures are the works of Raphael, Titian and Correggio; there are also some fine Caravaggios; among the sculptures the young Bernini's David, and Apollo and Daphne, excel any of the antique ones, or for that matter Canova's celebrated rendering of Pauline Bonaparte as Venus. The remarkable thing about this is that most of these outstanding works formed part of Cardinal Scipione Borghese's original collection. Evidently he possessed an unerring eye for works of art; and not only for the paintings of great masters of the past like Raphael and Titian. He bought with equal enthusiasm Caravaggio's pictures which had been refused by those who had commissioned them, and was one of the first to recognise the genius of young Gian Lorenzo Bernini.

One cannot help wondering what Cardinal Scipione would have made of the main hall of his villa today; to our present taste its combination of coloured marbles, frescoes and sculptures is a trifle overwhelming. The third-century mosaics discovered in one of the Borghese estates at Torrenuova are, however, interesting if gruesome. They represent the famous games in the arena in all their savage cruelty—mailed gladiators fighting one another and with ferocious animals. From their diversified physiognomy, it is evident that these are actual portraits; possibly even portrayals of real combats. The first letter of the Greek word for death (*thanatos*), the θ, beside those who have been worsted in combat, signifies that they had been condemned to death by the terrible 'thumbs down' gesture of the watching crowd. The names given beside most of the figures are evidently *noms de guerre*; one of them, Licentiosus, was obviously well-calculated to appeal to a certain type of Roman woman, like the Senator's wife who ran away with a gladiator called Sergius whom Juvenal pilloried in some caustic verses.

In the first room on the right (room I), Pauline Bonaparte queens it as she must so often have done—in slightly less revealing dress—in this same villa. So many stories have been told about this statue (No. LIV), which is Canova's masterpiece, that one wonders how many are really true and how many, in the Roman phrase, *ben trovato*. Certainly in her youth, when the statue was executed, her reply 'Oh, but the studio was heated', to the lady who asked how she could have posed thus, seems to be in character. But apparently the legend that her husband, who was remarkably broad-minded about her behaviour, was so jealous of her statue that he kept it locked up, is not founded on fact. Later in life, after they had separated, it was Pauline who remonstrated with him for letting people see it, as she said she had meant it to be for his pleasure alone. The resulting seclusion of his greatest work was something Canova found hard to bear; but on occasion he was allowed to show it to a select few. This he preferred to do at night, by the light of a single candle. When the gallery is open on summer nights (Note. Formerly, this was a regular weekly practice, unfortunately suspended for the present.), it is well worth asking the attendant to see the statue by *chiar di luna* (moonlight). All the other lights in the room are switched off, and Pauline appears faintly illuminated as by the light of the moon; an effect which would probably have appealed to the sculptor.

In the next room (room II), it is Bernini's 'David' (No. LXXVII) that dominates the scene. This was specially executed for his patron Cardinal Scipione, in 1623–4, when the sculptor was only 25; the head is a self-portrait. With its almost incredible sense of vigour and movement, this figure represents a revolution in art; as one of the earliest baroque statues it presages the change of taste which was to sweep all Europe. Again in the following room (room III), Bernini's 'Apollo and Daphne' (No. CV), made in the year following the 'David', instantly rivets our attention to the exclusion of all else. The group is intended to be seen from the left-hand side. The Barberini arms of an eagle and a dragon are sculpted in relief on each side of the base, beneath Latin inscriptions. That on the left, with the eagle, is from Ovid. That on the right, with the dragon, was composed by Cardinal Scipione for a friend of his, in order to draw a Christian moral from the pagan legend. The lines are a warning against the pursuit of pleasure, which even if attained bears bitter fruit like Daphne's laurel. *Bon viveur* that he was, Cardinal Scipione could not entirely escape from the somewhat prudish Counter-Reformation world in which he lived, whose art forms had originally been dictated by the Council of Trent. The group can also be seen at night by *chiar di luna* lighting.

Passing through a small room which was originally a chapel, we find ourselves in the resplendent *Sala degli Imperatori* (room IV). Though again somewhat overwhelming, this room is a perfect period piece, representing a truly Roman taste for splendour, characteristic of the eighteenth century. Although the same artists were responsible for the decoration as in the great hall, here the prevailing tones of the porphyry and ala-baster—exemplified in the seventeenth-century busts of the Roman emperors from which the room takes its name—pro-vide a unity which there is lacking. This room also contains two of Bernini's works; one is a small bronze of 'Neptune and Triton' (a recent acquisition, numbered differently, No. 7386), very similar to the large marble group of 1620 now in the Victoria and Albert Museum in London. The other is the 'Rape of Proserpina' (No. CCLXVII), of 1621-2; although displaying great technical virtuosity—note the hand of Pluto sinking into Proserpina's soft flesh—this shows that Bernini had not as yet escaped from the mannerist past; some authori-ties even see his father's hand in the composition.

The next room (room V) contains the 'Sleeping Herma-phrodite' (No. CLXXII); this is not the famous one of the original collection, which was among the sculptures sold by Prince Camillo to Napoleon and is now in the Louvre; but a much restored later copy of the Hellenistic original. In this room there is also a fine Greek archaic head of a girl of the sixth century BC (No. CLXXXI, the bust is a Roman addi-tion); also a supposed bust of Sappho (CLXXIV), copied from a Greek one of the fifth century BC.

Works by Bernini father and son stand in the following room (room VI). In the centre is Pietro Bernini's 'Aeneas and Anchises' (No. CLXXXII); against the wall stands Gian

Lorenzo's unfinished 'Truth' (not numbered), which was to be part of a large group representing Truth being unveiled by Time. This figure lacks the fire of Bernini's other works, and in fact it was undertaken at a time of profound discouragement for the artist. After the death of his great patron the Barberini Pope, Urban VIII, in 1644, Bernini failed to find favour with the Pamphilj successor, Innocent X—there was no love lost between the Barberini and Pamphilj families. His brilliant design for the 'Fountain of the Four Rivers' in the Piazza Navona, however, resulted in Bernini's return to papal favour. Later he had neither the time, nor possibly the inclination, to finish the group. This formerly stood in his own house in the Corso and, as the inscription indicates, he wished that it should serve as an admonition to his descendants, to whom it still belongs.

In the centre of room VII stands the group of a young man on a dolphin (No. CC), believed to have inspired Raphael's design for the figure of 'Jonah and the Whale' which we saw this morning in the Chigi chapel of S. Maria del Popolo. It dates from early in the second century AD and was probably intended for a fountain; the satyr's head is a later addition. In the same room there is a fine Greek archaic statue of a young woman (No. CCXVI). Although also ancient, the head is from another statue and has been much restored. A nineteenth-century restoration has greatly altered the character of the 'Dancing Satyr' (No. CCXXV), standing in the centre of the next room (room VIII). Originally he would have held a double flute instead of cymbals; even so the mischievous charm of the Greek bronze original, of the school of Lysippus, still lives in this Roman copy.

We now retrace our steps to the Sala degli Imperatori, where a door in the far left-hand corner leads to the staircase and the upper floor. Here twenty rooms, some of them quite small, house the famous Borghese collection of pictures. The first room we enter (No. IX, opposite the top of the stairs) contains some of the most important pictures in the collection. No less than three Raphaels; a 'Deposition' (No. 369), signed and dated 1507, was commissioned by Atlanta Baglioni, as a memorial of her son who had been killed in a struggle to gain power in Perugia. The portrait of 'An Unknown Man' (No. 371) was for long believed to be by Holbein; but the removal of overpainting confirmed Raphael's authorship, as given in the old inventories. The portrait of 'A Young Woman' with a little unicorn (No. 371) had also been painted over to represent St. Catherine; again restoration revealed its true authorship, particularly the beautiful handling of the red velvet and the jewel. The 'Madonna and the Child' with the three vases of flowers behind her (No. 348) is by Botticelli; even if it is not one of his great works, it possesses all his spontaneous charm. This room also contains a beautiful Pinturicchio 'Crucifixion' (No. 377), showing St. Christopher fording the river with the Child on his shoulder, and a lovely Italian landscape in the background.

Room X contains the curious Cranach 'Venus' with Cupid holding a honeycomb (No. 326). One of the many variations on this subject painted by the artist; it also formed part of Cardinal Scipione's original collection. The rest of the pictures in this room are by Italian artists of the fifteenth and sixteenth centuries; notable among them is the Andrea del Sarto 'Madonna and Child with St. John the Baptist' (No. 334).

We now return to the stairs and the three small rooms on the right. The first of these (room XI) is also, with the exception of three small landscapes, devoted to the work of Italian artists of the fifteenth and sixteenth centuries. In it are two strikingly different pictures by Lorenzo Lotto. One, a superb self-portait (No. 185), shows him as a bearded man in black velvet. There is a strange melancholy about the picture, enhanced by the curious motif of a tiny skull lying among jasmine flowers and rose petals under his right hand. The other is a touchingly homely 'Virgin and Child with Saints' (No. 193); but here again the artist has introduced a strange symbol—a pierced heart with the letters IHS, which the Bishop on the left holds out to the Child. In the same room is Girolamo Savoldo's lovely 'Tobias and the Angel' (No. 547), whose marvellous tones of silver grey and red make an instant appeal.

The next room to contain a really outstanding group of pictures is No. XIV; these are of a later period, being mostly seventeenth-century works. Facing us at the far end of the room is Domenichino's 'Diana' (No. 53), familiar from so many reproductions. Cardinal Scipione was so enamoured of this picture that he had it removed by main force from the artist's studio. Time has confirmed his judgment; it is one of the most famous pictures in the gallery. Time has also confirmed his judgment of Caravaggio's 'Madonna of the Palafrenieri', or 'Madonna of the Serpent' (No. 110). Because of its uninhibited realism, the canons of St. Peter's refused to allow the Confraternity of the Palafrenieri, who had commissioned it in 1605, to hang it in their chapel in the basilica. Caravaggio had his revenge when the favourite nephew of the pope bought it and hung it in a place of honour in his own collection. Though artistically not on a par with this last, two very early works by Caravaggio, hanging by the window are of interest. The 'Boy with the Basket of Fruit (No. 136) resembles the famous one in the Ambrosiana in Milan, while the other, also with a basket of fruit, but known as 'Il bacchino malato' (the young Bacchus, ill) (No. 534), is said to be a self-portrait painted when the artist had malaria. Of far greater power is the 'David with Goliath's Head' (No. 455); according to an old inventory Goliath's head was also a self-portrait. Almost unrecognisable as a work of Caravaggio, owing to retouching during the last century, is the 'St. John the Baptist in the Desert' (No. 267) hanging on the opposite wall. This room also contains several sculptures by Bernini including a portrait bust of Cardinal Scipione (No. CCLXV). Of greater historical than artistic interest is Bernini's terracotta model for the proposed equestrian statue of Louis XIV; ultimately this proved to be yet another disappointment, like the rest of his French projects.

Room XV contains a fine Rubens 'Deposition' (No. 411), executed during his stay in Rome in 1605. Also two interesting Bernini self-portraits, as a young man about 1625 (No. 554) and another painted about twelve years later (No. 545). In the next room (room XVI) there is a picture of a sleeping 'Venus' by Savoldo (No. 30), with a wonderful Italian landscape at sunset in the background. After room XVIII, which contains some remarkable Dutch pictures, we come to room XIX, where Correggio's 'Danae' (No. 125) overwhelms us with its wonderful rendering of white draperies and flesh tints. The light from the golden shower, into which Jove transformed himself in order to penetrate Danae's tower, bathes the whole picture with its radiance. The picture had a more adventurous career than most of the others in the gallery; it was commissioned by the Duke of Mantua as a gift for the Emperor Charles V, on the occasion of his coronation at Bologna. It journeyed to Prague and then to Stockholm; Queen Christina brought it back to Rome, but it did not remain there; subsequent journeys took it to London and to Paris. Finally it was bought by Prince Borghese in 1823 for 285 pounds and brought back to his family palace in Rome. The other outstanding picture in the room is Dosso Dossi's mysterious 'Circe' (No. 217 on the opposite wall), dressed in robes of almost oriental brilliance, with a turban on her head. Cardinal Scipione appears to have been particularly attracted by the work of this artist, as no less than six pictures by him, and three by his brother, hang in the room. Although Dossi was born in 1489 and died in 1542, there is an extraordinarily modern, almost impressionist, quality about some of the details of his work, particularly the light falling upon trees and the sheep in the 'Madonna and Child' (No. 211), also in the background of the 'Diana and Calisto' (No. 304).

Finally we come to the last room (room XX); in it hangs the greatest treasure of the whole collection—Titian's 'Sacred and Profane Love' (No. 147). The picture is so familiar as to need no description; though no reproduction prepares one for the wonderful colour and the warm clear light which gives the picture its atmosphere of tranquillity. It is known to have been painted about 1512 for the Aurelia family, whose arms appear on the classical sarcophagus which serves as a fountain; but the interpretation of the subject is a mystery which has exercised many minds. At different times the picture has been called 'Venus and Medea', 'Beauty Adorned and Disadorned', 'Heavenly and Earthly Love'. What seems to be certain is that it is an allegory of spring; it is now believed that it represents an episode from Francesco Colonna's strange dream romance, the *Hypnerotomachia of Poliphilo*— the same book from which the curious motif of Bernini's 'Elephant' with the obelisk upon his back—which we saw in the Piazza of the Minerva—was also taken. Having reached the culmination, as it were of the whole gallery, it seems an anticlimax to speak of anything else; but two other very fine Titians—'S. Dominic' (No. 188) and 'Venus Blindfolding Love' (No. 170)—also hang in the room.

During our walk or drive across the Villa Borghese Park we should make a point of seeing the Piazza di Siena, a grassy hippodrome surrounded by magnificent stone pines, where the Horse Show is held annually in May, and the Giardino del Lago, a charming landscape garden with an artificial lake and picturesque 'Temple of Aesculapius'. The entrance to the Giardino del Lago is not far from a *rond point* which has to be traversed in order to reach a road, bordered with fine *Magnolia grandiflora*, which we must not miss as it is the only one which connects the Villa Borghese with the **Pincio Gardens**, by means of a viaduct. Once across the viaduct we find ourselves in a wide avenue, the Viale dell' Obelisco. The obelisk from which this takes its name is not really an Egyptian one, but a Roman pastiche originally designed for the Emperor Hadrian, to commemorate his favourite Antinous, who was drowned in the Nile in AD 131. It was re-erected here by Pius VII in 1822.

Although the Pincio Gardens we see today were only laid out early in the last century, in classical times the hill was famous for its gardens; its present name being derived from the late imperial Pincian palace, where Belisarius lived in 537. Originally it was simply known as the Hill of Gardens, the most renowned of these being the Gardens of Lucullus, who was the first man to convert its slopes into a magnificent series of terraces in the Roman style. Probably it was here that Lucullus played his famous trick on Cicero and Pompey, when they asked to take pot luck with him, telling a slave to prepare dinner in the Apollo room. Unknown to his friends, this was the pre-arranged signal for a sumptuous banquet to the tune of 50,000 drachmas.

We now continue to the end of the Viale dell' Obelisco and a right turn brings us out on to the great terrace known as the **Piazzale Napoleone I**. This commands one of the most famous views in Rome, dominated by the cupola of St. Peter's, seen slightly to the left across the river. We can also see, farther to the left, the domes of several of the churches which we have visited during our walks; conspicuous among them are S. Carlo al Corso in the foreground, and S. Giovanni dei Fiorentini and S. Andrea della Valle in the distance. Still farther to the left, the high tower of the Palazzo del Senatore on the Capitol is just visible beside the conspicuously white Vittorio Emanuele Monument. Closer at hand, in the midst of the old city, the great hump-backed dome of the Pantheon can be seen unromantically silhouetted against the gasometer in the far distance.

The evening is the classic hour for a stroll on the Pincio,

aptly described by Miss Thackeray in the last century as then appearing in 'a fashionable halo of sunset and pink parasols'; when all the church bells are ringing for the Ava Maria. Incidentally, for non-Roman Catholics, the frequent pealing of Roman church bells may require some explanation. Light sleepers may well have been awakened by their ringing for early Masses at 7 a.m.; these continue at intervals through the morning till midday, when they ring again for the Angelus. Comparative silence then reigns among church bells— though monastery ones may toll in the interval—until the evening and the Ava Maria; to be followed, one hour after darkness, by the last peals announcing the final service of *Un' Ora di Notte* (the first hour of the night).

Turning our backs on the Piazzale Napoleone I, we now take the road sloping down the hill, the Viale Trinità dei Monti, which is shaded by fine old ilex for most of its length until we arrive at the **Villa Medici.** Just before we reach the villa we see a column with an inscription commemorating the fact that Galileo was imprisoned there from 1630 to 1633 by order of the Inquisition. Close by is the gate to the **Gardens of the Villa Medici,** but as these are now unfortunately only open on Wednesday mornings from 9 to 11 a.m., we will have to return to see them on that day.

When Galileo was imprisoned in the Villa Medici, it belonged to the grand dukes of Tuscany, having been purchased by Cardinal Ferdinando de' Medici in 1580. It was designed by Annibale Lippi for Cardinal Ricci in 1544; the austere façade, which we see from the street, having remained unchanged since that date.

The beautiful fountain standing in front of it originally had a Florentine lily in the centre. This was replaced by the existing stone cannon ball after Queen Christina of Sweden had tried her hand at firing one of the cannons of the Castel S. Angelo. Instead of aiming harmlessly into the air, the queen let fire at random, hitting the Villa Medici; the ball was placed in its present position as a memento of her somewhat erratic marksmanship.

Since it was purchased by Napoleon in 1803, the Villa Medici has housed the French Academy, the doyen of all the foreign schools of art and archaeology in Rome. This was founded in 1666, by Colbert, by order of Louis XIV; originally the *pensionnaires du Roi*, as they were called, were lodged near S. Onofrio on the Janiculum; later they moved to Palazzo Salviati in the Corso. Some of the greatest names in French artistic life have been associated with the Academy, from Poussin and Le Brun who were consulted by Colbert at its foundation, to Vernet and Ingres who were among its directors; while Subleyras, Natoire, Boucher, Fragonard, Prud'hon, Berlioz and Debussy were numbered among its many famous *pensionnaires*.

We now enter the garden by the gate on the left of the villa and, after climbing a steepish slope, find ourselves on the edge of the great *bosco*. Though the planting here, and in the garden generally, has considerably changed its aspect, the ground plan is the same as when it was first laid out. In this the Villa Medici is unique in Rome, and it is fascinating to think that we are treading the self-same paths as Velazquez, who lived here in 1650 and painted the two exquisite little garden pictures now in the Prado. John Evelyn, too, was here in 1644, but for once was more interested in the famous sculptures which the garden then contained than in its planting; most of these were subsequently transferred to Florence.

Today four-fifths of the garden are taken up by the *bosco*, where hedged walks lead in stately fashion to small pavilions and other view points, beneath the welcome shade of stone pines and immemorial ilex. Their intersections widen out to form circular spaces in characteristic Renaissance style; these are punctuated by marble herms and lined with low stone benches, forming in fact the typical background of the *fête champêtre* beloved of French eighteenth-century artists. A large open space and parterres lie directly behind the house itself; this is in accordance with the Renaissance idea of symmetry, which required a built-up area to be balanced by an open space. The garden façade of the villa was greatly altered by Cardinal Ferdinando de' Medici, who relieved its severity by the insertion of classical reliefs. Many of these came from Cardinal della Valle's collection, which he had bought in 1584. The fragments with the exquisite garland swags, between the windows on the left and right, recall those of the Ara Pacis. The statue of Mercury standing in the fountain before the loggia, so much admired by John Evelyn, is in fact a copy of Giambologna's original, which had also migrated to Florence. The one really important sculpture remaining in the garden is the head of a statue of Meleager; standing by the loggia which supports the terrace on the right, this is attributed to Scopas; the body is modern. Behind this a flight of steps leads to a shady terrace walk, with a superb view over the garden. From here a path, traversing a smaller *bosco*, brings us to the little artificial mount, crowned in Evelyn's day with a summer house and fountain.

On leaving Villa Medici, we continue along the Viale Trinità dei Monti, arriving shortly at the church from which it takes its name. The church of **Trinità dei Monti** was originally built as the conventual church for the monastery of the Minims of St. Francis of Paula; it was begun in 1495. When he was in Rome in the previous year, King Charles VIII of France gave 347 golden scudi for its construction. Successive popes, kings of France and cardinals subscribed to its building and to that of the monastery. The striking façade, with its twin belfries, was not completed for another century. The interior of the church is of particular interest to students of the work of Daniele da Volterra, as it contains two large works by his hand of the 'Assumption' and 'Deposition'; these are, however, very badly damaged. In 1828, convent and church were given by King Charles X to the Order of the Sacré Coeur, to whom they still belong.

The church of Trinità dei Monti is one of the landmarks of Rome; this morning we saw it soaring up above the Piazza di Spagna, as the culminating point in the whole of that fascinating townscape; now we look down over the Spanish Steps to an almost equally dramatic view of the city. In the foreground is the Roman obelisk, made in the Egyptian style for the Gardens of Sallust; this was re-erected here in 1789 by Pius VI. We now turn left into the little piazza by the Hassler Hotel. Directly in front of us, on the corner separating the Via Sistina from the Via Gregoriana, is a house with a delightful little rounded portico. This is believed to have been designed by Filippo Juvara in 1711, for the widowed Queen Maria Casimira of Poland. The house itself is said to have been built in the sixteenth century by the artist Federico Zuccari; the door of its main Via Gregoriana façade is made to represent the face of a monster. The famous German archaeologist Winckelmann lived here later in the eighteenth century, so did Angelica Kauffman; it is now the seat of the Hertziana Library. Salvator Rosa, whose romantic landscapes made such an impression on English travellers, lived and died in the house next door in 1673. In fact Via Gregoriana probably holds the palm, even in Rome, for the number of famous people who have lived there at one time or another. These include Francesco da Volterra, Poussin, Sereux d'Agincourt, Gregorovius, Lamartine, Francesco Crispi and d'Annunzio.

We now turn down the Via Sistina—the only part of Sixtus V's road leading to S. Maria Maggiore still to bear his name; after Piazza Barberini it is called Via Quattro Fontane, and after the Via Nazionale, Via Agostino Depretis. The second turn on the left, the Via dei Cappuccini, will bring us to the Via Veneto exactly opposite the church of S. Maria della Concezione and the Cappuccini cemetery.

Until 1887, when the beautiful Villa Ludovisi was destroyed to make way for the Via Veneto and the Ludovisi quarter, the Cappuccini church stood in a quiet cul-de-sac surrounded by gardens—a much more suitable setting for a Capuchin monastery than the hurly-burly of today. But with typically Roman philosophic attitude to the changing world about them, the friars have evidently decided to 'make up on the swings' what they have lost in the way of peace and tranquillity—their macabre cemetery under the church is, strangely, one of the tourist draws of Rome.

Very few tourists today go to the church to see anything else, but in Victorian times Guido Reni's 'St. Michael Trampling on the Devil' (in the first chapel on the right) was one of the sights of Rome. According to a malicious legend, the face of the devil is a portrait of Innocent X, who was apparently hated by the artist. This would not be impossible, as the church was peculiarly a Barberini preserve; there was so little love lost between the two families that when the Pamphilj pope was elected, two of the Barberini cardinals fled to the court of France. A painting portraying their reception there by Louis XIV as a child formed part of the family collection. S. Maria della Concezione was designed by Casoni, and built about 1624, for Urban VIII's older brother Cardinal Antonio Barberini, who was a Capuchin friar. He seems to have been of a very different type from the rest of his family, who were renowned for their prodigality and love of splendour. His tombstone—which is let into the pavement before the main altar—bears no name or title; simply the Latin epitaph '*hic jacet pulvis cinis et nihil*' (here lie dust, ashes and nothing). For all his austerity, Cardinal Antonio possessed the family capacity for recognising genius when he saw it—and the personal humility to award it its due. When young John Milton came to Rome in 1638, he was introduced to the cardinal by the Vatican librarian, the learned Lucas Holsteinius. Milton was invited to a musical party at the Palazzo Barberini, where the cardinal did him the signal honour of coming personally to the door to meet him, again accompanying him when he left. The recent discovery in the Barberini archives of the original thank-you letter which the poet addressed—in elegant Latin—to the cardinal on this occasion casts an interesting light on Milton's character. Milton himself later published a slightly amended version of this letter; it was a great deal less fulsome in its thanks than the one he really wrote to Cardinal Antonio.

A door to the right of the main altar leads to a lobby from which stairs descend into the five chapels of the crypt, arranged as a cemetery. The earth was brought here from the Holy Land, and originally the friars were actually buried in it. When it was full, their remains were disinterred to make room for their successors; the bones of no less than 4,000 of them cover the vaults and walls with a macabre baroque decoration. Niches contain the entire skeletons of some of the most devout brethren, enveloped in their cowled robes. Burial here was considered to be a great honour; among the bones one sees one or two children's skeletons—they are the remains of scions of noble families who died in infancy.

The Cappuccini church had other claims to fame, however, during the last century. Then the people attributed to the friars the magical power of being able to foretell the winning numbers of the lottery. One of them, Friar Pacifico, was so expert that he was known to all and sundry as 'the wizard'. A constant stream of 'penitents' filled the church; they were in fact the city's gamblers hoping for a tip; things came to such a pass that Pope Gregory XVI (1831–46) himself had to intervene. Poor Friar Pacifico was forbidden ever again to exercise his magic gift, and was banished from Rome. He was accompanied by a large crowd to Piazza del Popolo; there, by an adroit play upon words, he managed to combine a tearful speech of farewell to Rome with the announcement of the five winning numbers of the next lottery.

This jovial friar would have felt very much at home in the **Via Veneto** today—he liked the gay life, pretty women and his food; as everyone knows, the street has now become the centre of the gay night life of the city. Not all of it, however; the smart part begins at the corner of the Via Boncompagni and stretches to the Porta Pinciana. There is yet another distinction: the left-hand pavement—where Rosati's and the Café de Paris are—is the 'Italian' side; the right-hand one—with Doney's—is foreign and predominantly American. From sunset on a summer evening to one or two in the morning, this short stretch of street presents an even gayer and more lively scene than the Champs Élysées. This is due to the heat of the day when everyone who can stays indoors; and to the Italian—particularly the age-old Roman—love of strolling up and down to gossip and see and to be seen in one's best clothes.

CHAPTER TWELVE

The Corso to Palazzo Barberini

❧

TODAY again we begin our expedition from the familiar ground of Piazza Venezia. It will include a rather mixed bag of sights, but it illustrates perhaps better than any of our previous walks the infinite variety of Rome. The monuments we shall see range in time from the great fourth-century Baths of Diocletian and early Christian monuments, such as the Basilica of S. Agnese fuori le Mura, to Renaissance and baroque palaces and churches; including Palazzo Barberini, the Quirinal, S. Andrea al Quirinale, S. Carlo alle Quattro Fontane, and two small private art collections as well as two of the great national ones. Such, however, are the complications of the opening hours of the various galleries and palaces that it will not be possible to take in all the minor ones on the same day. The Colonna gallery is only open on Saturday mornings; that of the Accademia di S. Luca on Mondays, Wednesdays and Fridays; whereas the state rooms of the Quirinal palace are visible on Thursday afternoons. All these, however, are really of specialised interest; the connoisseur can take his pick of which individual one he wants to see, while the ordinary traveller would be well advised to concentrate his energies on the two great sights—the Barberini Gallery in the morning and the Museo Nazionale Romano in the Baths of Diocletian in the afternoon.

Turning our backs on the Piazza Venezia, we walk down the right-hand side of the Corso, past the somewhat forbidding neo-Florentine façade added to the Palazzo Odescalchi in the last century, and find ourselves in the little enclave of the Piazza di S. Marcello in front of the church of the same name. The church of **S. Marcello** now appears as one of Rome's most elegant baroque creations; but the concave façade is simply an addition made by Carlo Fontana in 1682–3, the origins of the church itself date back to early Christian times.

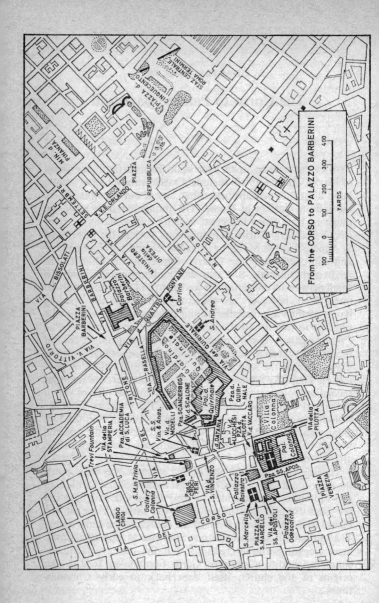

From the CORSO to PALAZZO BARBERINI

According to legend, S. Marcello was originally built over the *Catabulum* or stables of the central post office where the Emperor Maxentius condemned Pope St. Marcellus I (308–9) to work in a menial capacity. An office of this kind certainly did exist in this area of what was then the Via Lata; and the church was already old in 418. But S. Marcello has suffered so many subsequent reconstructions that today it appears as a predominantly baroque building; though it contains a fine gilded ceiling of the sixteenth century and some interesting Renaissance tombs. The most striking is that of Cardinal Michiel and his nephew Bishop Orso, on the left of the main door. The cardinal was poisoned in 1503 in Castel Sant' Angelo, by order of Alexander VI; his effigy is seen reclining in the central arch of the joint tomb, which is attributed to Jacobo Sansovino. Just below, his nephew is portrayed lying on a bier, beneath which are stacked piles of books; a memorial of the 730 precious codices which he bequeathed to the church. In the Middle Ages S. Marcello faced in the opposite direction, the apse probably stood where the door now is, on the Corso side. It was here in 1354 that the body of Cola di Rienzo hung for two days and two nights, until it was taken to the Augusteum and burnt by the Jews.

Leaving S. Marcello, we turn back along the Corso for a few paces, then turn left up the **Via dei SS. Apostoli**, which brings us into the long narrow piazza of the same name. The rather dilapidated palace on the near corner (No. 49) with the name Balestra above the door, was built in 1644 for the Muti-Papazzuri family; but its most famous occupants were the exiled Stuarts. Pope Clement XI (1700–21) rented the palace as a home for the Old Pretender and his Polish bride, Maria Clementina Sobieska. Here in the last week of December, 1720, their son Charles Edward was born; and here after so many tragic vicissitudes he finally returned to die in January 1788. As the end drew near, the wail of the bagpipes playing 'Lochaber no more' echoed through the candle-lit rooms of the Roman palace; and the man who had once been Bonnie Prince Charlie wept remembering the high hopes and terrible end of the '45. At the age of 75 his brother Cardinal Henry beggared himself by giving his entire fortune to the pope to help pay the enormous indemnity demanded by the invading Napoleon, and had himself to flee for his life. Later, though comfortably provided for by a Hanoverian pension, Henry

IX—as he styled himself—never returned to live in the palace which was haunted by so many tragic memories of his family.

Architecturally, the Palazzo Balestra is overshadowed by the other buildings in the piazza—Benini's fine Palazzo Odescalchi on the right, and the **Basilica of the SS. Apostoli** and Palazzo Colonna on the left. Like S. Marcello, the basilica appears today as a mixture of Renaissance, baroque and even neo-classical styles; but in fact it originally dates from the sixth century. But the old church was finally knocked down and rebuilt by Carlo Fontana early in the eighteenth century. The only relics of the original church to have been preserved are eight spirally fluted columns in the Chapel of the Crucifix in the far right-hand corner; though some fine Renaissance tombs of Della Rovere and Riario cardinals have also survived. Several members of both of these related families were closely connected with the basilica, and built palaces on either side of it. That of Cardinal Giuliano Della Rovere (afterwards Pope Julius II), which resembles the Palazzo Venezia, still stands on the left. It is possible that Julius was also responsible for the addition of the fifteenth-century double portico, which constitutes the most impressive feature of the basilica's façade. Today this is something of an architectural pot-pourri; the upper arches were walled in to make windows by Carlo Fontana, and a neo-classical finish provided for the rest by Valadier in 1827. About 1475 a new choir was added to the church, decorated with a singularly beautiful fresco of the 'Last Judgment' by Melozzo da Forli, fragments of which are preserved in the Vatican Gallery and the Quirinal.

If it is a Saturday morning we can now visit the **Gallery of Palazzo Colonna**, entrance at 17 Via della Pilotta, by taking the Via del Vaccaro to the Piazza della Pilotta and turning right into the Via della Pilotta. Before the state and private apartments of Palazzo Doria were opened (previously only the gallery was on view), this was of far greater interest as a sight than it is now, as it was then the only private Roman palace to open some of its rooms as well as the picture gallery to the public. Now, however, it very definitely ranks far behind; but about half an hour will be sufficient to make a rapid tour. Apart from the very fine gallery itself—one of the largest in Rome—only three other small rooms are visible. Unfortunately the effect of these has been largely spoilt by the introduction of highly polished modern marble floors, whose excessive lustre detracts from the faded charm of their baroque decoration and furnishing. The pictures include some family portraits of historic interest, such as that of Vittoria Colonna, the poetess friend of Michelangelo (No. 65); another of Marcantonio Colonna, who was awarded a 'Roman triumph' for his part in the victory of Lepanto (No. 66); and Marie Mancini, Louis XIV's first love who married a seventeenth-century Prince Colonna (No. 224). Artistically the most important pictures are a fine group of landscapes by Poussin (Nos. 105, 106, 108, 120, 128, 130, 132, 133, 134, 136, 139 and 140); a 'Narcissus' by Tintoretto (No. 70); a superb Veronese portrait of 'An Unknown Man' (No. 170); a portrait of Guidobaldo di Montefeltro attributed to Melozzo da Forli (No. 216); the charming primitive 'Madonna del Roseto' by Stefano da Verona (No. 221); and Annibale Carracci's 'Pranzo di un contadino' (a peasant eating beans) (No. 164).

We now turn back along the picturesque **Via della Pilotta**, bridged at intervals by small viaducts connecting the Colonna palace with the gardens ascending the Quirinal Hill. Here, according to medieval legend, stood the tower from which Nero watched Rome burn. Here also, according to a somewhat fanciful fourth-century author, Elagabalus's women's senate sat to discuss such weighty matters as social precedence, who might travel in a litter or coach and who might wear gilded and jewelled shoes. Both stories are connected with a mysterious building known to medieval pilgrims as the emperor's table (*mensa imperatoris*), and later as the Torre di Mesa; probably part of the ruins of Aurelian's Temple of the Sun, remains of which still exist in the gardens.

We cross the **Piazza della Pilotta**, which, like the street, owes its name to a ball game of classical origin, known as '*pilae triagonalis*' from its three players. This was also very popular in Rome in the seventeenth and eighteenth centuries. The whole of the right side of the square is occupied by the modern Pontifical Gregorian University. From here we continue along the Via dei Lucchesi, pausing for a moment to enter the church of S. Croce e S. Bonaventura dei Lucchesi, where two nuns in pale blue and white kneel motionless before the altar in perpetual adoration of the blessed sacrament. Their silent devotion is curiously at variance with the setting, for the baroque decoration of the church—with brocade-curtained galleries like opera boxes—recalls rather the mundane piety of Longhi's '*Nuns' parlour*'.

The Via di S. Vincenzo now brings us to one of the sights of Rome—the famous **Trevi Fountain**—where the entire wall of a palace has been turned into a baroque fantasy of gods and goddesses, tritons and dashing steeds, set among wild rocks, wind-blown trees and a leaping, glistening, rushing cascade of water. One's first reaction is that it is strange to find so vast a decorative fountain designed for so small a space, filling practically all of the little square. On further reflection, however, one realises that it is precisely to this apparent disproportion that it owes so much of its effect. Our surprise at finding this fantastic waterscape tucked away among small back streets adds greatly to our pleasure; although the fountain is world-famous, we enjoy the sensation of personal discovery. This is the secret of its charm and that of much of old baroque Rome; it is also one of the reasons why the modern sectors of the city, built or 'opened up' by the Haussmann and fascist schools of town planning during the last ninety years, appear dull by comparison.

It is most generally agreed that the fountain takes its name from the three streets—the *tre vie*—which meet in the little piazza. The water, however, comes (now once weekly—it is pumped back out of the basin into a tank), from Agrippa's aqueduct, the Acqua Vergine, built in 19 BC. According to legend a young girl—hence the *vergine*, some say her name was Trivia—first showed its source to some thirsty Roman soldiers. These springs rise near Salone, only fourteen miles away from Rome. The aqueduct is therefore the shortest of the ancient ones; this, and the fact that it runs mainly underground, made it the easiest to repair when Martin V started to try and put Rome on its feet again in 1447. After repairing the aqueduct he erected a very simple fountain, more or less on the site of the present one, but facing towards the Piazza dei Crociferi. In the seventeenth century Urban VIII restored the fountain, making the Romans pay for the work by a tax on wine; Pasquin reflected disgusted local feeling in the quip: 'After a thousand taxes on wine, Urban now refreshes the Romans with plain water.'

In fact it was only three centuries later, in 1762, that the fountain of Trevi was finally completed in its present form. Its actual erection took thirty years from the day in 1732 when Clement XII selected Nicola Salvi's project from among those of many other famous architects. Salvi died before the fountain was finished, and Giuseppe Pannini modified his original plans to a certain extent, substituting the allegorical statues of 'Abundance' and Salubrity of the Air' for Salvi's projected Agrippa and the Virgin Trivia; these stand in the niches to the right and left of the central group of 'Ocean' with his chariot.

The Romans have always considered the Acqua Vergine the best, as it is certainly the softest, of their local waters; until the present pumping system was installed, choosy English residents would keep a couple of demi-johns of Trevi water in the house for tea-making. Possibly this was the reason why in the last century it was said that the traveller who drank the fountain water would return to Rome—there is a similar superstition about the waters of the Nile. When exactly the custom of dropping a coin into the fountain replaced this rite it is difficult to say; though this also has very ancient origins in connection with wishing wells and religious shrines. Today, thanks largely to the world-wide publicity given to this custom by a popular film, the Trevi fountain brings in quite a handsome tribute of the currency of all nations. This is officially reserved for charitable institutions; though a good deal of surreptitious 'cleaning' of the fountain is carried on by the urchins of the neighbourhood if the policeman isn't looking.

The inconspicuous little baroque church of S. Maria in Trivia or dei Crociferi, in the small piazza on the left of the fountain, also has a long history. Originally its name was S. Maria *in synodochio*; this commemorated Belisarius's foundation of a *xenodochio* or hospice on this site, as an act of penance for sending Pope St. Silverius into exile in 537. The hospice survived until the eleventh century; a late medieval inscription inserted into the wall of the existing church in the Via Poli commemorates Belisarius's pious foundation.

Now is the moment for us to see the Gallery of the **Accademia di S. Luca** (entrance at No. 77 Piazza Accademia di S. Luca). A 'university' or confraternity of artists already existed in Rome towards the end of the fifteenth century; its seat was attached to a small church dedicated to St. Luke—the patron saint of painters—near S. Maria Maggiore. In 1577, Gregory XIII officially constituted an academy of *beaux arts*, naming it in memory of the old 'university' the Accademia di S. Luca and thus founding the existing institution. During the course of the centuries the academy has changed its seat several times; in 1932 it was transferred to its present one—the Palazzo Carpegna on the corner of the Via della Stamperia, by the Trevi fountain. This palace is chiefly remarkable for the unusual inclined spiral ramp, which Borromini designed in place of a staircase. This can be seen at the far end of the entrance hall; though its initial curve is ingeniously camouflaged by a stucco decoration of garlands. (The earliest of its kind in Rome was built by the Emperor Hadrian in his second-century mausoleum on the other bank of the Tiber.) The convenience of such a ramp in a Roman palace of the seventeenth century will be more readily appreciated when it is realised that water from the Trevi fountain was still carried upstairs, in barrels on the backs of mules, to the upper floors of the Vatican Palace until well into the nineteenth century.

But to return to the academy's picture gallery, a tour of which occupies about half an hour. The collection is a somewhat heterogeneous one, made up chiefly of paintings which were either the work of the academicians themselves or presented by them. Most of these were not princely collectors with ample means, but connoisseurs who appreciated the finer points of works of art, even if their authors did not bear famous names known to the general public. The collection is, therefore, definitely a specialised one; nevertheless it includes a Raphael fresco, three paintings attributed to Titian, a Rubens and the only picture by Piazzetta in Rome.

If we have been to see either the Colonna Gallery or that of the Accademia di S. Luca, it will now probably be somewhere about a quarter to eleven. During the summer months, from 2 May to 30 September, we must hurry on if we are to see the churches of S. Andrea al Quirinale and S. Carlo alle Quattro Fontane, and the Barberini Gallery before this last closes at one o'clock. In winter, when the Barberini Gallery is open all day till 4 p.m., or if we have seen neither of the small galleries, we will now have a little time to spare to explore a picturesque corner of old Rome, before proceeding with our main itinerary.

Turning back along the **Via della Stamperia**, on our left (No.8) we see what appear to be the windows of an old print shop. This is the Calcografia di Stato founded by Clement XII in 1738; it contains a collection of more than 20,000 original

copper plates of famous Roman engravers, including those of
Piranesi. Facing us, on the corner of the Via del Lavatore and
Via di S. Vincenzo, stands the soberly dignified baroque
church of SS. Vincenzo e Anastasio. This was rebuilt in 1630
by Martino Longhi the Younger for Cardinal Mazarin. The
lictor's *fasces* below the cardinal's hat is neither an ancient
Roman nor a fascist symbol, but formed part of the Mazarin
arms. In the crypt beneath the church are preserved the
hearts and viscera—removed for embalming—of many of the
popes from Sixtus V, who died in 1590, to Leo XIII, who
died in 1903. SS. Vincenzo and Anastasio is the parish church
of the Quirinal Palace where most of them lived.

We now turn left behind the church, up the narrow Vicolo
dei Modelli, off the Via di S. Vincenzo. The Vicolo took its
name from the number of artists' models—the ones who used
to parade on the Spanish Steps—who lived there. This brings
us into the picturesque little **Piazza Scanderbeg**, called after
the Albanian patriot, George Castriota, admiringly nicknamed Skanderbeg, or Prince Alexander, by the Turks, who
were forced to recognise this guerrilla leader as Lord of
Albania and Epirus. It is said that Paul II (1464–71) offered
Skanderbeg lodging in Palazzo Venezia during his visit to
Rome in 1466–7, but that the gallant soldier preferred to live
in the house of an Epirote friend in this square. According to
an eyewitness description Skanderbeg 'came with but few
horses, in poverty.' His stay here is commemorated by a
portrait painted over the door of the house (Nos. 116, 117).
Neither the portrait nor the house can be contemporary, as the
latter plainly dates from the eighteenth century. This is confirmed by the date, 1744, which appears under Skanderbeg's
portrait, showing him as an old man with a white beard (he
was over 60), wearing a scarlet cap and robes. The picture was
probably repainted when the house was rebuilt or restored in
the eighteenth century.

Before returning to our main itinerary, it is worth while
making a few minutes' detour up the **Via dello Scalone**—one
of Rome's least known street staircases—which leads to the
left off the Vicolo Scanderbeg to a disused door of the Quirinal
Palace. It brings us to a quiet sheltered corner, far from the
noise of traffic, commanding a view down the Via della
Panetteria to the colourful market under the Quirinal wall.
Returning to Vicolo Scanderbeg, a steep ascent brings us out

from under an arch into the Via della Dataria, called after an office of the papal government which was lodged in a palace in the street.

Well into Pius IX's reign (1846–78), this side of the Quirinal Hill was approached by a rough path, set among tufa rocks and flourishing vegetation, providing a highly picturesque contrast to the palace and the famous colossal marble statues of horses on the top. Its transformation, to provide a carriage road, was entrusted to the architect Virginio Vespignani; it cost the vast sum of 350,000 scudi. On the day of its opening, Pius IX, who regarded the result with a critical eye, asked the unfortunate Vespignani how much it would cost to put it back as it formerly was.

A steep flight of steps leading out of the top of the Via della Dataria now brings us into the **Piazza del Quirinale**; this is definitely one of the sights of Rome. Surrounded on three sides by palaces, its fourth is open to one of the most magnificent views over the city, stretching as far as the great dome of St. Peter's in the distance. In the midst of the great paved piazza stands the striking group of the 'horse tamers' or 'Castor and Pollux' and their steeds; since time immemorial these have been one of the landmarks of the city. They are colossal Roman copies of some Greek original which probably adorned the neighbouring Baths of Constantine, and are part of the small group of statues which have never been buried. The names of Phidias and Praxiteles are a subsequent, and erroneous addition made when the statues were moved by Sixtus V (1585–90). They were finally placed in their present position by Pius VI (1775–99) when the obelisk from the Augusteum was erected beside them; the fountain was added by Pius VII (1800–23); its basin is familiar from many old pictures of the Forum, where it was used as a cattle trough. The statues were mentioned in all the medieval guides to Rome, and woven around with wonderful legends. The Englishman, Master Gregory, who saw them in the twelfth century, said that then a marvellous statue of Venus stood nearby; some have been tempted to think that this was the Capitoline Venus which was later found not far away. Because of the statues, the Quirinal Hill has for centuries also been called Monte Cavallo. In the tenth century they also provided a sobriquet for one of the Crescenzi family, known as *Crescentius Caballi marmorei* (Crescentius of the marble horse); at this period it was not unusual for Roman families to be named after the ancient monuments which stood near their homes.

Through the centuries, the Quirinal Hill—which was the Sabine stronghold among the original seven hills of Rome—has been the home of many famous men. Cicero's friend Pomponius Atticus—to whom his famous letters were addressed—probably lived where the church of S. Andrea now stands. Somewhere on the farther slopes the epigrammatist Martial lived, very inelegantly in a room with a broken window; complaining constantly—just as we do—of the appalling Roman noise.

Rather appropriately, the Quirinal stables were built in the eighteenth century on the site where Crescentius of the Marble Horses' medieval fortress once stood. In the latter part of the fifteenth century this area was given over to private houses and gardens. Here two of the most distinguished humanists of the period then lived: Platina—whom Sixtus IV made first Prefect of the Vatican Library—and Pomponius Laetus. Pomponius was a redoubtable character—a distinguished bibliophile, classicist and antiquarian, the friend of Cardinal Raffaele Riario (who built the Cancelleria with the proceeds of his gambling), in whose palace Pomponius was the first to revive classical drama in Rome. Pomponius also founded his own academy, whose meetings were held in his house; here poets were crowned in classical style with bays picked in his own garden. The atmosphere of these meetings was definitely pagan, and, according to Pope Paul II's (1464–71) spies, republican. For alleged participation in a conspiracy against this pope, Pomponius and Platina were imprisoned in Castel Sant' Angelo, but in the end were released for lack of evidence.

The papal stables are the striking-looking buildings opposite the Quirinal Palace, designed by Alessandro Specchi for Clement XII (1730–40). The high wall next door to them, with the attractive door and steps, enclosed the upper reaches of the Colonna gardens. Across the street, standing in its own walled garden, is the Pallavicini-Rospigliosi Palace. This was originally built in 1603 for Cardinal Scipione Borghese by Giovanni Vasanzio (also the architect of the Villa Borghese). In the garden stands the **Rospigliosi Casino of the Aurora** (see Appendix for opening times; contrary to what is said in most guide-books, the gallery is *not* open). This was a tremendous tourist draw in the last century, when everyone went into raptures over the work of Guido Reni, whose finest painting they considered this to be. The somewhat flamboyant Palazzo della Consulta, next door, was designed by Ferdinando Fuga in 1734 for Clement XII, to house one of the papal courts.

The **Quirinal Palace** (see Appendix) was begun in 1574 by Gregory XIII as a summer residence for the popes. It was not finally completed until the reign of Clement XII, but the Vatican had such a bad reputation for its unhealthy situation that already in 1592 Clement VIII had moved to the Quirinal. It was the papal residence until 1870, when it became that of the kings of Italy; as it is now of the presidents. The site is a superb one. This is not surprising as it was originally chosen by Cardinal Ippolito d'Este for his town palace and gardens, once as famous as those he made at Tivoli. A succession of great architects, beginning with Flaminio Ponzio and including such names as Domenico Fontana, Carlo Maderno, Bernini and Fuga, at various times worked on the palace. Owing partly perhaps to its great size, and partly to its always having been an official residence, it lacks the charm of the great family palaces.

The Renaissance severity of the main façade is lightened by a graceful door designed by Bernini. This leads to the vast porticoed courtyard with the clock tower, which does indeed form an impressive spectacle when floodlit for big receptions. On such occasions the six-foot cuirassiers of the guard, dressed in crimson and blue gala uniforms with steel helmets topped with horses' tails, stand sentry on the grand staircase and in the gilded and chandelier-lit staterooms. Then the palace comes to life and makes a very different impression from when seen in cold blood, as it were, by the tourist.

In fact this part of the Quirinal has never really been lived in for nearly a century, both the kings of Italy and the presidents preferring the smaller and more homely palazzetto, at the far end of the long barrack-like wing overlooking the Via del Quirinale. This last is known as the *manica lunga* (the long sleeve); it was built to house the cardinals during papal elections—in far greater comfort than that which they now enjoy on similar occasions in the Vatican. Before 1870 the actual conclaves were held in the Cappella Paolina, built in exactly the same shape, and to the same dimensions, as the

Sistine chapel. This has a fine stucco ceiling; it was consecrated in 1611.

One of the principal sights of the Quirinal is the fragment of Melozzo da Forli's 'Last Judgment', from the SS. Apostoli; a superb Christ in glory surrounded by countless little angels, which is nevertheless somewhat overpowered by the ornate gilt decoration of the grand staircase. One of the most spectacular salons—the *sala degli specchi* (the hall of mirrors)—contains some fine Murano glass chandeliers. There is an attractive chinoiserie salon (rare in Rome). The traveller should also watch out for such details as the exquisitely fine coloured mosaics in some of the fireplaces; these originally came from—of all unexpected places—Hadrian's villa near Tivoli.

During the last century the Quirinal was the scene of some stirring events; it was from here that Pope Pius VI in 1799 and Pope Pius VII in 1809 were deported by Napoleon's orders. It was also from the Quirinal, a few days after Rossi's murder in the Cancelleria, that Pius IX was forced by an insurrection to flee from Rome to Gaeta in 1848. It required considerable cunning and audacity to carry through the plan, as the palace was carefully guarded and watched by hostile civic guards—the Swiss guards having been disbanded a few days previously. However the French Ambassador, the Duc d'Harcourt, and the Bavarian Minister, Count Spaur, were party to the plan. The Duc d'Harcourt requested a private audience, and remained reading the papers aloud in the pope's study to simulate conversation while the pontiff made good his escape. It was some time before the ruse was discovered. During the winter Garibaldi and Mazzini arrived, and the short-lived Roman Republic was declared. It was only some time after its fall, in April 1850, that Pius IX returned to Rome, but not to live in the Quirinal.

We now continue down the Via del Quirinale, which runs beside the *manica lunga* wing of the palace. Not far along on the right a singularly graceful semicircular flight of steps and portico lead up to the small oval baroque church of **S. Andrea al Quirinale**. This was designed by Bernini in 1658 for Cardinal Camillo Pamphilj, for the novices of the Jesuit order. So often in Rome in the fervour of the Counter-Reformation, baroque additions or decorations were superimposed upon existing churches for which in fact they were basically unsuited, with the result that to those of us who are not baroque specialists this style sometimes appears more or less as a kind of ornamental veneer, obscuring much that was infinitely more interesting in the original building. Fortunately here for once, in S. Andrea (and later in S. Carlo in the same street), we see two churches that are the work of masters, built and decorated as they originally designed them. The result is a revelation of extraordinary beauty and harmony; though small in size, the interior of S. Andrea conveys a remarkable feeling of grandeur. This is aided and abetted by the deep rich tones of the marbles in the shadowy body of the church, from which—by skilful lighting effects—our eyes are irresistibly drawn to the figure of St. Andrew above the main altar niche. Following his upward gestures our eyes are again led into the soaring light and space of the dome. In spite of its small size, S. Andrea took twelve years to complete.

At the far end of the Via del Quirinale is the cross-roads known—from four charming baroque fountains—as **Le Quattro Fontane**. This is probably the highest point of the Quirinal Hill and, if the traffic is not too thick, it affords delightful views in four directions: back along the Via del Quirinale to the obelisk and marble horses of the Quirinal; in the opposite direction along the Via XX Settembre (20 September was the day when Italian troops entered Rome in 1870), to the monumental Porta Pia; on the right to the obelisk and apse of S. Maria Maggiore; and on the left across the Piazza Barberini and up the Via Sistina to the third obelisk of Trinità dei Monti.

On the right-hand corner of the cross-roads stands the church of **S. Carlo alle Quattro Fontane** (see Appendix). This was Borromini's first architectural commission after twenty years spent as a stone-cutter, builder, draughtsman and architect's assistant. The adjoining monastery for the Spanish Discalced Trinitarians was begun in 1634 and the church four years later. It was completed in 1641, except for the façade which was only finished in 1667. The site is a small and awkward one; it is said that the area of the church itself is no bigger than that occupied by one of the piers which support the dome of St. Peter's. Nevertheless Borromini's design was immediately recognised as something remarkable; the Procurator General of the Order reported that many foreigners arriving in Rome tried to obtain copies of the plans; these included Germans, Flemings, Frenchmen, Spaniards and even Indians. He added that 'in the opinion of everybody nothing similar with regard to artistic merit, caprice, excellence and singularity can be found anywhere in the world'.

Today at first it is perhaps a little difficult to understand why the church should have been considered so revolutionary, except for the dome. The answer lies in the fact that Borromini was a builder and an architect first and foremost, unlike his Renaissance predecessors and baroque contemporaries who were just as much at home as sculptors or painters. Their conception of architecture was the humanist one based on the proportions of the human body, whereas he was chiefly concerned with geometrical form. As a result, Borromini's buildings were often regarded as bizarre and strange—they are in fact much more cerebral and subtle than those of his Roman contemporaries. It is noticeable that he found many more disciples in Piedmont and northern Europe than in Rome.

As with S. Ivo alla Sapienza, its unusual shape is one of the most striking characteristics of S. Carlo; this is roughly a diamond with convex curves in place of diagonal lines. Columns line the walls, framing the entrances to small chapels, cloisters, etc. The plan draws its inspiration from the great domed hall of the Piazza d'Oro in Hadrian's villa. What is really remarkable is the transition from this strangely shaped body of the church to the oval dome, which seems to be suspended in space above it. This impression is achieved by the series of windows which surround the dome's base, but are practically concealed by a wreath of ornamental foliage. They flood the curious coffering of octagons, crosses and hexagons with an intense light; the coffers diminish in size towards the lantern, thus increasing the apparent height of the church. Curiously enough, the buildings in Rome which most resemble the effect of this extraordinary dome are ultra-modern ones—the Palazzo and Palazzetto dello Sport, designed by Pier Luigi Nervi for the Olympic Games of 1960. The swaying curving movement of the body of S. Carlo is repeated in the façade, also in the campanile. By contrast the famous cloisters, in spite of their diminutive size, are sobriety personified, except for the fact that the central court repeats in embryonic form something of the church's curious shape.

It is unfortunate that S. Carlo and S. Andrea al Quirinale

stand, practically, within a few paces of each other; so that within the space of half an hour we can study two outstanding works of the two great architectural rivals of seventeenth-century Rome whose personalities are so clearly reflected in these churches. Bernini, brilliant son of a successful father, sophisticated and assured, the master of rich spectacular effect; Borromini, brought up in a hard school, a nervous recluse who ultimately committed suicide but, who, nevertheless, boldly challenged the accepted canons of his time and whose work still possesses a disturbing power to make one think and wish to penetrate the ideas behind it.

We have not yet finished with the rivalry between this famous pair. A short distance down the Via delle Quattro Fontane we see the **Palazzo Barberini,** upon which they both worked: Borromini from its inception in 1625 as draughtsman to his uncle, Carlo Maderno, and after Maderno's death in 1625 as Bernini's assistant until the palace was practically finished in 1633. There has been a good deal of argument as to how much of the palace's design can be attributed to Maderno and how much to Bernini; with a few reservations also in favour of Borromini. It is now fairly generally considered that although the building was far from complete when Bernini took over, Maderno's basic plans were adhered to, the new architect making only a few alterations. The rectangular staircase on the left was certainly designed by Bernini; the oval one on the right by Borromini. Bernini probably altered considerably, if he did not actually design, the great central portico with the double row of large windows above which is the outstanding feature of the palace. Note the ingenious device of the artificial perspective surrounding these on the top floor, designed to preserve the symmetry of the whole, while allowing for smaller windows proportionate to the size of the rooms on the upper storey. An attractive and unusual feature of this portico is that it diminishes in size—from the seven arches of the exterior façade, to five and then to three—as it approaches the delightful oval vestibule in the centre of the building.

Possibly more than any other palace, Palazzo Barberini represents the apogee of the splendour of life in baroque Rome. As we have seen, it was begun in 1625, on the site of an old Sforza palace, two years after the accession of the family Pope, Urban VIII. Some idea of Urban's conception of his role as a Maecenas may be judged from his remark to Bernini after his election: 'It is a piece of luck for you, Cavaliere, to see Cardinal Maffeo Barberini Pope, but far greater is our good fortune that the lifetime of Cavaliere Bernini should fall into our pontificate.' This is as significant of an attitude to life as the phrase attributed to Leo X: 'Let us enjoy the papacy, since God has given it to us.' Although it dates from 1656 (twelve years after Urban's death), the picture we saw in the Museo di Roma of the pageant given by the Barberini in honour of Queen Christina evokes perhaps better than anything else the pomp and circumstance of this fantastic world. The pageant was held in a theatre, especially constructed for the occasion, to the left of the palace. All the young bloods of the great Roman families—the Santacroce, Massimo and Barberini themselves—participated. They and their horses were caparisoned in red and blue embroidered with gold and silver, the riders wearing enormous ostrich-feather headdresses each of which alone cost 200 scudi. Carrying flaming torches in their hands, they indulged in mock battles with amazons, followed by a procession of tremendous baroque allegorical cars filled with graces, cupids and musicians, while choirs sang symphonies and trumpets blared.

In 1949 the palace was sold by the Barberini to the Italian State; not long afterwards it was decided to employ the main staterooms to house the **Rome National Gallery** (see Appendix for opening times). Although this is not its correct title, the collection of pictures is usually colloquially referred to as the Barberini Gallery; and indeed some of the pictures do come from the family collection, notably Raphael's famous 'Fornarina', which was already hanging in the palace in 1642.

Originally, the Rome National Gallery was called the National Gallery of Ancient Art; it was founded in 1893 when the government bought the Corsini Palace in Trastevere, and its owners gave the art collections it contained to the State. This original nucleus, which continued to be housed in the Corsini Palace, was gradually expanded by purchase and gifts: Duke Giovanni Torlonia's collection and that of the Monte di Pietà being added to it in 1892; the Colonna-Sciarra one in 1896; a large purchase from the Chigi collection in 1918; part of the Barberini collection in 1949; and, finally, in 1962, the Duke of Cervinara's bequest. The number of pictures in the collection now exceeds 1,700; those dating from the thirteenth to the end of the sixteenth century are hung in Palazzo Barberini; those of the following two centuries in Palazzo Corsini. In time it is hoped that the entire collection will be housed in the Barberini Palace.

At the time of writing there is no catalogue listing the pictures in room order; nor are the rooms or pictures numbered. The only catalogue on sale is arranged in alphabetical order under the artists' names, necessitating a good deal of patient turning of pages in order to 'read up' the contents of each room. It is hoped that the pictures will soon be numbered and that these numbers will be added to a new edition of the catalogue. The pictures now in Palazzo Barberini fill seventeen rooms; those numbered 1 to 14 contain pictures from the Rome National Gallery Collection dating from the thirteenth to the sixteenth century. The Cervinara bequest occupies rooms 15 and 16; room 17 being devoted to new acquisitions. When the whole collection is assembled in the palace, the Cervinara pictures will be transferred to the second floor, where a suite of rooms with elegant eighteenth-century decorations will provide a very suitable setting.

Beginning our tour of the gallery, room 1 (first on the left) contains a small but fine collection of primitives; notable among them is G. Baronzio's 'Scenes from the life of Christ'. The paintings in room 2 date mainly from the fifteenth or early sixteenth centuries; they include two 'Annunciations', one by Fra Angelico, the other by Filippo Lippi; also a 'Madonna and Child' attributed to Piero della Francesca (on loan); and Piero di Cosimo's 'Magdalen', which in spite of the saintly attributes is believed to be a portrait. The outstanding picture of Room 3 is Bartolomeo Veneto's 'Portrait of an Unknown Man', with a curious hat and checkered sleeves, familiar from countless reproductions. In the same room hangs Antoniazzo Romano's 'St. Sebastian', represented between two donors; the figures are portrayed against a singularly lovely sky and landscape, in which Monte Soracte is easily recognisable. Room 4 contains works from the second half of the fifteenth and the early sixteenth century.

No easel pictures hang in room 5; but it contains G. F. Romanelli's (and pupils) designs for tapestries representing scenes from the life of Urban VIII. Recently transferred here, these are the only seventeenth-century works now included in this part of the collection. Room 7 contains works of the sixteenth century. Room 8 is notable for some fine portraits; particularly Parmigiano's famous one of 'Stefano Colonna'— a striking dark bearded man in armour. In the centre of room 9 stands what is undoubtedly the best-known picture in the gallery—Raphael's famous portrait of the 'Fornarina'. Although the history of this picture is documented as far back as 1595, it will come as a surprise to most that several eminent authorities doubt that this is a work of Raphael; instead they attribute it to his favourite pupil Giulio Romano. Others have also denied that it is a portrait of Margherita the baker's daughter (in Italian a baker is a *fornaio*), considering rather that it represents either the famous Imperia or her rival Beatrice of Ferrara. Nevertheless, Raphael's name appears on the bracelet or ribbon on the lady's left arm. What few people notice, and indeed it is indistiguishable in most reproductions, is that the background of the picture is entirely made up of the green plants beloved of Renaissance gardeners—bays, myrtles and so on.

In the same room as the 'Fornarina' hangs a curious grisaille picture of a 'Pietà', attributed to the same artist that painted the famous Manchester 'Madonna' in the National Gallery in London. Its similarity to Michelangelo's 'Pietà' in St. Peter's strikes one at once. It is interesting to note that originally this picture was attributed to Luca Signorelli and believed to have inspired Michelangelo. However, more modern critics now consider that the opposite was the case; the artist taking his inspiration from one of Michelangelo's preliminary drawings for the Pietà. Closer inspection reveals many differences between the picture and the sculpture.

Room 10 contains what is probably the second most famous picture in the collection—Tintoretto's 'Christ and the woman taken in adultery'. In the same room hang two small but striking El Greco's—the 'Adoration of the shepherds' and the 'Baptism of Christ'. Until recent cleaning, when the varnish which gave a false warm tone to the pictures was removed, these were believed to be small replicas of two larger works. However, now that their true colour and free spontaneous brushwork is revealed, at least one critic considers that, instead, they were small preliminary studies for the larger works, one of which is now in the Prado. A portrait of Philip II of Spain, attributed to Titian, hangs in the same room.

A 'Venus and Adonis' by Titian, in room 11, whose remarkable beauty has also been revealed by recent cleaning, is similar to the one in the Prado, which the artist painted for the Emperor Charles V in 1554. This picture was so popular that several replicas were made, a custom not uncommon in the fifteenth and sixteenth centuries; this particular one subsequently belonged to Queen Christina of Sweden. With room 12, the Italian section of this part of the collection ends. In this room hang three pictures by Garofalo, two of which— 'King Picus being transformed into a woodpecker' and the 'Vestal Claudia and the statue of Cybele'—were inspired by incidents in Ovid's poems. The latter illustrates a pagan 'miracle' whereby the gods' intervention proved the chastity of the Vestal Claudia.

The next two rooms contain some remarkable works by Flemish and German artists. Notable among them are Quentin Massys' beautiful portrait of 'Erasmus' (room 13); and a copy, probably by Hans Hoffman, of Dürer's famous drawing of a hare; the original is in the Albertina in Vienna. In room 14, we come unexpectedly face to face with a Holbein portrait of 'Henry VIII', attired in the clothes he wore for his marriage to Anne of Cleves on 6 January 1540. Some critics deny that this is the work of Holbein; but in any case it is similar to the Windsor Castle portrait.

Rooms 15 and 16 contain the pictures left to the City of Rome by the Duke of Cervinara in 1960. They are nearly all the works of French eighteenth-century artists such as Lancret, Boucher, Fragonard, Hubert Robert and Greuze. There is also a striking 'Madonna and Child' by the Italian Renaissance painter Bartolomeo Montagna, two Guardis and two pictures by Bernardo Bellotto. Passing through room 17 we find ourselves in the great hall of the palace with the famous ceiling frescoed by Pietro da Cortona. This is baroque decorative painting in the grandest manner, remarkable at this early date—it was executed between 1633 and 1639—for the superabundant vitality of the composition, which seems to burst out of the *trompe l'oeil* architectural frame instead of being confined within it.

As examples of the rapid evolution in decorative painting, it is interesting to compare this ceiling with the one executed by Annibale Carracci only thirty years before which we saw in the Palazzo Farnese. Here the colouring is sumptuous, but many will prefer the delicate charm of Cortona's later work, which we have also already seen in the Palazzo Pamphilj. The composition of the Barberini ceiling is called the 'Triumph of Glory' or the 'Triumph of Divine Providence'. With a wealth of allegorical conceits, it represents Divine Providence receiving a starry crown from Immortality; with one hand Providence points towards a flight-formation of bees soaring through the heavens encircled by a garland of bays: bees, most conveniently, being both the symbol of divine providence and the heraldic one of the Barberini family.

It will now be one o'clock; for good Tuscan food we should try Nino's at 52 Via Rasella, a street leading out of the Via Quattro Fontane opposite the Palazzo Barberini gates, beside what was until recently the Scots College (it has now moved out to Marino). Or for a cup of coffee and a sandwich the Bar Quattro Fontane just on the left-hand corner of the farther side of Quattro Fontane (Nos. 124–5). There are plenty of good trattorias and snack bars nearby, but these are most convenient if we wish to remain in the area with the idea of seeing the Quirinal Palace on a Thursday. If we have finished earlier or want to get on with the next stage of our itinerary we would do well to walk along the Via XX Settembre and turn right into the Via V.E. Orlando. Here almost opposite the Grand Hotel is Canepa, a most useful institution comprising a first-rate restaurant, a *rosticceria*—where you can get hot food served quickly at the counter or have it packed for a picnic—and a bar with good snacks, all strung out along the street.

However, we should not leave the palace without taking a glimpse at two of the most charming monuments of what was the Barberini 'precinct'. These are Bernini's two famous fountains in the Piazza Barberini—the Tritone, or triton, and that of the bees. The **Fontana del Tritone**, from which the adjoining street takes its name, was the first designed by Bernini, about 1637. His use of travertine instead of the customary marble was something new; so too was the massive realism of the triton sitting astride the scallop shell, blowing a conch. This is not just a poetical rendering of a classical scene; not so many years ago in the Tuscan archipelago one could see of an evening fishermen sitting astride the prows of their boats blowing a conch shell to summon their crew for a night's fishing; almost any one of them might have served as Bernini's model.

The companion **Fontana delle Api** (fountain of the bees), standing on the corner of the Via Veneto, is less conspicuous but no less delightful. Here again the water falls into an open scallop shell, where the heraldic Barberini bees have alighted to take a drink. Once there was an inscription stating that the fountain had been erected in the twenty-second year of Urban VIII's pontificate; it was put up a few weeks before the twenty-first anniversary of his accession, thus anticipating the event. The superstitious Roman populace saw in this an evil omen; there was so much talk that the last figure of the Latin numeral XXII was chiselled away one night—too late; Urban died on 29 July, exactly eight days before the twenty-second year of his pontificate began.

CHAPTER THIRTEEN

Museo delle Terme [di Diocleziano]
to S. Agnese fuori le Mura

❦

OUR afternoon begins with the biggest sight of the day—the Museo Nazionale Romano or **Museo delle Terme** di Diocleziano. Here the great national collection of antique sculpture, painting and art—founded after the unification of Italy in 1870—is housed in the imposing ruins of the Baths of Diocletian, begun by Maximian in AD 298, continued by Diocletian and completed seven or eight years later. This is one of the most, if not the most, enjoyable museums in Rome. Not only is one's pleasure undisturbed by clock-watching for that awful Roman lunch 'hour' which always seems to interrupt one unawares when most interested—returning after four hours' interval the mood is inevitably lost. But above all it is the setting which so enormously increases our enjoyment; this is no modern institutional building, but the halls and gardens of one of the greatest bathing establishments of the ancient world. In other words the type of setting for which many of the sculptures and mosaics were originally intended. For the Romans the baths were not just a place in which to take a 'Turkish' bath and swim, or enjoy exercise and gossip; they also housed libraries and magnificent art collections. It is true that two of the gardens we see today are in actual fact cloisters built into the ruins. But, with their colonnades and fountains set among the green of clipped box, ivy and bay trees, they are highly reminiscent of classical gardens; if indeed not directly derived from them. On a fine day nothing could be more pleasant than to take time off from our itinerary to sit for a while in the sunshine and blessed peace of these gardens. So give yourself a good allowance of time—two to two and a half hours—in which to see the Museo delle Terme, as it is more familiarly called.

If we have not seen the smaller galleries during our morning's walk, we may have arrived in the vicinity of the museum by about midday. In this case we would be well advised to take a

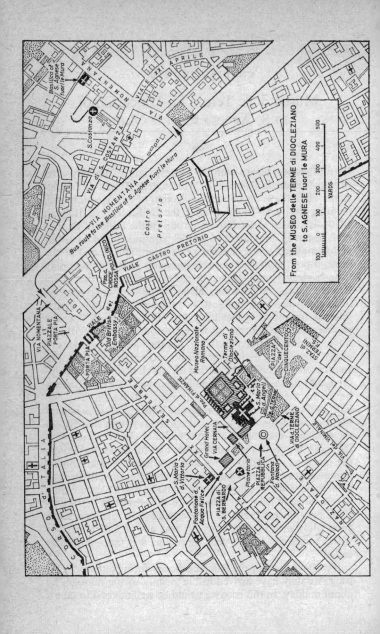

From the MUSEO delle TERME di DIOCLEZIANO
to S. AGNESE fuori le MURA

100   0   100   200   300   400   500
YARDS

quick look at the church of **S. Maria degli Angeli** before it closes; the entrance is exactly opposite the Fontana delle Naiadi in the centre of the Piazza della Repubblica, better known by its old name of Piazza Esedra.

This church should if possible be seen just before or after the Terme, certainly on the same day, as it gives a better idea than anything else in Rome of what a great Roman bath originally looked like. In 1561, Pius IV commissioned Michelangelo to convert the central hall of the *frigidarium* into a church. Unlike his eighteenth-century successor, Vanvitelli, Michelangelo treated the classical ruins with the greatest respect. Making the minimum number of alterations, he used the vast central part of the *frigidarium* as the nave, creating an entrance at the eastern end in what is now one of the halls of the museum. Enormous though it is, the area used for the church occupies only about half of the *frigidarium* building, which formed the central block of the Terme, the whole area of which was some 130,000 square yards. The *frigidarium*, or cold room, measures 300 by 88 feet, and is 92 feet high; it was flanked by four small covered pools and other halls whose uses are now unknown. On its northern side, the walls of this vast building rose out of the waters of a great swimming pool, 3,000 square yards in area. With its marble columns and sculptures this must have presented a tremendous spectacle, some vestiges of whose past grandeur still live for us in the drawings of Piranesi.

In 1749, the Carthusian monks who then owned the church and monastery among the ruins got Vanvitelli to transform the church. The main door was moved to the ruined *calidarium*, or hot room, where it now is. From here we pass through a circular hall—the old *tepidarium*, or warm room—into what is now the vast transept but which was originally the *frigidarium* and Michelangelo's nave. Even these eighteenth-century alterations and the decorations of the period have been unable to rob this superb building of its majesty. Eight of the original great rose-red granite columns support a rich classical entablature; though Michelangelo was forced to raise the floor level by some six feet, their height is still forty-five feet, their diameter five feet three inches. Above them rises the stupendous vaulting of the original ceiling; Vanvitelli's apse, on the far side, is a poor thing by comparison. Moreover in building it he destroyed the façade of the *frigidarium*, which until then had been visible almost in its entirety, though the small cloister of the monastery had been previously built over much of the ancient swimming pool.

Emerging from the church we now turn left along a path leading across a small public garden. Skirting the red brick walls of the Terme, just before we turn left down some steps to the museum entrance, we get a charming glimpse of pleasures to come—at the end of an alley we can look through two of the halls of the baths to the greenery and graceful fountain of one of the museum's three gardens. The Terme collection is so large that even the admirably succinct catalogue on sale has a text of 175 pages; so here we will content ourselves with a brief general description of each section, pointing out the most important objects, and warmly recommend those who wish to make a more detailed study to invest in the late Professor Aurigemma's excellent catalogue.

Unlike the other great Roman collections, that of the Museo delle Terme is neither an old nor a personal one, though it includes the famous Ludovisi family collection bought in 1906. According to its original terms of reference, promulgated in 1889, the museum was to be the repository of all antique works of art of high artistic or historic importance found within the City of Rome; this has now been extended to cover works in this category irrespective of their provenance. Thus the exhibits have for the most part been discovered during the last eighty years; though there are exceptions such as the Ludovisi collection and the ex-Lancellotti discobolus, which last was found in 1781 but was only included in the collection in 1958. Apart from such world-famous sculptures as the Ludovisi throne, the 'Niobid' from the Gardens of Sallust, the 'Girl of Anzio', the bronze 'Pugilist' in repose, the 'Venus of Cyrene', the 'Ephebe of Subiaco' and the 'Anzio Apollo', in the pictures of the 'Garden of Livia' and from the Roman villa at the Farnesina, the Terme possess the most important collection of antique painting after that of Naples National Museum.

The first seven halls of the museum are in fact so many rooms of the ancient *frigidarium* block of the baths. Although they would originally have been covered with marbles and mosaics their mellow Roman brickwork now makes an admirable setting for the sculptures, mosaics and sarcophagi which they contain. The museum is renowned for having the largest collection of sarcophagi in the world, many of them are arranged in these halls, particularly halls I, II and III.

In the centre of the floor in **hall IV** is an entertaining mosaic from Collemancio (No. 51) portraying pygmies hunting hippopotamus and crocodiles. This seems a curious subject for a classical mosaic from what is now Umbria, though it was apparently popular, as similar paintings and mosaics have been found elsewhere. But what is more surprising to anyone who has seen pygmies today in the heart of the Ituri forest in the Congo is the extraordinary veracity of the portrayal of their physique and colouring—their large heads, prominent buttocks and light brown colour, so different from the tall slender Negro tribes who live around them. Still today the pygmies are noted huntsmen, tackling even elephants with their primitive weapons. How, one wonders, did the Roman artist know all this? The answer probably is that the link was Egypt—a papyrus, dating from two thousand five hundred years before Christ, recorded that an Egyptian expedition 'to the land of the trees which lies beyond the land of Punt' had brought back a dancing dwarf for Pharaoh's entertainment. Still today the Ituri pygmies are as famous among the surrounding Negro tribes for their dancing as for their prowess as hunters.

In the same hall are a notable polychrome mosaic of a whirling wheel (No. 52); part of the dedicatory inscription of the Baths of Diocletian (No. 53); the striking colossal statue of the 'Kore' or 'Artemis of Ariccia' (No. 54); and a small tetra-style temple of the Corinthian order of the second century AD (this is partly restored). To the right and left of this last are two fine sarcophagi of the latter half of the second century AD; on that on the left is represented the meeting of Dionysus and Ariadne (No. 58); on the one on the right, a cavalry battle between Romans and Barbarians (No. 57). The wonderful polychrome mosaic of the Nile which was formerly the show-piece of hall v has now been returned to its original home in the Temple of Fortune at Palestrina.

In the centre of the floor of **hall VI**, we come face to face with some of the famous charioteers of ancient times in a mosaic dating from the fourth century AD (No. 88). The central figure with the palm is the winner—Aëri of the Greens, the site of whose barracks we may recall having seen at the Cancelleria. The horse on the left of his *quadriga* is also named—Itala; this is because the team's victory was largely dependent upon his efforts. In the *quadriga* or four-horse chariot, only the two centre horses were actually harnessed to the shaft; the two outside ones were loosely attached by traces (*funi* or ropes), and these were the ones who really bore the brunt of the race —particularly the one on the left, as he was the closest to the *metae*, that marked each end of the central spina of the circus; if in cornering at high speed he came too close, the whole *quadriga* might crash; if he swung out too far, valuable yards might be lost or a collision with another chariot occur. No Derby or Grand National winner today achieves the fame of these horses, whose names were known throughout the length and breadth of the Empire. Their charioteers, too, enjoyed a popularity that excelled any film or television star or football hero; to it was added the thrill of danger of their calling. Many of them died young, but the echo of their fame reaches us still in mosaics like this and in poems such as Martial's on the death of Scorpus, who won more than two thousand races as many years ago. In the same hall are several fine sarcophagi; notably one of the second century AD with Bacchic scenes (No. 94).

The next point of interest on our itinerary is **hall VIII**—this is really an open space, once occupied by the huge open-air swimming pool of the baths. Subsequent building has obscured practically all that remains of this once-magnificent sight; but on our left we can still see two (one curved and one rectangular) of the original five recesses which gave the effect of the *scenae frons* of a theatre to this façade which was mirrored in the pool. Passing through the fine double apsed hall (**hall IX**) with a large Egyptian-style sarcophagus in the centre, we come to **hall X** where two Roman tombs have been reconstructed. That on the left (No. 125), of Gaius Sulpicius Platorinus, contains some beautiful small urns. In it was buried a young girl, Minatia Polla, whose head we will see later in the museum; also Antonia Furnilla, grandmother of Titus's beautiful daughter Julia, whose elegant head we admired in the Capitoline Museum.

We now pass into **hall IX**, where among many fine mosaics we see on the far wall a number of fragments of a long inscription in small lettering. These are the Acts of the Arval Brotherhood, dating from about AD 59-60; only part of the inscription is here, the rest being in the Vatican Museum. This inscription demonstrates yet again the extraordinary continuity of Roman life; for it recounts the part played in religious processions by this confraternity, who existed specifically for taking part in them.

It was in fact a pagan predecessor of the Christian *Arcicon-fraternità del Gonfalone*—whom we met during our walk down the Via dei Banchi Vecchi—and so many of their *confrères* in medieval and Renaissance Rome.

Retracing our steps through hall X, we find ourselves in a charming little garden, actually sited where the ancient Romans once strolled along the tree-lined walks of Diocletian's Baths. The elegantly pavemented semicircular recess opening out of the far side was not a nympheum or ornamental garden pavilion but a *forica* or public lavatory (a thirty-holer as 'the Expert' would have termed it). This was formerly adorned with statues standing in niches in the wall nearest the garden.

By a door on the left-hand side of the garden we now enter the museum proper, where the administration has thoughtfully provided a bar with a comfortable place to sit down. The museum is divided into five sections of which three are absolute 'musts' for even the most hurried tourist; these are the Ludovisi-Boncompagni Collection in the small cloister; the series of halls numbered I to VIII on the ground floor; and the nine rooms on the first floor containing the frescoes from Livia's Villa at Prima Porta (often called her 'Garden Room'), the paintings and stuccoes from the Roman Farnesina Villa and two rooms of very fine mosaics. Of less importance—though they contain the wonderful head of the dying Persian and the famous sleeping Hermaphrodite—are the five small rooms immediately beside the entrance, also the sculptures and mosaics in the 'Michelangelo' cloister.

The **Ludovisi collection**, like several of the other great Roman family collections, was begun by the nephew of a pope; in this case Cardinal Ludovico Ludovisi, whose uncle reigned as Gregory XV from 1621 to 1623. Some of the sculptures were discovered in the vast grounds of the now-vanished family villa which occupied the site of the famous classical Gardens of Sallust and subsequently gave its name to the quarter round the Via Veneto. This was the case with the famous 'throne'—only discovered in 1887; other sculptures were bought from various older collections. Owing to many of these works having come to light two hundred and some even five hundred years ago, some have been considerably restored and polished in accordance with bygone fashion, which does not accord with our ideas today. However they thus also provide an interesting object lesson in the history of taste. The museum authorities have wisely decided to preserve the unity of the collection, exhibiting it in the delightful small cloister of the old Carthusian monastery.

In the cloister itself are five sculptures of outstanding interest—four of the greatest treasures stand in a small room opening out of it. Turning to the right on entering the cloister, we find, about the middle of the wall, a large statue of the Athena Parthenos (No. 180). This is a copy, made in Roman times by a Greek sculptor, of Phidias's colossal chryselephantine statue of Athene, which stood in the Parthenon in Athens. The original statue was nearly twelve metres high and made of ivory and gold; the goddess's left hand rested on a shield, on her right one stood a small statue of Victory on a column. The draperies and weapons of the original were of gold which was later removed. Here the mistaken modern restoration of Athene, especially of her arms, has greatly altered her appearance; but part of the Greek copyist's name can still be seen on the folds of her peplum near the ground on the left. The curious 'platform' sandals were common to the Greeks, Etruscans and Romans.

As we walk around the cloister, facing us at the corner is a striking group of a Galatian stabbing himself after having killed his wife (No. 190). The tragic scene reminds us of the 'Dying Gladiator' in the Capitoline Museum; and indeed it is a copy of part of the same famous group of bronzes erected in 197–159 BC by two kings of Pergamon, Attalus I and Eumenes II, to celebrate their victories over the Galatians. Here again the man's right arm and the woman's left one were added during restoration.

A little farther along is a graceful statue of a Satyr pouring wine (No. 194); this again is a marble copy of an original Greek bronze—probably the work of Praxiteles. The bunch of grapes and the horn are the restorer's additions; the original would have been holding a jug and cup.

At last we come to the little cell on the right which contains the Ludovisi 'throne' (No. 197). This wonderful work of Greek sculpture, dating from the fifth century BC, may have been an altar or part of an altar, but is more generally believed to have served as a throne for a goddess, possibly the famous Aphrodite of Eryx (the modern Erice in Sicily). This Aphrodite was the protectress of sailors, universally venerated throughout the Mediterranean, whose cult was of great antiquity. Her statue is known to have been brought to Rome in 181 BC. The great throne or altar stands facing the wall; originally it would probably have had a pointed back and metal additions. Several interpretations have been given to the famous relief, but the most likely seems to be that here we see the Goddess of Love being born of the sea foam—an aspect of her life that would have been particularly suitable for portrayal in her sanctuary at Erice. The myth itself is beautiful enough to the imagination; but here it lives before our eyes in all the sparkling beauty of a Mediterranean dawn. One can almost see the crystal drops falling from the goddess's hair and diaphanous drapery that—still wet from the sea—clings to her body as she rises from the waves. All the joy and surprise of life are mirrored in her up-turned face, as smiling she stretches up her arms to the two nymphs who raise her out of the depths on to the pebbled shore. It is a thing unique, never to be forgotten; and to the writer at any rate the most beautiful sculpture in Rome. Beautiful too, but not of this unique transcendental quality, are the two figures on either side of the throne; one a naked *hetaera* playing the double flute, the other a draped and veiled woman making an offering of incense. Again various interpretations have been advanced to explain the significance of these two reliefs; one that they represent two aspects of love—the pure one of a bride, the sensual one of a *hetaera*—the other that these were two priestesses of the cult of Aphrodite.

In the same cell, to the right and left of the Ludovisi throne, stand two colossal heads of goddesses; that on the right is the Ludovisi Hera or Juno (No. 198), much admired by Winckelmann, Goethe and Schiller. Seen in this dim light it has an undoubted majesty, but it reflects the cold classicism of the early Empire—not the pulsating life of Greece—whose taste seems to have had so much in common with that of the neo-classicists of the late eighteenth and early nineteenth centuries. Looking from this to the Ludovisi throne we can so well understand what a revelation the first sight of the Elgin marbles must have been to Canova.

Opposite, and infinitely more to our taste today—though she would scarcely have appealed to the neo-classicists—is a colossal head of Aphrodite, Hera or Artemis (No. 199). Like the Ludovisi throne, this was the work of a Greek sculptor, made in Sicily (or Southern Italy) in the fifth century BC; though the head dates from the beginning of the century, the throne from about 460-450 BC. Small holes on the forehead, ears and neck indicate that the head was adorned with metal ornaments; a drapery of metal or some other material also probably fell to the neck at the back. This goddess was an acrolith, or statue—the visible parts of whose anatomy, only, were of stone—as those of the chryselephantine ones were of ivory. The framework of the body was probably made of wood, covered over with draperies of some other material, possibly of metal. Some authorities have advanced the theory that this was the head of the Aphrodite of Erice, brought to Rome in 181 BC; possibly even the deity that sat upon the Ludovisi throne. Others have discounted this on the ground that the two sculptures are of different marbles. The head has been restored to a certain extent.

Almost concealed in the shadows to the left of the door lies the 'Head of the Sleeping Fury' or 'Erinys' (No. 200). Strangely enough this used to be known as the Ludovisi Medusa but, although the locks are tumbled and disordered, they are definitely hairs not serpents; they cling to the head as if wet with sweat. It is believed that this is a fragment of a relief, formerly at Delphi or on the sepulchre of Agamemnon, which represented the three Furies lying asleep, exhausted after a race. The head, whose nose has been restored, dates from the late Hellenistic period; in spite of the delicacy and beauty of his treatment, the artist has succeeded in conveying the feeling of the fire which slumbers here.

Before passing on to the other major works of art, we should not miss a charming minor one, which formerly stood in the small room. This has now been more suitably placed on the left of the door leading into the cloister garden opposite (No. 202). It was in fact a Roman garden ornament—a picturesquely twisted marble tree trunk, wreathed with vines and ivy, and hung with little masks and tambourines; probably it formerly supported a small statue. A little farther along on the right is the Ludovisi Ares—a handsome young soldier-god with curly hair seated resting against a rock, with his shield beside him. The statue is considered to be a rather free copy of a bronze by Lysippus; the smiling cupid at the warrior's feet was the copyist's addition.

The group of 'Orestes and Electra' (No. 220), standing about the middle of the next wing of the cloister, provides another excellent example of changing taste; this was greatly admired by the neo-classicists. On the evidence of the artist's signature (on the stele behind Orestes's left leg), this is known to have been the work of a pupil of the Neo-Attic school, to whose founder we owe the Ludovisi Hera. No doubt in time the wheel of fortune will come full circle, bringing this style again to favour; it is salutary to recall that Augustus Hare dismissed Borromini's masterpiece, St. Ivo alla Sapienza, as 'a ridiculous church'. In the far right-hand corner of the cloister stands a sarcophagus with a grand battle scene (No. 229); this reminds us that classical Rome could also produce its own brand of 'baroque' art. The heroic figure of the commander—with arm outstretched and cloak blowing in the wind—might well have served as a model for some sculpture of the seventeenth century, instead of dating as he does from some 1,400 years earlier. Almost hidden in the corner behind this is a superb Roman portrait bust (No. 231), whose austerity bespeaks some figure of the late Republic. Some consider this to be a portrait of Julius Caesar, others see in it Scipio Africanus.

We now leave the Ludovisi Collection and—crossing the entrance hall—come to the eight halls which house the most important sculptures of the main collection. Passing through the first oval hall, we see two charming pieces of garden sculpture; a fountain basin of the first century AD (No. 254) on the left, and on the right a rhyton (a vessel shaped like a drinking horn), also once part of a fountain of a slightly earlier period. We now come to **hall II**, called after the works which it contains —mostly copies of Greek sculptures of the fifth century BC— the Hall of Art of the Severe Style. As if to belie this somewhat forbidding title, the first thing we see on entering is a delightful marine mosaic in the centre, whose many colours glow more brightly for being covered with a veil of clear water. The most famous sculpture in the room is the 'Tiber Apollo' (No. 262), so called because it was found in the bed of the river in 1891. This is believed by some authorities to be a copy of a bronze by Phidias, given by the Athenians for the sanctuary of Delphi as a thank-offering for the famous victory over the Persians at Marathon in 490 BC. Other notable sculptures in the room are the 'Aura' or 'Nereid', with the swirling draperies, of about 400 BC (No. 265); the strangely static 'Dancing Girl' in a short chiton, of the middle of the fifth century BC (No. 268); the 'Pelophorus', or 'Peplus wearer', of about 480 BC found in the Piazza Barberini (No. 296); and the Palatine Juno, of the school of Phidias (No. 271). In all but the last of these four female figures the torso is practically all that remains; the Juno is complete except for the head and part of the arms.

We now come to the most important room in the whole museum, **hall III**; appropriately known as the Great Hall of the Masterpieces. Every single one of the fifteen sculptures which it contains can be definitely considered as such; they are moreover most beautifully displayed, so that it is possible to examine every detail in excellent lighting. On entering we find ourselves between two copies of the famous bronze 'Discobolos of Myron'. That on the right (No. 277), known from its place of discovery as the 'Discobolos of Castel Porziano', is of a slightly earlier date; possibly from the reign of Hadrian (AD 117–38). The head and a good deal of the limbs of this copy are missing, but its full effect is felt if one sits down on the small stool on the right of the door; from this lower position the poised energy of the whole composition strikes one with the impact of living force—one feels that at any moment the stone athlete will come bounding forward.

The famous 'ex-Lancellotti Discobolos' on the left (No. 288, which during the last war was sold to Hitler contrary to Italian law and is now the property of the State) is one of the best preserved statues to have come down to us from antiquity; it was found on the Esquiline in 1781. This remarkably perfect copy of the Greek original is believed to have been made at some time during the period of the Antonine dynasty—that is between AD 161 and 193. Evidence of the precise care with which the copy was made is shown by the *cornetti* (little horns) to be seen in the hair above the forehead of the statue, showing that the exact proportions of the original were preserved in the copy by the point system. The statue is so perfect that it is a joy to behold from any angle.

Immediately on either side of the door are two heads—an Apollo on the right (No. 276), and on the left the 'Goddess of Butrinto', called after the ancient city of that name in Albania where she was found (No. 289). While examining these heads we should also turn to look at the statue known as the 'Apollo of Anzio' (No. 286), standing on the left in the centre of the hall, as—especially owing to the treatment of the hair—they belong to a style called after this statue 'the type of the Apollo of Anzio'. The Apollo itself is a first-century Roman copy of a Greek bronze of the fourth century BC.

We now come to one of the most famous statues in the collection, indeed in all Rome—this is the 'Niobid' (No. 278), found on the site of the Gardens of Sallust—the Roman historian who lived from 86 to 34 BC. This beautiful and appealing statue of a young girl—one of the fourteen children of Niobe—is the original work of a Greek sculptor, dating from between the years 460 and 430 BC; probably it once formed part of the decoration of the pediment of a temple. She is portrayed just after being struck in the back by one of the arrows of Apollo or Diana. According to myth, this son and daughter of Latona avenged Niobe's slighting reference to their mother's only having two children—as compared to her own fourteen—by shooting them all with arrows; Niobe, petrified by her sorrow, turned into a rock. Two other figures from the same group had previously been found before this one was discovered in 1906; they are a dead boy and a fleeing girl, now in the Glyptothek Ny-Carlsberg in Copenhagen. The tragic fate of Niobe and her children was a fertile source of inspiration for classical sculptors, particularly in Greece, in the fifth century BC. Until they were removed to the Uffizi in 1775, the Niobe and her children of the Villa Medici were one of the sights of Rome, though these were only Roman copies. So is the 'Ephebe' of Subiaco, standing nearby (No. 280); this is believed to have formed part of another Niobe group; it was found in the ruins of Nero's villa at Subiaco in 1884.

There could be no greater contrast to the tragic dying Niobid than the statue of the 'Venus of Cyrene' which stands beside her (No. 279). Here the goddess is represented in all the glory of her youth and beauty, just after she has risen from the foaming waves that gave her birth. Her missing arms would have been raised to wring the water out of her wet hair; her robes, carelessly flung over a dolphin with a fish in its mouth, remind us of her recent emergence from the sea. The statue is most generally believed to be a copy of a Greek bronze, the work of a sculptor of a slightly earlier period than Praxiteles; others consider that it dates from a much later period and belongs to one of the schools of Asia Minor. The Venus was discovered after a storm in the Baths of Cyrene in 1913, apparently quite by accident—it is said by two army officers taking a walk. One of them carried a stick which struck something hard in the sand as he paced along. The other was curious and went back to see what it was, and so she was found.

The last in the line of statues standing on the right is the Torso Valentini, of a hero or athlete (No. 281). During the last century this was 'restored' by the addition of head, arms and legs, to represent 'Diomede Fleeing from Troy'. Freed of these accretions, the torso is now believed by some to be Pythagoras's statue of Philoctetes, walking with difficulty because he is wounded; this idea is based on the forward stooping position of the figure. Others place a different interpretation on this stance, believing the statue to have been another discus thrower. Both schools of thought, however, consider that the sculpture dates from the first half of the fifth century BC.

Standing on either side of the door at the far end of the hall are two heads; the small one on the right representing 'Hypnos' or 'Sleep' (No. 282), is of exquisite beauty; it is attributed to Praxiteles and was found in Hadrian's villa. That on the left (No. 283) bears some resemblance to Praxiteles's head of Eubuleus; it is a copy of a work of the fourth century BC.

We now come to the two famous bronzes discovered in 1884 on a building site in the Via Quattro Novembre, just beyond the Colonna Palace. The first may be a portrait statue of a ruler (No. 234), represented leaning on a spear like Lysippus's renowned rendering of Alexander the Great. Some believe that it is a Seleucid prince of the Royal House of Syria —possibly Demetrius I Soter, who as a boy was held hostage in Rome in 175 BC. Others consider that it may represent Pollux after his victory in a boxing match against King Amycus of the Bebrycians. The statue dates from the middle of the second century BC and would have had eyes inset in natural colouring, like other figures of this type.

Next to this imperious-looking youth sits the exhausted figure of a middle-aged boxer overcome with fatigue after a match. The brutal realism of the work is striking, far removed from the usual classical idealisation of an athlete. Sunk in lethargy, the boxer raises his battered head as if half stupefied to answer some unexpected call. The work is signed—on one of the straps of the *cestus*, or protective covering of the left hand; the name is Apollonius, son of Nestor, of Athens, also the author of the famous Belvedere torso in the Vatican. Some authorities think that the boxer formed a group with his neighbour and is in fact the vanquished Amycus, King of the Bebrycians. Others consider instead that it is a portrait statue of Clitomachus of Thebes, one of the winners of the Olympic Games of 200 BC.

Both bronzes are in a remarkable state of preservation owing to the mysterious circumstances in which they were found. On the authority of the great archaeologist Lanciani, who was an eye-witness of the boxer's excavation, there is no doubt that the statue had been hidden with the greatest care. It was found seated on a stone capital in a trench specially opened under the Temple of the Sun, afterwards filled with sifted earth in order to preserve the sculpture from injury. This trench was situated eighteen feet below an ancient concrete floor on the steep hillside of the Quirinal which rises at the corner of the Via Quattro Novembre, where the Casa dell' Aviatore now stands. Who hid the sculptures, and when and why, is one of Rome's many mysteries.

After the 'Apollo of Anzio' comes the 'Anzio Girl' or 'Sacrificial Servant' (No. 287). This extraordinarily lovely statue was discovered in 1878 when a violent storm carried away part of the wall of the ruined imperial villa or palace at Anzio, the ancient Antium. By an extraordinary stroke of good fortune, the head and naked right shoulder, which are a separate piece worked in a finer marble, were recovered in the following year. The statue had originally stood in a niche at the end of a large hall of the villa. The girl's whole attention is fixed on three mysterious objects which she is carrying on a tray; they are a roll of cloth, a bay twig and what was evidently some sort of vessel or box with claw feet, only one of which remains. It seems that these must have had some religious significance and, as the girl wears no wreath and her head is not covered in any way (as a sacrificing priestess's would have been), it is believed that she was some sort of sacrificial servant.

Apart from the look of serious concentration on the young face, one of the greatest charms of the Anzio girl is the careless arrangement of the draperies—the rough woollen cloak hitched up into a thick roll round her hips, as Mediterranean peasant women still do with their heavy skirts today. The contrast between this and the soft folds of the crinkly stuff of the chiton is particularly effective, especially at the back. According to some authorities the statue is undoubtedly a

Greek original of the beginning of the Hellenistic period; others consider, from the way in which the marble is worked, that it is an antique copy of an early imperial Roman bronze; in either case it is a thing of rare and eloquent loveliness.

The following room, hall IV, is remarkable for the gaiety and grace of its Hellenistic sculptures, like the 'Dancer' from Hadrian's villa (No. 294) and 'Charis' or 'Grace' (No. 293), both on the right. There are also several charming seated feminine figures, but the one that takes the palm is the 'Sea Goddess' or 'Tyche' (No. 296) seated pensively on a throne, with the most delicious baby triton beside her.

We now turn left into the very small hall V, containing two altars, with delightful reliefs, of the first century AD. The free naturalistic treatment of the plane branches of that on the left (No. 309) remind us of the popularity of this tree in Roman gardens; the umbrella carried by one of the sacrificing *camilli* on that on the right (No. 310), of the antiquity of its use in religious ceremonial. The next room, hall IV, is dominated by the statue of Augustus as 'Pontifex Maximus'; again one is struck by the extraordinary beauty and calm majesty of the face. The more so as this room is filled with Roman portrait sculptures of every age and type; varying from the plump round face and curls of young 'Minatia Polla' (No. 315) to the striking elderly woman (No. 314). In this room also stands a head of 'Nero' (numbered both 322 and 618) which has recently been moved here. The square head and low forehead present a remarkable contrast to the fine features of Augustus; this is considered to be the best likeness of Nero in existence. Farther on stands the austere figure of the 'Chief Vestal', found in their house in the Forum. It is interesting for its detailed portrayal of a vestal's dress, particularly her style of hair dressing, which was also that of Roman brides; though in place of the vestals' purple-edged white *suffibulum*, rather like a hood, brides wore a flame-coloured veil.

In the circular hall VII, another remarkably fine series of portrait heads are grouped round an altar from Ostia, dated 1 October, AD 124 and decorated with scenes from Roman legends (No. 331). The portraits include Hadrian, reigned AD 117–38 (No. 326) and his wife Sabina (No. 327); Vespasian, reigned AD 69–79 (No. 324); Nerva, reigned AD 96–8 (No. 325); Antonius Pius, reigned AD 138–61 (No. 328); and Lucius Verus, reigned AD 161–9 (No. 329). The next small room, **hall VIII**, is the last in the series containing the most important sculptures in the museum. Its showpiece is the superb, but fragmentary, sarcophagus, found comparatively recently near Acilia (No. 330). The treatment of the solemn procession of 'philosophers' or 'poets' who surround the sarcophagus is masterly. Both the sculptural technique and the hair-style of the single female head date the work to some time in the second half of the third century AD. But what, one wonders, does the scene represent? Who is the single beardless boy among so many solemn men? Who the woman? Unfortunately the answers to these questions are unlikely ever to be forthcoming. Delightfully naïve and simple by comparison is the sarcophagus opposite (No. 331), adorned with reliefs of pastoral scenes. The rendering of the animals, particularly the ponies, would be the delight of any child. This room also contains a fine head of the Emperor Gallienus who reigned from AD 253 to 268.

From here we climb the stairs, turn left in a small lobby and left again in the long gallery containing the stucco decorations from the Farnesina villa. We now find ourselves in what is probably the most charmingly decorated room that has come down to us from antiquity—the garden one from the Empress Livia's villa at Prima Porta. These frescoes, which were discovered in 1863, were skilfully detached from the walls of the villa—where they were being ruined by damp—and transferred to the museum in 1951. In the villa itself they adorned a sunken room with a barrel vault decorated with *stucchi*, of which the remaining fragments have been brought here. In her study of the birds and flowers represented in the frescoes, Lady Gabriel suggested that this underground or semi-underground room might have been made as a shelter for Augustus, who apparently was terrified of lightning. It seems more likely, however, that it was one of those sunken chambers—of which other examples exist in the imperial palace on the Palatine and in Hadrian's villa—used as refuges from the fierce midday heat of Italian summers.

If this were the case, nothing could have been more skilfully designed to give an impression of fresh coolness than this painted garden and orchard, alive with the flitting life of song birds and backed by the impenetrable green of bosky thickets. If the artist was not Ludius himself, who Pliny tells us invented this style of *trompe l'oeil* garden painting during

Augustus's reign, he was in any event a great one. The play of light and shade, the birds hovering over the fruit-laden branches of quince and pomegranate, the pink damask roses, iris, violets and poppies present an enchanting garden scene very different from the cold formality which one is inclined to imagine reigned in Roman gardens. A light criss-cross fence of canes, such as were still used in Italian Renaissance gardens, separates the spectator in most realistic fashion from flowers and trees growing in a grass border. In its turn this simple garden is separated from the orchard by a low wall. In one corner a small bird-cage is painted standing on the wall, looking for all the world as if it had just been left there by one of the empress's serving maids, so natural and lifelike is the whole scene.

The Prima Porta villa does in fact seem to have been a favourite country retreat of the imperial couple; Augustus's liking for the simple life—his homespun clothes and games of knuckle bones—were not just political propaganda. According to Suetonius the villa rejoiced in the homely name of *ad gallinas* when Livia went to live there just before her marriage to Augustus, an eagle flying over her dropped a white hen (*gallina*) in her lap; it held a twig of bay in its beak. The hen proved to be such a terrific layer that the villa took its name from her and her progeny. The slip of bay was planted and ultimately became the grove from where the laurels were picked to crown the brows of the Caesars at their triumphs.

We now return to the rooms which contain the wonderful series of stuccoes and paintings from a Roman villa discovered on the Tiber bank in the Farnesina garden in 1879. If some authorities are correct in their theories, this building was the scene of a very different type of imperial romance from the long domestic association of Augustus and Livia. They believe it may have formed part of the villa 'across the Tiber' where Caesar kept Cleopatra as his mistress—to the horror of staid Roman republicans of the old school and the shocked delight of the city's gossips. Writing some 150 years later, that master of the titillating anecdote, Suetonius, related how the two of them would sit up feasting until dawn. This, however, was during Caesar's Egyptian expedition where he first met and was captivated by Cleopatra, who already at the age of 20 dreamed of a world empire—was she not a Ptolemy, descended from a successor of Alexander the Great? Cleopatra was four years older when she came to Rome at Caesar's invitation, bringing with her Caesarion, the son she said was his. She was in Rome when Caesar was murdered, and stayed on for a month; willing to gamble her life if need be—for the Romans hated her—against the chance that in the ensuing chaos her son might be accepted as heir. It seems unlikely, but there might have been a chance; it is revealing that Augustus had Caesarion murdered, but had Cleopatra's children by Mark Antony—who were no danger to him—brought up and educated according to their rank.

Whether Cleopatra actually lived there or not, this Roman villa on the Tiber bank had several rooms decorated in what is called the Egyptianised style. This cannot be regarded as evidence that they were specifically decorated for her, as this style was popular in Augustan times. Egyptian subjects were then fashionable in Italy; much as they were in France and Europe generally in the early nineteenth century after Napoleon's Egyptian campaign. The exact date of the Farnesina Roman Villa is in fact a matter of argument, some authorities holding to the theory that it dates from Julius Caesar's time and was in fact his; others that it was a public building, and others again that it was of the time of Augustus. Before looking at the paintings, we return to the long hall through which we came to Livia's garden room; this contains the exquisite stucco decorations from the vaulted ceilings of three rooms in the villa. These have been pieced together from some thousand fragments, and are conveniently displayed at eye level, so that we can examine closely their extraordinary delicacy and freedom of execution. The first stuccoes (No. 360) came from a small room (*cubiculo*) whose walls were covered with an extraordinarily rich painted decoration on a red ground. What strikes us first about the stuccoes is the lightness and sureness of touch with which the artist worked in his fast-drying medium. Later we notice the strange resemblance of some of the scenes—especially the one showing a landscape with small houses and bridge—to those on a willow-pattern plate.

The stuccoes from Cubicolo E (No. 361), whose walls were impressively decorated with painted *trompe l'oeil* architecture, are suitably heavier and more 'classical' in style; the winged victory holding a helmet is particularly beautiful. In Cubicolo E (No. 362) the stuccoes were lighter and gayer; again in some of them we are reminded of the *chinoiserie* style. They would have formed an appropriate accompaniment to the mural decoration, again on a red ground, which included love scenes.

Turning to the room at the end on the left we now come to the paintings themselves. They belong to the styles classified by archaeologists as the 'second Pompeian style' of architecture in perspective; the third of 'Egyptianised' style; and the fourth style of architectural illusionism. In style and subject the paintings are closely related to Hellenistic art, especially of Alexandria. In the first small room are the paintings from Cubicolo E, in the second Pompeian style; particularly charming is a detail of a young woman seated, pouring scent into a small bottle. Then follows **hall II**, with the superb paintings from Cubicolo B (No. 365), the picture in the central frame represents the nymph Leucothea with little Dionysus on her lap. In a frame on the left wall is a striking Aphrodite enthroned, with Eros standing before her; on some other fragments Egyptian motifs—such as the sistrum and the sparrowhawk—are to be seen.

The next large room, **hall III**, contains paintings on a black ground from the large hall C in the Farnesina villa (No. 366). Most of the landscapes which originally filled the spaces between the slender columns and caryatids have disappeared; but the painted frieze above the garlands is artistically the most important part of the villa decoration to have survived. Executed with extraordinary delicacy and grace, they are believed to represent scenes of the Egyptian King Bocchoris giving judgment; he was apparently regarded as an Egyptian Solomon. In the centre of the hall stands the graceful bronze figure of the Tiber 'Bacchus' (No. 567). This was found in 1885 in the bed of the river not far from the Farnesina. Paintings from the *cryptoporticus* of the villa stand by the windows of this and the other rooms.

We now come to **hall IV** and the paintings from Cubicle D of the villa (No. 368). Here again Aphrodite reigns among love scenes, including one of a young bride seated on the marriage bed beside her husband. For once we know the artist's name—scratched on a column in Greek letters are the words 'Seleucus made it'. With **hall V**, which contains more fragmentary pictures from the rest of the villa, our tour of the paintings end. We retrace our steps to the landing at the top of the stairs, where there are two rooms containing a fine collection of polychrome mosaics.

Descending the stairs, we find ourselves back in the entrance hall, close to the door leading into the 'Michelangelo' cloister. If it is a fine day, this is the perfect moment for a breath of fresh air and a quiet walk in the garden, or simply to sit and sun ourselves and look at the view. Although the cloister was traditionally attributed to Michelangelo, it is now generally considered that he had no hand in its making. An inscription on the pilaster nearest the door records the date of its completion—1565—a year after the great man's death. In the centre of the garden a graceful fountain bubbles in the shade of four cypresses; this was built in 1695; one of the cypresses—a hoary old veteran supported by iron bands—was planted at the same time.

However, we have yet to see the five smaller halls of sculpture before we leave the museum and continue on our way. These are situated just to the left of the museum entrance as we face it on our way out. The outstanding works are the Dionysus from Hadrian's villa (No. 449 in **hall 3**), a Roman second-century copy of a Greek bronze; and the 'Sleeping Hermaphrodite' (No. 471 in hall 4), a Roman copy of a Hellenistic work. Like statues of Priapus, those of Hermaphrodites were often used as garden ornaments, because their symbolism of the male and female elements also signified fertility. In the same room is a beautiful head of a 'Sleeping Nymph' (No. 472) of honey-coloured marble; this came from Nero's villa at Subiaco. Last but not least—in fact the finest sculpture in this part of the museum—is the wonderful head of the 'Dying Persian' (**hall 4** No. 473). This is perhaps even more moving than those of the Galatian killing his wife (in the Ludovisi Collection) or the 'Dying Gaul' (on the Capitoline); certainly it was copied from the same group at Pergamon.

The last hall (**No. 5**), devoted to statues in coloured marbles, is dominated by a colossal seated goddess of imperial times (No. 478) (the head is a modern addition in plaster). Behind this is a polychrome mosaic of the four seasons (No. 479), represented by women's heads which surprise us by their modernity; they date from the fifth century AD. On the left is a small equestrian statue of a boy (No. 481). This has so gay and lifelike an appearance that one might almost imagine it was a toy; but in actual fact it was a funerary statue, possibly even used as an urn for the child's ashes (both horse and rider are hollow), placed outside the tomb. This sculpture dates from late imperial times and was found in a hundred fragments near Acilia, in 1928.

Emerging from the Museo delle Terme, we can now spare a few moments to examine its surroundings before catching the bus to S. Agnese. The large piazza in front of it, now called after the Republic, is still more generally known as Piazza dell' Esedra, the semicircle of buildings on its far side having been erected on the site of the great stepped niche, or *exedra*, which had served as a grandstand for watching athletic displays in the grounds of Diocletian's Baths. The vast area covered by the baths is really only brought home to us when we realise that parts of them still exist on the corner of Via del Viminale and in Piazza S. Bernardo, where a circular hall has been converted into the church of the same name.

But to return to the Piazza Esedra, where the striking fountain in the middle was once the cause of a good deal of friction. It was originally opened by Pius IX on the 10 September 1870; probably the last public work ever to be inaugurated by a pope, as the armies of united Italy entered Rome ten days later. At that time the fountain simply consisted of jets of water; later this was considered not to be sufficiently dignified for its commanding position and the sculptor Rutelli was commissioned to carry out the sculptural groups that now adorn it. It is said that the models for the curvaceous naiads wrestling with marine monsters were two sisters, well-known musical comedy stars of their day. Certainly the liberal display of their charms aroused a furore when the fountain was ready for its opening in 1901. So heated was public opinion that the ceremony was delayed indefinitely; until one night a group of young men tore down the concealing scaffolding, and the fountain was thus unceremoniously inaugurated. Many tales are told about the fountain. One of the most appealing is that in their old age the two sisters used every day to take a walk to 'their' fountain which reminded them of the gay days of their youth; and that once a year Rutelli would travel to Rome from his native Sicily to entertain them to dinner.

En route for S. Agnese, we now have the choice of taking the 37 bus from the Via Cernaia (to the left of S. Maria degli

Angeli), or the 60 from Piazza S. Bernardo. In order to reach this last we again pass the Grand Hotel and the **Fontanone dell' Acqua Felice**, the first of the great monumental fountains of Rome to be built in modern times—as part of the town-planning schemes of Sixtus V. In 1585 the pope had restored Alexander Severus's old aqueduct sufficiently to supply his own villa on the Esquiline. Two years later the fountain was inaugurated, causing such severe criticism of the central figure of Moses that the sculptor, Prospero da Brescia, is said to have died of a broken heart. It was in fact completed by another hand, because the pope was in such a hurry to press on with his plans for what—remarkably in the sixteenth century—he intended to make the industrial quarter of Rome. Sixtus had already built granaries, flour and fulling mills in the area; one wonders what the neighbours in those days thought of this arbitrary encroachment on their amenities? Previously this part of Rome had been given over to stately villas such as that of Rabelais's host, the French Ambassador, Cardinal du Bellay.

For our bus journey to S. Agnese, we should allow about half-an-hour; the distance is under two miles and except at the rush hours, we should do it in less. Our journey will take us past the historic **Porta Pia**, flanked on the right by the old British Embassy, on the left by Pauline Bonaparte's villa, now the French Embassy to the Holy See. The main block of the gate on this side was built to Michelangelo's designs for Pius IV in 1561. It was by breaches in the walls on either side of this gate that the armies of united Italy entered Rome on 20 September 1870; the building now houses the Bersaglieri Museum. In those days the open spaces of the Roman campagna stretched right up to the walls, with here and there fine villas bordering upon the Via Nomentana.

Today as we speed along the wide Via Nomentana, the prosperous suburbs give us no hint of such a recent past, let alone that of early Christian times. It comes as a definite surprise, as we get off the bus just before the traffic lights by the Via di S. Costanza, to realise that the **Basilica of S. Agnese fuori le Mura**, whose inconspicuous apse we see beside the road on the left, has been a place of pilgrimage since the first half of the fourth century. Already, at the church of S. Agnese in Agone in the Piazza Navona, we have visited the supposed site of the saint's martyrdom; here we find what was undoubtedly the place of her burial. The year 304 is believed to be the date of St. Agnes's martyrdom, which is said to have taken place on 21 January. The famous episode of her loosened hair covering her nakedness is mentioned in the inscription which St. Damasus had put over her grave; this was discovered in 1728, and is still preserved on the stairs leading down to the basilica.

The cult of this virgin martyr quickly achieved great popularity in Rome. Thus it is not surprising to find that within fifty years of her death a member of Constantine's family had built a basilica over her tomb. Its foundation has usually been attributed to Constantia, the daughter of Constantine the Great. The latest archaeological opinion, however, now attributes it to his grand-daughter of the same name, daughter of his son Constantine II; this Constantia lived in Rome from 337 to 350. A sepulchral inscription dated 349, still preserved in the church, proves that it was already in existence by that date.

To reach the Basilica of S. Agnese, we enter the courtyard of the adjoining convent, cross it and turn right down a long staircase, whose walls are covered with inscriptions (St. Damasus's is at the end), and find ourselves in the narthex. The church we see today was built by Honorius I (625–38) over the one founded by Constantia. Its curious site—half buried in the hill—is explained by the fact that, like its predecessor, it was built right into the catacombs in which St. Agnes was buried. Excavations beneath it, made during this century, have shown that the site of the original church was cleared by cutting right into the hill and the network of catacombs, which still surround Honorius's existing building. His basilica, with its galleries which give access from ground level, was probably thus designed partly for convenience, but also because galleries such as these were common in Byzantine churches, and the architect is believed to have been Greek. Several early Roman basilicas were erected in this style, usually over the tombs of saints, the other best known example is S. Lorenzo fuori le Mura.

In spite of several restorations, S. Agnese is one of the rare Roman churches which has best preserved the appearance—and the atmosphere—of a very ancient Christian place of worship. Seeing it thus, with the mellow afternoon light softly filtering down over its antique columns, we can most easily ignore the somewhat jarring nineteenth-century frescoes, and concentrate our attention on the wonderful seventh-century mosaic. Here St. Agnes looks very slim and young in her elaborate Byzantine court dress, embroidered with the phoenix symbol of immortality. She is portrayed against a field of gold, with the sword of martyrdom at her feet. On either side of her stand Pope Symmachus, who restored Constantia's first church and Honorius I who built this one. A dedicatory inscription, with Honorius's monogram, relates that for the building he expended 252 pounds of silver.

Below this, the apse is still lined with its contemporary marble decoration; in it stands an ancient episcopal throne. The altar canopy dates from 1614; but it is probable that the four very beautiful supporting porphyry columns date from the seventh century. St. Agnes's statue on the altar was made in the sixteenth century out of an antique work in alabaster. Beneath it lie her remains and those of her foster sister or freedwoman St. Emerentiana, who was stoned to death when found praying by her tomb. Here, on 21 January each year, two lambs decked with ribbons and flowers are blessed. They are then taken to the Pope for a further blessing before being handed over to the Benedictine nuns of S. Cecilia in Trastevere, who make the patriarchs' and archbishops' palliums from their wool.

After re-ascending the stairs, we turn left down a little path which leads us to the church of **S. Costanza**. In this quiet and peaceful corner stands what was originally the tomb of the Princess Constantia who built the Basilica of S. Agnese. Later this was transformed into a baptistry; in 1254 it was consecrated as a church and dedicated to a St. Costanza, not the princess, but a nun. Its circular shape is reminiscent of the great Roman pagan tombs; and indeed in the decoration of this very early Christian building the pagan and Christian worlds meet and mingle. The exquisite mosaics which adorn the vaulting—among the earliest of their kind to survive—are in effect more classical than Christian. The background is white, as in the ancient Roman pavement mosaics; the ornamental designs are either geometrical or floral. These last are composed of vine tendrils or sprays of fruit and flowers, interspersed with birds, amphorae and other purely secular motifs. Small semi-draped cupid-like figures alternate with traditional scenes such as the vintage, executed in wonderfully delicate colours with here and there the sparkle of gold.

These are probably the most beautiful mosaics in Rome; graceful and free in their design and execution but—apart from the possible Biblical associations of the fruitful vine— absolutely devoid of Christian content. Evidently they are of so early a date that no formula associated with Christian iconography had yet been evolved for this type of decoration. It is said that the two busts in the centre of the compartments, decorated with vine tendrils, to the left and right of the door, are portraits of Constantia and her husband. The great porphyry sarcophagus of Constantia (the original, which stood opposite the door, is now in the Vatican Museum) provides an interesting early example of the adaptation of pagan symbols to Christian use; it is covered with reliefs of sheep and peacocks—whose flesh was supposed to remain uncorrupt—also vintage scenes. The mosaics in the niches are of much later date—probably of the fifth or seventh centuries; they represent the donation of the keys and Christ giving peace (probably originally the law or Gospel) to the world. Even these, however, are bordered by exquisite garlands of fruit and foliage.

The circular nave with the mosaics is separated by a beautiful double ring of columns from the central domed space. Originally the dome, too, was covered with even more wonderful mosaics, of which drawings have come down to us in the sketch-book of the sixteenth-century artist Francisco d'Hollanda, now in the Escorial. These show water-side villa scenes, divided into compartments by caryatids who—like Daphne— merged into the green branches of trees. The Christian content of this exquisite decoration may at first glance seem doubtful, resembling as it does similar scenes in Pompeian paintings and the Farnesina stuccoes. But, as we have seen, no specific Christian iconography had yet been evolved; and possibly this was an attempt to portray the River Jordan, which subsequently became a favourite subject in church mosaics. This marvellous work of art of the fourth century was destroyed twelve centuries later to make way for the existing frescoes.

We must now return to the Via Nomentana and our bus, as we have yet one more church to see before our day's itinerary is ended. For this the 60 bus is preferable, as it passes

Piazza S. Bernardo; on the corner of which and Via Venti Settembre stands the church of **S. Maria della Vittoria**.

Begun in 1605 by Carlo Maderno for Paul V, this church was originally dedicated to St. Paul. Its dedication was changed after the gift of a picture known as the Madonna of Victory—hence the church's name. This was found in 1620, unscathed among the ruins of the Castle of Prague, by the triumphant Catholic armies who had defeated the Protestant forces of Frederick of Bohemia. The picture was subsequently destroyed by fire in 1833. The façade of the church was built between 1624 and 1626 by Giovan Battista Soria for Cardinal Scipione Borghese, who paid for the work in exchange for the famous statue of a Hermaphrodite (now in the Louvre). The statue was discovered in their garden by the Carmelites of the adjoining monastery; in spite of its value the find must have posed rather an embarrassing problem for the good friars, but its happy solution by Cardinal Borghese left all parties contented.

The interior of the church is one of the richest examples of baroque decoration in Rome. One uses the term 'decoration' advisedly here, as there is a world of difference between the effect of this church—where it is a subsequent addition—and that of S. Andrea al Quirinale and S. Carlo alle Quattro Fontane, which we saw this morning. Nevertheless S. Maria della Vittoria contains one of the most famous baroque compositions in Rome—Bernini's Cornaro chapel in the left transept, built between 1645 and 1652. Today hardly a book on Rome appears without a photograph of this work, which is regarded as one of Bernini's great achievements, especially for his ingenious use of concealed natural lighting effects (these are seen at their best in the afternoon).

Looking at the chapel we are instantly reminded of the fact that not only was Bernini the master of dramatic effect but was actually also a dramatist and producer—one of his own plays has recently been discovered in Paris where he himself is said to have acted before Louis XIV. This is not only because members of the Cornaro family are seen—in what can only be described as theatre boxes—on either side of the chapel, watching the dramatic climax of St. Teresa's vision and mystical union with Christ, but also from the way in which this last is presented. The sculptural group, which has all the effect of a *tableau vivant*, appears as if suspended in space on a cloudy firmament; it is illuminated by golden rays and the whole composition vividly recalls prints and descriptions of seventeenth-century theatrical productions that have come down to us. The saint is portrayed with eyes half-closed and open mouth, the angel holding the arrow as a boy with a smile, half compassionate.

Needless to say such a presentation of a mystical experience has aroused very different reactions at different periods. Augustus Hare quoted Mrs. Jameson's shocked Victorian 'the head of the St. Teresa is that of a languishing nymph, the angel a sort of Eros . . . the whole has been significantly described as a parody of divine love. The vehicle, white marble, its place in a Christian church—enhance all its vileness.' Her French contemporary Taine thought 'Bernini's St. Teresa adorable . . . the angel, the most beautiful page of a great lord who comes to bring joy to too-tender a vassal.' With sceptical eighteenth-century realism, his compatriot President de Brosses remarked: 'If that is divine love, I know what it is.'

CHAPTER FOURTEEN

S. Lorenzo fuori le Mura to S. Giovanni in Laterano

IN chapter XIII, with S. Agnese fuori le Mura, we made our first real expedition into the world of early Christian Rome. From now on this aspect of the city will fill an increasing amount of our time, as we explore the outer areas of the ancient city, both within and without the Aurelian walls. At first glance it may seem odd that many of the early Christian sites are to be found in such a definitely defined topographical area; however, when we think back to the urban configuration of classical Rome, the reason at once becomes evident. Much of the area we have explored up to now was occupied by the monumental centre of the city—the *fora*, temples and baths or the arenas and porticoes of the *Campus Martius*. It was in the narrow strip of land sandwiched between these and the great imperial parks and estates encircling the city that the bulk of the population actually lived. During the third century, when Christianity was gaining many converts, this residential area was already established on either side of the 'Servian' wall (in reality built after the burning of the city by the Gauls in 387 BC). As we know, the Christian meeting-places of this period were in private houses—many of which afterwards became the first churches of Rome—the famous *titoli*, or titular churches we still know today. Outside the Aurelian walls, which the emperor of that name (who reigned from AD 270–5) built as a defence against the threatened barbaric invasions of his day, lay most of the pagan cemeteries and Christian catacombs. Here too, after the age of persecution was over, arose the oratories and the type of church known as a '*basilica ad corpus*' (basilica at the body), built over the tomb of a particularly venerated martyr or saint.

The exploration in this chapter will take us to see one of the most famous of these last, S. Lorenzo fuori le Mura; three of the great basilicas—S. Giovanni in Laterano, S. Maria Maggiore and S. Croce in Gerusalemme (the first a Constan-

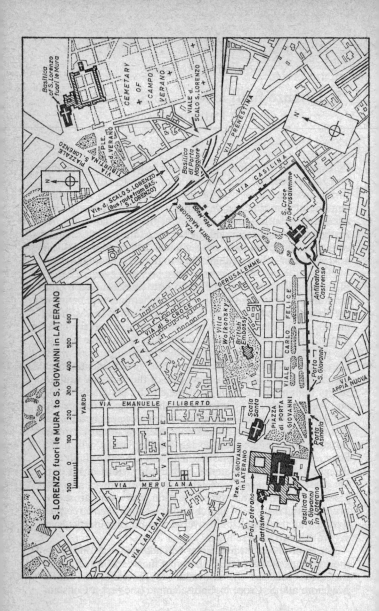

S. LORENZO fuori le MURA to S. GIOVANNI in LATERANO

tinian foundation; the last built into a hall of his mother, St. Helena's, palace); and three of the ancient *tituli*. By way of complete contrast, we will also see the palace of early Christianity's greatest enemy—the notorious Golden House of Nero, the ruins of which lie buried close by.

We start off by the 66 bus from Largo del Tritone—at the middle of the Via del Tritone by the tunnel. Passing through the tunnel under the Quirinal Palace and up the Via Nazionale, this takes us past the Piazza della Repubblica or Esedra, and the Naiad fountain—familiar from yesterday's excursion —to the Piazza Cinquecento in front of the main Stazione Termini, one of the best modern buildings in Rome. If there is not too much traffic, a quick glance to the right may enable us to see the venerable relic of the Servian wall bordering on the left side of the cantilevered glass porch of the station. A sharp right turn brings us into the Viale del Castro Pretorio, the terminus for many provincial buses, named after the barracks of the Praetorian Guard, whose site on the left of the road is still a military establishment. Passing the Air Ministry, our route continues down the Viale Pretoriano, dignified by a fine stretch of the Aurelian wall bordering its left-hand side. But shortly a left turn down Via dei Ramni takes us into the hurly-burly and somewhat sordid surroundings of the initial stages of the Via Tiburtina, the road to Tivoli.

If we started off at 9 a.m., when there is a comparative lull in the traffic, in less than three-quarters of an hour we should have arrived at our stopping place of Piazzale San Lorenzo, easily recognisable from the soberly dignified medieval façade and campanile of the **Basilica di S. Lorenzo fuori le Mura**, visible among trees on the right. Since 1830 all Catholics who die in Rome—with the exception of the pope, cardinals, certain prelates and sovereigns and princes of royal houses— are usually buried in the huge Campo Verano cemetery which has grown up round S. Lorenzo. The last ten years have also seen the increasing development of an industrial area along the Via Tiburtina beyond. Thus today it is hard to believe that some eighty years ago this venerable basilica still slumbered in peaceful isolation.

S. Lorenzo is at one and the same time one of the strangest and most fascinating of Roman basilicas. Externally, it is perhaps very much what we would expect—beside a low hill a thirteenth-century porticoed façade and campanile rise out of a mass of monastic buildings. There is a particularly charming view, down an avenue of limes, on the right, to the recently restored exterior of Clement III's cloister, built between 1187 and 1191, with graceful six-light windows. In the church portico are thirteenth-century frescoes of the life and martyrdom of St. Lawrence and legends associated with it; the tomb of Italy's great post-war statesman, Alcide De Gasperi; and a late classical sarcophagus with vintage scenes, in which Pope Damascus II is said to have been buried in 1048.

Before entering, it would perhaps be as well to outline the building history of this strange church which has mystified generations of scholars and archaeologists, as it was only finally revealed by the excavations and restorations resulting from bomb damage during the last war. Together with Pope Sixtus II, St. Lawrence suffered martyrdom in the year 258, under the Emperor Valerianus; he was buried on 4 August in the cemetery of Cyriaca in the Agro Verano district beside the Via Tiburtina. According to tradition, during the reign of Pope St. Sylvester (314–35) Constantine built a basilica over the site; this gave access to the saint's tomb in the catacombs below. Subsequently several popes were buried in the same catacombs; and Sixtus III (432–40) remodelled and redecorated the sanctuary. Between 579 and 590, Pelagius II built an entirely new basilica, which inscriptions praised as being spacious and well-lit and giving improved access to St. Lawrence's tomb. In 1148 the ciborium for the high altar was made and signed by the stone-masons Johannes, Petrus, Angelus and Saxo; between 1187 and 1191 Clement III built the cloister. In 1191 or 1192, Cardinal Cencio Savelli remodelled and redecorated St. Lawrence's tomb. As Pope Honorius III, between 1216 and 1227, he added to Pelagius's basilica.

Today Honorius's basilica really serves as a nave, relegating to Pelagius's old one the function of a long high chancel, with St. Lawrence's tomb enclosed in a crypt-like chapel beneath. As we enter, we are impressed by the sober dignity of the antique Ionic columns rising from the cosmatesque pavement, the delicate mosaics of the ambos and the graceful ciborium. But these are common to many other Romanesque churches in Rome and elsewhere; it is only as we ascend the chancel steps, that the greater richness and mystery of Pelagius's basilica becomes apparent. On three sides huge fluted Corinthian columns of precious *pavonazzo* marble support an entablature of antique fragments; above them rise the shadowy arcaded galleries. A dim light filters through the windows of pierced marble, to illuminate Pelagius's sixth-century mosaic on the inner face of the great central triumphal arch. In it he is portrayed standing beside St. Lawrence (the smaller figure without a halo on the left), offering a model of his church to Christ, enthroned in majesty, wrapped in imperial purple robes and seated upon an orb. Sadly, this old basilica is now laterally divided in two by the chancel. But from the episcopal throne at its far end, and in the shadows of St. Lawrence's crypt beneath, we can still conjure up some idea of how it looked in the sixth century.

A small subterranean chapel opening out of the left aisle of Honorius's basilica is dedicated to St. Cyriaca, in whose cemetery St. Lawrence was buried. Its present decoration dates from the seventeenth century; but before that there was a thirteenth-century chapel, and before that possibly an earlier one still. A little farther on steps lead down into the aisle of Pelagius's basilica, which ends in the funerary chapel of Pius XI (1846–78)—a typical nineteenth-century interpretation of medievalism. Traversing this and the other aisle of the old basilica, we find ourselves at the entrance to the sacristy, leading in turn into the cloister. The garden has not yet quite recovered from the work involved in the recent restorations. But the peace of past centuries still fills its surrounding arcades while shafts of sunlight stream down between the classical and medieval columns, which are so appropriately mingled in this place where memories of pagan, early Christian and medieval Rome are fused together.

It comes as something of a shock to emerge again into the twentieth century, and board the ED bus in the Piazzale S. Lorenzo *en route* for the Porta Maggiore, S. Croce in Gerusalemme and S. Giovanni in Laterano. From 1 October to 2 May we should continue directly on to either of these latter; but during the summer months if we are interested in the origins of early Christian church architecture and the art of Roman stucco decoration we should descend from the tram at Porta Maggiore in order to see that mysterious building known as the **Basilica di Porta Maggiore** (at the time of writing the Basilica is closed indefinitely for restoration).

We now have a short time to examine the Porta Maggiore

itself; one of the most imposing of its kind, built by Claudius in AD 52, but really originally forming part of the Claudian aqueduct. Conduits of both the Acqua Claudia and the Anio Novus were concealed in it; an inscription also records Vespasian and Titus's restorations; later it was incorporated into the Aurelian walls. The double arches of the gate lead to the ancient Via Prenestina (the road to Palestrina) and the Labicana or Casilina (the road to Cassino). The famous Baker's Tomb, with its round stone ovens and charming frieze representing all the phases of bread-making at the end of the republican era (note the donkey propelling the mill on the left), stands just outside the gate. It was erected by his wife Atinia in memory of Marcus Vergilius Eurysaces, who was evidently a baker with a very big business.

A maze of tram lines and a high brick-faced railway embankment on the left greet us as we turn from the Baker's Tomb to look for the Basilica di Porta Maggiore. Its entrance is the door where the brick embankment juts out into the Via Prenestina on the left; a strange environment for the sanctuary of an ancient mystic sect. In fact its discovery in 1916 caused no little worry to the archaeologists and railway engineers; here, within a few feet of the many railway lines leading to the Roman terminus, was a building of incalculable archaeological and artistic interest which had survived almost intact for 2,000 years. It lay, however, at a considerable depth—14 metres below the permanent way—and great pains and layers of concrete were expended to preserve it from damage and vibration caused by passing trains. All of this partly explain the remarkably discouraging regulations with which the authorities have seen fit to hedge it around; still, the site is off the beaten track, and the basilica itself is not a sight calculated to attract the 'Rome in a day' mass of tourists; but it is of tremendous interest to students of art and archaeology.

It is believed that the basilica dates from the first century of the Empire and was the meeting-place of members of one of the mystic sects, possibly the Neo-Pythagoreans, who believed in the transmigration of the soul. With the materialism consequent upon increased wealth and power, the old Roman state religion had lost much of its grip during the last years of the Republic. Augustus reinstated it, but afterwards as a result of the expansion of the Empire and trade many oriental cults were introduced into Rome and received with enthusiasm by those who longed for a warmer and more personal religion which held out some promise of a life hereafter.

What astonished the discoverers of the basilica was its similarity in form and decoration to the early Christian ones—the apse and aisles and the stucco reliefs of praying figures with hands outstretched in the ancient fashion. The full meaning of other scenes represented in these exquisite stuccoes, which cover the vaulted ceiling and much of the walls, has, however, never been completely elucidated. Many of the subjects are drawn from Greek mythology, such as 'The Rape of Ganymede' in the centre of the vaulted nave. Or that of the apse, which is variously interpreted to represent 'Venus and Adonis', or 'Sappho and Phaon', symbolising the soul's journey through the purifying waves to the underworld. Others obviously represent cult symbols such as the relief of garlands and streamers reverently placed upon a table. But what possible religious significance, one wonders, could be attributed to such scenes as children playing ball games and the curious relief of the pygmy and a woman, apparently feeding two small wild cats, portrayed among palm trees with other mysterious figures. The subject matter of many of the decorations of the basilica is indeed an enigma; but this need not interfere with our enjoyment of their exquisite grace and almost perfect state of preservation. Here for once we see this type of Roman art of the first century in its original beauty and surroundings; a circumstance that enables us much more clearly to picture how those of the Farnesina villa (which we saw at the Terme yesterday, and to which they are closely related), must once have looked, and to imagine the richness of Nero's Golden House whose ruins we will shortly be seeing.

During the winter months, if we have been lucky with the traffic and not taken too long over our journey to and from S. Lorenzo, we have the choice of first seeing S. Croce in Gerusalemme—which is open till 1.30 p.m. and will only take about quarter of an hour—and then walking on to S. Giovanni in Laterano; or of going straight on by bus to the latter. Time is the essence of our decision, as the opening and closing hours of the most important things we want to see at S. Giovanni are more than usually complicated—the Baptistry closes at midday, the Cloister and Scala Santa half an hour later; the basilica itself is open all day.

As **S. Croce in Gerusalemme** comes first on our route, and as

with luck we may be able to fit it in then, we will treat our
itinerary in that order. S. Croce is one of the most surprising
churches in Rome—its façade and oval vestibule of 1743 are
among the most delightfully light rococo creations in the city.
Its interior appears to be almost wholly baroque except for
some fine antique columns, a cosmatesque pavement and a few
Renaissance details. But actually recent archaeological investigation has revealed that the entire body of the church formed
part of an imperial palace built somewhere between AD 180
and 211. Its other title—the Basilica Sessoriana—does indeed
afford a clue to this surprising fact; the *Palatium Sessorianum*
is known to have been owned by Constantine's mother, St.
Helena, between the years 317 and 322. Moreover, throughout
the ages this church and the chapel named after her have been
associated with the legend of St. Helena's discovery of the true
Cross.

Some time between the years 313 and 361 this great hall of
the Sessorian palace was converted into a basilica; communicating with it are two small rooms which also formed part of
the palace. One of these has for centuries been known as the
chapel of St. Helena, the other was dedicated at the end of the
fifteenth century to St. Gregory. By the middle of the fourth
century both the basilica and chapels would have been isolated
from the palace, as it was no longer considered suitable for
churches to form part of a lay dwelling as they often had in the
original *tituli*. The palace itself, however, continued for long to
exist as an imperial possession; in the year 500 Theodoric is
still recorded as having ordered the execution of an officer
there. By the middle of the fourth century the basilica had
been donated by Constantine or, more probably, by one of his
sons to the Church; it is possible that the relic of the Cross
already formed part of this donation. The legend of Helena's
finding of it dates from the second half of the fourth century.
But it is remarkable that Eusebius—the Bishop of Caesarea—
to whom Constantine related his vision of the Cross, which he
adopted as his symbol, never mentioned the empress's discovery of the relic. Between 425 and 444, some hundred years
after St. Helena's death, the Emperor Valentinian III decorated her chapel with mosaics, which included portraits of his
mother, Galla Placidia, his sister Honoria, and himself.

Although there are classical ruins on both sides of S. Croce
(those on the right are known as the Anfiteatro Castrense and

believed to have been the private amphitheatre of the imperial palace), no sign of its ancient origins are visible when we enter it today. Still the church contains some Renaissance treasures; notably a beautiful water stoop, with fishes carved in relief inside; also Jacobo Sansovino's fine tomb of Cardinal Quiñones (the Emperor Charles V's confessor) in the apse. The apse itself is decorated with a charming late fifteenth-century fresco attributed to Antoniazzo Romano, portraying the legend of St. Helena's finding of the true Cross, rediscovered during the restoration of the basilica in 1492. Relics of this were found walled into a niche above the apse; presumably for safety, as the history of many of Rome's famous relics show them to have been very vulnerable to sack and theft. The fragments of the Cross and other relics are now preserved in a modern chapel whose entrance is at the far left end of the church near the apse. Also in the chapel is a fine miniature Byzantine mosaic of Christ.

A door in the wall beside the apse opens on to a sloping flight of steps leading down to the chapel of St. Gregory, one of the rooms of the Sessorian palace. This is now practically subterranean, reminding us of the rise in levels in Rome since classical times, as the floor level of this and the communicating chapel of St. Helena was originally that of the basilica and the whole palace.

We now enter the chapel of St. Helena; facing us, above the altar (at which only the Pope and titular Cardinal may say Mass), is an antique statue, converted by the addition of the Cross and a new head and hands to represent the empress. According to legend, this chapel was once her bedroom; more probably it was her private chapel, possibly even the place in which the relic of the Cross was originally kept. No evident trace of Valentinian III's mosaics now remain; but for once we cannot really regret them, as the Renaissance ones which have replaced them are of such extraordinary beauty (these are best seen by morning light; such artificial lighting as there is, is poor; the switch is on the left of the far door). Some consider that Melozzo da Forli—who is believed to have designed the existing mosaics just before his death in 1494—preserved some semblance of the original design in his own. Be that as it may, looking at the glowing colours—particularly the blues against the gold ground—we have little doubt that this is a masterpiece in its own right; possibly the last in the long tradition of mosaic as a fine art. The cardinal represented kneeling beside St. Helena was the donor, Cardinal Carvajal, who also had the long inscription made on coloured tiles recording the rediscovery of the relic of the Cross; this is now on the walls of the staircase that leads us back to the basilica.

On leaving S. Croce, we walk along the wide tree-lined boulevard of the Viale Carlo Felice, past the monumental bronze statue of St. Francis of Assisi, and find ourselves in the Piazza di Porta S. Giovanni. This last is quite a modern gate, made by Giacomo della Porta for Gregory XIII (1572–85); but beside it rise the rounded towers of the ancient Porta Asinara. The whole piazza is dominated by Alessandro Galilei's imposing façade of the **Basilica di S. Giovanni in Laterano**, built in 1736. (The basilica is open from 6.30 a.m. to half an hour before sunset, on Sundays till 8.30 p.m.; the Cloister from 9 a.m. to 12.30 p.m. and from 3 to 6.30 p.m. shut on Sundays; the Scala Santa from 5 a.m. to 12.30 p.m. and from 2.45 to 7.30 p.m.; the Baptistry from 8.30 a.m. to midday and from 3.30 to 7 p.m. in summer, from 3 to 4.30 p.m. in winter.)

In view of these varied closing hours—complicated even for Rome!—we would be wise to make first for the Baptistry to be sure of seeing it before midday. To reach it, we turn right in front of the basilica—skirting the modern Lateran Palace, built as a summer residence for Sixtus V by Domenico Fontana in 1586, on the site of part of the old 'Patriarchate', official residence of the popes since the days of Constantine. Until 1963 this housed the famous collections of the Christian, Profane and Ethnological Missionary Museums. They are now in process of transference to a new building in the Vatican in order to make way for the offices of the Vicariato. We now find ourselves in the **Piazza di S. Giovanni in Laterano** in the midst of which rises the oldest and tallest obelisk in Rome. Dating from the reigns of Tutmes III and IV in the fifteenth century BC, it originally stood before the Temple of Ammon in Thebes, was brought to Rome by Constantius II in AD 357, and raised in the Circus Maximus. In 1587 it was found there in three pieces, and was placed in its present site in the following year by Sixtus V, as one of the ornaments of his network of new roads.

Another result of Sixtus V's town planning was the destruction of the old Patriarchate or Pontifical palace. Although this had become practically uninhabitable since the papal residence in Avignon, Sixtus's action in destroying it has since been regarded as an unpardonable act of vandalism. Certainly, judging from sixteenth-century drawings, and the Sancta Sanctorum—the private chapel of the popes above the Scala Santa, which is the only part of it to have survived—the venerable palace must have contained many treasures.

The exact topography of the palace is difficult to establish (though there is an interesting model in the Museo di Roma); but the actual residence of the popes seems to have stood on the area between where the Scala Santa is today and the basilica. Here was the famous loggia from which Boniface VIII announced the first Holy Year of 1300; a scene which was afterwards recorded in a fresco executed by Giotto in the loggia itself, of which a fragment is now preserved in the basilica. Opening out of this was the *aula Concilii* in which papal elections took place. Before the palace stood the famous bronze equestrian statue of Marcus Aurelius, preserved here because it was believed to represent Constantine. In this palace too there was the great triclinium of Leo III built just about the time of Charlemagne's coronation in 800, where a mosaic decoration illustrated the divine division of the spiritual and the temporal power between pope and emperor, with portraits of Leo and Charlemagne. It was in this room that the popes entertained the emperors to a banquet after their coronation; its ruins survived until the seventeenth century, together with the much damaged mosaics in the apse. These were heavily restored (according to some completely remade after the original design) and can still be seen in the building to the right of the Scala Santa.

Crossing the Piazza di S. Giovanni in Laterano to the far left-hand corner, we pass one end of the transept of the basilica. The belfries and the small window above the Renaissance portico are all that we can now see of the medieval building. In one of the belfries hangs the oldest bell in Rome, dating from 968. In a chapel on the left of the portico is a statue of Henry IV of France, a reminder of his gift of the Abbey of Clairac to the Chapter of the Lateran. We now come to the Baptistry, long believed—on the basis of medieval legend—to have been the scene of Constantine's baptism by Pope Sylvester I. In actual fact this event took place at Achiron, near Nicomedia, shortly before the emperor's death in

337. The Baptistry occupies the site of the baths of the *Domus Faustae*—the 'House of Fausta', Constantine's second wife, who was a daughter of the Emperor Maximinian. This palace had originally belonged to the Laterani, a rich patrician family, from whom it was confiscated by Nero, when Plautius Lateranus was executed for taking part in the conspiracy of Piso. The house seems to have brought fatality to its owners. Fausta too was executed by Constantine's orders; she was suffocated in the hot room of a bath—the accepted Roman method of tactfully eliminating someone involved in a serious domestic scandal. Fausta is believed to have deceived Constantine into having Crispus—his son by another wife—executed on the false charge of having tried to violate her. Crispus's death ensured that Fausta's own sons, Constantine II and Constans, would succeed to the Empire.

This domestic tragedy did not, however, take place in the *Domus Faustae*, as the empress did not die till 326 or 327; and already in 313 Pope Melchiades had convoked a synod there. After the synod the first service of baptism was held in these baths; later Constantine built a circular baptistry on the site. This was replaced by the existing octagonal building in Sixtus III's reign (432–40).

We now enter the Baptistry by a door opposite the original one. In the centre is a large round enclosure, formerly used for baptisms by immersion. In the middle of this stands a bath-shaped green basalt urn, now used as the font. In this on the night of 1 August 1347 Cola di Rienzo took a bath before his public appearance as a knight, when he summoned the pope and sovereigns of Europe to appear before him. Eight porphyry columns stand around the double font, supporting an architrave with an inscription of Sixtus III's time; above this, smaller white marble columns rise to support the dome. Excavations in the pavement reveal traces of the earlier baptistry and the original pavement of the antique baths.

The Baptistry is surrounded by four chapels. That on the right is dedicated to St. John the Baptist; although originally built in the fifth century it was redecorated in the eighteenth. The only object of special interest it now contains are the famous bronze musical doors—when moved they emit a harmonious sound—believed to have come from the Baths of Caracalla. Opposite the present entrance is the chapel of SS. Rufina and Seconda, the original narthex of the building. In the apse on the left is a singularly lovely mosaic of the fifth century with a design of acanthus scrolls on a blue ground, sparkling here and there with gold. In 1153 or 1154 Anastasius IV placed the relics of SS. Rufina and Seconda in the opposite apse, from which all trace of the original fifth-century mosaic of peacocks and pastoral scenes has now unfortunately disappeared.

Both of the foregoing chapels can be seen without difficulty; but in order to penetrate into the other two the assistance of the somewhat unwilling guardian is necessary, as they are both locked. The next in order is the chapel of S. Venanzio, originally the vestibule of the baptistry; dedicated as an oratory by the Dalmatian Pope John IV (640–2), to his father's patron and co-national St. Venantius. John IV's mosaic decoration still survives; rough in workmanship, it indicates the decadence of the arts in seventh-century Rome. Nevertheless it is effective and interesting, not only for the portrait of Pope John IV (on the left in the apse), but because it is a record of contemporary history. To the ordinary observer, the rows of saints on either side of the apse would appear to be a normal form of church decoration; on closer observation, however, it emerges from the inscriptions above that they are all Dalmatians. Some authorities regard this as a votive record of the recent end of the Istrian schism; but Emile Mâle in his fascinating book *Rome et ses Vielles Eglises* gives another explanation. In the middle of the seventh century, what is Yugoslavia today was overrun by the Slavs, the original inhabitants taking refuge in the islands and the ruins of Diocletian's palace at Split. Their compatriot John IV did what he could to help them, ransoming some and sending an envoy to rescue the relics of his country's martyrs of the age of persecutions from the cemetery at Salona. He then prepared this oratory to receive their remains. As we will see later in our excursions, this is not the only historical event to be recorded in Roman church mosaics. The fourth, and most beautiful, chapel is dedicated to S. John the Evangelist. It was built by Pope St. Hilary (461–8); the ceiling is still covered with his exquisite mosaics. On a blue ground, the lamb is portrayed in the centre of the vault, surrounded by a lovely garland of lilies and other flowers (be sure to make the guardian turn on the light as otherwise much of the detail is invisible).

Leaving the Baptistry, we would be well advised to retrace

our steps across the piazza to the **Scala Santa**, in order to see it before we enter the basilica, as it may be closed by the time we come out. The Scala Santa was the principal ceremonial staircase of the old Patriarchate; it is traditionally identified with the stairs ascended by Christ in Pontius Pilate's palace in Jerusalem and brought to Rome by St. Helena. This tradition, however, is believed to date only from the eighth or ninth century. When he destroyed the old Lateran palace, Sixtus V had the stairs removed from their previous position and installed here; they lead up to the Sancta Sanctorum or chapel of S. Lorenzo. This was originally the popes' private chapel in the old palace. Thus the stairs and the chapel are the only surviving remains of the Patriarchate, originally built on the site of the Domus Faustae, and probably begun during the reign of Pope St. Sylvester I (314–35) after the Empress Fausta's death.

Owing to its removal in the sixteenth century, the Scala Santa today conveys no feeling of great antiquity; the steps themselves are covered with wood, and are ascended by Roman Catholics on their knees. On either side are two other staircases also leading to the Sancta Sanctorum, which takes this name from an inscription appearing on the architrave within—*Non est in toto sanctior orbe locus* (in the whole world no place is more sacred than this)—also repeated by Sixtus V on the exterior of the building. The phrase refers to the many relics preserved in the chapel; notably the revered *acheiropoieton* (not painted by human hands) picture of Christ. This is covered with silver, and hangs above the altar. It is not definitely known when this painting was brought to Rome, but it is believed to have come from Constantinople at the time of the iconoclastic persecutions. Certainly the picture was already in Rome by 752; in that year Pope Stephen II himself carried it in procession through the city to invoke divine protection against the Lombards. Right until the end of the sixteenth century the picture was annually carried in procession to S. Maria Maggiore on the day of the Assumption, with pauses on the way, during which the painted feet were washed with water scented with basil. It is believed that this ceremony was instituted by Sergius II (844–7) in order—in the manner of a passion play—for Christ to greet the Virgin, newly assumed into heaven. A similar ceremony still takes place in Tivoli on 15 August; but the Roman one had to be abandoned owing to quarrels about precedence among participants in the procession. Some authorities believe the picture is a copy of one preserved in the church of S. Bartolomeo degli Armeni in Genoa, brought there from Edessa in 1308 by Basilian monks fleeing from the Armenian massacres. In both pictures, the head as far as the beard is painted on canvas and the rest on wood; both are remarkable examples of the oriental type of picture known as *acheiropoieton*, derived from a common prototype.

What little of the Sancta Sanctorum can be seen through the gratings of the windows reveals its extraordinary beauty. As it stands it is the work of Roman mosaic artists of the cosmatesque school, made in 1278 by order of Pope Nicholas III. Unfortunately the marble panelling of the lower part of the walls is covered with red brocade hangings; but above them, in twenty-eight Gothic tabernacles, are medieval paintings of popes and martyrs. The white marble altar has doors with reliefs of the heads of SS. Peter and Paul, and thirteenth-century inscriptions of Innocent III and Nicholas III.

We now return to the main entrance of the **Basilica di S. Giovanni in Laterano**. Twenty-three architects took part in the competition of 1732 for the honour of being the designer of its new façade; the palm was only awarded to Alessandro Galilei's surprisingly—for the period—classical elevation after the jury of academicians had been involved in intrigues of truly Byzantine intricacy and duration. The inspiration is, of course, derived from St. Peter's, but here the openings of the great benediction loggia provide a greater contrast of light and shade. The fifteen gigantic statues—which are such a Roman landmark, being visible as far away as the Janiculum—represent Christ, SS. John the Baptist and John the Evangelist, also twelve doctors of the Church.

The portico, alas! no longer commands the beautiful view over the campagna to the Sabine and Alban hills; hideous modern suburbs have robbed it of this, its great redeeming beauty, in the eyes of Augustus Hare. Trenchant, as usual, in his firm disapproval of the baroque, he described Borromini's conversion of the interior as a hideous modernisation. It is interesting to compare this nineteenth-century view with Professor Wittkower's, that here Borromini showed 'an inexhaustible wealth of original ideas and an uninhibited imagination'. One is tempted to wonder what further re-assessment of the basilica's architectural merits or demerits will be forthcoming in the next hundred years. But if we ourselves share neither view—simply finding it a rather cold though impressive church—we must remember that from the very beginning it was an official, we might almost say representa-tional, building, created as the cathedral of the seat of the papacy. As such the basilica had no associations with the faith and suffering of the age of persecutions, as did most of its contemporaries. It was built by Constantine over the barracks of the *Equites Singulares*, the emperors' private guards. More-over it has suffered through the ages more than almost any other of the great basilicas. The original fourth-century building, dedicated to the Saviour (SS. John the Baptist and the Evangelist were a later addition), was practically destroyed by the Vandals and restored by Leo the Great in the fifth century. It was ruined by an earthquake in the eighth century and rebuilt in the ninth; twice burnt down in the fourteenth century and twice restored. Thus when in 1646 Borromini was commissioned to carry out yet another restoration little of the original structure can have remained.

Once again, owing to the inopportune opening and closing hours of the cloister, we should not linger now to examine the basilica. A quick glance at the famous central antique bronze doors—brought here from the Senate House in the Forum—and at the closed one on the extreme right, only opened during holy years, is all we can allow ourselves for the moment, for we must press on to see the **Cloisters** before they shut at 12.30. Their entrance is through a small door at the end of the left aisle, just before the transept. There is no diversity of opinion about the artistic importance of the cloisters; they are univer-sally agreed—together with those of S. Paolo fuori le Mura—to be the most beautiful examples of their kind in Rome; a masterpiece of that school of mosaic artists known as the Cosmati. An inscription in the middle of the part of the cloister opposite the door records that they were the work of the two Vassallettos, father and son, among the most famous artists of the Cosmatesque school. They were built between 1222 and 1230. The full beauty of the mosaics is best appre-ciated from the garden, where a ninth-century well stands at the crossing of the paths. From here the many-coloured fragments of marble and sparkling gold of the twisted columns and frieze glow brilliantly in the sunlight, set off by the dark green of the box hedges. The capitals are exquisite and varied, some of them being adorned with stone garlands. The frieze too has an infinity of sculptured motifs; strange affronted beasts and birds, a very lifelike owl and—above the second column of the left-hand arcade—an oddly Picasso-like head, in which profiles and full face merge into one.

Relics of the medieval basilica are ranged round the cloister walls. Among the tombstones, reliefs and mosaics is a beautiful antique white marble *sella curule* (curule chair), framed in a cosmatesque setting; this was used in the old basilica as the papal throne. Its existence here reminds us of that other antique seat of red marble which formerly stood in the portico of the basilica and is now in the Vatican Museum. This classical *chaise percée*—known as the *sedia stercoraria*—was used during a curious ritual which preceeded the popes' 'taking possession' of the temporal power in the basilica; this gave rise to many innuendos and legends and was finally discontinued by Julius II in 1503. Until then the popes remained seated on the chair, while a verse from the first Book of Samuel was chanted (Chapter II, Verse 8): 'He raiseth up the poor out of the dust, and lifteth up the beggar from the dunghill, to set them among princes, and to make them inherit the throne of glory.' In Latin the dung-hill is translated as *stercora*; but how this became associated with the pontiffs' assumption of the temporal power and their simultaneous distribution of largesse to the watching crowds is a mystery whose origins are lost.

We now return to the basilica to continue our tour of it in peace, as it at least does not shut until half an hour before sunset. It is probably simplest to retrace our steps to the main entrance and begin from there. In the double aisle on the right, on the first left-hand pillar we come upon the central fragment of Giotto's fresco of Boniface VIII proclaiming the first holy year of 1300. A little farther on, on the right, is the Torlonia chapel; the last Roman family chapel to be made (in 1850). Built against the next pillar on the left is a surprisingly modern monument to Pope Sylvester II (999–1003), set up in 1909 by a Hungarian, to commemorate this pope's award of the iron crown to St. Stephen I the first Christian king of Hungary. Incorporated into the monument is an inscription, possibly part of the 'magician Pope' Sylvester II's original tomb from the old basilica, it is said to sweat and emit the sound of rattling bones before the death of a pope.

In the chapel in the transept at the end of this aisle there stood formerly the tomb of Lorenzo Valla. He was buried here in spite of the fact that his researches had proved that the document purporting to record Constantine's donation to Pope Sylvester I of the Lateran and all Italy and the West was a forgery (it was probably made by one of the entourage of Stephen II in the eighth century). On the right in the chapel is a late fourteenth-century relief in a cosmatesque setting; it is a portrait of Boniface IX (1389–1404). Just to the left of this chapel is the tomb of one of the greatest popes of the Middle Ages, Innocent III, who died in Perugia in 1216; his remains were brought here in 1891 by order of Leo XIII. It was in the basilica during Innocent's reign that St. Dominic and St. Francis of Assisi first met; Innocent's approval of the foundation of their orders is recorded among the events of his life, portrayed in the modern frescoes on the right of the presbytery.

In 1884 Leo XIII extended and enlarged the presbytery and the apse, having recomposed in this last the mosaic made between 1288–94 by Jacopo Torriti and Jacopo da Camerino for Nicholas IV. The figure of this pope, as donor, appears beside that of the Virgin; those of the two artists, shown very small, among the prophets grouped around the windows below. Although this mosaic was restored and enlarged during its removal in the last century, and it itself only dates from the thirteenth, some believe that its iconography is based on that of the original Constantinian mosaic of the fourth century. The head of Christ at the summit of the apse recalls the legend of his visionary appearance on the day of the basilica's consecration in the presence of Constantine and Pope St. Sylvester I. Some authorities think that the actual legend drew its inspiration from the original mosaic itself, where for the first time in a great Roman church the head of the Saviour—to whom it was then dedicated—was portrayed for all to see.

In the middle of the transept stands the papal altar, where only the pope can say Mass; it contains a wooden table upon which St. Peter is believed to have celebrated Mass. Above it rises a fine Gothic canopy, made for Urban V in 1367, this was restored during the Renaissance. In the curtained space, the heads of SS. Peter and Paul are preserved in silver reliquaries.

These are not the original gem-studded ones made for Urban V, which were stolen in 1434 and rediscovered but finally disappeared at the end of the eighteenth century—stolen by French republicans at the time of the Revolution. The existing reliquaries are approximate copies of the originals. At the foot of the altar, within the sunken area of the *confessio*, is a fine bronze relief, marking the tomb of Martin V. This pope's return to Rome on 30 September 1420 (three years after his election which ended the great schism) began the period of the city's reconstruction and Renaissance glory. As recorded in the inscription, '*temporum suorum felicitas*' (his were times of happiness).

The tomb of Leo XIII (1878–1903), which was transferred in 1924, is on the left of the presbytery. We continue past this and the chapel of the Sacrament at the end of the transept, notable for its gilded altar, and continue down the double aisle. Here the Corsini chapel (the last beside the entrance) contains (on the left) the tomb of the Medici Pope, Clement VII 1523–34); he lies in a magnificent porphyry urn taken from the Pantheon.

We can now board the 85 or 88 bus from Piazza S. Giovanni in Laterano (the stop is at the far end of the zebra crossing by the Lateran palace), which will take us by way of the Via Merulana and the Via Labicana to the Colosseum and the Parco di Traiano. Or, if we have had to retrace our steps to see S. Croce in Gerusalemme, which fortunately only shuts at 1.30 p.m., we take the ED (this stop is on the right of the piazza as we come out of the church) bus from there to the Colosseum. In fine weather, the Parco di Traiano has many pleasant corners in which to eat a picnic lunch, and a little bar in a kiosk at the far end of the Viale Domus Aurea. For a smart and rather luxurious lunch, the Domus Aurea Restaurant on a high terrace above the Viale Serapide has a fine view and much to commend it. For more modest requirements, the little Trattoria di Nerone on the corner of the Via dei Terme di Tito (just beside where the Viale del Monte Oppio enters the park) is an excellent choice.

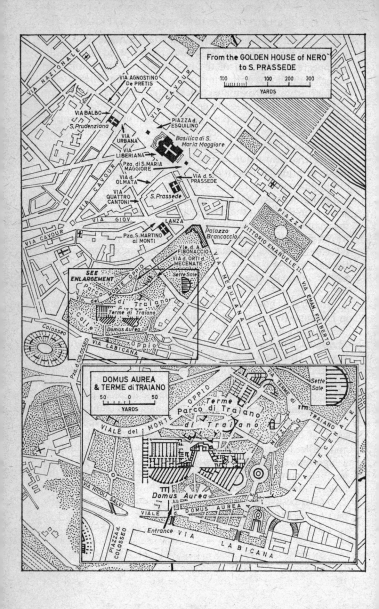

CHAPTER FIFTEEN

The Golden House of Nero to S. Prassede

THE hatred that Nero inspired in the Roman people kept his memory green right into the Middle Ages, when legend associated the ruined tower in the Colonna gardens and the Torre delle Milizie with the story of his fiddling while Rome burned. Various sites were attributed to his famous palace the **Domus Aurea** or **Golden House** (closed for repairs at the time of writing) which was said to have been built at places as far apart as the Vatican, the Lateran and the 'Temple of the Sun' on the Quirinal. Curiously enough, when some of its buried rooms actually were discovered at the end of the fifteenth century no one had the slightest idea that they had stumbled on the remains of the fabulous palace. They believed instead that they were grottoes—caves or underground rooms—part of the palace or baths of Titus whose name was still correctly associated with the Esquiline area. Their painted decoration did, however, create a sensation; antiquarians and artists rushed to study them. Still some thirty years later—between 1517-19— they provided the inspiration for Raphael and Giovanni da Udine's famous decorations in the Vatican *Loggie*, executed in the 'grotesque' style called after them. Nevertheless the rooms remained half filled with rubble—the fifteenth- and sixteenth-century artists were let down into them on a rope and were able to scratch their names on the ceiling—and it was only in the early nineteenth century that systematic excavation was begun; by then, however, their true nature had been recognised.

The palace upon which Nero's own comment was 'Good, now I can at last begin to live like a human being!' did not find much favour with his successors, and no one seems to have had many regrets when the palace was devastated by fire in AD 104. After this Trajan—continuing the Flavian emperors' policy, begun with the building of the Colosseum, of returning to the Roman people the land which Nero had expropriated—

levelled part of the palace, filled in the rest, and built his famous public baths on the site. Finally Hadrian destroyed practically the last visible vestige of the famous building when in AD 121 he erected the Temple of Venus and Rome on the site of its vestibule at the eastern end of the Forum.

It is interesting to note, however, that a relic of the gardens still survives—the remains of a nympheum, with walls bordering on the modern Via Claudia, on the slopes of the Coelian Hill. The landscaped gardens—whose artificiality so enraged Tacitus—stretched from here to what is now the Via Merulana, near the Lateran, to the Palatine and, probably, as far as the Forum of Augustus beside the present Via dei Fori Imperiali. It was the seizure of this vast tract of land—laid bare by the famous fire of AD 64—and its conversion into a private park in the heart of the city, that infuriated the Romans; more even than the sybaritic luxury of the palace itself. Judging from the strictures of Vitellius and the descriptions of Suetonius the palace seems to have been designed more for luxury than comfort. Sea-water, as well as sulphur-water from Tivoli were piped into its baths; part of its interior was decorated with mother-of-pearl and gems; dining-rooms had fretted ivory ceilings through which flowers could be scattered. In other rooms ceilings were fitted with a system of pipes for spraying scents and the place was called the Domus Aurea (the Golden House) because the main façade was covered with gold.

It is a far cry indeed from this magnificence to what we see today. Just round the corner from the 85 and 88 bus stop at the end of the Labicana is one of the main entrances of the Parco di Traiano or Colle Oppio; turning into it we find ourselves in the Viale della Domus Aurea. The first turn on the left brings us to a little garden below the high curved wall of the Baths of Trajan. Here a dark door and stairs lead down into shadowy rooms and passages, which their Renaissance discoverers may well be forgiven for believing formed part of some mysterious troglodyte annexe of the ancient baths; though when it was built—with spacious courts and colonnades facing south—the Golden House must have been full of sun and light. The whole of this vast labyrinth of rooms and passages is now not only buried in the earth (its excavation is not yet complete), but over and in front of it were built the massive substructures of the Baths of Trajan.

As a result the layout of the palace is not at all easy to understand; its details are in fact of specialised interest, but certain aspects—such as the famous octagonal room believed to have been the principal dining-room, and some of the paintings—hold an appeal for most of us; especially on a blazing summer day when it is the coolest place in Rome. The well-equipped traveller will, however, come armed with a torch with a powerful beam and opera glasses, as Fabullus's famous paintings are in general notable more for their delicacy than for the suitability of their scale for the immensely high rooms; many of them are in fact very difficult to see. In the main they belong to what is called the fourth Pompeian style, which consists of delicate architectural *trompe l'oeil* framing small landscapes with figures, astonishingly impressionist in the freedom of their execution. There is one basic difference between these paintings and those of Pompeii; there a red ground was preferred, here in Rome a white one. Viewing the tenuous grace of this decoration we are not surprised to recall that Pliny obviously regarded Fabullus as a rather affected aesthete—describing how he wore his toga even when standing on a scaffolding to paint. Nero, however, must have been a whole-hearted admirer, as although he employed two architects for the Golden House—Severus and Celer—Fabullus is the only artist whose name has come down to us. He spent so much time on its decoration that Pliny said that the palace had become the prison of his work. It was also filled with master-pieces of Greek sculpture, especially the portico which extended the entire length of the main façade and the adjoining rooms. The Laocoön, which Pliny mentioned as being in the palace of Titus, was probably originally part of Nero's col-lection; it was found by de Fredi in 1506 in a room under his vineyard near the Baths of Trajan.

The Golden House arouses more varied opinions than almost any other sight in Rome. Some find it absolutely fas-cinating, while to others it is depressing and gloomy; so the time it will occupy in our itinerary is more than usually a matter of personal taste. However there are certain things we should not fail to see. These include the rooms grouped round the famous one known as the 'Sala della Volta Dorata' (the room with the gilded vault); the gilded and painted ceiling is considered to be Fabullus's masterpiece. This was the great entrance hall of the palace, opening out of a recessed court in the centre of its main façade; it would probably have enjoyed a magnificent view over the valley with the artificial lake, where the Colosseum now stands. On the other side of this room we find ourselves in the great *cryptoporticus*, known since the Renaissance; it was here that Raphael and other artists came to study the paintings—their names can still be seen scratched on the ceiling. To the right, at the beginning of the *cryptoporticus*, is the library, the only room in the whole palace whose function is known beyond any doubt, owing to the wall niches used as bookcases. Passing through this and other rooms we come to the famous octagonal hall, lit like the Pantheon by an opening in the middle of the ceiling. Rooms fan out from this in three directions. One of them contained a water staircase, down which water must have cascaded over glittering mosaics as in the mauresque palaces of Granada, Sicily and Kashmir. Even robbed as they are of their decoration, we cannot but appreciate the extraordinary beauty of this set of rooms. Was this great octagonal hall the famous dining-room that Suetonius described as having a roof which 'revolved slowly, day and night, in time with the sky'. This is a question which has intrigued generations of scholars. Before starting on our way back through the palace, we must take a momentary glimpse at a painted room with an apse beyond the octagonal hall; it was here that de Fredi is said to have found the Laocoön.

Returning to the entrance of the Golden House, we now have the choice of strolling across the **Parco di Traiano**—a pleasant park laid out around the ruins of Trajan's Baths—to the church of S. Martino ai Monti. But this last only re-opens at 4 p.m., and if our tour of the Golden House has been brief we may have time on our hands. In this case we can take the 5 tram from the Colosseum to the Basilica of S. Maria Maggiore, which fortunately stays open all day. However, as the walk across the park is pleasant and can be continued for the short distance to S. Maria Maggiore, we will treat our itinerary in this way, taking in S. Martino ai Monti *en route*.

After leaving the Golden House, we climb the steps to the terrace on top of the ruins of the Baths of Trajan, strike out across the park, traversing the Via degli Orti di Mecenate (the site of the famous gardens of Maecenas), and continue along the Viale A. Fibonacci. This brings us into a wide car road, the

Viale del Monte Oppio. Shortly after this Viale leaves the park, it is bordered on the right by the high wall of the gardens of the Palazzo Brancaccio which encloses the 'Sette Sale', the ruins of the water tanks that supplied the Golden House and the Baths of Trajan.

A short way farther along the Viale del Monte Oppio we find on the left a small piazza dominated by the church of **S. Martino ai Monti**. The eighteenth-century façade does not prepare us for the fact that its origins date back to the early Christian *titulus Equitii*, over which St. Sylvester I (314–35) built a church. This was restored and enlarged before Pope Symmachus (498–514) constructed the body of the existing church, dedicating it to St. Martin of Tours and Pope St. Sylvester. However if we walk round the right side of the church into the Via Equizia, we will see that it is built right into the ruins of some ancient building; the great tufa blocks of the foundations probably formed part of the Baths of Trajan—one of the old names of the church was S. Martino in Thermis.

With the exception of some fine classical columns, the interior of S. Martino contains little to remind us of its great antiquity. It owes its splendid gilded Renaissance ceiling to St. Carlo Borromeo, whose motto 'Humilitas' appears in the decoration. Poussin's brother-in-law, Dughet, painted most of the frescoes between 1645 and 1650. At either end of the right wall are two sixteenth-century paintings of great historical interest, which show old St. Peter's and St. John Lateran as they were in medieval times. In the view of St. Peter's (at the far end near the altar), the great bronze pine cone now in the Belvedere Courtyard, is seen in the foreground.

The high altar of S. Martino is raised above a crypt which contains the relics of many martyrs whose names, as the ancient dedication says, 'are known only to God'. From here stairs lead down to what are believed to be the remains of the original third-century *titulus*, possibly part of the house of Equitius. Access is, however, very difficult, as the doors are locked and no one ever seems to be available to accompany visitors who would like to see these interesting early Christian remains.

Leaving S. Martino ai Monti by the far door on the right of the high altar, we find ourselves at the top of a steep flight of steps looking down on a little piazza dominated by two high medieval towers. The piazza is called after the church S. Martino ai Monti; the towers after the fortress of the Capocci family, of which they formed part in medieval times. From here we make our way to S. Maria Maggiore by way of the Via Quattro Cantoni, past a charming old baroque palace to the Via dell' Olmata, which brings us into the Piazza di S. Maria Maggiore. In the centre of the piazza rises a huge column, brought here from the Basilica of Maxentius by Paul V.

The **Basilica of S. Maria Maggiore** ranks fourth among the great patriarchal basilicas of Rome, and is one of the 'seven churches' that since time immemorial have been one of the chief objects of pilgrimage in the city. The others are St. John Lateran, St. Peter's, St. Paul's and S. Lorenzo fuori le Mura, S. Croce and S. Sebastiano. In view of this, it comes as a surprise to many travellers to find that S. Maria Maggiore has no connection with the period of persecution, or even with that of Christianity's triumph under Constantine. It is in fact now known to have been built by Sixtus III (432–40); not, as its other title of Basilica Liberiana—and legend—would have it, by Pope St. Liberius (352–66). Liberius did build a basilica on the same Esquiline Hill; it is with this long-vanished church that the charming legend of his dream vision of the Virgin commanding him to build a church where the snow fell on the night of 5 August should be associated, and not as it usually is with S. Maria Maggiore.

It is now generally considered that Sixtus III chose to build S. Maria Maggiore on the Esquiline because in his time many Roman women still frequented a temple of the mother-goddess Juno Lucina, which also stood on the hill. Apart from the customary practice of substituting a Christian cult for a pagan one, Sixtus's dedication of his magnificent new church to the Virgin Mary was inspired by the findings of the Council of Ephesus of 431. These condemned the Patriarch Nestorius's theories as to the two natures of Christ—the human and divine—as heresy; also his contention that the Virgin was only the mother of the human Christ, and could not therefore be called the Mother of God. The Council recognised that her supernatural splendour raised her above all created things; and from that moment her cult developed enormously, her festivals were instituted, and churches were dedicated to her all over the Christian world. When we enter the basilica, we will see that the mosaics with which Sixtus decorated it were specially designed to commemorate this momentous occasion.

As the famous Roman scholar Silvio Negro once put it, S. Maria Maggiore confuses the ordinary traveller 'by the contrast between what they see outside, and what they find within'. As a matter of fact this could be applied to many other Italian churches, but in reverse order; very often their exteriors may be medieval or Renaissance, while inside they are baroque. S. Maria Maggiore is almost completely eighteenth-century outside (it was encased in a shell, as it were, by Ferdinando Fuga in 1741-3); while the interior is the only example of a basilica built in the classical style to have survived in its integrity among the great patriarchal ones of Rome. St. Peter's and St. Paul's Without the Walls have been rebuilt; St. John Lateran, S. Lorenzo fuori le Mura and S. Croce completely transformed. On entering S. Maria Maggiore we are at once struck by this fact; the superb Renaissance ceiling (said to have been gilded with the first gold brought from the New World) and the beautiful cosmatesque pavement appear as mere incidents in the dominating classical harmony of the whole building. This impression is chiefly due to the rows of magnificent classical columns lining the nave; their proportions and spacing accord exactly with the canons of Vitruvius, as do the proportions of the nave itself. Curiously enough this perfect harmony is largely due to Fuga's work of restoration in the eighteenth century, contemporary documents record the fact that he gave to the rather heterogeneous assortment of columns then standing in S. Maria Maggiore their present uniformity. He pared down those that were too thick, shortened the longer ones and provided them all with their existing bases and Ionic capitals.

Along the walls above the architrave are set thirty-six mosaic panels, representing scenes from the Old Testament. All but a few of these near the door (which are modern replicas) date from the time of Sixtus III; though the fact that they have at some time been moved has led some experts to believe that they might be of an earlier date or have come from another building. Their colouring and workmanship are exquisite; but their size, and the fact that they are placed so high, makes them very difficult to study in detail (here again opera glasses come in very useful).

Fortunately we do not encounter the same difficulty in the blaze of gold and colour of the mosaics surrounding the high altar. Those in the triumphal arch, which rises above it, represent the Annunciation and the main events of Christ's childhood. It is here that Sixtus III's intention of glorifying our Lord's divinity, and the Virgin Mary as the Mother of God, is clearly shown; in some of the scenes portrayed he even resorted to the apocryphal gospels in order further to stress these themes. In the top left-hand corner of the arch the Annunciation is portrayed with hitherto unparalleled splendour. The Virgin appears enthroned and dressed in the robes of a Byzantine princess, with diadem and jewels; the dove hovers above her head and she is surrounded by angels. In the midst of all this grandeur a homely note is struck by the fact that she is in the act of spinning—a basket of purple wool lies beside her. This is in accordance with the apocryphal legend that Mary was in the service of the Temple; and is seen here preparing the wool for the veil of the Holy of holies.

To the right of this group is a scene illustrating the theme of Christ's divinity. Joseph is seen looking rather worried, conversing with an angel. It is a representation of the dream in which he was told that Mary had conceived by the Holy Spirit. Below this, Christ is shown being adored by the Magi: not in the customary fashion as a baby on his mother's knee, but as a child seated alone in splendour on an imperial throne, with a small cross on his forehead as well as a halo. Beneath this is the Massacre of the Innocents. On the right of the arch, below the Presentation in the Temple and Joseph's dream warning to fly into Egypt, the scene of the Holy Family's arrival there is also portrayed according to the apocryphal gospels—possibly that of the pseudo-Matthew. According to this, all the idols in the temples of the city of Sotinen fell down when the Holy Family arrived; and the city governor came out to worship the Christ child. Here we see Jesus accompanied by angels, with a cross on his forehead, being welcomed by an obsequious governor and his train. Below, the Magi are seen being received by Herod. Crowning the whole composition, at the summit of the arch, is an empty throne surrounded by saints; this is a symbol of the invisible but ever present God.

Sixtus III's original apse was not separated from the

triumphal arch, as is the existing one. A new apse was built by Nicholas IV (1288–92), the pope who added so much to the beauty of the Lateran. Here again in S. Maria Maggiore he employed the same Franciscan, Turriti, who had worked on the mosaics in the apse of the Lateran. Here, as there, this artist probably adhered very closely to the design of the original fifth-century mosaic. The foliage scrolls in the apse resemble those of the fifth-century mosaics in the chapel of SS. Rufina and Seconda in the Lateran Baptistry; the River Jordan, with its boats, swans and fishes, the portrayal of the same subject in the apse of the Lateran Basilica. The only thing which has certainly been changed is the great central motif of the coronation of the Virgin. In Sixtus III's original mosaic in the apse this was probably portrayed in the old style, showing the Virgin with Christ as a child on her knee, with a hand emerging from heaven, holding a crown over her head. Here, enlarging further upon the theme of Sixtus III's mosaics, the Virgin is presented in far greater glory, enthroned side by side with Christ. Three insignificant human figures appear kneeling between the saints and angels on the right and left; they are Pope Nicholas (on the left) and the brother Cardinals, Giacomo and Pietro Colonna, who helped to defray the cost of this enormous work.

Although the mosaics constitute the greatest apparent glory of S. Maria Maggiore, it has long been famous for three other things. These are the *acheiropoieton* picture of the Madonna, the relic of the holy crib, and the oratory of the *presepio* or Christmas crib. The oratory of the *presepio* is known to have been associated with the church for far longer than the other two; its existence is documented as early as the reign of Theodore I (642–9), when S. Maria Maggiore was also known as '*Beata Maria ad Praesepe*'. This small chapel, which stood outside the church and was built to resemble the grotto of the Nativity at Bethlehem, was seen and described by the English pilgrim St. Winnibald, who visited Rome between 721 and 723. In medieval times it must have been a veritable treasure-house; successive popes filled it with gifts such as a gold and jewelled statue of the Virgin and Child weighing five pounds, an altar covered with gold, and gates of pure silver. It was here until 1870 that the popes celebrated the first of the three Masses on Christmas Eve; as Gregory VII did in 1075, when he was seized and carried off by the supporters of the Emperor

Henry IV, he was soon liberated by the Romans and had his revenge at Canossa.

Like S. Maria Maggiore itself and so many other Roman churches, the chapel of the *presepio* was looted of its valuables during the sack of Rome in 1527. Although the gold and the jewels then vanished, it was still an artistic treasure of the first order, as at the end of the thirteenth or the beginning of the fourteenth century it had been decorated by Arnolfo di Cambio. Unfortunately when Sixtus V (1585–90) commissioned Domenico Fontana to build the Sistine chapel (which forms the transept to the right of the nave) he also ordered him to transfer the oratory of the *presepio* to a new site beneath it. The result was a disaster, in spite of Fontana's elaborate plans (of which accounts and drawings still exist), and his having encased the entire oratory in a wooden scaffolding, it collapsed. The mosaic ceiling and marble pavement were reduced to fragments; only the walls, altar and some of the sculptures were saved. These now stand in a dark subterranean grotto beneath the Sistine chapel; the gate at the top of the steps leading down to it is closed (ask in the sacristy for someone to open it; this is usually easier in the afternoon) and few travellers even know of its existence.

Nevertheless Arnolfo's statues representing the scene in the Bethlehem stable are among the most beautiful of their kind, and one of the greatest treasures of S. Maria Maggiore. They are about half life-size—the original Madonna and Child have been replaced by sixteenth-century figures. But in the rest, in Joseph's pensive stance, in the reverent figures of the three kings and the gentle gaze of the ox and ass, all the poetry and mysticism of medieval Christianity still lives and breathes. Just to look at them is an unforgettable experience; but it makes one regret even more bitterly the fact that all the rest of Arnolfo's work was sacrificed to its incorporation into the Sistine chapel which stands above.

When we return to it, the gilding and grandeur of Sixtus's chapel somehow feel oppressive; though we must recognise that richness was the declared aim of this pope's artistic policy. In it he was actuated by two ideas—one, that as churches are an earthly imitation of heaven, they should contain the most priceless treasures; the other, that by destroying the ruins of pagan Rome he was benefiting Christian Rome. The chapel is filled with marbles looted from the monuments of ancient Rome and decorated with mannerist paintings of the period, which were heavily restored in 1870.

On leaving the Sistine chapel, we should continue up the right aisle in order to see the beautiful tomb of Cardinal Consalvo Rodriguez (on the right). This was made at the end of the thirteenth century by the famous Giovanni di Cosma; it contains a fine mosaic of the Virgin and Child. We now return to the nave, where beneath the high altar (made by Vespignani in 1864) a statue of Pius IX (1846–74) is seen kneeling before the reliquary of the holy crib. This last is exposed on the 25th of each month, and on Christmas Eve is carried in solemn procession round the basilica which is most beautifully illuminated for the occasion.

The first mention of the existence of a relic of Christ's crib in Rome comes in an eleventh-century inventory; but as this list also mentions the Ark of the Covenant as being preserved in the Lateran, its veracity is more than doubtful. The earliest reliable mention of the crib's existence at S. Maria Maggiore is contained in a letter which Petrarch addressed to Clement VI in Avignon in 1345. In trying to persuade the pope to return to Rome, Petrarch listed among the sacred treasures of the city the crib of S. Maria Maggiore. The relic consists of five pieces of wood, linked together by metal bands; upon one of the pieces is some writing in Greek. Believed to date from somewhere between the seventh and ninth centuries, this inscription is a curious list of what appear to be artistic religious subjects. Among other things it mentions St. Demetrius of Thessalonica, St. Eustace and the stag, and martyrs mounted on horses; how this writing ever came to be there is a mystery.

From the high altar we now turn left into the Pauline chapel, adorned with customary Borghese magnificence by Paul V. It was built in 1611, the decoration being completed five years later. Practically all the sculptors then living in Rome contributed to the work; among the more gifted was Pietro Bernini, father of the famous Gian Lorenzo. Unfortunately one of the least significant was commissioned to execute the sculptures on the tombs of Paul V and Clement VIII. If none of these artists were masters, their lack of inspiration was partly compensated for—in contemporary eyes at least—by the richness of the materials employed. The main altar is a mass of jasper, agate, amethyst and lapis lazuli; in its midst is enshrined the famous *acheiropoieton* picture of the 'Madonna and Child'.

This beautiful picture in the Byzantine style is usually described as dating from the twelfth or thirteenth century; but modern authorities now believe that it was painted some four centuries earlier. It is from the dome of this chapel that a shower of white flower petals flutters down every year on 5 August, in memory of the legendary snow-fall which is said to have occurred on that day in the fourth century, which led to Pope Liberius's building of his basilica on the Esquiline.

Continuing down the aisle on this side, we come to the Sforza chapel (nearest to the door); this was built by Giacomo della Porta between 1564–7, some believe to plans drawn up by Michelangelo. The gates are usually closed, but its serene beauty can be appreciated even when glimpsed through them. We now emerge from the basilica by the same door as we came in; turning to the left, if we find the iron gate on that side open, we should enter the courtyard there to see the curious monument which it contains. At first glance this appears to be a cross surmounting a normal column; on looking closer we see that the 'column' bears a curious resemblance to the elongated barrel of an old cannon.

The story of this monument is as curious as its appearance. It was erected in 1595 (with an inscription commemorating the fact), to celebrate Henry IV of France and Navarre's conversion to the Roman Catholic Church two years previously—the event that gave rise to his famous *mot* 'Paris is worth a Mass'. Possibly this lighthearted quip was reported to Clement VIII; at any rate that stern disciplinarian himself composed the inscription, referring in rather austere terms to the 'Absolution' of the man who had now become the 'Most Christian King'. This word absolution was regarded by the French as offensive to their national dignity as it implied their king's submission to the pope. However, it is said that the French abbot of the nearby Abbey of St. Anthony, before which the monument originally stood, upheld his monarch's independence by the ready wit which he applied to its design. For a normal column he substituted the elongated barrel of a cannon, executed in marble, inscribing upon it Constantine's famous '*in hoc signo vinces*'. The first Christian emperor's motto referring to his victory under the sign of the Cross was, of course, unexceptionable—but when applied to a cannon in the name of Henry IV, it could well be interpreted as an allusion to that martial monarch's military power! In spite of this

Clement VIII's inscription apparently continued to rankle; it was finally removed by order of Clement IX in 1688, as the result of a *rapprochement* with Louis XIV. In the ensuing exchange of courtesies, Louis also graciously agreed to the destruction of a monument recording an attack on the French ambassadress by the papal Corsican guard in 1662; its erection had been one of the acts of reparation then demanded by the French king.

Returning to the Piazza di S. Maria Maggiore, and skirting round the basilica, we find ourselves standing at the foot of the gracefully curved flight of steps leading down from it into the Piazza dell' Esquilino. From here there is a fine view down the Via Agostino Depretis (as this end of the Via Sistina is now called), bounded at both ends by obelisks. That nearest us is one of the pair which originally adorned the Augusteum; the one in the far distance stands before the church of Trinità dei Monti. Traversing the piazza, we take the second turn to the left into the Via Urbana, which follows the line of the ancient *Vicus Patricius*; in classical times a smart residential street lined with the mansions of senators and patricians.

A short way down on the right, well below the level of the road, we see what appears to be a nineteenth-century church built in medieval style. Only the fine romanesque campanile and some reliefs round the door betray that fact that this is the ancient church of **S. Pudenziana** dating in fact from the fourth century. For long S. Pudenziana was believed to be the oldest place of Christian worship in Rome; according to legend it had been built over the house of the Senator Pudens, where St. Peter lived for seven years with this one of his first Roman converts, and his daughters SS. Prassede and Pudenziana. Research has, however, revealed very definite discrepancies between this legend and such facts as are also available as a result of archaeological excavation.

When S. Pudenziana was subjected to a thorough examination by archaeologists shortly before the last war, it was found that the whole building—right up to the clerestory— had formed part of some baths built in the second century AD, about a hundred years after St. Peter's death; also that these baths had been converted to form the existing church at the end of the fourth century. These discoveries confirmed dedicatory inscriptions which had previously existed in the church, which stated that the work of conversion had been carried out in the reign of Pope St. Siricius (384–99) at the expense of Illiceus, Leopardus and the Presbyter Maximus; also that they had paid for the decoration which was completed in the reign of St. Innocent I (401–17).

Fifth-century documents refer to the church as the *titulus Pudentianae*; it was only in the eighth century that it was called S. Pudentiana; and it is now believed that its Apostolic foundation was attributed to it by a mistaken interpretation of a passage in the *Liber Pontificalis* in later centuries. Be that as it may, S. Pudenziana is one of the most ancient churches in Rome; and what is more, still retains its wonderful mosaics dating from the first years of the fifth century.

Like most early churches, S. Pudenziana originally had a portico; this was unfortunately destroyed when the church—which was in a ruinous state—was restored by Cardinal Enrico Caetani, the work being completed in 1588. Fragments of the door frame, which probably dated from the restoration of Pope Hadrian I (772–95), are still preserved in the nine-teenth-century façade. They consist of ancient columns and a sculptured frieze portraying SS. Prassede and Pudenziana dressed as empresses with crowns; Pudens is shown as a senator; and S. Pastor with a tonsure and attired in papal robes.

As we see it today, the body of the church is largely the result of Cardinal Caetani's restoration. This involved the removal of the medieval choir, the building of pillars to re-inforce the columns introduced in medieval times, the re-decoration of a side chapel which had formed part of the Roman baths (now known as the Caetani chapel), and, sadly, a reduction of the fifth-century mosaic by cutting off its edges. A fascinating and tantalising discovery was recorded by Francesco da Volterra as having been made during this work of transformation. Somewhere under the pavement the work-men found fragments of a Laocoön, larger in size than the one in the Vatican. They only extracted two pieces—a leg without a foot and a fist—which were subsequently given to Francesco da Volterra and afterwards stolen from him, greatly to his chagrin, as he believed them to have belonged to the original work and that the Vatican one was only a copy. Sad to relate, subsequent excavations have revealed no more fragments.

None of these alterations have dimmed the splendour of the wonderful fifth-century mosaic which is the glory of the church. The first thing which strikes us is the lightness and delicacy of its colouring. The predominating pale blue of the sky, the softly glowing gold of Christ's robes and the mellow red tiled roof of the semicircular portico before which Christ, SS. Peter and Paul and the Apostles (whose number was reduced during the Caetani restoration) are grouped. The world of classical art still lives in this wonderful mosaic; the Apostles are living persons—they seem to be portraits—and not yet the orientalised hieratic figures they were later to become in religious art. The classical world is also still evident in the leafy crowns which SS. Prassede and Pudenziana hold over the heads of SS. Peter and Paul; it is noticeable that Christ alone among all these figures has a halo. For all its magnificence, there is a lightness—a gaiety almost—about the composition which was characteristic of early Christian art, but was later to disappear under the oriental influence of Byzantium.

Before leaving S. Pudenziana, we should examine the classical ruins to be seen behind the apse (they can be reached from the left aisle). Then, once outside the church, turn out of the Via Urbana into the Via Depretis; from where the first turn on the left, into Via Balbo, will bring us to a curious brick passageway extending on to the left-hand pavement. Here we can actually walk through what was once one of the upper storeys of the second-century Roman baths; their walls go down to a depth of more than six yards below the pavement. Returning to the Piazza dell' Esquilino, we continue up the Via Liberiana on the right of S. Maria Maggiore, and, after crossing the end of the Via dell' Olmata, dive into the narrow Via di S. Prassede. If by now we feel like a restful cup of tea or coffee and a wash, there is a convenient tea room on the left of the street.

Opposite, an old wall and a rather inconspicuous door is all that we see of the church of **S. Prassede**. This is a side entrance, which brings us into the right aisle of this, one of the most moving and appealing of Roman churches. S. Prassede is rich in art treasures, but on entering it is not so much this that strikes us, as the sensation of being in a well-loved parish church, where for the last eleven centuries people have come with their load of cares and sorrows, and gone away refreshed. The church we see was built by St. Paschal I (817–24), who had been a priest of the original *titulus* mentioned in the list drawn up at Symmachus's Council of 499. The author of his life (written only twenty-two years after his death) says that Paschal built a new church not far from the old one; a statement which has caused considerable argument among archaeologists, some of whom aver that what is now the parvis was the site of the original *titulus*; others that it must have been farther away.

According to legend, the original *titulus* was built above the house where S. Prassede sheltered persecuted Christians, twenty-three of whom were discovered and killed before her eyes. She collected their blood with a sponge and placed this in a well where she herself was afterwards buried. In the centre of the nave, a circular porphyry slab with an inscription is said to mark the spot; the sponge is also said to be preserved with the relics of SS. Prassede and Pudenziana in a chapel under the high altar.

The great artistic treasure of the church is the chapel of S. Zenone (on the left of the aisle where we entered). It is the most exquisite little mosaic-decorated chapel in Rome, whose medieval name 'the garden of paradise' is easily understood. Its entrance is adorned with black granite columns and a lovely antique marble urn, surrounded by a semicircular mosaic portraying Christ and the Apostles, the Madonna and Child, SS. Pudenziana and Prassede and other saints. Its interior is a soft blaze of gold dimly glittering in the subdued light. The whole of the upper walls and vault are covered with mosaics; on this last, four angels, poised on azure spheres, hold aloft a garland surrounding the head and shoulders of Christ. In the arches, SS. Peter and Paul stand beside the empty Seat of Judgment; Christ, the Virgin and saints figure in the others. In a niche on the left, the Virgin's head is seen between that of SS. Prassede and Pudenziana; the mysterious woman's head with the square halo of a living person is that of Theodora, mother of Paschal I, who built this chapel during her lifetime and later had her buried here. In another niche, to the right of the chapel, is preserved a fragment of a column of rare oriental jasper; this was brought back from the East during the Crusades by Cardinal Giovanni Colonna. It is believed to be part of the column to which Christ was bound when he was scourged.

As we emerge from the chapel, we should look closely at the pier in the nave with the monument dedicated to the memory of a prelate called G. B. Santoni. This is one of Bernini's earliest recorded works, executed when he was about 19. We may also wonder which among the others inspired Browning's 'The Bishop Orders His Tomb'. We now make our way down to the far end of the nave. Its construction is rather curious; at intervals the familiar colonnades of a Roman basilica are interrupted by piers supporting great arches; these were built to reinforce the old church. In the centre of the beautiful cosmatesque pavement, we see the porphyry slab marking S. Prassede's well; from here we get a fine view of the mosaic decoration of Paschal I's triumphal arch above the high altar. We cannot help being struck by the difference between this ninth-century work and that of S. Pudenziana; here the classical technique and style has been superseded by that of Byzantium. The theme represented is that of the heavenly Jerusalem of the Apocalypse, with Christ in the middle, flanked by the Virgin, St. John the Baptist, S. Prassede, Moses, Elijah and the Apostles. Before them, a crowd of saints and martyrs and the host of the elect proceed towards the jewelled walls of the city of Jerusalem.

The inspiration for the mosaics in the apse is derived from the wonderful mosaic in SS. Cosma e Damiano in the Forum. Here again we see the same blue heavens, the same palm trees of paradise; and Christ again arrayed in golden classical robes—scroll in hand—descending cloudy stairs. But instead of SS. Cosma and Damiano, here SS. Peter and Paul present to Christ the sisters SS. Prassede and Pudenziana attired in Byzantine court dress. The influence of Byzantium, together with a decline in the arts in eighth-century Rome, had combined to give a hieratic rigidity to the figures. This is however set off by delightfully human details, such as the friendly hands of SS. Peter and Paul, placed on the sisters' shoulders as if to dispel their timidity. It is noticeable, too, that although Christ and SS. Peter and Paul wear classical sandals, as in the earlier mosaic, the contemporary figure of Paschal—holding a model of his church and portrayed with the square halo of the living—wears thonged slippers, remarkably like those used by Italian peasants of certain mountain provinces today. The arch above the apse is adorned with a charming garland of lilies and other flowers, with Paschal's monogram in the centre.

Although by Roman standards S. Prassede is not so very

old, something in its atmosphere seems to take us back to the simplicity and faith of past ages. This is most strongly felt on Easter Eve at the ceremony of the kindling of the fire. Then the whole church is plunged in darkness, while the officiating clergy bless and light the great paschal candle from the flames of a brazier in the star-lit parvis. Unlike the great basilicas, the service here is not attended by large crowds; but for this very reason it is infinitely more moving. As the small procession—usually a very mixed group of men and women of all conditions of life—forms up behind the cross and wends its way up the nave by the light of the single great candle, one experiences the feeling of returning to the shadowy world of the catacombs, where long ago just such groups must have gathered together.

Gradually the church is filled with tiny points of light, as each member of the congregation lights his or her candle from the flame of the great paschal one; and the priest intones the words *lumen Christi*. Finally, when the procession reaches the altar, the whole church is filled with a blaze of glorious colour as every light is turned on to illuminate the gilded splendour of the mosaics, and the first words of the Exultet ring out in the hushed church. In Easter, Rome is the scene of many impressive religious ceremonies, but few are as moving as this.

CHAPTER SIXTEEN

S. Clemente to the Basilica of Maxentius

❧

OUR excursions to date have led us through many and varying aspects of Roman townscape; but today and tomorrow we are going to see yet another one—perhaps best defined as 'a classical landscape with churches'. For we are now coming to the Coelian Hill, one of the few areas within the Aurelian walls to have retained something of its uniquely Roman pre-1870 character. Right up to the unification of Italy, the town occupied only a tiny proportion of the vast area enclosed by the walls; the rest was filled with a picturesque medley of parks, gardens and vineyards dotted with the ruins of antiquity and the churches which had grown up among them, since the days of Constantine.

We set out from Piazza Venezia, boarding the 88 or 85 bus in front of Palazzo Venezia; after passing the Colosseum, this puts us down in Via di S. Giovanni Laterano, near the **Basilica of S. Clemente**, which stands on the left on the corner of the Piazza di S. Clemente. Archaeologically this is one of the most interesting churches in Rome. It is also one of the most appealing; to a great wealth of art and treasures is added the atmosphere of a much-loved church, upon whose care and maintenance no pains have been spared. Here too the traveller is welcomed with a warm Irish brogue by the Dominicans, who are a fount of information about the complicated building history of their church. This consists of three successive places of Christian worship, built one on top of the other between the first and twelfth centuries, and includes a well-preserved Mithraeum. S. Clemente has been in the care of Irish Dominicans since 1667; it was due to the enterprise and adventurous spirit of Fr. Mullooly and his successors that the excavations, begun in 1857 when archaeology as a science was in its infancy, revealed that the church's origins go right back to the days of early Christianity.

A *titulus Clementis* figured in the list of churches drawn up

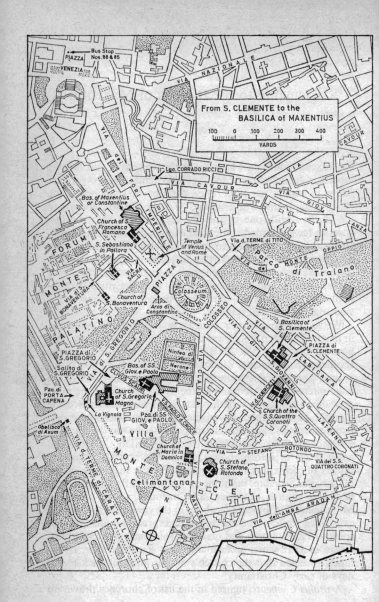

From S. CLEMENTE to the
BASILICA of MAXENTIUS

100   0   100   200   300   400
YARDS

at the Roman Council of 499. This would have been the church dedicated to Pope St. Clement I (88–97?), which was built during the reign of Pope Siricius (384–99) over the filled-in courtyard and ground-floor rooms of a first-century mansion. The mansion had belonged to a man also named Clement, possibly a relation of the Consul-Martyr Titus Flavius Clemens; it seems fairly certain that part of the house had been used as a place of Christian worship from the end of the first or the beginning of the second century. The existing basilica was built in the eleventh century on top of the fourth-century church, still occupying exactly the site of the original first-century house; though it now stands sixty feet higher, so greatly has the level of the land risen since classical times.

Coming in from the Via di S. Giovanni in Laterano, we enter S. Clemente by a side door. At first glance the church appears to be a typical example of eighteenth-century baroque; but a few paces into the nave bring us face to face with one of the most perfect medieval church interiors in Rome. Framed by rows of antique columns, and set in the midst of a beautiful cosmatesque pavement, the choir enclosure is walled with panels of white and coloured marbles. These are decorated with the early Christian symbols of the fish, dove and vine, exquisite for the purity and simplicity of their workmanship. The choir was the gift of Pope John II (535–55); it was transferred from the lower pre-existing church when the present basilica was built towards the end of the eleventh century. It is believed that the church had to be rebuilt because the earlier one was severely damaged when Robert Guiscard and his Normans sacked this part of Rome in 1084; certainly it was about this time that the older church was filled in and the new one built above it.

The nave of the new church was narrower than that of the old one, and the choir had to be slightly altered to fit it. At the same time the high medieval pulpit was added on the left, together with the beautifully decorated mosaic paschal candlestick. These high pulpits with their adjoining candle-sticks are particularly characteristic of medieval central and southern Italian churches. They probably owe their design to the local custom of reading the *Exultet* (which follows the kindling of the fire on Easter Saturday) from a long illumin-ated scroll. On these scrolls, the subjects mentioned in the Exultet were illustrated by lively miniatures, usually painted upside-down in relation to the text; so that as the deacon intoned the verses, the congregation could watch this medieval form of 'moving pictures' slowly descending from the pulpit.

Unlike the choir, the high altar has been remodelled several times. The *confessio*, or martyr's tomb beneath it—said to contain the relics of SS. Clement and Ignatius—dates from 1868; the columns supporting the canopy, from the fifteenth or sixteenth century. The canopy itself, however, may well be contemporary with the choir, and have been transferred from the earlier church. The anchor which is so conspicuously displayed on the front may mystify those who are not familiar with the legends of St. Clement. The real St. Clement, who was the fourth pope, was described by second-century writers as being a contemporary of SS. Peter and Paul. Certainly he wrote a celebrated and authoritative letter on church matters to the Christian community of Corinth, which was read publicly with the scriptures in 170, and was still being read there in the sixth century. Modern research has revealed that St. Clement's literary style indicates a Jewish background; it is thought that he may have been a liberated slave in the household of Domitian's cousin, the martyred Titus Flavius Clemens. Apart from this, little is known about St. Clement's life or death; but it did not prevent his becoming the subject of many legends, or a fourth-century writer from composing an apocryphal description of his life and 'Acts'. According to these St. Clement was banished by Trajan (98–117) to work in the mines of the Crimea, where he made so many converts that he was martyred by being bound to an anchor and thrown into the sea. Later the water miraculously receded, revealing his body laid in a tomb built by angels. The body was recovered, buried on an island, and in the ninth century was translated by the missionaries SS. Cyril and Methodius to Rome. At the place of his martyrdom, however, the sea continued to recede annually for some time, providing a fruitful source of miracles. One of these, and scenes from the 'Acts', are illustrated by frescoes in the lower church, which we will see later.

It is believed that much of the decoration of the apse behind the high altar was inspired by, if not exactly copied from, that of the original fourth-century church below. Certainly the episcopal throne was brought from there; the word 'martyr' seen on its back is a fragment of Siricius's original dedicatory inscription in the fourth-century church. The name of Cardinal Anastasius, the builder of the present basilica, is also recorded here. On the wall above is a superb twelfth-century fresco of 'Christ, the Virgin and Apostles', whose warm tones of red and yellow form a perfect foil for the predominating blue, green and gold of the magnificent mosaic in the semi-dome. This mosaic, which is the culminating glory of the whole church, recalls with its exquisite foliage scrolls the small fifth-century one we saw in the Lateran baptistry. Although here the ground is gold—typical of the later Byzantine style of mosaics—it is believed that the design and possibly even some of the original *tesserae* were taken from the original one in the fourth-century church.

Before leaving the altar area, we should also study the aumbry or wall-tabernacle on the right, one of the most beautiful of its kind in Rome. This was given in 1299 by Giacomo Caetani, titular Cardinal of the Church. A relief shows him kneeling beside his uncle Boniface VIII, to the left of the Virgin and Child, providing an indication that the whole aumbry was probably the work of Arnolfo di Cambio, as the pope's head is a miniature copy of Arnolfo's portrait of him in the vatican grottoes.

The other great artistic treasures in this part of S. Clemente are the frescoes in the chapel of S. Catherine of Alexandria (at the far end of the left of the aisle, on the right of the door by which we entered). These date from the first half of the fifteenth century and have recently been restored. During the work the artist's preliminary sketches were discovered on the wall beneath. These were removed and now hang on either side of the adjacent door beside Sassoferrato's Madonna, which closely resembles that of the National Gallery in London. Previously the frescoes were attributed to Masaccio; now they are more generally assigned to Masolino da Panicale, though some authorities believe that both artists had a hand in the work.

The frescoes on the left of the chapel represent legendary scenes from the life of St. Catherine of Alexandria—her dispute with learned doctors, her missionary work and conversion of the Emperor Maxentius's wife, who was executed in consequence; also the miracle of St. Catherine's being freed from death on the wheel by an angel, her ultimate decapitation, and her body being carried by angels to Mount Sinai, where the famous monastery called after her still stands. The Crucifixion above the altar is the work which is most closely associated with Masaccio's name; as he died in 1428 or 1429, it is probably the earliest in the series. The paintings on the right wall represent scenes from the life of St. Ambrose of Milan. As we turn right on emerging from the chapel, we shall see a fine picture of St. Christopher, the patron saint of travellers, many of whom in the past have scratched their names, prayers and dates upon the painting. Some of these graffiti date from the second half of the fifteenth century.

Before making our way down into the shadowy depths of the lower church and excavations beneath it, it is pleasant to rest for a moment in the sunlight of the colonnaded medieval forecourt, the only one of its period to have survived in Rome. Like the basilica itself, this stands directly above its fourth-century predecessor; the gate leading into it from the Piazza di S. Clemente is really the main entrance to the church. On the outside this is surmounted by a distinctive overhanging porch which now looks charmingly picturesque, but it had a far grimmer function in the Middle Ages. Then it formed part of the defences of the church and monastery, like the machicolations of a castle. Evidently Cardinal Anastasius who built it had no intention of being caught napping by another Robert Guiscard.

Returning to the basilica, we pass through the vestibule on the right and descend into the fourth-century church. At first it is very difficult to imagine it as such; walls subsequently built to support the nave and aisles of the eleventh-century basilica have resulted in its appearing rather as a series of four long passages of varying width. Its height too has been diminished by the new basilica's having been partly sunk into its filled-in remains. But if it is very difficult to gain an overall impression of the whole, most skilfully placed lighting affords us every now and then evocative glimpses of an ancient column, a sarcophagus, a sculptural fragment or a painting. Seen thus they seem to emerge out of the shadowy past as they must once really have done to Fr. Mullooly when he broke through the outer wall not far from where we entered and started to dig his way back through the refuse of centuries to discover S. Clement's early Christian origins. Fr. Mullooly must have been a remarkable man, for even in those early days of archaeology he had the foresight to commission artists to make copies of the frescoes in which all the pristine freshness of their colour, just as they were discovered, was recorded (three copies now hang in the vestibule through which we pass to reach the lower church). It seems strange to the layman, but paintings such as these appear to survive centuries of burial in damp earth almost unscathed; while a hundred years' exposure to the air has caused them to fade disastrously.

Turning sharply to the right as soon as we reach the bottom of the steps, some way along the long narrow passage which was originally the right-hand aisle of the church, we come upon the first of these paintings. Set back in a small niche, it appears—and was for long believed to be—a fifth-century picture of the Virgin and Child. Considerable interest has, however, been aroused by the recent suggestion that it is in fact a contemporary portrait of Justinian's Empress Theodora, who died in 548.

Retracing our steps we again find ourselves in the long passage leading straight from the foot of the stairs. This was the narthex of the old church; it lies directly beneath the forecourt we lately left. One of the frescoes here—a ninth-century 'Last Judgment'—has been removed and now hangs in the atrium of the sacristy. The two remaining frescoes on the opposite wall date from the eleventh century and are of considerable importance in the history of painting. They were the gift of Beno de Rapiza and his wife Maria Macellaria, represented together with their children beneath the right-hand fresco, which portrays one of the miracles recounted in the apocryphal 'Acts of St. Clement'. This last is a curious composition, showing a child in a curtained pavilion, with fish swimming above and to one side of it; on the left are a kneeling woman and a religious procession. The painting represents the miraculous survival of a child who was carried away when the waves returned to cover St. Clement's tomb after its annual exposure. He was found there alive and well when the sea ebbed again the following year. The other fresco portrays the translation in 868 of St. Clement's relics from St. Peter's to this church. It will be recalled that the relics were believed to have been brought back from the Crimea by SS. Cyril and Methodius. We now enter the nave, which has been much reduced in size by the walls built to support the upper church. Immediately on the left of the door is another fresco in which Leo IV is shown with the square halo of the living on the left of the picture. The nave contains other ninth-century frescoes, chiefly of New Testament subjects; also one of 'Christ's Descent into Limbo'. However, these are not considered to be of such importance as the two eleventh-century ones on the left wall.

It must be admitted that the subject of the last fresco calls for lively treatment; the story is a very funny one, especially for a pious legend. Two panels—set one above the other— illustrate the story of Sisinnus, a jealous pagan husband, who followed his wife Theodora to a church where St. Clement was officiating. In the upper panel, Sisinnus is seen arriving and being struck blind and deaf as a result of his unworthy suspicions. In the lower one St. Clement is seen visiting Sisinnus's house and curing him. It also shows the ungrateful man giving vent to his rage and ordering his servants to bind the saint and his companions and to drag them away. However, Providence intervened with unusually humorous results, making Sisinnus and his henchmen mistake some columns lying on the ground for St. Clement and his entourage. They are seen struggling with these unwieldy objects; while the accompanying inscription records Sisinnus' vituperative commands. 'Go on, you sons of harlots, pull!' he shouts. 'Pull away, Gosmari and Albertel. You, Carvoncelle, get behind with a lever.' Possibly it was not thought suitable to dignify such highly-coloured language by rendering it in Latin, so the vernacular was used instead for this reason. The inscription is of very great importance as being the earliest one known to have been written in Italian.

At the far end of the nave there is a modern altar standing in the apse; this last is not, however, that of the original fourth-century church, but a smaller one built to support the apse of the new church above. A door on the right leads into the old and far larger apse; this is one of the very few parts of the fourth-century church to stretch beyond the confines of the house of Clemens, which lies beneath. It was specifically designed to do so, and it is not the only example of its kind in Rome; another possibly even more striking one occurs in S. Prisca on the Aventine, the reason being that in the house adjoining that of Clemens there existed a centre of Mithraic worship. At one time Mithraism was viewed as a rival of Christianity—it was protected by Commodus and Diocletian. Even after the disestablishment of the pagan cults in 382, it was still powerful as the chief religion of the rank and file of the western legions. Mithraism was only finally crushed by Theodosius's victories over Maximus and the legions at Siscia in 388, and Arbogastes and the Franks on the Frigidus in 394. The following year it was formally outlawed. Shortly after this, the clergy of St. Clement's must have acquired the now abandoned Mithraic temple; and when they built their new church, they extended the apse so that it stood above the spot where one of the last rites of paganism had been celebrated.

A door leads from this apse into a long narrow passage, formerly part of the nave, but now separated from it by the wall built to support the basilica above. On the wall immediately to the left of this door is another ninth-century fresco of 'Our Lord's Descent into Limbo' to free just souls who had died before the redemption.

Continuing a short distance down the passage, we turn through a door to the right, cross the nave, and find ourselves in the left aisle. At the far end of this, beside what is believed to be the tomb of St. Cyril, steps lead down to the level of the temple of Mithras and the original house of Clemens. Both these large adjoining blocks were constructed towards the end of the first century, over the filled-in remains of even earlier buildings devastated by Nero's famous fire of AD 64; they were separated from one another by a narrow alley. The 'Mithraic' house was a typical Roman *insula* or block of flats, in which some ground-floor rooms were adapted to this form of worship, about the end of the second century. At the same time the characteristic cave-like *triclinium*—for the consumption of the religious banquet, which formed an important part of the Mithraic ritual—was built in the courtyard of the *insula*.

Turning left and then right at the bottom of the stairs, we find ourselves at the entrance to a room which served as the vestibule of the temple. It is believed that this was reserved for the initiates; remnants of seating provided for them and some fine stucco decoration still survive. Far better preserved, however, and far more evocative is the *triclinium* across the passageway on the left. With its vaulted ceiling covered with small stones in imitation of a cave, and its rocky grotto at the far end, this might well be mistaken for one of those underground nympheums which served as refuges from summer heat in Roman palaces and villas. In actual fact the whole design was dictated by the curious creed of Mithras, a god born of a rock, who at Apollo's command killed the bull which was the symbol of fertility. In this struggle Mithras was helped by a snake and a dog but betrayed by a scorpion, which spilled some of the bull's precious blood—from which all things living were created—and thus introduced evil into the world. The scene showing Mithras plunging a knife into the bull's back is portrayed on the altar now at the far end of the *triclinium*, though it probably formerly stood in the room of the initiates. After his victory, Mithras banqueted with Apollo, and was conveyed in his chariot to heaven. The ritual banquets held in the Mithraic *triclinia* commemorated this event. Other gods such as Helios, Selene and Serapis were associated with the cult; reliefs of the first two are also to be seen in this Mithraeum.

Mithraism was a highly moral religion strictly limited to men, loyalty and fidelity being regarded as the ultimate virtues; it also held out hope of a life hereafter. In view of the recent discovery of a Mithraeum in the heart of the City of London, it is interesting to note that it was the British legions who revolted after the disestablishment of the pagan cults in 382, electing as their leader Maximus, who fought paganism's penultimate battle against the Christian Theodosius in 388.

Not all of the Mithraic *insula* beneath S. Clemente has yet been excavated, but a room leading out of the end of the passage on the right is believed to have been the 'school' or instruction room for postulants; in it are seven niches with graffiti, thought to represent the seven stages of initiation. Beside this is an iron door leading to a tunnel, built in 1912-14 to carry off the water—whose flow has been constantly audible ever since we descended into the lower levels—to the Cloaca Maxima, some seven hundred yards away beside the Colosseum. This water, which flooded the Mithraeum for forty years after Fr. Mullooly's excavations of 1870, runs in the external tufa wall of Clemens's house, some thirty feet below the Via di S. Giovanni in Laterano. It is not known if this is a relic of some ancient aqueduct, or simply the canalisation of some underground spring; but the supply is pure and plentiful and was used by the Dominicans during the water shortages of the last war.

Returning to the vestibule of the Mithraeum, and entering the small room on the left, we cross the narrow alley which once separated it from the house of Clemens. After descending a few steps we find ourselves at last in this Christian dwelling of the first century. Very little of Clemens's house has so far been excavated; but it is known that the few rooms which have, bordered on the great courtyard over which the nave of the fourth-century basilica was built. Passing through them in the dim light and silence—broken only by the sound of the running water—is a rather eerie experience; and inevitably one wonders what dramas of fear and courage, of faith and despair, of sorrow for the ordeal and death of beloved martyred friends and relations they must have witnessed during the period of persecutions.

Our exploration of S. Clemente will probably have occupied the best part of three-quarters of an hour, much of it spent underground, so a short climb to the breezier heights of the Coelian Hill will not come amiss. To get there we cross Via di S. Giovanni in Laterano to the Via dei Querceti, take the first turn to the left, and find ourselves in Via dei SS. Quattro Coronati. Walking up it we pursue exactly the opposite route to that taken in the old days by the papal cavalcade on the '*possesso*' on its way to the Lateran; and thereby hangs one of the most fabulous tales of Roman folklore. The papal cavalcade proceeded up the Via dei SS. Quattro Coronati to this point, then changed over to the Via di S. Giovanni in Laterano, because in the lower part of the street there was a house known to the Roman populace as that of 'Papessa Giovanna'. Some fragment of a classical relief, showing a woman with her breast bared and a child in her arms, marked the spot; this was removed and the whole house pulled down by order of Pius IV in 1550. How it came to be associated with the fantastic legend, or perhaps even gave rise to it, is not known. But the fact remains that for centuries the Romans told the story of how an Englishwoman called Joan succeeded in being elected as Pope John VIII. Her portrait, entitled 'Johannes VIII, a woman of England', even survived among the papal portraits in Siena Cathedral for 200 years, until Clement VIII ordered its removal in 1592 and the substitution of that of Pope Zacharias (741–52).

The legend dates from the twelfth century, some three hundred years after the beautiful Joan was believed to have succeeded to Leo IV (847–55). According to it, she first disguised herself as a monk in order not to be separated from her lover, who was a Benedictine. Together they travelled the world, going to England, and to Athens, where they studied philosophy at the famous schools. Here the lover died, and Joan went on to Rome, where her brilliance and profound knowledge of philosophy and theology opened all doors before her. She acquired another lover, but this did not quench her ambition to become pope. She was duly elected, but at the very moment when she was on her way to take possession of the temporal power in the Lateran, Joan gave birth to a child in the Via di S. Giovanni in Laterano. Both she and it were killed by the outraged populace and buried by the roadside.

As we crossed the Via dei Querceti we caught a glimpse of the ponderous mass of what at first appears to be a medieval castle on the hill. This is the fortified Abbey—the only one in Rome—of the **Quattro Coronati**; often used in medieval times as a temporary papal residence or as a lodging for important guests. The approach is steep, but finally some steps on the right bring us out on to a small open space before the tower which rises above the dark medieval door of this massive building—now shared by a home for deaf and dumb children and an enclosed order of nuns. Two successive courtyards lead us to the door of the church of the SS Quattro Coronati (open from 10 a.m. to 12.30 and from 3 to 7 p.m.). This was for long believed to have been founded in the sixth or possibly even in the fourth century, and to have been associated with the *titulus Aemiliani*, which existed in this area in the time of Gregory the Great (590–604). Recent research has, however, proved that the existing church was built during the reign of Leo IV (847–55), gravely damaged by the Normans in 1084, and reconstructed on a smaller scale by Paschal II (1111–16).

Leo's original church was a large one, extending right over the inner courtyard which originally formed part of its nave. When Paschal II rebuilt it in the twelfth century he only utilised half of the space; hence the disproportion between his church, with its short nave and aisles, and Leo's enormous original apse. Paschal also added the upper galleries. Although it is not architecturally outstanding, with its cosmatesque pavement and double arcades supported by ancient columns this silent and isolated church has tremendous atmosphere. But its chief beauty is the exquisite little cloister (to enter ring the bell by the door on the left and make a small offering to the attendant nun), carried out as a work of devotion by Roman thirteenth-century sculptors and masons in memory of their martyred predecessors. The peace and calm of another age dwells in this beautiful place, filled with the scent of flowers and the music of the little fountain that gurgles in its midst. This last is unique in Rome, in that it dates from the twelfth century; it probably formerly stood in the courtyard in front of the church.

The Quattro Coronati has yet another treasure in store for us before we leave. This is the chapel of S. Silvestro, which still belongs to the confraternity of sculptors and stone-cutters. The entrance is on the left of the outer court as we come out. The door is often locked, but the key can be obtained by ringing the bell and asking for it at the grated window of the enclosed convent on the same side of the inner court; it will come out on a turn-table, and must be returned. The chapel of S. Silvestro was dedicated in 1246; its walls are decorated with remarkably well-preserved frescoes illustrating the legend of Constantine being cured of leprosy by Pope St. Sylvester I. It is interesting to note that here, still in the middle of the thirteenth century, the Byzantine influence on painting was so strong in Rome.

We now set out on a walk which takes us past some of the most picturesque and charming corners of our 'classical land-scape with churches'; though even here the growth of modern Rome has made itself felt within the last few years. We con-tinue along the Via dei Quattro Coronati, as it leads straight out before the church, and find ourselves at its far end facing the romanesque portico of the old **Hospital of S. Giovanni**. This was built in the Middle Ages as a *dépendence* of the Lateran Palace. Here we turn sharp right down the Via di S. Stefano Rotondo which begins as a fairly modern-looking street, but gradually merges into the past, bordered as it is on the right by the mellow brickwork of the Claudian aque-duct, and on the left by hospital gardens enclosing medieval ruins. The walk is particularly attractive in spring, when wistaria trails its mass of lavender-coloured flowers over the old walls.

At the far end of the street on the left, we find the church of **S. Stefano Rotondo** (from the writer's twenty years' experience, this is the most capricious in its opening hours of any Roman church; for years it was hermetically closed for repairs, after being open for a short while. At the time of writing it is again closed for repairs). As a matter of fact the church is well worth looking at also from the outside; standing back from the road, its warm brick walls and mellow tiled roof are framed in the green of a shady garden. The mere fact that it has been closed for so many years causes the ordinary traveller to pass it by; even today it possesses something of that tranquil seclusion that so attracted the composer Palestrina in the sixteenth century. It was in a small house in the surrounding vineyards that he composed the sacred music which Pius IV compared to 'the concerts of the angels'.

Possibly because of its circular shape, most unusual in a Roman church, S. Stefano was for long believed to have been erected over the remains of the round central building of Nero's great market, the *macellum magnum*. In actual fact it was built by Pope S. Simplicius (468–83); and many believe that its design was inspired by that of the church of the Holy Sepulchre at Jerusalem.

When S. Stefano was built, it consisted of a series of three circular concentric naves, separated from one another by rings of antique columns. Innocent II (1130–43) introduced a series of transverse arches, also supported by ancient columns, in order to reinforce the vault. Unfortunately in his restoration of 1450, Nicholas V walled in the outer ring of columns, greatly reducing the size of the church and altering its effect. Finally, at the end of the sixteenth century, this outer wall was covered with a terrifyingly realistic series of frescoes of the most famous and well-established scenes of early Christian martyrdom. It is to be hoped that when S. Stefano is really ultimately restored this outer wall will be removed, revealing its original beauty which can only be guessed at today.

Among the chapels now surrounding S. Stefano the first on the left contains an antique marble seat, said once to have served as the episcopal throne of St. Gregory the Great. Farther on is the chapel of SS. Primus and Felician, made by Theodore I (642–9), to which he translated their relics from the Catacombs of the Via Nomentana—the earliest recorded instance of what was later to become a common practice. In the apse, the two saints are represented in a mosaic, standing on either side of a jewelled cross surmounted by the head and shoulders of Christ, somewhat similar in style to that of St. John Lateran. Pope Theodore was a Greek whose family lived in Jerusalem; some authorities believe that he had represented here the cross which Constantine had set up on the summit of Golgotha, that he would have known in childhood before it was looted by Chosroes in 614.

Emerging from Via di S. Stefano Rotondo into the roar of traffic in the Via della Navicella, we see before us yet another charming view of our 'classical landscape with churches'. An imposing gate on the left leads into the **Villa Celimontana**, now a public park, but formerly the famous Villa Mattei. In the foreground is the delightful boat fountain known as the *Navicella*, copied for Leo X (1513–21) from a classical one, which was probably a votive offering. Behind it rises the elegant Renaissance façade of S. Maria in Domnica; and to the right of this a superb medieval portal and the Arch of Dolabella, dating from AD 10.

Explanations of the origin of the name of the church of **S. Maria in Domnica** are varied. According to some authorities it is derived from that of a family—Domnica was the name of a Byzantine family, which may have had a Roman branch. But the most generally accepted theory is that it is a corruption of *dominicum*, a word applied in early Christian times to a church. According to legend, S. Maria in Domnica was built over the house of St. Cyriaca, a pious matron of the third century. However, the existing church dates from the reign of St Paschal I (817–24), the founder of S. Prassede. It was restored by Leo X early in the sixteenth century, when the fine porticoed façade, attributed to Peruzzi, was added.

The first thing that strikes us on entering the church, is the ample width of the nave, which is dominated by Paschal's superb ninth-century mosaic in the apse. Most unusually in a mosaic of this kind, our overwhelming impression is of the setting; the green and flowering garden of paradise in the midst of which the Virgin and Child sit enthroned. They are surrounded by an angelic host, whose sky-blue haloes are repeated an infinity of times, disappearing into the distance. Pope Paschal himself is seen kneeling before the Virgin, holding one of her scarlet-slippered feet in his hands. As in the mosaic of S. Prassede, he appears as quite a young man with the square halo of the living. The Virgin carries in her left hand the *mappa*, or fashionable fringed handkerchief of a Byzantine court lady.

As in S. Prassede, Paschal's monogram is inscribed at the summit of the apse; a Latin poem, inscribed in gold letters on a blue ground, celebrating his offering, appears at the base of the mosaic. After having enjoyed the extraordinary beauty of this mosaic, it is sad to have to say that this is the first Roman church we have encountered in which recent hideous modern alterations to the altar and sunken *confessio* mar the dignity and splendour of the whole composition.

On leaving S. Maria in Domnica we turn left, and find ourselves in front of the beautiful medieval gateway adorned with mosaics. Here Christ is portrayed on a gold ground, with a black and white man on either side of him. An inscription records the names of Magister Jacobus and his son Cosmate—the original 'Cosmati' after whom this whole school of Roman mosaic workers was called. The gate once led in to the great Hospital of St. Thomas, founded by S. Giovanni di Matha, who also originated the Trinitarian Order in the reign of Innocent III (1198–1216). The primary object of the order was to ransom Christian slaves—hence the black and white men represented over the door. It is said that Giovanni di Matha died in 1213 in the room with the small windows above the **Arch of Dolabella** on the right. This last was built in AD 10 by the Consuls P. Cornelius Dolabella and Caius Julius Silanus, possibly on the site of one of the gateways of the old Severian wall. Nearby on the right are the ruins of Nero's extension of the Claudian aqueduct, built to supply the imperial palace on the Palatine. On the other side of the arch we find ourselves in a narrow road called after St. Paul of the Cross, lined by high garden walls. A short way along on the right we may catch a glimpse into the garden of the Passionist Congregation of St. Paul. This is a delightful old-fashioned '*orto*' with lavender hedges and oleanders surrounding plots of tomatoes and lettuce; no one would for a moment imagine that it had once formed part of the gardens of Nero's Golden House. But in fact it occupies the site of one of the nympheums of these famous gardens, for which he partially demolished the temple that his mother had dedicated to the memory of his stepfather Claudius.

The street widens out into the **Piazza di SS. Giovanni e Paolo**, one of the most fascinating of its kind in Rome. Looking around it we realise that there is practically not a building in sight dating from later than the Middle Ages. The ancient porticoed church rises before us; on our right a beautiful romanesque campanile soars up out of a mass of monastic buildings, which in their turn rest upon the great stone blocks of a classical ruin. To the left, a narrow street passes under a series of medieval arches, affording us a glimpse of the green Palatine Hill beyond; its name—the *Clivus Scauri*—has remained unchanged for some two thousand years. It is a place in which time seems to have stood still; in fact it is one of the few corners of Rome where a medieval pilgrim would have little difficulty in recognising his whereabouts.

The piazza takes its name from the **Basilica of SS. Giovanni e Paolo**, dating from the fifth century or even earlier. This is almost certainly the same church as the *titulus Pammachii* listed in 499, whose name was changed to SS. Iohannis et Pauli by 535. This was confirmed by a fifth-century inscription formerly existing in the church, which gave the name of Pammachius as its founder. We know from the writings of St. Jerome, who was a friend of his, that Pammachius was a senator who played a great part in public life until the death of his wife. After this he gave all his money to the poor, retired into monastic seclusion, and died in 410—the year in which Alaric sacked Rome. It is believed that Pammachius built the church some time before his death, possibly during the reign of St. Damasus (366–84).

In Rome we have by now become accustomed to seeing churches whose foundations may date back even further than this; but what is surprising about SS. Giovanni e Paolo—and what astonished even the archaeologists responsible for its recent restoration—was the fact that under the accretions of subsequent centuries they found Pammachius's original building. The five large walled-in openings with classical columns, which we see high up on the façade, formed part of this original church. These were repeated at ground level; two of the supporting columns can still be discerned behind the portico.

Excavations beneath the church (carried on intermittently between 1887 and 1958) have shown that two Roman houses below—dating from the second and third centuries—had been united under Christian ownership and used as a place of burial. This was absolutely exceptional within the confines of the city of Rome, where very ancient laws expressly forbade the cremation or burial of any but the Vestal Virgins and, later, members of the imperial family. Nevertheless, a steep staircase had subsequently been built giving access from the church to a shaft, at the bottom of which lay three graves. In another part of one of the Roman houses other tombs were discovered in a similar shaft and in a room above it. Both these burial areas had been connected by stairs with the basilica which was subsequently built above; and the shafts prolonged so that they projected through its pavement. These were, in fact, 'cataract tombs' like the one built by Constantine in the *confessio* of St. Peter's. The fifth-century church of SS. Giovanni e Paolo was, therefore, a basilica *ad corpora*, built to shelter this evidently much-revered place of Christian burial.

Such are the findings of archaeology; we will now see how they compare with tradition. The earliest record of the martyrs SS. John and Paul occurs in a sixth-century account known as the 'Passion'. According to this, they had been officers at the court of Constantine, and guardians of his daughter Constantia. Upon the emperor's death (in 337) John and Paul had retired to private life on the Coelian. Julian the Apostate, after his accession (in 360), recalled them to military service at his court; compliance would have been tantamount to a denial of their faith, refusal meant death. Bravely awaiting the inevitable sentence in their own home, the two saints were found there by the captain of Julian's Guard. Upon their refusing to sacrifice to a pagan god, they were there beheaded and secretly buried on the night of 26–27 June in the year 361. A later version of the 'Passion' states that in their last moments the martyrs were assisted by the priest Crispus, the cleric Crispinianus and the matron Benedicta, who were afterwards discovered praying at the martyrs' tomb and beheaded, their bodies also being subsequently buried in the same place. It was over this spot that the Senator Byzantis began to build a basilica, which was completed by his son Pammachius.

The whole of this story has been the subject of much learned controversy. However, in one of the shafts which formerly connected the place of burial with the floor of the church there are paintings, including the portrayal of a martyrdom by beheading, of two men and a woman. These pictures were executed in the ancient Hellenistic style, without preparatory drawings. Thus it is evident that, whoever they may have been, the tombs of these martyrs early became an object of veneration, resulting in the careful preservation of the houses in which they stood, and the subsequent building of the basilica which sheltered and gave access to them.

The recent restoration of the exterior of the basilica revealed that it cannot long have survived exactly as Pammachius built it. Gashes and splintering of the columns of the five great openings high up on the façade (now walled in), are believed to have been the results of the fury of Alaric's sack in 410. These were converted into ordinary windows shortly afterwards, and the first of the supporting arches constructed across the *Clivus Scauri*. Further restorations and additions were made in the eleventh and twelfth centuries. These included the building of the existing monastery and campanile, the addition of the church portico with its strange gallery above, the addition of more supporting arches over the *Clivus Scauri* and the decorative arcade, which is such a striking external feature of the apse. Much of this work was carried out by Honorius III, who was careful still to mark the spot to the right of the centre of the nave known as the *locus martyrii* (place of martyrdom), which lies almost immediately above the painted shaft leading to the tombs of the three martyrs far below.

The result of the 1948–52 restorations, which cleared away the accretions of successive centuries, has been to reveal the exterior of the basilica much as Honorius left it. The interior of the basilica, however, now bears no sign of resemblance to its original early Christian or even medieval state. It is now a typical eighteenth-century late baroque church with one unfortunate exception. In 1911 the plain white walls were painted over to imitate coloured marbles. The only existing reminder of the character and function of the original basilica is a small railed-in space to the right of the centre of the nave marking approximately the *locus martyrii*. Here each year on 26–27 June—as the last survivor of a time-honoured Roman custom once common to many basilicas—a mosaic of flowers is laid in memory of the martyrdom of SS. John and Paul.

The spot is not strictly the true one; a glass disk set into the floor near by, now enables us to look down into the painted *confessio* in the shaft above the three martyrs' tombs, while, by a door on the right of the church, we can descend into the original Roman houses below. In one is the famous painted room, decorated with *orantes*, figures praying with their arms outstretched in the ancient fashion; in the other pagan frescoes have been revealed, which were covered over when it too became part of that Christian burial ground and place of worship to which the Basilica of SS. Giovanni e Paolo owes its existence.

Leaving the Piazza of SS. Giovanni e Paolo, we now descend the *Clivus Scauri*; not forgetting to look back after we have passed the arches, in order to enjoy the highly picturesque view of the colonnaded apse, framed by cypress trees. We now turn left and see before us the church of **S. Gregorio Magno** rising at the top of an imposing flight of steps. To the English this is the most important of Roman churches. According to tradition, it was from the monastery which he founded here, on the site of his ancestral home, that Gregory the Great (590–604) dispatched St. Augustine on his mission to convert England.

It was on the site of this monastery that Gregory II (715–31) built a church, dedicating it to his great predecessor and namesake. This was completely transformed; externally in 1629 by G. B. Soria for Cardinal Scipione Borghese, internally in 1734 by F. Ferrari. This is the building we see today, of which the fine baroque façade is considered to be Soria's masterpiece but gives no indication of its early origins. However, the existing forecourt occupies the site of the ancient parvis and some interesting tombs from the earlier church are preserved there. Among them is that of Sir Edward Carne, who came several times to Rome between 1529 and 1533, as one of Henry VIII's envoys who attempted to gain the pope's consent to the annulment of Henry's marriage to Catherine of Aragon. Carne returned to Rome as Mary's ambassador; wisely remaining there after Elizabeth's accession, he became warden of the English hospice, ending his days in the city in 1561. Another English tomb in the forecourt is that of Robert Pecham, also a religious exile; he died in 1569.

The most curious monument in the forecourt is the one in the far left-hand corner, now containing the remains of Canon Lelio Guidiccioni, who died in 1643. This beautiful tomb had originally been made for Imperia, the famous courtesan; it bore an elegant Latin inscription which read 'Imperia, a Roman courtesan who, worthy of so great a name, offered an example of beauty rare in mankind. She lived twenty-six years and twelve days, and died in 1512 on the fifteenth of August.'

Except for a fine cosmatesque pavement and some antique columns, the interior of S. Gregorio now also appears as a typical baroque church. However, in St. Gregory's chapel (in the far right-hand corner) there is an exquisite fifteenth-century altar with reliefs portraying scenes from his life, also a beautiful painted altar-piece of the same period. Leading out of this is another chapel, believed to have been Gregory's own cell; in it are preserved the stone upon which he is said to have slept and his episcopal throne—a fine classical marble seat (there are some beautiful reliefs on the side facing the wall).

Through a door on the left of the church we enter the Salviati chapel; this contains a curious old picture of the Virgin, which is said to have spoken to St. Gregory; also a fine fifteenth-century gold and white altar. Here we can ask the sacristan to show us the three chapels, picturesquely set among cypresses to the left of the church. These are dedicated to St Andrew, S. Sylvia and S. Barbara and contain important frescoes by Domenichino and Guido Reni. The central chapel of S. Andrew is believed to stand on the site of Gregory's original oratory dedicated to this saint. That on the right is dedicated to Gregory's mother, St. Sylvia; while in the one on the left is preserved what is believed to be the table at which Gregory himself daily served meals to twelve poor men; verses record the legendary appearance of an angel who once brought their number up to thirteen. Until 1870 the popes annually followed Gregory's example by personally serving thirteen pilgrims here on Maundy Thursday.

Leaving S. Gregorio, we turn left down the Salita of the same name, and then sharply to the right; past a delightful little Renaissance pavilion known as the Vignola. Opposite us rises the famous fourth-century obelisk of Axum brought here from Abyssinia by Mussolini in 1937; and the ultra-modern glass-fronted conference hall of the Food and Agriculture Organisation of the U.N. We now follow the wide tree-lined Via di S. Gregorio, which traverses the valley between the Coelian and Palatine Hills. It was on the left-hand side of this, at the foot of the Palatine, that Septimius Severus built the curious edifice known as the *Septizodium* or *Septizonium*. This was decorated with fountains, and resembled the *scenae frons* of a Roman theatre; his contemporaries said that he built it to impress his fellow Africans arriving in Rome by the Appian Way. Much to the sorrow of the Romans, the remains of this fantastic building were pulled down by Sixtus V in 1585–90. As we walk along the Via di S. Gregorio, on our left the Palatine appears as a further extension of our 'classical landscape with churches', with S. Bonaventura and St. Sebastiano in Pallara picturesquely sited in their gardens on the top.

Just before the Arch of Constantine we turn left out of the Via di S. Gregorio, up the Via Sacra—whose ancient paving is still extant—to the top of the little hill crowned by the Arch of Titus; from where there is an excellent view of the Forum. Turning left again, we find ourselves in the **Via di S. Bonaventura**, a little country road, bordered by trees and old stone walls; shortly we come to an old gateway on the left. If this is closed, at any time between 7 a.m. and sunset we can ring the bell on the left and enter one of the most unexpected and delightful corners of old Rome. This is the Palatine as our ancestors knew it—in the midst of an enchanting little flower garden, complete with vine arbour, clumps of acanthus, and masses of daffodils, violets, lilies and roses in season, rises the little tenth-century chapel of S. Sebastiano in Pallaria. Beside it in a charming little medieval house lives the parish priest— surely one of the most fortunate of his kind.

Built on the site where St. Sebastian's martyrdom is believed to have taken place in Diocletian's reign, this chapel was also known in early times as S. Maria in Palladio. It stands above the ruins of the temple in which the Syrian Emperor Elagabalus assembled all the most sacred objects in Rome— including the famous Palladium, normally kept by the Vestals —to do honour to his black stone idol, the oriental god Elagabal. The ultimate fate of the Palladium is unknown, but it is significant that the memory of what was probably its brief sojourn here—Elagabulus's mad reign only lasted four years—was sufficient to give its name to the whole area.

The remainder of the road leading to the church of S. Bonaventura is picturesque; but if we are pressed for time, we would be wise to retrace our steps to the Via Sacra. On the far side of this rises a curious mass of buildings, conspicuous for a Romanesque campanile on the left, and on the right for classical ruins surrounded by clipped evergreens. This is all that is left of the Temple of Venus and Rome, once the largest in the city, designed by Hadrian and dedicated by him in AD 135. We have already noted the emperor's originality as an architect at the Pantheon; this temple was no exception —its double sanctuaries were placed back to back, a circumstance unique in Italy. We can still see the coffered apse of the one dedicated to Venus, facing towards the Colosseum. The shrubs clipped in circular form suggest a hypothetical reconstruction of the temple's vast colonnades, which were built over the vestibule of Nero's Golden House.

Continuing round the platform upon which the temple stands, past the monastery which has been built into its ruins, we come to the church of **S. Francesca Romana**. This traces its origins back to an eighth-century oratory dedicated to SS. Peter and Paul, erected in honour of a miracle related in the apocryphal 'Acts of Peter'. According to this legend, Simon Magus (the same as mentioned in Acts of the Apostles viii, 9–24, from whom the word Simony is derived) met SS. Peter and Paul in Rome in the reign of Nero and challenged them to a competition in levitation in the Forum. By his magic arts Simon did indeed succeed in flying up into the sky, but crashed to earth and was killed as a result of the prayers of the two Apostles that his chicanery might be revealed. This oratory contained—as the existing church still does—two stones said to bear the impress of the knees of the Apostles as they prayed.

Half-way through the tenth century, the oratory was incorporated into a church known as S. Maria Nova; built to take the place of the sixth-century S. Maria Antiqua, then crumbling under the decaying ruins of the Palatine on the other side of the Forum. It was here in 1421 that S. Francesca Romana founded her congregation of Oblates and was herself later buried. Since her canonisation in 1608, the church is most usually called after her. It was completely converted to the baroque style between 1600 and 1615; externally the only visible trace of the medieval church is the fine twelfth-century campanile, which we saw from the Via Sacra.

The interior too is now almost entirely baroque, glittering with gold and brilliant coloured marbles; in the apse is a charming twelfth-century mosaic, probably executed by the same artists as that of S. Clemente. The Virgin is enthroned in the centre, with the Christ child in her arms; it is interesting to note that here also she is seated on the same type of oriental lyre-backed throne as in the ninth-century frescoes of S. Maria Antiqua.

S. Francesca Romana contains another exceedingly interesting, in fact unique, example of early Christian art. This is the fifth-century encaustic picture of the Virgin and Child (now in the sacristy) which was discovered in 1950 when the picture was restored. Beneath repainting of the last century, a beautiful twelfth-century picture was first discovered (this now hangs over the high altar); beneath this again was found this unique example of easel painting of the fifth century. Over the sacristy door hangs a picture of considerable interest to English travellers. Attributed by some to Perin del Vaga, this shows Reginald Pole in conversation with Paul III. It must have been painted before Pole was created a cardinal for having written a book condemning Henry VIII's divorce in 1536, as he is shown here dressed in black. The design of the *confessio* is attributed to Bernini, beneath it is the crypt in which the body of S. Francesca Romana is preserved (it is exhibited on the ninth of each month).

Emerging from S. Francesca Romana, we are confronted by the brick walls of the Basilica of Maxentius or Constantine, which we originally saw when exploring the Forum on our first day's walk. As this vast pile is now used in summer as an open-air concert hall, it is not accessible from the Forum enclosure and therefore comes more conveniently into today's exploration. Centuries of use as a quarry have reduced this enormous building to about a third of its original size, though the three remaining coffered vaults exercised a great influence upon Renaissance architects. Its building was begun by Maxentius between the years 306–312; it was later completed by Constantine with certain alterations—notably the addition of the apse facing the Forum, which contained his own colossal statue.

Like all Roman pagan basilicas, that of Maxentius was intended to serve as a law court and for the conduct of business affairs. It was in fact the last of its kind to be built in Rome; its design is typical of the architectural style of late imperial times. In fact the construction does not at a l resemble our usual conception of a classical building, especially that of a basilica. Here the great colonnaded porticoes of the older type of basilica have been replaced by a vast rectangular brick-faced concrete building, whose enormous vaulted aisles are supported by six huge piers, evidently inspired by the halls of the baths of Caracalla and Diocletian. This type of construction, like the nearby Senate House, was in fact typical of the functional architecture of the later Empire. What we see today are simply the bare bones of the building; originally its interior would have been rich in marble panelling and stucco decoration. As we have seen, one of the great Corinthian marble columns which stood beside the piers was set up in front of S. Maria Maggiore. One of its fellows travelled farther at the end of the eighteenth century, when it was given to the Russian Empress, Catherine the Great, and raised in what was then St. Petersburg. In Renaissance times, and right into the last century, the basilica was called the Temple of Peace, in mistake for Vespasian's long-vanished temple of that name which stood in his nearby forum. Like the real Temple of Peace, the basilica was believed to have been the repository of many treasures, including the seven-branched candlestick and the loot of Jerusalem.

The existing main entrance to the Basilica of Maxentius brings us out into the Via dei Fori Imperiali, from where we have a choice of two familiar lunching places. Either we can return to the Trattoria Angelino ai Fori, in the Largo Corrado Ricci just across the way. Or, in order to be nearer the Colosseum and the beginning of our afternoon's walk, we can go to the little Trattoria di Nerone in the Via Terme di Tito.

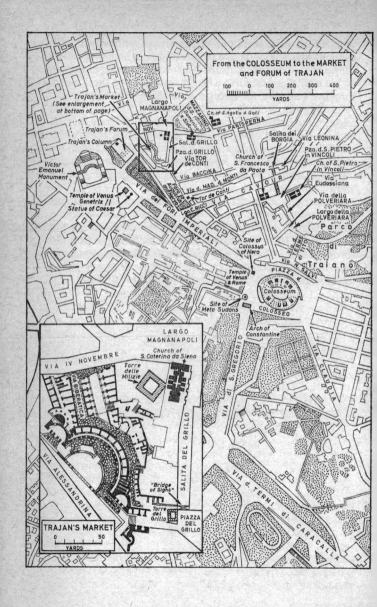

From the COLOSSEUM to the MARKET and FORUM of TRAJAN

100   0   100   200   300   400
YARDS

Trajan's Market (See enlargement at bottom of page)

Largo MAGNANAPOLI

NOV.

Trajan's Forum

Trajan's Column

Victor Emanuel Monument

Temple of Venus Genetrix Statue of Caesar

Sal. d. GRILLO
Pza. d. GRILLO
Via TOR de CONTI

Via BACCINA

VIA del FORI IMPERIALI

Via d. MAD. d. MONTI

Tor de Conti

Lgo. C. RICCI

VIA CAVOUR

Ch. of S. Agata d. Goti

Via PANISPERNA

Salita dei BORGIA

Via LEONINA

Pza. d. S. PIETRO in VINCOLI

Ch. of S. Pietro in Vincoli

Church of S. Francesco da Paola

via Eudossiana

Via della POLVERIARA

Largo della POLVERIARA

Parco

di

Traiano

Site of Colossus of Nero

VIA di S. GREGORIO

Temple of Venus & Rome

Site of Meta Sudans

PIAZZA d.

Colosseo

COLOSSEO

Via d. N. SALVI

PIAZZA

Arch of Constantine

VIA CLAUDIA

VIA d. TERMI di CARACALLA

LARGO MAGNANAPOLI

VIA IV NOVEMBRE

Church of S. Caterina da Siena

Torre delle Milizie

VIA BIBERATICA

VIA ALESSANDRINA

SALITA DEL GRILLO

"Bridge of Sighs"

Torre del Grillo

PIAZZA DEL GRILLO

TRAJAN'S MARKET

0   50
YARDS

CHAPTER SEVENTEEN

The Colosseum to the Market and Forum of Trajan

❧

AT intervals during our morning's walk we have caught glimpses of the **Colosseum**, dominating all around it; now at last we are going to explore this greatest remaining monument of ancient Rome. The Colosseum has been one of the 'sights' ever since it was built in the first century; though as far as we know, it was not so called for another six or seven hundred years. The first mention of the name occurs in a chronicle attributed to the Venerable Bede, quoting the famous proverb which says that as long as the Colosseum stands, so will Rome; when Rome falls, so will the world. In the *Mirabilia* and other medieval guide-books the great arena was naturally woven around with legends of every kind, the most common being that it was once covered with a great brass dome.

In ancient times the Colosseum was known as the Flavian Amphitheatre, after the three emperors of that dynasty who had a hand in its making. The first was Vespasian, who conceived the idea of thus returning to the Roman people some of the land which Nero had expropriated for the Golden House. The building was not finished when he died in AD 79. It was inaugurated by his son Titus in the following year; but it was only finally completed during Domitian's reign (AD 81–96). Both as a feat of engineering and a work of architecture, the Colosseum merits all the praise that has been showered on it during the centuries. Like the Great Pyramid, it is one of those buildings about which one can produce sheaves of statistics; but of all the known facts, two perhaps, more than any others, bring home to us the genius of its builders. First, that this vast mass of stone—originally a third of a mile in circumference—was raised on the marshy ground left after the draining of the lake in the gardens of the Golden House, an achievement which would tax the ingenuity of modern engineers. Secondly, that it was designed so as to enable a potentially unruly crowd of some 50,000 to enter, find their seats and disperse with ease by its eighty *vomitoria* or exits.

Architecturally, the inspiration for the Colosseum was obviously drawn from the Theatre of Marcellus. Like it, the orders of the half-columns on the arcades are Doric at ground level, Ionic on the first floor and Corinthian on the second; the Theatre of Marcellus is believed also formerly to have had a Corinthian second storey. The Colosseum has yet one more, consisting of a plain wall with Corinthian pilasters. In each alternative compartment formed by these last there is a small window; the intervening blank spaces were decorated by Domitian with now vanished bronze shields. The projecting corbels here were used as supports for masts, from which were stretched strips of awning to shade the arena—this operation was carried out by sailors of the imperial fleet. One of the things which mystifies most travellers is that the great stone blocks of the building are pitted with holes; these were made in the Middle Ages, when the metal cramps holding the stones together were pillaged. The enormous admiration which the Colosseum aroused among Renaissance and later architects—among other things it was the source of inspiration for the loggias of Palazzo Venezia, the courtyard of the Farnese Palace and, probably, the façade of the Cancelleria—did not prevent its being used as a quarry right up to the eighteenth century. It was only in the nineteenth century that the work of preservation was begun, by Pius VIII (1800–23) buttressing the crumbling outer wall. This was continued by later popes and the French administration, who also began to weed out the luxuriant vegetation which had established itself throughout the building. Though, according to Augustus Hare, in 1840 the arena of the Colosseum was still like 'an English abbey, an uneven grassy space littered with masses of ruin, amid which large trees grew and flourished'. After 1870 all vegetation was extirpated, and the cells beneath the arena— used in ancient times to house the animals and equipment— were excavated. As Hare said, this was 'much regretted by lovers of the picturesque'—and botanists. Two books had been written on the flora of the Colosseum which numbered 420 species, some alleged to be exotic importations, whose seeds had been introduced with the animal fodder in classical times.

Probably at no other period in its history was the Colosseum so much admired as by the romantics of the last century. Contemporary literature and letters are filled with descriptions of it seen by moonlight; but none so famous as that of Byron in 'Childe Harold':

> Arches on arches! as it were that Rome,
> Collecting the chief trophies of her line,
> Would build up all her triumphs in one dome,
> Her Colosseum stands . . .

If this picturesque aspect of the ruined Colosseum dominated the romantics, the other side of the coin did sometimes appear; in 'Manfred' Byron wrote 'But the gladiator's bloody circus stands'. These thoughts were uppermost in Dickens's mind, who, although he considered it 'the most impressive, the most stately, the most solemn, grand, majestic, mournful sight conceivable', was nevertheless overwhelmed by the thought of the horrors it had witnessed.

How the heirs and descendants of the austere and sober Romans of the early Republic ever came to be so debauched is a mystery, and not only to us. Juvenal (AD 42–125), the originator of the phrase 'bread and circuses', first used it in a tirade against his contemporaries' pursuit of the most vicious sensations and pleasure. This he attributed to the imperial system of dictatorship, which robbed them of any part in the government and all sense of responsibility, substituting instead the monthly dole of food to 150,000 idlers at the Portico Minicius, and free entertainment on a scale which the world has never seen before or since; it is estimated that for each working day during the year in imperial times the Romans enjoyed a day's holiday.

Emerging from the Colosseum, on the side facing the Temple of Venus and Rome, if traffic permits, we shall see the sites of two once-famous monuments marked in the road. Some travertine slabs at the beginning of the Via dei Fori Imperiali mark the spot to which Hadrian moved the Colossus of Nero, that stood formerly in the vestibule of the Golden House. This was of gilded bronze, some 150 feet high; it was dragged to the site by twenty-four elephants. After Nero's death it had been transformed into a sun god; later the face was probably altered to resemble various other emperors. According to tradition, the colossal bronze head we saw in the Palazzo dei Conservatori on the Capitol is a relic of the ultimate edition of this versatile statue, disguised as one of the sons of Constantine. It was still standing in 334; according to early medieval legend it was destroyed by Pope Sylvester I (314–55)—Gregory the Great (590–604), given in the twelfth- and fourteenth-century accounts, seems a more likely candidate.

Nearer the Arch of Constantine, a circular mark set into the ancient Roman pavement shows where the ruins of the Meta Sudans stood until 1936. This was a curious cone-shaped fountain, surmounted by a bronze ball pierced with tiny holes through which the water seeped or sweated (*sudare* is the verb to sweat in Italian). It was originally built by Titus and restored by Constantine. The fountain stood almost directly before the **Arch of Constantine**; erected in 315 by the Senate and people of Rome to commemorate the emperor's victory over Maxentius in 312 at the Milvian Bridge—the victory which followed upon his vision of the Cross and the words 'in this sign thou shalt conquer'. The same economically utilitarian spirit that diversified the career of Nero's colossus was active in the construction of Constantine's arch. Of the many sculptures adorning it, only the reliefs immediately above the two smaller arches, and the roundels and two lower ones on the ends, were actually made for it; all the rest were taken from earlier monuments. The degeneration of the arts in fourth-century Rome is clearly evident in the rough workmanship of these, which show Constantine speaking to the Romans, distributing *tesserae*, his triumph and his victory at Susa; also poor Crispus's triumph (on the side towards the Palatine). The other—much finer—reliefs were taken from monuments of Trajan, Hadrian and Marcus Aurelius.

In medieval times the arch was known as *Arco de Trasi*; this is believed possibly to have been a corruption of *Traci* or Thracians, from the figures of barbarians—Thracians or Dacians, from a monument of Trajan—which stand above the columns (these last were also plundered, from a monument of Domitian). The great reliefs of battle scenes, appearing high up on the ends and inside the central arch, were also probably taken from an arch dedicated to Trajan; while the eight very fine rectangular reliefs on both sides of the attic represent scenes from the life of Marcus Aurelius. Finally, the eight beautiful roundels above the small arches, representing scenes of hunting and sacrifices to the gods, are believed to date from

Hadrian's reign. Although many of the heads on these were later changed, one of the emperor's favourite, Antinous, is still recognisable. It may seem strange that sacrificial scenes, representing such pagan gods as Apollo, Hercules, Sylvanus and Diana, should be included in the triumphal arch of the first Christian emperor. But it should be borne in mind that in 315 Constantine was a pagan himself; also that the pagan power was still strong, particularly in Rome. Twenty-two years were to pass before Constantine's baptism; in the meantime—able politician that he was—his cautious attitude was well summed up in two words of the dedicatory inscription. This states that he had triumphed by '*instinctu divinitatis*' (divine stimulus) and the greatness of his mind; no further qualification of the 'divine stimulus', whether Christian or pagan, is given.

Turning our backs on the Arch of Constantine, we circumnavigate the Colosseum on the Parco di Traiano side, where to the right of the entrance to the Metropolitana, or Underground, we see a flight of steps. These lead to the Via Niccolo Salvi, from which we continue up the now familiar Via delle Terme di Tito and turn left at the top. This brings us to the spot where the Via and Largo della Polveriera meet, the former affording us a charming view towards S. Francesca Romana and the Basilica of Maxentius. The intervening lowlying land was in ancient times known as the *Carinae*; a name still recorded in the little church of S. Maria in Carinis. This area is of great topographical inportance in the history of the nearby church of **S. Pietro in Vincoli**, as the Temple of Tellus is known to have stood there, from which the urban prefecture of Roman times took its name of *in Tellure*. This contained both a tribunal and a prison, and somewhere near by was a building later known as the *Macellum martyrum* (literally the slaughter-house or place of massacre of the martyrs), where Christian martyrs were believed to have been tortured. The Via Eudossiana now brings us to the Piazza di S. Pietro in Vincoli, in front of the church. S. Pietro in Vincoli was originally known as the *titulus Eudoxiae*, as it had been built by Sixtus III (432–40) with money given by the Empress Eudoxia to house the chains which had bound St. Peter during his imprisonment in Jerusalem. To these were later added those with which St. Peter was believed to have been bound in Rome. Many authorities believe that the Roman set of chains probably came from the prisons of the nearby urban prefecture, which was still in use in the fifth century, and for a considerable time to come, This would explain why the church was not built on the site where St. Peter may have been imprisoned, but simply near by.

The chains themselves were mentioned at the Council of Ephesus in 431; as a result of their fame, the cult spread far and wide. Many churches of St. Peter in Chains arose, often containing as a relic filings from the chains in Rome; one such is known to have existed as far away as Numidia (Algeria). S. Pietro in Vincoli was rebuilt in the eighth century by Hadrian I; and again during the reign of Sixtus IV (1471–84), by his nephew Cardinal Guiliano Della Rovere, whose titular church it was. The severely beautiful porticoed façade of this period still stands; so, rather surprisingly, does part of Guiliano's cardinalate palace, on the left. It was in the garden behind that he placed his collection of classical sculptures—including the 'Apollo del Belvedere', the 'Venus Felix' and 'Hercules and Antaeus'—which, when he became Pope Julius II, he transferred to the Vatican.

The interior of S. Pietro in Vincoli still preserves its old basilical form, with twenty ancient fluted columns, with Doric capitals, dividing the aisles. It is one of the great tourist sights of Rome, but to the writer one of the saddest. The old pavement has recently been replaced by a dazzlingly highly polished travertine floor whose overwhelming brilliance destroys the harmony of the building. Fortunately it is rare in Rome today to find a church restored with such a lack of taste. But then S. Pietro in Vincoli has almost lost the atmosphere of a church; with rows of charabancs outside the door, conducted parties streaming in their dozens up the nave, and guides giving their lectures, where, one wonders, could the ordinary person find the peace to say the shortest of prayers?

It is the church's misfortune—one cannot view it in any other light—that it contains one of Michelangelo's masterpieces, the famous Moses on Julius II's tomb. As is well known, what we see is only a fragment of the great monument as Michelangelo planned it to stand in St. Peter's—other sculptures are in Florence and in the Louvre. It was placed here in 1544, long after the pope's death, the troubles that the unfinished monument cost Michelangelo caused him to refer to it as 'the tragedy of the tomb'. The proud Julius would no doubt have echoed his words if he could have seen the pathetic little effigy of himself, by Maso del Bosco, which surmounts it. Still, nothing can take away from the majesty of Moses: descended from Sinai with the tables of the law under his arm, to find the Israelites worshipping the golden calf. All the '*terribilità*' (the terribleness) of Michelangelo's genius is there, allied to his consummate mastery of technique. Though the arms are criticised for being too large, the veins and sinews stand out on them as if the statue were pulsatingly alive with rage. The artist's individuality is illustrated by his substitution of a satyr's horns for the traditional rays of light on Moses' forehead.

Like other famous Roman statues, the Moses has its own legends; some true, some probably invented. Michelangelo is said to have spent six months in the mountains above Carrara looking for exactly the right piece of marble; and to have thrown his hammer at the statue's bare knee (there is a mark) shouting at it to speak. In the beard he is said to have portrayed both Julius and himself in profile. His own head is not difficult to distinguish in the lock immediately under the lip; that of the pope is larger and more indefinite, and only visible in certain lights—in the luxuriance of the trailing locks. The rest of the monument is by Michelangelo's pupils—though he himself is believed to have had a hand in the two beautiful statues of Leah and Rachel on either side of the Moses.

Not many people look at anything else in the church except Julius's tomb and the relic of the chains, which are preserved in a bronze and crystal reliquary under the high altar. It does, however, contain other treasures: notably a beautiful fourth-century sarcophagus in the *confessio* behind the altar, discovered in 1876. This is internally divided into seven compartments and is believed to contain the relics of the seven Maccabees, brought from Antioch during the reign of Pelagius I (556–61). In the left transept there is an imposing gilded baroque organ; and farther down the aisle on this side, a fine mosaic of St. Sebastian. Over an altar nearer the door is a fine 'Deposition' by Pomarancio. Close to this is the tomb of Cardinal Cusano, with coloured reliefs by Andrea Bregno. Just beside the door is the tomb of the Pollaiuolo brothers, with a fresco of the plague in Rome in 1476, attributed to Antonio Pollaiuolo. This is particularly interesting for the picture it gives of the Roman landscape at that time.

Standing on the steps looking over the Piazza S. Pietro in Vincoli, our attention is arrested by a tower near the far corner; this is known as the **Torre dei Borgia**. It is now incorporated into the group of monastic buildings attached to the church of S. Francesco da Paola, which faces in the opposite direction. Church and monastery were built in the seventeenth century on the site of the garden of the adjoining palace, to which the tower was attached. The history of the site goes back into the dim past. The stairs which descend in a tunnel under the palace to the Via Cavour are said to have been built on the site of the *Vicus Sceleratus*, where according to legend the early Roman Queen, Tullia, drove her chariot over the body of her father Servius Tullius. Though now renamed after S. Francesco da Paola, the subsequent history of the steps is scarcely less sinister; they are far better known as the Salita dei Borgia. Not all authorities are agreed upon the subject, but the grim palace above is most generally regarded as having been the one in whose garden Vanozza Cattanei gave a dinner on the fatal night of 14 June 1497. It was after this that her eldest son the Duke of Gandia was murdered. Certainly the stairs, in their dark tunnel, and the sinister-looking door which opens out of it have all the atmosphere of ancient evil and intrigue. Today the palace houses the Istituto Centrale del Restauro, where Italy's national art treasures are restored, but its origins are said to date back to the eighth-century palace of the Bishops of Tivoli.

In Augustus Hare's day the steps continued right across where the Via Cavour now runs, into the Via Leonina; looking back from here—traffic permitting—we get an impressive view of the palace and the steps. We turn left in the Via Leonina, continuing down the Via Madonna dei Monti; which follows the course of that very ancient Roman Street the *Argiletum*.

We now come to the vast truncated stump of the Tor de' Conti, once one of the greatest of its kind. Petrarch described it as being 'unique in the whole city' before it was ruined by the earthquake of 1348. The tower was built early in the thirteenth century by Innocent III, as a state fortification for protecting this area; more or less for policing the route of the papal processions on their way to the Lateran. But as even such a powerful pope as Innocent depended in those times on his relations for protection, it soon became a family appanage of the Conti di Segni—from whom he sprang—and still bears his name today.

Vasari said that the architect was Marchionne d'Arezzo. In any case its creator built a formidable fortress, for even after earthquake and pillage two segments of it and a fragment of a third were still standing at the end of the sixteenth century. In its prime the tower must have been similar to, but a good deal higher than, the Torre delle Milizie is today.

We now proceed along the **Via di Tor de' Conti**, one of the most picturesque in Rome, bordered on the left by the massive ancient wall which formed the boundary between the Forum of Augustus and the populous quarter of the *Suburra*. As we walk along, every now and then we catch glimpses of the forum itself, seen through ancient arched entrances; the first of these is known as the Arco dei Pantani.

In Italian *pantano* is a muddy or marshy place: affording a clue as to why this area only again began to be built over at the end of the sixteenth century; it was infested with malaria. After this, however, it became a popular district forming a warren of narrow streets and alleys with here and there a fragment of a classical building, until Mussolini's clearance of the imperial *fora* in 1932–3. At that time many picturesque corners of old Rome diappeared; notably Via Bonella which ran from the Arco dei Pantani to the church of SS. Luca and Martina, beside the Curia. Fragments of the Forum of Augustus, the Temple of Mars Ultor and the Forum of Nerva, appeared among its houses; also the remains of what in medieval times was believed to have been an arch dedicated to Noah.

The Via di Tor de' Conti terminates in the even more picturesque **Piazza del Grillo**, in which stand the palace and tower of the same name, linked by a 'bridge of sighs'. The tower, which was built in 1223, originally also belonged to the Conti, passing later to the Carboni family. It was bought in 1675 by Marchese Cosmo del Grillo, whose inscription EX MARCHIONE DE GRILLIS still appears at the top. The marquis built the adjoining baroque palace, which contains a theatre and delightful little garden of the period.

On the opposite side of the Piazza del Grillo is the entrance to the Casa dei Cavalieri di Rodi which is the seat of the Italian Priory of the Order of Malta. Although from this side the building looks somewhat severe, it is in fact of great interest. It was built into the ruins of the Forum of Augustus in the twelfth century, and remodelled in the fifteenth. This reconstruction was undertaken by Cardinal Marco Barbo, nephew of Paul II, who is believed to have employed the same architect and artists as for the Palazzo Venezia. On the ground floor one of the porticoes of Augustus's Forum is perfectly preserved within the building; it is now used as a chapel. Above there is a fine Renaissance hall, with stairs leading to a beautiful portico of the same period. This is the loggia which we saw, illuminated, from the Capitol, on our first night in Rome; it affords wonderful views over the entire area of the forum.

We now start up the steep **Salita del Grillo**, passing beneath the 'Bridge of Sighs' between the palace and the tower. At the top we find ourselves in the triangular Largo Magnanapoli, with the high walled enclosure of the Villa Aldobrandini on our right. Beside this—on the right—runs a street with the curious name of Via Panisperna, about the origins of whose name there are many theories. The dull—and probably correct —one is that it was called after two families whose names were Panis and Perna; the more picturesque theory, that it originated in a dole of bread and ham, 'Pane e Perna', distributed by monks at the church of S. Lorenzo farther along the street. This church was believed to have been built on the site of St. Lawrence's martyrdom on the gridiron.

Closer at hand there are no less than three churches: S. Caterina da Siena, on the left-hand corner of the Salita del Grillo, built in 1630; SS. Domenico e Sisto, with an impressive baroque façade rising from a steep flight of steps on the right of the Via Panisperna; and on the corner of this street and Via Mazzarino, S. Agata dei Goti or 'in Suburra', on the border of the ancient Suburra district. Although to look at it one would never imagine so, this church dates from the middle of the fifth century; having been founded by Ricimer. an Arian Suebe, who became Patrician of Rome.

We now return to Largo Magnanapoli and the Via IV Novembre where the **Torre delle Milizie** towers up behind the entrance of Trajan's market. This tower, the most remarkable of its kind to have survived, at least to its second storey, was built by Gregory IX (1227–41). It formed part of a heavily fortified area, belonging later to the Annibaldi; in 1301 it passed to Boniface VIII and so to his family the Caetani. Their ownership of it was not undisturbed; after its seizure by the Emperor Henry VII on the occasion of his far from peaceful coronation in 1312, it was returned to this Ghibelline family. Ruins of their castle can still be seen in the enclosure of Trajan's market and forum.

We now enter the **Mercati Traianei** from the Via IV Novembre; it will lead us in turn to the **Foro Traiano**. Trajan's great group of buildings comprising his forum and markets, was designed by the famous Apollodorus of Damascus, and built at the beginning of the second century. Its creation brought to fruition a long-cherished plan for joining together the two great monumental centres of Rome—that of the *fora* (of which it was the last to be built) and the *Campus Martius*. Until then these areas had been separated by a narrow ridge which ran from the Quirinal Hill to that of the Capitol; the height of this ridge is still marked today by the summit of Trajan's Column (42 metres).

The function of the markets were two—the obvious practical one of a commercial centre, and the architectural one of shoring up the side of the Quirinal Hill, out of which the great apse or exedra of the forum had been cut. Immediately after its construction, Trajan's forum with its temple, libraries and markets was already considered to be one of the wonders of the classical world, even after the building of the new Imperial capital Constantinople. When the Emperor Constantius II came to Rome in 356, he regarded the forum with amazement, admitting that he could never hope to equal it. He thought, however, that he might erect the statue of a horse like the one of his great predecessor's equestrian monument which stood in the vestibule. Whereupon the Prince Hormizdas, who formed part of his entourage, said: 'First, Sire, command a like stable to be built, if you can.'

Possibly owing to the fact that it was the last to be built, and no doubt also to the soundness of its construction, Trajan's forum appears to have stood up to the ravages of time better than the others. It was in good condition during Theodoric's reign (454–526). According to his biographer, Gregory the Great (590–604) was so moved by the sight of a bronze relief in the forum, representing Trajan awarding justice to a widow whose son had been killed, that he prayed for the soul of so just a man to be freed from hell. When the pope returned to St. Peter's, he had a vision in which he was told that Trajan's soul had been freed by his intercession, but that he was not to pray for any more pagans! Other versions of the legend say that Gregory was given the choice of three days of purgatory or earthly pain and sickness, as the price of the emperor's salvation; he chose the latter, and never again enjoyed good health. From a poem of Venantius Fortunatus, a Bishop of Poitiers who died in 609, we know that in his day the Romans still gathered in Trajan's forum—possibly in one of the libraries—to listen to Virgil being read aloud.

Entering the markets from the Via IV Novembre, we are really coming in by the back door. But as this is by far the best preserved part of the complex mass of buildings; as the view over the *fora* is so superb; and as—last but not least at the end of an energetic day—we shall be going downhill all the way, perhaps this is the most advantageous way in which to conduct our exploration. We enter the market by a great vaulted hall, with rows of small shops or offices ranged in two tiers on either side. This was probably a bazaar or market for some specialised type of goods. It owes its remarkable state of preservation to the fact that it was incorporated into a convent; though it was also restored during the 1932–3 excavations. From the far end we descend a staircase leading to the Via Biberatica; a medieval corruption of *pipera*, the Latin word for pepper—an expensive but much sought-after ingredient of Roman sauces—from which this street of the spice shops took its name.

Retracing our steps, we find ourselves in the top row of the three tiers of similar shops which line the great exedra overlooking Trajan's forum. Broad staircases—some of them original Roman ones—connect the three storeys, each of which is protected by a shady portico facing on to the forum. Although these Roman shops now stand stark and empty, it is not difficult to imagine the busy scene which they must have represented in ancient times. In some of them a small drain in the middle of the floor indicates that they were oil or wine shops, which would then have been filled with great amphorae containing the famous vintages celebrated by the classical authors: the produce of the vineyards of Falernum, or the Rhaetian wine of Augustan fame, both so strong that they were diluted and cooled by the addition of snow.

Standing cheek by jowl with these would have been the

flower shops with garlands ready prepared for banqueting, hanging outside the door. Also shoe-shops, embroiderers, and perfumers and druggists, whose wares were advertised by notices similar to our patent medicine advertisements. We know that such a medley of shops existed in Galba's *horrea* which covered an area of three acres; in fact these great Roman markets might well be compared with a modern department store.

But now, as we pace through the deserted streets and galleries, some lizards and a few stray cats sunning themselves on the warm stones are the only living creatures we are likely to encounter. Or, in the height of summer, butterflies hovering over the blossoming oleanders which frame such delightful glimpses of the Torre del Grillo and the Casa dei Cavalieri di Rodi.

Finally we reach the level of the forum itself. To tell the truth this comes as something of an anti-climax. Whereas the small shops are so remarkably preserved, Trajan's great forum —that wonder of the world which was once surrounded by marble colonnades leading up to a vast basilica, libraries and temple—is now divided into two sunken enclosures which bear absolutely no relation to the original layout. Still, we should walk to the far left-hand corner of the enclosed space in front of the exedra, where a tunnel will bring us out among a forest of broken columns. This is all that remains of the huge Basilica Ulpia (once the size of St. Paul's Without the Walls) which reached nearly to the Victor Emanuel Monument on one side, and on the other to the Via IV Novembre.

But at least one monument remains unscathed to remind us of former glories; this is **Trajan's Column**, which soars up into the evening sky, scarcely changed since it was built in the year 113. A fine inscription, above the door at the base, records that it was erected by the Senate and people of Rome to the Emperor Caesar Nerva Trajan Augustus, to show how high the hill had been which had stood in its place. The marvellous reliefs covering the whole of the shaft represent scenes during the emperor's campaigns against the Dacians in 101–3 and 107–8. They include some 2,500 figures, providing a mine of information about Roman and barbaric arms and methods of warfare. The base is covered with reliefs of trophies of Dacian weapons; the funerary chamber inside it once contained Trajan's ashes, which were laid to rest in a golden urn. The emperor's statue which stood on the summit was replaced by that of St. Peter in 1587.

A short flight of steps in the corner of the enclosure nearest to the Victor Emanuel monument brings us back to modern street level before the twin churches of S. Maria di Loreto and SS. Nome di Maria. This is the site of one of Trajan's libraries for Greek and Latin books—which formerly stood on either side of the column. It is also a good vantage point from which to study the reliefs on the column, before we continue down the modern Via dei Fori Imperiali. This was made at the time of the clearance of the area in the nineteen-thirties; it traverses all the imperial *fora*, a good deal of whose ruins must still lie buried beneath it and the surrounding gardens. Modern copies of the statues of the emperors who made the *fora* stand close by under the trees.

On the opposite side of the road we see Julius Caesar, just beside the sunken ruins of the **Temple of Venus Genetrix**, which dominated his forum. The building we see was Trajan's restoration of the original temple, which was dedicated in 46 BC. It was made by Julius Caesar as a votive offering for his victory at Pharsalus, two years before; the *Julia gens* claimed to be descended from Venus—hence the dedication. Caesar covered the breast of Arcileus's statue of the goddess with British pearls; he also made her an offering of six collections of cameos and engraved gems. His own equestrian statue stood in front of the temple; the horse was a work of Lysippus, plundered from an equestrian monument to Alexander the Great. Only a small portion of a fourth-century reconstruction of the porticoes still exists; they are to be seen on the far side of the temple.

Returning to the gardens on the other side of the Via dei Fori Imperiali, behind Augustus's statue, we see the remains of the **Forum of Augustus**, backed by the monumental wall which divides it from the Suburra and the Casa dei Cavalieri di Rodi. Between the two great exedrae stands the Temple of Mars Ultor (Mars the Vindicator), erected to commemorate Augustus's victory at Philippi, where Caesar's murder was avenged by the defeat and death of Brutus and Cassius. This temple, too, must have been filled with treasures—Augustus is known to have presented valuable pictures and jewels to the Temple of Concord; naturally he would have done the same here.

Not far from the statue of Augustus stands that of Nerva; it occupies a site just to the left of the remains of his forum. This was known either as the **Forum of Nerva** or the **Forum Transitorium**, as it connected the other *fora* with that of Vespasian. It was built over part of the old *Argiletum*, which led from the original Roman Forum to the Suburra. Not a great deal of it is visible; though the Temple of Minerva—now reduced to a ruined podium—was almost complete until the seventeenth century; Paul V plundered its marbles to build the Fountain of the Acqua Paula on the Janiculum in 1612. To the right, standing against the boundary wall, are two Corinthian columns—an old Roman landmark, known as the *Colonnacce*. One of Piranesi's famous compositions shows these much as they appeared until 1930, half buried beside Via Bonella. Above the columns is a relief of Minerva, and a delightful frieze, showing women going about their household work; Minerva, or Athene, was the presiding deity of such tasks. It seems odd that this fragment, which appears to be part of a porticoed entrance to some building, was built right up against the boundary wall of Nerva's forum. In fact it formed part of an ingenious piece of architectural *trompe l'oeil*—probably designed by Rabirius who built the Flavian palace on the Palatine. This was intended to give an illusion of greater width to the long narrow forum. In front of the *Colonnacce* we can see traces of the paving of the *Argiletum*, over which it was built; and near by, the remains of 'Noah's Arch'—medieval legend made him one of the founders of Rome.

Vespasian's Forum and **Temple of Peace** once covered the whole of the surrounding area where the Via Cavour now joins the Via dei Fori Imperiali. In the temple were kept the spoils of Jerusalem, brought back by his son Titus. Of the Forum and Temple of Peace little now exists except a fragment built into the foundations of the Tor de' Conti, a broken column lying in the grass near the entrance to the Roman Forum, and a few pieces of marble paving. Only the library has survived, incorporated into the church of SS. Cosma e Damiano.

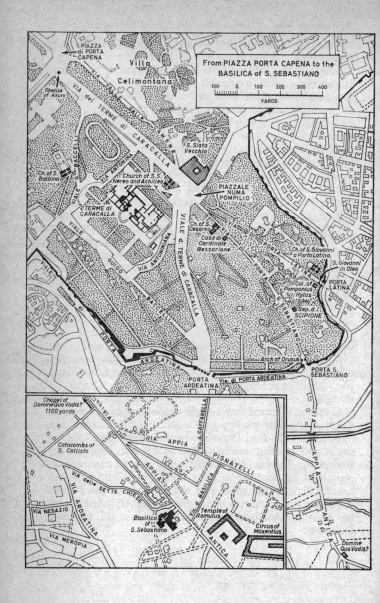

From PIAZZA PORTA CAPENA to the
BASILICA of S. SEBASTIANO

100   0   100   200   300   400
YARDS

PIAZZA di PORTA CAPENA

Villa Celimontana

Obelisk of Axum

VIA DELLE TERME DI CARACALLA

VIA VALLE DELLE CAMENE

S. Sisto Vecchio

Ch. of S. Balbina

Church of S.S. Nereo and Achilleo

TERME di CARACALLA

VIALE GUIDO BACCELLI

VIA ANTONINA

PIAZZALE NUMA POMPILIO

Ch. of S. Cesareo

Casa di Cardinale Bessarione

VIALE d. TERME di CARACALLA

VIA ANTONINIANA

Ch. of S. Giovanni a Porta Latina

S. Giovanni in Oleo

PORTA LATINA

Col. of Pomponius Hylas

Sep. d. SCIPIONE

VIALE di PORTA ARDEATINA

VIA di PORTA SAN SEBASTIANO

VIA DI PORTA LATINA

Arch of Drusus

PORTA ARDEATINA

Via di Porta Ardeatina

PORTA S. SEBASTIANO

VIA APPIA

Chapel of Domine Quo Vadis? 1100 yards

Catacombs of S. Callisto

VIA APPIA

Via d. CAFFARELLA

PIGNATELLI

VIA APPIA

VIA delle SETTE CHIESE

VIA ARDEATINA

VIA NESAZIO

VIA MEROPIA

Basilica of S. Sebastiano

Via di BASILICA

Temple of Romulus

Circus of Maxentius

VIA APPIA ANTICA

VIA APPIA ANTICA

Domine Quo Vadis?

CHAPTER EIGHTEEN

Piazza di Porta Capena to S. Sebastiano

❧

TODAY'S excursions are *par excellence* a journey into the classical landscape beloved of eighteenth-century artists and travellers. From beginning to end we will be travelling along the Old Appian Way, still for the most part lined with cypresses and the ruins of classical tombs and villas. Even today one sometimes sees great white oxen plodding their way along it; or the picturesque wine carts from the Alban Hills, said to have been designed by Michelangelo. Nor will churches be lacking; no Roman road is so rich in early Christian associations as this. According to legend, after his escape from the Mamertine prison, it was here that St. Peter saw Christ on the spot now marked by the chapel of *Domine Quo Vadis*. Here too are the most famous early Christian cemeteries, from which all the others later took the name of catacombs.

Starting off from Piazza Venezia by the 89 or 90 bus, our route takes us past the *Circus Maximus* to the **Piazza di Porta Capena**, where we will recognise the obelisk of Axum standing in front of the F.A.O. building. The piazza, now one of the busiest cross-roads in Rome, is called after the ancient Porta Capena, the gate in the Servian wall leading to the Old Appian Way. The **Via Appia**, the first of the great consular roads, was completed in 312 BC by Appius Claudius the Censor, who also built the first aqueduct. Straight as a die, the old road traverses the campagna to the Alban Hills; Appius Claudius probably only 'modernised' this first part, extending it to Capua; later it reached to Brindisi in the heel of Italy. Little now remains of the Porta Capena, and the part of the Via Appia within the Aurelian wall is doubly disguised as a modern motor-way called the Via delle Terme di Caracalla. But the narrow old **Via della Valle delle Camene**, parallel to it on the left, takes us even further back into Roman history. It is called after the valley, sacred wood and fountain of the Camene, where the vestals came to draw the water for their

lustrations. This road borders on the walled park of the Villa
Celimontana, where another spring—the legendary meeting-
place of King Numa Pompilius and the Nymph Egeria—
really rose; later we shall see its very picturesque namesake.
Appropriately, the bus puts us down in the **Piazzale Numa
Pompilio**, in whose centre stands a delightful little circular
medieval shrine whose original dedication has long been
forgotten.

On the left rises a picturesque group of monastic buildings,
with a baroque church and fine medieval campanile; this is
S. Sisto Vecchio. For all its baroque appearance, the church
is believed probably to have been built on the site of the *titulus
Tigridae*, mentioned in documents of the fifth century and
during the reign of Gregory the Great. Certainly the core of
the existing building and the campanile date from Innocent
III's time; his successor, Honorius III, gave it to St. Dominic.

Standing among the trees opposite S. Sisto is the little
church of **SS. Nereo e Achilleo** (ring the bell on the right of the
door for the *guardiano*; a small tip should be given). Modest
though its outward appearance is—dating from Cardinal
Baronius's restoration of 1597—this is one of the oldest and
most famous titular churches of Rome. Moreover, it is unique
in that it was called *titulus fasciolae*, not after its original owner,
but after a legendary event in the martyrdom of St. Peter.
According to this, after his escape from the Mamertine prison,
while St. Peter was fleeing along the Appian Way, the bandage
(*fasciola*) that he had wrapped round the sores on his leg
caused by his chains, dropped off at this particular spot. This
story is first mentioned in the Acts of SS. Processus and
Martinianus; but it is a fact that the *titulus fasciolae* already
existed in 377; this is attested by an inscription in St. Paul's
Without the Walls. In accordance with later custom, in the
sixth century the church had been dedicated to the martyrs
SS. Nereus and Achilleus, who were buried about a mile and
a half away in the catacomb called after them and St. Domitilla.

Though seldom visited, SS. Nereo e Achilleo is one of the
most appealing of Rome's small churches. Its interior is a
wonderful palimpsest of styles, ranging from the eighth to the
sixteenth century. Thanks to the wishes of its last restorer,
the antiquarian Cardinal Baronius, it has not been subsequently submerged by baroque renovations. The apse and the

triumphal arch date from the reign of Leo III (795–816); this last is still decorated with mosaics of the period, with the 'Annunciation', 'Madonna and Child' and 'Transfiguration'. In the 'Annunciation', the Virgin is shown spinning, as in the mosaics in S. Maria Maggiore.

Sixtus IV (1471–84) restored Leo's building, and it is probable that the characteristic fifteenth-century octagonal columns in the nave date from this time. The walls of the nave are covered with frescoes of Apostles and martyrs by Pomarancio, executed during the reign of the Aldobrandini Pope, Clement VIII (1592–1605), one of whose kinsmen lies buried beneath an elaborate inlaid marble slab in front of the choir. On either side of this stand a beautiful medieval pulpit and Renaissance paschal candlestick, both brought from St. Paul's Without the Walls. The pulpit rests on an enormous porphyry pedestal found in the Baths of Caracalla. The lovely cosmatesque choir, with four large candlesticks, dates from the thirteenth century. Behind the altar is a fine episcopal throne, inscribed on the back with part of the homily delivered by Gregory the Great in the basilica built above the tombs of SS. Nereus and Achilleus. The church also contains some interesting classical remains, including two small altars standing on either side of the apse. These are adorned with winged figures which retain some traces of their original polychrome colouring. The wide cornice in the apse also appears to have been adapted from some ancient building; on it strange mask-like faces merge into surrounding foliage.

Emerging from SS. Nereo e Achilleo, we turn right into the Piazza Numa Pompilio, where we find a small path leading from the beginning of the Via Antoniniana up to the large open space in front of the **Terme di Caracalla**. Begun by Septimus Severus in 206 and inaugurated by his son Caracalla eleven years later, the baths were completed by Elagabalus and Alexander Severus. They continued in use until the Goths cut the aqueducts which supplied them, in the sixth century. They were the second largest in the city, being able to accommodate 1,600 bathers at a time, as opposed to the 3,000 capacity of Diocletian's Baths, built a century later. But, judging from subsequent finds, they were more luxurious; the gems of the Farnese collection of marbles were all discovered there, also the fountain basins in the Piazza Farnese and the mosaics of boxers in the Lateran collection. Apart from a few fragments, nearly all trace of the decoration has now disappeared.

The older among us who are not classical scholars will probably retain vague memories from our history lessons that the luxurious baths were among the causes which led to Rome's 'Decline and Fall'. This was certainly Gibbon's opinion. Modern authors, with their minds conditioned by contemporary recognition of the need for community centres, and life, see things in a different light. M. Jérôme Carcopino, in his *Daily Life in Ancient Rome*, considers that the baths 'brought immense benefit to the people'; Miss Shearer in her *Marvels of Ancient Rome* describes them as 'immense club houses'. Whichever view one takes, there is no doubt that these great public baths were an essentially Roman invention, and that they played an enormous part in the life of the city.

Although the two main components of the baths—the *thermae* or bathing establishment, and the *palestrae* or places for exercise—bore Greek names and their origins were Greek, the idea of amalgamating them, adding libraries and art galleries, and putting the whole thing at the service of the people, was Roman.

Originally both sexes seem to have used the bath at the same time indiscriminately. Later they were segregated, the women bathing before the men; though both were allowed to exercise in the *palestrae*. These games and exercises, consisting of many kinds of ball games, playing with hoops and wrestling (there were even women wrestlers), usually preceded the bath.

The bath itself was a long and complicated business, beginning with the *sudatoria*—small hot, dry rooms which provoked sweating. This was continued in the *calidarium*—a large hot room, whose atmosphere was moistened by a great tub of hot water with which the bathers douched themselves. It was then that the *strigil*, or scraper, was applied; either for a fee by the bath attendants or, in the case of rich people, by their own slaves. Next came the first stage of the cooling down process in the *tepidarium*, a large hall of temperate atmosphere. Finally there was the plunge into the cold waters of the *frigidarium* pool; followed, for the rich, by a rub down with scented woollen cloths.

In the Terme di Caracalla we first enter the *frigidarium*, most of whose area was taken up by the swimming pool;

round the walls were ranged the *apodyteria* or dressing-rooms. Next to this is the *tepidarium*, flanked at either end by *palestrae*. A second smaller *tepidarium* follows, before we reach the great ruined apse which was once part of the circular *calidarium*. Today this last is used in summer as the stage for outdoor performances of the opera. Some idea of its vast size may be judged from the fact that in the elaborately set performances of *Aida*, with a cast of hundreds already on the stage, there is still room for a four-horse chariot to be driven on, turned, and driven off again. Beneath the vast mass of ruins exist the almost equally vast 'service quarters'—the stoking rooms, furnaces and storerooms—and the underground passages where slaves and bath attendants scurried to and fro out of sight of the bathers. Surrounding all this were the gardens, a stadium, libraries, lecture-rooms, shops and porticoes, where the crowds of bathers sauntered and gossiped These were also, of course, frequented by less reputable members of society such as pimps and panders and ladies of the town; nor have these last entirely deserted the environs of the Terme di Caracalla today.

Before continuing with our main itinerary, we can make a detour by way of the Via Antoniniana to see the church of **S. Balbina** (usually entered from the ex-monastery on the right, now an old people's home). Unfortunately, at the time of writing the church has recently been closed for what are said to be extensive repairs, as it is in a dangerous condition. For some time at any rate—let us hope not for twenty years' duration as at S. Stefano Rotondo—its interior is unlikely to be visible. This is a pity, as S. Balbina contains one of the finest cosmatesque tombs in Rome, that of Cardinal Surdi, brought from St. Peter's; it dates from 1291 and is signed by Giovanni di Cosma. Framed by cypresses, the church has a dignified Renaissance portico rising above a wide flight of steps; but, as its medieval campanile indicates, it is a good deal older, originally dating from the fourth or fifth century. It was built over some classical ruins; probably the *Domus Cilonis*, the palatial home of Septimius Severus's friend L. Fabius Cilo.

Returning to the Terme di Caracalla, we traverse the Piazza Numa Pompilio and find ourselves at the beginning of the **Via di Porta S. Sebastiano**; which is the name given to another tract of the Via Appia, within the Aurelian wall. This is a delightful corner, with the Via di Porta Latina branching off to the left, both roads bordered by high-walled gardens giving them a countrified aspect. Nowadays it seems almost impossible to believe that this was how some three-quarters of the area within the Aurelian wall looked until 1870. The whole of the Via Veneto quarter, that of the station and the Castro Pretorio, to say nothing of the Aventine, Coelian and the surroundings of the Lateran and S. Croce, were all then filled with parks and gardens and traversed by country lanes.

A little way along the Via di Porta S. Sebastiano on the right is the church of **S. Cesareo**. This is another ancient church which was restored during the reign of the Aldobrandini pope, Clement VIII (1592–1605). The family coat of arms, of stars and bend dexter embattled on both sides, has been adopted as the principal decorative motif of the beautiful wooden ceiling, gilded and painted in tones of blue and terracotta. The dignified Renaissance façade is attributed to Giacomo Della Porta; but the great charm of the church lies in the lovely cosmatesque choir, pulpit and altar. Behind this last is a fine episcopal throne with serpentine columns. According to some authorities S. Cesareo was built into the ruins of classical baths; it is interesting to note that the mosaic on the floor behind the altar, with its black and white representation of sea monsters, is of the type usually encountered in such buildings.

To the left of S. Cesareo, an old door with a grille affords us a delightful glimpse of an old-fashioned garden; where fragments of antique sculpture stand among box parterres, and the glittering waters of a small fountain cascade down an old terracotta urn. It is the kind of vista that usually tantalises by its inaccessibility; who, one wonders, is the fortunate being that lives in such an enchanted spot? and how could one possibly explore it? For once our curiosity is easily satisfied, and the reality even more charming than one might have imagined. This is the garden of the **Casa del Cardinale Bessarione**. Although it is not definitely known that the great Greek humanist who died in Italy in 1472, ever really lived in the house, it is a perfect example of the type of suburban retreat recommended for a man of letters by his contemporary, Leon Battista Alberti.

We enter by a gate a short way farther along the Via di Porta S. Sebastiano. The little house, with its crossed mullioned

windows and frescoed loggia, is unique in Rome. Until shortly
before the war it was an inn; but restoration then revealed not
only the original *quattrocento* door frames and fire-places, but
also some most delightful painted wall decoration. In the first
large room, which we enter from the loggia, this takes the
form of garlands with fluttering ribbons, suspended from
trompe l'oeil corbels; in another smaller room, of an overall
pattern of acanthus leaves and pomegranates. These and all
the other rooms have been charmingly arranged with contemporary paintings, pottery and furniture. Altogether this
enchanting little house and garden presents an evocative picture of the simplicity and charm of life in early Renaissance
Rome.

Continuing along the Via di Porta S. Sebastiano, some way
farther along on the left, we find the entrance to the **Sepolcro
degli Scipioni** (Tomb of the Scipios; one sometimes has to
wait a few moments even during the opening hours; if the
custodian is already showing another party round, the gate is
shut). The tomb was discovered in 1780, naturally arousing
tremendous interest, as the Scipios were one of the greatest
families of Republican Rome. For generations they had led
her armies and played an outstanding part in history, even
before the renowned Scipio Africanus defeated Hannibal at
Zama and his daughter Cornelia achieved tragic fame as the
mother of the Gracchi.

Although we no longer see the tomb by candle-light as
travellers did in the last century, there is an empty sadness
about the place. As we walk along these shadowy passages,
inevitably we wonder how many families existing in the world
today will be remembered more than two thousand years from
now? But the very immortality which they achieved seems to
add to the sadness of the place. Here lay Lucius Scipio
Barbatus, consul in 298 BC and conqueror of the Samnites and
Lucania. His son, consul in 259 BC and conqueror of Corsica
and Algeria. Scipio Hispanis and Scipio Asiaticus—the con-
querors of Spain and Asia Minor. But the great Scipio
Africanus was buried at Liturnum in 183 BC—a voluntary
exile from what he considered to be Rome's base ingratitude.

Our ticket of admission to the tomb of the Scipios also gains
us admission to a small Christian tomb and some nearby
columbaria, which, according to Augustus Hare, were in his
time in the care of an 'extortionate' custodian. What is a great

deal more interesting, however, is the **Columbarium of Pomponius Hylas,** which is the most perfectly preserved of any in existence (entrance to this is also covered by the same ticket, but as it is some way away a tip is advisable). To reach it, the *guardiano* will take us up a path beside his own house, which it is interesting to observe is built immediately above a modest Roman dwelling of similar type. We cross the Orti degli Scipioni—a pleasant little public park, spoilt as usual in Rome by neglect—to the entrance on the Via di Porta Latina. Just beside this, a door gives on to a steep staircase leading down into the *columbarium*, which was discovered intact in 1831.

With all its mosaic, stucco and painted decoration in mint condition, the tomb of Pomponius Hylas does not in the least resemble the usual monotonous 'dovecote' (*columbarium* is the Latin for dovecote) used in the first century AD to house the funerary urns of those who had been cremated. It is interesting to note that the great archaeologist Nibby believed that Pomponius built this tomb as a commercial speculation, no doubt offering as a further guarantee of its reliability that he himself intended to have his own ashes placed there.

Before we turn back across the Orti degli Scipioni, we have time to look at yet another charming corner of this peaceful oasis of old Rome. To reach it we have to cross the far from peaceful Via di Porta Latina; but before doing so, we must pause for a moment to look at the delightful little Renaissance chapel on the right of the Porta Latina. This goes by the curious name of **S. Giovanni in Oleo** (St. John in oil). According to legend it stands on the spot where St. John was boiled in oil, from which 'he came forth as from a refreshing bath'; an event which is said to have occurred before he went to Patmos. An earlier chapel is said to have existed on the site; the present one was built during the reign of Julius II (1503–13) at the expense of a Frenchman, Benoît Adam. Some attribute its design to Bramante; but there is no doubt that it was restored by Borromini, who added the charming terracotta floral frieze.

Crossing the road we turn right down a cul-de-sac, at whose end rises the church of **S. Giovanni a Porta Latina.** This is perhaps the most picturesque of old Roman churches; a tall conifer shades an ancient well standing in the forecourt, classical columns support the medieval portico, and a superb twelfth-century campanile soars up into the blue sky. S. Giovanni was originally built by St. Gelasius I (482–96), rebuilt by Hadrian I in 772 and reconsecrated by Celestine III in 1191; subsequently it was restored several times. Nevertheless the interior preserves the rare simplicity of its very early origins. Beautiful antique columns of varying styles line the aisles; these lead to two minor apses, flanking the main one, in the oriental fashion. A most unusual feature in Rome, the main apse is pierced by three windows; but rarer still, all three apses are polygonal on the outside. A soft golden light filters through the thin sheets of selenite in the windows, illuminating some faded but exceedingly interesting twelfth-century frescoes.

We now retrace our steps across the Orti degli Scipioni and catch the 118 bus, whose stop is conveniently, though one feels rather inappropriately, placed opposite the entrance to the Tomb of the Scipios. This soon brings us to the **Porta S. Sebastiano**, the most imposing in the whole vast circuit of the Aurelian wall. Immediately before it stands the 'Arch of Drusus', in reality built as part of one of the aqueducts; by whom is not certain. The Porta S. Sebastiano was originally called the Porta Appia; it was rebuilt in the fifth century by Honorius, and restored in the following century by both Belisarius and Narses. It is flanked by two high medieval towers, and is most impressive when viewed from the Via Appia outside. Once the gate is passed, this famous road is finally called by its ancient name; and almost at once we see on either side ruins of the tombs for which it has always been famous. These are now interspersed with petrol pumps and notices such as 'Dancing Quo Vadis'; inspired, one hopes, rather by the title of the film, but in any case very indicative of the new Italy, whose miracles tend to be commercial.

Very shortly afterwards we come to the place where the Via Ardeatina forks off to the right. During the last war some caves bordering on it were the scene of the slaughter of 335 innocent people by the Germans. One of the finest memorials erected in this century marks the spot; the caves themselves bear a tragic resemblance to the catacombs, the last resting place of so many martyrs of an older but no more cruel world. It is with something like relief that we return to ancient history and get off our bus at the **Chapel of Domine Quo Vadis** (just before the fork), which according to tradition marks the spot where Christ appeared to St. Peter as he was escaping from Rome during Nero's persecution. In his astonishment he uttered the famous words '*Domine quo vadis?*' (Lord whither goest thou?) to which Jesus replied, 'I go to Rome to be crucified a second time', and disappeared. St. Peter understood, and returned to Rome to face his martyrdom. The church contains a replica of the stone said to be marked with the footprints of Christ; the original is in S. Sebastiano. A little farther along on the left, in the fork of the Vicolo della Caffarella, there is a charming little circular chapel standing in a yard. This was built by Cardinal Pole, who believed that St. Peter's vision may have occurred at this second fork, and wished to mark the spot.

Over a gate in the angle between the Via Appia and the Via Ardeatina we will have seen a large notice indicating that this is the entrance to the **Catacombs of S. Callisto** or S. Calixtus. For cars this is the correct entrance, but when travelling by bus it is wiser to stay on it to the stop at the secondary entrance, farther along the Via Appia, as from there it is a much shorter walk to the catacombs themselves. In winter, if we have been fairly brisk about our sight-seeing, and it is not later than 11.30, now is the moment to go and see these catacombs. In summer, when at the height of the season there are often crowds waiting to take their turn among the conducted parties—no one is allowed into the catacombs alone—we should probably be wise to continue on the bus to the stop in front of the Basilica of S. Sebastiano.

Here we have the choice of several things to see. Nearby there are the ruins of the Temple of Romulus, the Circus of Maxentius and the tomb of Cecilia Metella, and, of course, the **Basilica of S. Sebastiano** and its **Catacombs**; also the choice of two trattorias for luncheon. As the catacombs of S. Sebastian do not seem to attract such crowds, we will probably still have time to see them and the basilica before they close at midday. After that it is a matter of individual choice whether we wish to loiter around the neighbourhood until the catacombs of S. Calixtus open again at 3 p.m., or set out immediately after our meal to explore the Via Appia. For the first kilometre to the Osteria Belvedere, we can take the bus; after that the rest has to be done on foot; it is a little over a kilometre to the beginning of the most interesting monumental part, which stretches for three kilometres. After that we can turn left along a side road, that brings us to the Via Appia Nuova; this distance is about a kilometre. Here we can catch a bus from the Capannelle Race Course, which brings us into Rome by the main railway station.

Except in the heat of summer, we would probably be well advised to take this course, as on a fine day the walk is exceedingly picturesque. But in doing so, we will probably have to make up our minds to see only one or other of the catacombs, or return on another day. In the heat of summer we will probably find it more enjoyable to eat a protracted lunch in a shady trattoria and do a little sight-seeing near by, followed by a visit to the Catacomb of S. Calixtus (from where we can take the bus direct to the Osteria Belvedere). Later we can take a short stroll, when it is cooler, along the Via Appia; but in doing so we shall miss the most interesting part. As most travellers come to Rome during the summer, we will treat the expedition in this order, continuing along the whole length of the Via Appia; though all but the most energetic should be warned that this would entail a walk of over three miles at the end of a day's sight-seeing.

As visits to both the Catacombs of St. Sebastian and St. Calixtus can only be made in parties that are accompanied by well-qualified English-speaking guides, it would be superfluous to give a detailed itinerary of either. But a note on the origins of these early Christian cemeteries may not come amiss; also a brief summary of their individual features and history will assist those who wish to see only one catacomb to make their choice. However, as it is more than likely that either or both of them will be visited after the luncheon interval, we will defer this to the afternoon's itinerary and in the meantime concentrate our attention on food. For those who are feeling extravagant, the Ristorante S. Callisto (on the little hill to the left before the Basilica of S. Sebastiano: there is an entrance from the piazzetta in front of the church) provides a beautiful view. Those who want to eat well but not so expensively will find the Trattoria Archeologica, a little beyond the church on the left, an excellent choice both in summer and winter. Here one can eat *pollo allo spiedo* (grilled chicken) according to the season, either in a shady arbour or beside a roaring fire. Those who have had the forethought to bring a picnic will find some hospitable fields bordering on the lanes in the area.

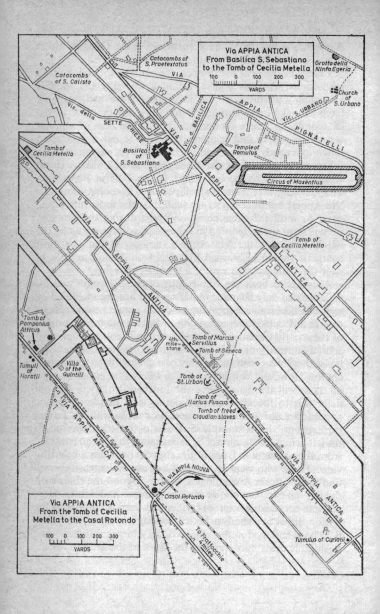

Via APPIA ANTICA
From Basilica S. Sebastiano
to the Tomb of Cecilia Metella

100   0   100   200   300
YARDS

Catacombs of
S. Praetextatus

Catacombs
of S. Calisto

Grotta della
Ninfa Egeria

Church of
S. Urbano

Vic. della

VIA

VIA

APPIA

Vic. S. URBANO

PIGNATELLI

SETTE CHIESE

Vic. d. BASILICA

APPIA

Tomb of
Cecilia Metella

Basilica
of S. Sebastiano

Temple of
Romulus

Circus of Maxentius

Tomb of
Cecilia Metella

VIA

APPIA

ANTICA

ANTICA

Tomb of
Pomponius
Atticus

Tomb of Marcus
Servilius
Tomb of Seneca

4th
mile-
stone

Tumuli
of
Horatii

Villa
of the
Quintili

Tomb of
St. Urban

VIA

Tomb of
Ilarius Fuscus

APPIA

Tomb of freed
Claudian slaves

ANTICA

VIA

Acqueduct

VIA APPIA NOUVA

APPIA

ANTICA

Casal Rotondo

Via APPIA ANTICA
From the Tomb of Cecilia
Metella to the Casal Rotondo

100   0   100   200   300
YARDS

To Frattocchie
4¼ miles

Tumulus of Curiatii

CHAPTER NINETEEN

S. Sebastiano, the Catacombs and the Old Appian Way

❦

THERE are various interpretations of the origins of the word *catacumbas*, from which catacomb is derived. All authorities seem to be agreed that the first syllable *cata* is derived from the Greek preposition *kata* meaning near or beside; but the *cumbas* presents a problem. Some identify it with the Greek *kumbé* or *kumbos* and Latin *cumba*, meaning a valley or combe; others consider that it should be associated with the conception of lying or sleeping, as in our word recumbent, derived from the Latin *cumbere*, to lie. But however it may have originated, there is no division of opinion about the fact that *catacumbas* has since time immemorial been applied to the early Christian cemetery beneath the **Basilica of S. Sebastiano**; or that all other such Christian burial places were subsequently called catacombs after it. The catacombs are entered by a door to the left of the basilica and tours of them are conducted by the monks.

The Catacombs of St. Sebastian owe their great interest to two things: that they were the only ones whose existence was never forgotten, and continued to be an object of pilgrimage through the Middle Ages to modern times; also that the bodies of SS. Peter and Paul are believed to have been hidden in them for forty years after Valerian's persecution of 258. Excavations carried out between 1915 and 1925 to discover possible archaeological confirmation for this tradition brought some interesting results. Hitherto evidence had been limited to fourth- and fifth-century sources, such as a poetic but somewhat vague inscription composed by Pope St. Damasus and a martyrology; also seventh-century pilgrims' guides, like the *Salzburg Itinerary*. From these it appeared that the Apostles' bodies had been placed here in the year when Bassus and Tuscus were consuls; in other words the year 258.

The excavators discovered beneath the church the remains

of a *triclinia*—a kind of open-air shelter of the type in which the Christians held the funerary *agape* or *refrigerium*, a meal given for the benefit of the poor. The walls of this building were covered with *graffiti* (scratched inscriptions) invoking SS. Peter and Paul; or recording, for example, that 'in honour of Peter and Paul, I, Tomius Caelius, have made a refrigerium'. These inscriptions—which are of a type familiar to archaeologists in many sanctuaries and places of pilgrimage—date from the third century: thus confirming the tradition that what were believed to be Peter and Paul's relics were placed in the catacomb in 258, and remained there for forty years. This is the conclusion reached by many authorities on the subject; though some maintain that the translation occurred earlier, and contest it, chiefly on the grounds that until the Lombard and Saracen invasions the relics of Christian martyrs were not usually moved from their resting place. During the excavations three very interesting tombs of the second century were also discovered, originally pagan, one at least of which is believed also to have been used by Christians.

The Basilica of S. Sebastiano was built in the first half of the fourth century, and dedicated to the Apostles. In the Middle Ages the name of St. Sebastian was added, which finally supplanted the early dedication. According to tradition, St. Sebastian was an officer of the imperial household who, during the persecution of Diocletian in 303, was condemned to be shot to death with arrows. He fell wounded, and was taken into her house and cured by a pious widow called Irene. Nevertheless he was subsequently executed, and his body buried in the catacomb by St. Lucina. Until its restoration in the seventeenth century, stairs led down from the basilica to this tomb, which had been decorated with cosmatesque mosaics by Honorius III.

The Basilica of S. Sebastiano as we see it today is entirely baroque. The depredations and neglect of centuries had reduced it to a state of ruin by the seventeenth century, when Cardinal Scipione Borghese commissioned Flavio Ponzio to restore it. The work was completed by Giovanni Vasanzio (the architect of Villa Borghese), who designed the façade and is said himself to have carved the fine polychrome wooden ceiling. Although all traces of the old church have vanished, with its white walls and spacious proportions the existing basilica gives an impression of calm dignity; while Antonio

Giorgetti's recumbent statue of St. Sebastian (in the chapel on the left over the original subterranean tomb) is a masterpiece of its kind. Opposite it, in a reliquary in a chapel on the right, is the stone said to bear Christ's footprints, found on the site of the chapel of Domine Quo Vadis.

On the corner of the Vicolo delle Sette Chiese, leading out of the Via Appia beside S. Sebastiano, is a gate with a notice saying that this is yet another entrance to the Catacombs of *S. Callisto* or *S. Calixtus*. This entrance, however, is not always open, and if we wish to curtail the time spent walking we can take the bus from S. Sebastiano to the other entrance we passed earlier on the Via Appia. From here it is only a few steps to the entrance of the catacombs themselves, which are planted around with cypresses and flowers.

The Catacombs of St. Çalixtus are vast—among the largest in Rome; they were excavated at four different levels at various periods after the first half of the second century. Originally they were five separate places of burial—the crypts of Lucina, the cemetery of St. Calixtus proper, that of St. Soter and those of Balbina and Basileus. In time these separate burial grounds were joined together to form this one vast catacomb.

What puzzles many travellers is how it was possible for these miles of galleries to be excavated—not only here but in the catacombs all round Rome—and thousands of Christians to be buried in them during the age of persecutions, which lasted intermittently from the time of Nero to within a few years of the Declaration of Milan in 313. It might have been imagined that as the Christians buried their dead—at a time when most pagans were cremated—these members of a proscribed sect might have been prohibited from doing so; or at least that their cemeteries would have been profaned and closed. The reason why they were not is to be found in one of the oldest Roman laws, which made any tomb or place of burial sacrosanct. The law also allowed the bodies of those who had suffered the death sentence to be given to relations or friends for burial, though a magistrate's permission was necessary for this.

We have already seen with what tremendous importance the Romans surrounded everything connected with burial, and how in the poorer classes this gave rise to burial clubs. Also how great families, such as the Scipios, had their own tombs.

Both these aspects of Roman burial customs assisted the early Christians in creating their own cemeteries, where they were buried together according to their own rites. It would have been comparatively easy for a Christian community to pose as a burial club; and easier still for patricians such as Pomponia Graecina or members of powerful families such as Flavius Clemens and his wife Domitilla (who were cousins of Domitian) to make tombs ostensibly intended for their families and household, but which in reality were the resting-place of their fellow Christians.

But, one may ask, why did the Christians choose to be buried in underground galleries? At one time it was thought that the custom originated from the fact that the *arenile*—old quarries and sand and gravel pits—afforded concealment. Now it is generally considered that by excavating galleries beneath them, the original private cemeteries could be made to accommodate many more graves. Certainly it is astonishing how many *loculi*—shelf-like compartments in which the bodies were laid without coffins, enveloped in two shrouds between which was a coating of lime—have been fitted into a small area. In fact the catacombs of St. Calixtus trace their origins from the private burial ground of the Cecili family, the ashes of whose earlier pagan members were laid to rest in *columbaria* on the ground above. These catacombs were called after St. Calixtus, because before he became Pope in 217, his predecessor, Zephyrinus, had entrusted him with the administration of this cemetery—the earliest known to have belonged to the Church. By the time St. Jerome (340–420) was a boy, the catacombs were already a place of pilgrimage and wonder. although people were still buried there. At least at S. Sebastiano burials continued during the fifth century, the latest known tomb being that of a *fossor* or grave-digger, dated 508. They remained a place of pilgrimage for centuries—pilgrim guides like the seventh-century *Salzburg Itinerary* gave detailed descriptions of them. But, like the Roman campagna generally, the catacombs suffered greatly from the barbaric invasions. Even more serious damage occurred in 756, when they were sacked by Aistulf's Lombards, who were then besieging Rome. But most terrible of all were the Saracen incursions of 846–7 when St. Peter's, St. Paul's Without the Walls and the whole of the country round Rome was devastated. As a result of these inroads and that of an even more insidious enemy—malaria—the campagna became a desert, and successive popes pursued the policy of transferring to the city churches the relics which were in the most exposed sites. By the ninth century another and less-expected influence had come to disturb these venerable resting-places of the early Christians. The translation of relics had by then become a general practice, not only to the Roman churches, but to the rest of Europe. Nor was this always carried out with due ecclesiastical sanction; a veritable traffic had begun in which tomb-robbers played their part; the catacombs were pillaged to supply these treasures that were coveted by the whole Christian world.

In view of all this, it is not surprising that men ceased to venture much outside the walls of Rome unless they went in company, like the bands of pilgrims who still wended their way to the now fortified monastery of S. Sebastiano. The rest of the campagna became a desert, and in the general ruin the very sites of the other old burial grounds were forgotten. It is true that in 1462 Ranuccio Farnese, with Abbot Ermete of Pisa and some of his monks, penetrated into part of the Catacombs of St. Calixtus, and that some hundred years later Antonio Bosio got lost while exploring those of St. Domitilla. But these were isolated incidents. So little was known and remembered about the catacombs that when in 1854 De Rossi, the father of Christian archaeology, told Pius IX that he had found the tombs of the early popes at St. Calixtus, the pope would not believe him and chaffed him about his 'dreams'. But Pius was moved to tears when the same afternoon De Rossi showed him the fragmentary inscriptions which he had found in the Crypt of the Popes in the Catacombs of St. Calixtus. Piecing them together with his own hands, Pius asked, 'Are these really the tombstones of my predecessors who repose here?' De Rossi could not resist getting a little of his own back and smilingly replied, 'But it's all a dream, Holy Father, all a dream.'

De Rossi's discovery of the Crypt of the Popes gives the Catacomb of St. Calixtus possibly a greater religious and historical interest than any other in Rome. Here it is not a matter of conjecture based on careful examination of ancient documents; the tombstones of five popes who reigned between 230 and 283 are there for all to see. They were St. Pontian (elected in 235), who was deported to work in the Sardinian mines and died there in 235; St. Anterus, who only reigned for forty days and died in 236; St. Fabian, elected in 236, and martyred on the persecutions of Decian on 20 January 250; St. Lucius I, who reigned from 25 June 253 to 5 March 254, spending part of this time in exile; and St. Eutychian, who reigned from 275 to 283. On the basis of an inscription placed here later by Pope St. Damasus, it is believed that St. Sixtus II was also buried in this crypt, together with four deacons —Gennarus, Magnus, Vincent and Stephen. Sixtus suffered martyrdom in the cemetery of St. Calixtus on 6 August 258. Two other martyrs of the same persecution—the deacons Felicissimus and Agapitus—were buried in the nearby cata-combs of Praetextatus. Three other third-century popes—SS. Stephen, Dionysius and Felix I—are also believed to have been buried in the crypt, as well as eight bishops, including Bishop Optatus of what is now Biskra in Algeria. Many of these funerary inscriptions are written in Greek—St. Anterus and St. Sixtus were both of that nationality.

Next door to the Crypt of the Popes is that of St. Cecilia, in which it is believed that the body of this young martyr was found by Pope Paschal I in 821 (some authorities consider that it was in the catacombs of Praetextatus), before he transferred it to the church of St. Cecilia in Trastevere. Throughout the centuries the cult of St. Cecilia has rivalled that of St. Agnes in the veneration it aroused first among the Romans and later throughout medieval Europe. All know the story of her martyrdom as related in the *Passion*, which was however written many centuries later. How this high-born Roman maiden and St. Urban converted her husband, St. Valerianus, and his brother to Christianity. How she lived with Valerianus in chastity, and was guarded by an angel, until his martyrdom for refusing to sacrifice to idols. How she herself suffered martyrdom: first by attempted suffocation in the *sudatorium* of the baths of her house in Trastevere, during which she sang the hymns that made her the patron saint of Music; then, on being found still alive, she was ordered to be beheaded, the execu-tioner striking in vain three times; she survived for a few days to convert many by her teaching. These events are sometimes attributed to the reign of Marcus Aurelius, sometimes to the time of Commodus or Septimius Severus. It is now considered to be more likely that St. Cecilia's martyrdom took place during the persecutions of Diocletian in 303, and that the St.

Urban who converted her husband and brother-in-law was a bishop, not the Pope Urban I who reigned from 222 to 230. St. Cecilia's husband, St. Valerianus, and his brother Tiburtius were buried in the nearby Catacomb of St. Praetextatus. In the ninth century their relics, together with hers and those of St. Urban, were placed under the high altar of the church of St. Cecilia in Trastevere. When the sarcophagus containing her body was opened during Clement VIII's reign (1592–1605) she was found swathed in golden robes. Maderno, who then saw her, made the famous statue of which a copy now lies in the saint's crypt in the catacombs of St. Calixtus.

The two crypts of the popes and St. Cecilia are the places of greatest religious and historical importance in these catacombs. Though to students of early Christian art, as to the ordinary person the crypts of the sacraments are of tremendous interest—with their third-century paintings of New Testament scenes and early Christian symbols, such as the baskets of bread signifying the Eucharist, the fish, the symbol of Christ, and Jonah and the whale symbolising death and salvation. As might be expected, these are not the work of great artists; but they must have been carried out with infinite love and faith, probably by the friends and relations of those who lie buried nearby. Like the inscriptions on the tombs themselves they are all pervaded with a sense of happiness—one might almost say gaiety—and of absolute confidence in the peace in which their dead now rested. These are the things that take away from that 'horror of the darkness' which St. Jerome also felt when he explored the catacombs. That reminded him of those words of the prophet 'they descend alive into hell' and made him quote Virgil's 'The very silence fills the soul with dread'. He too probably felt a certain sense of relief when he emerged again into the sunlight of the Via Appia.

If we have contented ourselves with visiting only one catacomb, or have to wait until they open at three o'clock, we may now have the time to make a short detour to see the church of **S. Urbano** and the **'Grotta della Ninfa Egeria'**; both are really remains of the Villa of Herodes Atticus. The traveller should be warned that it is necessary to cross private property to get there, and permission may not always be forthcoming; also that the going to 'Egeria's Fountain' is rough. However, for those who are interested in Roman and English landscape garden design, and in seeing Roman ruins in the same state as rejoiced the hearts of Claude Lorraine and our own eighteenth-century ancestors, it is well worth trying to reach this delectable spot. We set out, either down the Via Appia Pignatelli (which branches off the Appia Antica to the left, shortly after the second entrance to the catacombs of St. Calixtus); or by taking the little Vicolo della Basilica (the first turning on the left after the Basilica of S. Sebastiano). In the latter case, when this joins the Appia Pignatelli, we turn right, and some way along we will see a small road turning off to the left with a notice saying 'Strada Privata'. Until recently this led to some peasants' cottages; now a villa has been built, whose owner's permission must be sought in order to walk the few paces which separate it from the church of S. Urbano.

This enchanting little building, formerly known as the Temple of Bacchus, from an altar of that god found near by, was in reality probably a garden pavilion of the villa of the fabulously rich Herodes Atticus. It is remarkable for its extraordinary state of preservation—it is complete right up to the roof—due to its having been converted into a church in the ninth or early tenth century, when the Corinthian columns of the portico were walled in. At that time the building was believed to have been frequented by St. Urban, who, according to the Passion of St. Cecilia, had hidden in the nearby catacombs of Praetextatus.

Though unlikely, this could have been true, as Herodes Atticus lived in Rome during the reigns of Antoninus Pius (138–61) and Marcus Aurelius (161–80). He was professor of rhetoric to Marcus Aurelius and became Consul in 143. The story of Herodes's wealth beats any fairy tale. That which he inherited, his father had found as buried treasure near the Acropolis in Athens. Shortly after he came to Rome Herodes fell in love with a beautiful heiress—Annia Regilla—and she with him. Though her brother strongly disapproved of her mésalliance with an unknown foreigner, they married and lived happily until the birth of Annia's fifth child, after which she died suddenly. Her brother then saw his chance, and accused the distraught husband of murder. After a public trial Herodes was acquitted; no one apparently had ever imagined he could be guilty, and his mourning for his beloved wife became legendary. It is said that he even stripped his houses of their coloured marbles, replacing them with a variety of grey; while the Roman wits wondered how his cooks dared serve white beans at table in a home where everything was shrouded in mourning of the deepest dye. Annia was laid to rest in a tomb in the vast villa grounds; for long it passed under the mistaken name of the Temple of Divus Rediculus (the God who made Hannibal return on his tracks, not of ridicule); it still stands on the other side of the valley.

Even though the church of S. Urbano should by now be thoroughly exorcised of pagan ghosts—it is covered inside with eleventh-century frescoes of saints and martyrs—one cannot help feeling that it is a haunted spot. Seen on a summer evening, with a crescent moon rising in a clear sky, it is almost impossible to believe that such a place could have survived into the twentieth century. If Annia and Herodes no longer walk there, then one feels that the spirits of the sixteenth-century humanists must. For in their day the 'Egeria's Grotto' near by was a place of pilgrimage for artists and writers, who believed that this was the place of her meetings with Numa Pompilius.

They may be forgiven for their mistake, as it is one of the strangest and most evocative places in the Roman campagna. A rough path leads across the fields down into the valley; the ruins of ancient terraces are barely discernible under the brambles; rushes whisper in the bed of the invisible stream whose rippling fills the still air. At the bottom we turn left along an old farm road, over-grown with grass and bushes; suddenly we see a real classical grotto, with a spring of clear ice-cold water gushing from a niche, just as it must have done for centuries. Ivy hangs in festoons over the arched entrance of the high vaulted room, which has been built into the hill-side; ferns grow in the crevices of the niched walls; for a moment we are tricked into the belief that the nymph herself lies reclining at the far end. It is the cover of a classical sarcophagus, put there, it is said, during the sixteenth century, when the grotto was restored and became a popular subject with artists. No one ever seems to come here now; the wilderness which surrounds it has preserved it inviolate; it is to be hoped that it will long continue to do so.

Returning to the Via Appia Antica by way of the Via della Basilica, we find next upon our route the **Temple of Romulus**.

This high-walled enclosure, with a modern house in the centre, was not dedicated to the founder of Rome, but to Maxentius's son who died at an early age in 307. Remains of his circular tomb can be seen behind the house. On the far side, standing at an angle to it, rise the impressive ruins of the Circus of Maxentius. This is the best preserved of Roman circuses; in it even such details as the amphorae used to lighten the load in the construction of the vaults can still be seen. The circus, which was designed for chariot races, is 482 metres long and 79 wide; it could accommodate 18,000 spectators. It was here that the obelisk of Diocletian (now in the Piazza Navona) was found; it had been used as one of the ornaments of the spina —the central dividing wall—whose ruins we can still see. A race involved seven turns round the circus, and great dexterity was required of the charioteer and the inside horse in rounding the two ends of the spina.

On the top of the hill beyond is one of the famous landmarks of the Roman campagna—the **Tomb of Cecilia Metella**. It may seem strange that in such a masculine society as that of ancient Rome a woman could have had so magnificent a tomb; almost rivalling in its size, and resembling in shape, those that Augustus and Hadrian built for the imperial dynasties. Byron was not quite right when he described Cecilia as 'the wealthiest Roman's wife'. She was in fact the daughter-in-law—not the wife—of M. Licinius Crassus the triumvir, the Rothschild of the late Republic, who made a fortune out of buying up cheaply the property of the victims of Sulla's proscriptions. It was Crassus the triumvir who financed Julius Caesar in his early days. Apart from this, and the fact that she was the daughter of Quintus Metellus Creticus, nothing is known about the life of Cecilia Metella.

Still, Cecilia won posthumous fame. The whole of the district surrounding her tomb was known for centuries as Capo di Bove, from the classical frieze with bulls' skulls which we can still see near the top. It was due to her, or at least to the fact that her sorrowing relations built her such a large and solid tomb at a strategic point commanding the Appian Way, that the old road preserved its character and many of its monuments. In 1300 the Caetani Pope, Boniface VII, gave Cecilia's tomb to his relations, who made it into a stronghold that enabled them to control the traffic on the Via Appia and exact tolls from travellers. As a result, this tract of the road

Trajan's Column. The reliefs, which illustrate his campaign against the Dacians in what is now Rumania, provide a wonderfully detailed documentation of Roman military works. In the background in the church of SS Nome di Maria

Top left The Arch of Constantine, built in 315 to celebrate his victory over Maxentius at the battle of the Milvian Bridge

Below left The entrance hall to the Palazzo Farnese, whose beautiful proportions are due to Sangallo's interpretation of Vitruvius. The Palace was begun by Sangallo in 1514, continued by Michelangelo, and completed by Giacomo della Porta in 1589

The Roman Palace

Top right The courtyard of the Palazzo della Cancelleria, built around 1500

Below The courtyard of Palazzo Spada. Begun in 1550, its exuberant stucco decorations presage the baroque

Below right A wing of the Doria gallery, completed in the eighteenth century, with Bernini's bust of Innocent X at the far end

A detail of the Creation of Man from Michelangelo's frescoes on the ceiling of the Sistine Chapel

The Sarcophagus of the Bride and Bridegroom in the Etruscan Museum at Villa Giulia

The Ludovisi Throne in the Museo delle Terme

The statue of Augustus in the Vatican Museum

Michelangelo's Pieta in St Peter's

The cloister of St Paul's Without The Walls, begun in the twelfth century and completed in 1214. This is a supreme example of the work of the school of Roman mosaic artists known as the Cosmati

The Cloister of S Giovanni dei Genovesi, the finest fifteenth-century cloister in Rome. Beyond the characteristic octagonal columns of the period is a beautiful old garden planted with orange trees, jasmine and scented herbs

Cabs waiting for a fare in the Piazza of St Peter's

was deserted for the Via Appia Nuova, which leads to the gate by St. John Lateran. It was only in the last century that the long-deserted road was cleared and its monuments weeded out and restored as we see them today.

The rough walls standing on either side of the road by Cecilia's tomb formed part of the Caetani fortress; they also built about 1300 the now ruined Gothic church, dedicated to St. Nicholas. Just beyond this is the Osteria Belvedere, the terminus of the bus service, from where we must continue our exploration on foot. For the next kilometre or so the road is lined with cypresses; as yet there are few tombs or ruins, but this stately avenue provides an appropriate prologue to the monumental part which is to follow. Here on summer nights in the light of a full moon it is not so difficult to imagine those funerary processions which must have passed this way so often in pagan times, with their weeping mourners and attendants wearing the funerary masks of revered ancestors, accompanied all the way by the weird music of the flutes. Or the vast pile of some great family tomb illuminated by the flames of the funerary pyre leaping skywards, and the smoke eddying and swirling above the dark cypresses.

Just after the fourth milestone—that is four miles from the old Porta Capena where we began our morning's walk—stand the remains of the Tomb of Marcus Servilius (on the left). From now on for the next three kilometres the road is lined on both sides by tombs, ruins, fragments of reliefs and statuary. This is the most picturesque part of the old road, whose charm we largely owe to the imagination of Canova, who as early as 1808 conceived the then revolutionary idea of leaving as many sculptural fragments and inscriptions as possible at the site on which they were discovered, instead of removing them to museums. The fragments and inscription of Marcus Servilius's tomb, found in 1808, he had arranged on a modern building, which he had erected for the purpose.

A little farther along on the same side is the so-called **Tomb of Seneca**. According to Tacitus, on the day of his death Seneca had returned from Campania and halted at a villa four miles outside Rome. There he was dining with his wife and two friends, when Nero sent Gavius Silvarus, a colonel of his guard, to question his old tutor. The emperor hoped to gain evidence of Seneca's participation in Piso's conspiracy; the old man defended himself with pride and frankness, but the inevitable death sentence followed. Gavius could not bring himself to convey the message personally, and sent one of his staff officers to tell Seneca that he must die. As a last farewell to his friends Seneca said, 'I leave you my one remaining possession, and my best: the pattern of my life.' His wife chose to die with him, and in stoic Roman fashion they both opened their veins. Owing to his age, Seneca bled slowly; in order to conceal his agony and not witness that of his wife, he asked her to go into another room. To the end his bravery and his clarity of mind did not desert him, and he died dictating a dissertation to his secretaries. It is doubtful if the tomb we see, with a marble relief of the death of Atys, is really the one where the great philosopher was buried in the year 66; but the Via Appia was the main route from Campania, and it stands near the fourth milestone from Rome, so his remains must have lain near by.

A little farther along on the right is the so-called **Tomb of St. Urban**; this dates from the time of the Antonines; a tower was erected on the top of it in the Middle Ages. Farther along on the right is another tomb of the same period, that of Ilarius Fuscus, distinguishable by a relief of five family portrait busts. The funerary inscriptions of freed slaves of the imperial Claudian house have been affixed to another ruin nearby. The road continues, flanked by numerous tombs and ruins on either side, until we reach what is perhaps the most picturesque stretch in its whole extent. On a slight incline it deviates slightly, evidently in order to avoid two very early tombs which must have existed even before the road was built. One of these—a grass-covered mound shaded by stone pines, with a circular tower on top—is said to be the tomb of one of the legendary Curiatii. According to Dionysius of Halicarnassus the famous duel between the Horatii and Curiatii took place five miles from Rome; it is supposed to have occurred in the reign of Tullus Hostilius, during the war with Alba Longa (673–642 BC).

The view from here is extraordinarily beautiful, with pine trees and cypresses fringing the road, whose grassy verges are covered with flowers in spring, when acanthus unfolds its graceful leaves beside sculptured fragments. Here and there traces of the ancient pavement have been uncovered; their dark polished stones gleam in the sun and, straight as a die, the old road pursues its course to the distant Alban Hills. A little farther along on the left are the ruins of an extraordinary tomb, shaped like a giant mushroom. The strength of its stone core is such that it has resisted centuries of spoliation, when the surrounding stones were removed, giving it this odd shape. Near by are two more grass-covered tumuli, known as the tombs of the Horatii. On the left is the tomb of Marcus Cecilius, with a hospitable inscription of thanks and good wishes to those who visit his tomb. Somewhere near by Cicero's friend T. Pomponius Atticus was buried in 32 BC.

Beyond this are the imposing remains of one of the great villas that once also lined the Via Appia; this is the **Villa of the Quintili**. The whole of the area between here and the Via Appia Nuova—more than a kilometre away—is sown with the ruins of this vast estate. We can still see the remains of terraces, cisterns, aqueducts, a hippodrome and amphitheatres scattered through the fields. The large building giving on to the Via Appia Antica was a nympheum (turned into a stronghold in the Middle Ages), which must have served as a formal entrance hall to this palatial residence. Unfortunately the gate to this is now closed; formerly it was possible to see the remains of the fountains and water channels that cooled the nympheum, and trace the aqueduct that fed them to a great vaulted cistern. The splendour of the villa was such that it excited the cupidity of the Emperor Commodus, who had its owners Condianus and Maximus Quintilius proscribed and put to death although they were brave soldiers and well-known authors of books on agricultural subjects. A strange tale is told about Sextus, the son of one of them, who it seems was in Syria when his father and uncle died, and managed to fake his own death in an accident. Commodus's agents investigated the rumours of his survival, and several young men who resembled Sextus were killed, possibly the real Sextus among them. During the reign of Commodus's successor, Pertinax a young man appeared in Rome declaring that he was the lost heir and giving pretty good proofs that he was. He was unmasked, however, by the emperor himself, who addressed him in Greek, a language that Sextus knew well; the impostor's complete ignorance of it proved his downfall.

After the Villa of the Quintili the roadside is almost bare, except for fragments of statues lying among the aromatic *mentuccia* (*Mentha peperita*) and wild fennel that burgeon there in spring. But in the distance we already see the *Casal Rotondo*—the largest circular tomb in the whole length of the Via Appia. Strangely enough it is not known for whom this was erected; though for long it went by the name of Cotta's tomb, because the archaeologist Canina found a fragmentary inscription with the name near by. This and broken pieces of decorative reliefs have been attached to a wall built close by. Some fortunate person has evidently succeeded in obtaining a lease of the tomb and renovated the ruined house which stands on top. One envies him the wonderful view over the Campagna and the wilder reaches of the Via Appia, with its ruined villas and medieval watch-towers stretching away into the far distance. There we turn down the road to the left and about a kilometre's walk brings us to the Appia Nuova and the Capannelle Race Course where we catch the bus back to Rome. Those who can give a whole day to the Via Appia Antica, and provide themselves with a picnic lunch, can explore these its wilder and more romantic reaches; but the walk is a long one—another six kilometres or so, to the Osteria delle Frattocchie, where the old road joins the Via Appia Nuova. Near Frattocchie stands an old tower known as *il Torraccio*, and the ruins of *Bovillae*. This was the native town of *Julia Gens*, where Julius Caesar had his ancestral estates.

After Frattocchie the old road merges with the new, but is no less historic for that; fringed still by antique tombs—but also modern villas—it pursues its unswerving way to Albano. Here even the Roman engineers had to give way before the forces of nature, as represented by the Alban Hills; but as soon as the road debouches into the plains again—the famous Pontine Marshes—it returns to its dead straight course. Just before this it passes through Cisterna, where the Caetani own a farm called *Le Tre Taverne* (the Three Taverns); the road continues to Fàiti, whose ancient name was Forum Appii. Those names seem familiar, and if we look at the New Testament (Acts xxviii, verse 15) we will see why. It reads: 'And so we went onwards to Rome. And from thence, when the brethren heard of us, they came to meet us as far as Appii Forum and the Three Taverns; whom when Paul saw, he thanked God, and took courage.' We began our morning's walk with legends of St. Peter; since then we have explored a small part of the old road that, as these words reveal, was to have an importance in world history of which Appius Claudius can never have dreamed when he built it in 312 BC.

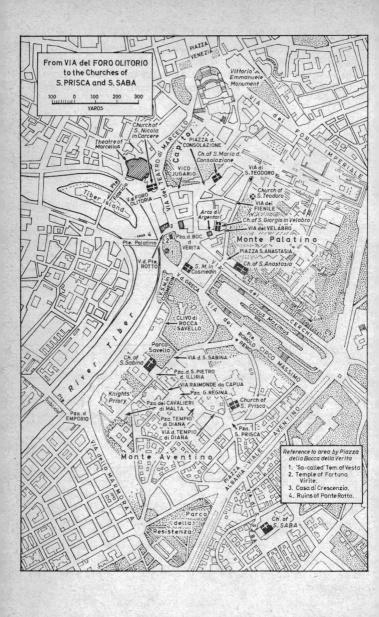

From VIA del FORO OLITORIO to the Churches of S. PRISCA and S. SABA

100   0   100   200   300
YARDS

PIAZZA VENEZIA

Vittorio Emmanuele Monument

VIA del FORI IMPERIALE

Church of S. Nicola in Carcere

Theatre of Marcellus

Pte. Fabricio

Tiber Island

V.d. FORO OLITORIA

Pte. Palatina

Capitol

PIAZZA d. CONSOLAZIONE

Ch. of S. Maria d. Consolazione

VICO JUGARIO

VIA di S. TEODORO

Church of S. Teodoro

VIA dei FIENILE

Arco d' Argentari

Ch. of S. Giorgio in Velabro

VIA del VELABRO

Pza. d. BOC. d VERITA

Monte Palatino

PIAZZA S. ANASTASIA

Ch. of S. Anastasia

V.d. Pte. ROTTO

S. M. in Cosmedin

V. d. GRECA

River Tiber

VIA S. MARIA in COSMEDIN

CLIVO di ROCCA SAVELLO

Circus Maximus

VIA del CERCHI

Pte. ROMOLO e REMO

VIA del CIRCO MASSIMO

Parco Savello

Ch. of S. Sabina

VIA d. S. SABINA

Pza. d. S. PIETRO d. ILLIRIA

VIA RAIMONDE da CAPUA

Knights' Priory

Pza. G. REGINA

Church of S. Prisca

Pte. Sublicio

Pza. d EMPORIO

Pza. dei CAVALIERI di MALTA

Pza. TEMPIO di DIANA

VIA d. TEMPIO di DIANA

Pza. S. PRISCA

VIA del MARMORATA

Monte Aventino

PIAZZA ALBANIA

VIALE AVENTINO

Parco della Resistenza

Ch. of S. SABA

Reference to area by Piazza della Bocca della Verita

1. 'So-called' Tem. of Vesta
2. Temple of Fortuna Virile.
3. Casa di Crescenzio.
4. Ruins of Ponte Rotto.

CHAPTER TWENTY

Via del Foro Olitorio to S. Prisca and S. Saba

TODAY'S sight-seeing is quite frankly a mixed bag. Starting off with the area on which the oldest Roman market—the *Forum Boarium*—and its close neighbour—the *Forum Olitorium*—stood, we continue via temples and churches to the Aventine, perhaps the most picturesque and peaceful of the seven hills. The afternoon will take us to the Protestant Cemetery, where Keats's body and Shelley's heart lie buried; to the Pyramid of Cestius; the Testaccio (hill of the potsherds); and to the second greatest Christian Basilica in Rome, S. Paolo fuori le Mura (St. Paul's Without the Walls). After this, the energetic can take a bus tour of the E.U.R., originally designed for Mussolini's international exhibition of 1940 (that never took place); it has now become a garden suburb surrounding the very fine Palazzo dello Sport and other buildings made for the Olympic Games of 1960.

Again this morning we start off from the Piazza Venezia; but this time a short walk down the **Via del Teatro di Marcello** (which passes to the right of the Vittorio Emanuele Monument) brings us to the beginning of our itinerary. Just after we have passed the great bulk of the Theatre of Marcellus on the right, we see a picturesque group (on the left of the road) of a medieval house and some ruined fragments of classical porticoes. The house, which dates from the twelfth or thirteenth century, may at one time have belonged to the Pierleoni; certainly it stood within the bailiwick of that redoubtable Jewish family who in the Middle Ages even produced an anti-pope, Anacletus II (1130–8). According to some authorities one of the neighbouring porticoes may have been the *porticus Minucia* where indigent Romans received their monthly dole—the bread of Juvenal's '*panem et circenses*'. It seems a likely supposition, as the other portico is thought to have been that of the wheat merchants—the *porticus dei frumentari*.

As the name of the **Via del Foro Olitorio**—the very short street on the right leading to the Tiber bank—indicates, the whole of this area was once occupied by the Forum Olitorium, the vegetable and fruit market of ancient Rome. Like the Roman Forum itself, this began as a simple market, but eventually became a monumental centre surrounded by temples and other public buildings. Some traces of the former can still be seen embedded into the walls of the picturesque old church of **S. Nicola in Carcere** standing a little to the left of the Theatre of Marcellus. Although internally the church has little to interest us, its exterior is one of the most perfect examples of a Roman architectural palimpsest. It is built on the site of three temples of Republican times, which are believed to have been those dedicated to Janus, Juno Sospita and the Temple of Hope, built during the desperate days of the first Punic war (264–241 BC). The podium and some of the columns of the Temple of Hope can be seen on the right of the church, beside the campanile, which is really the stump of a medieval tower. The mannerist façade should probably be attributed to Giacomo della Porta, who restored the church in 1599. It is incorporated into the Temple of Juno Sospita and is known to have been used as a Christian place of worship since 1128. The appellation '*in carcere*' (in the prison) for long resulted in the site being confused with that of the Mamertine prison—which was, of course, on the other side of the Capitoline Hill—but a prison does seem to have existed here in the eighth century.

Continuing along the Via del Teatro di Marcello, lined here by large modern blocks of offices of the municipal administration, we are approaching one of the most ancient sites in Rome—the Forum Boarium or cattle market, which existed even before the Roman Forum and the foundation of the city. In this area stood some very ancient temples, notably that of Fortune and the *Mater Matuta* (the Dawn Mother), traditionally said to have been built by Servius Tullius, and certainly dating from the end of the sixth or the beginning of the fifth century BC. The Forum Boarium later became an important commercial centre with a port on the Tiber.

We now turn up the Vico Jugario to the left, so called in memory of the *Vicus Jugarius* of classical times, that led from this area to the Forum by way of the Temple of Saturn. This brings us to the Piazza della Consolazione, in front of the church of S. Maria della Consolazione, with an imposing façade built at the beginning of the last century. The adjoining buildings formerly housed the Ospedale della Consolazione—a pious institution whose origins went back before the year 1000.

We now branch right, down the Via dei Fienile, and find ourselves in the very picturesque **Via di S. Teodoro** called after the circular church of that name, nestling at the foot of the Palatine Hill. This is the first we shall see of a group of churches of very ancient foundation associated with the period when representatives of the Byzantine emperors still lived in and around the imperial palace on the Palatine, using it as a kind of Viceregal Lodge. S. Teodoro was built into the ruins of the great store-houses or *horrea* that stood between the Forum and the Tiber. Its foundation is usually considered to date from the seventh century; it contains the remains of a mosaic of that period representing Christ seated upon an orb, as in S. Lorenzo fuori le Mura. Practically all the rest of the church dates from Nicholas V's restoration in the fifteenth century—in 1705 Carlo Fontana converted the old cemetery in front into a semicircular forecourt.

We now continue along the Via di S. Teodoro to the right; at the end (on the left) we find a picturesque little piazza dominated by the church of **S. Anastasia**. The foundation is a very early one, dating back to the original *titulus Anastasiae*, created by Anastasia—possibly a member of Constantine's family—and later dedicated to the martyred saint of the same name. S. Anastasia was for long the imperial parish church, owing no doubt to an aristocratic founder and its vicinity to the Palatine; in order of precedence it ranked after St. John Lateran and S. Maria Maggiore. A tombstone which existed in the church until the fifteenth century afforded evidence of how late the imperial palace near by had been kept in repair, and was regarded as an official residence of the Byzantine emperors. It recorded that one Plato, who died in 686 (he was the father of Pope John VII) had been keeper of the palace and restored its great staircase.

It was at S. Anastasia that the popes celebrated at dawn the second of the three Christmas masses; it still holds a very special place in the Christmas celebrations of the Roman Church, 25 December being the saint's feast day and anniversary of her martyrdom. Some authorities see in this a connection with its situation near to the spot where the *Lupercal* is known to have been; believing that here, as in so many other places, the Roman Catholic Church pursued its policy of substituting a Christian celebration for a pagan one—the birth of Christ for the birth of Rome. The remains of an *insula* of the first century can still be seen in the vaults beneath the church; otherwise it is difficult today to find any other sign of its great antiquity. It was restored in the thirteenth and fifteenth centuries, prior to the complete conversion of the interior in 1636 and the erection of the existing façade in 1722. S. Anastasia does, however, contain what must be one of the most modern church inscriptions in Rome —in the centre of the nave—stating that in the reign of John XXIII, at the time of the Vatican Council II, its titular Cardinal McIntyre, Archbishop of Los Angeles in California, had it restored with the aid of members of his diocese.

As is graphically shown by an old print in the portico of S. Anastasia, in the days when the church was built it must have been completely overshadowed by the vast structure of the **Circus Maximus**. While we regard with horror the Romans' passion for the gladiatorial combats in the Colosseum, their enthusiasm for horse and chariot racing brings a kindred feeling. Anyone who now enjoys a day at the races would probably have felt quite as much at home in the Circus Maximus as at the Derby, and very much impressed by Roman skill with horses. The religious ceremonial would come as something of a surprise, but the presence of the emperor and the *Pompa Circensis* have their modern parallel in the Royal procession at Ascot. Betting had its devotees then as now, though few losers today would go quite so far as the disgusted Romans who engraved the losing favourite's name on a piece of bronze, accompanying it with curses and consigning it to the infernal gods at the bottom of their tombs. Still, win or lose, the Romans loved their horses; as at least one inscription to Polydoxus from his owner Pompeianus, that still exists at Constantine, bears witness. What probably more than anything else would surprise the modern race-goer is that the Romans rode without stirrups; also that races might alternate with other feats of equestrian skill, reminiscent of the Cossack displays and tent pegging. But all of these were mere hors d'oeuvres or intermissions between the really great events of the day—the chariot races.

The opening of the Circus Maximus races—which might last as long as fifteen days, with twenty-four races each day—must have been a tremendous spectacle. The great arena in its heyday held a crowd of at least thirty thousand, all dressed in their best—especially the feminine element. Ovid in his *Art of Love* advised young women to make the best of their opportunities on these occasions. The emperor, with his family and court, would have been seated in the imperial box, which still juts out towards the circus from the Palatine. The presiding magistrate—wrapped in purple robes with an ivory baton surmounted by an eagle in his hand and crowned with a golden wreath of laurels—gave the signal for the start by dropping a white napkin into the arena. As it touched the glistening golden sand, the rope which was extended between two statues of Hermes in front of the *carceres* (the enclosures in which the chariots waited) fell; and the race was on. The progress of the various laps was signalled to the crowd by moving seven large wooden eggs on the central spina; later bronze dolphins were also employed for this. The chariots would have belonged to one of the four factions—the whites and the greens, who were usually allied; and the blues and the reds, who were also partners. It is believed that in the case of *quadriga* races no more than four took part in the Circus Maximus, but for the smaller chariots there could have been as many as twelve, as that was the number of the *carceres*.

The winner would be rewarded with a large cash prize, but even the losers among the crowd might hope to get something. The emperors would often make a largesse of packets of food, purses of money, or tickets like those in our raffles, where the lucky number might bring the winner a house, a ship or even a farm. The arcades outside the circus—which resembled those of the Colosseum—were filled with shops and taverns, where the winners could celebrate or the losers drown their sorrows. They were also the haunt of less respectable elements such as soothsayers and prostitutes.

All this, of course, is a description of the Circus Maximus as it appeared at the height of Rome's prosperity and imperial power; its beginnings and its end were very different. Somewhere about 400 BC it was an open marshy valley, in which the first wooden *carceres* were built in 326 BC. The last games were held in the circus by Totila the Ostrogoth, in AD 549. Practically all we can see of the Circus today is an open grassy valley, in whose midst the gardens department of the municipality has marked the spina by a grassy bank, planted with shrubs and cypresses. The *carcere* and the consul's box stood at the end nearest to us; of them no trace remains. A few ruins and a medieval tower still stand at the far curved end of the elongated horse-shoe, whose shape served as a pattern for the other circuses that arose throughout the Roman world. The tower is all that remains of the great fortresses of the Frangipane—one of the most powerful families of medieval Rome, who turned the Colosseum into a castle. Here the devout Jacopa of that name received St. Francis of Assisi on his last visit to Rome. He gave her a present of a lamb, the symbol of innocence and meekness, possibly as a gentle hint that the lady might at least imitate this last characteristic of the animal; because of her forceful character the saint was apt to refer to her as *Brother* Jacopa!

We now retrace our steps to where the Via del Velabro turns out of the Via di S. Teodoro. It runs into a hollow, known since ancient times as the *Velabrum*. Whereas in Roman times this must have been a lively commercial centre—the Arch of Janus at the far end is of the type built over a busy cross-roads as a shelter and meeting place for merchants—today it is one of the quietest and most picturesque corners of old Rome. The arch itself dates from the late Empire, probably the reign of Constantine; and like his triumphal arch was made up of older fragments.

Nearer to us, on the right, stands the lovely romanesque church of **S. Giorgio in Velabro**. This was built at the end of the seventh century over an even earlier church dating from the fifth or the beginning of the sixth century. The portico and campanile date from the twelfth century; but the sobriety and the curiously irregular shape of the church inside reveal its very early origins (it was skilfully restored in 1926). On summer days the doors stand wide open, revealing a wonderfully cool and tranquil interior; the chief impression is of variations on the theme of grey—of antique columns, stone altar, canopy and weathered wood ceiling. The altar and canopy are of the thirteenth century, the former being relieved by a little discreet cosmatesque mosaic; this and a fresco in the apse (attributed to the school of Cavallini) are the only notes of colour in the whole church. The altar contains part of St. George's skull, said to have been found in the Lateran Palace and brought here in processional state by Pope Zacharias (741–52). Before leaving, we should examine the elegant small classical arch, the **Arco degli Argentari**, to the left of the church portico. This was built by the money-changers in honour of Septimius Severus, his wife Julia Domna and his two sons Geta and Caracalla, who are shown in the reliefs in the act of making a sacrifice. After Geta's murder by Caracalla his name and effigy were removed.

As we emerge from the Via del Velabro we see on our right a street with the curious name of **S. Giovanni Decollato** (St. John beheaded). As a matter of fact this is the not unsuitable dedication of the chapel belonging to the Arciconfraternità della Misericordia, a confraternity founded in 1488, whose self-imposed task was to give religious and material aid to condemned criminals in their last moments; also to afford them decent burial. This confraternity still exists, and has in its possession a box containing herbal medicines, a bottle for aromatic vinegar (the equivalent of smelling salts) and a metal cup and flask (containing one imagines something stronger), with which these pious brethren accompanied the unfortunates on their last journey.

It is strange how certain localities seem to be fraught with tragedy. Near the **Piazza della Bocca della Verità**, which we now enter—once the site of the Forum Boarium—stood the terrible classical prison and place of execution known as the *Doliola*. In the eighth century there was another prison here called the *Carcer ad Elephantum* after the nearby elephant fountain. Finally, in the last century the piazza was used for public executions—a photograph of one of these is preserved in the Rome Museum.

It is not surprising in view of this that the area came to be regarded with superstitious dread. In medieval times this was chiefly associated with the famous Bocca della Verità (the mouth of truth), really a classical drain-covering in the form of a great face with open mouth in the portico of the church of S. Maria in Cosmedin. In the Middle Ages the Bocca della Verità was used for a sort of trial by ordeal to see if people— particularly wives suspected of unfaithfulness—were telling the truth. It was thought that if anyone told a lie while holding their right hand in the open mouth the terrible stone jaws would close, cutting off their fingers.

The church of **S. Maria in Cosmedin** is one of the most admired and best known to foreigners of all Rome's ancient churches. This is probably partly due to the fact that it was one of the first to have been restored to the simple dignity of its ancient origins, in 1894–9. The old name for the church, *S. Maria de Schola graeca*, reveals its origin. It was built in the sixth century to serve the Greek colony, whose numbers were latter swollen by the arrival of refugees fleeing first from the Arab invasions and later from the iconoclasts. *Schola*, as we will recall, meant an association or confraternity, which could be the members of a foreign colony as well as a guild of artisans. The church was built on the site of the *Statio Annonae*, the seat of the central food distribution organisation of classical Rome. Some of the columns of the ancient building are still to be seen in the church. Various interpretations have been put upon the word *Cosmedin*, but it is now generally believed to recall the *Kosmidion* of Constantinople. S. Maria was enlarged in the eighth century, from which period dates a marble mosaic of *opus sectile* in front of the altar. The very fine cosmatesque pavement, choir and paschal candlestick are, however, of the twelfth century, the episcopal throne and beautiful altar canopy from the thirteenth—this last was executed in 1294 by Deodato, son of the famous Cosma. The portico, where the Bocca della Verità now stands, and the superb campanile were built in the twelfth century.

Crossing to the other side of the road, we pass a delightful fountain, made in 1715; its tritons, rugged rocks and shell-basin were obviously inspired by Bernini. Before us in an open grassy space rise two charming little Republican temples, the circular one is usually erroneously called the Temple of Vesta, the rectangular one the Fortuna Virilis. Both were built about 100 BC or even earlier and it is not definitely known to what gods they were dedicated. Climbing the steep flight of steps leading up to the portico of the second, we are struck by how small a space the actual *cella* occupied in a classical temple. Empty as it is, this gives perhaps a clearer perception than any other building in Rome of what a pagan temple looked like—its great height in relation to its size is remarkable. Evidently none of these antiquarian preoccupations enter the mind of the enterprising woman photographer who with sound commercial acumen has selected this temple as her pitch for taking souvenir portraits and family groups of visitors to Rome.

Looking from here across the brief Via di Ponte Rotto, we

see the **Casa di Crescenzio**, one of the few medieval Roman houses to have survived. This it probably owes to the belief that it was once the home of Cola di Rienzo, who claimed descent from the famous family of the Crescenzi. In actual fact—as the long inscription on the façade states—it was built by one Nicolò, son of Crescenzio and Theodora, who wished to renew the ancient magnificence of Rome. Obviously this was the reason why he embedded classical fragments as decoration into the walls of his house, and with twelfth-century brickwork tried to reproduce the effect of a classical portico. The house was also popularly known as that of Pontius Pilate: this is now believed to have been due to the fact that medieval passion plays are known to have been acted in the area, and this rather grand building was selected to serve as Pilate's palace. A nearby inn was known as 'Caiffa' or the house of Caiaphas.

We now return to S. Maria in Cosmedin, cross the Via della Greca and set off down the Via di S. Maria in Cosmedin towards the Aventine. Not far along on the left we come upon the Clivo di Rocca Savella—a steep walled path and steps leading up to the **Parco Savello**. This is a charming small public garden, filled with orange trees, occupying the walled area of the old Savelli fortress which some authorities believe stood on the site of Emperor Otto III's (983–1002) palace. From here there is a fine view over Rome, with the cupola of St. Peter's looming impressively in the distance. We traverse the park to its far corner, where a door in the wall leads us into the quiet little Piazza di S. Pietro d'Illiria, shaded by lime trees and refreshed by a clear fountain. On one side of this stands the church of **S. Sabina**; the only one in Rome apart from S. Anastasia to have its closing hours thoughtfully displayed on the door.

To the writer, this is the finest of Rome's ancient churches. The outside is of the starkest simplicity; in the interior the severe majesty of the fifth-century basilica stands revealed in all its grandeur. Probably in no other Roman church are superb proportions and a magnificent array of twenty-four matching Corinthian columns allied to such a flood of golden light as pervades the whole of this splendid building. S. Sabina, whose name has not been changed from that of the original *titulus*, was built over the site of a Roman house by Peter of Illyria between 422 and 432. The whole body of this original church has survived the centuries, and was restored almost to its pristine state by Muñoz in 1936–8. At that time, when the windows which had been walled up were reopened, some of the ninth-century *transennae* or frames used for holding the selenite (which then took the place of glass) were found. These have been restored (and the selenite replaced); so too has the ninth-century choir. A flat wooden ceiling—similar to that which would have existed in the fifth-century church—has been reintroduced. S. Sabina is often cited as the earliest Roman example of the use of an arcade, as opposed to an architrave, above the columns separating the nave from the aisles. The *opus sectile* decoration of coloured marbles on the clerestory dates from the fifth century; so does the long dedicatory mosaic inscription in gold on a blue ground, above the main door. The severe female figures on either side of this personify the church as represented by conversions from the Jewish and pagan religions.

Thus S. Sabina as we see it today is a fifth-century church with ninth-century additions. The only exceptions to these two periods in the body of the church are Zuccari's sixteenth-century fresco in the apse (which follows roughly the design of the original mosaic), the painted roundels of saints above it, and the representations of the symbolic holy cities on either side. These were executed at the time of the restoration, to replace mosaics of these subjects known previously to have existed there. There are, of course, tombs of later periods; notably the mosaic one (the only one of its kind in Rome) of Muñoz da Zamora, a General of the Dominicans who died in 1300. There are also two side chapels; one dedicated to St. Hyacinth, with sixteenth-century frescoes by the Zuccari brothers (off the right aisle) and the chapel of St. Catherine of Siena (off the left aisle), both of which are of a later period.

S. Sabina is now usually entered by the side door from the Piazza di S. Pietro d'Illiria; but before leaving we must make our way to the main door, which opens out of the portico joining the church to the Dominican monastery, on the left of the square. In a severely classical frame here we find what must certainly be the oldest carved wooden doors in existence; they date from the fifth century. The decoration takes the form of panels illustrating incidents from the Old and New Testaments, worked in high relief in the style of the paleo-Christian sarcophagi. The representation of the Crucifixion is one of the earliest known. On request to one of the Dominican friars (who is generally to be found in the vicinity of the door), it is usually possible to see St. Dominic's own cell in the priory (now a chapel); also the beautiful cloister, dating from the thirteenth century.

We now continue along the Via di S. Sabina to the **Piazza dei Cavalieri di Malta**, one of the most charming and original of its kind in Rome. It was designed by the famous engraver Piranesi in the second half of the eighteenth century. With its small obelisks and trophies of arms (imitating those of antiquity) and its tall cypresses, this square resembles one of the artist's own drawings. To the world in general, however, it is better known for the famous view through the keyhole of the door leading into the Knight's Priory, on the right. Peeping through this we see the dome of St. Peter's beautifully framed by an avenue of trees. The Priory is the residence of the Grand Master of the Order.

Depending upon how long we have taken up to now with our explorations, we next have a choice of sights. If it is not yet much later than eleven o'clock, we may be able to fit in both the churches of S. Prisca and S. Saba before they close at twelve. If it is later than that we will only be able to see one. On Mondays, Wednesdays and Fridays from 10 to 11.30 a.m. we can see the well-preserved mithraeum beneath S. Prisca (though an ancient titulus the church itself is of little interest), or press on to the picturesquely medieval S. Saba. If we decide on the latter, we return to the Piazza S. Pietro d'Illiria, turn right down the Via Raimondo da Capua, and halfway down catch the 94 bus for S. Saba.

For S. Prisca, we continue down Via Raimondo da Capua, cross the Piazza Giunone Regina (called after the temple of that name which stood near by), and walk down the Via del Tempio di Diana.

We now come to the Piazza S. Prisca, the quaint little church of **S. Prisca** stands high up on the left corner of the square. Although the existing church rises on the site of the fourth-century *titulus Priscae*—traditionally associated with the house of Aquila and Prisca, mentioned in the Epistles of St. Paul—it is of little architectural interest today. However, before 1952, the monks of the adjoining monastery had spent several years excavating below the church in the hope of discovering the original early Christian meeting house. They were unsuccessful, but in that year two Dutch archaeologists took over the work and completed the excavation of the mithraeum, which was known to exist. Here, as in S. Clemente, it was found that in the fourth century the triumphant Christians had built the apse of their new church right above the shrine of Mithras. Evidently the Christians and Mithraic communities, who had hitherto existed side by side, had been at daggers drawn. When the Christians gained possession of the mithraeum, they smashed the statues and hacked at the painted walls with axes.

Plain evidence of the fury of this attack was found by the Dutch archaeologists as they carefully sieved the earth with which the mithraeum had been filled. Fragments of the stucco statues of Mithras and Serapis—which had miraculously survived centuries of burial—were collected and pieced together, and the damaged painted walls restored. Today the mithraeum is one of the best preserved and lit in Rome; particularly interesting for the unique frescoes showing the seven stages of initiation into the cult, on the left wall. Here too is a representation of the sacred banquet, whose participants partook of bread, wine, and the flesh of some sacrificial animal. On the right wall is a painting—the only one found to date in a mithraeum—of the great Roman sacrifice of the *suovetaurilia*, of a ram, a bull and a boar.

Our bus to S. Saba will take us past all these sites and across the wide Viale Aventino where it joins Piazza Albania, stopping in the quiet little Via di S. Saba that climbs the hill known as the Piccolo Aventino on the other side. The setting of the church of **S. Saba** comes as a complete surprise after the modern residential quarters we have traversed on the way. The tree-lined road and walled garden before the church look much the same as in the eighteenth-century prints; but now, thanks to careful restoration in 1909, the arches of the charming and unusual fifteenth-century loggia have been unblocked. The portico beneath is filled with sculptural fragments, illustrative of S. Saba's long and varied history, since its foundation in the seventh century, as the church attached to a monastery for Oriental monks, who had fled from the Persian and Arab invasions of Palestine. Of that period, or a little later, there is a most interesting relief (in the left corner) of a horseman with a falcon.

S. Saba was for long believed to have been built over the

house of St. Sylvia, the mother of Gregory the Great; but this has not been confirmed by excavation. This, instead, revealed an oratory of the seventh century, with some remarkable fragments of painting which are now preserved in the passage leading to the sacristy. The existing church was built above the oratory some time during the tenth century, the campanile in the eleventh, but most of the decoration dates from the thirteenth. This last is recorded in an inscription above the beautiful cosmatesque main door, which states that it was made during the reign of Innocent III (1198–1216) by Master Jacopo, father of the famous Cosma. Of this period too are the superb mosaic pavement and the remains of the beautiful choir, now standing against the right wall of the church. As might be expected in a church originally built for Oriental monks, S. Saba has three apses in the Greek style; in the central one rises the beautiful altar canopy, supported by antique columns. Originally the apse was decorated with mosaics; these were replaced in the sixteenth century by paintings, which may repeat the original decorative theme, but are of no artistic interest. Below, however, just behind the altar, is a very fine Crucifixion of the thirteenth century; while the triumphal arch above has a delightful fifteenth-century Annunciation executed for Pius II's nephew, Cardinal Piccolomini.

On the left-hand side of the church is a short fourth aisle, with some interesting thirteenth-century frescoes of episodes in the life of St. Nicholas of Bari. These include a scene which to some might appear to be a curious decoration for a Christian church—it shows three young ladies lying naked in bed. For those unfamiliar with the legends of St. Nicholas, it should be explained that they were three maidens of good family whose penniless father (seen on the right of the painting) was in despair as he saw no future for his dowerless daughters but a life of vice. St. Nicholas (seen looking through the window at the back with a bag in his hand) was aware of their predicament; one night he threw a bag of gold through their window, thus providing the girls with a handsome dowry enabling them to marry, and becoming the prototype of our own Santa Claus.

By now, whichever way we have arranged our itinerary, we will be feeling ready for luncheon. Unfortunately neither the Aventine proper nor the Little Aventine are well supplied with restaurants. So we must either return to Via di S. Prisca, where we can eat rather expensively at Apuleius in a reconstructed Roman house of the first century. The only alternative is to make our way to Piazza Albania, traverse the small public garden called the Parco della Resistenza, and try our luck among the bars of the Via della Marmorata and the adjoining streets. In fine weather this is one of the occasions when a pocket-sized picnic lunch is useful.

CHAPTER TWENTY-ONE

The Pyramid of Cestius to the Tre Fontane

❦

WHEREVER we may have lunched, the point of departure for our afternoon's itinerary is the **Piazza di Porta S. Paolo**. After S. Sebastiano, the Porta San Paolo is perhaps the finest in the Aurelian wall; the best view is from the outside, where the Pyramid of Gaius Cestius rears its 120 feet above the wall. Built as his tomb by this wealthy praetor, who died in 12 BC, the monument would have been one of the last things St. Paul saw when he was led to his execution by the Ostian Way since, of course, in the year 62 the walls would not have existed—they were only built two centuries later. On the side facing towards the city, the gate is still as Aurelian built it, with the addition of a medieval shrine; the outer face, with its great defensive towers, was the work of Belisarius. The gate, originally known as the Porta Ostiense, has for centuries been called after St. Paul, as the road passing through it leads to his basilica.

We now return by the little Via Raffaele Persichetti, named after a school-teacher who was killed in the abortive resistance to the German occupation of Rome on 8 September 1943. The adjacent Parco della Resistenza also commemorates this episode. From here we turn left down the Via Caio Cestio to the **Protestant Cemetery**, whose entrance is a little way along on the left (if the gate is shut ring for the *guardiano*). The cemetery should really be called the non-Catholic cemetery, as members of the Orthodox Church and non-Catholic Italians are also buried there. A cemetery should be a sad place, but somehow this is not; perhaps it is because to northerners it feels so familiar. Here in the midst of Rome, with its flowers and its trees, it still has something of the simplicity of an English country churchyard. Nor need Cestius's pyramid take away from this impression; in the Sussex village of Brightling the eccentric Squire Jack Fuller built a tomb for himself exactly like it. Most people go to the Protestant Cemetery to

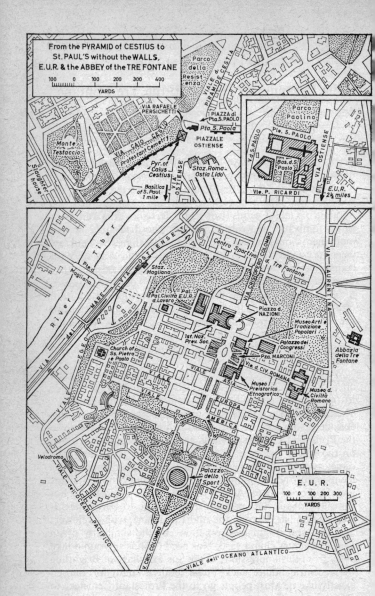

From the PYRAMID of CESTIUS to
St. PAUL'S without the WALLS,
E.U.R. & the ABBEY of the TRE FONTANE

100   0   100   200   300   400
YARDS

Parco
della
Resistenza

VIA RAFAELE
PERSICHETTI

PIAZZA di
Pta. S. PAOLO

Pta. S. Paola

PIAZZALE
OSTIENSE

Monte
Testaccio

VIA CAIO CESTIO

Protestant Cemetery

Slaughter
house

Pyr. of
Caius Cestius

Basilica
of S. Paul
1 mile

VIA OSTIENSE

Staz. Roma-
Ostia Lido

Parco
Paolino

V. di S. PAOLO

Ple. S. PAOLO

Bas. d. S.
Paolo

VIA OSTIENSE

Vle. P. RICARDI

E.U.R.
2½ miles

Tiber

River

Pte. d.
Magliana

VIA OSTIENSE

Centro
Sportivo

VIA CRISTOFORO C. Tre Fontane

VIA LAURENTINA

Staz.
Magliana

VIA DEL MARE

VIA EGEO

Pal.
Pal. Civiltà E.U.R.
d. Lavoro

Piazza d.
NAZIONI

Museo d.
Tradizione
Popolari

1st. Naz.
Prev. Soc.

Palazzo dei
Congressi

Abbazia
della Tre
Fontane

Church of
Ss. Pietro
e Paolo

VIALE

Pza. MARCONI

Vle. d. CIV. ROMANA

VIALE

ASIA

Museo
Preistorico
Etnografico

Museo d.
Civiltà
Romano

VIALE

EUROPA

VIALE

AMERICA

Velodromo

VIALE dell' OCEANO PACIFICO

Palazzo
dello
Sport

E.U.R.

100 0 100 200 300
YARDS

V. CRIS. COLOMBO

VIALE dell' OCEANO ATLANTICO

see Keats's tomb and the spot where Trelawney buried Shelley's heart.

Leaving the cemetery, we continue along the Via di Caio Cestio to the left; at the end we see a curious green hill rising like a hump, it is the **Monte Testaccio**. This used to be one of the sights of Rome and must have been one of the gayest and most delightful places in the city; now, surrounded as it is by dreary suburbs, no one would want to linger more than a few minutes to view it as a curiosity. The hill takes its name from the word *testa* meaning a potsherd; in fact the whole of this not inconsiderable eminence—45 metres high and 850 round —was built up out of the fragments of broken amphorae. In classical times, wine, oil, wheat and other commodities were imported by ship into Rome in these vessels. They were unloaded at the river port known as the *Emporium*—which stood near the Piazza dell' Emporio at the end of the Via Marmorata, itself the site of a deposit for imported marbles—and their contents were stored in great warehouses near this spot. Potsherds seem to be practically indestructible; other ancient cities have their 'Hill of the Potsherds'—notably the Kom al Shoghafa, above the catacombs at Alexandria. The hill is surmounted by a cross; in medieval times it was a place of pilgrimage, marked by the stations of the Cross. Then the surrounding meadows were the scene of the famous Testaccio 'games'. Tremendous civic ceremonial preceded bull-baiting and the savage pursuit of unfortunate pigs, which were dismembered by young men armed with swords; the pieces were then taken home to eat.

We now retrace our steps to the Porta di S. Paolo, where the 18 or 23 bus take us to the **Basilica di S. Paolo fuori le Mura**. As regards surroundings, St. Paul's is the Cinderella of all the great Roman basilicas; the gas works, general markets and a desolately poor quarter fringe the dusty road leading up to it. Admittedly the Via della Conciliazione has little to commend it architecturally as an approach to St. Peter's; but at least it is well kept, and one feels that something could be done to improve the road to St. Paul's. This is all the more sad when one reflects that in the eighth century the magnificent portico still existed that stretched from the Porta di S. Paolo to the basilica.

Nor is the exterior of the church either imposing or attractive; Augustus Hare described it as looking 'like a very ugly railway station'. Externally the existing building dates entirely from the reconstruction after the fire of 1823; it was completed in 1854, not a very fortunate period artistically speaking. The tragedy of the fire was all the greater because, alone among the great basilicas, St. Paul's had stood almost unchanged since it was begun by the three Augusti—Valentinian II, Theodosius and Arcadius—and completed by Honorius early in the fifth century. This great building—the largest Christian church until the building of new St. Peter's—replaced the smaller basilica built by Constantine over the Apostle's tomb.

Although its position beside the Tiber, outside the walls, rendered the basilica more vulnerable than any other to attack and pillage (it was sacked by the Saracens in 846 and fortified by John VIII in 880), its very isolation contributed to the old building's preservation from change and 'restoration'. As malaria gained its deadly hold, the surrounding countryside became a desert and John VIII's once flourishing fortified village, Giovannipoli, fell into ruin. When Hildebrand first came as a monk to the adjoining monastery in the eleventh century only a few dissolute brethren remained, and the grazing flocks would wander into the basilica. Needless to say when he became abbot, Hildebrand changed all that; he re-introduced the stern monastic rule, restored the church and in 1070 welcomed the gift of some splendid bronze doors. These were made in Constantinople and inlaid with silver; they were presented by Pantaleon of Amalfi, one of a family who evidently made a habit of such gifts—the doors of the church at Monte Cassino and in the Apulian shrine of Monte Sant'-Angelo also came from them. Though practically destroyed by the fire of 1823, the doors are still preserved in a small room of the cloister. Though the doors were preserved, unfortunately more of the ruined basilica was destroyed after the fire than was strictly necessary. Practically all that now remains of it are the restored mosaics on the triumphal arch and apse, the paschal candlestick and the canopy over the main altar.

Still, as we enter the basilica (usually by a door at the end of the left transept) we cannot help being impressed. Its vast size, the forest of great columns dividing the nave from the four aisles, and the silence which reigns in its shadowy spaces, do convey a feeling of monumental grandeur. Like all neo-classical recreations the building has something of a chill about it; but it probably gives us a clearer impression of what the pagan basilicas—from which the early Christian ones were copied—were really like, than any other building in Rome. The whole world contributed to the rebuilding of St. Paul's. Mohammed Ali of Egypt sent columns of oriental alabaster, the Tsar Nicholas I the malachite and lapis lazuli which adorn the altars at either end of the transept; 185 bishops from all over the world attended its consecration.

During the excavations which preceded the rebuilding, the architects dug deep under the shrine of the *confessio* and found there an iron grating (probably like the one protecting St. Lawrence's tomb at S. Lorenzo fuori le Mura) covering St. Paul's tomb, which was of the type built in the first century. This was surrounded by many tombs both Christian and pagan, these last going back as far as the end of the Republican era. In fact, if in 1823 the architects had been in possession of the same technical means as the archaeologists who excavated the shrine under St. Peter's during the last twenty years, no doubt they would have laid bare a very similar necropolis to that which we can now see at St. Peter's. Accounts of St. Paul's martyrdom vary, but according to the second-century author, Tertullian, he was beheaded at the Aquae Salviae (now the Tre Fontane), not far away. According to tradition, his body was then claimed by the pious matron Lucina, who buried it in her family tomb in a vineyard by the Ostian Way. Constantine afterwards encased the body in a double sarcophagus of marble and bronze.

Above this spot now rises Arnolfo di Cambio's beautiful altar canopy, which according to an inscription was made by him and his partner Pietro (probably Pietro Cavallini) in 1285. This stands framed in the triumphal arch, whose mosaics were presented by Galla Placidia. Her name is recorded in the inscription running round the arch; that of Honorius, who completed the basilica, and Theodosius, who begun it, are seen above. The mosaics on the inner face of the arch are the work of Cavallini; those in the apse were made about 1220, mosaic workers being specially summoned by Pope Honorius III from Venice for the purpose. All of these mosaics have, of course, been much restored. To the right of the apse begins the famous series of mosaic roundels with portraits of the popes which continues round the whole basilica. These are, of course, modern reconstructions, though some of the original portraits on the right-hand wall survived the fire; these were removed and are now in the adjoining monastery.

Curious, and typically Roman, tales are told about the fire. It occurred when Pius VII lay dying; but before then the people had noticed that there was no more room for another papal portrait in the old basilica for Pius's successor. Filled with superstitious dread, remembering the events following upon the French Revolution, and Pius's own arrest and enforced residence in France at the hands of Napoleon, they wondered what fresh cataclysm was to come. During the night of 16 July the sick pope himself was troubled by strange dreams of some disaster coming to the Church of Rome. He had begun his religious life as a monk at St. Paul's, and the basilica was very dear to him. When the sad news of its destruction reached the Quirinal, it was kept from him; he died shortly afterwards without knowing.

If Pius could return today to St. Paul's, apart from the mosaics and the altar canopy the only thing he would recognise inside the church would be the huge paschal candlestick—the grandest of its kind—that, looking rather like some classical triumphal column, stands by the corner where the right transept joins the nave. It dates from the twelfth century, and is signed 'I Nicholas de Angelo with Pietro Bassalecto completed this work'; the Bassalectos or Vassallettos were one of the most famous Roman families of mosaic workers.

The one place where Pius would still feel completely at home is the **cloister**; by some miracle this, the most beautiful in all Rome, escaped untouched by the holocaust. Begun under the Abbot Pietro of Capua (1193–1208) and finished in the time of Abbot Giovanni (1212–26), it is believed to be the work of the same Pietro Vassalletto who collaborated in making the paschal candlestick and worked in the Lateran cloister. The cloister of St. Paul's is, however, not only richer and better preserved, but it seems as if, both at its creation and today, greater love and personal attention had been lavished on it. There are charming little individual notes, such as the small sphinx-like animals couchant between the columns. The columns themselves are of a bewildering variety of form and colour; some carved in cream marble, twisting like serpents; others so richly encrusted with gold and red and black that one can scarcely see the basic stone for the mosaics; some slim and straight, others corkscrewed like Jacobean furniture;

they have one thing in common—their exquisite workmanship.

But in Rome by now we are becoming accustomed to the architectural glories of cloisters, some well, some not so well preserved; what is usually missing is the garden—rough grass and box hedges is all we often find, if that. At St. Paul's at last we find a real cloister garden, obviously tended and loved by the monks themselves (the only one to compare with it is at the Quattro Coronati). Roses massed in neat beds line the grass plots, well-trimmed bays provide accents of dark green in the centre, while feathery papyrus waves in the fountain. Filled with the scent and colour of growing things, which was also an integral part of their design as their creators saw it, the cloisters of St. Paul's live as a place of spiritual repose, and not just as another architectural wonder on a tourist itinerary.

On leaving St. Paul's we may feel we would like to call it a day; but as it should still be quite early for anything but a winter afternoon, we may wish to explore further. There are two widely divergent possibilities before us; either we can take the 123 bus from its terminus in front of the basilica and make a tour of the ultra-modern E.U.R. quarter, or we can take the 223 from the same place, which will bring us close to the Trappist monastery of the Tre Fontane—believed to have been the site of St. Paul's martyrdom.

The first expedition is of very considerable interest to the student of modern architecture. Many of the buildings intended for Mussolini's 1940 exhibition suffer from the pompous rigidity of Fascist architecture at its worst, but some really remarkable sports installations were made there for the Olympic Games of 1960. Pre-eminent among these is Nervi's great **Palazzo dello Sport**, crowning the hill at the far end of the central vista of the Via Cristoforo Colombo. Really to be appreciated this should be seen from inside, where the enormous dome of prefabricated concrete elements spreads out like a huge sun-flower. The effect of the exterior has been somewhat spoilt by the addition of a sort of glass cummerbund, necessitated by air conditioning. Several interesting museums are now also housed at the E.U.R.; notably that of the Civiltà Romana, with its excellent model reconstruction of ancient Rome, and its facsimiles and reconstructions of Roman art and architecture throughout the Empire. There is also the museum of the Arti e Tradizioni Popolari, and shortly there will be the Pigorini Ethnographical Museum which is in the process of being transferred there. All these museums are of considerable but specialised interest, and are only open in the morning; so that at least one expedition must be made specially to see them. For the expert on any of these subjects, this should definitely be one of their Roman itineraries.

Nothing could be a greater contrast to the E.U.R., with its brash modernity, crowded carways and vast glass-fronted blocks, than the **Trappist Monastery of the Tre Fontane**. Although it lies literally almost a stone's throw down the hill to the east of the E.U.R. (with a car both can easily be seen together), this is another world. The bus stops just beyond the gate in the Via Laurentina, but the place is unmistakable; an open gate in an old rustic wall leads to a tree-shaded drive. This terminates before a fine fortified medieval gate that stands invitingly open.

Within the most perfect peace and silence reigns in a little garden filled with classical fragments, broken only by the cooing of some fan-tail pigeons and the musical sound of water flowing into an old sacrophagus. There is a feeling of another world about the whole place; the doors of three churches are always open (from 6 a.m. to 8 p.m. in summer, till 7 p.m. in winter). **SS. Vincenzo e Anastasio**, the Abbey church which faces us as we enter, dated originally from the seventh century. It was built by Honorius I and restored by Honorius III in 1221—most of what we see today dates from that period. From there we walk along a path shaded by ilex and bordered by thickets of hibiscus and Japanese medlars, to the church of **S. Paolo alle Tre Fontane**. This was originally built in the fifth century over what is believed to be the scene of St. Paul's martyrdom, where the three springs flowed. It was rebuilt by Giacomo della Porta in 1599 and superficially no trace of the original church is to be seen; though St. Paul is said to have been bound to a column standing in a corner. In the middle of the floor is a fine classical polychrome mosaic of the four seasons, from Ostia Antica. Retracing our steps we see on our left the church of **S. Maria Scala Coeli**. This takes its name from a vision which St. Bernard is said to have had here of an angel leading a soul from purgatory up a flight of steps to heaven; it was also rebuilt by della Porta in 1582.

Altogether the scene is very different from that described by travellers in the last century, when this was considered to be the most melancholy spot in the whole campagna. Then 'a few pale monks ridden by malaria' could only live in the ruined monastery for a few months in the year. In 1868 the monastery lands were given to the Trappists, who set about their reclamation, draining the marshes and planting eucalyptus trees, which were considered a sovereign protection against the mysterious germs of the malaria. From these trees the monks still make a noted liqueur, which is on sale in a little shop in the gate-house. They are also famous for their chocolate and honey. But their most useful product to anyone who lives in Rome and suffers from headaches when the scirocco blows is the aromatic vinegar—*Aceto Galenico*—compounded from some ancient formula with herbs and spices. It is indeed a sovereign remedy, much appreciated by the Romans; who, with several hundred years of experience behind them, greatly prize what they call '*roba dei frati*' (the friars' medicaments). It feels something of an anti-climax to return to our 223 bus, changing at St. Paul's Without the Walls to the 23 bus, which will put us down just beside the Tiber island and the Via del Foro Olitorio, where our morning's walk began.

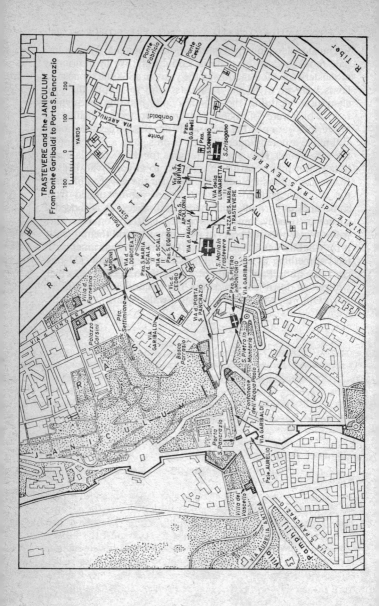

CHAPTER TWENTY-TWO

TRASTEVERE and the JANICULUM
From Ponte Garibaldi to Porta S. Pancrazio

100   0   100   200
YARDS

R. Tiber

Ponte Fabricio

Ponte Cestio

VIA ARENULA

Garibaldi

Ponte Garibaldi

Ponte Sisto

River Tiber

VIALE di TRASTEVERE

Pza. G.G.Belli

S.SONNINO

S.Crisogono

Vic.d.S. RUFINA

VIA della LUNGARETTA

Pza.S. APOLLONIA

VIA d. PAGLIA

PIAZZA di S. MARIA in TRASTEVERE

S.Maria in Trastevere

Pza.S.MARIA d.SCALA

VIA d. SCALA

Vic.d. CEDRO

Pza.S.EGIDIO

MARONI

VIA d. DOROTEA

Vic.d. Fornesina

Villa Fornesina

LUNGARA

Pta. Settimiana

Palazzo Corsini

VIA GARIBALDI

Bosco Patrizio

VIA di PORTA S. PANCRAZIO

Pta. S. PIETRO in MONTORIO

S. Pietro in Montorio

VIA GARIBALDI

J A N I C U L U M

T R A S T E V E R E

Fontana e S. Pietro in Montorio

Fontanone dell'Acqua Paola

Porta S. Pancrazio

Villa del Vascello

Pza. S. PANCRAZIO

Pte. AURELIO (VIA GARIBALDI)

VIA AURELIA ANTICA

VIA S.PANCRAZIO

Pamphili

Trastevere and the Janiculum

❧

ACCORDING to themselves, the inhabitants of Trastevere are the only real Romans descended from ancient classical stock; but this must be taken with a grain of salt. As early as the first century AD sailors from Ravenna were established there, whose job it was to work the awnings of the Colosseum. Later, owing to its close connection with the Port of Ostia, Trastevere became increasingly polyglot, the home of Oriental commercial communities, especially Jews. This still held good in the Middle Ages, owing to the river port of the Ripa Grande; though the Jews soon migrated across the Tiber, their place was filled by other foreigners—including northerners—who came by water and the Via Aurelia. Reminders of Trastevere's maritime past still exist in the Piazza dei Mercanti and the church and hospice of S. Giovanni Battista dei Genovesi, built in 1481 for Genoese sailors.

Possibly because of its hybrid population this quarter across the Tiber was for long regarded as an independent entity; until the fourteenth century it was a separate *rione*, its people and the Romans of the other bank regarding each other almost as foreigners. Still in the last century a real Trasteverino would boast that he had never crossed the Tiber! Something of this spirit survives: families will count the generations they have been resident in Trastevere; their dialect is more pronounced than that of the other bank and until 1870 was markedly different. Trastevere is in fact the stronghold of Roman dialect poetry—two piazzas and two streets have been named after dialect poets. It has too its own special *festa*—*Noiantri*—held in July, now a wonderful mixture of ancient and modern; with fairy-lights festooning the streets, fireworks, open-air cinemas, concerts, mandolin serenades, dancing in the piazzas, and boat and swimming races in the Tiber. Nineteen centuries ago, in his *Fasti*, Ovid described a very similar Trastevere festival, then celebrated on 24 June.

Thus, even if the Trasteverini cannot really lay claim to ancient Roman descent, they have every justification for regarding their quarter as the stronghold of Roman popular custom and tradition. For the traveller it holds the added attraction of being perhaps the least affected of all the old *rioni* by the new Italy of the commercial miracle; even in the middle of the morning it is usually still possible to saunter through the *vicoli* without imminent fear of being crushed between rows of parked cars and headlong traffic. This comes as a very welcome change after the hurly-burly of the Largo di Torre Argentina and the Via Arenula, that lead us to the Ponte Garibaldi. Already from this bridge we catch a glimpse of two conspicuous monuments of Trastevere—the statue of the poet Gioacchino Belli and the Torre degli Anguillara, standing in the Piazza G. Belli. Top-hatted and frock-coated in marble, the poet is represented leaning against one of the classical herms of the Ponte Quattro Capi. A rich marriage provided the wherewithal for Belli's sartorial elegance but bourgeois comfort did not stifle the satirical wit of this the most famous of Rome's dialect poets. The Torre degli Anguillara was the home of one of Trastevere's most noted families, it dates from the thirteenth century and is the only one of its kind to have survived in the district.

On the opposite corner of the adjoining Piazza Sidney Sonnino (called after an Italian statesman of the First World War) and the Viale Trastevere we see the church of **S. Crisogono.** As its fine Romanesque campanile indicates, this church is very much older than Soria's restrained baroque façade of 1626 would lead us to suppose. It is in fact one of the ancient titular churches of Trastevere mentioned at the council of 595, though the main body of the existing church was built in 1123 by Giovanni da Crema (Honorius II's legate in England). A more famous titular of the church was Stephen Langton, Archbishop of Canterbury, who defied both King John and the redoubtable Innocent III in the struggle over Magna Carta.

The interior of S. Crisogono presents the familiar Roman mixture of a Romanesque basilica with baroque decoration. Antique granite columns support a trabeation ornamented with motifs from the Borghese arms—Cardinal Scipione of that family having financed Soria's restoration. Contrasting with the superb thirteenth-century cosmatesque pavement is a blue and gold baroque ceiling; in the centre of this is a copy of

Guercino's 'Triumph of S. Crisogono'—the original is now in London. In the apse behind the triumphal arch—which is supported by the two largest porphyry columns in Rome—there is a fine small mosaic picture of the Madonna and Child with SS. Crisogono and James; this dates from the end of the thirteenth century and is attributed to the school of Cavallini. Those interested in paleo-Christian remains should now go to the sacristy at the end of the left aisle of the church. From here it is possible to descend into the excavations which have revealed part of the ancient *titulus*, apparently the converted hall of a large building of the fourth century, with frescoes dating from the eighth to the eleventh century (a small offering towards the cost of light should be made).

Leaving S. Crisogono by the side door on the right, we now make our way down the Via della Lungaretta; one of the ancient thoroughfares of Trastevere, dating from classical times, which was restored and given its present name during the reign of Julius II (1503–13). A short way along on the right, looking down the Vicolo di S. Rufina, we catch a picturesque glimpse of the romanesque campanile of the little church of **SS. Rufina e Seconda**. The campanile is one of the oldest in Rome, dating probably from early in the twelfth century.

A little way farther along on the right we come upon the **Piazza S. Apollonia**. A not very distinguished little square and rather mystifying as to name, as the only church now standing in it is dedicated to S. Margherita; it may, however, have witnessed the last chapter of a great romance. The church of S. Apollonia formerly stood opposite that of S. Margherita, beside a convent for women tertiaries of the Franciscan order. This was installed in an old palace of the Pierleoni and until the second half of the sixteenth century was not an enclosed convent in the ordinary sense. Apparently one of the functions of the tertiaries was to provide a home for repentant women, and on 18 August 1520 they there received Margherita, the daughter of a baker called Francesco Luti. Some authorities believe that this Margherita was none other than Raphael's famous *Fornarina*—the baker's daughter—whom he loved for so many years and used as his model for the Sistine Madonna, the 'Veiled Woman' of the Pitti and the audacious portrait we saw in the Barberini gallery. Probably it will never be known for certain if this baker's daughter, who found refuge in the Piazza S. Apollonia just four months after Raphael's death, and the *Fornarina* were one and the same person. But to add to the mystery, there is a tradition that Raphael's last work—the famous 'Transfiguration' in the Vatican gallery, in which the *Fornarina* is said to be represented—was painted in a house in this same square.

The Via della Lungaretta now debouches into the **Piazza di S. Maria in Trastevere** which is *the* piazza and heart and core of the whole *rione*; one of those delightful meeting-places of all and sundry, for gossip or a glass of wine, that add so greatly to the enjoyment of life in any Italian town. And what more beautiful setting could one ask in which to while away an idle hour than this? The sparkle of the fountain is matched and repeated by the glittering gold mosaics of the church, at festivals both are illuminated, providing a magical scene. It is said that church and fountain are the oldest of their kind in Rome; scholars have engaged in learned battle to prove the rights and wrongs of this. Also to provide scientific explanations for the ancient legend which says that on this spot, on the day that Christ was born (or thirty-eight years previously), a fountain of pure oil sprang from the earth, signifying the grace of God thus diffused upon mankind.

A small street leading out of the right-hand corner of the piazza is still called Via della Fonte d'Olio in honour of this event. According to Eusebius, it rose at the *Taberna Meritoria* (a hospice for veterans) and flowed from there all day to the Tiber. Others interpret the *Hospitium* or *Taberna Meritoria* as referring to an early Christian meeting house, whose use was sanctioned by Alexander Severus (reigned 222–35). What is certain is that the story of the fountain of oil and the *Taberna Meritoria* have been associated with this site since classical times.

Supporters of the theory that the church of **S. Maria in Trastevere** is the oldest in Rome, point to the fact that in imperial times Trastevere was a centre for Oriental, and particularly Jewish people, and attribute its foundation to the Christian meeting place said to have been founded by Pope St. Calixtus I and sanctioned by Alexander Severus. It is a matter of historical fact that Pope St. Julius I completed or rebuilt a church on this site in 341–52 and that in the list of titular churches compiled at the council of 499 it appears as *titulus Juli*, in that of 595 as *titulus Juli et Calisti*; it is therefore certainly one of the oldest churches in Rome. Pope St.

Calixtus I's association with the area is not limited to his legendary foundation of this church. Another one dedicated to him stands in the small Piazza di S. Callisto round the corner; this is linked to S. Maria by the large Palazzo di S. Callisto which is Vatican property. The palace is believed to stand on the site of the house where St. Calixtus was imprisoned and scourged. He is said to have been martyred by being flung from one of its windows into a well in the courtyard below in the year 222.

The church of S. Maria was restored by John VII and Hadrian I in the eighth century and rebuilt more or less as we see it today by Innocent II (1130–43), who came of a famous Trastevere family, the Papareschi. There has been considerable argument as to whether the beautiful mosaic on the façade dates from about the time of Innocent II or from the following century. The later date is now more generally accepted, and the figure of one of the donors who appear at the Virgin's feet is by some identified with a canon of the church who died early in the fourteenth century. The ten female figures which appear on either side of the Virgin have also been the subject of controversy, some authorities maintaining that they represent the wise and foolish virgins and others that they do not.

In the portico of the church, which is an addition made by Carlo Fontana in 1702, there are some interesting sarcophagi and reliefs. Notable among them are the sarcophagus with the heraldic lion of the Papareschi family and sculptural fragments of the eighth and ninth centuries from the choir of the old church. The beautifully sculptured stone cornices of the three doors were evidently taken from classical buildings of the middle period of the Empire. Although it was begun in 1140 and completed in 1148, the interior of the church gives the impression of being a great deal older. The use of classical fragments as brackets on the trabeation, and the trabeation itself—as opposed to arches—recalls early Christian basilicas such as S. Lorenzo fuori le Mura and S. Maria Maggiore.

Inevitably we are reminded more of S. Maria Maggiore than of any other Roman basilica, because the mosaics, which are the outstanding beauty of both churches, are devoted to the glorification of the Virgin. Her enthronement in the semi-dome of the apse is of particular interest: it is the earliest known example (it dates from shortly after the church's completion in

1148) of the portrayal of this scene showing the Madonna seated beside Christ on his throne; that of S. Maria Maggiore was made a century and a half later. The mosaic is contemporary with those of S. Clemente and S. Francesca Romana and shares certain details of their design. Here, as in S. Francesca Romana, the throne is of the ancient lyre-shaped type and, as in S. Clemente, there are the sheep and, on either side of the apse, prophets bearing scrolls. In S. Francesca Romana too there were once prophets like these, with caged birds hanging beside them. To the uninitiated these might appear to be a purely decorative feature; in actual fact they signify that, in having taken on human form in the Virgin's womb, Christ became a prisoner of the sufferings of the flesh for our redemption, like a bird imprisoned in a cage.

The outstanding artistic achievement of this superb mosaic is, however, the masterly portrayal of the two central figures—especially the ethereal beauty of the Madonna's face and the majesty of Christ. This last recalls the Pantocrators of Greece and Sicily; reminding us that this Renaissance of mosaic as an art in twelfth-century Italy was due to the introduction of Byzantine masters. On either side of the central figures, stand ranged SS. Peter, Julius, Cornelius, Calepodius, Calixtus and Lawrence, because their relics were preserved here; in the left corner Innocent II is seen carrying a model of his church.

Immediately below this twelfth-century mosaic is a series of thirteenth-century ones, representing scenes from the life of the Virgin; these are a major work of Pietro Cavallini. Starting from the left, the six panels show the birth of the Virgin, the Annunciation, the birth of Christ (just below the Virgin is a small building labelled *Taberna Meritoria,* from which flows a viscous stream of oil), the arrival of the three Magi, the Presentation in the Temple and the Assumption of the Virgin (her soul is represented as a small figure which Christ holds in his arms). In the centre of the apse immediately below these panels is another mosaic by Cavallini, showing the Madonna and Child encircled by a rainbow, with SS. Peter and Paul presenting the donor, Bertoldo Stefaneschi, a member of yet another famous Trastevere family whose arms with crescent moons may be seen at the base of the panel.

The altar canopy, which was remodelled in the last century, is supported by four fine porphyry columns; in the steps, between it and the paschal candlestick on the right is a small fenestella opening on to the spot where the famous fountain of oil is said to have gushed forth. Looking back from here we have a good view of the beautiful cosmatesque pavement and the singularly fine gilded ceiling. This last was designed by Domenichino in 1617, who painted the picture of the Assumption in the centre. This artist was also responsible for the design of the winter choir, a chapel to the right of the apse. High above the door is to be seen a shield with the old British royal arms, quartered with the fleur-de-lis and with a crescent moon in the centre. This is surmounted by a royal crown and a cardinal's hat and indicates that the chapel was restored in the eighteenth century by Cardinal Henry of York.

In the Altemps chapel, on the other side of the apse, is an interesting fresco representing the Council of Trent. This chapel also usually contains a precious eighth-century picture of the Madonna (undergoing restoration at the time of writing). As we emerge from the chapel we see the tomb of Cardinal Pietro Stefaneschi who died in 1417. He was the last of his house, one of the six Roman families who were hereditary guardians of Veronica's veil or *Volto Santo* and whose origins can be traced back to the eighth century.

We now turn left into Via della Paglia and right into **Piazza S. Egidio**; looking back we see a picturesque view of the side and old entrance of S. Maria in Trastevere. Formerly on the left of this square rose the great towered stronghold of the Stefaneschi. Now the only reminder of the baronial families of old Rome is the charming early Renaissance palace of the Velli opposite, where a coloured tile with a bear holding a rose, indicates that it is Orsini property. Taking the left-hand street out of the far end of Piazza S. Egidio, we pass the Vicolo del Cedro.

We now come to **Piazza S. Maria della Scala**, so called after the church of that name on the left. This was built in 1592 to the design of Francesco da Volterra to house a miraculous picture of the Virgin, which previously adorned an adjoining street staircase. At the end of the square is the famous **Farmacia di S. Maria della Scala**, the last of the old Roman conventual pharmacies to survive; it is still administered by the Carmelite monks of the adjoining monastery. Until not long ago the old pharmacy, dating back to the beginning of the seventeenth century, was still in use. Now the shop is a modern one on the ground floor, but on request the monks will take visitors to see the original one upstairs. In the passage leading to it stand great marble urns formerly used to store the famous Theriaca, a compound of many herbal and other ingredients preserved in honey or syrup. Nero's physician, Andromachus of Crete, is said to have invented a fearsome compound of this name as an antidote for poison; vipers' heads continued as one of its ingredients until comparatively recent times. The brimstone and treacle of Victorian England was derived from it; a mild herbal variety is still sold in the pharmacy as a cure for stomach ache.

In the same passage hang two pictures of Fra Basilio, a monk who lived from 1726 to 1804, whose fame as a herbalist spread far beyond the confines of the Papal States. In 1802 he was honoured by a visit of no less a person than Victor Emanuel I of Savoy and Sardinia. Fra Basilio was the inventor of many of the herbal medicines still sold in the pharmacy, notably the *Acqua Antipestilenziale* now used for stomach disorders and the *Acqua di S. Maria della Scala* or *Antisterica*, for soothing headaches. Several of the objects seen in the background of the picture, showing Fra Basilio teaching his students, can still be seen around the place, including some curious obelisks, crosses and trees made of glittering crystalline salts.

There is little doubt that the delightful decoration of the old pharmacy dates from Fra Basilio's day—the elegant walnut cupboards, with their carved and gilded pilasters, the glass cases with gilt baroque pedestals, housing a remarkable collection of eighteenth-century glass phials and bottles from Murano and Bohemia; also the fine Italian majolica jars. The walls of the storeroom are entirely lined with painted cupboards, decorated with portraits of Hippocrates, Galen and other great figures in the history of medicine. These contain scores of boxes, each with a painted label denoting its herbal contents. Fra Basilio's own herbal—dated 1755—is preserved here. It contains 230 varieties of herbs, dried, pressed and mounted in a highly decorative style; the therapeutic qualities of each are indited in exquisite script on the opposite page.

Continuing along the Via della Scala, we come to a crossroads where the Via Garibaldi leads up the hill on the left, the Via di S. Dorotea towards the river on the right, and Alexander VI's picturesque Porta Settiminiana spans the street in front of us. The little church of S. Dorotea, in the street of the same name, has, however, two lasting claims to fame. It was here that the Counter-Reformation movement first began, as a result of the activities of the Compagnia del Divino Amore. This counted among its members the future Carafa Pope, Paul IV (1555–59), S. Gaetano da Thiene and the humanist Sadoleto. Here also, in two small rooms beside the sacristy, S. Guiseppe Calasanzio founded the first free popular school in Rome in 1587. A narrow street turning to the left, called the Vicolo Moroni, has two branches; that turning to the left again is a cul-de-sac terminated by the high brick walls of an early medieval house where the Moroni family lived in the fourteenth century. Returning to the Via di S. Dorotea and traversing the little Piazza di S. Giovanni della Malva, we find ourselves in a picturesque piazza, the fountain on the right we have already seen from the Ponte Sisto, which stands opposite.

Retracing our steps to the Porta Settiminiana, we find ourselves looking down the **Via della Lungara**; begun by Alexander VI (1492–1503) and completed by his successor Julius II; it runs parallel to the Via Giulia across the Tiber. An ivy-covered gate, a little way along on the right, opens on to one of the most charming sights in Rome—**the villa and gardens of the Farnesina**. This also houses the Gabinetto Nazionale delle Stampe (roughly corresponding to the Print Room of the British Museum).

Today the villa that Baldassare Peruzzi built between 1508 and 1511 for Agostino Chigi is wrapt in the sunlit peace of its green garden. Only the music of its small fountain, and from time to time the staid receptions of the Accademia dei Lincei (the most renowned of Italian learned bodies), disturbs its tranquillity. It must have looked very different in the sixteenth century when Agostino Chigi made it the rendezvous of all the rank and fashion, the greatest artists and poets, the most beautiful women, the most learned philosophers of his day.

Knowing this, at first glance we are somewhat surprised that Peruzzi did not depart further from his customary sobriety when designing a building for such a purpose. But we should bear in mind that we now come in by what was originally the back entrance; to get the right effect we should quickly traverse the small hall to the famous Loggia of Psyche. The arches are now glassed in, but originally on their arrival here the guests would have found themselves in a loggia opening directly on to the garden. The entire decoration of this magnificent gallery was intended to give the impression of an open pergola, garlanded with fruit and flowers and shaded by superb tapestries. Peruzzi and Raphael designed it thus—as if the garden pergolas, decked ready for a summer banquet, reached right into the house. It is therefore one of the earliest examples of the interpenetration of house and garden which was the ideal of the Renaissance villa.

Although Raphael drew up the overall scheme for the decoration of the loggia, he did not himself execute it. The two great 'tapestries' in the ceiling—representing the Council of the Gods and Cupid and Psyche's wedding banquet—are attributed to Francesco Penni and Raffaellin del Colle. The incidents representing Psyche's adventures in the heavens while Venus was waging jealous war upon her, painted in the vaults, are believed to be the work of these two artists and Giulio Romano. Only one figure, that of one of the Graces (with her back turned, in the group in the corner to the right of the door) is attributed to Raphael himself. The beautiful garlands surrounding all these motifs are the work of Giovanni da Udine. They are almost unique in decorative work of this kind in that the fruit, flowers and vegetables are botanically recognisable. Julius II's arms in the centre of the ceiling recall the almost unheard-of honour that this pope accorded Agostino Chigi by allowing him to quarter the della Rovere arms with his own.

The theme of Psyche's adventures was drawn from Ovid's *Metamorphoses* and the *Golden Ass* of Apuleius; this last had lately been republished with a commentary by one of Agostino's friends. The decoration of the loggia was never completed according to Raphael's plans, which included Psyche's adventures on earth represented as painted tapestries 'hanging' on the walls now covered instead with architectural *trompe l'oeil* decoration of the seventeenth century. The ceiling is known to have been finished by 1 January 1517, more than two years before Raphael's sudden death. The fact that Raphael never completed the decoration for so liberal a patron and friend as Agostino Chigi, though his designs for it are known to have existed, has given rise to many legends. In his life of Raphael, Vasari was evidently giving credence to one of these, when he said that Raphael was so distracted by a love affair—presumably with the *Fornarina*—that he neglected his work; he also said that Agostino Chigi finally allowed the lady to live with Raphael in the villa.

A hundred years after Raphael's death the future Chigi Pope, Alexander VII (1655–67), actually confirmed and elaborated this story in a biography of his forebear Agostino. According to this, Raphael made so little progress, also with his work in the Vatican Stanze, that Leo X asked Agostino to use his influence with the artist. The wily banker had the lady kidnapped and hidden, pretending that she had found another love. For a while Raphael worked assiduously, then became melancholy and his labour slackened. Finally Chigi was reduced to 'discovering' the object of Raphael's affections and allowing her to live with him.

Raphael did, however, complete one work in the villa—the famous Galatea—in the loggia of that name leading out of the Loggia of Psyche. Formerly this was also an open gallery giving on to the garden; now the arches have been walled up and windows inserted in their place. The grace and life implicit in every line of the triumphant Galatea, as she drives her scallop-shell chariot and team of dolphins over the waves, makes us regret even more that Raphael took so little part in the actual execution of the adventures of Psyche. The fresco is most generally believed to have been painted in 1511, in an interval between the execution of the Stanza della Segnatura and that of Heliodorus in the Vatican. Pressure of these more exacting tasks would therefore explain the appearance of this one fresco as an isolated motif among the work of many other artists. Originally the decoration of the gallery was to have been divided into mythical scenes connected with the sea on the walls, and with the air for the ceiling. Now it is admittedly a rather curious and not altogether harmonious assortment of different subjects and periods. Sebastiano del Piombo painted the Polyphemus (whose blue tunic Agostino Chigi had added later for the benefit of a prudish lady), also the lunettes. There has been a good deal of discussion as to whether the gigantic head in one of these last was by Sebastiano del Piombo or Peruzzi. It is now more generally attributed to Peruzzi; the myth of its being by Michelangelo has been exploded. The decoration of the ceiling is also by Peruzzi; what is not generally very well known is that the large astral motifs show the position of the planets and constellations on 1 December 1446, the day of Agostino Chigi's birth, and therefore represent his horoscope in pictorial form. The land-scapes on the walls are attributed to Gaspard Dughet; they were executed in the seventeenth century after the villa had been bought by the Farnese.

Before leaving the ground floor we should see the small room at the other end of the Loggia of Psyche; this has a fine decorative frieze attributed to Peruzzi. Then, after climbing the stairs, we find ourselves in what must have been the main living-room of the villa, known as the Salone delle Prospettive. Its decoration by Peruzzi is one of the earliest Renaissance examples of *trompe l'oeil*. Between the great painted porphyry columns of the simulated loggias at either end of the room, we catch enchanting glimpses of Trastevere and the Borgo at the beginning of the sixteenth century. It is possible to identify such familiar landmarks as the Porta Settiminiana, the campanile of S. Maria in Trastevere and S. Spirito in Sassia.

Leading out of this room is the Stanza delle Nozze di Alessandro con Rossana, Agostino Chigi's own bedroom, decorated with scenes from the life of Alexander the Great. Some think that the frescoes were executed at two different periods, the earliest—and best—having been generously com-missioned in 1509–10, when poor Sodoma was smarting with shame at having been superseded by Raphael in the decoration of the Vatican Stanze. Something of his gratitude must have informed the artist's hand as he worked; the scene of Alexander's marriage to Roxana is considered to be Sodoma's masterpiece. Possibly of a later and less happy period is the scene showing Alexander with the family of Darius. The representation of Bucephalus, on the opposite wall, is certainly not by Sodoma, though the paintings on either side of it are. This has led to the supposition that when Agostino Chigi's great bed (decorated with gold and ivory and precious stones) was moved, before the villa was sold to the Farnese, the space was filled in by an unknown hand. Indeed the Chigi splendour of this villa did not last for long. As a result of family quarrels and bad administration Agostino's great fortune was soon dispersed, his treasures sold, and in 1579 or 1580 the house itself was bought by the Farnese. Hence its present name, distinguishing it from the great Farnese palace on the opposite bank of the Tiber, to which it was to have been joined by a bridge. When the new river embankment was built in 1879, a classical villa was discovered, of which we saw the painted and stucco decoration in the Museo delle Terme.

We now cross the Via della Lungara to the **Palazzo Corsini**, where the seventeenth and eighteenth-century sections of the **Galleria Nazionale d'Arte Antica** are temporarily housed pending transfer to the Palazzo Barberini. The palace also contains (though it is not yet on show at the time of writing) the famous Odescalchi collection of arms and armour; this too will ultimately be transferred to the Palazzo Barberini. More permanent denizens of the palace are the Accademia dei Lincei and its famous library, the Caetani Foundation, also the beautiful Corsini library, consisting of a series of rooms giving on to a garden terrace with a fine view of the Janiculum.

The Palazzo Corsini, whose long and graceful façade is one of Fuga's most distinguished works, was built between 1732–6 for the family of Clement XII (1730–40) on the site of the old Riario palace. This earlier building was the home of Caterina Sforza and Queen Christina of Sweden. Caterina came to live here after her marriage to Girolamo Riario in 1477. She was at the height of her beauty, which was said to 'glow like the sun and rival the lilies', but she had the misfortune to incur the enmity of the Borgias. In 1500 she returned to Rome as Cesare's prisoner and was incarcerated in the dread Castel S. Angelo; there she might have remained for life if the Borgias' French allies had not so much admired her courage as to insist on her liberation. Queen Christina lived in the Palazzo Riario from 1662 until her death in 1689, filling it with her wonderful art collections and making it the intellectual centre of Roman life. From the meetings of wits and savants gathered there was born her own Accademia Reale, the predecessor of the famous Arcadian Academy whose meeting-place we shall shortly see.

As the Galleria Nazionale di Arte Antica is only temporarily housed in the palace, we will not enter into a detailed description of the twelve rooms in which it is displayed, but simply make a note of the most famous works. The collection was founded by Cardinal Neri Corsini in the eighteenth century, and given by representatives of that family to the Italian State in 1883. Since then it has been greatly added to and includes a large number of outstanding works of Flemish and other foreign artists as well as of Italians of the seventeenth and eighteenth century. The most famous pictures by

Italian artists include Caravaggio's Narcissus and St. John the
Baptist, Guido Reni's 'Beatrice Cenci', Baciccia's portrait of
Bernini, several portraits and landscapes by Salvator Rosa, a
fine group of views of Rome by Pannini and of Venice by
Canaletto. Works by foreign artists include a Madonna and
Child by Murillo, a St. Sebastian by Rubens, a 'Repose in
Egypt' by Van Dyck, a snow scene by J. Breughel the younger,
and three works by Vouet, including 'Christ turning the money
changers out of the Temple'. Of particular interest to students
of baroque decoration, are Andrea Pozzo's small preparatory
oil sketches for the frescoes of the nave and *trompe l'oeil* dome
of the church of S. Ignazio.

If by now it is somewhere about midday, we have just the
time to fit in two more sights before the Roman lunch and
siesta hour descends upon us. These are the garden of the old
Arcadian Academy, or Bosco Parrasio, the church of S.
Pietro in Montorio and Bramante's famous Tempietto. The
first is very little known, because not everyone is aware that it
is possible to gain access to it. Although a national monument,
the Arcadia is now a private house, whose owners fortunately
are not always in residence. Strictly speaking only the garden
is visible to the public, but as in order to reach it one has to
pass through the dining-room, we should hurry in order to get
there as early as possible.

To reach the **Arcadia or Bosco Parrasio**, we return to the
Porta Settiminiana and turn right up the Via Garibaldi, which
climbs the steep slope of the Janiculum. Half-way up the hill,
just where the Via Garibaldi curves sharply to the left, we see
a large gate inscribed Bosco Parrasio, affording a glimpse of a
delicious garden. The gate is never open and to get inside we
must take the steep Via di Porta S. Pancrazio, on the left;
some way up on the right is a small iron door (No. 32, ring the
bell and ask to see the garden). We pass through the beautiful
circular dining-room, so excellently proportioned that it is
difficult to realise that it is some thirty feet high. This meeting
place of the Arcadians was built in 1725. The avowed aim of
the academy was to exterminate bad taste and free Italian
poetry from the 'barbarism' of the seventeenth century. As
symbols of classical purity all members took the names of
Arcadian shepherds, adopted the pipes of Pan and a fir branch
as their badge, and named their meeting-place after the grove
sacred to Apollo. The design of the garden has been associated

with the name of the architect of the Spanish Steps. Understandably so, as, with the exception of the delightful little amphitheatre in front of the house, it takes the form of a graceful baroque staircase wending its way through a wood. The perfect season in which to see it is April, when the giant wistaria covering the convex façade of the house is in full bloom, filling the amphitheatre with its heady scent. Here the Arcadians met in summer to read their literary compositions.

But we must not linger too long in this delightful place if we are to see S. Pietro in Montorio before it closes at one. To reach this church, we retrace our steps down the Via di Porta S. Pancrazio and, just beyond a small fountain on the right, we find a steep path punctuated by flights of steps that bring us out on to the terrace in front of the church. This affords us one of the most celebrated views of Rome. Across the red-tiled roofs of Trastevere we see the green oases of the Palatine and Aventine; in the far distance the statues on the portico of St. John Lateran are silhouetted against the blue of the Alban Hills. Appropriately enough for such a wonderful spot, the cloister beside the church of **S. Pietro in Montorio** contains one of the most exquisite architectural creations in the world—the **Tempietto del Bramante**.

The purity of line and harmonious proportions of this small circular temple convey such an effect of grandeur that they belie its actual dimensions. Framed in the shadowy arch of the cloister, the Tempietto glows golden against the blue of the sky, looking for all the world like some precious reliquary set upon a heavenly altar. This is precisely what its creator intended, for the Tempietto marks the spot which was once believed to be the most sacred in Rome—the place of St. Peter's crucifixion. This idea is said to have originated in a curious interpretation of the tradition that St. Peter had been crucified *inter duas metas*, between two *metas*; these were the tall posts that marked either end of the spina of a classical circus (in this case actually, of course, the Vatican circus). In shape these *metas* were something between an obelisk and a very much elongated pyramid—a great deal smaller and thinner, but nevertheless somewhat resembling the Pyramid of Cestius. For centuries this last had been known as the Meta of Remus and another building, which stood near the Vatican, as the Meta of Romulus. Apparently it was calculated that the site of S. Pietro in Montorio was equidistant between the two, and therefore was the true *inter duas metas* of tradition. A much older church, dedicated to St. Peter, is known to have existed on the site.

The existing church of S. Pietro in Montorio was built for Ferdinand and Isabella of Spain in 1481 to the plans of Baccio Pontelli. Its sober and dignified façade is now attributed to the school of Bregno. The nave is lined with chapels, notable for works of art dating principally from the sixteenth and early seventeenth centuries. Most famous is Sebastiano del Piombo's 'Flagellation' in the first chapel on the right, recently restored. In the next chapel is Pomarancio's 'Madonna della Lettera', in the apse and on the wall above this are Peruzzi's 'Coronation of the Virgin' and the 'Four Virtues'. The semicircular chapel forming the right transept was designed by Vasari, who also painted the 'Conversion of St. Paul' (the figure in black on the left is a self-portrait). This chapel contains two fine tombs by Ammannati. In the central apse, which was seriously damaged during Garibaldi's defence of the Roman Republic of 1849, Raphael's 'Transfiguration' hung from 1523 to 1809. It then formed part of Napoleon's loot, but was returned to the Vatican, where it now is; its place has been taken by a copy of Guido Reni's 'Crucifixion of St. Peter'. Although there is no inscription to commemorate the fact, Beatrice Cenci was buried under the steps of the altar after her execution in 1601. Also buried in the church are the Earls of Tyrone and Tyrconnel who fled to Rome after an unsuccessful conspiracy against Queen Elizabeth. The penultimate chapel on the left, of the Raimondi family, is of particular interest as one of Bernini's first essays in the use of concealed natural lighting. The sculptured marble frieze of roses and small birds is curiously classical in feeling for the seventeenth century.

By now it will probably be one o'clock and food and a rest will be uppermost in our minds. For this we have a choice of several alternatives. Either we can make our way back down the steps to Via Garibaldi and enjoy a copious Trastevere meal at Antica Pesa (No. 18) or at Romolo's beside the Porta Settiminiana (No. 8 Via di Settiminiana). Both have gardens, and Romolo—as befits the house in which Raphael is said to have courted the *Fornarina*—is the more elegant. Otherwise we can continue a little farther on our itinerary, turning right up the hill beyond S. Pietro in Montorio, where another tract of the Via Garibaldi will lead us past the monumental

Fontanone dell'Acqua Paola, built in 1612 by Giovanni Fontana for Paul V with stone plundered from the Forum of Nerva. This brings us to the **Porta S. Pancrazio**, immortalised in history by Garibaldi's heroic defence in 1849. On the left-hand corner of the Piazzale Aurelio, outside the gate, is the modest little Trattoria Gianicolo. But for Garibaldean enthusiasts, Scarpone (big boot)—a short way along the Via S. Pancrazio (to the left of the Villa Pamphilj)—is an alternative. This was the Casa Giacometti, which served as the base from which the *Bersaglieri* attacked the French stronghold of the Casino dei Quattro Venti. Today Scarpone is a restaurant, but its name is said to be derived from the nickname of 'big boots' that Garibaldi gave to its owner.

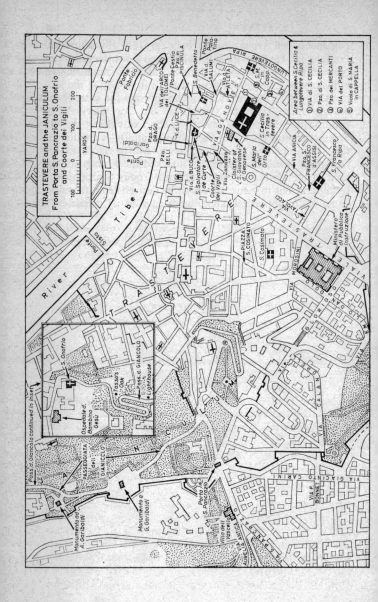

CHAPTER TWENTY-THREE

Trastevere and the Janiculum [continued]

❧

WORLD history has moved at such a pace during the last century that today few foreign travellers realise that the busy road fork outside the Porta S. Pancrazio was in 1849 the scene of the desperate battle between Garibaldi and the French forces, during the 'Hero's' defence of the short-lived Roman Republic. This is the spot of which Trevelyan wrote, 'It was here that Italy bought Rome . . . here at the San Pancrazio Gate, in 1849, that her claim on Rome was staked out and paid for; twenty-one years passed and then in 1870 the debt was acquitted.'

On the summit of the rise between the Via S. Pancrazio and Via Aurelia Antica, in what are now the grounds of the Villa Pamphilj, stands a triumphal arch which marks the site of the Casino dei Quattro Venti of the Villa Corsini. It was up the drive leading to it that the Garibaldini and Bersaglieri made charge after desperate charge in the face of the gun-fire of the French forces who were ensconced in the villa, in those days an impregnable site and the military key to Rome. Some cannon balls, relics of the battle, are still to be seen embedded in the rustic rockwork surrounding the gate of the Villa Pamphilj. On the right of the Via S. Pancrazio, leading up to it, stand the ruins of the Villa del Vascello, left thus as a memorial to General Medici's heroic defence of this outpost. Here he defeated all the French forces' attempts to dislodge him; the ruin of this once-beautiful villa was only finally evacuated at dawn on 30 June—the day after the feast day of SS. Peter and Paul—that saw the end of the battle.

After 1870 the summit of the Janiculum to the north of the Porta S. Pancrazio was laid out as a park; in this setting stand monuments to Garibaldi, his heroic wife Anita, and the men who fought with him in 1849, including John Peard, the English Garibaldino. To enter it we pass through the gate to the left of the Porta S. Pancrazio. Here on the left of the road stands a reminder of an older Rome, the façade of a small house which is believed to have been that of Michelangelo, brought here in 1930, during Mussolini's clearance of the slopes of the Capitol; of all incongruous things it now masks a water cistern.

A short walk under the plane-trees of the Passeggiata del Gianicolo brings us to the great open space where Garibaldi's statue stands. The view from here is superb; looking at it we are reminded of his own description of Rome as 'the greatest theatre in the world'. Continuing our walk, we pass the statue of Anita Garibaldi, portrayed with only slight dramatic licence on a rearing horse, holding a baby with one hand and brandishing a pistol in the other. Farther along on the right is the lighthouse presented to Rome by Italians living in Argentina, whose beam flashes the red, white and green of the Italian colours over the city at night. Here too there is a superb view and, a little farther along, a conveniently-placed snack bar where good *Espressos* are served. Just beyond this a flight of steps provides a short cut to the dried stump of an ancient evergreen oak with withered branches carefully supported by iron bands. This is Tasso's Oak, the tree beneath which this tragic poet used to sit in 1595 dreaming of past glories as he approached his end. Beside it rises a fine grove of cypresses, screening from view a charming little amphitheatre; this can be entered from a path on the right at the foot of the steps. Here S. Filippo Neri, who died in the same year as Tasso, is said to have instructed his Filippini in music and sacred drama.

Continuing down the Passeggiata del Gianicolo to the corner, and dodging the traffic as it roars up the hill, we cross over to what is still one of the most poetic spots in all Rome, the church and cloister of S. Onofrio. This was founded in 1419 by the Blessed Nicola da Forca Palena as a hermitage for monks of the Hieronymite Order and dedicated to the Egyptian hermit St. Onophrius. Something of the peace associated with its origins still dwells here; on the terrace in front of the church a fountain murmurs in the shade of ilex trees, where stone seats invite contemplation of the beautiful view. A graceful L-shaped Renaissance portico connects the church and monastery. In it are the tomb of its founder and frescoes of the life of St. Jerome by Domenichino. At the right end is a charming baroque shrine of the Rosary, dating from

1620. A low passage leads from the portico into the beautiful and severely simple fifteenth-century cloister; the lower arcade is supported by antique columns, the upper one with the characteristic octagonal ones of the period. The frescoes representing incidents in the life of St. Onophrius are mainly the work of Cavalier d'Arpino. On the first floor the cell where Tasso died is preserved as a museum. In the gallery leading to it is a beautiful lunette of the Madonna and Child in a Della Robbia frame; formerly believed to have been the work of Leonardo, this is now attributed to his pupil Boltraffio; it was executed in 1513. It is comforting to think that after so many tragic vicissitudes, Tasso found a peaceful end in a place of such beauty and tranquillity, though he died on the day before his triumphant coronation with the poet's laurel crown was to have taken place on the Capitol.

The 'dim religious light' of the church's interior is well suited to the almost Gothic lines of its main structure, but the richness of the Renaissance glows in the gold of the frescoes adorning the apse. On the authority of Vasari these are attributed to Peruzzi, though the influence of Pinturicchio is evident in some of them. They represent God the Father, the Birth of Christ, the Flight into Egypt, the Coronation of the Virgin, and the Virgin and Child enthroned; surrounded by the Apostles, saints, sybils and angelic musicians. By the first chapel on the right is Tasso's monument, erected some two and a half centuries after his death.

Emerging from S. Onofrio, if we are lucky we will catch the small 41 bus which stops in the Via del Gianicolo by the Hospital of the Bambino Gesù a little farther down the hill. But as it only runs every quarter of an hour, we may have some time to wait. The bus brings us back along the Passeggiata del Gianicolo, passes the Porta S. Pancrazio and ends up where the Via G. Carini crosses the Via Fratelli Bonnet. From this last we can take the 75 or 44 bus which will bring us back by way of Via Calandrelli and Via Dandolo down the hill to Trastevere. We get off at the Ministero della Pubblica Istruzione, on the corner where the Via E. Morosini (called after one of the heroes of the defence of the Roman Republic) meets the Viale Trastevere.

Before crossing this wide thoroughfare, we should turn back along the Via Morosini towards the Piazza S. Cosimato. Just within the piazza on the right we see the picturesque tenth-century porch of the church of S. Cosimato. This is closed, as the church now forms part of a hospice for old people and is not accessible to the public. It is, however, possible to see the two delightful cloisters; the entrance—a modern one with a porter—is a little farther back on the same side. A path traversing a small garden brings us to a fine, large Romanesque cloister, dating from the eleventh or twelfth century. There are some interesting fragments of paleo-Christian and medieval reliefs affixed to the wall on the side of this cloister leading into the second one. This last is a dignified example of the fifteenth-century architecture, with octagonal columns.

Retracing our steps to the Viale Trastevere, we cross over to the Via Tavolacci, which brings us to the Piazza S. Francesco d'Assisi, dominated by the imposing but restrained façade of the church of **S. Francesco a Ripa**, added at the time of Mattia de' Rossi's reconstruction of 1682–89. The little Via Jacopa dei Settesoli, leading into the piazza on the right, recalls the tradition that the church was founded by St. Francis of Assisi's friend, the redoubtable Jacopa Frangipane. Her family was often nicknamed de Settesoli, from their ownership of the Septizonium, of whose name this was a medieval corruption.

In actual fact S. Francesco a Ripa was founded by Count Pandolfo dell' Anguillara in the thirteenth century, beside the hospice of S. Biagio where St. Francis lodged when he came to Rome. The hospice was given to the Franciscan Order by Gregory IX in 1229. Today the church is chiefly a place of pilgrimage for art historians because one of Bernini's famous latest works—the statue of the Blessed Ludovica Albertoni—lies in the last chapel in the left aisle. The statue is placed above and behind the altar and, in contrast to the shadowy chapel in front, is dramatically lit by a concealed side window. It was executed in 1674, some thirty years after the Raimondi chapel, which we saw in S. Pietro in Montorio this morning. Thus these two works illustrate Bernini's first essay and one of his ultimate achievements in this use of light, for which he was so famous.

A much older treasure of S. Francesco a Ripa is a near-contemporary portrait of St. Francis himself, painted in the thirteenth century. This is attributed to the school of Margaritone d'Arezzo and is said to have been commissioned by the devoted Jacopa Frangipane. The picture hangs in what is believed to have been the cell in which St. Francis lived in the old Hospice of S. Biagio, later converted into a chapel. To see it we must ask in the sacristy—to the left of the main altar. A passage, with some interesting Anguillara tombstones and a steep stair, brings us to the chapel. In 1603 this was enlarged by the addition of the adjoining cell; in 1698 the whole place was redecorated with wooden panelling and baroque draperies. Though these last are at variance with St. Francis's own austerity, the little chapel is imbued with that indefinable spirit of peace and tranquillity which seems to be inseparable from any place in which he lived. On either side of St. Francis are two portraits of famous members of his order—St. Anthony of Padua and St. Louis of Toulouse. As the golden fleur-de-lis of the background of this last picture indicate, this saintly bishop was a member of the French royal family. The son of Charles II, the Angevin King of Naples, and nephew of St. Louis, he died in Rome at the age of 23 in 1277 and was canonised in 1317.

Emerging from S. Francesco a Ripa, we take the Via Anicia, named after that famous medieval Roman family from which both Gregory the Great and St. Benedict are supposed to have sprung. We pass the church of **S. Maria dell' Orto**, built in 1566; the fine façade is crowned with obelisks. A little farther along on the left of the Via Anicia we see a brown door (No. 12) with a plaque indicating that it belongs to the Pia Società di S. Giovanni Battista dei Genovesi. This is the entrance to the famous cloister (ring the bell for the *guardiano*) designed by Baccio Pontelli for the Genoese sailors' hospice. It is without doubt the finest fifteenth-century cloister in Rome. Stately octagonal columns support the double loggias surrounding it; in the centre stands an old well almost concealed by cascading jasmine. Here for once the beauty of superb architecture is enhanced by a well-kept garden, filled with orange trees, sweet-smelling herbs and flowers. Evidently this garden has long been cherished; a Latin inscription on the fifth column to the right of the door records the fact that the first palm tree to be grown in Rome in modern times was planted here in 1588 by Antonio Lanza of Savona.

Turning right down the Via dei Genovesi, we turn right again into the narrow little Via di S. Cecilia; which brings us to the piazza of the same name in front of the church of **S.**

Cecilia in Trastevere. Traditionally this very ancient titular church is said to have been founded by Pope St. Urban I (222–30) over the house where St. Cecilia lived with her husband St. Valerianus; here also she is said to have undergone the first stage of her martyrdom, by attempted suffocation in the *sudatorium* of the baths. As we have seen in the chapter on the catacombs, it is now more generally believed that St. Cecilia's martyrdom should be dated to the persecutions of Diocletian in 303. Unfortunately restoration of the crypt (which was undertaken at the end of the last century and the beginning of this) has rendered archaeological examination of the early church and the Roman house beneath it more than ordinarily difficult. However, the ruins of classical buildings—including baths—are still visible under the whole area.

The existing church was built by Paschal I (817–24) but has been much altered. Originally it had galleries like those of S. Lorenzo and S. Agnese fuori le Mura, which were erected over the tombs of their titular saints. Possibly the fact that Paschal I rediscovered St. Cecilia's body and brought it to be buried here (together with those of St. Valerianus, St. Tiburtius and St. Urban) caused him to imitate these ancient basilicas.

When Cardinal Sfondrati, titular of the church, had St. Cecilia's tomb opened in 1599, her body was found lying on its side, wrapped in a golden robe; on her neck were the wounds made by the three blows of the executioner's sword, which had also failed to kill her. Clement VIII came to see the body and Stefano Maderno made a drawing of it from which he afterwards executed the beautiful statue that lies beneath the altar. St. Cecilia came of a patrician family and married into one—her husband is believed to have been a member of the ancient Valerii family. This would account for the first attempt to have her quietly done away with, by suffocation in the baths of her own house, like Constantine's guilty wife, Fausta; also that she was apparently eventually executed there, on 22 November, which is celebrated as her feast day.

A beautiful enclosed garden lies before the church; in the middle is a huge classical marble vase, employed as the centrepiece of a fountain, just as it may once have adorned the peristyle of the domus of the Valerii. Yellow jasmine and the sky-blue flowers of plumbago, growing in old raised beds, cover the garden walls; children play round beds of lilies and clipped bays, while their mothers sit gossiping round the fountain. Suitably in such a Roman setting, the church of S. Cecilia itself is a perfect architectural palimpsest. The façade was added by Fuga in the eighteenth century. It rises above a medieval portico with antique columns; the mosaics of the architrave date from the twelfth century, as does the towering campanile. Within the portico is Cardinal Sfondrati's fine tomb designed by Stefano Maderno.

As usual, Augustus Hare did not take kindly to architectural palimpsests, his acid comment upon the interior of the church was that 'it was miserably modernised in 1725'. Apparently in order further to strengthen the building, its ancient columns were encased in piers in 1823. However, the result is that of a not unpleasing church of the eighteenth century, with a fresco of the 'Apotheosis of S. Cecilia', by Sebastiano Conca, in the centre of the ceiling. Still, remembering that the wall above the door was once covered with a fresco of the Last Judgment by Cavallini, and that traces of further decoration by his pupils have been found on the walls of the nave, one is inclined to agree with Augustus Hare and bitterly to regret the good intentions of the eighteenth-century renovators. Fragments of Cavallini's fresco were discovered in 1900, behind the stalls and panelling of a gallery above the door; this is used by the nuns of the adjoining convent which is an enclosed order. It is possible to enter the gallery between 10 and 11 a.m. on Tuesday and Thursday mornings. It is worth every effort to get even a hurried glimpse of the fresco, as it is unique—the only major relic of Cavallini's painting in existence—and of extraordinary beauty. In the centre Christ sits enthroned in a mandorla, surrounded by angels in richly jewelled Byzantine robes, whose fluttering wings range in colour from delicate shades of cream and amber, through gradations of pink and rose to deepest crimson. Above them, sitting in solemn majesty, are the Apostles and saints, predominantly robed in tones of grey and blue. There is a power and richness in the whole composition that astonishes us, especially when we consider that it was executed as early as 1293.

Fortunately other remains of the old church still survive. On the right of the door is the fine tomb of Adam Easton, titular cardinal of the church, who died in 1398; curiously, the royal arms of the Plantagenets appear on the tomb. On the left of the door is an even more beautiful tomb, that of Cardinal Forteguerri, who died in 1473, by Mino da Fiesole; this was at one time dismantled but was reconstructed in its present position in 1891. Passing the first chapel on the right, we enter a narrow passage, charmingly decorated with landscapes by Pomarancio and Paul Brill. It brings us to what is traditionally said to have been the *sudatorium* or *calidarium* of the baths where St. Cecilia was immured for three days during the attempt to kill her by suffocation. Fragments of ancient terracotta pipes, of the type employed by the Romans in their baths, are to be seen lining the walls; above the altar is Guido Reni's picture of the saint's decapitation.

Returning to the church we see through a grille on the right the chapel of the Ponziani family, to which S. Francesca Romana's husband belonged. This has been restored quite recently, when the frescoes of the school of Pinturicchio were discovered on the vault and others attributed to Antonio da Viterbo on the walls. There follows the chapel of the Relics, designed by Vanvitelli; this can also be seen through a grille from the aisle or entered by a door farther along on the right by a 'Madonna and Child' by Perugino. At the end of the aisle is a fresco of the twelfth or thirteenth century representing Paschal's discovery of the body of St. Cecilia.

Above the main altar stands Arnolfo di Cambio's superb canopy, dating from 1283; beneath it lies Stefano Maderno's infinitely beautiful and touching statue of St. Cecilia. In the apse behind the altar is Paschal's ninth-century mosaic, in which he had himself represented as being presented to Christ in heaven by St. Cecilia herself; he is seen on the left bearing a model of his church, the other figures are SS. Peter, Paul, Agatha and Valerian. We must now find the custodian to accompany us if we wish to descend into the crypt and see the classical ruins below it. As the crypt was completely redecorated in what has been described as a 'sumptuous Byzantine style' in 1899–1901, if time presses we would probably be wise to continue with our itinerary.

Emerging from S. Cecilia, we make for the Piazza dei Mercanti opposite; on the left corner is a charming medieval house, recently restored. The name of the piazza is a reminder of the days when the Ripa Grande—the main river port of

Rome—maintained Trastevere's ancient connection with the sea. The little Via del Porto at the far end affords us a delightful glimpse of the Aventine across the river. Leaving the piazza we turn down the narrow Vicolo di S. Maria in Cappella, on the left.

The Vicolo takes its name from the charming little Romanesque church of **S. Maria in Cappella**, at the far end on the right. This was dedicated in 1090 and was then known as S. Maria ad Pineam. The miniature campanile is among the oldest in Rome. In the fifteenth century the church was attached to a hospice founded by S. Francesca Romana's father-in-law. Subsequently the site passed through many hands until, in the seventeenth century, it came into the possession of Donna Olimpia Pamphilj, Innocent X's sister-in-law, who made a riverside pleasure-garden beside the old church. Two hundred years later her descendants built a hospice for the aged poor, enclosing the old garden in its midst. This still exists and is a typically picturesque corner of old Trastevere, with neat vegetable plots surrounded by potted orange and lemon trees, oleanders, plumbago and old-fashioned flowers (no one seems to mind if one walks in to take a look).

In front of the church of S. Maria in Cappella we now turn down the Vicolo di Augusto Jandolo and find ourselves back in the Via dei Genovesi. From here we turn right into a *vicolo*, diminutive even for Trastevere, called dell' Atleta. The name records the discovery here in 1849 of the famous 'Apoxyomenos', an athlete using a strigil, copied from an original of Lysippus—which is now one of the treasures of the Vatican Museum. On the left of the *vicolo* is a fine fortified medieval house.

The Vicolo dell' Atleta ends in the Via dei Salumi, called after the warehouses where the sausage-makers stored their *salumi*, sausages of the salami or Bologna type. Two other *vicoli* lead out of this street right in front of us, that on the left has no name, but looking down it we catch a glimpse of the charming old **Piazza in Piscinula**. This takes its name from the ruins of some classical baths, which probably still exist under the uneven surface of the square. The baths are said to have belonged to the family of the Anici; in the late Middle Ages St. Benedict was believed to have been a scion of this noble house (in actual fact he was the son of a modest farmer of

Norcia) but the tiny church of S. Benedetto in Piscinula, on the left, perpetuates the legend.

The façade of the church dates from the seventeenth or eighteenth century but, as usual, the campanile betrays a very much earlier origin. This is surely the smallest and one of the most charming in Rome. To see inside the church, we ring the bell of the convent door on the right. This is usually answered by a very endearing old nun, who leads one through a tiny vestibule to see a little chapel, said to have been the cell in which St. Benedict himself lived. This has a vaulted ceiling supported by antique columns in the corners, and a cosmatesque pavement. The charming old church is built on the basilica plan, with ancient columns dividing its tiny nave and aisles. Behind the altar is a fourteenth-century painting of St. Benedict enthroned; on the altar itself is an early fifteenth-century Venetian Madonna and Child, with saints (a small offering should be made).

On the opposite side of the piazza rises the picturesque Casa dei Mattei. Though basically medieval with some attractive fourteenth-century windows, the house also has loggias and crossed-mullioned windows of the following century; it was restored quite recently, after having been used as an inn of the poorest type, suitably called The Spendthrift. The building was, however, the original home of the Mattei, before they moved across the river to the magnificent palaces beside the Fountain of the Tortoises. Possibly the reason why the family finally abandoned their ancestral home for ever is to be found in an appalling series of murders, terminating in a homicidal brawl which occurred there in 1555.

From the far end of the Piazza in Piscinula we now turn left, away from the river, up a steep incline which probably covers the ruins of some classical mansion. Before us looms another medieval house, with an arch, beneath which the street passes, taking from it the name of **Via dell' Arco dei Tolomei**. The house is now an orphanage, but once it was the home of the famous Sienese family that boasted of its descent from the Ptolemies of Egypt and did indeed come to Italy with Charlemagne. Its most notable member, who lived in Rome during the sixteenth century, was Claudio, a poet and epigrammatist; he belonged to the same famous humanist circles as Castiglione, Navaghero and Trissino.

Under the Arco dei Tolomei there is a rare survival of the

old abbreviated form of that institution to which Vespasian unwittingly gave his name. According to Suetonius's account, the emperor would have been the first to regret the disappearance of the *Vespasiani*, as the reason why they are called after him is that he derived a considerable income from this unexpected source. Again, according to Suetonius, this first of the Flavians was very attached to money. Suetonius's story casts an amusing light on the characters of both the emperor and his son, Titus. Apparently Titus complained to his father about the tax which he had placed on the sale of the contents of the city's urinals (this was used for fulling woollen cloth). Vespasian handed his son a coin, which had been part of the first day's takings, and asked him if it smelt. 'No, Father,' came the surprised reply, 'That's odd,' said the emperor, 'it comes straight from the urinal.'

After the Arco dei Tolomei, we turn right up the Via dei Salumi, cross the Via della Luce and continue along the picturesque Vicolo del Buco. This winds past a medieval house, round the Romanesque apse of the little church of S. Salvatore de Curte, the last part of whose name was for long a mystery, whose elucidation we will shortly find. This brings us to the Piazza del Drago and the Vicolo Zanazzo—named after yet another Roman dialect poet. Where these two streets meet in the tiny Via di Monte Fiore we see a high blank wall. This conceals the **Coorte dei Vigili** or the barracks of the seventh cohort of the ancient Roman fire brigade. The ruins were discovered only in 1866, but evidently the memory of their existence had been perpetuated in the otherwise inexplicable name of the neighbouring church of S. Salvatore de Curte. The walls of the barracks are covered with curious pictures and graffiti; many of these last include the words *sebaciaria fecit*, an allusion to the illuminations for public festivals with *fiaccole* (metal bowls of grease with a wick, such as are still used today), which was apparently included among the firemen's duties.

The barracks are close to Piazza Belli where we began our morning's walk; they date from the reign of Augustus, Ovid's contemporary. So, in more ways than one, we have returned to our point of departure; for in conservative Trastevere—that stronghold of popular custom and tradition—the procession for the modern festival of *Noiantri* starts from just near here. As it goes on its way beneath festive arches blazing with electric light, accompanied by the blare of the band and the shouts of the populace, one cannot help but wonder if the ghosts of those ancient Roman *vigiles* of the seventh cohort mix with the throng—they would probably feel very much at home there.

CHAPTER TWENTY-FOUR

The Vatican Palace and Museum

❧

THE **Vatican Museum** (opening hours p. 564) contains the largest collection of antique art in the world. In addition there is the Museo Sacro, illustrating the evolution of Christian usage of the applied arts from the paleo-Christian period to the eighteenth century, also a notable Pinacoteca or picture gallery; to these will shortly be added the former Lateran collections of Sacred and Profane Art, also the Ethnological Missionary Museum. It is, of course by the way of the Vatican Museum that we gain entrance to those parts of the Vatican Palace which are open to the public; these include the Sistine Chapel, the Borgia Apartment, the Raphael Stanze and Loggie, the chapel of Nicholas V and part of the famous library. (Research students wishing to work in the library enter by the Porta S. Anna in the Via di Porta Angelica; they must bring written credentials.)

In terms of the importance of the collections, the number of the exhibits and the area required to house them, the Vatican Museum is a formidable sight to tackle. If our enjoyment is not to be impaired by mental indigestion and physical exhaustion we would be wise to divide our exploration of it between two visits at least. The first (to be made preferably on a Monday morning, when the Italian state museums are closed) should include what might be called the more intimate or palace aspect—the Sistine Chapel, the Borgia Apartment, the Raphael Stanze and Loggie, the Museo di Arte Sacra and the library, all of which are grouped close together and serve as an opportune reminder that the Vatican Museum is the oldest regal art collection in Europe—the Pope's example being later followed by other sovereigns. The itinerary should then be completed by a visit to the Pinacoteca, where many of the finest works are coeval in period with the parts of the palace which we have just seen. This itinerary will serve as an excellent introduction to our afternoon's visit to St. Peter's, as the history of the palace and the basilica, and the person-

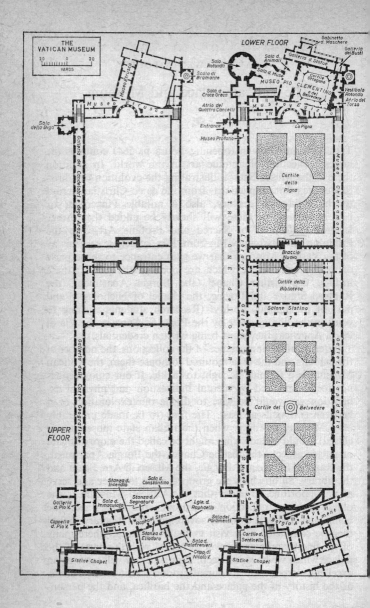

THE VATICAN MUSEUM

20   0   20
YARDS

LOWER FLOOR

Gabinetto d. Maschere
Galleria d. Statue
Galleria dei Busti
Sala Rotonda
Scala di Bramante
Sala d. Animali
Sala d. Muse
MUSEO PIO
Cortile Ottagono
CLEMENTINO
o. del Belvedere
Vestibolo Rotondo
Atrio del Torso
Sala a Croce Greca
Atrio del Quattro Cancelli
MUSEO EGIZIO
Entrance
La Pigna
Museo Profano

Museo Etrusco
Museo Etrusco

Sala della Biga

Galleria dei Candelabri e degli Arazzi

Cortile della Pigna

STRADONE dei GIARDINI

Library Gallery
Museo Chiaramonti

Braccio Nuovo

Galleria delle Carte Geografiche

Cortile della Biblioteca

Satone Sistino
7

UPPER FLOOR

Cortile del Belvedere

Galleria Lapidaria

9

Museo Sacro

10
11
13

Stanza d. Incendio
Sala d. Constantino
Galleria d. Pio V.
Sala d. Immaculata
Stanza d. Segnatura
Lgie. d. Raphaello
Cappella d. Pio V.
Raphael Stanze
Stanza d. Eliodora
Sala d. Palafrenieri
Capp. di Nicolo V.
Sala dei Paramenti
Sala dei Paramenti
Sala d. Palafrenieri
Borgia Apartment
Cortile d. Sentinella

Sistine Chapel

Sistine Chapel

alities of popes and artists involved in their creation, are closely linked. The second visit should be exclusively devoted to the vast collections of antique art of the Vatican itself and, when the new museum is completed, of the Lateran as well. It would be advisable to time this second visit for a weekday, other than a Monday, as we can then go in the afternoon to see Castel S. Angelo (which is closed on Mondays) and the Borgo. However, for the convenience of those who may be able to make only one visit, the whole palace and museum will be dealt with in one chapter.

From the centre of Rome the best means of transport to the Vatican is the 64 bus, which starts at the Stazione Termini and stops in the Via Nazionale, Piazza Venezia, Largo di Torre Argentina and many other places *en route*. Its terminus is in the Piazza della Città Leonina, from where we follow the Vatican City walls (keeping them on our left) along the Via di Porta Angelica, Piazza del Risorgimento and Via Leone IV; turning left out of this last into the Viale del Vaticano, we find the imposing museum entrance a short way up on the left. Although opera glasses (which are very useful for studying details of the Sistine Chapel ceiling) may be taken into the museum, it is as well to remember that *cameras must be left behind in the cloak-room*; also that women should bring some sort of jacket or cardigan if they are wearing a sleeveless or very short-sleeved dress, as otherwise they may not be able to enter. For practical reasons this is also advisable, especially in spring and autumn when the vast museum rooms are of a much lower temperature than the sunny streets outside; in winter a warm coat is welcome.

As the Sistine Chapel is one of the principal sights in Italy, those who wish to see it in comparative peace, especially at Easter and during the crowded summer months, are advised to go straight to it on their arrival at 9 a.m. From the museum there are several ways of reaching it; the most usual is from the Sala dei Paramenti, to the left of the far end of the long library gallery and the Museo Sacro, on the lower floor of the museum. The chapel of Pius V, on the second floor at the far end of the Galleria dei Candelabri e degli Arazzi and the Galleria delle Carte Geografiche, is also sometimes used as an alternative. The museum authorities vary entrances in accordance with the number of visitors, so the best thing to do is to ask on your arrival which entrance is being used and make straight for it; the large conducted parties tend to arrive later in the day, generally having begun their itinerary with the museums.

If we are on our first visit to the Vatican, it is with some surprise that we emerge from the lift or the remarkable double circular ramps, which take the place of a staircase, to find ourselves in an open gallery facing on to a garden. But the buildings which now house the bulk of the Vatican collections are in fact the galleries that Bramante designed for Julius II (1503–13) to enclose the famous garden of the Cortile del Belvedere. Originally the Cortile della Pigna and the present Cortile del Belvedere, which we see on our left as we walk along the library gallery, were joined by stairs and ramps to form one great garden. The sculpture gallery of the Braccio Nuovo and Sixtus V's great library hall, known as the Salone Sistino, were unfortunately built over this central part of the garden, dividing it into two. All that now remains to remind us of what an English traveller, William Thomas, described in 1549 as 'the goodliest thing of this world' are the niche in the Cortile della Pigna, containing the great classical bronze pine-cone (whose discovery near S. Maria sopra Minerva gave its name to the whole quarter) and the semicircular steps at the far end of the Cortile del Belvedere. These last were designed for use as the auditorium of an outdoor theatre.

Firmly disregarding even the most enticing sights *en route*, a brisk walk of some ten minutes (it is about half a kilometre) from the museum entrance, brings us to the **Sistine Chapel**. More, probably, has been written about this great hall-like chapel than any other building in the world; but in fact no description, picture or photograph conveys the impact which it makes. Perhaps the first, and in the end the most lasting, impression that one carries away, is of the contrast between the golden-cream light and space and the exquisite feeling of harmony engendered by the ceiling as opposed to the deep blue darkness and turmoil of the 'Last Judgment'.

This impression in fact provides the key to the artistic history of the chapel. It was built for Sixtus IV (1473–84) by Giovannino de' Dolci, the walls were also decorated during his reign by the greatest artists of the period, including Botticelli, Ghirlandaio, Pinturicchio and Signorelli. The themes of the paintings were selected in accordance with the old medieval conception of the division of the world into three epochs—the first, before God gave the Law to Moses; the second that of the Law as given to Moses; the third, the period of grace, dating from the birth of Christ. The second and third of these epochs were represented in the fifteenth-century frescoes painted on the walls of the chapel, showing scenes from the life of Moses and Christ. When Julius II finally persuaded Michelangelo to paint the ceiling, he decided to complete the series, choosing as his theme the first epoch—before the Law—hence the famous portrayals of the Creation, the birth of Eve, the Fall and so on. Michelangelo painted the ceiling between 1508 and 1512, at the height of the Renaissance, in a world still filled with optimism and classical ideals of beauty; thus these frescoes are the culmination of all that had gone before in the creation of the chapel. In 1527 came the terrible sack of Rome, and with it the end of this aspect of the Renaissance world.

The 'Last Judgment' was the product of a totally different environment and the way of thought, especially in the mind of its creator. When Michelangelo began it twenty-two years had passed since he had finished the ceiling, only seven since the sack of Rome. To his contemporaries, and especially to him, the sack had seemed like the end of the world and a certain manifestation of the wrath of God. The reformation of the Church was the main aim of Paul III, who, immediately after his accession in 1534, confirmed Michelangelo's commission to paint the 'Last Judgment'. During the seven years in which he worked upon it, Michelangelo was also caught up in the movement for spiritual regeneration. Through the medium of his universal genius, the thoughts and aspirations of these two totally different worlds, and the spiritual travail that separated them, have set their seal upon the chapel.

It seems almost symbolic that the jewel-like *opus Alexandrinum* pavement of the Sistine Chapel should hark back to the medieval past of the Cosmati. While from this base, as it were, we follow almost a century's evolution of the work of Italy's greatest artists as our eyes travel up the walls to the ceiling, finally coming to rest upon the 'Last Judgment'. Ideally we should catch our first glimpse of this tremendous vision through the exquisite marble screen, sculptured by Mino da Fiesole, Andrea Bregno and Giovanni Dalmata. Here again it could be truthfully said that 'the classic Renaissance achieved its conscious aim to emulate classic Antiquity'; the

garlands might have been designed for Augustus's Ara Pacis—
Sixtus IV's arms reveal that it belongs to the fifteenth century.

All the warmth, the humanity, the love of intimate personal
detail and allusions to current events and personalities characteristic of early Italian Renaissance painting appear in the
scenes of the lives of Christ and Moses frescoed on the two
side walls. These characteristics are particularly noticeable in
the series illustrating the life of Moses. The panel representing
Pharaoh being drowned in the Red Sea in fact alludes to the
papal victory at Campomorto in 1482 and includes portraits
of Roberto Malatesta, Virginio Orsini and the pope's nephew
Girolamo Riario. In the same way the 'Punishment of Korah,
Dathan and Abiram' is portrayed against a background of
contemporary Rome, showing the Arch of Constantine and
the ruins of Septizonium. The panels on this wall are as
follows: Moses and his wife in Egypt; the circumcision of
their son, by Pinturicchio and his pupils; the burning bush,
with Moses killing the Egyptian and driving the Midianites
from the well, also the daughters of Jethro, by Botticelli;
Pharaoh drowned in the Red Sea, attributed to Cosimo Rosselli
or Domenico or Benedetto Ghirlandaio; Moses on Sinai and
the worship of the golden calf by Cosimo Rosselli; the punishment of Korah, Dathan and Abiram, by Botticelli; Moses
giving the rod to Joshua and the death of Moses, by Luca
Signorelli and Bartolomeo della Gatta.

The scenes from the life of Christ on the opposite wall begin
with his Baptism, by Pinturicchio or Perugino; there follow the
Temptation, by Botticelli (in this last the artist has portrayed
the façade of the Hospital of S. Spirito); the Calling of SS.
Peter and Andrew, by Domenico del Ghirlandaio; the Sermon
on the Mount, by Cosimo Rosselli and Piero di Cosimo; the
Donation of the Keys, by Perugino (the fifth figure on the right
is a self-portrait); the Last Supper, by Cosimo Rosselli. On
the end wall (opposite the Last Judgment) Domenico del
Ghirlandaio's Resurrection and Francesco Salviati's S.
Michael protecting Moses' body were repainted at the end of
the sixteenth century by Arrigo Fiammingo and Matteo da
Lecce.

Originally the ceiling of the Sistine Chapel was simply
painted blue and covered with gold stars. The story of its
transformation into one of the most sublime artistic creations
of all time is largely that of the personal relationship between

two titanic figures of the Renaissance—Michelangelo and Julius II, whom two great historians, Gregorovius and Burckhardt, described as 'the greatest Pope since Innocent III' and as 'the saviour of the Papacy'. Burckhardt's summing up of this relationship could scarcely be bettered. He wrote: 'Probably the alternations of merciless pressure and unmeasured vituperation with the frankest indulgence and kindness which characterised the relations between Julius and Michelangelo were the means of obtaining more from him than any other treatment would have done'.

His admiration of Michelangelo's 'Pietà' (now in St. Peter's) caused Julius to summon its author to Rome in 1505 to design his tomb. Michelangelo spent six months in Carrara selecting the marble for the sculptures and set up a studio in Rome only to find that the pope had changed his mind, becoming more interested in the rebuilding of St. Peter's; he wished Michelangelo to paint the ceiling of the Sistine Chapel. After several attempts to see Julius, in order to come to some settlement, especially for the quantities of marble he had ordered, Michelangelo fled in a rage to his native Tuscany because a mere lackey had turned him out of the Vatican. Couriers were sent to fetch him back, but neither these nor the pope's letters, nor the admonitions of the Florentine authorities succeeded in getting Michelangelo to return. It was only after Julius II's conquest of Bologna, in 1506, that Michelangelo was made to go there by the Gonfaloniere Soderini; he said later: 'I was forced to go with a halter round my neck'.

Soderini tried to soften the blow by giving Michelangelo a letter of introduction to his Cardinal brother at the papal court. It is a revealing document, both his summing up of Michelangelo's character and his future. Soderini wrote: 'The bearer of these presents will be Michelangelo the sculptor, whom we send to please and satisfy His Holiness. We certify that he is an excellent young man, and in his own art without peer in Italy, perhaps even in the universe. It would be impossible to recommend him more highly. His nature is such that he requires to be drawn out by kindness and encouragement; but if love is shown him and he is well treated, he will accomplish things which will make the whole world wonder.'

Michelangelo was 31 at the time of this momentous encounter with Julius. At first things did not go well, the pope receiving the sculptor's lame apologies with hauteur. But when Cardinal Soderini started to make excuses, on the lines that artists like Michelangelo had never been taught manners, Julius rounded on him in a fury, saying: 'You venture to say what I would never have dreamed of saying, get out of my sight you miserable ignorant clown'. Michelangelo was pardoned and commissioned to make a gigantic bronze statue of the pope for the church of S. Petronio in Bologna; not a welcome task for one whose medium was marble, it took him sixteen months.

Barely was this work completed, in March 1508, when the summons from Rome arrived to paint the ceiling of the Sistine Chapel. Bramante's jealousy was probably behind this astonishing idea of the pope's of commissioning a sculptor to execute this tremendous work in fresco. It is said that Bramante, who was a bitter rival of Michelangelo's instigated it in the belief that he would either refuse—because he had little or no experience in this branch of art—or would accept and make a failure of it. Michelangelo, whose heart was still set upon making Julius's monumental tomb, did indeed do all he could to evade the commission; then, seeing that the pope was adamant, he accepted. Astonishingly—but when was Michelangelo not astonishing—he proposed doing far more even than Julius asked. Instead of contenting himself with fulfilling the original plan of painting the twelve Apostles in the lunettes and covering the ceiling with a decorative design, Michelangelo proposed painting the whole ceiling. The pope gave his willing assent.

Possibly at this stage even Michelangelo became alarmed at his own temerity. Without experience he had taken on the greatest work of fresco the world had ever seen, in a chapel already decorated by masters of this art, with his rival waiting hopefully for his downfall. Prudence, and the custom of the day, indicated that he should call in assistants. Seven answered his summons, but after a short trial he sacked the lot; locking the door of the Sistine Chapel, he started on his Herculean task alone.

This was in the summer of 1508. At the end of the year Raphael, Bramante's protégé, began to paint Julius's private apartment—the *stanze*—only a few yards away across the Cortile Borgia. For years these rivals, so diametrically opposed in their art and in their characters, worked almost side by side; each must have had the other constantly in mind, each strove to his utmost and each produced a masterpiece. It was impossible that they should not sometimes meet. It is said that once when passing Raphael, surrounded by his helpers, Michelangelo called out: 'Where are you going, surrounded like a provost?' calling forth the retort: 'And you, solitary like an executioner?' Nevertheless, modern art critics consider that Raphael paid the lonely giant the 'sincerest form of flattery' by introducing a single figure painted in his style (possibly even a portrait of Michelangelo) into the centre of his 'School of Athens'; also that the ceiling of the Sistine Chapel had a great influence upon Raphael's subsequent work. The story goes that Bramante, who also had a key to the chapel, took Raphael to see the half-finished frescoes in the summer of 1511 and that Raphael tried to get the commission to finish them.

His biographer, Condivi, said that Michelangelo complained bitterly to Julius II of the wrongs done to him by Bramante and Raphael and that Julius told him to go on with his work undisturbed, and showed him special favour. Certainly in 1511 Michelangelo went to see the pope, who was campaigning near Bologna, but the most pressing reason was probably his lack of money. The financial drain of Julius's wars resulted in Michelangelo's never getting paid. During the following winter he wrote to his brother: 'I tell you I have not got a *grosso* (a Tuscan coin worth threepence), I could well say that I go naked and barefoot; nor can I get paid the rest of my fee until I have finished my work.'

'When will you finish?' was in fact the pope's constant refrain. In his impatience Julius took no account of the almost superhuman task which this one man had undertaken—more than 10,000 square feet to be painted by a single hand. For months Michelangelo lay on his back on the scaffolding, with paint dripping on to his face and into his eyes. The strain on his physique was such that for long he could not read a letter unless he held it above him, tilting his head backwards. Still, this extraordinary man could laugh, somewhat bitterly, at his hardships, writing satirical verses describing the effects of the appalling discomfort upon himself and his art.

But when Julius came to see Michelangelo in the winter of 1509–10, climbing up the highest ladder, where Michelangelo had to give him a hand, he seemed completely to disregard the difficulties; all he could ask was: 'When will you finish?'

'When I can,' came the terse reply. In 1511 Julius was back with the same question. Though his own fortunes were then at so low an ebb that he had to pledge the papal diadem to Agostino Chigi for ready cash, Julius could not resist having half the scaffolding taken down to see what had been finished. Finally, in the autumn of 1512, when his usual question brought the usual reply, the pope turned in fury upon Michelangelo saying: 'Do you want me to have you thrown down from the scaffolding?' Probably it was only a threat but, knowing his patron's temper, Michelangelo had the scaffolding taken down although he had not completed the finishing touches of gold and ultramarine. The pope noticed this and said that the figures would look poor, to which Michelangelo replied: 'Those who are painted here were *also* poor.' It was a spirit that Julius could appreciate; indeed Michelangelo had grounds—for more than four years of anguished creation, for months of unremitting toil and hardship, the greatest artistic genius of the modern world was paid 3000 ducats. Centuries later another genius, Goethe, said that no one who had not seen the Sistine Chapel can have a complete conception of what a single man can accomplish. But its creator saw things in a different light. Humbly he signed his work, not with his own name, but with an inscription ascribing the honour of its completion to God, the alpha and omega, through whose assistance it had been begun and ended. (This was either unknown or forgotten for centuries; it is beside the figure of the Prophet Jeremiah, who is clothed in sackcloth.)

Beginning from the altar, Michelangelo's series of great compositions in the centre of the vault represent: the Separation of Light and Darkness, the Creation of the Sun and Moon, the Creation of Trees and Plants, the Creation of Adam, the Creation of Eve, the Fall and Expulsion from Paradise, the Sacrifice of Noah, the Flood and the Intoxication of Noah. Jonah is represented on the spandrel above the altar; Zechariah on that at the other end of the chapel. On the spandrels above the side walls, prophets and sibyls alternate; on the left (beginning from the altar end) are Jeremiah, the Persian Sibyl, Ezekiel, the Eritrean Sibyl and Joel. On the right wall (beginning from the altar end) are the Libyan Sibyl, Daniel, the Cumean Sibyl, Isaiah and the Delphic Sibyl.

On *trompe l'oeil* plinths, situated above and on either side of the prophets and sibyls, are the famous naked decorative figures known as the *ignudi* (these support triumphal garlands and painted bronze medallions). The joyous life and verve of this part of the composition bespeaks the Renaissance spirit, so much at variance with the sombre majesty of the Last Judgment. The triangular ressaults, in the corners of the chapel, are filled with scenes from the Old Testament. In those to the right and left of the altar are the Brazen serpent and Ahasuerus, Esther and Haman. At the other end of the chapel, Judith and Holofernes (on the right) and David and Goliath (on the left). In the lunettes and ressaults above the windows on the side walls are portrayed family groups representing the genealogy of the Virgin.

If the ceiling of the Sistine Chapel at once elicited a universal chorus of praise, echoed continually down the centuries, this was definitely not the case with the **Last Judgment.** Even before its official inauguration in 1541, this gigantic composition divided public opinion into opposing camps—those who saw in it a supreme masterpiece and those who regarded it as offensive to religious feeling. Needless to say connoisseurs of art—such as the Farnese Pope, Paul III, during whose reign it was painted—have always recognised its greatness (so curiously enough did Fynes Moryson who saw it in 1594); but among lesser spirits it has even aroused violent antagonisms. The incident related of Paul III and his master of ceremonies, Biagio da Cesena—which occurred when the fresco was not yet finished—admirably illustrates these two attitudes. Biagio criticised the nude figures as being indecent; Michelangelo retaliated by introducing his portrait into the composition (it is in the extreme bottom right-hand corner). With ass's ears and a serpent coiled round his loins, Biagio is portrayed as Minos—the cruel judge of souls in hell. The unfortunate man begged the pope to command the removal of the portrait, but Paul replied: 'I might have released you from purgatory, but over hell I have no power.' His further unspoken comment upon other detractors was to commission Michelangelo to paint the nearby Pauline Chapel.

Paul III's successors were not so appreciative; Paul IV, the Carafa Pope of the Inquisition (1555–9), called the Last Judgment a 'stew of nudes' (in the pejorative Renaissance sense of the word stew meaning a public bath). During Pius IV's reign, in 1564, orders were given for breeches or loincloths to be painted over some of the figures; Daniele da

Volterra, who carried out the order, was known ever after as *il braghettone* (the breeches-maker). More artistic bowdlers were employed by Gregory XIII (1572–85) and Clement VIII (1592–1605); this last pope wanted to have the whole fresco whitewashed. Apart from the nudes, the painting was criticised because Christ was portrayed (as in paleo-Christian art) without a beard and as a young man. One observer even saw heresy in the fact that, while the figure of St. Bartholomew (to the right of Christ when looking at the picture) was portrayed with a beard, none appears on his own flayed skin which he is holding. The terrible and tragic face represented on the skin is, in fact, Michelangelo's self-portrait; the convulsed features reflect the spiritual crisis through which he was passing owing to the world tragedy as he saw it and his contemporaries' lack of comprehension.

The head of St. Bartholomew is in fact a portrait of Pietro Aretino. Why Michelangelo should have seen fit to represent a saint and martyr with the head of the brilliant but licentious satirist is a mystery which has exercised many minds. Aretino's and Biagio da Cesena's are not the only portraits among the hundreds of figures which throng the Last Judgment. Dante and Savonarola are represented, also Julius II, Clement VII and Paul III. As well as his enemies and these great historical figures, Michelangelo included portraits of three of his friends: Tommaso de' Cavalieri, his faithful servant Urbino and, surprisingly, a woman—Vittoria Colonna. Michelangelo was more than 63 when he met Vittoria, and later he mourned her death with the words '*morte me tolse uno grande amico*' using the masculine form of the word (*amico*) for the friend whom death had carried away, as if this woman of remarkable intellect had been a man (and not the last love some romantic novelists would prefer). When Michelangelo first met Vittoria Colonna he had already begun the Last Judgment and they saw much of each other while he was working on it. Sharing as they did deep religious convictions and a passionate desire for church reform, it is not surprising that Michelangelo should have included Vittoria's likeness in this great work that expressed so much of his own religious feeling.

Here in the Last Judgment it is the *terribilità* (terribleness) that so impressed his contemporaries which dominates Michelangelo's art to the exclusion of all else. He has portrayed the *dies irae*—the day of wrath—with Christ as the inexorable judge standing on the clouds. The only note of tenderness is the Virgin's figure; the Apostles and prophets, ranged on either side, are portrayed with elemental force. In the centre of the composition angels sound the last trumpet to wake the dead, who are pictured in the left-hand corner; more angels raise those among them who are to be saved. On the other side of the picture, damned souls descend in chaos to Charon, waiting with his fateful barque to ferry them to Minos and the underworld. It is a scene of tragic grandeur, once beheld never to be forgotten.

It is of course in the Sistine Chapel that the cardinals meet in conclave for the election of each new pope. Their canopied thrones are ranged along the walls while the voting continues —the voting papers being placed on a chalice. After each scrutiny the papers are threaded on a silk cord and burnt in an iron stove which stands by the wall at the far end of the chapel. Until the two-thirds majority required to elect a pope is reached, voting papers from each ballot are burnt with damp straw, thus producing black smoke, visible to the crowds waiting in the Piazza of St. Peter's, warning them that so far no pope has been elected. Finally, when the two-thirds majority has been reached, the canopies over the thrones of all but the newly-elected pope are lowered. Dry straw is then mixed with the ballot papers, making the white smoke that announces to the world the election of the new pope (after the election of John XXIII, the majority of the two-thirds plus one vote, which had previously been required, was changed to the simple two-thirds). During the conclave a whole area of the Vatican Palace surrounding the Sistine Chapel is walled off, and living accommodation for the cardinals kitchens, etc., are arranged in the neighbouring rooms.

If we emerge from the Sistine Chapel into the Sala dei Paramenti, the **Borgia Apartment** is reached by taking the other door on the same side of the Sala and crossing the adjoining small room. The Borgia Apartment should in any case be the next sight on our itinerary as, apart from the chapel of Nicholas V, its decoration dates from an earlier period than the other rooms we shall see. In fact the whole area of the Vatican Palace, except for the Borgia tower, was built or reconstructed by Nicholas V (1447–55) as part of the great extensions he planned for both the palace and St. Peter's. After his accession in 1492, the second Borgia Pope, Alexander

VI, had this suite of six rooms on the first floor of the palace decorated by Pinturicchio and his assistants; the work was finished in 1495. This was the private papal apartment also used by Julius II, before the completion of the *stanze* which he commissioned Raphael to decorate on the floor above.

Except for the last room, the Borgia Apartment seems surprisingly small for a sovereign's dwelling; but in fact this was customary at that time. Most of the rooms actually lived in by Renaissance potentates in Italy—like those of the doges in their vast palace in Venice or the personal apartments in the ducal palaces of Mantua and Urbino—are remarkably small. Possibly because of this, the Borgia Apartment does not have that museum atmosphere common to most historic places constantly open to the public. This strange feeling of intimacy is probably due even more to little details, like the gaming boards—for Three Men's Morris and so on, that someone has scratched into the stone window-seats of two of the rooms. The painted decoration too incorporates so many of the Borgia family badges that the whole apartment has been described as 'a store-house of heraldry'. These badges are not great official coats-of-arms, but personal or family insignia, much favoured during the Renaissance. Constantly recurring among them are the double crown of Aragon—a reminder that Calixtus III, Alexander VI's uncle, originally came to Italy as secretary to Alfonso of Aragon—and the Borgias' own wavy pennant-like flames or garbs. These badges seem to set the seal on the Borgia possession of the rooms, particularly the third one which was Alexander's study, where his treasure was discovered after his death. Heightening even further this uncanny impression of rooms still tenanted from long ago are the portraits of Alexander and his children, incorporated by Pinturicchio among the allegorical and biblical figures which throng the frescoed decoration.

The frescoes themselves give a particular character to the apartment; the liberal use of gold and the jewelled enrichments recall the pages of an illuminated manuscript, reminding one of the medieval world that was not so far removed from the fifteenth century. The first two rooms are more austere; they take their names of Sala delle Sibille and del Credo from the Sibyls and the Apostles bearing scrolls upon which they were believed to have composed the Creed before they separated to go about their mission of converting the world.

The third room, known as the Sala delle Scienze e delle Arti Liberali, which was largely the work of Pinturicchio's pupil Antonio da Viterbo, is immensely rich. This, one feels, probably reflects as much the personal taste of the patron as that of the artist, as it was Alexander VI's study.

The Sala dei Santi, the fourth room, is even more richly decorated with frescoes, which are considered to be Pinturicchio's major work. On the ceiling the heraldic Borgia bull and the double crown are constantly repeated in the decorative borders of pictures representing the myths of Isis, Osiris and the Egyptian bull-god Apis; this last being, of course, yet another reference to the family arms. The Egyptian theme is continued in the frescoes representing the lives of saints, from which the room takes its name. Two of the major compositions illustrate St. Anthony and St. Paul the Hermit in the Egyptian desert; also St. Catherine of Alexandria disputing with the philosophers before the Emperor Maximian. In this last picture there are several contemporary portraits; the central figure of St. Catherine—a beautiful young girl with long fair hair—is believed to be Alexander VI's daughter, Lucrezia Borgia. The man in oriental dress standing by the emperor is Andrew Palaeologos, on the extreme left Pinturicchio has included his own self-portrait, while on the right of the picture the mounted Oriental is the unfortunate Prince Djem (brother of the Sultan Bayezid II) believed to have been poisoned later by the Borgias.

Of equal splendour is room V, the Sala dei Misteri della Fede, called after Pinturicchio's frescoes of the mysteries of the faith—the Annunciation, Nativity, Epiphany, Resurrection, Ascension, Pentecost and Assumption—which decorate the walls. In the picture of the Resurrection, Alexander VI is portrayed in profile, kneeling with his pearl-covered papal diadem beside him. It is a portrait of terrifying realism. The handsome young soldier standing near by is said to represent the infamous Cesare, and a young Roman the brother he murdered, the Duke of Gandia.

This Sala dei Misteri della Fede is the room which is believed to have been the Borgia Pope's dining-room; the mere thought conjures up some sinister visions. The adjoining room, the last and largest of the series, known as the Sala dei Pontifici, is now used as the cardinals' dining-room at the time of the papal elections. It was here, on 29 June 1500, that Alexander

VI narrowly escaped with his life when the ceiling collapsed; this was rebuilt for Leo X (1513–21) and decorated with stucco and frescoes by Giovanni da Udine and Perin del Vaga. On the walls are a fine series of Flemish sixteenth-century tapestries; one of the doors is a good modern copy of wooden *intarsio* work by Damiano da Bergamo. The room also contains some interesting bronzes and terracottas, including Bernini's model for the tomb of Alexander VII in St. Peter's.

Returning to the Sala delle Sibille, we find a small door on the left and some stairs leading to the Raphael Stanze on the second floor. On the way up we catch a picturesque glimpse of the Swiss Guard on duty in the Cortile della Sentinella—through which ambassadors pass when coming to present their credentials and to be received in audience by the pope. At the top of the stairs is the little private chapel of Urban VIII.

The Raphael Stanze consist of only four rooms, situated immediately above the inner part of the Borgia Apartment. The two central ones—the Stanza della Segnatura and the Stanza di Eliodoro, which are considered to contain Raphael's greatest work—were respectively the pope's private library or study and his bedroom. It is said that Julius II's dislike of living in the Borgia Apartment, with its decoration that was a constant reminder of an unloved predecessor, prompted his decision to have these rooms on what was then the top storey of Nicholas VI's building, redecorated for himself. Perugino, Baldassare Peruzzi, Sodoma and Lorenzo Lotto were then entrusted with completing the decoration, which had been begun in the previous century by Piero della Francesca, Signorelli, Bartolomeo della Gatta and Bramantino. A little of the work of some of the fifteenth-century artists, and of Sodoma's school, still survives on the ceilings of the Stanza della Segnatura and the Stanza di Eliodoro. But all the rest was swept away when, towards the end of 1508, Julius II decided to entrust the entire decoration of the rooms to Bramante's young compatriot from Urbino, Raffaello Sanzio, then barely twenty-six years old.

As Raphael began with the Stanza della Segnatura, we would be wise also to begin our exploration of the *stanze* there, passing through the first room—the Stanza dell' Incendio—to reach it. Unlike the other *stanze*, which take their names from their painted decoration, the Stanza della Segnatura is so called because the decrees of the ecclesiastical Court of the Segnatura were signed there by the pope. Thus the theme of the paintings, the famous 'Disputation of the Sacrament' and the 'School of Athens', have no relation whatsoever to the name of the room. This is in itself somewhat misleading, but what is even more so is the fact that 'Disputation of the Sacrament' is a misnomer based on an erroneous seventeenth-century interpretation of Vasari. In fact the great fresco really represents the Triumph of the Church or of Religious Faith and Truth; while the 'School of Athens', on the opposite wall, illustrates the Triumph of Scientific Truth.

This juxtaposition of works portraying a religious concept and a philosophical one, represented by classical learning, was typical of the Renaissance world; particularly of the neo-Platonism of Marsilio Ficino and of the court of Urbino, which Raphael had known in his youth. Briefly, the three themes illustrated in the paintings of the Stanza della Segnatura are Truth, Goodness and Beauty. On the walls, Truth is illustrated by the 'Disputation of the Sacrament' and the 'School of Athens'; on the corresponding sides of the ceiling the idea of Truth is personified by two female figures in roundels, representing Theology and Philosophy. On the wall, with the window facing towards the Cortile dei Pappagalli, Goodness is interpreted by a painting of the virtues, Fortitude, Prudence and Temperance. Justice is illustrated by Gregory IX delivering the Decretals to Raymond of Penafort and Justinian giving the Pandects to Trebonianus; she is also personified, in a roundel on the ceiling, holding a sword. Finally, Beauty is represented on the wall (with the window facing towards the Belvedere Court), by the famous painting of the Parnassus, and personified as Poetry in the adjoining roundel on the ceiling.

In the centre of the ceiling, the crossed keys of Nicholas V's arms are surrounded by dancing angels, attributed to Bramantino; the small historical and mythological paintings in the interstices of the roundels to the school of Sodoma. Of the rest of the ceiling decoration, three of the small rectangular allegorical scenes with *trompe l'oeil* gold mosaic backgrounds are believed to be by Raphael himself.

The 'Disputation of the Sacrament' was the first of the great frescoes executed by Raphael in the decoration of the *stanze*. It is divided into two parts by a cloudy barrier. In the upper one God the Father appears, surrounded by a glory of angels and cherubs, above Christ enthroned with the Virgin and St. John the Baptist on either side of him. Ranged in a semicircle round this central group are the figures of the elect, drawn from the Old and New Testaments; only those of the New Testament have haloes. Looking at the painting and proceeding from left to right, on the left-hand side are St. Peter, Adam, St. John the Evangelist, David, St. Stephen and Jeremiah. On the right-hand, reading from right to left, are St. Paul, Abraham, St. James (or possibly St. Matthew), Moses, St. Lawrence and St. George or Judas Maccabaeus.

Forming a link between this upper sphere and the lower part of the composition, representing the Church Militant, are the Dove of the Holy Spirit and four cherubs holding the Gospels, from which rays descend to an altar where the Blessed Sacrament is displayed in a monstrance. Grouped around the altar are the Latin fathers of the Church, popes, cardinals, bishops and theologians. Among the group on the left (looking at the picture) are St. Gregory the Great with a manuscript inscribed *L. Moralium*; next to him is St. Jerome with his lion and a volume of his letters. On the other side of the altar, St. Augustine is seen dictating to a secretary, with a copy of his *De Civitate Dei* at his feet. Near by are St. Ambrose, St. Thomas Aquinas and the Franciscan St. Bonaventura, canonised in 1482 by Julius II's uncle Sixtus IV. In fact, apart from idealised representations of great Church figures, the composition also includes portraits of historic and contemporary personages such as Dante and Sixtus IV (seen on the right), Fra Angelico (on the extreme left) and possibly Bramante (leaning over the balustrade). It is believed that the vast blocks of stone (evidently the beginnings of a monumental building, behind the group on the right of the picture) suggests Julius II's plan for the rebuilding of St. Peter's. This pope's name appears in the embroidery on the altar-cloth.

Although the composition of the 'Disputation of the Sacrament' has always been regarded as masterly, some individual figures and small details such as the use of plaster and gold leaf, and the names of saints appearing in their haloes, indicate that Raphael had not yet quite broken away from the influence of Perugino and the Tuscan school of the previous century. All trace of this has, however, vanished in the 'School of Athens' on the opposite wall; here the figures move freely in the halls of a great classical basilica, whose splendour gives us a foretaste of what the new St. Peter's was to be. According to Vasari, the architectural part of the design, which is based on a profound knowledge of classical monuments, Raphael owed to Bramante. The two central figures are Plato and Aristotle. Significantly, in view of the neo-Platonic inspiration of the room's decoration, Plato stands in the place of honour on the right, pointing to heaven with one hand, and holding his *Timaeus* in the other (some believe that the head is a portrait of Leonardo). Aristotle appears with his *Ethics* in one hand, gesturing, with the palm of the other turned downwards to the earth, signifying his more earthly and concrete philosophy.

Many of the figures can be recognised, both as representations of classical masters of philosophy and science, as well as portraits of contemporary personages. Particularly interesting is the group on the left (looking at the picture) in which Pythagoras is portrayed seated, reading a book. A youth beside him holds a tablet upon which Raphael has represented in an ingenious diagram the whole system of the Pythagorean harmonic scale. These figures are not far removed from that of Plato carrying his *Timaeus*, in which he described the harmony of the universe on the basis of Pythagoras's discovery of the ratios of musical consonances. Thus, even in what might appear to be small incidental details, the basic philosophical theme of the painting is carried on.

Recognisable in the same group—Epicurus, crowned with vine leaves; the small boy beside him is a portrait of Federico Gonzaga—at that time held a hostage by Julius II. Next comes the turbaned head of Averroes, the Moslem commentator of Aristotle; the tall fair youth in a white robe near by is sometimes identified as Julius's nephew, Francesco Maria Della Rovere. Strangely enough the identity, even as a classical philosopher, of the conspicuous figure holding a tablet and apparently talking to Pythagoras, has never been established. There is little doubt, however, that the pensive figure in contemporary dress, seated on the steps, is a portrait of Michelangelo, representing Heraclitus the pessimist. In view of Michelangelo's own character this personification is appropriate, though the figure did not appear in Raphael's original cartoon and was evidently an afterthought; significantly it is painted in Michelangelo's own style, possibly after Raphael had seen part of the ceiling of the Sistine Chapel in 1511.

The semi-recumbent figure, of Diogenes the cynic, links the two groups in the foreground. In that on the right, Euclid (really a portrait of Bramante) expounds a problem to his pupils. The inconspicuous gold letters R.U.S.M., on the neck-band of Euclid's tunic, are of particular interest; they represent the words *Raphael Urbinus Sua Manu*, in fact Raphael's signature. Behind Euclid stands Ptolemy the geographer, portrayed with a crown because he was believed to be related to the royal dynasty of Egypt. In his hand he holds a terrestrial globe, while Zoroaster the astronomer, beside him, holds a celestial one. Just to the right of these two figures is Raphael's self-portrait, beside that of an older man with a flat cap, thought to be Sodoma. On the other side of the picture the faun-like profile of Socrates is easily recognisable; he is seen counting on his fingers the propositions of a syllogism, facing Alexander the Great, who is arrayed in shining armour.

Inevitably, in the painting representing Gregory IX giving the Decretals to Raymond of Penafort (beside the window facing in to the Cortile dei Pappagalli), this thirteenth-century pope is given the features of Julius II. Beside him stand the Cardinals Giovanni de' Medici and Alessandro Farnese (the future popes Leo X and Paul III). It is believed that this composition and that of Justinian delivering the Pandects owe more to the hands of Raphael's pupils than his own. The beautiful lunette above, representing the Virtues, is, however, undoubtedly Raphael's own work.

In the famous Parnassus (above the window on the opposite wall), there are many portraits. Some have even sought to identify Apollo himself with Giacomo Sansecondo, a musician of Julius II's court; also the head of one of the Muses with that of the Fornarina. However, among the procession of poets who ascend and descend the hill, many personifications and contemporary portraits are definitely recognisable. Prominent among them are Sappho, Homer, Virgil and Dante on the left (looking at the picture) and Raphael's contemporaries Castiglione, Boccaccio and possibly Antonio Tebaldo, on the right.

The adjoining Stanza di Eliodoro takes its name from Raphael's dramatic rendering of Heliodorus's expulsion from the Temple in Jerusalem, as described in the (for Protestants apocryphal) second Book of Maccabees. The paintings on the other walls represent St. Peter's delivery from prison, the meeting of Attila with St. Leo the Great, and the Mass of Bolsena, where the miraculous bleeding of the host resolved the officiating priest's doubts on transubstantiation. It is most generally agreed that these incidents from Biblical and other sources were personally chosen by Julius II to illustrate the intervention of providence in defence of the Church and, by allusion, certain aspects of his own life.

However, as the frescoes were executed during the years 1512–14, they were continued during the papacy of Leo X (1513–21). Some believe that this pope commissioned the 'Deliverance of St. Peter' as referring to his own escape from imprisonment by the French in 1512. Certainly, after his accession Leo X ordered Raphael to transform the 'Meeting of Attila and St. Leo' into an allegory of the Battle of Ravenna, at which he himself had been present in the previous year. Leo's own portrait was then substituted for that of Julius II, as the head of St. Leo. This has had the rather confusing result of making Leo X's plump features appear twice in the same painting—as the saintly pope and as a cardinal of his entourage. The picture was so far advanced when Julius II died that Leo's portrait as cardinal was already there; apparently Raphael or an assistant simply repeated it as pope.

The 'Expulsion of Heliodorus', the 'Miraculous Mass of Bolsena' and the 'Delivery of St. Peter' (this last particularly for its marvellously contrasted light effects), are considered to be among Raphael's greatest works, especially remarkable for his newly-acquired mastery of colour (the group of Swiss Guards is admired as the best example of this). But the 'Meeting of Attila and St. Leo' is not on a par with these, and is largely the work of his assistants. The design for the decoration of the ceiling in this room, with its faded *trompe l'oeil* tapestries, is by Raphael, but it was executed by another hand.

We now return to the first of the *stanze*—that of the Incendio—where the hands of Raphael's assistants are even more clearly evident in the decoration. This room was painted between 1514 and 1517, for use as the pope's dining-room. It seems likely that Leo X was himself responsible for the choice of the subjects, as they represent scenes from the lives of two saintly popes of the same name of the eighth and ninth centuries —Leo III and Leo IV. The Stanza dell' Incendio takes its name from the fresco (on the wall opposite the window) of the great fire (*incendio*) which occurred in the Borgo in 847, threatening St. Peter's itself. According to the *Liber Pontificalis* its progress was arrested by Leo IV making the sign of the cross; here, naturally, Leo IV is portrayed with the features of his distant successor Leo X.

Another episode in the life of Leo IV, the naval battle against the Saracens at Ostia in 849, provides the subject for the fresco on the wall opposite the main entrance; this is believed to be largely the work of Giulio Romano.

We now return across the Stanza della Segnatura and the Stanza di Eliodoro to the Sala di Costantino. Although this last is included under the title of the Raphael *stanze*, Raphael himself had practically no hand in the design or execution of its decoration; his contribution was limited to some sketches for details of the Battle of the Milvian Bridge (on the main wall facing the windows) and allegorical figures. All the rest is the work of Guilio Romano, Giovan Francesco Penni and other assistants. Begun in 1517 during Raphael's lifetime, the decoration of this room was halted during Hadrian VI's short reign and completed in 1524 under Clement VII. Although the scenes representing the baptism of Constantine, the Battle of the Milvian Bridge, the apparition of the Cross and the donation of Constantine are executed in a grand manner and on a vast scale, the magic which—even by remote control—Raphael seems to have been able to exercise over his assistants is totally lacking here. The room is in a curious way a memorial to the spirit that had fled; looking at it, and comparing it with the rest of the *stanze*, we can better understand the appalling sense of loss that Raphael's premature death produced in his contemporaries.

By a door at the far right end of the Sala di Costantino we reach the Sala dei Palafrenieri—a large room divided by pillars —whose decoration now chiefly dates from the reign of Gregory XIII (1572–85), though the ceiling is of an earlier period and bears many of the Medici heraldic devices such as the three feathers, the three rings and the yoke with the letter N. A door in the far right-hand corner of this room brings us to the chapel of Nicholas V. This is so small and so hidden away that it is often missed by travellers, nor do many of the large conducted parties come here; but it is one of the most exquisite things in the Vatican Palace, indeed in all Rome. Fra Angelico painted it between 1447 and 1449 for the humanist Pope Nicholas V, whose private chapel it was.

Especially after the splendours of the Borgia Apartment and the *stanze*, the chapel comes as a complete contrast; it seems as if some lingering influence of the gentle spirits and simpler world of this pope and his artist dwell here still. Scenes from the life of St. Lawrence fill the upper part of the walls; in them the saint and Sixtus II (portrayed with the sensitive features of Nicholas V) appear robed in softly muted tones of rose and blue. Garlands of bay leaves and flowers divide this series of frescoes from those, representing the life of St. Stephen, in the lunettes above; while the Evangelists float on clouds among the golden stars of the blue painted vault.

We recross the Sala dei Palafrenieri and take a door on the right out of the Sala di Costantino into the Loggie di Raffaello, overlooking the Cortile di S. Damaso. Raphael contributed as an architect to the design of this loggia, which had been begun by Bramante before his death in 1514; the work was completed in 1518. Raphael is believed to have drawn up the general scheme for the decoration of the whole loggia and to have made sketches for the paintings in the first eight vaults (coming from the far end, which is the proper entrance of the gallery). These, together with the stucco decoration, were executed by his assistants, notably Giovanni da Udine, Giulio Romano, Giovan Francesco Penni and Perin del Vaga. Of the thirteen vaults, the painted decoration of the first twelve is devoted to Old Testament subjects, many of them similar to those executed by Michelangelo in the ceiling of the Sistine Chapel. As a result the two ceilings are popularly known as the 'Bible of Michelangelo' and the 'Bible of Raphael.'

However, the loggie are even more famous for the 'grotesque' decoration in stucco and painting which drew its inspiration from the classical decoration of this type lately discovered among the Roman ruins—particularly those of the Golden House of Nero. For grace, charm and fertility of invention, this gay and delightful decoration of the Loggie di Raffaello has probably never been equalled; the bright sunlight and fresh air of this enchanted gallery make a delightful interlude before we turn to our exploration of the Vatican Museum.

We now retrace our steps to the Sala dell' Incendio, cross the adjoining Sala dell' Immacolata—with its nineteenth-century frescoes celebrating the promulgation of the dogma of the Immaculate Conception—and traverse the upper chapel and gallery of St. Pius V. This brings us to the very imposing Galleria delle Carte Geografiche. The walls of this vast gallery were painted between 1580 and 1583 by Antonio Danti (from information provided by his geographer brother Egnazio), with maps of all the regions of Italy. The effect is exceedingly decorative and for students of Italian topography the gallery is of particular interest. From the windows there are beautiful views of the Vatican gardens. We now return to the Stanza dell' Incendio and the stairs to the lower floor of the museum. On our way, we should pause for a moment to enter a room on the left of the Gallery of St. Pius V; this contains the famous Chiaramonti Niobid, formerly in the Cortile del Belvedere, which dates from the fourth or third century BC.

The stairs leading from the chapel of Urban VIII now bring us back to the first room of the Borgia Apartment; from here we start our exploration of the **Museo Sacro** and the library, which we glimpsed in passing, on our way to the Sistine Chapel. Traversing the Sala dei Paramenti, we find ourselves in the lower chapel of St. Pius V, where it is hoped that part of the Treasure of the Sancta Sanctorum will soon be arranged. This consists of objects of ivory, enamel and precious metals, brought from the Sancta Sanctorum near the Lateran in 1906. Textiles from the same chapel will be arranged in a room leading out of the Sala dei Paramenti; in this room there will also be a notable embroidered *opus anglicanum* cope of the end of the thirteenth century.

Artistically speaking, the most important object among the treasures of the Sancta Sanctorum is a large enamelled cross. Some authorities identify this with a cross which once belonged to Pope St. Symmachus (489–514) that was used as a reliquary for a fragment of the True Cross. It is in fact hollow, and when it was examined during this century, was found to contain balsam. From an inscription on the sides other authorities date the cross to the reign of Paschal I (817–24).

The **Treasure of the Sancta Sanctorum** also includes what must be one of the most remarkable collections of early textiles in existence. This comprises religious vestments, of wool or linen, which may be dated to somewhere between the first and third centuries of our era. Of very early date too are the *linteamina* or *brandea*—small fragments of stuff which were soaked in the blood of martyrs. What is not generally known is that this custom of conserving blood-soaked cloths is classical in origin. The blood of gladiators killed in the arena was thus preserved in pagan times, as was that of loved relatives, long before this custom was practised at the martyrdom of saints.

Of considerably later date—ranging from the fifth to the eighth centuries—are fragments of fine silk stuffs, which were probably gifts or offerings to the Sancta Sanctorum. These are also *brandea*—not in the sense that they were steeped in the blood of martyrs—but because they had been placed in contact with some sacred object, a custom common in the Middle Ages. Many of the textiles included in the treasure are of Oriental origin, such as the Coptic stuffs dating from the fourth and fifth centuries; there are also Byzantine, Sassanid and Syrian textiles.

We now come to the three rooms (Nos. 10, 11 and 12 on plan) housing the older sections of the Museo Sacro, which was founded by Benedict XIV in 1756 to illustrate the development of the applied arts for specifically Christian use. In actual fact some of the earliest exhibits are not Christian, they were included in the museum because they were found in the catacombs at a period when it was still believed that all catacombs were necessarily Christian places of burial. The collection in general includes glass, enamels, ivories, gold and silver work, dating from the second to the eighteenth century.

In order to study the Museo Sacro in chronological order we should begin with the farthest room (No. 10); this contains glass vases, cups and bottles dating from the first to the fourth century; also reliquaries and other sacred objects, including a disk believed to portray the oldest portrait of SS. Peter and Paul. However, by far the most striking exhibits are two cases containing the gold glasses, which are in the second room (No. 11 on plan), these date from the third to the fifth century. Many of these were in fact not specifically designed for Christian usage at all, but were simply glass bowls, plates or goblets decorated with fine gold. Often they were made specially as wedding presents—especially those decorated with portraits of a husband and wife. When their owners died, these glasses were embedded in the plaster in which the bodies were enclosed, as an ornament and a means of identification. The earliest of these glasses are usually of the finest workmanship; two particularly notable examples are the portrait of a husband

and wife on what was the bottom of a white glass plate, and the medallion of blue glass with the head of a man named *Eusebi Animadulcis*. But the most striking—and very famous —example of this exquisite work is the one inscribed *Dedali Ispetua Pie Zeses* (in the case on the right). On it are portrayed all the various activities of a shipwright's workshop, executed in minute and perfect detail; it is fascinating to note that the saws and other tools are the same as those used by Italian carpenters today. The gold glasses in the case on the left are unmistakably Christian; many of them are adorned with religious subjects and portraits of SS. Peter and Paul. Though the quality of the workmanship is variable in some of these, the heads of the two saints remain true to type: St. Peter being portrayed with curly hair and a very bushy beard; St. Paul, bald, but with a longer and straighter one.

The third, and largest room (No. 12 on plan) contains the collections of ceramics, enamels, ivory and silver and gold. The ceramics are mainly Italian Renaissance ware; the enamels range in date from the second or third century to the seventeenth, and come from many countries. Some of the ivories even date from pagan times, others are as late as the eighteenth century; they are of very varied provenance. The gold and silver, mainly French, Genoese and German crosses and chalices, dates mostly from the sixteenth and seventeenth centuries. In the fourth case on the left is a 'golden Rose'. Originally this was the traditional papal gift to the prefects of Rome; later the privilege was extended to crowned heads, churches and cities, whom the popes particularly wished to honour.

In the next case some very large rings, with what are obviously imitation stones, catch the eye; these are the famous 'Fisherman's rings' or seals of several popes. After the death of a pope his personal seal, which was of great state importance, was broken so that it should not fall into unauthorised hands—hence the imitation stones which have here been inserted in their place. Curiously enough the earliest of these rings was that of an anti-Pope at the time of the Great Schism—Count Robert of Savoy (1378–94); the rest belonged to Nicholas V (1447–55), Pius II (1458–64) and other fifteenth- and sixteenth-century popes. The last case on the left contains a remarkable collection of ivories. Some of the very early Christian ones are Egyptian, others are Byzantine and two caskets are even

Moslem, having been made in Palermo during the Arab occupation of Sicily.

Retracing our steps, we take the door leading to the left into the **Sala delle Nozze Aldobrandini** (No. 13 on plan). This room is called after one of the best-known classical paintings in existence. Familiar from countless reproductions, this wedding scene is believed to be a copy of a famous painting by the Greek artist Aetion, of the time of Alexander the Great, representing Alexander's marriage to Roxana. It was discovered in 1605 on the Esquiline, and was kept in the Villa Aldobrandini (hence its name) until 1818, when it came into the possession of the Vatican Library. In the same room are the first-century frescoes of Ulysses's adventures in the land of the Laestrygons, also found on the Esquiline, in 1848; these are remarkable for the almost impressionist freedom of style of the Hellenistic artist. The room also contains a third-century painting known as the 'Heroines of Tor Marancia'; a charming first-century fresco of a procession of children, from Ostia, and an interesting painting of a cargo boat being loaded in the third century. In fact gathered together in this small room are some of the most remarkable and well-preserved examples of antique painting in the world.

We now emerge into the long Galleria di Urbano VIII (No. 9 on the plan); this contains an interesting but somewhat miscellaneous collection of objects. Notable are some globes and two early maps, dating from 1528 and 1529, showing America; what are now the United States are variously named as 'Terra dei Bacalaos' and 'Nova Gallia'. The next two rooms (both marked 8 on plan) are both called Sala Sistina after Sixtus V; in the second is a facsimile of the Hungarian regalia and a wooden contrivance of most extraordinary aspect. This is the machine, invented by Bramante, for affixing the great papal seal or *bollo* to important official documents; in fact the origin of those papal 'bulls' which appeared so frequently on the pages of our school history books.

In the first of the two small ante-rooms before the vast Salone Sistina of the **Vatican Library** (No. 7 on plan) we see the library's largest and smallest codices—a thirteenth-century Hebrew Bible and the Masses of St. Francis and St. Anna, of the sixteenth century. Although a library had existed in the old Lateran Palace, the real founder of the Vatican Library was Nicholas V; when he became Pope in 1447 there were only 340 books, when he died there were 1,200; it is in fact the oldest of the Vatican collections. The library was so enormously increased by successive popes that the old Floreria beneath the Borgia Apartment was no longer capable of holding it. Sixtus V (1585–90) then commissioned Domenico Fontana to design the existing building, that divided the Cortile del Belvedere in two, creating this enormous hall which is decorated with paintings illustrating the progress of Sixtus V's Roman town-planning. Today the Salone Sistina is used to display some of the most beautiful and interesting codices and documents from among the library's vast collection of 60,000 codices and 7,000 incunabula. The actual library, manuscript room and archive, in which scholars work, are on the floor below.

The codices on exhibition are clearly labelled so that it is not necessary to give a detailed list. Among the most famous are three copies of Virgil's works, dating from the fourth and fifth centuries, one with a portrait of the poet; among the most curious is Frederick II's illustrated book of falconry of the thirteenth century. Several Exultet rolls, which we have mentioned in connection with the high pulpits in Roman medieval churches, are to be seen on the far side of case 4; this also contains an Anglo-Saxon Gospel of the eighth century. In the next case is a tenth-century copy of the famous classical Roman cookery book of Apicius. Case No. 7 contains drawings by Michelangelo and his poems written in his own hand; also drawings by Raphael. In case No. 9 are autograph poems of Petrarch, letters of St. Thomas Aquinas, Michelangelo, Raphael and Martin Luther. Also, surprisingly, Henry VIII's love letters to Anne Boleyn, ending 'your loyal friend'; these are bound in a small book and constitute striking evidence of the capacity of the papal intelligence service in the sixteenth century. The case also contains a signed copy of Henry's famous book *Assertio Septem Sacramentorum*, for which he received the title of Defender of the Faith, borne by his successors ever since.

Leaving the library, we make our way along the vast **gallery**, divided into a series of halls, named after Alexander VIII (1689–91) and Clement XII (1730–40), to the general museum entrance known as the Atrio dei Quattro Cancelli. From here we proceed to the **Pinacoteca** or Picture Gallery by following the covered passageway towards the entrance building, turning left there, and then right, we come to the door of the Pinacoteca—a separate building which was erected in 1932, standing in the garden, from where there is a fine view of the dome of St. Peter's.

Curiously for Italy, the picture gallery is one of the later Vatican collections, having been founded by Pius VI (1775–99). It is, however, remarkable for its early works—the oldest picture dates from the eleventh century—in fact the collection of primitives and paintings of the fifteenth century is one of the most extensive in Rome. In their haste to reach the Raphael room (of the famous tapestries) many of the conducted parties seem to ignore all this; also they remain unaware of the fact that since 1960 the Pinacoteca has started to collect (in room XVII) the works of contemporary artists such as de Chirico, Utrillo, de Pisis and Rouault. The outstanding works in **room I** (devoted to primitives and Byzantine paintings) are Margaritone d'Arezzo's portrait of St. Francis of Assisi, a Last Judgment of the Roman Benedictine School of the eleventh century (the gallery's oldest picture), also Boniface VIII's cope of thirteenth-century *opus Anglicanum* embroidery.

Room II (Giotto and his school) contains the famous Stefaneschi polyptych painted by Giotto for the altar of the *confessio* in Old St. Peter's. On the near side Christ is seen enthroned in the centre with the donor, Cardinal Stefaneschi, kneeling at His feet; on either side are represented the martyrdoms of SS. Peter and Paul. That of St. Peter is particularly interesting as it shows the medieval interpretation of St. Peter's crucifixion *inter duas metas*; St. Peter is seen crucified upsidedown between the Pyramid of Cestius and the Meta Romuli. This last was evidently in fairly good condition when Giotto painted the picture at the end of the thirteenth century or the beginning of the fourteenth. On the top of the Meta Romuli there is a tree, probably an allusion to another Roman tomb near by, called in the Middle Ages the Terebinthus Neronis—the Terebinth (*Terebinthus pistacia* or Chian Turpentine tree) of Nero. On the other side of the polyptych St. Peter is seen enthroned, with Cardinal Stefaneschi holding up before him a miniature reproduction of the whole polyptych, framed in a beautiful Gothic frame which no longer exists. In the same room are some fine works of Pietro Lorenzetti (170), Bernardo Daddi (174) and Lorenzo Monaco (196–201), also a very appealing series of the life of Christ and other subjects (124–32) by Giovanni di Paolo.

Two outstanding works in **room III** are Fra Angelico's 'Madonna and Child with Saints' (No. 253), also his 'Scenes from the life of St. Nicholas of Bari' (Nos 251–52); in Gentile da Fabriano's 'Miracles of St. Nicholas' (Nos. 247–50) the ship on the green sea is particularly beautiful. There is also a lovely Filippo Lippi triptych (No. 243). **Room IV** contains two famous works of Melozzo da Flori—the fresco of Sixtus IV nominating Platina prefect of the Vatican Library (No. 270); between the pope and the kneeling Platina stands Cardinal Giuliano Della Rovere (the future Julius II), the other figures are Della Rovere and Riario relations. In the last century the fresco was transferred from the wall of the old Vatican Library on to canvas. In the same room are fragments from Melozzo's great fresco of the Ascension, from the apse of the church of the SS. Apostoli (Nos. 269A–269O); the angelic musicians are remarkably beautiful. Notable among the paintings by fifteenth-century artists, in **room V** is Francesco del Cossa's 'Miracles of S. Vincenzo Ferrer' (No. 286), one of the very rare examples of this artist's work in Rome. Among the collection of polyptychs in **room VI** there is a fine signed Pietà by Crivelli (No. 300). The outstanding work of **room VII** (devoted to Perugino and Umbrian painters of the fifteenth century) is Perugino's 'Madonna and Child with Saints' (No. 317).

Room VIII (the large one at the far end of the building) is entirely devoted to celebrated works of Raphael; these include the marvellous group of tapestries, woven in Brussels from his cartoons for the Sistine Chapel, where they were first hung in 1519. Of the original ten cartoons, seven are preserved in the Victoria and Albert Museum in London; four other sets of the tapestries exist, in the Palazzo Ducale of Mantua, the Kaiser Friedrich Museum in Berlin and at Hampton Court. Of the three most famous paintings in the room, the 'Coronation of the Virgin' (No. 334) is the earliest; painted when Raphael was only 20, it was his first great composition. The 'Madonna of Foligno' (No. 329) was commissioned as a votive offering by Sigismondo Conti and painted between 1512 and 1513.

But Raphael's greatest work shown here is the 'Transfiguration' (No. 333) that was unfinished when he died and was hung above his bier as he lay in state. In the wonderful figure of Christ, rising heavenwards in a glow of dazzling light against the stormclouds louring over Mount Tabor, Raphael's genius triumphantly reasserts itself. Miraculously almost, all the signs of fatigue and lack of inspiration that had been accumulating during the last years have vanished here. The picture, which was commissioned in 1517 by Cardinal Guilo de' Medici (the future Clement VII) for the Cathedral of Narbonne, was completed in its lower half by Giulio Romano and Giovan Francesco Penni.

The most fascinating work in **room IX** (devoted to artists of the sixteenth century) is Leonardo's curious monochrome of St. Jerome (No. 336). Although it is unfinished and in poor condition, it is one of the few of Leonardo's pictures that have always been accepted as an authentic work. In the same room is a beautiful Bellini Pietà (No. 290). The major works in **room X** are Titian's 'Madonna and Child with Saints' (No. 351) and Paris Bordone's 'St. George' (No. 354). **Room XI** contains works of artists of the later sixteenth and early seventeenth century; in **room XII** are two masterpieces of the seventeenth century—Caravaggio's wonderful 'Deposition' (No. 386) painted in 1602–4 for the Chiesa Nuova, and Domenichino's 'Communion of St. Jerome' (No. 384), painted in 1614. Of the remaining rooms, No. **XV**, which is devoted to portraits, contains three outstanding works—Titian's portrait of the Doge Niccolo Marcello (No. 445), Carlo Maratta's Clement IX (No. 460) and, surprisingly, Lawrence's fine portrait of George IV (No. 448). **Rooms XVI** and **XVII** contain modern and contemporary works, including Manzù's bust of Pope John XXIII.

Our tour of the Pinacoteca should conclude our first morning's exploration of the Vatican Museum; for those who may not have very much time at their disposal in Rome, we will continue with what should really be another day's itinerary—the great collections of classical art. These can conveniently be divided into six sections: the Museo Pio Clementino, containing many of the most important exhibits; the Museo Chiaramonti; the Braccio Nuovo, with the famous 'Augustus of Prima Porta'; the Museo Profano of the library, a perfect example of a small eighteenth-century museum setting; the Museo Egiziano, interesting but not of equal importance to the London and Paris collections; all of these are on the lower floor. On the upper floor are the Sala della Biga and the Galleria dei Candelabri, also the Museo Etrusco principally noted for the gold treasure of the Regolini-Galassi tomb and the bronze 'Mars of Todi', but not on the scale of the Villa Guilia Museum. Adjacent to this is a new section, opened in 1960, containing original Greek sculptures, including some fragments from the Parthenon. To these will be added within the next few years all the Lateran collections of classical and paleo-Christian art, as well as the Ethnological Missionary Museum. The new building which is to house them, near the Pinacoteca, is in the course of construction at the time of writing.

The foundation of the Vatican collection of classical sculpture was laid in the first years of the sixteenth century, when Julius II transferred the finest works (which had been displayed in the garden of his Cardinalate palace beside S. Pietro in Vincoli) to the small private garden that Bramante had designed for him in the central court of Innocent IV's old Villa Belvedere. Although much changed, Julius II's garden still exists in the Cortile del Belvedere; it is now more generally known as the Cortile Ottagono. This is surrounded by the halls of the Museo Pio Clementino, still maintained, more or less, in the style in which they were arranged for two eighteenth-century popes—Clement XIV and Pius VI. The Museo Chiaramonti came into being during the reign of the pope of that family, Pius VII (1800–23). The charming little Museo Profano of the library was begun by Clement XIII in 1767, and completed by his successor Pius VI. The Etruscan and Egyptian Museums were founded by Gregory XVI in 1837 and 1839 respectively; though the former has lately been rearranged. From this it is evident that the Vatican Museum has become, during the course of the centuries, not only a museum for the display of classical art in all its branches, but also a museum of the various styles and fashions in museum arrangement—the most varied and extensive of its kind in the world.

From the Atrio dei Quattro Cancelli (the general internal entrance to the museums), we turn left up a flight of steps and find ourselves in the first room of the **Museo Pio Clementino,** called from its shape the Sala a Croce Greca. This and the two following halls—the Sala Rotonda and the Sala delle Muse—constitute a perfect example of the neo-classical museum style of the eighteenth century. In them mosaics, sarcophagi, statues and reliefs—often much restored and polished—are grouped together with an eye to the general effect irrespective of period, and in an architectural setting which was believed to reproduce a classical background similar to that in which they would originally have been seen.

The most striking exhibits in this room are the two superb porphyry sarcophagi of the fourth century. That on the right was probably intended for Constantine the Great himself— the war-like reliefs presuppose a man's place of burial—but in actual fact it was used for his mother, St. Helena; it was found in her tomb near the Via Casilina. On the wall behind is the rest of the inscription of the Arval brothers, of which we saw part in the Museo delle Terme. We have already seen a facsimile of the other sarcophagus, in S. Costanza near the Via Nomentana, originally the tomb of Constantine's granddaughter, Constantia. Here in the original sarcophagus we are again struck by the paleo-Christian adaptation of such classical scenes as the vintage.

The most interesting statue in the Sala a Croce Greca is inconspicuously placed behind this sarcophagus, to the left of the window (No. 567). In it we see an austere-looking woman, her hair bound by a simple band and done up in an uncompromising bun; of the supreme intelligence of the face there can be no doubt, but such is its forcefulness that it might be that of a man—and yet this is known almost certainly to be a portrait of Cleopatra. The body—which is derived from some Greek model of the fifth century BC—is not hers but, from its striking similitude to her coinage, there is little doubt that the head is.

We now come to the Sala Rotonda, the most effective of Simonetti's neo-classical settings. In the centre of this room, beneath a dome with coffering inspired by that of the Pantheon, is the superb porphyry fountain found on the site of the Baths of Titus and the Golden House, which afterwards stood in the garden of the Villa Giulia. It rises in the centre of the beautiful polychrome mosaic from Otricoli, with groups of marine gods and scenes of Greeks battling with centaurs. Ranged around the walls are busts of emperors, empresses and gods, including the famous Jove of Otricoli (No. 539), copied from an original work of the fourth century BC. In niches, decorated with gilded shells and painted Pompeian red, statues are seen to considerable effect.

Certainly the colossal gilded bronze Hercules (No. 544) from Pompey's Theatre (dating from the end of the first century BC or the first of our era, and a rare survivor of its kind), looks very effective when seen across the room from the entrance. In the next niche (to the right) is a celebrated statue of Ceres (No. 542), copied from a Greek original of the fifth century BC. Next to her is the famous Antinous (No. 540), a fine statue of Hadrian's favourite, who was drowned in the Nile in AD 130; he is portrayed here as Bacchus.

We now turn to the right into the Sala delle Muse, so called from the striking group of Apollo and the muses placed in the central octagonal part of this room; these statues were inspired by Greek models of the third century BC and found in a villa near Tivoli. The room also contains many portrait busts of famous Greek philosophers and writers copied from Greek originals of the fourth century BC. Among the most striking are Plato (No. 519, the inscription Zenon is erroneous), Euripides (No. 521), Demosthenes (No. 506), Epicurus (No. 498, from a third-century original) and Homer (No. 512, from a fifth-century BC original).

The next room, a large rectangular hall, is known as the Sala degli Animali; it was created during the reign of Pius VI to house an extraordinary collection of animal sculptures which are largely the work of Francesco Antonio Franzoni, who lived from 1734 to 1818. Although a few of these are original, or fragments of original, classical works, they have been heavily restored in a style reminiscent of Landseer. The room does, however, contain the well-known statue of Meleager (No. 40), with a boar's head and a dog, copied from a work of Scopas of the fourth century BC, there are also some very fine polychrome mosaics of the second century.

A door on the left leads us into the Galleria delle Statue; this was extended by Pius VI, but the further end of the room formed part of Innocent VIII's original fifteenth-century Villa del Belvedere; his arms appear in the vault and the walls are decorated with rather damaged frescoes of the school of Pinturicchio. Against the end wall (immediately on the left on entering) is the beautiful 'Sleeping Ariadne' (No. 414), found in 1503 and formerly believed—from the asp bracelet on her arm—to be Cleopatra. This Hellenistic work of the second or third century BC formed part of Julius II's original collection of statues; it was arranged by Bramante as a fountain in the pope's private garden in the Villa del Belvedere. Other important statues in the gallery are the 'Apollo Sauroctonus' (No. 264) or Apollo the lizard-killer, a copy of a bronze by Praxiteles; a Satyr in repose (No. 406) also a copy of Praxiteles; the delightful Eros of Centocelle (No. 250), a copy of a Greek original of the fourth century BC, probably really representing Thanatos; a Hellenistic Triton or marine centaur (No. 253); the Apollo Citaredo (No. 395) a copy of an original of the fifth century BC. Finally, the Amazon of the Villa Mattei (No. 265); this has been badly restored and the head belongs to another statue and the figure should be holding a lance not a bow, but it is a copy of one of the three amazons of Ephesus sculpted by Polycleitos, Phidias, Cresilas and Phradmon for a competition, as recorded by Pliny. The gallery also contains the famous Barberini candelabra (Nos. 412 and 413 on either side of the 'Sleeping Ariadne'). These date from the second century and were found in Hadrian's villa; they are considered to be the finest of their kind. Judging from representation on classical reliefs, these beautiful sculptured candelabra were used in the manner of *torchères*, as supports for flaming bowls of oil or fat, like the *fiaccole* still used for festive illumination in Rome today.

A door at the far end of the Galleria delle Statue leads into the Galleria dei Busti, made for Clement XIV by throwing together four small rooms of Innocent VIII's Belvedere. The gallery is divided by columns and arches into four sections, mostly devoted to portrait busts. Notable among the imperial portraits in the first section are the young Augustus (No. 39), Caracalla (No. 292), and a remarkable Julius Caesar (No. 376). In the third section at the far end, is the well-known Verospi statue of Jove seated (No. 326), before him is a curious marble celestial globe with the signs of the zodiac (No. 341). Hidden away in a corner on the left is an interesting statue of a woman praying with hands outstretched (No. 352), believed to be a portrait of Augustus's wife, Livia.

Retracing our steps to the other end of the Galleria delle Statue, opposite the entrance we find a door leading first into a small vestibule and then into the Gabinetto delle Maschere. This is called after the delightful polychrome mosaics with theatrical masks, from Hadrian's villa, let into the floor. Here stands a copy of Praxiteles's famous 'Venus of Cnidus', in which for the first time (in the fourth century BC) he dared to represent the goddess naked, bending slightly forward as if about to step into a bath. Beside one of the windows stands a curious antique chair of red marble; it is the famous *chaise percée* or *sedia stercoraria* that formerly stood in the Lateran.

Retracing our steps to the centre of the Sala degli Animali, we find the entrance of the Cortile Ottagono or Cortile del Belvedere. Although the setting has been very much altered and is now surrounded by porticoes, this still contains the Laocoön, Apollo di Belvedere and Venus Felix, which belonged to Julius II's original collection. After so many great halls and galleries it is a joy to be in the open air again, to seat oneself on the edge of the fountain, ringed round with clipped evergreens, and to pause for a while before examining in detail the masterpieces of sculpture which the court contains.

Actually, if we have chosen our seat well, the central fountain is the perfect place from which to see the recent re-arrangement of **the Laocoön** in its original form, and to compare it with a cast (on the left) of what it looked like for centuries, owing to Montorsoli's mistaken restoration made about 1532–5. It does not require the eye of an expert to recognise the infinitely more harmonious line of the pyramidal grouping now restored to the original, by the replacement of the curved right arm of Laocoön himself and the removal of the one which Montorsoli had added to one of his sons.

F. Magi's book, relating the history of this restoration, reads almost like a detective story. The newly reattached arm of the Laocoön was found in 1905 in a marble cutter's shop in the Via Labicana by the archaeologist Pollak, who soon recognised that it belonged to the group. However, nothing was done about it until 1957, when the fragments of what were at first believed to be another Laocoön were found in a cave near Sperlonga; and an examination of the Vatican group was decided upon. Investigation soon revealed that Pollak had been right, but that in the sixteenth century someone, probably Michelangelo, had started on a further restoration, beginning to make another arm (now attached to the back of the plinth upon which the group stands), and cutting away a good deal of the right shoulder of the central figure in order to make it fit. Fortunately, a sixteenth-century bronze copy of the group, made for François I, still exists in the Louvre; this reproduced the Laocoön in its original un-restored state. From a cast made of this bronze it was possible to reconstruct the missing piece of shoulder and to reattach the Pollak arm in its original position. Thus we see the Laocoön today in more perfect condition than it has appeared at any time since the fall of the Roman Empire.

The Laocoön was discovered by De Fredi on 14 January 1506 and Julius II sent Giuliano da Sangallo to see it; he went carrying his small son, Francesco, on his shoulders, accompanied by Michelangelo. Sixty-one years afterwards the son recounted how 'directly my father saw the statue he exclaimed "this is the Laocoön mentioned by Pliny" '. The discovery created a sensation, prospective purchasers were legion but in March of the same year Julius II acquired the group by granting De Fredi and his son an annual charge of 600 gold ducats upon the tolls of the Porta S. Giovanni for their lifetimes. Michelangelo and Cristoforo Romano 'the finest sculptors in Rome' were instructed by the pope to examine the group to try to establish if it was indeed the one that Pliny mentioned as being made of a single block of marble. This early attempt at archaeology resulted in their discovering four joints in the stone, but so skilfully concealed that they came to the conclusion that Pliny might have been justified in making such a mistake. The group, executed in Greek marble, is the work of Agesander and his sons Athenodorus and Polydorus, of Rhodes; according to modern expert opinion it dates from the second century BC. It represents the legend of Laocoön, a priest of Apollo, who warned the Trojans against the dangers of the famous wooden horse and, together with his sons, was suffocated by two great serpents who came out of the sea at Apollo's command.

In the corner opposite the Laocoön (on the same side of the court) is the equally famous 'Apollo di Belvedere', also part of Julius II's original collection; this was found in the fifteenth century at Grottaferrata. It is a copy of a Greek original of the fourth century BC, probably a bronze by Leochares; Apollo is represented as he steps forward to see if the arrow he has just loosed has met its mark. The next corner contains three statues by Canova, made in 1800 to fill the gap left by classical works taken to France by Napoleon as a result of the Treaty of Tolentino; the central figure is the famous Perseus. Under the portico, in the centre of the wall, is the beautiful Hermes (formerly known as the Belvedere Antinoos), probably representing 'Hermes psychopompos', who led souls into

Hades. Probably made during Hadrian's reign, it is a copy of a work of Praxiteles. In the corner at the far end is the Venus Felix and Cupid; the body is a copy of Praxiteles's Venus of Cnidus, the head a portrait of a Roman lady of the second century. On the plinth is an inscription stating that the statue was dedicated to Venus Felix by Sallustia and Elpidus.

We now cross the Cortile del Belvedere to the door in the wall between the Apollo and the Perseus, and find ourselves in the Vestibolo Rotondo. In the centre of the adjoining room on the left stands the Atleta Apoxyomenos, which was found in the Vicolo dell'Atleta in Trastevere in 1849. It is a unique copy of a fourth-century BC bronze of Lysippus, which Pliny records as being in Rome in his day; the original was made in honour of a victorious athlete; he is portrayed using the strigil to remove the dust and oil with which he had covered himself before the match. The statue is thus placed in the centre of the room because it can be equally admired from any angle. Among other sculptures in the same room is an altar dedicated by Augustus in 12 BC, with a representation of the prodigious sow of Laurentum, mentioned in the *Æneid*, that produced thirty piglets.

We now cross the Vestibolo Rotondo to the cruciform Atrio del Torso on the far side; in the centre of this stands the famous 'Torso del Belvedere', signed by Apollonius, son of Nestor, of Athens. This sculptor lived in Rome at the end of the Republic; the bronze boxer of the Museo delle Terme is also by him. This marvellous fragment of a figure seated on the skin of some wild animal is believed to represent Hercules. It was found at the beginning of the sixteenth century, arousing tremendous admiration among artists, especially Michelangelo, upon whom it had a profound influence. Against the wall in the same room is the sarcophagus of L. Cornelius Scipio Barbatus, Consul in 208 BC, the earliest of the family to be buried in the tomb by the Via Appia Antica where we saw a replica of this sarcophagus.

A steep flight of steps leads down from the Atrio del Torso to the long gallery which forms the first section of the **Museo Chiaramonti.** The two others are the Galleria Lapidaria (its continuation, which can only be seen by special permission) and the Braccio Nuova, built at a right angle to the main gallery (parallel to the library) and connecting it with the galleries on the other side of the main Cortile del Belvedere.

Although this gallery was originally arranged for the Chiaramonti Pope, Pius VII (1800–23), according to Canova's advice, it did not then look as it does today. Subsequent finds have resulted in what can only be described as appalling overcrowding, which produces a feeling of confusion and exhaustion in the beholder. For the specialist there is, of course, much of tremendous interest; for the layman too, many individual exhibits would appeal for artistic or historical reasons if only they could be viewed separately. This vast gallery is divided into fifty-nine compartments (identified by Latin numerals); those with little time to spare should, however, not miss a fine portrait of a Roman of the end of the Republic (compartment XIX, No. 13), a fragment of a Greek relief of the fifth century BC, representing Penelope (compartment XXII, No. 16), and the portrait of a lady of the Julio-Claudian family (compartment XLVII, No. 15).

At the end of the Chiaramonti gallery we turn right into the **Braccio Nuovo,** built between 1817 and 1822 for Pius VII by Raphael Stern. Although the cold nineteenth-century neoclassicism of the setting may not appeal to all of us today, this gallery has preserved the dignity which has been entirely lost by overcrowding in the previous one. Along the walls the most important statues are ranged in niches, alternating with busts placed on pedestals and brackets, the pavement is inlaid with antique mosaics, the barrel vault coffered in the classical style. Half-way down, the gallery is interrupted by a large hall with an apse, on the left; this is built over the central part of the upper terrace of Bramante's original great Cortile del Belvedere garden, which was joined to the lower court by a series of stairs and ramps.

Among the most interesting sculptures in the first part of the gallery is a charming statue of Silenus holding the infant Bacchus in his arms (in the third niche on the right, No. 11), a copy of a work of Lysippus. On the same side is the famous statue of Augustus from Prima Porta (fourth niche on the right, No. 14); this was found in 1863 in Livia's villa *ad Gallinas,* from which the painted garden room of the Museo delle Terme also came. Augustus is portrayed at about the age of forty; the statue is considered to be the best portrait of him in existence. The reliefs on the armour are almost as fine as the portrait itself; in the centre of the cuirass is represented the scene of the Parthian King returning to Tiberius, in

20 BC, the Roman military insignia of the eagle which Crassus had lost thirty-three years earlier. The small cupid, seated on a dolphin, beside Augustus's right leg, is not mere decoration, but a reference to the Julian family's fabled descent from Venus. In the last niche on the right, before the central hall, is a beautiful figure formerly believed to personify Modesty; it is in fact a copy of Philicus of Rhodes' statue of Mnemosyne —the mother of the Muses—of the third century BC.

On the left-hand side of this part of the gallery the most famous sculpture is the 'Spear-bearer' (in the third niche, No. 123), a copy of a bronze by Polycletus of the second half of the fifth century BC, considered to be his masterpiece and the result of years of study of the proportions of the human body. Near by is an interesting portrait head of the Arab Emperor Philip (No. 121), who held the reins of power for five years during the troubled period after the murder of Caracalla, when ten emperors were murdered in the space of thirty-six years. In the next niche is the torso of an athlete of the fifth century BC, to which the head of Lucius Verus has been added (No. 120). There follows a copy of Praxiteles's Satyr in repose (No. 117), inferior to that of the Capitoline Museum; a statue of Claudius (No. 114); and the Pallas Athene from the Giustiniani collection, this last is a copy of a bronze of the end of the fifth or the beginning of the fourth century BC.

We now arrive at the central hall where, in the midst of the large apse on the left, lies the gigantic recumbent figure of the Nile (No. 106). With a sphinx beside him, he is surrounded by emblems of fertility, such as a cornucopia of grapes, a bunch of corn and sixteen *putti* climbing all over him (these last are much restored). On the back of the base is a Nilotic scene of pygmies hunting crocodiles and hippopotami among the great seed pods of the *Nelumbo nucifera*, the Lotus of the Nile. In the apse, behind the Nile, stands a cruelly revealing portrait bust of Mark Anthony (No. 89) and a beautiful one of Marcus Aurelius when young (No. 94).

At the time of writing on the right of the hall are two bronze peacocks still retaining some traces of gilding. These are the famous birds found in Hadrian's tomb, which normally stand on either side of the gigantic bronze pine-cone in the Cortile della Pigna. In 1575 the pine-cone stood under, the peacocks above, a stone canopy in front of Old St. Peter's as they had been since the Middle Ages; the pine-cone was there in Dante's day as he mentioned it in the *Divina Commedia*. It is possible that these originals may remain here and be replaced in the Cortile della Pigna by replicas, in order to save them from exposure to the weather. In the gallery beyond the central hall there is a remarkable portrait bust of a Roman of the Augustan age (at the far end on the right, No. 53), and, in the last niche on the right, a fine copy of a masterly bronze of Demosthenes by Polyeuctus of 280 BC. Opposite him is a copy (much restored by Thorwaldsen) of the wounded Amazon (No. 67), with which Polycletus is believed to have won the competition held in Ephesus in the fifth century BC. Also on the left (No. 85, in the niche nearest the central hall) is a copy of a severe but striking statue of Artemis in a long robe; the original was of the fourth century BC.

We now emerge from the far end of the Braccio Nuovo to find ourselves back again in the long library gallery, which we saw on our way to and from the Sistine Chapel and the Borgia Apartment. On this ocassion, however, we did not have the time to study the charming little Museo Profano of the library, at the far end of the gallery near the Atrio dei Quattro Cancelli (No. 1 on the first-floor plan). This was designed by Luigi Valadier for Clement XIII in 1767, to house the Vatican collection of medals; it is quite a small room and, by comparison with the great sculpture galleries, seems almost like the salon of a private house. Its great charm lies in the fact that its eighteenth-century décor is complete, right down to the cases of rare Brazilian wood designed by Valadier, though it was only completed during the reign of Pius VI (1775–99). The cases contain chiefly small Etruscan and Roman bronzes and Roman ivories. The most interesting exhibit, however, is the fragment (the head and arm in case III on the right) of a small chryselephantine, or gold and ivory, statue of Athena, believed to be an original Greek work of the fifth century BC. It will be recalled that Phidias's famous statue of Athena in the Parthenon, of which we saw a copy in the Museo delle Terme, was chryselephantine.

Leaving the Museo Profano, we mount the stairs which lead to the Sala a Croce Greca, where we began our exploration of the collections of classical art, but now we continue to the upper floor and the **Sala della Biga**, which stands directly above the Atrio dei Quattro Cancelli. The marble-lined room was designed by Camporese for Pius VI, as a setting for the *biga* or racing chariot with two horses, from which it takes its name. This group was composed in 1788 out of classical fragments by the same sculptor, Franzoni, who was responsible for so many of the exhibits in the Sala degli Animali. Here again he added considerably to what already existed; only the body of the chariot itself and part of the right-hand horse are ancient, and they did not originally form part of the same group. The chariot had been used for centuries as the episcopal throne of the church of S. Marco; it dates from the first century and had probably formed part of a chariot which was a votive offering; nevertheless it must be admitted that the general result is effective.

Ranged round the walls of the room are some remarkable statues, notably a bearded one of Dionysius (No. 608) of the beginning of the fourth century BC; the Greek inscription with the name of Sardanapalus is a later addition. There is a very fine first-century statue of an old Roman making a sacrifice (No. 612), magnificently swathed in his toga. Also two statues of discus throwers—in one (No. 615) the athlete is seen measuring the terrain in paces; this is a copy of a fifth-century BC bronze by Polycletus's son Naucydes; the other (No. 618) is a copy of Myron's famous bronze. Possibly the most fascinating exhibits, for the light that they cast on the details of chariot racing, are the three small third-century sarcophagi (Nos. 609, 613 and 617). Suitably, the last statue in the room (No. 619) near the door on the left is that of a winning charioteer bearing the palm (the head has been added).

Outside the Sala della Biga, we turn right into the Galleria dei Candelabri. The decoration here is the latest in period of any of the great galleries, dating from the reign of Leo XIII (1878–1903). The gallery, of course, takes its name for the series of superb candelabra ranged in pairs on either side of the dividing arches; the first two pairs, dating from imperial times, came from the churches of S. Costanza and S. Agnese; of the third pair, the beautiful spiral one on the right with doves on the base came from Otricoli. In general the gallery is notable for fine sarcophagi, urns and vases. Most appealing among the former for its human interest is a small boy's sarcophagus (No. 20 just on the right inside the door), showing him reclining by a pile of books, with his pet dog lying scratching itself beside him. There are in fact many statues of children in the gallery; one playing with nuts (No. 18 on the right of the door), small satyrs looking at their tails (Nos. 37–40), a boy with a goose (No. 66), a most charming little Greek girl running (No. 5) and finally, a delightful little Negro slave carrying toilet articles (No. 32).

Retracing our steps to the top of the stairs, we turn right into the **Museo Gregoriano Etrusco**, founded by Gregory XVI in 1837. This is most famous for the wonderful treasure found in the 'Regolini-Galassi' tomb at Cerveteri in 1837, dating from about 650 BC. In it lay the body of a man, probably a *lucumo* or chief, with his chariot, bed and throne; also that of a lady, covered with jewels, probably his wife; and a prince or warrior with his arms and chariot. With these three persons were buried vessels and plate of silver and silver gilt, pottery and ordinary kitchen implements; all of these are exhibited in room 2a of the museum, immediately after the first room, the Sala dei Sarcofaghi. The following three rooms, 3a, b and c, are devoted to bronzes; including the famous 'Mars of Todi'—an armour-clad figure of the fourth century BC. On the edge of the cuirass is an inscription which says 'Ahal Trutitus gave this'. Room 4a contains an interesting collection of funerary urns. In room 5a is the Guglielmi collection, mostly from Vulci, given to Pius XI in 1937; in room 6a is a beautiful collection of jewels; room 7a is devoted to terracottas. There follows the Antiquarium Romanum, with terracottas, bronzes and glass of various periods and provenance. From Saletta II of this, one passes into Sala 9a, containing the Falcioni collection, from the Viterbo region, including an exquisite gold diadem and ear-rings. In the last small section of the Antiquarium, Saletta III, is a beautiful bronze head of a Roman emperor of the third century, crowned with laurels. Traversing room IIa, which contains bronzes of the imperial period, we come to the top of the famous Scala di Bramante, but before descending it we should not miss a recent addition to the museum (opened in 1960)—a small but very beautiful collection of original Greek sculptures. There are only two little rooms; they are distinguished not only for their content, but also for the effective use of natural lighting.

Sala 12 a.a. contains a fine fragment of a relief of the fifth century BC, of a horseman, as well as an Attic relief of dancing nymphs of the fourth century BC and other fragments. In Sala 12 a.b. is the superb Stele del Palestrita, an Attic sepulchral relief of the fifth century BC, showing an athlete in profile, with his young attendant, who is holding out towards him a jar of oil with which to rub himself before the contest. In the same room are some important fragments from the Parthenon, including the head of Athena's horse, from the temple's west pediment, also the head of a young man with a basket and the head of Erichthonius. The collection is completed by a notable head of Athena and a very appealing one of a mule.

A corridor leads from here to the Staircase of the Assyrian reliefs, bringing us to the collections of Italic and Attic vases. Alternatively we can return to the Scala di Bramante, which is really a circular inclined ramp, that returns us to the lower floor and the Museo Gregoriano Egizio, the last stage of our itinerary. The windows on the way down the Scala di Bramante afford some interesting views over Rome, and the last one a particularly charming glimpse of the Fontana della Galera, with its bronze seventeenth-century galleon floating in the middle of a large pool.

The Egyptian collection of the Vatican was begun by Pius VII, but the real founder of the museum was Gregory XVI (1831–46). The false Egyptian style of the setting will appeal to few today. Nevertheless it contains some interesting sculptures, notably the head of a pharaoh of the eleventh dynasty (2054–2008 BC) Mentuhotep IV (No. 28 in room 11), also a colossal statue of Rameses II's mother, Queen Mutuy (No. 22 in the same room), and the small statue of a priest, Udja-hor-resent (No. 196 in room IV) who, according to an inscription on the statue, witnessed Cambyses taking the city of Sais in 525 BC. Possibly the most fascinating section for visitors to Rome is room III where Roman imitations of the Egyptian style are exhibited. These were mostly found in Hadrian's Villa; evidently this emperor's Oriental travels exercised something of the same influence upon contemporary taste as Napoleon's Egyptian campaign some seventeen centuries later.

Within a few years it will be possible to continue from the Museo Egiziano, by way of the Atrio dei Quattro Cancelli and the covered passageway (which now leads only to the Pinacoteca), to the new museum containing the **Lateran Collections.** These consist of the Museo Profano founded by Gregory XVI (1831–46), the Museo Cristiano founded by Pius IX in 1854 and the Museo Missionario Etnologico, founded by Pius XI in 1926 with the exhibits of the Missionary Exhibition of Holy Year 1925. The decision to transfer these collections from the Lateran Palace, in order to make way for the offices of the Vicariato, was made by John XXIII towards the end of his reign. There is no doubt that it will greatly benefit the tourist to find all the great papal collections gathered together in one place; especially as the fine arts of the Museo Cristiano will now be housed close to the applied arts of the Museo Sacro.

Although it is the smallest, the **Museo Cristiano** has the greatest human interest. The collection of paleo-Christian sculpture includes the famous, and exceedingly rare, statue of the 'Good Shepherd' that owes so much of its inspiration to the beautiful 'Hermes Kriophoros', which we saw in the Museo Barracco. Another interesting statue, that of St. Hippolytus, has now been transferred to the library entrance reached from the Porta S. Anna. This martyred saint, who died about 235, is believed to have been the first anti-pope; a list of his writings is inscribed in Greek on the chair upon which the statue is seated, also a sixteen-year cycle of his invention for discovering the date of Easter. The Museo Cristiano is also famous for its paleo-Christian sarcophagi and its large collection of inscriptions of the same period.

The **Museo Profano** also has a number of notable inscriptions and a rather heterogeneous collection of sculpture and mosaics; consisting partly of an overflow from the Vatican Museum and partly of objects found during the nineteenth-century excavations. These include two colossal statues of Tiberius and Claudius and two copies of famous Greek works —one of Sophocles, of which the original dated from the fourth century BC, and one of Marsyas after a work by Myron. The reliefs include two beautiful Greek originals, an Attic one of Medusa, probably dating from the fifth century BC, the other of Bacchic scenes, of the neo-Attic school, dating from the first century BC. Important among the Roman reliefs is one of the first century AD, with personifications of the Etruscan cities of Tarquina, Vulci and Vetulonia. Others, portraying funerary rites, come from the tomb of the Haterii. There are also portrait busts of members of the family. The collection includes two outstanding mosaics. One is the delightful *asaroton* or unswept pavement, copied from a famous Greek original which was at Pergamon. On it are scattered the remains of a banquet—fruit, fish-bones, the leg of a chicken and so on—the border is made up of masks, vases and tableware. Though infinitely less appealing, the other mosaic is of considerable interest for the portrayals of pugilists and their equipment; it was found in the Baths of Caracalla.

The **Museo Missionario Etnologico** is vast; it includes not only interesting documentation of the history of Roman Catholic missions, but also illustrates the life and customs of the countries in which they have been, and are still, active. These range in area from Tibet to New Guinea and from South Africa to the New World.

The question of where to eat will by now be uppermost in the minds of even the most ardent sight-seer. Pierdonati in the Via della Conciliazione 39, beside the Columbus Hotel, combines good food with the setting of a fifteenth-century palace and is well placed for continuing our afternoon's expedition to St. Peter's. Marcello, 87 Borgo Pio, is more modest but also conveniently placed; while the Moorish restaurant, Taverna Negma, in the Borgo Vittorio, caters for more exotic tastes and maintains the Borgo's old cosmopolitan tradition. As might be expected in an area so frequented by foreign tourists, bars where one can have a cup of coffee and sandwiches are plentiful in and around the Via della Conciliazione; on a fine day it is pleasant to sit outside and watch the world go by, but many of them also have indoor tea rooms.

CHAPTER TWENTY-FIVE

The Borgo and St. Peter's

❧

IF we are able to devote two days to our exploration of the Vatican, St. Peter's and the Borgo, we will be able to allow ourselves a fairly leisurely luncheon before going on to a choice of sights—either St. Peter's or the Borgo. If, however, time presses and everything has to be fitted into one day, we would be well advised to begin with the principal sight of the Borgo, **Castel S. Angelo**, except on Mondays when it is closed, as there is a bar where one can lunch in the summer months and at St. Peter's the treasure and the grottoes are closed between 1 and 2 p.m. and 1.30 and 2.30 p.m. respectively.

For the hurried and somewhat tired tourist, Castel S. Angelo has another advantage; although its history is closely connected with them, intellectually it is a great deal less demanding than either the Vatican Palace or St. Peter's, thus making a lighter interlude. In spite, or possibly because, of its sinister history as a state fortress and prison, the castle is the most popular sight in the city among the Romans; evidently it exercises the same sort of attraction as the Tower of London for family outings. This is not only due to its blood-curdling associations. Thanks to models, collections of arms and gifts of Renaissance furnishings, the ordinary visitor takes away with him a clear picture of what the castle probably looked like at various stages in its 1800 years' existence, and particularly at the peak of its importance during the Renaissance period.

By far the most interesting and picturesque route from the Vatican to Castel S. Angelo is by way of the Via dei Corridori and Borgo S. Angelo, which form one continuous street bordering on the famous *passetto* or fortified corridor that connects the Vatican Palace with the castle. The Via dei Corridori begins in the Largo del Colonnato, just between the Colonnade of the Piazza of St. Peter's and the Piazza della Città Leonina, where two arches have been pierced through the thickness of the *passetto*'s supporting wall. According to

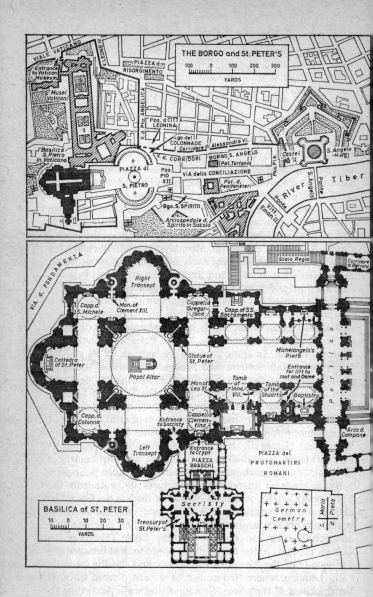

THE BORGO and St. PETER'S

100   0   100   200   300
YARDS

VIALE VATICANO · V. LEONE IV · PIAZZA d. RISORGIMENTO

Entrance to Vatican Museum

Musei Vaticani

V. d. Pta. ANGELICA

Pza. d CITTÀ LEONINA

Lgo. del COLONNADE · Corridore di Alessandro VI.

Basilica S. Pietro in Vaticano

V. d. CORRIDORI · BORGO S. ANGELO · Pal. Torlonia

PIAZZA di S. PIETRO · Pza PIO XII · VIA della CONCILIAZIONE · Pal. d. Penitenzieri

Bgo. S. SPIRITO

Arciospedale d. Spirito in Sassia

Pza. PIA · Ponte Vitt. Eman. II · Castel S. Angelo · Ponte S. Angelo · River Tiber

Vitt. Eman.

BASILICA of ST. PETER

10   0   10   20   30
YARDS

VIA d. FONDAMENTA

Scala Regia · Corridore d. Bernini

Right Transept

Capp. d. S. Michele · Mon. of Clement XIII.

Cappella Gregoriana · Capp. of SS. Sacramento

Cattedra of St. Peter

Statue of St. Peter

Michelangelo's Pietà

Papal Altar

Entrance for lift to roof and Dome

Mon. of Leo XI. · Tomb of Innoc. VIII.

Tomb of the Stuarts · Baptistry

Capp. d. Colonna

Entrance to Sacristy

Cappella Clementina

Portico

Arco d. Campane

Left Transept

Entrance to Crypt

PIAZZA BRASCHI

PIAZZA dei PROTOMARTIRI ROMANI

Sacristy

Treasury of St. Peter's

German Cemetery

S. Maria d. Pietà

some, the *passetto* was built by Nicholas III in 1277, according to others by the anti-pope John XXIII (1410–15); it was repaired by the Borgia Pope, Alexander VI, later in the fifteenth century. The narrow corridor in the thickness of the wall is surmounted by a battlemented walk; this fortified escape route enabled Clement VII to take refuge in Castel S. Angelo at the time of the sack of Rome in 1527.

At the far end of the Borgo S. Angelo we turn right into the Piazza Pia, from where we get a fine view of the great castle, towering up the river bank, and the **Ponte S. Angelo** with its Bernini angels. The three central arches of the bridge are ancient, remains of the Ponte Elia which was called after the Emperor Publius Aelius Hadrianus, to whose great family tomb it led. Hadrian began to build the mausoleum in AD 135; only three years before his death, the remains of his predecessor Trajan had been buried beneath his column; after the death of his predecessor Nerva, there was no more room in the imperial tomb built by Augustus on the other side of the Tiber. Hadrian's tomb was completed in 139 by his adoptive son and successor, Antoninus Pius. The square base was surmounted by a circular edifice 20 metres high; as in Augustus's tomb this was crowned by a conical mound of earth planted with trees. Concealed in the centre of the earth mound was a tower-like structure which, emerging at the top, served as a base either for a four-horse chariot, a colossal statue of Hadrian or, according to some, the great bronze pine-cone now in the Vatican. The base and the circular edifice were covered with Parian marble, columns and colossal statues alternated around its circumference; the vast building stood in the midst of a garden enclosed by a bronze railing.

Hadrian's tomb was only used as an imperial mausoleum for sixty years; in 271 it was included in Aurelian's walls. In 326, with the foundation of Constantinople, Rome ceased to be the imperial residence and in 337 Constantine died a Christian. In 410 Alaric sacked the tomb like the rest of Rome and in 537, during Witigis's siege, the defending garrison smashed the statues on the mausoleum, flinging the fragments down on the besieging Goths. Thus Hadrian's tomb made its début as a fortress, in fact the fortress which was to be the military key to Rome for more than a thousand years.

A further important event in its history occurred fifty-three years later, in the first year of Gregory the Great's reign. Rome was then decimated by plague and the pope ordered forty processions to make their way through the city to intercede for God's help. People fell out of the ranks, dying by the wayside, as men and women, priests and children marched through the empty streets. Just as Gregory was about to enter St. Peter's, he saw a vision of the Archangel Michael, on the summit of what was left of Hadrian's tomb, sheathing his sword. The pestilence then ceased, a chapel was built on the spot where the archangel had appeared, and it is from this event that the castle takes its name.

The door by which we enter the Castel S. Angelo is the same as that of the original tomb, though now, once inside, we find ourselves in an uncovered area which in classical times would have been enclosed by the tomb's square base. From here some steps descend into the vaulted vestibule, leading into the heart of the great circular mass. Here the museum authorities have arranged four models of the building, showing what it looked like during various phases of its existence. The first is a reconstruction of the original tomb; the second, all that is left of this today, stripped of modern additions; the third and fourth models show the castle as it appeared during the reigns of Alexander VI (1492–1503) and Urban VIII (1623–44). On the left beyond these one can see the bottom end of a lift shaft, built for Leo X (1513–21), who was very fat; on the right is the original inclined ramp, leading to Hadrian's funerary chamber. In classical times this was paved with black and white mosaic, of which a few traces remain, and was ventilated by four shafts that must have traversed the earth mound. The last but one of these was converted in medieval times into the terrible bottle-necked dungeon of S. Marocco in which, according to his memoirs, Cellini was so fortunate as to spend only one day.

Hadrian's inclined ramp ends where Alexander VI's *cordonata* or gently graded staircase begins; running at right angles to the ramp, it cuts diametrically across the great central circular mass of the building. Until 1822 the whole of the middle part of the *cordonata*, which traverses the central burial chamber in mid-air, was a wooden drawbridge that, when raised, would have completely isolated the garrison and papal apartment from the outside world. Attackers would have had to scale the walls of the funerary chamber to gain access to the rest of the *cordonata*, which leads to the upper levels of the castle. The *cordonata* now turns left and brings us to the very picturesque Cortile dell' Angelo or delle Palle, so called after Raffaello da Montelupo's marble angel and the piles of cannon balls it contains. The angel formerly stood on the summit of the castle, but was replaced by van Verschaffelt's existing bronze one in 1753. On the right of the court are a series of rooms containing a collection of arms ranging in period from the Bronze Age to modern times. Facing us at the far end of the court is the façade, designed by Michelangelo, for Leo X's chapel, and an open stair leading to the papal apartment on the upper storey.

A door on the left of the court leads into a series of rooms named after the various popes for whom they were decorated. The first two are called the Sale di Clemente VIII; the larger of these has a magnificent stuccoed chimney-piece and the Aldobrandini pope's arms in the centre of the ceiling. To the left of the door leading into the next room is a stone head of Paul IV (1555–9) which was found in the bed of the Tiber; probably it is the same one that was dragged through the streets of Rome on the day of the death of this Carafa pope, who was so much hated by the populace. The following room, which is known as the Hall of Justice after the court that sat there in the sixteenth and seventeenth centuries, and from Perin del Vaga's frescoed 'Angel of Justice', stands immediately above Hadrian's funerary chamber and was part of the original Roman building. From here we pass into the Sala dell' Apollo, charmingly decorated with grotesques for Paul III in 1547; it contains a fine collection of arms. A door at the far end on the right leads into Leo X's chapel, another on the left into two rooms called after Clement VII, who lived there during the sack of Rome; one has a fine frieze painted by Giulio Romano. Opening out of a passage beside these two rooms is a short stair leading to Clement VII's bathroom. This is the most delightful little place, gaily decorated with grotesques by Giulio Romano; its walls were heated from behind, in the ancient Roman manner, by hot air piped up from furnaces below which also supplied hot water for the marble bath.

The passage now brings us to the Cortile di Alessandro VI, also known as the Court of the Oil Well or of the Theatre, from the storage places for oil beneath it and the theatrica performances given there in Renaissance times. The distinguishing feature of this court is, however, the beautiful wellhead with the Borgia arms of Alexander VI. Ranged round the right-hand side of this courtyard, at a lower level, are a series of gloomy cells known as the *prigioni storiche*. Legend associates these with the places of confinement of Giordano Bruno, Beatrice Cenci and her stepmother and Cardinal Carafa, who was strangled in the castle in 1561. Tradition also asserts that in the last prison there are still traces on the wall of Cellini's charcoal drawing of 'God the Father, Christ and Angels', which he executed while imprisoned there. Modern experts incline to the opinion that Cellini was more likely to have been incarcerated in one of the rooms opening directly on to the court, which has a fire-place, as in his memoirs he specifically mentions that he was able to melt both metal and wax in the fire in his own cell. At the same level as the *prigioni storiche* are vast storerooms for oil and grain, capable of holding 22,000 litres of the former and 3,500 quintals of the latter.

A stair from the far end of the Cortile di Alessandro VI now brings us out on to the open walk which surrounds the whole of the vast central circular block of the original tomb. The views over Rome and the lower parts of the castle itself are superb, particularly when seen framed by the arches of Paul III's nearby loggia, built by Antonio da Sangallo the Younger in 1543. It must have been from this side of the castle that poor Clement VII mourned as he watched the smoke rising from his beloved villa on the slopes of Monte Mario during the sack of Rome—the beautiful villa that Raphael had designed for him and Giulio Romano and Giovanni da Udine had decorated, filling its gardens and woods with fountains; it still exists under the name of Villa Madama (though not generally open to the public, permits are obtainable from the Ministero degli Affari Esteri).

Continuing along the walk, we find an excellent bar, where in summer meals are also served. Here all feeling of a Roman tomb or Renaissance prison is far away, comfortable seats are ranged along the walk, which is gay with potted oleanders and here and there a creeper-covered pergola. Nevertheless, Augustus Hare mentions in his *Walks in Rome* that in his day cells on this roof were still used as prisons 'in which prisoners suffer terribly from the summer sun beating on their flat roofs'. Probably it is one of these that is now arranged as the cell of a political prisoner during the reign of Gregory XVI (1831–46). Half-way round the walk we come to another loggia, directly overlooking the Ponte S. Angelo. This was designed by Bramante for Julius II and commands an even better view than that of Paul III.

We now ascend the few steps leading from the loggia to the Papal Apartment, which was arranged for Paul III (1534–49). This would, of course, only have accommodated the pope in a time of emergency; normally it may well have been used by the castellan. It is believed that the man directly responsible for its superb decoration was Tiberio Crispo, mentioned by Vasari as a connoisseur of the arts who greatly embellished the castle. The first room, known as the Sala Paolina, is the most magnificent; its splendid frescoes were begun by Perin del Vaga and his assistants, and completed by Pellegrino Tibaldi. The paintings represent scenes from the Old Testament and the life of St. Paul and of Alexander the Great. The Archangel Michael is seen sheathing his sword in the middle of the wall opposite the door. To the right is an amusing *trompe l'oeil* door, seen half open with a figure climbing a flight of steps: it was painted thus to correspond with the real steps leading up from the door at the other end of the wall. There has been some argument as to the identity of the personage seen looking through another *trompe l'oeil* door to the right of the entrance. According to legend this black-robed figure was Beatrice Cenci's advocate, but, as she was tried and executed some fifty years after the room was painted, this is not possible. Modern authorities believe that it is a portrait of Fulvio Orsini, an illegitimate son of this ancient house who was an intimate friend of Paul III and drew up the plan of subjects for the decoration of this room.

A door at the far end on the right leads into the Camera del Perseo, so called from the beautiful frieze painted by one of Perin del Vaga's assistants; in it scenes from the myth of Perseus alternate with maidens seated beside unicorns—these last were the heraldic emblem of the Cardinal Castellan, Tiberio Crispo. Through the generosity of the Contini Bonacossi family and Cavaliere Mario Menotti, this and the following room have been beautifully furnished in sixteenth-century style, the Camera del Perseo as a reception-room and the adjoining Camera di Amore e Psyche as a bedroom. complete to the smallest detail of bed-linen with exquisite needle-point lace. Both rooms contain a remarkable collection of pictures, including works by Carlo Crivelli, Bartolomeo Montagna and Lorenzo Lotto.

Returning to the Sala Paolina, steps and a narrow curving passage—charmingly painted with grotesques—lead us into the magnificent library. This also is superbly decorated in the grotesque style. Leading out of the far end of the library are two rooms, known from motifs in their decoration as the Camera dell' Adrianeo and the Camera dei Festoni. Both of these have been filled with a remarkable collection of Renaissance furniture and pictures by the Contini Bonacossi family; these include works by Francesco Bissolo, Ercole Grandi, Dosso Dossi and Poussin. In the Camera dei Festoni hangs an interesting picture of Cardinal Gozzadini receiving the Old Pretender at Imola in 1717; the pale blue of his Garter ribbon looks strange to modern eyes, though this was the original colour of the Order.

A short stair leads from here to three small rooms above Paul III's loggia; the central one is usually known as La Cagliostra, as the notorious Count Cagliostro is said to have been imprisoned here in 1789. The rooms on either side also contain interesting works of art.

Returning to the library, and crossing to the other side, we find ourselves in one of the most interesting places in the castle. It is a circular room, which formed part of Hadrian's original building, and was adapted by the popes as a strongroom for their secret archive (only transferred from here to the Vatican in 1870) and as their treasure chamber. The Renaissance cupboards for the archive still line the walls; in the centre of the room stand three massive fourteenth-century treasure chests that must have once housed the gold and jewels and the most precious relics of the papacy. A narrow staircase, built in the thickness of the original Roman wall, leads up past yet another circular room of Hadrian's great mausoleum, to the terrace on the summit of the castle. Above the battlements, behind us, van Verschaffelt's colossal baroque Archangel stands sheathing his sword; before us is one of the most magnificent views in Rome. This terrace is the setting of the last scene in *Tosca*, appropriately Roman in its grandeur.

Returning to the Piazza Pia, the much criticised Via della Conciliazione opens up before us. Named after the conciliation between Church and State achieved by the Lateran

Treaty of 1929, this wide thoroughfare (which was begun in 1936 and completed for Holy Year 1950) has replaced the two old streets of the Borgo Vecchio and the Borgo Nuovo divided by the famous spina—a narrow row of houses called after the spina of classical circuses. Half-way up the Via della Conciliazione stand two old palaces, that still recall something of the former picturesque approach to St. Peter's. On the right the **Palazzo Torlonia** appears as a miniature Cancelleria; it was built between 1496 and 1504 and is attributed to the same architect, Andrea Bregno. Until the Reformation this was the seat of Henry VIII's Embassy to the Holy See. Immediately opposite, another fifteenth-century palace recalls the style of the Palazzo Venezia. Originally built for a Della Rovere Cardinal, this was for long known as the **Palazzo dei Penitenzieri**; it is now a hotel. It is well worth while walking into the courtyard to admire the beautiful well-head, with the Della Rovere arms, and the fine porticoes.

Returning to the Via della Conciliazione, we should now make a slight detour down the Via Scossacavalli to the Borgo S. Spirito. On the far side of this street we see the long arcaded wall of the **Arciospedale di S. Spirito in Sassia**, whose original predecessor, the *burgus Saxonum*, gave its name of burgh or borgo to the whole of this quarter. The foundation of the Saxon borgo is usually attributed to the King Ine of Wessex who abdicated in order to take up residence in Rome in 726.

During Leo IV's reconstruction of the Borgo after the fire, the church of S. Maria in Saxia was built in 850, on the site of the existing church of S. Spirito in Sassia; King Burgraed of Mercia was buried there in 874. By the middle of the eleventh century the church owned houses, workrooms and a cemetery, but a hundred and fifty years later, although the church and hospice were endowed with vineyards and land, the institution had ceased to flourish. In fact it was reduced to such a state of poverty that the energetic Pope Innocent III expropriated it in 1201, creating instead a general hospital whose administration he entrusted to Guido of Montpellier, founder of the Order of S. Spirito.

The existing Hospital of S. Spirito in Sassia, with its characteristic octagonal drum, was built by Sixtus IV between 1473–8; it still forms part of the modern hospital. The adjoining *ospedaletto* contains an interesting museum of the history of medicine from Roman times (a special permit is necessary to see this, obtainable at Lungotevere in Sassia No. 3). Continuing to the right along the Borgo S. Spirito, we come to the **Palazzo del Commendatore** (No. 3), formerly the residence of the director of the hospital; this was built between 1567–71; it has a fine porticoed court with a delightful ornamental clock. The Biblioteca Lancisiana, a library devoted to the history of medicine, is housed in the palace.

On the corner next to the Palazzo del Commendatore is the church of **S. Spirito in Sassia**; sadly this now bears no trace of its early English associations. It is, however, a fine Renaissance building, the main body of which was rebuilt after the sack of Rome in 1527 to the design of Antonio da Sangallo the Younger; the façade was completed during Sixtus V's reign (1585–90). The short Via dei Cavalieri del S. Sepolcro, opposite the church, brings us back into the Via della Conciliazione, and the **Piazza di S. Pietro**, Bernini's architectural masterpiece, begun and completed during the reign of the Chigi pope, Alexander VII (1655–67). Looking at it, it seems impossible that something so beautiful and so vast could have been designed and built in such a short time; then it is brought home to us that it is probably due largely to this that the piazza is a masterpiece—it was designed and carried out by the genius who conceived it; very few great architectural projects have been so fortunate, St. Peter's itself among them.

Rather surprisingly, the two beautiful fountains were not built at the same time: that on the right was erected for Paul V (1605–21), the other by Bernini in 1677. Between the fountains and the obelisk two round slabs of stone are set into the paving; standing on either of these the observer receives the impression that the piazza is outlined by a single, instead of a quadruple, file of columns. The other stone slabs, with rather worn inscriptions, set into the pavement round the obelisk, are a compass of winds.

The obelisk is the earliest monument in the piazza; it was in fact the first obelisk to be raised in modern times. Formerly it stood near the sacristy to the left of St. Peter's. In 1586 Sixtus V ordered Domenico Fontana to remove it to its present site; the work was carried out by 900 men and 140 horses with the aid of forty-four windlasses; it took more than four months. At the last moment it nearly ended in tragedy: when with superhuman efforts the huge stone was gradually being raised into position, for one terrible moment it remained stationary, the ropes were giving way. Dead silence reigned as the pope had ordered that under pain of death no one was to utter a sound during the dangerous operation of raising the obelisk; suddenly a voice called out: '*Aigua ae corde*' (in Genoese dialect 'water on the ropes'). The man who dared to break the silence and save the situation was Bresca, a sailor of Bordighera, who knew that this would cause them to tauten and shrink. As a sign of his gratitude Sixtus V commanded that henceforth the palms used in St. Peter's on Palm Sunday should come from Bordighera.

The obelisk is now crowned by the Chigi emblem of a star resting on five small mounts, surmounted by a cross; a relic of the Cross is contained within this device. In medieval times, when the obelisk stood beside St. Peter's it was believed that Caesar's ashes had once rested on the top, enclosed in a golden urn. Throughout the ages it had been one of the great landmarks of Rome. Even after its removal by Sixtus V, its former site was marked because right up until 1940 it was believed that it had stood on the spina of Nero's circus, the scene of the terrible martyrdom of so many Christians as described by Tacitus, and traditionally that of St. Peter himself. However, the recent excavations under St. Peter's clearly showed that the walls of Constantine's original basilica had not, as was formerly believed, been built over Nero's circus, but in fact on virgin soil. The obelisk is generally described as being that mentioned by Pliny as having been one of two made by Nencoreus, son of Sesostris, brought from Egypt to Rome and erected in the Circus of the Emperors Gaius, or Caligula, and Nero. It does indeed still bear Gaius's dedicatory inscription to the memory of his two predecessors Augustus and Tiberius, but the failure to find any trace of the circus under St. Peter's has posed an archaeological problem to which the answer has not yet been found.

On our way towards St. Peter's we should spare a moment to take even a distant glance at the wonderful ceremonial entry that Bernini provided for the Vatican Palace. The **Portone di Bronzo** opening on to it is reached through the inner right-hand end of the great curved colonnade. Through this door we get a vista of the long Corridore del Bernini leading to his famous *trompe l'oeil* **Scala Regia** in the far distance. Here, by the ingenious introduction of two rows of columns, diminishing in size as they recede, Bernini's genius evoked an air of sumptuous grandeur in what is in reality a steep and irregularly shaped stair.

We now ascend the delightful series of shallow steps, some curved and some taking their shape from this trapezoidal part of the piazza, that lead to the **Basilica of St. Peter** (details of opening times for St. Peter's, the treasure and the grottoes, together with advice on how to obtain the permit to view the Preconstantinian Necropolis are given in the Appendix).

The façade and nave of St. Peter's, both designed by Carlo Maderno, who was appointed architect in charge of the basilica in 1603, have been criticised possibly more than any other major work of architecture; the façade for being too long in relation to its height and the nave for obscuring the view of the dome from the piazza. In fact both faults were due to circumstances beyond Maderno's control. The façade as he planned it consisted only of the central section, which stands back a little and is reached from the raised part of the piazza; the two slightly projecting bays at either end, with high arched openings, are in fact the lower storeys of towers which Paul V later decided to have built and were not completed when he died in 1621. In 1637 Urban VIII accepted Bernini's project for raising these towers to a considerably greater height than was originally intended. One of them was actually built, but the walls beneath began to give way, and it had to be taken down, with the unfortunate result that the two tower bases have remained, looking like unwanted extensions of the façade.

In the same way, the addition of the nave—which transformed Bramante's original, and Michelangelo's later, plans for a church built in the form of a Greek cross into a Latin one—was imposed upon Maderno by Paul V. This was largely owing to liturgical reasons, but the pope also yielded to the pressure of opinion which considered that the whole of the area of the original Constantinian basilica should be covered by the new one. Thus the portico of the existing church rises somewhere about the middle of the site of the atrium of Constantine's basilica, while the far wall of the chapel containing Michelangelo's Pietà stands roughly on the line of the ancient façade.

The new basilica was consecrated on 18 November 1626, believed to be the one thousand three hundredth anniversary of dedication of its predecessor; though modern archaeological opinion places the building of the main body of Constantine's church approximately between the years 322 and 337, the year in which he died, and it was completed by his son. As in the other ancient basilicas, like S. Agnese and S. Lorenzo fuori le Mura, which were erected over cemeteries, the site was a difficult one; at the south-east corner the platform upon which the basilica was erected was raised 35 feet, in the northwest one it was levelled by cutting into the Vatican hill. Upon this base rose a lofty church with a five-aisled basilical nave, similar to St. Paul's Without the Walls. Constantine's nave reached as far as the present crossing beneath the dome, from here the transept stretched out to where the existing transept arms begin; the walls of the old apse still stand beneath the far side of the modern papal altar. As in St. Paul's Without the Walls and S. Maria Maggiore, the apse and clerestory were adorned with mosaics; a record of the former was made at the time of its destruction in 1592. Practically the only relics of the old basilica to have been preserved in the new one are six elaborately sculptured spiral marble columns. Four of these formerly supported the canopy above the shrine of St. Peter; that in the Constantinian church consisted of a box-like marble and porphyry structure enclosing an earlier monument; this stood on the chord of the apse (these columns were placed by Bernini in the galleries under the dome).

About the year 590, the deacon Agilulf came to St. Peter's and gave a vivid description of what he saw in it to Gregory of Tours, who wrote it down. After stating that St. Peter was buried 'in the Temple formerly called Vaticanum', he described the Constantinian shrine and said that in it there was a small window through which a man could push his head and pray for anything he wished, while letting a weighted piece of cloth down into the shrine itself. The cloth was then regarded as a sacred token, and if the suppliant's prayer was to be granted it would weigh more after it had been pulled up again than it had previously done.

Not long after Agilulf's visit either Pelagius II (579–90) or, more probably, Gregory the Great (590–604), carried out considerable alterations in and around the shrine of St. Peter. The whole of the apse was filled by a raised presbytery, that extended a short distance into the transept of the church; beneath this a semi-circular passage was made, of which the existing parts are now known as the covered Confessio. Stairs led up from a recessed space in the centre of the presbytery to an altar with a new canopy above. This altar was in fact the top of the Constantinian shrine, from which its own canopy had been removed. In the centre of the recessed space a small arched opening gave on to a niche adorned with a mosaic of Christ; this came to be known as the Niche of the Pallia, from the custom of placing there the woollen *pallia* (long strip-like vestments), previous to their bestowal upon newly-appointed or consecrated archbishops.

At Julius II's command Bramante began the ruthless destruction of the old building; in 1506 the foundation stone of the new one was laid and 2,500 workmen began the great piers of the crossing. In all the subsequent vicissitudes of the building—and, to quote James S. Ackerman, 'Almost every major architect in sixteenth-century Rome had a hand in the designing of St. Peter's' (*The Architecture of Michelangelo*, Zwemmer 1961)—they have remained the constant factor in the superlative grandeur of its design. After years of deliberation Julius and Bramante had produced a project of unprecedented magnificence, summed up in the phrase 'the Pantheon raised upon the Basilica of Constantine' (in this case of course the Basilica of Constantine and Maxentius by the Forum). With its low dome and centralised plan this church would have somewhat resembled S. Sophia in Constantinople. The great arches connecting the piers were completed in 1511; they were coffered in the classical Roman style. Ackerman believes that it was Bramante's rediscovery of the ancient Roman building technique of making strong concrete walls faced with brick that enabled him to plan on so vast a scale and with such fluidity. But, such is the irony of history, Bramante was really laying the foundations for the triumphal accomplishment that his hated rival, Michelangelo, was to achieve in the eyes of posterity.

Julius II's death in 1513, and Bramante's in the following year, brought a temporary halt to the building of the basilica. During the next two decades architect succeeded architect but, owing to the political and financial situation of the papacy, not much progress was made. Finally, in 1539, Paul III took matters in hand and ordered Sangallo to prepare a new model. This took seven years and cost as much as an ordinary church; not very surprisingly, as he planned an exceedingly complicated building. Some progress was made with this, but in 1546 Sangallo died and was replaced—most unwillingly—by the 71-year-old Michelangelo.

His disinclination, combined with age and fame, enabled the great man to dictate the terms of his contract; in acceding to them perhaps Paul III ruefully recalled Leo X's dictum that Michelangelo was 'frightening' and that 'one cannot deal with him'. In any case the new architect succeeded in getting *carte blanche*—he was given a completely free hand with the design and administration, he was in fact allowed to alter or destroy any existing part of the building. Still, posthumously, Bramante received his due, while Sangallo was castigated. Michelangelo himself wrote: 'One cannot deny that Bramante was as worthy an architect as any in ancient times. He laid down the first plan of St. Peter's, not full of confusion, but clear and pure, full of light. . . . And it was regarded as a beautiful thing.'

In essence Michelangelo's transformation of Sangallo's plan was to remove the complicated and fussy outer additions and ambulatories, reducing the building to an even more simple basic form than that of Bramante; while he suggested the effect of a Latin cross and nave by slightly extending the eastern end of the basilica. Although, as we have seen, Maderno's nave definitely changed the ground plan to a Latin cross, as Ackerman says: 'The Basilica today owes more to Michelangelo than to any other architect'.

The extraordinary thing is that to the world at large Michelangelo's name is chiefly associated with the design of the dome (in fact considerably altered by della Porta) whereas his great surviving contribution was to the body of the church. There is a practical reason for this: the parts of St. Peter's that were completed according to Michelangelo's plans are not normally seen by the public, as they face on to the Vatican gardens. Only those who are so fortunate as to penetrate beyond the sacristy can see and appreciate the full beauty and flowing lines of Michelangelo's design, the majesty of his gigantic order of pilasters—recalling those of the Senator's Palace on the Capitol—and the windows that Vasari described as being 'of varied form and awesome grandeur'.

The dome, on the other hand, is visible to all, and its drum—with its paired columns and lovely garlands—was indeed built according to Michelangelo's plans. But the curve of the great cupola is different; as far as we can judge his ultimate intention was to build a lower and more rounded one, surmounted by a proportionately loftier lantern. Thus, as we enter St. Peter's today, we must not be surprised if it appears to us almost as a typically baroque church. The higher dome, with its changed lighting effects, and above all the subsequent mannerist and baroque decoration have here almost completely obscured the legacy of Michelangelo.

As we pass through the great central portal, we will recall that it is from the window of the benediction loggia above that the twenty-nine popes who have been elected since it was built first gave their Apostolic blessing. Inside the portico, of the five great doors facing us that on the extreme right is the holy door, only opened every quarter of a century during Holy Year, when the Pope himself knocks on it with a silver hammer, making a tiny metallic note that through microphones now echoes around the whole basilica. The gleaming bronze doors in the centre were made by Filarete by command of Eugenius IV, for Old St. Peter's; the work occupied the artist for twelve years—from 1433 to 1445. Eugenius was the pope who presided over the famous Council of Florence in 1439 which sought to bring about the union of the churches in the face of the Turkish threat. The Emperor John Palaeologos came to it with the Orthodox Patriarch of Constantinople, also representatives of many of the other Oriental churches, including—to everyone's astonishment—some Ethiopian monks. The council and other scenes from Eugenius's life are represented in reliefs placed above and below the great figures of SS. Peter and Paul on the door; in them the Emperor John Palaeologos is distinguishable by his extraordinary long pointed hat, not very different from those Italian university students wear today. The Ethiopian monks, wearing turbans and long flowing robes, but with recognisably African features, are seen kneeling before Eugenius and making a visit to Rome, in the relief under the figures of St. Peter and Pope Eugenius on the right of the door. Beneath this again, the martyrdom of St. Peter is represented *inter duas metas*—as taking place in a classical setting, midway between the Pyramid of Sestius and the Meta Romuli. The main panels of the door are surrounded by foliage decoration framing a variety of motifs.

After we have entered the church, we should not forget to look at the back of the doors where, low down on the right

one, we will find Filarete's 'signature'. The central seven
figures are easily recognisable as Filarete and his assistants
executing what seems to be a joyous dance with the tools of
their profession in their hands (Filarete is the leader on the
right). There is some doubt as to the interpretation of the
somewhat shaggy dog-Latin inscription above them, as it is
full of mistakes and colloquialisms; but it is generally accepted
to mean that while others got the money and credit for his
work, Filarete at least had the fun of it. Even more cryptic are
the two figures at either end, one seated on an ass and the
other on a camel, playing the pipes; so far no scholar has been
able to arrive at an explanation of their significance.

Filarete's bronze doors are shortly to be joined by three
other modern ones, of which the first pair on the left are
already installed. Like the designer of the other two, which are
not yet ready, Giacomo Manzù was one of the winners of a
competition held in 1947. The main subjects of his composition
are the Death of Christ and the Death of the Virgin, but on the
back the sculptor has included a relief of the Vatican
Second Ecumenical Council and of Pope John XXIII conversing with Cardinal Rugambwa of Tanganyika; obvious
parallels to Filarete's reliefs of the Council of Florence and
the Ethiopian monks who came to Rome on 10 October
1441. Another and much more momentous date in October—
the 11th of that month in 1962—is also commemorated by
another work by Manzù in the portico. This is an outsize
representation of John XXIII's coat-of-arms in the pavement,
executed in inlaid marbles in what—for its august surroundings—is a remarkably modern style; it records the opening of
the Second Vatican Council.

The statues of sainted popes, gilding, *stucchi*, several
inscriptions, an equestrian statue of Charlemagne (in the far
distance on the left), made in 1725 by Agostino Cornacchini to
balance Bernini's one of Constantine (which is only visible on
the right when the doors to the Scala Regia are open), combine to give typically baroque splendour to the portico. But
before leaving it, we should look above the central portal
giving on to the piazza. There, scarcely distinguishable among
the shadows, is all that restoration has left of Giotto's famous
mosaic of the Navicella—the barque which is the symbol of
the Church. On the right Christ is seen walking upon the
waters and, almost invisible beneath Him is the donor,

Cardinal Stefaneschi, who gave the mosaic to Old St. Peter's in 1298.

Pushing aside the heavy padded leather curtain, we now enter the basilica. At first, to be frank, we are disappointed; we have heard so much about its stupendous size that we expect this to strike us all at once. Only gradually does it dawn upon us—as we watch people draw near to this or that monument, strangely they appear to shrink, they are, of course, dwarfed by the scale of everything in the building. This in its turn overwhelms us. Many also find the grandeur of gold, marbles and mosaics oppressive, but it must be borne in mind that St. Peter's was built as the setting for great festivals, canonisations and papal functions; then and then only does it really come into its own.

When the vast nave and aisles are crammed to overflowing with people of every race, the tribunes filled with gorgeous uniforms and women in black mantillas, and the shining halberds and helmets and orange and purple slashed uniforms of the Swiss Guard flash out among the crowd, the whole basilica is filled with an electric current of anticipation as everyone awaits the arrival of the Pope. He is preceded by a long procession, opened by a Minimite friar carrying a bunch of flowers on a staff; like English judges' posies, this is a relic of the days when herbs were believed to be disinfectants against plague. Then follow representatives of all the religious orders, prelates and the canons of the great papal basilicas, the silver mace bearers attired in ruffs and flowing Renaissance coats. Even more picturesque are the Privy Chamberlains, with cloak and sword, in black costumes of the type which we associate with Henry VIII; the letters C. S. on their gold chains signify *cubiculum secretum*, the Latin title of their office which goes back to early medieval times.

At last the Pope himself comes into sight, surrounded by the Guard and fan bearers waving the great ostrich-feather *fiabella*, shaped like palm leaves, said to have originated with religious services held in the catacombs. Four prelates hold the canopy high above the Pope's head as he is borne on the shoulders of four red-robed *sediari* (chair bearers) in the gestatorial chair. This picturesque and practical custom seems to have originated when, after the period of Avignon and the Schism, a fifteenth-century pope was nearly crushed by the welcoming crowd outside the Lateran; his attendants then lifted him in a chair on their shoulders for all to see. The order of the procession is still the same as that of the papal caval-cades which formerly rode through the city at great festivals; then as now the rear is brought up by the Noble Guard, splendid in scarlet uniforms and shining helmets with flowing black horse tails.

If we have not been so fortunate as to be present in the basilica on one of these great occasions, we must try for a moment to conjure up the scene in our imagination, as its colour, pageantry and human warmth will cast a glow over the somewhat formidable serried ranks of monuments that now confront us. The least conspicuous and, historically, one of the most interesting, is the great circular porphyry slab, which lies in the pavement right in front of the central door. On this on Christmas night of the year 800, Charlemagne knelt for his coronation as the first Emperor of the West since the deposition of Romulus Augustulus in 476; formerly the slab lay near the altar of Old St. Peter's. The first two arches on either side of the nave belong to Maderno's prolongation of the basilica; some idea of its size is brought home to us by brass tablets in the pavement giving the comparative length of other great churches: of these St. Paul's in London is the largest. A great deal of the decoration of this part of the basilica was designed by Bernini, notably the stucco alle-gorical figures in the spandrels of the arches and the marble decoration of the pillars, where *putti* uphold palm-wreathed portraits of early popes and the papal tiara and keys. The Pamphilj dove at the top and bottom of each panel and the fleurs-de-lis above indicate that the decoration was carried out for Innocent X.

At the base of the last pillar on the right the famous **Bronze Statue of St. Peter** sits enthroned. Formerly believed to be a work of the fifth century, this is now dated to the thirteenth and attributed to Arnolfo di Cambio. It is in any case a master-piece, implicit with dignity in every line, and one of the most beautiful things in the whole basilica; the gorgeous robes and jewels with which the statue is clad on the feast day of SS. Peter and Paul can only detract from its majesty. A mosaic medallion portrait of Pius IX, placed on the wall above the statue in 1871, records the fact that he was the first pope who exceeded the twenty-five years of St. Peter's pontificate which, according to an old tradition, would never be excelled; in fact Pius's successor, Leo XIII, reigned from 1878 to 1903.

We now find ourselves in the central crossing, standing beneath the vast sweep of the dome, of which the soaring height dwarfs everything else in sight. Light streams in from the encircling windows of the dome, glancing sunbeams illuminate the grey of marble, the glitter of gold and the dull gleam of bronze. This is the dominant colour theme of one's first impression and, in memory over the years, it is probably the most lasting. They are the materials from which Bernini wrought some of his greatest works that stand in this part of the basilica; the statue of S. Longinus with the lance—for which Bernini made twenty-two studies—is in the niche at the base of the first of Bramante's piers on the right. The balconies high up on all four piers were also designed by him; it is here that he installed the six spiral marble columns from Old St. Peter's and it is from these balconies that at Easter and other great feasts the chief relics are displayed—the Sacred Lance, which is believed to have pierced Christ's side as he hung on the Cross, the largest fragment of the Cross, and the *Volto Santo*, or Veronica's veil, said to have received the imprint of Jesus' face on his way to Calvary. Statues of St. Helena, St. Andrew and St. Veronica stand at the base of the piers below the balconies where the relics associated with them are exhibited.

It must be admitted that not all the decoration of this part of St. Peter's approached Bernini's standard; guides are wont to dwell enthusiastically upon the vast size of the mosaics in the pendentives and the cupola, noting that St. Mark's pen (in one of the roundels of the pendentives) is a metre and a half long. Certainly the scale is remarkable, but few would be prepared to argue with Wittkower's description of the mosaics in the dome as 'trite representations in mosaic of Christ and the Apostles, half-figures of popes and saints, and angels with the instruments of the Passion'. They were designed by Clement VIII's favourite artist Cavaliere d'Arpino, and took from 1589 to 1612 to execute.

Even Augustus Hare, who was not a Bernini enthusiast, was not prepared to criticise the grandeur of the great bronze **Baldacchino** which he raised—to the same height as that of Palazzo Farnese—above the papal altar at which only the Pope celebrates Mass, facing the congregation. Looking at the huge canopy, one is reminded of the fantastic splendour of that ephemeral type of architecture which, especially in seventeenth-century Italy, was designed for the decoration of churches, piazzas and palaces to celebrate such varied occasions as the canonisation of a saint, the triumphal entry of a pope or the birth of a royal heir. Possibly Bernini felt that the joy of great feasts, associated with the enduring qualities of bronze, most appropriately expressed the sentiments experienced in such a place. But the design of his *baldacchino* has a much more curious association: all its baroque splendour cannot obscure the fact that its basic form resembles that of the much more modest canopy which surmounted the shrine of St. Peter in the Constantinian basilica. From the *Liber Pontificalis*, and a casket found in Pola in 1906, we know that this was supported by serpentine marble columns and had a curved open canopy above, but Bernini could not possibly have been aware of it.

These columns themselves have an interesting history. The original six, which Constantine had brought from Greece, date from the second century AD and probably came from some classical building near Constantinople. To these Gregory III added another six, of similar period and design, when he placed a new screen before St. Peter's shrine in the eighth century. So striking was their aspect that not only were they much copied, especially for paschal candlesticks, but they became the subject of legend. In the Middle Ages they were believed to have come from the Temple of Apollo at Troy; by the fifteenth century they were nothing less than the columns of Solomon's Temple, against one of which Christ leaned while disputing with the doctors. After considerable damage by pious relic collectors, this one is now kept behind the grille in the same chapel as Michelangelo's Pietà; two others flank the altar on the right in the chapel of the Blessed Sacrament, these last are the ones which inspired Bernini's design of the *baldacchino*.

The *baldacchino* took more than ten years to make and, as everyone knows, it aroused the most famous pasquinade of all—*quod non fecerunt barbari, fecerunt Barberini* (what the barbarians didn't do, the Barberini did), because it was said to have been made from bronze beams taken from the portico of the Pantheon. It was inaugurated on 28 June 1633 on the eve of the feast of the SS. Peter and Paul by the Barberini pope, Urban VIII, whose heraldic bees swarm among the bay leaves of the columns. There is a legend that the *baldacchino* was commissioned by Urban VIII as a thank-offering for the safe survival of a favourite niece, who nearly died in giving birth to a child. This is substantiated by some curious reliefs appearing on the marble pedestals which support the bronze columns. Here the escutcheons upon which the Barberini bees are emblazoned are surmounted by a series of heads, all but the two facing the nave representing a woman's face with varying expressions of pain, and other details are also said to have a gynaecological significance, while on the last pedestal on the right there appears a smiling baby's face.

Stretching out before the *baldacchino* is the horseshoe-shaped area of the sunken open **Confessio**, surrounded by a balustrade upon which ninety-five gilded lamps burn perpetually. The rich marble and intarsio decoration of the Confessio was designed by Maderno and completed in 1615. Two curving flights of steps lead down to the floor, which is on a level with the '*sacre grotte*' or crypt of St. Peter's. Strangely in so sacred a spot, the only floral decoration is usually a rather melancholy potted palm. In the centre is Canova's kneeling statue of Pius VI, who is buried beneath. Facing the statue, directly beneath the papal altar, is the heavy gilded grille which conceals the sixth-century Niche of the Pallia which has survived all the subsequent vicissitudes of the building history of St. Peter's. Though much restored, the original mosaic of Christ is still there. Before it, the floor of the niche is covered by a gilded bronze plaque, with a cross in the centre, flanked by the keys and surmounted by the papal tiara; at the bottom the dove of the Pamphilj Pope, Innocent X, indicates that the plaque was laid down during his reign (1644–55). In the right-hand angle of the cross is a small door opening on to a shaft, the same down which the deacon Agilulf, and countless other pilgrims, lowered their *brandea*.

Until 1940 little or nothing was known about what lay below this spot which marks the traditional last resting-place of St. Peter. The Renaissance architects had recorded the existence of pagan tombs discovered beneath Constantine's church during the building of the new basilica, but that was all. In 1939, when the preparations for the tomb of Pius XI were being made in the '*sacre grotte*', Pius XII decided to have the floor of the crypt lowered in order to make it more spacious.

While the work was in progress, portions of the pavement of the Constantinian basilica were discovered as well as the remains of Christian and pagan tombs. The pope then ordered the complete excavation of the whole crypt, including—which was absolutely unprecedented—the archaeological examination of the area of the shrine behind the Confessio. The work continued until 1949; two years later the official Vatican report *Esplorazioni sotto la confessione di San Pietro in Vaticano eseguiti negli anni 1940–1949* was published. As its title indicates, this was solely concerned with the excavations under and around the shrine behind the Confessio of St. Peter's and is a work intended for scholars rather than the general public.

However, this was followed in 1956 by one of the most fascinating books ever written on an archaeological subject, *The Shrine of St. Peter* by Jocelyn Toynbee and John Ward Perkins (respectively Professor of Classical Archaeology at Cambridge and Director of the British School at Rome). In this book, which is based on the Vatican report, the authors have made the history and the discovery of the pre-Constantinian necropolis or cemetery found beneath St. Peter's come vividly alive for the general reader, both in its Christian and pagan aspects. Normally it is open to the public by special permission; the visit is always made in small parties accompanied by highly-qualified guides. The building history of the site is, however, so complicated that the *Shrine of St. Peter* is of the greatest assistance to the ordinary traveller in understanding it, and I am much indebted to this book for the short description which follows, for the benefit of those who may not have the same good fortune as I had in being able to see the excavations themselves.

Very briefly, what the excavators found under the crypt of the existing basilica, and Constantine's earlier one that preceded it, was a cemetery resembling that of the Isola Sacra near Ostia. The tombs were mostly pagan ones dating from the second and third centuries of our era. Many have preserved their original painted stucco, and mosaic decorations in all their brilliant colour, as fresh as if they had been made yesterday, instead of having been buried ever since Constantine levelled the area to build his basilica. This is in fact one of the best preserved Roman burial grounds in existence, and a very beautiful sight.

In the western part of this cemetery, among poorer and earlier places of burial, rise the remains of a monument or *aedicula*, which is generally accepted by scholars to be the 'trophy' of St. Peter, described by the priest Gaius as already standing on the Vatican Hill about the year 200 (Gaius's description is recorded in Eusebius's *Ecclesiastical History*). This *aedicula*, and the wall of which it is part are dated by archaeologists approximately to the period AD 160–70; there is ample evidence to show that it was very carefully sited to mark a precise spot. The *aedicula* consisted of three niches, one above the other, the lowest apparently being an arched recess forming part of the foundations of the wall below ground level; the other two were contemporary with the wall itself, being built into it, with a small table-like stone shelf, supported by colonnettes, separating them. It is the central one of these three niches that, slightly modified, continues to exist as the Niche of the Pallia, above which rises the papal altar and baldacchino of St. Peter's.

It was this *aedicula* which Constantine had enclosed in his box-like marble and porphyry shrine that, with its canopy, formed the architectural focus and *raison d'être* of his whole church. The shrine was profaned and rifled at some later date in the Middle Ages, probably during the Saracen incursion of 846. Very clear evidence of this destruction was found by the excavators, on the *aedicula* itself and beneath it; in fact practically all that remained below was an empty hole that, from its dimensions, might well formerly have contained a casket. The only discovery which might be interpreted as relics were some bones found in a recess beneath the wall into which the *aedicula* was built. These the excavators stated were human, though no authoritative scientific pronouncement has yet been made about them.

After examining the evidence, both from archaeological and literary sources, that the *aedicula* was built on the site of St. Peter's grave, or possibly of his martyrdom, the authors of *The Shrine of St. Peter* conclude as follows: 'Although it is not certain that the *aedicula* marks the site of an earlier grave, the hypothesis that it did so explains much that is otherwise obscure; and that although there is nothing to prove that this grave was that of St. Peter, nothing in the archaeological evidence is inconsistent with such identification.'

Although the Niche of the Pallia is concealed behind the

gilded grille in the Confessio, we shall see later that the back of Constantine's marble and porphyry shrine, which enclosed the *aedicula*, is still visible in the Cappella Clementina from the Grotte Nuove part of the crypt; while from the excavations of the pre-Constantinian cemetery it is possible to see the wall of which the *aedicula* forms a part.

As we have been looking at the Confessio and Baldacchino, our eyes have been irresistibly drawn beyond them to Bernini's glory surrounding the **Cattedra of St. Peter**; this is exactly what the artist intended. The designs of the Baldacchino and Cattedra are, as it were, interdependent, the first serving as a frame through which the other is intended to be seen, though their actual creation was separated by a period of years—the Cattedra only being begun in the reign of Alexander VII (1655–67). The so-called Cattedra of St. Peter, which we do not see, is an ancient wooden chair with ivory ornamentation, dating from Carolingian times; this was traditionally said to have been used by the Apostle. It is encased in Bernini's bronze throne with gilded reliefs that is raised above the altar of the central apse. Surrounding and supporting the throne are Bernini's bronze statues of four of the great Doctors of the Church; the two in front, wearing mitres, are SS. Ambrose and Augustine representing the Latin Church, those behind are SS. Athanasius and John Chrysostom, of the Greek one. Over and above this group, clouds, gilded rays and a mass of angelic figures are entwined, providing a frame for the central window in which the dove of the Holy Spirit hovers in the brilliance of the Roman sunlight without.

On either side of the Cattedra chapel are two of the finest papal tombs in the basilica; that on the right was designed by Bernini for Urban VIII. Here again bronze, marble and gilding are combined to produce an effect of great richness; the marble figures represent Charity and Justice, while the hand of Death is seen writing the pope's name on a marble slab, and bronze Barberini bees appear to rest for a moment on the monument before taking their last flight. Paul III's monument, on the left, is considered to be the masterpiece of Guglielmo della Porta; it was designed between 1551 and 1575. The tomb is flanked by allegorical figures of Justice and Prudence which are said to be portraits of this Farnese pope's sister—the famous Giulia Bella—and his mother, Giovanella Caetani. The classical features and bare feet are about all that can now be seen of the formerly nude Justice, whose beauty was such that it aroused an unhealthy infatuation; the figure is swathed in metal draperies.

In order to make a systematic tour of the basilica we would be wise to return to the beginning of the right-hand aisle, where the first chapel contains the most famous work of art in the whole building—Michelangelo's **Pietà**, the only sculpture that he ever signed. Jacopo Galli, Michelangelo's banker friend, negotiated this very important commission for the young sculptor (he was only 24) with the French Ambassador, Cardinal Jean Bilhères de Lagraulas. Galli promised that the group would be 'the most beautiful work in marble in Rome today': few men have kept their word better. The contract was signed on 27 August 1498; it stipulated that the sculpture should be finished a year from that date, the price to be 450 golden ducats. Barely visible through the grille on the right of the chapel is the Colonna Santa, one of the spiral columns from the Constantinian basilica which was believed to have been the one against which Christ leaned in the Temple of Solomon.

Continuing along the right aisle, we see almost immediately on the left the monument of Queen Christina of Sweden, who is one of the few women to have been buried in St. Peter's. She died in Rome in 1689, having lived there for a great deal of her life after her abdication and her conversion to Roman Catholicism; the monument is by Carlo Fontana. Opposite, on the right, is the monument of Leo XII (1823–9). Farther up the aisle, on the adjoining pier on the left, is the monument to Countess Matilda, of Canossa fame; although she died in 1115, the monument was designed by Bernini.

The large and splendid Cappella del SS. Sacramento comes next on the right. Here the beautiful wrought-iron gate is the work of Borromini, the gilded bronze pyx on the central altar is by Bernini, its design was inspired by the Tempietto del Bramante; above it hangs Pietro da Cortona's 'Trinity'. On either side of the altar on the right of this chapel are the two marble columns from the Constantinian basilica that gave Bernini his idea for the Baldacchino. Immediately beyond the chapel, on the right of the aisle, is the eighteenth-century monument of Gregory XIII, the Boncampagni pope who reformed the calendar in 1582, substituting the one called after him for the ancient Roman Julian calendar; a relief on the sarcophagus recalls this event. Immediately opposite, on the left of the aisle, is the severely simple monument of Gregory XIV. According to legend the poverty of its style is due to the fact that gold and jewels to the value of 15,000 *scudi* were ground up to provide a miraculous potion to cure the pope's illness; without success, however, as he reigned for only a few months in 1590.

Having reached the end of the aisle, we now turn right into the Cappella Gregoriana, designed by Giacomo della Porta in 1583. Above the altar facing us is the little twelfth-century 'Madonna del Soccorso' from Old St. Peter's. We continue into the right transept where, as in most of the rest of the basilica, the altars are surmounted by mosaic copies of famous pictures—that on the right is taken from Poussin's 'Martyrdom of St. Erasmus', while the original is in the Vatican Pinacoteca. Continuing towards the western end of the basilica, we see Clement XIII's celebrated monument by Canova. It stands above a door on the right leading to the Cappella di S. Michele.

Traversing the basilica, between the Baldacchino and the Cattedra, we see facing us in the far corner the Cappella della Colonna, with the tomb of St. Leo the Great beneath the altar on the right. Above this is Algardi's famous relief of St. Leo's meeting with Attila. Two early medieval popes, SS. Leo II and Leo III, are buried beneath the altar on the left, while the body of Leo XII (1823-9) actually lies beneath the pavement in the centre (though his monument is the one we have already seen in the right nave: the Latin inscription 'Least among those to inherit so great a name' was dictated by the pope himself shortly before his death.

Traversing the left transept we come to the Cappella Clementina. Like the Cappella Gregoriana, on the opposite side of the basilica, this was also the work of Giacomo della Porta. Above the altar facing us is the neo-classical monument of Pius VII. This was erected in 1823; it is the work of Thorwaldsen and was commissioned by Cardinal Consalvi, who was much criticised for having employed a Protestant artist. It is in fact the only part of St. Peter's made by non-Catholic hands.

We now come to the left aisle, where, immediately on the right, is the monument of Leo XI, designed by Algardi. The relief on the sarcophagus portrays the scene when the pope, who was then still Cardinal Medici, witnessed Henri IV's renunciation of the Protestant faith. The roses and the words *sic floruit*, inscribed on the ends of the plinth, refer to this pope's very short reign of twenty-four days. Farther down the aisle, on the left, is the beautiful fifteenth-century bronze tomb of Innocent VIII, designed by Pollaiuolo. This is the only papal monument from Old St. Peter's that was transferred to the new one, possibly because, in the seated effigy the pope is shown holding in his hand the relic of the sacred lance, given to him by the Sultan Bajazet II.

Built into the next pier on the left is the monument designed by Canova to mark the spot in the grottoes below where the three last members of the royal House of Stuart lie buried. On it are portrait busts of the 'Old Pretender' and 'Bonnie Prince Charlie' in armour, Henry in his cardinal's robes beneath two winged genii, holding reversed torches, convey something of the tragedy of those three lives. Queen Elizabeth the Queen Mother came to see the monument when she was in Rome and paid for the restoration of the tomb. On the wall opposite, a mosaic portrait of Maria Clementina Sobieska looks down from her baroque monument at that of her husband and sons; she died of tuberculosis at the age of 33 and was also buried in St. Peter's. The last chapel on the right is the baptistry; the font, which is the cover of an antique porphyry sarcophagus formerly believed to have been that of Hadrian, has a bronze cover designed by Carlo Fontana.

Having completed our tour of the basilica itself, the question of what to see next really depends on the time of year. In the hot summer months we would be wise to continue with the Treasury and the Grottoes, reserving to the last our visit to the roof and cupola; though there is nearly always a breeze on the roof, the climb in the interior of the dome to the lantern above can be something of an ordeal in hot weather. To see the Treasury, we retrace our steps past Pius VII's monument to the part of the basilica between the Cappella Clementina and the left transept, where we find the sacristy door on the left.

The sacristy, which is connected to the basilica by two open galleries, was built in the eighteenth century on the site of the Roman tomb that had been converted into a chapel and was known as the Cappella di S. Andrea or della Madonna della Febbre (Our Lady Protectress against Fever). A painting of the Madonna della Febbre (dating probably from the fourteenth century) is still preserved in the Sagrestia dei Beneficiati; it is enclosed in a beautiful frame by Donatello, dated about 1432.

The **Treasury of St. Peter's** is housed in an adjoining suite of rooms; it was sacked in 846 by the Saracens, again during the sack of Rome in 1527 and further diminished by the terms of the Napoleonic Treaty of Tolentino. Travellers should therefore not be surprised to find that most of the objects gathered there (which are clearly labelled) are comparatively modern. The one exception is the magnificent jewelled cross given by the Emperor Justin II, probably dating from the year 575. The famous blue and gold 'Dalmatic of Charlemagne' is of a much later date; guide-books usually attribute it to the tenth or eleventh century, but D. Talbot Rice in the *Art of Byzantium* (London 1959) dates it to the early fifteenth century. Other interesting exhibits of about this period are the fisherman's ring of Sixtus IV (1471–84) and two beautiful candelabra by Pollaiuolo. All of these are in the first room. In the second room are another fine pair of candelabra, attributed to Cellini, and an astonishing cross given to Pius X (1903–14); resting on a mass of uncut emeralds, it is smothered in glittering gems.

It must be admitted that many of the objects exhibited in the treasury are notable rather for their intrinsic value than their artistic worth, but there are others which are interesting for their associations. In this class are two chalices, one studded with diamonds that belonged to the last of the Stuarts, Cardinal Henry of York; the other, the first object to be made of platinum, was presented by Charles III of Spain to Pius VI (1775–99). The treasury also includes recent gifts, such as those made by heads of states who have been received in audience by the popes.

The Sacre Grotte Vaticane, or **Crypt of St. Peter's,** occupy the area between the floor of the basilica and the original constantinian one. Adjoining the crypt or grottoes are rooms in which are exhibited objects from the old Museo Petriano and finds from the 1940–50 excavations. To reach them we emerge from the basilica, turn sharply to the right and descend the steps to the Via dell' Arco delle Campane. Two Swiss Guardsmen are on duty at the Arco delle Campane, but will let one enter in order to see the Grotte. Traversing the

Piazza dei Protomartiri Romani, so called because it was believed to be on the site of Nero's circus (the Vatican obelisk formerly stood at the far end), we see on our left the entrance to the picturesque little German cemetery, whose origins date back to the eighth century. We now walk under one of the open passages leading to the sacristy and find ourselves in the little Piazza Braschi; the entrance to the Grottoes is on our right.

Before reaching the Grottoes themselves, we pass through six rooms, arranged more or less as a museum, containing relics of Old St. Peter's and some tombs. Room IV (on the left after the first three) is the most interesting. It contains mosaics and other fragments from the old church, including heads of St. Bernard of Clairvaux and of an angel, probably by Melozzo da Forli; also Arnolfo di Cambio's statue of Boniface VIII (1294–1303) and Paolo da Siena's Benedict XII (1303–4). In room VI is Pollaiuolo's magnificent monument to Sixtus IV (1471–84); the pope lies on a catafalque surrounded by reliefs personifying the cardinal and theological virtues, while the base is ornamented with female figures symbolising the arts and sciences.

Returning to the third room, from which stairs lead down to the recently excavated pre-Constantinian cemetery, a few steps bring us into the Sacre Grotte or crypt itself. This is divided into two sections, somewhat misleadingly named the Grotte Vecchie and the Grotte Nuove. In fact the Grotte Nuove were made first, between 1534 and 1546, when Paul III continued with the building of New St. Peter's; they lie beneath the crossing and dome of the existing church and take the form of a horseshoe-shaped passage with adjoining chapels, the inner wall of the curving part being the wall of the apse of the original Constantinian basilica. They are called the Grotte Nuove because they were decorated at a later period than the Grotte Vecchie. The Grotte Vecchie, on the other hand, date from 1606, when Paul V ordered the last remaining part of Old St. Peter's to be knocked down in order to make way for the nave of the new basilica; they stretch for a considerable distance beneath it. When, in 1939, the floor of the Grotte was lowered, workmen found traces of the pavement of the old Constantinian basilica at a depth of only 30 centimetres.

We enter the Grotte Vecchie first: they have the appearance of a normal crypt, with great piers dividing their area into a nave and two aisles; the entrance is roughly in the middle of the left aisle. Immediately on the right is the funerary monument of the first Borgia Pope, Calixtus III (1455–8). The next tomb but one is that of Nicholas Breakspear, the only Englishman to become a pope, who reigned as Hadrian IV from 1154 to 1159; he is buried in a fine antique red granite sarcophagus of the third century. Almost opposite is the tomb of the only emperor to be buried in St. Peter's, Otto II, who died in Rome in 983; he was interred in a simple paleo-Christian sarcophagus. In a niche at the end of the nave, on the right, is a statue of St. Peter which stood in the old basilica; the figure is a classical one of the third century, to which a head was added in the Middle Ages, possibly by Arnolfo di Cambio.

Continuing down the right aisle we come to the tomb of the much-loved late Pope, John XXIII; the pavement before it is always covered with flowers. The very beautiful altar at the end of the aisle is composed of fragments from the Orsini chapel of Old St. Peter's; it consists of a relief of the Madonna and Child flanked by SS. Peter and Paul and the figures of the Orsini Pope, Nicholas III (1277–80), and a cardinal; it is a fifteenth-century work by Isaia da Pisa.

By a door on the right we now enter the Grotte Nuove. Almost immediately on the right is the passage leading to the Cappella di S. Longino, excavated, like those of SS. Helena, Veronica and Andrew, into the bases of the great piers supporting the dome. After this, in a vaulted room on the right, is the magnificent monument of Paul II (1464–71), its creation occupied Giovanni Dalmata and Mino da Fiesole for something like ten years, Dalmata's allegorical figure of Hope is particularly famous, so are Mino da Fiesole's Faith and Charity. Continuing along the passage of the Grotte Nuove, we catch fascinating glimpses of the basilica and dome above, through grilles in the ceiling, and, through a door on the left, of the Confessio. The Cappella di S. Elena opens off to the right as we reach the curve and embedded into the wall on the left (that of the original Constantinian apse) are some fine reliefs which formed part of Sixtus IV's marble *baldacchino* in Old St. Peter's.

Half-way round the curve a vaulted passage (on the left) decorated with blue and gold *stucchi*, leads into the small cruciform **Cappella di S. Pietro** or **Cappella Clementina**, made by Clement VIII (1592–1605). To all outward intents and purposes this looks like a typical chapel of the period, but if we look carefully above the altar, we see a plain white marble slab with a strip of porphyry in the middle. This is the back of the Constantinian shrine enclosing the second-century *aedicula*, believed to mark the traditional burial place of St. Peter, which was discovered during the recent excavations. By his own wish Pius XII was buried in the chapel opening out of the Grotte Nuove opposite. Continuing along the passage, we pass the entrances to the Cappella di S. Veronica, also that of S. Maria in Porticu containing a ninth-century Madonna and Child and a fourteenth-century fresco attributed to Pietro Cavallini. A third chapel, opening off to the right, is called Cappella della Madonna della Febbre or delle Febbri, after the old one beside Old St. Peter's, it contains a fresco of the Madonna and Child from the original chapel. Just before we arrive at the entrance passage leading to the Cappella di S. Andrea, we see affixed to the wall an eighth-century mosaic of the Madonna and Child enthroned, with two praying figures.

We now re-emerge into the Grotte Vecchie and, passing into the nave, see the superb central altar with its relief of Christ, by Giovanni Dalmata, that came from the tomb of Nicholas V (1447–55). Continuing down the left aisle, among the papal tombs we find that of the last Stuarts; in all the Grotte contain the tombs of eighteen popes, one emperor and two queens. If we happen to have visited them when the lights are on in the excavated area beneath, we will also have been able to catch glimpses, through grilles in the pavement, of the pre-Constantinian cemetery that lies below.

We now cross to the far side of the right aisle where a door, opposite that in the left aisle by which we entered the Grotte, leads into three more museum rooms. The first of these, number VII, is largely devoted to inscriptions ranging in date from paleo-Christian times to the end of the fourteenth century. Two rooms on the left, which are thrown together to make room VIII, contain an interesting collection of paleo-Christian sarcophagi. The long passage leading to the exit and room X, by which we emerge from the Grotte, contain some interesting reliefs and classical fragments, including some very fine marble plaques, with floral ornamentation, of the Augustan period. Once again in the open air, we pass by way of the Vatican post office back into the Piazza of St. Peter's.

An expedition to the roof and dome is all that now remains

to complete our itinerary. Re-entering St. Peter's, we turn into the left aisle and, just after the baptistry, find the door on the left, underneath Clementina Sobieska's monument, leading to the lifts which take us to the roof. The sensations produced by the roof of St. Peter's are absolutely unexpected and extraordinary; the breeze, the light and air and the wonderful cloudscapes, combined with the undulating surface, give the impression of walking on the deck of a ship at sea—in fact this is highly appropriate, as a ship has since time immemorial been the symbol of the Catholic Church. It is, of course, a ship dreamed of in some fantastic never-never-land of Renaissance and baroque architectural fantasy, with the immense statues of the façade lining the 'rail' and domes of every size and description springing from the 'deck', culminating in the majesty of the vast central cupola. Nevertheless there is a feeling of a holiday spirit abroad among the visitors who pace to and fro, searching for the best vantage points from which to see and photograph the truly stupendous views. This is aided and abetted by the existence of a small *Espresso* bar and post office where one can buy picture postcards.

Two sets of stairs within the drum rise to the gallery that encircles the base of the interior of the great dome. This is 53 metres above the floor of St. Peter's and, possibly more than anything else, gives one an idea of the basilica's enormous size—the people walking in the crossing below look like ants. A narrow spiral stair and the more gradual curve of the *lumaca* di S. Andrea bring us to the second gallery beneath the lantern, 20 metres higher than the last. Finally, by a very narrow spiral stair, we reach the circular balcony on the outside of the lantern, with its fabulous circular view of all Rome.

Back once more in the piazza, we experience something of the same sensations of a mountaineer returning to his base: it seems strange to find all its varied life continuing as before. As the shadows lengthen, the piazza gradually empties of its transient population; only one group remains, the patient cabbies waiting for a fare. To those who know and love old Rome it is a joy to see them there, survivors from another age into the modern Italy of mechanised miracles. They provide a link between us and the countless thousands who have passed this way before. For they may well be descendants of those selfsame *vetturini* that occupy such a special place in travel literature, for the charmed moment when they reined in their horses and, pointing their whips, cried: 'Ecco Roma!' as the dome of St. Peter's first appeared on the horizon. *Ecco Roma* —here is Rome—this book has tried to interpret something of the magic that those words convey.

Appendix

❧

Places of Interest not Mentioned in the Text

CATACOMBS OF PRISCILLA 430 Via Salaria, open 9 a.m. to midday and from 3 p.m. to sunset.

CATACOMBS OF S. AGNESE (under the Church of S. Agnese fuori le Mura) 349 Via Nomentana, open 8 a.m. to midday and from 3 p.m. to sunset.

GALLERIA NAZIONALE D'ARTE MODERNA 135 Viale delle Belle Arti (state owned). Closed Mondays; open Sundays and half-holidays (see p. 547) 9 a.m.–1 p.m.; summer, 9 a.m.–1 p.m. and 4–6 p.m.; winter, 9 a.m.–1 p.m. and 4–6 p.m. Collection of painting and sculpture of European artists and sculptors of nineteenth and twentieth centuries.

GIARDINO ZOOLOGICO Villa Borghese, open 8.30 a.m. to sunset.

MUSEO DELLA CIVILTÀ ROMANA Piazza Agnelli E.U.R. (municipally owned). Closed Mondays; for holidays see p. 563. Sundays 9 a.m.–1 p.m.; weekdays 9 a.m.–2 p.m., also Tuesdays and Thursdays 5–8 p.m. A collection of *reproductions* illustrating the history of Rome and her influence in the world, including the model of Rome in imperial times.

MUSEO NAZIONALE DELLE ARTI E TRADIZIONI POPOLARI Piazza, Marconi E.U.R. (state owned). Closed Mondays, open Sundays and half-holidays (see p. 547) 9 a.m.–1 p.m.; summer and winter 9 a.m.–2 p.m. Collection illustrating Italian folklore, festivals, customs and costumes.

MUSEO PREISTORICO E PROTOSTORICO DEL LAZIO Piazza Marconi, E.U.R. (state owned). Closed Mondays. Open Sundays and half-holidays (see p. 547) 9 a.m.–1 p.m.; summer and winter 9 a.m.–2 p.m.

MUSEO DELLA VIA OSTIENSE Porta S. Paolo (state owned). Closed Mondays, open Sundays and half-holidays (see p. 547) 9 a.m.–1.30 p.m.; summer and winter 9 a.m.–1.30 p.m.

CONTEMPORARY ARCHITECTURE Apart from the famous Stazione Termini, of special interest are the following: Palazzo dello Sport and other installations for the Olympic Games of 1960 at the E.U.R., also the Palazzetto dello Sport and Stadio Flaminio near the Villaggio Olimpico, half-way down the Viale Tiziano, and the Stadio Olimpico at the Foro Italico.

ILLUMINATIONS The Romans excel in the art of floodlighting monuments, an increasing number of these are now illuminated every night; these include the Capitol and Forum (this last is not illuminated during the summer months when there is *Son et Lumière*), the Palatine seen from the Circus Maximus, the Colosseum, the Theatre of Marcellus, Castel S. Angelo, Fountain of Trevi, Fountains of Piazza Navona, Palazzo Farnese, Cancelleria, S. Maria in Cosmedin and many other important churches and palaces.

By Special Permit

VILLA DORIA PAMPHILJ 12 Via S. Pancrazio (Janiculum), permit obtainable from Amministrazione Doria Pamphilj, 5 Piazza Grazioli. Only great Roman seventeenth-century park existing largely unchanged, though partly landscaped in the nineteenth century.

VILLA MADAMA Via Macchia Madama (on slopes of Monte Mario above Foro Italico), permit obtainable from Cerimoniale, Ministero Affari Esteri (La Farnesina by Piazzale Maresciallo Diaz, Foro Italico). Villa originally designed by Raphael for Clement VII before he was Pope, partly completed by Antonio da Sangallo the Younger. Has superb loggia with stucco decoration by Giovanni da Udine and paintings by Giulio Romano, also small part of original garden.

General Information

ECCLESIASTICAL DRESS In Rome one sees representatives of every grade of the Roman Catholic priesthood, as well as representatives of all the religious orders, therefore a short note on some of them may be of help to non-Catholics. Cardinals normally wear soutanes with red piping and, usually, red socks (if they follow the rule, unlike the late

Secretary of State, Cardinal Tardini, who habitually wore a plain black soutane); bishops have similar piping of a magenta colour.

The seminarists are particularly colourful—The **Germans** and **Hungarians** wearing bright red soutanes (popularly known as *gamberi cotti* or boiled lobsters; this conspicuous dress is said to have resulted from their uproarious behaviour in times past). The **Spaniards** have a black soutane with a blue belt and a blue-striped collar, the **English** and **French** plain black soutanes, the **Scots** a purple soutane (presumably taken from their native heather, no one has ever dared attribute this distinctive colour to any other cause) with a red belt. The **Belgians** wear black soutanes with red seams, the **Poles** black with a green belt. The **Greeks** and **Ruthenians** a blue soutane with a red belt. **North Americans** wear black with blue piping and **South Americans** have in addition a blue belt. **Armenians** wear black with a red belt and seminarists of the **Propaganda Fide**, black with red piping and a red belt. The best place to see the whole gamut of seminarist costume is in the Piazza della Pilotta when the Pontificia Università Gregoriana closes about midday.[1]

CHURCH FESTIVALS The great church festivals are, of course, the same the world over, but the Romans gather particularly in the Piazza of St. Peter's on Palm Sunday, and in S. Anselmo on the Aventine to hear the Gregorian plainsong of the Benedictines at Tenebrae in Holy Week. The kindling of the holy fire on Holy Saturday is a magnificent ceremony in the great basilicas but a particularly touching one in the very old churches such as S. Prassede and S. Clemente; on Easter Sunday, of course, all pilgrims and all Rome gathers in the Piazza of St. Peter's for the Pope's blessing. Midnight Mass on Christmas Eve is celebrated with particular splendour at S. Maria Maggiore and S. Maria in Aracoeli and, again with great beauty, at S. Anselmo. From then until after the Epiphany in many Roman churches one can see the lovely old Christmas cribs, some of them dating from the eighteenth century. That of the Aracoeli is the most famous, but those of S. Marcello, S. Maria in Via and S. Carlo alle Quattro Fontane are small and beautifully arranged.

1. These rules were general until the last few years, but things are changing fast and already many of them are of purely historic interest.

Rome has, in addition, many religious celebrations which are uniquely hers, such as the blessing of the lambs on 21 January at S. Agnese fuori le Mura; the Mass celebrated in the private chapel of the Palazzo Massimo alle Colonne on 16 March to commemorate the miracle performed there by S. Filippo Neri; the feast of SS. Giovanni e Paolo, celebrated in the church dedicated to them on the Celio, when a mosaic of flowers is laid above the place of their martyrdom; and on 5 August, the feast of the 'Madonna of the Snow', in S. Maria Maggiore, where, during the celebration of Mass, white flowers shower down from the dome of the Borghese chapel in commemoration of the miraculous snow-fall on that day, to which the basilica's origins are traditionally attributed. In addition to the many other specially Roman feasts, the Collegium Cultorum Martyrum commemorates the memory of the martyrs on several occasions in the different catacombs, but particularly on the afternoon of 1 January in the Catacombs of Priscilla (by the Via Salaria) when they walk in procession with lighted candles chanting the Litany and the Te Deum.

CLOTHES Hot weather usually begins in Rome in mid-June and can last until the end of September, during this period only thin clothes are needed with a light wrap in the evenings. For October light woollen clothes and a light coat and mackintosh. From November to end March warm clothes and a heavy top-coat. April as for October, and in May some thin clothes as well. Except in the height of summer and depth of winter the most useful combination for women is a skirt, shirt and twin set, as the temperatures can change rapidly even between morning and afternoon. Long evening dresses are rarely worn in Rome except at Embassies and Opera first nights.

SHOES As walking is the only way to see Rome, bring a really comfortable pair of old shoes, preferably with a thick soft sole, as the streets are paved with small cobbles made of lava, which is as hard as iron, and museums and galleries with equally resistant marble. Crêpe rubber is best for winter, espadrilles for summer (addresses where they can be got are given in the shopping list). Ferragamo make a light inexpensive shoe with a wedge heel and thick sole, called 'Camping', ideal for all but winter walking. Even extensive English country walkers may find that they fall victim to the common tourist complaint, locally known as marble foot-rot. The chiropodist at the hairdressers Carlo e Carlo, 155 Via Veneto, is a past-master at curing this; he speaks English and has an English degree.

CURING ROMAN TUMMY More common in summer than in winter, this is usually due to the change in climate and food. Entero-Vioform (*entero-vioformio* in Italian) available in any chemist, and a light diet of boiled rice (*riso in bianco*), grated apple (*mela grattugiata*) and plenty of fresh lemon juice (*spremuta di limone*) usually does the trick, if not call a doctor. Names of chemists stocking English and American medicines are given in the shopping list. Insurance to cover your trip can be a sound investment.

PUBLIC HOLIDAYS Banks, offices and most shops are closed on the days listed below, but State-owned galleries, monuments, museums, etc are open in the morning except on New Year's Day, Easter, 1 May, 2 June, 15 August and Christmas, when they are also closed all day. For holiday closing of Municipal museums etc. see p. 563, for the Vatican museum, see p. 564.

New Year's Day; 6 January—Epiphany; 19 March—St. Joseph; Easter Monday; 25 April—Liberation Day; 1 May—Labour Day; 6th Thursday after Easter—Ascension Day; 2 June—Republic Day; 9th Thursday after Easter—Corpus Domini; 29 June—SS. Peter and Paul (Rome only); 15 August—Assumption; 1 November—All Saints; 4 November—Victory Day; 8 December—Immaculate Conception; Christmas Day; 26 December—St. Stephen's Day.

USEFUL ADDRESSES (N.B. In Italy the system of having several telephone lines listed under a single number does not usually obtain. Most of the addresses given here have several numbers, in some cases a great many, so consult the directory if the one given is engaged. Most telephone numbers are of six figures, though new ones may have as many as seven. Offices with a very large switchboard, like the American Embassy and the Questura, may have only three or four figures.)

ALITALIA (Reservations) 13 Via Bissolati—5454 or 483531. (Air Station Terminal) 36 Via Giolitti—460841

AMERICAN CHURCH 58 Via Napoli (corner of Via Nazionale)—463339

AMERICAN CONSULATE 121A Via Vittorio Veneto—4674
AMERICAN EMBASSY 119A Via Vittorio Veneto—4674
AMERICAN EXPRESS CO. 38 Piazza di Spagna—688751
ANGLICAN CHURCH 153 Via del Babuino—674357
AUSTRALIAN CONSULATE AND EMBASSY 26 Via Sallustiana—
482001
BEA and BOAC (Information and Reservations) 6a Via Nazio-
nale (Hotel Quirinale)—489956
(Air Station Terminal) 30 Via Giolitti—460841
BRITISH CONSULATE 12 Piazza di Spagna—689413/4 (if in case
of emergency there is no reply, ring the Embassy)
BRITISH EMBASSY Villa Wolkonsky, 25 Via Conte Rosso—
776551
BRITISH LEGATION TO THE HOLY SEE 91 Via Condotti—687479
BRITISH METHODIST CHURCH 3 Via Banco di S. Spirito—
6568314
BRITISH RAILWAYS 40 Via Torino—464861
CANADIAN EMBASSY 27 Via G.B. de Rossi—862433
CAR HIRE Automobile Club d'Italia (Servizio Turismo) 261
Via Cristofero Colombo—5796
CENTRAL POST OFFICE Piazza S. Silvestro
CHURCH OF SCOTLAND 7 Via XX Settembre—471627
COOK (THOMAS) AND SON 9 Via Vittorio Veneto—479441
GREAT SYNAGOGUE Lungotevere Cenci—564648
IRISH EMBASSY 9 Via del Circo Massimo—578243
ITALIAN STATE TOURIST ORGANISATION INFORMATION OFFICE
Stazione Termini—465461
LOST PROPERTY OFFICE Servizio Oggetti Rinvenuti, 11 Via F.
Negri—592189
PAN AMERICAN AIRWAYS (Information and Reservations) 77
Via S. Nicola da Tolentino, 46 Via Bissolati—476951
PAWN SHOP Cassa di Risparmio di Roma, 2A Piazza del
Monte di Pietà—474841
QUESTURA DI ROMA (Central Police Office) 15 Via S. Vitale—
4686
SAN SILVESTRO CENTRE (for English-speaking pilgrims) 41 Via
del Gambero—683219
SOUTH AFRICAN EMBASSY 4 Piazza Monte Grappa—312145
TWA (Reservations) 67 Via Barberini
(Terminal) 59 Via Barberini—471141

Hotels

Rome has more than 200 hotels divided into five categories: *di lusso* (luxury), first class corresponding to the French four star hotel; second class to the French three star; and third and fourth classes corresponding to the French two and one star ones. There are also more than 300 pensions divided into three grades. Practically all of these hotels and pensions are listed in the excellent *Annuario Alberghi d'Italia*, which is published annually by the Italian State Tourist Organisation and can be consulted in any of their offices. The minimum and maximum prices charged for rooms and full pension are also listed in the *annuario*; these are fixed annually for each category but do not include heating, air-conditioning, service (which varies from 15% to 20%), *taxe de séjour* and a general state tax on the whole bill (of from 1% to 3%), all of which are extras.

The short list of hotels and pensions which follows is the result of recommendations over a period of years, *but there are certainly many others in each category which are equally good*. Those situated in old Rome—roughly the area stretching from the Piazza del Popolo to the Forum, bounded by the Tiber on one side and the Pincio, Via Sistina, Via Quattro Fontane, Via del Quirinale and Via 24 Maggio—are marked with an asterisk. A few comments on particular character and situation are given. Light sleepers are warned that, especially in summer, Rome is noisy, and in hotels that do not have air-conditioning they should ask for an inside room.

Di Lusso

BERNINI BRISTOL 23 Piazza Barberini (has roof-top restaurant with fine view)

EDEN 49 Via Ludovisi (overlooks Villa Borghese and gardens on two sides)

FLORA 191 Via Vittorio Veneto (overlooks Villa Borghese)

GRAND HOTEL (LE) 3 Via Vittorio Emanuele Orlando

HASSLER-VILLA MEDICI 8 Piazza Trinità dei Monti (at top of Spanish Steps, roof-top restaurant, wonderful views)

HILTON (CAVALIERI) Via Michelini Tocci (on hill-top overlooking Rome, has garden and swimming pool)

First Class

BOSTON 47 Via Lombardia
DE LA VILLE 69 Via Sistina (has interior garden court)
ELISEO 30 Via di Porta Pinciana (overlooks Villa Borghese, has roof restaurant in summer)
* FORUM 25 Via Tor dei Conti (overlooks imperial *fora*, has roof restaurant)
MASSIMO D'AZEGLIO 18 Via Cavour
* MINERVA 69 Piazza della Minerva (overlooks piazza with Bernini elephant, has interior courtyards)
* NAZIONALE 131 Piazza Montecitorio
* RAPHAEL 2 Largo Febo (just by Piazza Navona, centre of picturesque old Rome, has roof garden)
* VALADIER 15 Via della Fontanella (near Piazza del Popolo and Pincio)
VICTORIA 41 Via Campania (overlooks Villa Borghese)

Second Class

* ANGLO-AMERICANO 12 Via Quattro Fontane (back rooms look on to garden of Palazzo Barberini)
* BOLOGNA 4A Via S. Chiara
COLUMBUS 33 Via della Conciliazione (restored historic palace, near St. Peter's with small garden)
DINESEN 18 Via di Porta Pinciana (overlooks Villa Borghese)
ESPERIA 22 Via Nazionale
* INTERNAZIONALE 79 Via Sistina
* PACE ELVEZIA 104 Via IV Novembre
* SANTA CHIARA Via Santa Chiara (just behind Pantheon)
* SENATO 73 Piazza della Rotonda (overlooks Pantheon)

Third Class

* CONDOTTI 37 Via Mario dei Fiori
* DELLE NAZIONI 36 Via delle Carrozze
* PORTOGHESI 1 Via dei Portoghesi
SANTA PRISCA 25 Largo Manlio Gelsomini (small, quiet, on Aventine)

Fourth Class

* IRIS 1B Via Madonna dei Monti

Pensioni

Class 1

LA RESIDENZA 22 Via Emilia (near Via Veneto)

* CASA PALLOTTI 64 Via dei Pettinari (near Ponte Sisto)

Class 2

* COSMOPOLITA 114 Via IV Novembre
* SCALINATA DI SPAGNA 17 Piazza Trinità dei Monti (at top of Spanish Steps, bed and breakfast only)
* SUISSE 56 Via Gregoriana

WALDORF 79 Via Boncompagni

Class 3

S. ANSELMO 2 Piazza S. Anselmo (quiet on Aventine)

WOODCOCK-GRAVINA 47 Via Capo d'Africa (Anglo-Italian ownership)

* ROSARIO 42 Via Sistina

Restaurants

There are over 3,000 restaurants and trattorias in Rome; everyone has their own preferences and many will wish to make their own discoveries. The following is a list of suggestions of those conveniently situated in the historic centre of Rome, in the fashionable Via Veneto area, or, especially for summer, among picturesque surroundings farther out. Several of these last are conveniently sited for luncheon on the walks which take the traveller farther afield, in this case a note is made of the chapter to which they apply. The categories of *** expensive, ** medium and * good trattorie necessarily cover a certain range of prices as no definite classification exists, notes as to general character and specialities are given wherever possible. Nearly all restaurants now close one day a week, unfortunately the days are liable to change and it is as well to ring up beforehand to make sure they are open.

***

31 AL VICARIO 31 Via Uffici del Vicario—672251. Candle-lit in Old Rome, Italian and international cuisine

GEORGE'S 7 Via Marche—489204. Italian and international cuisine, *pollo alla zingara*, Italian cheeses, excellent cellar (only Roman restaurant in top category with Michelin star)

HOSTARIA DELL' ORSO 93 Via Monte Brianzo—564221. Medieval hostelry where Montaigne stayed in heart of old Rome, Italian and international cuisine

**

ALFREDO 30 Piazza Augusto Imperatore—681672. Famous for *fettucine*

ALFREDO ALLA SCROFA 104 Via della Scrofa—650163. Famous for *fettucine*

CANEPA 84/86 Via Vittorio Emanuele Orlando—461040. Opposite Grand Hotel, good grills

L'ESCARGOT 34 Via dell' Umiltà—675891. French food and wine, Burgundy *vin ordinaire*

FONTANELLA BORGHESE 86 Via della Fontanella Borghese—683849. Tuscan specialities and wine

GIGGI FAZI 22 Via Lucullo—464045. Lively, Roman specialities

DA GUIDO 37 Via Aurora—481593. Specialises in Italian country food

HOSTARIA SS APOSTOLI 1 Via del Vaccaro—673897. Hors d'oeuvres including *scapece*

MEO PATACCA 30 Piazza de' Mercanti—586198 (always open). Old Trastevere, very lively, Roman specialities

PAPA GIULIO 19/20 Via Giulia—650655. Old Roman atmosphere, open fire

PASSETTO 14 Piazza Zanardelli—650569. Excellent Italian food

RANIERI 26 Via Mario de' Fiori—6791592. Quiet old-world charm, *cannelloni*

SANS SOUCI 20 Via Sicilia—489388. Hors d'oeuvres, cheeses

ULPIA 2 Piazza di Foro Traiano—689980. Overlooking imperial *fora*

*

ABRUZZI 129 Via Frattina—690067. *Fettucine con tartufi* or *funghi*

ANGELINO 37 Piazza Margana—681328. Picturesque piazza near the Capitol

DA ANGELINO AI FORI 4 Largo Carlo Ricci—6791121. With garden near Forum

ANTICA PESA 18 Via Garibaldi—509236. Trastevere, garden, *spaghetti alla poverella*

BATTAGLIA 48 Via della Colonna Antonina—683717. Venetian specialities, Valpolicella wine on draught

BUCO 8 Via S. Ignazio—673298. Florentine specialities

CHIANTI (AL) 17 Via Ancona—861083. Tuscan food and game

CORSETTI 27 Piazza S. Cosimato—509009. Trastevere piazza, *zuppa di pesce* and fish generally

GALEASSI 3 Piazza S. Maria in Trastevere—503775. Picturesque Trastevere piazza, Roman food

MASTROSTEFANO 94 Piazza Navona—651669. Most beautiful piazza in Rome, by Bernini fountain

NECCI 50 Piazza dell' Oratorio—670537. Candle-lit, open fire, *pasta al pesto*

NINO 11 Via Borgognona—675676. Tuscan food

PANCRAZIO 92 Piazza del Biscione—561246. Built into ruins of Pompey's theatre, Roman food

PICCOLO MONDO 39D Via Aurora—474595. Via Veneto area

ROMOLO 8 Via Porta Settiminiana—588284. Trastevere, garden, Roman specialities

Restaurants outside the centre, pleasant for eating out of doors in summer and convenient for itineraries

** ALLO ZOO DI ROMA Giardino Zoologico, Villa Borghese—879307. For Chapter 11

** APPIA ANTICA 125 Via Appia Antica—750391. For Chapter 19, garden with beautiful view, chicken

** APULEIUS 15 Via Tempio di Diana, Aventine—572160. For Chapter 21, ancient Roman setting and Roman specialities

** DOMUS AUREA Via del Monte Oppio—776097. For Chapters 15 and 16, in Parco di Traiano, terrace with beautiful view

** L'ESCARGOT 46 Via Appia Antica—5163791. French food and wine

** HORTI GALATEAE 5 Via Porta S. Sebastiano—753330. Quiet, in garden

* HOSTARIA L'ARCHEOLOGIA 139 Via Appia Antica—7880494. For Chapter 19, open fire in winter, garden for summer, *fettucine alla vaccara* and chickens on spit

* MARCELLO 87 Borgo Pio near St. Peter's—564462. For Chapter 25, courtyard
* NERONE Via Terme di Tito, beside Parco di Traiano. For Chapters 15 and 16, very simple little trattoria
* ORAZIO A CARACALLA 5 Via Porta Latina—751201. Typical Roman osteria and pizzeria for eating out under a pergola
* PIERDONATI 39 Via della Conciliazione 653557. For Chapter 25, in old palace near St. Peter's
** SCARPONE 15 Via S. Pancrazio, Janiculum—506120. For Chapter 23

Nightclubs and Dancing

For Winter

CABALA (above the Hostaria dell' Orso) 93 Via Monte Brianzo —564221

CAPRICCIO 38 Via Liguria—463370

CRAZY 25–32 Via Lazio—487242

JICKY CLUB 13 Via Vittorio Veneto—487198

OTTANTAQUATTRO 84 Via Emilia—471538

PIPISTRELLO 27A Via Emilia—474123

For Summer

CASINA DELLE ROSE Villa Borghese—864004

BRIGADOON Via Aurelia (12th Kilometre)—690009

Entertainments

OPERA The winter season at the Teatro dell' Opera, Via Viminale, telephone 463641, lasts from December to May, but in July and August open-air performances are given in the Terme di Caracalla, telephone 578300.

THEATRES Theatres are only open during the winter months and seasons are very short, often only lasting a few weeks. Consult *The Week in Rome* for what is on. A season of Classical Drama (in Italian) is given in July each year in the open air in the Roman Theatre at Ostia Antica; even those not fluent in Italian will enjoy this for the beauty of the setting. Sometimes at the end of July and beginning of August there is also a season of classical plays given in Greek.

MUSIC HALL The main Music Hall theatre is the Teatro Sistina, 129 Via Sistina, telephone 487090; here runs are usually longer, consult *The Week in Rome*.

CONCERTS From October to May the orchestra of the Accademia Nazionale di S. Cecilia gives afternoon concerts on Sundays and Wednesdays in the Auditorio Pio, 4 Via della Conciliazione. On Fridays there are concerts of chamber music in the Accademia di S. Cecilia, 6 Via Vittorio. In July and August the Accademia's orchestra gives open-air concerts on Tuesday and Friday nights in the Basilica di Massenzio by the Forum.

SON ET LUMIÈRE During the summer months there is a programme of *Son et Lumière* in the Forum every night but Tuesdays and Fridays, the entrance is by the Arch of Titus. N.B. *Bookings for all entertainments can be made through CIT and other agencies.*

MARKETS, FAIRS, SHOWS AND FESTAS Christmas Fair in Piazza Navona lasts all of Advent and until Epiphany.
Flea Market by Porta Portese, open every Sunday morning.
International Horse Show, Piazza di Siena, Villa Borghese, at end of April.
Noiantri Festa in Trastevere, second half of July.
Rose Show, Roseto di Roma, Via di Valle Murcia (Aventine), May to beginning of June.

Shopping

Although Rome is the capital it is not the best shopping centre in Italy for specifically Italian products; for this Florence is the ideal place for handicrafts, and Milan for manufactured ones. However, the most famous Italian firms have branches in Rome and it is also a centre for the great couturiers, some

of whom also have boutiques like Fontana at 6 Via S. Sebas-
tianello, and Gattinoni at 44 Via Sistina and 91 Piazza di
Spagna. Curiously, the old Roman tradition still obtains to a
certain extent of shops of a similar character being grouped in
the same street; thus the Via del Babuino and the Via dei
Coronari are *par excellence* the streets for antique shops, the
Via della Croce for delicatessen, and the Via Frattina, one of
the most attractive shopping streets in Rome, for costume
jewellery and accessories. The Via Condotti is the Bond Street
of Rome and, together with the Piazza di Spagna, the smartest
shopping centre, equalled only by the Via Veneto area. For
smaller and less expensive shops the small streets between the
Piazza del Parlamento and Piazza Montecitorio and the Via
della Scrofa is a good hunting ground. While for gay straw
handbags, sun hats, scarves and odds and ends STANDA and
UPIM (the local equivalents of Woolworths and Marks and
Spencer) are good.

Departmental Stores

LA RINASCENTE Piazza Colonna and Piazza Fiume
CIM 97C Via XX Settembre

English Books

LION BOOKSHOP 181 Via del Babuino

Chemists selling English and American medicines

CHIEFFO 47 Via Capo le Case
INTERNAZIONALE SCHIRILLO 129 Via Vittorio Veneto
LEPETIT 417–418 Via del Corso

Costume Jewellery

LUCIANA 93 Via della Vite

Espadrilles

BALANI 40 Via della Croce
CASA DELLE PANTOFOLE 30 Via della Rotonda

Glassware

NAVARRINI 507 Via del Corso (for Empoli and Murano glass)

Gloves

ANTICOLI 115 Via Tritone
PERRONE 92 Piazza di Spagna

Hairdressers and Instituts de Beauté

CARLO E CARLO 155 Via Vittorio Veneto
ELIZABETH ARDEN 19 Piazza di Spagna
EVE OF ROME 116 Via Vittorio Veneto

Handbags

GUCCI 8 Via Condotti
ROMANI 94 Via del Babuino

Hats

CANESSA 56 Via Sistina
VENTURI 84 Via Vittorio Veneto

Jewellery

BULGARI 10 Via Condotti
MASSONI 48 Largo Goldoni
VENTRELLA 168 Via del Corso

Lingerie

BELLINI 77 Piazza di Spagna
CERRI 89 Piazza di Spagna

Materials

COEN 36 Via del Tritone
GALTRUCCO 18/23 Via del Tritone

Men's Clothes

BATTISTONI 61A Via Condotti (across courtyard)

Pedicure

SIGNOR PENNA Carlo e Carlo, 155 Via Veneto

Ready-Made Dresses

GITER 11 Piazza Barberini
MYRICAE 36 Via Frattina

Shoes

FERRAGAMO 65 Via Condotti
FRATTEGIANI 50 Via Sistina
LUCARELLI 4E Via Borgognona

Sweaters

MILO 103 Via Sistina
SPAGNOLI 130 Via Veneto

Table Linen

BELLINI 77 Piazza di Spagna

Books on Rome

Among the works consulted the following are suggested for
further study:

Guide Books

The Tourist Club Italiano *Roma e Dintorni*, Milan, 1962, is an
absolutely first-rate guide book of the Baedeker type; the
small pale blue guide books to individual galleries and monuments issued by the Libreria dello Stato are usually written by
outstanding authorities and excellent. In most Roman
churches reliable guide books in Italian are now on sale.

Art and Architecture

J. S. ACKERMAN *The Architecture of Michelangelo*, London, 1961.

E. AMADI *Roma Turrita*, Rome, 1943.

M. ARMELLINI *Gli Antichi Cimiteri Cristiani di Roma e l'Italia*, Rome, 1893.

M. ARMELLINI *Le Chiese di Roma dal Secolo IV al XIX*, Rome, 1942.

C. D'ONOFRIO *Le Fontane di Roma*, Rome, 1957.

C. CECCHELLI *Monumenti Christiano-Eretici di Roma*, Rome, 1944.

C. CECCHELLI *I Mosaici di S. Maria Maggiore*, Turin, 1956.

C. HÜLSEN *Chiese di Roma nel Medio Evo*, Florence, 1927.

R. KRAUTHEIMER *Corpus Basilicarium*, Vatican, 1937.

M. LAZZARONI/M. L. A. MUÑOZ *Filarete Scultore*, Rome, 1908.

R. LEFÈVRE *Villa Madama*, Instituto Poligrafico dello Stato, Rome, 1964.

F. MAGI *Il Ripristino del Laocoonte*, Vatican, 1960.

E. MÂLE and D. BUXTON *The Early Churches of Rome*, London, 1960.

G. MASSON *Italian Villas and Palaces*, London, 1959.

G. MASSON *Italian Gardens*, London, 1961

P. PECCHIAI *La Scalinata di Piazza di Spagna*, Rome, 1941.

A. PETRIGNANI *La Basilica di S. Pudenziana in Roma*, Vatican, 1934.

D. REDIG DE CAMPOS *The 'Stanze' of Raphael*, Rome, 1963.

M. E. SCHERER *Marvels of Ancient Rome*, London/New York, 1956.

D. TALBOT RICE *The Art of Byzantium*, London, 1959.

P. TOESCA *Pietro Cavallini*, London, 1960.

C. DE TOLNAY *Michelangelo*, Princeton, 1947.

J. TOYNBEE/J. WARD PERKINS *The Shrine of St. Peter*, London, 1956.

R. WITTKOWER *Gian Lorenzo Bernini*, London, 1955.

R. WITTKOWER *Art and Architecture in Italy 1600–1750*, London, 1958.

General

A. HARE *Walks in Rome*, London, 1878.

J. FLEMING *Robert Adam and his Circle*, London, 1962.

J. D'HOSPITAL *Rome en Confiance*, Paris, 1962.

J. LEES MILNE *Roman Mornings*, London, 1956.

A. LYALL *Rome Sweet Rome*, London, 1956.

H. V. MORTON *A Traveller in Rome*, London, 1957.

S. NEGRO *Roma non Basta una Vita*, Venice, 1962.

G. B. PARKS *The English Traveller to Italy*, Rome, 1954.

R. RODD *Rome*, London, 1932.

STENDHAL *Promenades dans Rome*, Paris, 1893.

Etruscans

A. BOETHIUS, C. FRIES, E. GJERSTAD, K. HANELL, C. E. OSTENBERG, V. POULSEN, B. THORDEMAN, E. WELIN, E. WETTER *Etruscan Culture, Land and People*, New York, 1963.

J. HEURGON *La Vie Quotidienne chez les Etrusques*, Paris, 1961.

M. PALLOTTINO *The Etruscans*, London, 1955.

History

G. P. BAKER *Twelve Centuries of Rome*, London, 1936.

E. GIBBON *The History of the Decline and Fall of the Roman Empire*, London, 1963.

F. GREGOROVIUS *History of the City of Rome in the Middle Ages*, London, 1894–1902.

R. LANCIANI *The Golden Days of The Renaissance in Rome*, New York, 1906.

M. MICHELET *Memoires de Luther Ecrits par Lui-Même*, Paris, 1837.

L. VON PASTOR *The History of the Popes from the Close of the Middle Ages*, London, 1923.

J. A. SYMONDS *The Renaissance in Italy*, London, 1906–7.

Life in Ancient Rome

J. P. V. D. BALSDON *Roman Women*, London, 1962.

R. H. BARROW *The Romans*, London, 1960.

J. CARCOPINO *Daily Life in Ancient Rome*, London, 1961.

B. GUÉGAN *Les Dix Livres de Cuisine d'Apicius*, Paris, 1933.

G. HIGHET *Poets in a Landscape*, London, 1959.

R. LANCIANI *Pagan and Christian Rome*, New York, 1893.

Special Aspects

c. BANDINI *La Galanteria nel Gran Mondo di Roma nel Sette-cento*, Rome, 1930.

c. BANDINI *Roma nel Settecento*, Rome, 1930.

D. S. GALBRAITH *Papal Heraldry*, Cambridge, 1930.

U. GNOLI *Cortigiane Romane*, Arezzo, 1941.

U. GNOLI *Alberghi ed Osterie di Roma nella Rinascenza*, Rome, 1942.

c. L. MORICHINI *Degli Istituti di Publica Carità ed Instruzione e delle Prigioni di Roma*, Rome, 1842.

A. STEFANUCCI *Storia del Presepio*, Rome, 1944.

Topography

G. BARRACONI *Rioni di Roma*, Rome, 1905.

A. BOETHIUS *The Golden House of Nero*, University of Michigan, 1960.

F. CASTAGNOLI, C. CECCHELLI, G. GIOVANNONI, M. ZOCCA *Topografia e Urbanistica di Roma*, Bologna, 1958.

P. ROMANO *Roma nelle sue Strade e nelle sue Piazze*, Rome, 1950.

Museums, Galleries, Churches and Other Places of Interest Open to the Public

The times listed below are purely indicative. The opening hours of **state-owned museums etc.**, particularly, are subject to frequent and unpredictable alteration. Part or whole of these sights are also liable to be closed for restoration or staff shortages at any time for an indefinite period. Summer openings usually begin on 2 May and end on 30 September, but this is what the authorities concerned call *linea di massima*, which indicates that it is liable to fluctuation and summer openings may begin in June or last into October.

The **municipally-owned museums etc.** are usually only closed unexpectedly owing to staff shortages but they are also closed or open for a reduced period on certain municipal holidays as well as the national holidays; both are listed below. **The**

privately-owned galleries etc. are also more regular in their habits.

A current copy of *The Week in Rome* is helpful in spotting any recent changes in opening hours, but **the Reader has been warned, if you have no time to waste get your hotel hall porter to ring up first.** For these reasons the Museums etc. are grouped according to ownership. **They are followed by general indications as to the opening hours of churches.**

State-owned Museums, Galleries etc.

For full state holidays and religious and half-holidays see p. 547.

BASILICA DI PORTA MAGGIORE Closed indefinitely for repairs.

CASTEL S. ANGELO Shut Mondays. Open half-holidays 9.30 a.m.–1.30 p.m.; Sundays 8.30 a.m.–2.30 p.m.; summer 8.30 a.m.–2.30 p.m. winter 9.30 a.m.–4 p.m.

COLOSSEUM 10 a.m.–1 hour before sunset.

DOMUS AUREA Closed for repairs but when these are completed, summer 9 a.m. to one hour before sunset, winter 9 a.m.–4 p.m.

GALLERIA DI ARTE ANTICA (Palazzo Corsini) Shut Tuesdays. Open Sundays and half-holidays 9 a.m.–1 p.m.; summer, winter 9.30 a.m.–4 p.m.

GALLERIA BORGHESE Open Sundays and half-holidays 9 a.m.–4 p.m.; summer and winter 9 a.m.–4 p.m.

GALLERIA DI PALAZZO BARBERINI Shut Mondays. Open Sundays and half-holidays 9.30 a.m.–1 p.m.; summer 9 a.m.–1 p.m. and 4–6 p.m., winter 9.30 a.m.–4 p.m.

GALLERIA SPADA Shut Mondays. Open Sundays and half-holidays 9.30 a.m.–1 p.m.; summer 9 a.m.–1 p.m. and 4–6 p.m., winter 9.30 a.m.–4 p.m.

MUSEO DELLA VIA OSTIENSE, PORTA S. PAOLO Closed Mondays. Open Sundays and half-holidays 9 a.m.–1.30 p.m., summer and winter 9 a.m.–1.30 p.m.

MUSEO ETRUSCA VILLA GIULIA Shut Mondays. Open Sundays and half-holidays 9 a.m.–1 p.m.; summer and winter 8.30 a.m.–2.30 p.m.

MUSEO NAZIONALE ROMANO DELLE TERME Shut Mondays. Open Sundays and half-holidays 9 a.m.–1 p.m.; summer and winter 9.30 a.m.–4 p.m.

MUSEO PREISTORICO, COLLEGIO ROMANO Shut Mondays. Open

Sundays and half-holidays 9 a.m.–1 p.m.; summer and winter 9.30 a.m.–4 p.m.

PALAZZO SPADA STATE ROOMS Open Sundays 9 a.m.–1 p.m.; weekdays, if the Consigilio di Stato is not sitting late, 4–6 p.m.

PALAZZO VENEZIA Shut Mondays. Open Sundays and half-holidays 9 a.m.–1 p.m.; summer 9 a.m.–1 p.m. and 4–6 p.m., winter 9.30 a.m.–4 p.m.

PANTHEON 9 a.m.–6 p.m.

ROMAN FORUM AND PALATINE Open all week winter and summer from 9 a.m. to one hour before sunset.

TERME DI CARACALLA Open all week, summer 9 a.m. to one hour before sunset, winter 9 a.m.–4 p.m.

VILLA FARNESINA IN VIA DELLA LUNGARA Closed Sundays. Open 9 a.m.–1 p.m.

Municipally-owned Museums

Closed all day Monday and on following holidays:—1 January, 21 April, Easter Sunday, 1 May, 2 June, 29 June, 15 August, 25 December and Sundays when General and Municipal Elections are held.

Open Sundays and following holidays from 9 a.m.–1 p.m.:— 6 January, 11 February, the last day of Carnival, 19 March, Holy Thursday, Easter Monday, 25 April, Ascension Day, Corpus Domini, 28 September, 4th October, 1 November, 4 November, 8 December, 26 December, 31 December.

Open weekdays from 9 a.m.–2 p.m.; on Tuesdays and Thursdays, also open from 5–8 p.m. The Capitoline Museums only, on Saturdays also from 9–11.30 p.m.

The Museums are as follows:—

CAPITOLINE MUSEUMS
MUSEO DI ROMA
MUSEO DELLA CIVILTÀ ROMANA
MUSEO NAPOLEONICO
MUSEO BARRACCO

Municipally-owned Monuments

Closed Mondays and holidays as above, open Sundays and half-holidays as above from 9 a.m.–1 p.m. Summer (1 June–

30 September) 9 a.m.–1 p.m. and 3–6 p.m.; Winter (1 October–21 May) 10 a.m.–5 p.m.

The Monuments are as follows:—

ARA PACIS AUGUSTAE
FORUM OF CAESAR
FORUM OF AUGUSTUS AND CASA DEI CAVALIERI DI RODI
FORO TRAIANO
TORRE DELLE MILIZIE
CASA DI CARDINALE BESSARIONE AND THE TOMB OF THE SCIPIOS

The Vatican Museum

Closed Sundays and the following fixed feasts:—1 January, 6 January, 19 March, 1 May, 29 June, 14 and 15 August, 1 and 2 November, 8 December, 24, 25 and 26 December.

Closed also on the following movable feasts:—Ash Wednesday, Easter Saturday and Sunday, Ascension Day, 3 June (anniversary of death of last Pope, John XXIII), Corpus Domini, 24 June (name day of Pope Paul VI), 30 June (anniversary of Pope Paul VI's coronation). N.B. These last dates change with each Pope).

The museum is open on weekdays from 9 a.m.–1 p.m.

Privately-owned galleries, Palaces etc.

ACCADEMIA DI S. LUCA GALLERY Mondays, Wednesdays, Fridays 10 a.m.–1 p.m.

COLONNA GALLERY Saturdays 9 a.m.–2 p.m.

DORIA GALLERY AND PALACE Tuesdays, Fridays, Saturdays, Sundays, 10 a.m.–1 p.m.

ISTITUTO PER LA STORIA DEL RISORGIMENTO ITALIANO Closed Sundays. Saturdays 9 a.m.–1 p.m.; weekdays 9 a.m.–2 p.m.

KEATS-SHELLEY MUSEUM Closed Sundays. Saturdays 9 a.m. to midday; summer 9 a.m. to midday and 4–6 p.m., winter 9 a.m. to midday and 3–5 p.m.

PALAZZO FARNESE (Salon d'Ercule) Sundays 11 a.m. to midday.

PALAZZO PAMPHILJ (Pietro da Cortona Salon) The first and third Sundays in the month from 10.30 a.m.–1 p.m.

QUIRINAL PALACE Thursdays 3–5 p.m. *Bring passport.*

ROSPIGLIOSI CASINO AURORA First Saturday of month 10 a.m.
to midday and 3–5 p.m.

VILLA MEDICI GARDEN Open Wednesdays 9–11 a.m.

The Opening hours of Churches and Catacombs

Four of the great basilicas are open all day, though their
cloisters, treasures, etc. close for a time about midday.

S. PAOLO FUORI LE MURA 5.30 a.m.–7.30 p.m. The *cloister* from
9 a.m. to midday and 3–7.30 p.m. Shut on Sundays.

S. PETER'S 7 a.m. to half an hour before Ave Maria. The
lift to the roof functions from 8 a.m. to three-quarters of an
hour before Ave Maria. The *treasure* is open from 9 a.m.–
1 p.m. and from 2 p.m. to three-quarters of an hour
before the basilica closes. The *grottoes* are open from
7 a.m.–12.45 p.m. and 2.30 –5.45 p.m. The *Preconstantinian
Necropolis* below the grottoes can only be seen by special
permit obtained by personally taking a written request to
the administration offices of the Reverenda Fabbrica
(these are reached via the Arco delle Campane on the left
of St. Peter's; in winter the permit is usually granted within
a day or two, but during the crowded Easter and summer
seasons there is usually a minimum delay of a week).

S. GIOVANNI IN LATERANO Weekdays from 6.30 a.m. to half an
hour before sunset; on Sundays till 8.30 p.m. The *cloister*
from 9 a.m.–12.30 p.m. and 3–6.30 p.m., *shut on Sundays*.
The *Scala Santa* from 5 a.m.–12.30 p.m. and 2.45–7.30 p.m.
The *Baptistry* from 8.30 a.m. to midday and 3.30–7 p.m. in
summer and 8.30 a.m. to midday and 3–4.30 p.m. in winter.

S. LORENZO FUORI LE MURA 6 a.m. to midday and in summer
3–7.30 p.m.; 6 a.m. to midday and 3–4.30 p.m. in winter.

S. MARIA MAGGIORE 6 a.m.–8 p.m. in summer and to 7 p.m. in
winter.

*Other Churches' minimum hours of opening are from 9 a.m.
to midday and from 4–6 p.m., though many open much earlier in
the morning and stay open later at night, particularly on
Sundays. Some notable exceptions to this rule are as follows:—*
The churches of S. Cesareo and SS. Nereo and Achilleo
belong to the state and are, therefore, like museums, closed on
Mondays and state holidays; on Sundays and half-holidays

they are open from 9 a.m.–1 p.m.; summer 9 a.m.–1 p.m. and 3.30–6.30 p.m.; winter 9 a.m.–2 p.m.

S. CARLO ALLE QUATTRO FONTANE 6–11 a.m. and by ringing at the monastery next door (No. 23) until 12.30 p.m. or between 3.30–7 p.m.

S. COSTANZA 8 a.m. to midday and 3.30 p.m. to sunset.

S. CRISOGONO 6–11 a.m. and 3.30–7 p.m.

S. ELIGIO DEGLI OREFICI Custodian usually leaves his address in a note on the door.

S. GIOVANNI A PORTA LATINA 6.30 a.m. to midday and 4 p.m. to sunset.

S. GIROLAMO DELLA CARITÀ 6 a.m. to midday and 4.30–5.30 p.m.

S. IVO ALLA SAPIENZA Sundays 9.30 a.m. to midday. Otherwise ask the porter in the lodge on the right of the courtyard who has the key; if he is not around ask in the National Archive on the first floor. (A tip is appreciated by the porter.)

S. LORENZO IN LUCINA 6.30 a.m. to midday and 4.30–8 p.m.

S. LUIGI DEI FRANCESI 6.30 a.m. to midday and 3 p.m. to sunset.

S. MARIA DELL' ANIMA entrance in German Hospice, 20 Via della Pace, open all day.

S. MARIA DELLA PACE 7–8.30 a.m. At other times ask *guardiano* at 4 Vicolo dell' Arco della Pace, which is also the cloister entrance; a tip is expected.

S. PRISCA 6 a.m. to midday and 4.50–7 p.m.

S. SEBASTIANO 8.30 a.m. to midday and 3–6 p.m. in summer, 8.30 a.m. to midday and 2.30–5 p.m. in winter.

TRINITÀ DEI MONTI 10 a.m. to midday and 4–6 p.m. in summer, 10 a.m. to midday and 2–4 p.m. in w nter.

Catacombs

S. AGNESE (see p. 543).

S. CALLISTO and S. SEBASTIANO 9 a.m.–12 noon, 2 p.m.–sunset.

S. PRISCILLA (see p. 543).

Index

❧

The Index is in two sections: *a* persons (including their statues or memorials, tombs, etc., except in special cases); *b* places, streets, buildings and subjects. Churches, streets (*vie*), *palazzi* and squares (*piazze*) are grouped together (in their own alphabetical order) under those respective general headings in index *b*. The general heading *restaurants* covers only those which are mentioned in the body of the book, but not those listed on pages 551–4, as these latter will be readily traced from the list itself. Individual works of art (paintings, sculptures, etc.) are included only in a few special cases. Saints who are referred to 'for their own sake' are included in the Index of Persons, under their names; as titulars of churches they will be found under the general heading 'Churches' in index *b*. In alphabetisation no account is taken of the preposition *di* and its various combinations with the definite article (*del*, *della*, *dei*, *degli*, etc.); thus, 'Via della Pace' is treated as though it were 'Via Pace'.

a Index of Persons

Apollonius, son of Nestor, 284, 498
Appius Claudius, 48, 379
Apuleius, 440
Aragona, Tullia d', 176
Arcadius, Emperor, 424
Arcileus, 376
Aretino, Pietro, 191, 472
Ariosto, Lodovico, 100
Arpino, Cavaliere d', 451, 526
Asprucci, Antonio, 234
Astor, Viscount, 234
Attalus I, 278
Atticus, Pomponius, 403
Augustine of Canterbury, St., 356
Augustine of Hippo, St., 41
Augustus, Emperor, 32–3, 36, 40, 48, 57, 70–1, 116, 117, 287, 288, 289, 376, 499
Aurelian, Emperor, 299
Aurigemma, Prof., 274

Baciccia (G. B. Gaulli), 112, 444
Baglioni, Atlanta, 238
Bainbridge, Cardinal, 148
Balzac, Honoré de, 201
Barberini family, 102–3, 246–7, 527
Barberini, Cardinal Antonio, 246–7
Barberini, Cardinal Francesco, 140
Barbo, Cardinal Marco, 372
Barbo, Pietro, see Paul II, Pope
Baronio, 219
Baronius, Cardinal Cesare, 380
Baronzio, Giovanni, 266
Barracco, Giovanni, 126
Bartoli, Prof., 51
Basilio, Fra (herbalist), 438
Bassalecto, Pietro, 426
Baugin, 137
Bede, the Venerable, 363
Belisarius, 65, 255, 387, 421
Bella Giulia, see Giulia Farnese
Belli Gioacchino, 66, 192, 432
Bellini, Giovanni, 491
Bellotto, Bernardo, 268
Bembo, Cardinal Pietro, 104, 110, 175
Benedict, St., 457–8
Benedict XII, Pope, 536
Benedict XIV, Pope, 485
Benedicta, 354
Benjamin of Tudela, 66
Beno da Rapiza, 343
Berlioz, Hector, 244
Bernard, St., 428
Bernini, Gian Lorenzo, 91, 105, 167, 168, 171, 177, 196, 203, 204, 212, 213, 217, 235, 236, 237–8, 240, 260, 261, 264, 269–70, 297, 329, 334–5, 360, 414, 446, 452, 476, 516, 517–18
Bernini, Pietro, 203, 242, 329
Berthauld, L. M., 214
Bessarione, Cardinal, 384
Biagio da Cesena, 471
Bibiena, Maria, 104–5
Bibulus, C. Publius, 83
Bigio, Nanni di Bacco, see Nanni
Bilhères de Lagraulas, Cardinal Jean, 532
Bissolo, Francesco, 514
Boccaccio, Giovanni, 480
Bocchoris, 290
Boethius, Axel, 89
Boltraffio, 451
Bonaparte, Lucien, 192
Bonaparte, Napoleon, see Napoleon I
Bonaparte, Pauline, 183, 236
Bonaventura, St., 151
Boniface II, Pope, 116
Boniface IV, Pope, 58, 100
Boniface VIII, Pope, 309, 315, 341, 372, 400, 536
Boniface IX, Pope, 316
Borau, H., 152
Bordone, Paris, 491
Borghese, Camillo, 183, 233, 236
Borghese, Francesco, 234
Borghese, Marcantonio, 234
Borghese, Cardinal Scipione, 181, 231–6, 237, 241, 259, 297, 356, 392, 432
Borgia, Cesare, 115, 157, 475
Borgia, Lucrezia, 475
Borgia, Rodrigo, see Alexander VI, Pope
Borromini, Francesco, 136, 149, 155, 166, 167, 169, 171, 191, 193, 204, 262, 263, 264, 313, 314, 386, 532
Bosco, Maso del, 369
Bosio, Antonio, 205, 395
Boswell, James, 119
Botticelli, Sandro, 239, 464, 466
Boucher, Francois, 244, 268
Boveschi family, 191
Bracciolini, Poggio, 28, 29
Bramante, Donato, 145, 153, 154, 187, 195, 215, 245, 464, 468, 469, 478, 492, 494, 513, 518, 520
Bramantino, Bartolomeo, 476
Brazzà family, 172
Bregno, Andrea, 108–9, 145, 215, 369, 465, 515
Bresca, 517

b Index of Places and Subjects

Fontana Classics of History and Art

The Italian Painters of the Renaissance
Bernhard Berenson
Berenson's writings have profoundly influenced our approach
not only to Italian painting and sculpture, but to art criticism
and aesthetics in general.

The Renaissance
Walter Pater
'A splendid edition of Pater's most famous work, illustrated
with great skill and subtlety and introduced by an exemplary
essay from Sir Kenneth Clark.' *Observer*

Renaissance and Baroque
Heinrich Wölfflin
The first English translation of a pioneer work of wide in-
fluence. Introduced by Peter Murray.

Lectures on Modern History
Lord Acton
Introduced by Hugh Trevor-Roper, who discusses some of
the reasons why Acton's greatness is more apparent in our
times than it was in his.

A History of Europe
H. A. L. Fisher
'The last great survey of our European past.' GEOFFREY
BARRACLOUGH, *Observer*. 'A work which will be a classic to
future generations and will place Dr Fisher among our few
great historians.' HAROLD NICOLSON

Fontana History

The British Monarchy Series
This series describes the evolution of the British monarchy from the Saxon and Norman kings to George V—their personalities and lives, their influence on their ages. It comprises six volumes, each with twelve pages of photographs.

The Saxon and Norman Kings
Christopher Brooke
'An illuminating and imaginative reconstruction of what it really meant to be a king in Saxon and Norman times. The essential merits of this book are its lightness of touch and its firm grounding in scholarship.' *The Economist*

The Plantagenets
John Harvey
'A portrait gallery of medieval English sovereigns, illustrated with many splendid photographs. Learned, informative and entertaining.' PETER QUENNELL, *Daily Mail*

The Tudors
Christopher Morris
'Brilliant . . . Mr. Morris's flair for the apt point or quotation is remarkable.' J. E. NEALE, *History*

The Stuarts
J. P. Kenyon
'A sardonic, witty, yet scholarly book, written with splendid gusto.' *Sunday Times*

The First Four Georges
J. H. Plumb
'The vitality and frankness of a literary Hogarth. He is never dull or merely derivative.' *The Economist*

Hanover to Windsor
Roger Fulford
'As accurate as it is amusing, and conspicuously fair in its judgements.' *The Times Literary Supplement*

Fontana Modern Novels

Doctor Zhivago · *Boris Pasternak*

The world-famous novel of life in Russia during and after the Revolution. 'Doctor Zhivago will, I believe, come to stand as one of the great events in man's literary and moral history' *Edmund Wilson, New Yorker*. 'One of the most profound descriptions of love in the whole range of modern literature' *Stuart Hampshire, Encounter*

The Leopard · *Giuseppe di Lampedusa*

'Perhaps the greatest novel of the century' *L. P. Hartley*. 'Incontestably a masterpiece' *Listener*. '*The Leopard* has certainly enlarged my life . . . Reading and rereading it has made me realise how many ways there are of being alive' *E. M. Forster*

The Mandarins · *Simone de Beauvoir*

A magnificent satire by the author of "The Second Sex". '*The Mandarins* gives us a brilliant survey of the post-war French intellectual . . . a dazzling panorama' *Paul Johnson, New Statesman*. 'A superb document . . . a remarkable novel' *Iris Murdoch, Sunday Times*

Les Belles Images · *Simone de Beauvoir*

Her totally absorbing study of upper-class Parisian life. 'A brilliant sortie into Jet Set France' *Daily Mirror*. 'As compulsively readable as it is profound, serious and disturbing' *Queen*

Fontana Modern Novels

At Lady Molly's · *Anthony Powell*

The fourth novel in his famous "Music of Time" series, described by John Davenport in the *Observer* as 'the most exciting experiment in post-war English fiction.' 'I enjoyed *At Lady Molly's* even more than its predecessors, which is saying a lot' *Spectator*

What's Become of Waring · *Anthony Powell*

A hilarious parody of the English literary scene by one of our greatest living satirists. 'Exceedingly funny and brilliantly easy to read. Mr. Powell manages to convey a very agreeable friendliness and sympathy without any taint of sentimentality' *Maurice Richardson, Observer*. 'Brilliant and accomplished' *L. P. Hartley*

The Once and Future King · *T. H. White*

T. H. White's classic re-creation of the Arthurian Legend. 'A glorious dream of the Middle Ages as they never were but as they should have been' *New York Times*. 'A magnificent and tragic tapestry . . . Irresistible' *J. W. Lambert, Sunday Times*

The Gab Boys · *Cameron Duodu*

The perceptive novel of a group of young Ghanaians growing up under a new dictatorship. 'One of the most readable and instructive African books I've come across' *Observer*. 'Mr. Duodu lets off shafts at Civil Service corruption, the inadequacies of education and the absurdities of British life as seen by Africans . . . Distinctly entertaining' *Sunday Times*